# THE
# COLLINS
# SPURRELL
# WELSH
# DICTIONARY

# THE COLLINS SPURRELL WELSH DICTIONARY

HarperCollins*Publishers*

First published in this edition 1991

© **William Collins Sons & Co. Ltd. 1960**

© **HarperCollins Publishers 1991**

ISBN 0 00 433549-X

---

*revised in collaboration with/diwygiwyd mewn
cydweithrediad â'r*
Dr. David A. Thorne and the Department of Welsh
Language and Literature, St. David's University
College, Lampeter

Dr. David A. Thorne ac Adran Iaith a Llenyddiaeth
Cymru, Coleg Prifysgol Dewi Sant, Llanbedr Pont
Steffan

*editor/golygydd*
Anne Convery

---

*Printed in Great Britain by
HarperCollins Manufacturing, Glasgow*

# CONTENTS

# INTRODUCTION

The first Spurrell Welsh-English dictionary appeared in 1848 published by William Spurrell (1813–89) the Carmarthen printer and publisher. One of his sons, Walter Spurrell (1858–1934), joined his father in the business and the family firm published a series of distinguished Welsh-English, English-Welsh dictionaries and influential Welsh grammars during the latter part of last century and the first half of the present century. William Spurrell was advised by and well-acquainted with Daniel Silvan Evans (1818–1903), one of the father figures of Welsh lexicography, sometime lecturer in Welsh at St David's University College, Lampeter and the first professor of Welsh to be appointed by the University of Wales.

The Collins-Spurrell Welsh Dictionary was first published in 1960 and quickly became an essential tool of general reference for Welsh learners as well as those anxious to interpret literature. It was edited by Henry Lewis, Professor of Welsh Language and Literature at University College, Swansea. The staff of the Department of Welsh Language and Literature at St David's University College, Lampeter are happy to cooperate with the editorial staff at Collins to produce this latest edition of a famous dictionary.

D A THORNE

# THE WELSH LANGUAGE

MOST of the languages of Europe, and some of the languages of Asia, can be traced back to a common ancestor to which the name Indo-European is commonly given. From this ancestor were derived a dozen or so branches, one of which is called Celtic. This branch probably had its beginning in the upper Danube valley, and from there spread in many directions over Europe, and even to Galatia in Asia Minor. As the Celtic-speaking people became scattered, changes naturally occurred in the language, resulting in the growth of dialects. Of these the best known on the continent is that which was spoken in Gaul, to which the name Gaulish is given. Gaulish became extinct in the early Christian period, and was displaced by Latin.

In the meantime people speaking different forms of Celtic had crossed over from the Continent to the British Isles. One group established itself in Ireland. This is known as the Goidelic or Gaelic group, and from it descended the Irish language, which spread from Ireland to the Isle of Man, developing later to Manx, and also to Scotland, eventually becoming Scottish Gaelic. The other group prevailed in Britain and the language is called British or Brythonic or Brittonic. Prior to the Roman Conquest this language was spoken throughout what later became England, Wales and southern Scotland. It was from this descendant of the original Common Celtic language that ultimately sprang the Welsh, Cornish and Breton languages.

The language of the Goidelic group is referred to also as Q Celtic, and that of the British group as P Celtic. The reason for this is that the Indo-European consonant written 'qu' has given 'c' in the former and 'p' in the latter. An example is found in the forms corresponding to the English interrogative pronoun 'who', which in Irish is 'cia' or 'cé', in Welsh 'pwy', and in Latin 'quis'. It may be mentioned that Gaulish shows the same development as the British languages. Thus whereas the word for 'head, end' is in Irish 'ceann' (earlier 'cenn'), it is in Welsh 'pen', while the corresponding form is found in Gaulish 'penne' in a compound name.

One of the oldest poems in Welsh literature is a eulogy to Cynan Garwyn, son of Brochwel Ysgithrog. Cynan's son Selyf is known to have been killed as he led the Welsh in the battle of Chester about the year 615. The eulogy is attributed to Taliesin, whom persistent tradition acclaims as author of eulogies and elegies to princes in southern Scotland and northern England who struggled against the Saxon invader in the late sixth century. Another name that has been handed down from these early times is Aneirin, whose long poem *Y Gododdin* refers to a great tragic exploit at Catraeth, somewhere in the neighbourhood of Catterick. These early traditions have tenaciously persisted throughout the long story of Welsh poetic literature.

Recorded Welsh prose goes back to the early ninth century. The earliest remains are scanty, but it can hardly be contested that prose writing must have long preceded what little has had the good fortune to escape oblivion. It is free from the crudeness that would be expected from initial efforts, and the way in which difficult and somewhat abstruse material is expressed with clarity, economy and directness goes a long way to prove that the writers were inheritors rather than initiators. The splendour and exactness of medieval Welsh prose, quite apart from its literary content, is striking evidence of the mastery of the writers of the prose medium. These qualities appear not least in the unlikely realm of legal writing.

During its long history the Welsh language has naturally undergone changes, but far from the extent to which English, for example, has changed since the days of Chaucer. He was a contemporary of Dafydd ap Gwilym, but whereas Chaucer has to be practically translated into Modern English, Dafydd is using to all intents the same language as any present-day poet expressing himself in the same type of poem. Similarly, if most of the earlier prose literature were printed in accordance with modern orthographical usage, the reader would not experience excessive difficulty in comprehending it. There have been changes in syntax, and still more in vocabulary. Idiomatic expressions have become obsolete from age to age, and new ones have grown. But substantially the literary language has been strikingly uniform.

The vocabulary has naturally been greatly affected from time to time by contact with peoples speaking a different language. Like many other languages Welsh has rarely been afraid of borrowing words from foreign languages. In the period of Roman occupation, and later under the influence of the Church, hundreds of Latin words were borrowed and submitted to the same treatment as native words. The same is to a less extent true of the period of contact with Anglo-Saxons. Then came the influence of the Normans, followed ultimately by the great pressure of English. All these accretions have been from non-Celtic sources, but the Welsh vocabulary is not without borrowings taken from time to time from Irish.

The written, and especially the printed, literary language always tends to be more static and conservative than the spoken. This results in the retention in the literary language of forms which have long since vanished completely from everyday colloquial speech, thus giving the printed literary language a somewhat artificial appearance. But the spoken language also differs from area to area. Indeed a brook seems a sufficient barrier to create divergence in expression between the inhabitants on either side. It is well known that speakers of dialect in one locality can hardly understand compatriots speaking another dialect of the same language. To secure, therefore, that all speakers, of whatever dialects, should have access to all that is of value in enlightened minds, the standard literary language must retain a high level of permanence, but should also avoid pedantic rigidity and scholastic snobbery.

# NOTES ON THE PRONUNCIATION OF WELSH

## VOWELS

They are sounded, long or short, as the vowels in the English words given.

A      p*a*lm, p*a*t.
E      g*a*te (without diphthongization), g*e*t.
I      f*ee*t, f*i*t.
O      m*o*re, n*o*t.
U (1)   North Wales: like French *u* or German *ü* without rounding lips.
  (2)   South Wales: as I.
W     c*oo*l, f*u*ll.
Y (1)   In monosyllables generally, and in final syllables, as U (the 'clear' sound).
  (2)   In all but final syllables, and in **y, yr** (the), **fy** (my), **dy** (thy), **yn, yng, ym** (in), the adverbial **yn**, the preverbal and relative particle **y, yr** (**y'm, y'th** etc), **syr** (sir), **nyrs** (nurse), as English f*u*n, (the 'obscure' sound).

## DIPHTHONGS

(1)   Falling diphthongs, in which the second sound is consonantal: the two vowels have the sound noted above: **ae, oe, ai, oi**, the diphthong **ei** as English *by*, **aw, ew, iw, ow, uw, ŵy, yw**.

(2)   Rising diphthongs, in which the first sound is consonantal: **ia, ie, io, iw, iy**, ('obscure' y); **wa, we, wi, wo, wy**, ('clear' y), **wy**, ('obscure' y).

## CONSONANTS

Only such as differ from English need be noted.

CH   (following C in the alphabet), as Scottish lo*ch*.
DD   (following D in the alphabet), as *th* in English *th*is, brea*th*e.
F      as English *v*.
FF    As English *f*.
G     always as in English *g*o.
NG   (following G in the alphabet), as in English si*ng*. In some words (e.g. **dangos**), however, it is sounded *ng-g*, as in English lo*ng*er. Alphabetically this follows after N.
LL    produced by placing the tongue to pronounced *l*, then emitting breath without voice.
PH   (following P in the alphabet), as English *f*.
TH   always as th in English *th*in.

## ACCENT

Welsh words are generally accented on the last syllable but one. There are certain exceptions:

(1) The reduplicated personal pronouns **myfi, tydi, efe, efô, hyhi, nyni, chwychwi, hwynt-hwy,** accented on the final syllable.

(2) Verbs in **-(h)au, -(h)oi, -eu,** accented on the final syllable.

(3) A few dissyllabic words beginning **y** + consonant, accented on the final syllable.

(4) Certain polysyllabic words with a diphthong resulting in contraction in the final syllable, such as **Cymraeg.**

(5) Some late borrowings accented as in the language of origin, generally English.

## INITIAL MUTATIONS

Certain initial consonants are mutated under certain conditions, as shown in the following table. Only the radical form is given in the dictionary.

| SOUNDS | EXAMPLES | | | |
|---|---|---|---|---|
| | *Radical* | *Soft* | *Nasal* | *Spirant* |
| **p** | *p*ren | *b*ren | *mh*ren | *ph*ren |
| **t** | *t*ad | *d*ad | *nh*ad | *th*ad |
| **c** | *c*am | *g*am | *ngh*am | *ch*am |
| **b** | *b*aich | *f*aich | *m*aich | |
| **d** | *d*yn | *dd*yn | *n*yn | |
| **g** | *g*ŵr | -ŵr | *ng*ŵr | |
| **ll** | *ll*ais | *l*ais | | |
| **rh** | *rh*es | *r*es | | |
| **m** | *m*am | *f*am | | |

# ABBREVIATIONS

# BYRFODDAU

| | | |
|---|---|---|
| abbreviation | **abbr** | byfford |
| adjective | **adj** | ansoddair |
| adverb | **adv** | adferf |
| collective noun | **coll n** | enw torfol |
| colloquial | **col** | tafodieithol |
| conjunction | **conj** | cysylltiad |
| contraction | **contr** | cywasgiad |
| demonstrative | **dem** | dangosol |
| dual noun | **dn** | enw deuol |
| emphatic | **emphat** | pwyslais |
| exclamation | **excl** | ebychiad |
| feminine | **f** | benywaidd |
| grammatical | **gram** | gramadegol |
| imperative | **imper** | gorchmynnol |
| masculine | **m** | gwrywaidd |
| mutation | **mut** | treiglad |
| noun dual | **nd** | enw deuol |
| plural | **pl** | lluosog |
| pronoun | **pron** | rhagenw |
| preposition | **prep** | arddodiad |
| relative | **rel** | perthynol |
| singular | **sg** | unigol |
| verb | **vb** | berf |
| intransitive verb | **vi** | berf gyflawn |
| transitive verb | **vt** | berf anghyflawn |

# GEIRIADUR CYMRAEG A SAESNEG

## A

**a** *interrogative particle* ♦ *preverbal particle* ♦ *rel pron* who, that, which

**a, ac** *conj* and

**â, ag** *conj* as

**â, ag** *prep* with

**a** *excl* ah, oh

**ab, ap** *nm* son (*before name, in place of surname, like 'Mac', and 'Fitz'*)

**abad** (**-au**) *nm* abbot

**abadaeth** (**-au**) *nf* abbacy, abbotship

**abades** (**-au**) *nf* abbess

**abatir** (**-oedd**) *nm* abbey-land

**abaty** (**abatai**) *nm* abbey

**aber** (**-oedd, ebyr**) *nm* confluence; mouth of river, estuary; brook, stream

**aberfa** (**-oedd**) *nf* mouth of river, estuary

**abergofiant** *nm* forgetfulness, oblivion

**aberth** (**-au, ebyrth**) *nm* sacrifice

**aberthged** *nf* oblation; offering of fruits

**aberthol** *adj* sacrificial

**aberthu** *vb* sacrifice

**aberthwr** (**-wyr**) *nm* sacrificer

**aberu** *vb* flow into, disembogue

**abid** *nm/f* apparel; dress of religious order

**abiéc** *nm/f* alphabet

**abl** *adj* able; well-off

**abladol** *adj* ablative

**abledd** *nm* ability; plenty

**abrwysg** *adj* clumsy, drunken

**absen** *nm* absence; slander

**absennol** *adj* absent

**absennu** *vb* backbite, slander

**absennwr** (**absenwyr**) *nm* backbiter

**absenoldeb** *nm* absence

**absenoli** *vb* absent

**absenoliaeth** (**-au**) *nm* absenteeism

**abwyd, -yn** (**-od**) *nm* worm; fishing-bait

**ac, a** *conj* and

**academaidd** *adj* academic

**academi** (**-iau**) *nm* academy

**acen** (**-ion**) *nf* accent

**aceniad** *nm* accentuation

**acennod** *nf* accent mark

**acennu** *vb* accent, stress

**acenyddiaeth** *nf* accentuation

**acer** (**-i**) *nf* acre

**acrilig** *adj* acrylic

**act** (**-au**) *nf* act

**actio** *vb* act

**actor** (**-ion**) *nm* actor

**actores** (**-au**) *nf* actress

**acw** *adv* there, yonder

**ach** *excl* ugh

**ach** (**-au, -oedd**) *nf* degree of kinship; (*pl*) pedigree, ancestry

**aches** *nm* tide, flood; eloquence

**achlân** *adv* wholly, entirely

**achles** (**-oedd**) *nf* succour, protection; manure

**achlesol** *adj* succouring

**achlesu** *vb* succour, cherish; manure

**achlod** *nm* shame, disgrace

**achlust** *nm* rumour ♦ *adj* attentive

**achlysur** (**-on**) *nm* occasion

**achlysuro** *vb* occasion

**achlysurol** *adj* occasional

**achos** (**-ion**) *nm* cause, case

**achos** *conj* because, for

**achosi** *vb* cause
**achres** (-i, -au) *nf* genealogical table
**achub** *vb* seize, snatch; save, rescue. **a. y blaen** forestall. **a. y cyfle** seize the opportunity
**achubiaeth** *nf* salvation
**achubol** *adj* saving
**achubwr** (-wyr), **-ydd** (-ion) *nm* saviour, rescuer
**achul** *adj* thin, emaciated
**achwre, ach(f)re** *n* under-thatch, protection; covering, garment
**achwyn** *vb* complain ♦ (-ion) *nm* complaint, plaint
**achwyngar** *adj* querulous
**achwyniad** (-au) *nm* complaint, accusation
**achwynwr** (-wyr) *nm* complainer; complainant, plaintiff
**achwynyddes** (-au) *nf* complainant
**achydd** (-ion) *nm* genealogist
**achyddiaeth** *nf* genealogy
**achyddol** *adj* genealogical
**ad-** *prefix* very; second; bad, re-
**adail** *nf* building, edifice, structure
**adain, aden** (**adenydd**) *nf* wing; fin; spoke
**adamant** *nm* adamant, diamond
**adamantaidd** *adj* adamantine
**adar** *npl* (**aderyn** *nm*) birds, fowls. **a. drudwy, a. yr eira**, starlings. **a y to** sparrows
**adara** *vb* catch birds, fowl
**adardy** (-dai) *nm* aviary
**adareg** *nf* ornithology
**adargi** (-gwn) *nm* retriever, setter, spaniel
**adargraffiad** (-au) *nm* reprint
**adarwr** (-wyr) *nm* fowler
**adarwriaeth** *nf* fowling
**adarydd** (-ion) *nm* ornithologist
**adaryddiaeth** *nf* ornithology
**ad-dalu** *vb* repay, requite
**ad-drefnu** *vb* rearrange
**adeg** (-au) *nf* time, occasion, opportunity
**adeilad** (-au) *nm/f* building, edifice
**adeiladaeth** *nf* building; edification, construction
**adeiladol** *adj* edifying, constructive
**adeiladu** *vb* build, edify
**adeiladwr** (-wyr), **-ydd** (-ion) *nm* builder
**adeiledd** *nm* structure
**adeiniog** *adj* winged
**aden** (-ydd, **edyn**) *nf* wing (**adain**)
**adenedigaeth** *nf* regeneration
**adeni** *vb* regenerate
**adennill** *vb* regain, recover
**aderyn** (**adar**) *nm* bird
**adfach** (-au) *nm* barb; liver-fluke
**adfail** (-feilion) *nm* ruin
**adfeddiannu** *vb* repossess
**adfeiliad** *nm* decay, ruin
**adfeiliedig** *adj* decayed, in ruins
**adfeilio** *vb* decay, moulder
**Adfent** *nm* Advent
**adfer, -u, -yd** *vb* restore
**adferf** (-au) *nf* adverb
**adferfol** *adj* adverbial
**adferiad** *nm* restoration
**adferol** *adj* restorative; remedial
**adferwr** (-wyr) *nm* restorer
**adflas** *nm* after-taste, bad taste
**adfyd** *nm* adversity
**adfydus** *adj* adverse, miserable
**adfynach** *nm* renegade monk
**adfyw** *adj* half alive, half dead
**adfywhau** *vb* revive, reanimate
**adfywiad** (-au) *nm* revival
**adfywio** *vb* revive, resuscitate
**adfywiol** *adj* refreshing
**adg-** see **atg-**
**adiad** *nm* drake
**adio** *nm* addition ♦ *vb* add
**adiolyn** (**adiolion**) *nm* additive
**adladd, adlodd** *nm* aftermath
**adlais** (-leisiau) *nm* echo
**adlam** (-au) *nm* home; rebound. **cic a.** drop-kick
**adlamu** *vb* rebound
**adleisio** *vb* resound

**adlewyrch, -iad (-au)** *nm* reflection

**adlewyrchu** *vb* reflect

**adlewyrchydd (-ion)** *nm* reflector

**adlog (-au)** *nm* compound interest

**adloniadol** *adj* of *or* for entertainment

**adloniant** *nm* recreation, entertainment

**adlonni** *vb* entertain, refresh

**adlunio** *vb* remodel, reconstruct

**adnabod** *vb* know, recognize

**adnabyddiaeth** *nf* knowledge, acquaintance

**adnabyddus** *adj* known, familiar

**adnabyddwr** *nm* knower

**adnau (adneuon)** *nm* deposit, pledge. **ar a.** on deposit

**adneuo** *vb* deposit

**adneuol** *adj* depositing

**adneuwr (-wyr)** *nm* depositor

**adnewyddiad (-au)** *nm* renewal, renovation

**adnewyddu** *vb* renew, renovate

**adnewyddwr (-wyr)** *nm* renewer, renovator

**adnod (-au)** *nf* verse

**adnoddau** *npl* resources

**adolygiad (-au)** *nm* review

**adolygu** *vb* review

**adolygydd (-ion)** *nm* reviewer

**adran (-nau)** *nf* division, section, department

**adref** *adv* homewards, home

**adrodd** *vb* relate, recite

**adroddgan (-au)** *nf* recitative

**adroddiad (-au)** *nm* report; recitation

**adroddwr (-wyr)** *nm* narrator, reciter

**ads-** see **ats-**

**aduniad** *nm* reunion

**aduno** *vb* reunite

**adwaith (-weithiau)** *nm* reaction

**adweithiol** *adj* reactionary

**adweithydd (-ion)** *nm* reactor

**adwr** *nm* coward, churl

**adwy (-au, -on)** *nf* gap, breach; pass

**adwyth (-au)** *nm* evil, misfortune, illness

**adwythig** *adj* cruel; evil, baneful; sore, sick; harmful

**adyn (-od)** *nm* wretch

**adysgrif (-au)** *nf* copy, transcript

**adysgrifio** *vb* copy, transcribe

**addas** *adj* suitable, proper

**addasiad (-au)** *nm* adjustment, adaptation

**addasrwydd** *nm* suitableness, fitness

**addasu** *vb* suit, adapt, fit

**addawol** *adj* promising

**addef** *vb* acknowledge, own, admit

**addefiad** *nm* admission, confession

**addewid (-ion)** *nf* promise

**addfain** *adj* slender, shapely

**addfed** see **aeddfed**

**addfwyn** *adj* gentle, meek, mild

**addfwynder** *nm* gentleness, meekness

**addien** *adj* fair, beautiful

**addo** *vb* promise

**addod** *nm:* **wy a.** nest-egg

**addoed** *nm* death, hurt

**addoedi** *vb* delay, postpone, prorogue

**addoediad** *nm* prorogation

**addoer** *adj* sad, cruel; chilling

**addoldy (-dai)** *nm* place of worship

**addolgar** *adj* devout, reverent

**addolgarwch** *nm* devoutness, reverence

**addoli** *vb* worship, adore

**addoliad** *nm* worship

**addolwr (-wyr)** *nm* worshipper

**adduned (-au)** *nf* vow

**addunedu** *vb* vow

**addurn (-au, -iadau)** *nm* ornament, adornment

**addurnedig** *adj* decorated

**addurniad** *nm* ornamentation

**addurno** *vb* adorn, ornament

**addurnol** *adj* ornamental, decorative

**addurnwr (-wyr)** *nm* decorator

**addysg** *nf* education, instruction

**addysgiadol** *adj* instructive, educational

**addysgiaeth** *nf* instruction, training

**addysgol** *adj* educational

**addysgu** *vb* educate, instruct

**addysgwr (-wyr), -ydd (-ion)** *nm* educator, instructor, tutor

**aeddfed** *adj* ripe, mature

**aeddfedrwydd** *nm* ripeness, maturity

**aeddfedu** *vb* ripen; mature

**ael (-iau)** *nf* brow

**aele** *adj* sad, wretched

**aelgerth, -geth** see **elgeth**

**aelod (-au)** *nm* member, limb. **A. Seneddol** Member of Parliament

**aelodaeth** *nf* membership

**aelodi** *vb* become a member; enrol

**aelwyd (-ydd)** *nf* hearth, fireside

**aer (-ion)** *nm* heir

**aer** *nm* air

**aeres (-au)** *nf* heiress

**aerfa** *nf* slaughter, battle

**aerglo** *nm* air-lock

**aeron** *npl* fruit, fruits, berries

**aerwy (-au, -on)** *nm* collar, torque; neck-chain

**aes** *nf* shield

**aestheteg** *nf* aesthetics

**aesthetig** *adj* aesthetic

**aeth** *nm* pain, grief, fear, shock

**aethnen** *nf* aspen, poplar

**aethus** *adj* poignant, grievous, severe

**afal (-au)** *nm* apple

**afaleua** *vb* gather apples

**afallen (-nau)** *nf* apple-tree

**afan** *npl* (**-en** *nf*) raspberries

**afanc (-od)** *nm* beaver

**afiach** *adj* unwell, unhealthy, morbid

**afiachus** *adj* sickly; unwholesome

**afiaith** *nm* zest, mirth, glee

**afiechyd (-on)** *nm* disease, malady

**afieithus** *adj* mirthful, gleeful

**aflafar** *adj* harsh, unmelodious

**aflan** *adj* unclean, polluted, foul

**aflawen** *adj* fierce; sad, cheerless, dismal; awful

**aflednais** *adj* immodest, indelicate

**afledneisrwydd** *nm* immodesty, indelicacy

**aflem** *adj* obtuse

**aflendid** *nm* uncleanness; pollution

**aflêr** *adj* untidy, slovenly

**aflerwch** *nm* untidiness, slovenliness

**afles** *nm* disadvantage, hurt

**aflesol** *adj* disadvantageous, unprofitable

**afliwiog** *adj* pale, colourless

**aflonydd** *adj* unquiet, restless

**aflonyddu** *vb* disquiet, disturb, molest

**aflonyddwch** *nm* disturbance, unrest

**aflonyddwr (-wyr)** *nm* disturber

**afloyw** *adj* turbid; opaque

**afluniaidd** *adj* mis-shapen, deformed

**aflunio** *vb* disfigure, deform

**aflwydd** *nm* misfortune, calamity

**aflwyddiannus** *adj* unsuccessful

**aflwyddiant** *nm* failure

**aflwyddo** *vb* fail

**aflywodraeth** *nf* misrule, anarchy

**aflywodraethus** *adj* ungovernable, uncontrollable

**afon (-ydd)** *nf* river

**afonig** *nf* rivulet, streamlet, brook

**afradlon** *adj* wasteful, prodigal

**afradlonedd** *nm* prodigality

**afradloni, afradu** *vb* waste, lavish, squander

**afraid** *adj* unnecessary, needless

**afrasol** *adj* graceless, impious

**afreidiau** *nm* superfluity

**afreidiol** *adj* needless, superfluous

**afreol** *nf* misrule, disorder

**afreolaidd** *adj* irregular;
disorderly
**afreoleidd-dra** *nm* irregularity
**afreolus** *adj* unruly, disorderly
**afreswm** *nm* absurdity
**afresymol** *adj* unreasonable
**afresymoldeb** *nm*
unreasonableness
**afrifed** *adj* innumerable
**afrllad, -en (-au, -ennau)** *nf* wafer
**afrosgo** *adj* clumsy, unwieldy
**afrwydd** *adj* difficult, stiff,
awkward
**afrwyddineb** *nm* difficulty
**afrwyddo** *vb* obstruct, hinder
**afrywiog** *adj* perverse,
crossgrained, improper
**afrywiogrwydd** *nm* churlishness,
roughness
**afu** liver ♦ *nm/f* **a. (g)las** gizzard
**afwyn (-au)** *nf* rein
**affeithiad** *nm* affection (in
grammar)
**afflau** *nm* grip, hug, embrace
**affliw** *nm* shred, particle
**Affrica** *nf* Africa
**affwysol** *adj* abysmal
**ag** *conj* as ♦ *prep* with. see **â**
**agen (-nau)** *nf* cleft, chink, fissure
**agendor** *nm/f* gulf, abyss
**agennu** *vb* split, crack
**ager, agerdd** *nm* steam, vapour
**agerfad (-au)** *nm* steamboat
**agerlong (-au)** *nf* steamship,
steamer
**ageru** *vb* steam, evaporate
**agerw** *adj* bitter, fierce
**agor, -yd** *vb* open, expand
**agorawd (-au)** *nf* overture
**agored** *adj* open; liable
**agorfa (-oedd)** *nf* opening, orifice
**agoriad (-au)** *nm* opening; key
**agoriadol** *adj* opening, inaugural
**agorwr (-wyr), -ydd (-ion)** *nm*
opener
**agos** *adj* near, nigh
**agosaol** *adj* approaching

**agosatrwydd** *nm* intimacy
**agosáu** *vb* draw near, approach
**agosrwydd** *nm* nearness,
proximity
**agwedd (-au)** *nf* form; aspect;
attitude
**agweddi** *nm* dowry, marriage gift
**agwrdd** *adj* strong, mighty
**angall** *adj* unwise, foolish
**angau** *nm/f* death
**angel (angylion, engyl)** *nm* angel
**angen (anghenion)** *nm* need, want
**angenrheidiol** *adj* necessary,
needful
**angenrheidrwydd** *nm* necessity
**angerdd** *nm* heat; passion; force
**angerddol** *adj* ardent, intense,
passionate
**angerddoldeb** *nm* vehemence,
intensity
**anghaffael** *nm* mishap; defect,
flaw
**anghallineb** *nm* unwisdom,
imprudence
**angharedig** *adj* unkind
**angharedigrwydd** *nm* unkindness
**anghelfydd** *adj* unskilful, clumsy
**anghenfil (angenfilod)** *nm* monster
**anghenraid (angenrheidiau)** *nm*
necessity
**anghenus** *adj* needy, necessitous,
indigent
**angheuol** *adj* deadly, mortal, fatal
**anghlod** *nm* dispraise, dishonour
**anghoelio** *vb* disbelieve
**anghofiedig** *adj* forgotten
**anghofio** *vb* forget
**anghofrwydd** *nm* forgetfulness
**anghofus** *adj* forgetful, oblivious
**anghred** *nf* unbelief, infidelity
**anghredadun (anghredinwyr)** *nm*
unbeliever
**anghrediniaeth** *nf* unbelief,
infidelity
**anghrediniol** *adj* unbelieving
**anghredu** *vb* disbelieve
**anghrefyddol** *adj* irreligious

**anghrist** (-iau) *nm* antichrist
**anghryno** *adj* incompact, prolix
**anghwrtais** *adj* discourteous
**anghwrteisi** *nm* discourtesy
**anghydbwysedd** *nm* imbalance
**anghydfod** *nm* disagreement, discord
**Anghydffurfiaeth** *nf* Nonconformity
**Anghydffurfiwr** (-wyr) *nm* Nonconformist
**anghydnaws** *adj* uncongenial
**anghydsynio** *vb* dissent, disagree
**anghydweddol** *adj* incompatible
**anghyfaddas** *adj* unsuitable, unfit
**anghyfaddasu** *vb* unfit, disqualify
**anghyfamodol** *adj* uncovenanted
**anghyfanhedd-dra** *nm* desolation
**anghyfanheddle** (-aneddleoedd) *nm* desolate place
**anghyfanheddol** *adj* desolating; desert
**anghyfannedd** *adj* uninhabited, desert
**anghyfansoddiadol** *adj* unconstitutional
**anghyfartal** *adj* unequal, uneven
**anghyfartaledd** *nm* disparity
**anghyfarwydd** *adj* unfamiliar, unskilled
**anghyfeillgar** *adj* unfriendly
**anghyfiaith** *adj* foreign, alien
**anghyfiawn** *adj* unjust, unrighteous
**anghyfiawnder** *nm* injustice
**anghyflawn** *adj* incomplete
**anghyfleus** *adj* inconvenient
**anghyfleustra** (-terau) *nm* inconvenience
**anghyflogaeth** *nm* unemployment
**anghyfnewidiol** *adj* immutable
**anghyfraith** *nf* transgression, crime
**anghyfranogol** *adj* incommunicable
**anghyfreithlon** *adj* unlawful, illegal, illegitimate

**anghyfrifol** *adj* irresponsible
**anghyffredin** *adj* uncommon, rare
**anghyffwrdd** *adj* intangible
**anghyffyrddus** *adj* uncomfortable
**anghymedrol** *adj* immoderate
**anghymen** *adj* rash, coarse, untidy
**anghymeradwy** *adj* unacceptable
**anghymeradwyo** *vb* disapprove
**anghymesur** *adj* inordinate
**anghymharol** *adj* incomparable
**anghymharus** *adj* ill-matched
**anghymhendod** *nm* foolishness, indelicacy, untidiness
**anghymhwyso** *vb* unfit, disqualify
**anghymhwyster** *nm* incapacity, disqualification
**anghymodlon** *adj* implacable
**anghymwys** *adj* unfit, unsuitable
**anghynefin** *adj* unfamiliar
**anghynefindra** *nm* unfamiliarity
**anghynhyrchiol** *adj* unproductive
**anghynnes** *adj* odious, loathsome
**anghysbell** *adj* out-of-the-way; remote
**anghyson** *adj* inconsistent
**anghysondeb, -der** (-au) *nm* inconsistency
**anghysur** (-on) *nm* discomfort
**anghysuro** *vb* discomfort
**anghysurus** *adj* uncomfortable
**anghytbwys** *adj* unbalanced, lopsided
**anghytgord** (-iau) *nm* discord, dissension
**anghytûn** *adj* not agreeing, discordant
**anghytundeb** *nm* disagreement
**anghytuno** *vb* disagree
**anghywair** *adj* ill-equipped; discordant ♦ *nm* disrepair
**anghyweithas** *adj* froward, uncivil
**anghywir** *adj* incorrect, inaccurate, false
**anghywirdeb** (-au) *nm* inaccuracy, falseness
**anghywrain** *adj* unskilful; slovenly
**angladd** (-au) *nm/f* burial, funeral

**angladdol** adj funereal
**angof** nm forgetfulness, oblivion
**angor** (-au, -ion) nm anchor
**angorfa** (-oedd, -feydd) nf anchorage
**angori** vb anchor
**angylaidd** adj angelic
**angyles** (-au) nf female angel
**ai** adv is it? what? **a. e?** is it so?
**ai** conj or; either; if
**aidd** nm zeal, ardour, zest
**Aifft:** yr A. nf Egypt
**aig, eigiau** nf host, shoal
**aig** nf (late corrupt form) sea, ocean
**ail** adj second ♦ adv a second time, again
**ailadrodd** vb repeat
**ailadroddiad** (-au) nm repetition
**ailenedigaeth** nf rebirth
**aileni** vb bear again, regenerate
**Ailfedyddiwr** (-wyr) nm Anabaptist
**ail-law** adj second-hand
**aillt** nm vassal, villain, slave
**ais** npl (eisen nf) laths; ribs
**alaeth** nm wailing, lamentation, grief
**alaethu** vb lament
**alaethus** adj mournful, lamentable
**alarch** (-od, elyrch) nm swan
**alaru** vb surfeit; loathe
**alaw** (-on) nf lily; air, melody, tune
**Alban:** yr A. nf Scotland
**Albanwr** (-wyr) nm Scot
**alcali** (-ïau) nm alkali
**alcam** nm tin
**alcohol** nm alcohol
**alch** (-au, eilch) nf grate, grill
**ale** (-au, -on) nf aisle; gangway; alley
**algebra** nm algebra
**Algeria** nf Algeria
**Almaen:** yr A. nf Germany
**Almaeneg** nf German
**Almaenwr** (-wyr) nm German

**almon** nm almond
**aloi** (aloeon) nm alloy
**Alpau:** yr A. npl the Alps
**allan** adv out
**allanol** adj outward, external
**allblyg** adj extrovert
**allforio** vb export
**allfro** nm foreigner; foreign land
**allfudwr** (-wyr) nm emigrant
**allgarwch** nm altruism
**allor** (-au) nf altar
**allt** (elltydd) nf hill; cliff; wood
**alltud** (-ion) nm alien; exile
**alltudiaeth** nf banishment, exile
**alltudio** vb banish, exile
**allwedd** (-au, -i) nf key, clef (music)
**am** prep round, about; for; at; on ♦ conj for, because; so long as
**am** see ym
**amaeth** nm husbandman; agriculture
**amaethdy** (-dai) nm farm-house
**amaethu** vb farm, till
**amaethwr** (-wyr) nm farmer
**amaethwraig** nf farm-wife
**amaethyddiaeth** nf agriculture
**amaethyddol** adj agricultural
**amarch** nm disrespect, dishonour
**amau** vb doubt, suspect ♦ (-heuon) nm doubt
**ambell** adj occasional. **a. waith** sometimes
**amcan** (-ion) nm purpose, aim; guess. **ar a.** at random, approximately, at a guess
**amcangyfrif** vb estimate ♦ (-on) nm estimate
**amcanu** vb purpose; aim; guess
**amdo** (-oeau) nm shroud, winding-sheet
**amdoi** vb shroud, enshroud
**amdorch** (-dyrch) nf chaplet, wreath
**amddifad** adj destitute, orphan
**amddifadrwydd** nm destitution, privation

**amddifadu** *vb* bereave, deprive
**amddifaty** (**-tai**) *nm* orphanage
**amddifedi** *nm* destitution, privation
**amddiffyn** *vb* defend, protect, shield ♦ (**-ion**) *nm* defence
**amddiffynfa** (**-feydd**) *nf* fortress
**amddiffyniad** *nm* protection, defence
**amdiffynnwr** (**-ynwyr**), **-ynnydd** (**-ynyddion**) *nm* defender, protector
**amddyfrwys** *adj* mighty, rugged; marshy
**America Ladin** *nf* Latin America
**Amerig: yr A.** *nf* America
**amfesur** (**-au**) *nm* perimeter
**amgáu** *vb* enclose, shut in
**amgen** *adj, adv* other, else, otherwise; different. **nid a.** that is to say, namely
**amgenach** *adj, adv* otherwise; better
**amgueddfa** (**-feydd**) *nf* museum
**amgyffred** *vb* comprehend, comprise ♦ (**-ion**) *nm* comprehension
**amgyffrediad** *nm* comprehension
**amgylch** (**-oedd**) *nm* circuit; environs, surroundings. **o (oddi) amgylch** round about, about
**amgylchedd** *nm* circumference; environment
**amgylchfyd** *nm* environment
**amgylchiad** (**-au**) *nm* circumstance; occasion
**amgylchiadol** *adj* circumstantial
**amgylchu** *vb* surround
**amgylchynol** *adj* surrounding
**amgylchynu** *vb* surround
**amharchu** *vb* dishonour, disrespect
**amharchus** *adj* disrespectful, disreputable
**amhariad** *nm* impairment, damage
**amharod** *adj* unprepared, unready
**amharodrwydd** *nm* unreadiness
**amharu** *vb* impair, harm, injure,
damage
**amhendant** *adj* indefinite, vague
**amhenderfynol** *adj* irresolute
**amhenodol** *adj* indefinite
**amherchi** *vb* dishonour, insult
**amherffaith** *adj* imperfect
**amherffeithrwydd** *nm* imperfection
**amhersonol** *adj* impersonal
**amherth(y)nasol** *adj* irrelevant
**amheuaeth** *nf* doubt, scepticism
**amheugar** *adj* suspicious; sceptical
**amheuol** *adj* doubting, doubtful
**amheus** *adj* doubting, doubtful, dubious
**amheuthun** *adj* dainty, savoury ♦ (**-ion**) *nm* dainty, delicacy, treat
**amheuwr** (**-wyr**) *nm* doubter, sceptic
**amhlantadwy** *adj* childless, barren
**amhleidiol, amhleitgar** *adj* impartial
**amhoblog** *adj* sparsely populated
**amhoblogaidd** *adj* unpopular
**amhosibl** *adj* impossible
**amhriodol** *adj* improper
**amhrisiadwy** *adj* priceless
**amhrofiadol** *adj* inexperienced
**amhrydlon** *adj* unpunctual
**amhûr** *adj* impure, foul
**amhwrpasol** *adj* irrelevant
**amhwyllo** *vb* lose one's senses, go mad
**aml** *adj* frequent, abundant ♦ *adv* often
**amlder, amldra** *nm* abundance
**amlдduwiad** (**-iaid**) *nm* polytheist
**amlдduwiaeth** *nf* polytheism
**amleiriog** *adj* wordy, verbose, prolix
**amlen** (**-ni**) *nf* envelope, wrapper
**amlhad** *nm* increasing, increase
**amlhau** *vb* increase, multiply
**amlinelliad** (**-au**) *nm* outline
**aml-lawr** *adj* multi-storey

**amlochrog** _adj_ many-sided
**amlosgfa** _nf_ crematorium
**amlosgi** _vb_ cremate
**amlwg** _adj_ plain, clear, manifest, evident, prominent
**amlwreigiaeth** _nf_ polygamy
**amlwreigiwr** (-wyr) _nm_ polygamist
**amlygiad** (-au) _nm_ manifestation
**amlygrwydd** _nm_ prominence, limelight
**amlygu** _vb_ manifest, reveal, evince
**amnaid** (-neidiau) _nf_ beck, nod
**amneidio** _vb_ beckon, nod
**amnest** (-au) _nm_ amnesty
**amod** (-au) _nm/f_ condition
**amodi** _vb_ covenant, stipulate
**amodol** _adj_ conditional
**amrant** (-au, -rannau) _nm_ eyelid
**amrantiad** _nm_ wink, twinkling, second
**amreiniol** _adj_ unprivileged
**amrwd** _adj_ uncooked, raw, crude
**amryddawn** _adj_ versatile
**amryfal** _adj_ sundry, manifold
**amryfus** _adj_ erroneous, inadvertent
**amryfusedd** (-au) _nm_ error, oversight
**amryliw** _adj_ variegated; multicoloured
**amryw** _adj_ several, sundry, various
**amrywiad** (-au) _nm_ variant
**amrywiaeth** _nm_ variety, diversity
**amrywio** _vb_ vary, differ
**amrywiol** _adj_ sundry
**amser** (-oedd, -au) _nm/f_ time
**amseriad** (-au) _nm_ timing, dating, date
**amserlen** (-ni) _nf_ time-table
**amserol** _adj_ timely; temporal
**amseru** _vb_ time, date
**amserydd** (-ion) _nm_ chronologist
**amseryddiaeth** _nf_ chronology
**amseryddol** _adj_ chronological
**amwisg** (-oedd) _nf_ covering,
shroud
**amwisgo** _vb_ enwrap, shroud
**amwys** _adj_ ambiguous
**amwysedd** _nm_ ambiguity
**amyn** _conj, prep_ unless, except, but
**amynedd** _nm_ patience
**amyneddgar** _adj_ patient
**an-** _prefix_ un-, in-, de-, dis-
**anabl** _adj_ disabled
**anabledd** _nm_ disability
**anad** _adj:_ **yn a.** above all, more than
**anadferadwy** _adj_ irreparable
**anadl** (-au, -on) _nf/m_ breath
**anadliad** _nm_ breath, breathing
**anadlu** _vb_ breathe
**anadnabyddus** _adj_ unknown
**anaddas** _adj_ unfit, unsuitable
**anaddasu** _vb_ unfit, disqualify
**anaeddfed, anaddfed** _adj_ unripe, immature
**anaeddfedrwydd** _nm_ unripeness, immaturity
**anaele** _adj_ awful, direful; incurable
**anaesthetig** _adj_ anaesthetic
**anaf** (-au) _nm_ blemish, defect; wound
**anafu** _vb_ blemish, maim, hurt
**anafus** _adj_ maimed, disabled
**anair** (-eiriau) _nm_ ill report, slander
**anallu** _nm_ inability
**analluog** _adj_ unable
**analluogi** _vb_ disenable; disable
**anaml** _adj_ infrequent, rare ♦ _adv_ rarely, seldom
**anamlwg** _adj_ obscure, inconspicuous
**anamserol** _adj_ untimely, mistimed
**anap** (-hapon) _nm/f_ mischance, mishap
**anarchiaeth** _nm_ anarchy
**anarchydd** (-ion) _nm_ anarchist
**anarferol** _adj_ unusual, extraordinary
**anarfog** _adj_ unarmed

**anchwiliadwy** *adj* unsearchable

**ancr** *nm/f* anchorite, anchoress

**ancwyn** (**-ion**) *nm* dinner, supper; delicacy

**andras** *nm* curse; devil, deuce

**andwyo** *vb* spoil, ruin, undo

**andwyol** *adj* harmful, ruinous

**anedifeiriol** *adj* impenitent

**aneddfa** see **anheddfa**

**aneffeithiol** *adj* ineffectual

**aneglur** *adj* indistinct; illegible

**aneirif** *adj* innumerable

**anelu** *vb* bend, aim

**anenwog** *adj* unrenowned, ignoble, mean

**anerchiad** (**-au**) *nm* salutation, address

**anesboniadwy** *adj* inexplicable

**anesgusodol** *adj* inexcusable

**anesmwyth** *adj* uneasy, restless

**anesmwythder, -dra** *nm* uneasiness, unrest

**anesmwytho** *vb* be or make uneasy

**anesmwythyd** *nm* uneasiness, disquiet

**anewyllysgar** *adj* unwilling

**anfad** *adj* wicked, nefarious

**anfadrwydd** *nm* wickedness, villainy

**anfadwaith** *nm* villainy; crime

**anfadwr** (**-wyr**) *nm* villain, scoundrel

**anfaddeugar** *adj* unforgiving

**anfaddeuol** *adj* unpardonable

**anfantais** (**-teision**) *nf* disadvantage

**anfanteisiol** *adj* disadvantageous

**anfarwol** *adj* undying, immortal

**anfarwoldeb** *nm* immortality

**anfedrus** *adj* unskilful

**anfedrusrwydd** *nm* unskilfulness

**anfeidrol** *adj* infinite

**anfeidroldeb** *nm* infinity

**anferth** *adj* huge, monstrous

**anferthedd** *nm* hugeness, monstrosity

**anfodlon** *adj* unwilling

**anfodloni** *vb* discontent, dissatisfy

**anfodlonrwydd** *nm* discontent

**anfodd** *nm* unwillingness, displeasure

**anfoddio** *vb* displease, disoblige

**anfoddlon** *etc* see **anfodlon**

**anfoddog** *adj* discontented, dissatisfied

**anfoddogrwydd** *nm* discontentment

**anfoesgar** *adj* unmannerly, rude

**anfoesgarwch** *nm* rudeness, incivility

**anfoesol** *adj* immoral

**anfoesoldeb** *nm* immorality

**anfon** *vb* send, transmit, dispatch

**anfoneddigaidd** *adj* ungentlemanly

**anfonheddig** *adj* ignoble, discourteous

**anfoniad** *nm* sending, transmission

**anfri** *nm* disrespect, dishonour

**anfucheddol** *adj* immoral

**anfuddiol** *adj* unprofitable

**anfwriadol** *adj* unintentional

**anfwyn** *adj* unkind, ungentle, uncivil

**anfynych** *adj* infrequent, seldom, rare

**anffaeledig** *adj* infallible

**anffaeledigrwydd** *nm* infallibility

**anffafriol** *adj* unfavourable

**anffawd** (**-ffodion**) *nf* misfortune

**anffodus, anffortunus** *adj* unfortunate

**anffrwythlon** *adj* unfruitful, barren

**anffurfio** *vb* disfigure, deform

**anffurfiol** *adj* informal

**anffyddiaeth** *nf* atheism

**anffyddiwr** (**-wyr**) *nm* infidel, atheist

**anffyddlon** *adj* unfaithful

**anhaeddiannol** *adj* unmerited, undeserved

**anhaeddiant** *nm* demerit, unworthiness

**anhapus** *adj* unhappy, unlucky

**anhardd** *adj* unhandsome, unseemly, ugly

**anhawdd** *adj* hard, difficult

**anhawddgar** *adj* unamiable, unlovely

**anhawster** (**anawsterau**) *nm* difficulty

**anheddfa** (**aneddfaoedd**) *nf*, **-le** (**aneddleoedd**) *nm/f* dwelling-place

**anhepgor** (**-ion**) *nm* essential

**anhepgorol** *adj* indispensable

**anhoffter** *nm* hatred, dislike

**anhraethadwy** *adj* unutterable

**anhraethol** *adj* unspeakable, ineffable

**anhrefn** *nm* disorder, confusion

**anhrefnu** *vb* disorder, disarrange

**anhrefnus** *adj* disorderly, untidy

**anhreiddiol** *adj* impervious, impenetrable

**anhreuliedig** *adj* undigested; unspent

**anhrugarog** *adj* unmerciful, merciless

**anhuddo** *vb* cover (a fire)

**anhunedd** *nm* wakefulness, disquiet

**anhwyldeb** *nm* disorder, complaint, illness

**anhwylustod** *nm* inconvenience

**anhyblyg** *adj* inflexible, stiff, rigid

**anhydawdd** *adj* insoluble

**anhyder** *nm* distrust, diffidence

**anhyderus** *adj* diffident

**anhydrin** *adj* unmanageable

**anhydyn** *adj* intractable, obstinate

**anhyddysg** *adj* unversed, ignorant

**anhyfryd** *adj* unpleasant

**anhyfrydwch** *nm* unpleasantness

**anhygar** *adj* unpleasant, unamiable

**anhygoel** *adj* incredible

**anhygyrch** *adj* inaccessible

**anhylaw** *adj* unhandy, unwieldy

**anhynod** *adj* indistinctive; uncertain

**anhysbys** *adj* unknown; unversed

**anhywaith** *adj* intractable, refractory

**anial** *adj* desert, wild ♦ *nm* wilderness

**anialwch** *nm* wilderness

**anian** (**-au**) *nf* nature, instinct, genius

**anianawd** *nm* temperament, disposition

**anianol** *adj* natural

**anianyddol** *adj* physical

**anifail** (**-feiliaid**) *nm* animal, beast

**anifeilaidd** *adj* beastly, brutish

**anifeileiddio** *vb* animalize, brutalize

**anlwc** *nm* bad luck, misfortune

**anlwcus** *adj* unlucky

**anllad** *adj* wanton, lascivious, lewd

**anlladrwydd** *nm* wantonness, lewdness

**anlladu** *vb* wanton

**anllygredig** *adj* incorrupt, incorruptible

**anllygredigaeth** *nf* incorruption

**anllythrennog** *adj* illiterate

**anllywodraeth** *nf* misrule, anarchy

**annaearol** *adj* unearthly, weird

**annatodol** *adj* indissoluble, that cannot be undone

**annaturiol** *adj* unnatural

**annealladwy** *adj* unintelligible

**anneallus** *adj* unintelligent

**annedwydd** *adj* unhappy, miserable

**annedwyddwch** *nm* unhappiness

**annedd** (**anheddau**) *nf* dwelling

**anneddfol** *adj* lawless

**annefnyddiol** *adj* useless; immaterial

**annel** (**anelau**) *nm/f* trap; purpose, aim

**annelwig** *adj* shapeless, unformed; vague

**anner** (**aneirod, -i, -au**) *nf* heifer

**annerbyniol** *adj* unacceptable

**annerch** *vb* salute, greet, address ♦ (**anerchion**) *nm* salutation, greeting

**annewisol** *adj* ineligible, undesirable, unwelcome

**annhebyg** *adj* unlike, dissimilar

**annhebygol** *adj* unlikely, improbable

**annhebygolrwydd** *nm* improbability

**annhebygrwydd** *nm* unlikeness, unlikelihood

**annheg** *adj* unfair

**annhegwch** *nm* unfairness

**annheilwng** *adj* unworthy

**annheilyngdod** *nm* unworthiness

**annherfynol** *adj* endless; infinitive, infinite

**annhirion** *adj* ungentle, cruel

**annhosturiol** *adj* pitiless, ruthless

**annhuedd** *nf* disinclination

**annhueddol** *adj* disinclined, indisposed

**anniben** *adj* untidy, slovenly

**annibendod** *nm* untidiness

**annibyniaeth** *nf* independence

**annibynnol** *adj* independent

**Annibynnwr (-ynwyr)** *nm* Independent

**annichellgar** *adj* guileless, simple

**annichon, -adwy** *adj* impossible

**anniddan** *adj* comfortless, miserable

**anniddig** *adj* peevish, irritable, fretful

**anniddigrwydd** *nm* peevishness

**anniddos** *adj* leaky, comfortless

**annifeiriol** *adj* innumerable, countless

**anniflanedig** *adj* unfading, imperishable

**annifyr** *adj* miserable, wretched

**annifyrrwch** *nm* misery

**anniffoddadwy** *adj* unquenchable

**annigonedd** *nm* insufficiency

**annigonol** *adj* insufficient, inadequate

**annigonolrwydd** *nm* inadequacy

**annileadwy** *adj* indelible,

ineffaceable

**annilys** *adj* unauthentic, spurious, insincere

**annillyn** *adj* inelegant, clumsy

**annioddefol** *adj* unbearable, intolerable

**anniogel** *adj* unsafe, insecure

**anniolchgar** *adj* unthankful, ungrateful

**anniolchgarwch** *nm* ingratitude

**annirnadwy** *adj* incomprehensible

**annisgrifiadwy** *adj* indescribable

**annisgwyliadwy** *adj* unexpected

**anniwair** *adj* unchaste, incontinent, lewd

**anniwall** *adj* insatiable

**anniweirdeb** *nm* unchastity, incontinence

**anniwylliedig** *adj* uncultured

**annoeth** *adj* unwise, imprudent

**annoethineb** *nm* unwisdom, folly

**annog** *vb* incite, urge; exhort

**annormal** *adj* abnormal

**annos** *vb* incite, set (a dog) on

**annosbarthus** *adj* unruly, disorderly

**annuw, -iad (-iaid)** *nm* atheist

**annuwiaeth** *nf* atheism

**annuwiol** *adj* ungodly, godless

**annuwioldeb** *nm* ungodliness

**annwn, annwfn** *nm* the underworld; hell

**annwyd (anwydau, -on)** *nm* cold

**annwyl** *adj* dear, beloved

**annyledus** *adj* undue, wrongful

**annymunol** *adj* unpleasant, disagreeable

**annynol** *adj* inhuman, cruel

**annysgedig** *adj* unlearned

**anobaith** *nm* despair

**anobeithio** *vb* despair

**anobeithiol** *adj* hopeless

**anochel, -adwy** *adj* unavoidable, inevitable

**anodd** *adj* hard, difficult

**anoddefgar** *adj* impatient, intolerant

**anogaeth** (**-au**) *nf* exhortation
**anolrheinadwy** *adj* untraceable
**anolygus** *adj* unsightly
**anonest** *adj* dishonest
**anonestrwydd** *nm* dishonesty
**anorchfygol** *adj* irresistible; unconquerable
**anorfod** *adj* insuperable; unavoidable
**anorffen** *adj* endless, unending
**anorffenedig** *adj* incomplete, unfinished
**anorthrech** *adj* invincible
**anrasol** *adj* graceless
**anrhaith** (**-rheithiau**) *nf* prey, spoil, booty
**anrheg** (**-ion**) *nf* present, gift
**anrhegu** *vb* present, give
**anrheithio** *vb* prey, spoil, plunder
**anrheithiwr** (**-wyr**) *nm* spoiler, pillager
**anrhydedd** (**-au**) *nm* honour
**anrhydeddu** *vb* honour
**anrhydeddus** *adj* honourable
**anrhydeddwr** (**-wyr**) *nm* honourer
**ansad** *adj* unsteady, unstable
**ansadrwydd** *nm* instability
**ansafadwy** *adj* unstable; fickle
**ansathredig** *adj* untrodden, unfrequented
**ansawdd** (**-soddau**) *nm/f* quality, state
**ansefydlog** *adj* unsettled, unstable; fickle
**ansefydlogi** *vb* unsettle
**ansicr** *adj* uncertain, doubtful
**ansicrwydd** *nm* uncertainty, doubt
**ansoddair** (**-eiriau**) *nm* adjective
**ansoddeiriol** *adj* adjectival
**ansyber** *adj* untidy, slovenly
**Antartica** *nf* the Antarctic
**anterliwt** (**-iau**) *nm/f* interlude
**anterth** *nm* meridian, zenith, prime
**antur** (**-iau**) *nm* attempt, venture; adventure; enterprise. **ar a.** at random

**anturiaeth** (**-au**) *nf* adventure, enterprise
**anturiaethus** *adj* adventurous, enterprising
**anturiaethwr** (**-wyr**) *nm* adventurer
**anturio** *vb* venture, adventure
**anturus** *adj* adventurous
**anthem** (**-au**) *nf* anthem
**anudon** (**-au**) *nm* false oath, perjury
**anudoniaeth** *nf* perjury
**anudonwr** (**-wyr**) *nm* perjurer
**anufudd** *adj* disobedient
**anufudd-dod** *nm* disobedience
**anufuddhau** *vb* disobey
**anundeb** *nm* disunion
**anunion** *adj* crooked; unjust
**anuniondeb** *nm* injustice, iniquity
**anurddo** *vb* spoil, mar, disfigure
**anwadal** *adj* unstable, fickle, changeable
**anwadalu** *vb* waver, vacillate
**anwadalwch** *nm* fickleness
**anwar** *adj* wild, barbarous, savage
**anwaraidd** *adj* uncivilized, barbarous
**anwarddyn** (**-wariaid**) *nm* barbarian, savage
**anwareidd-dra** *nm* barbarity
**anwastad** *adj* uneven, unstable, fickle
**anwe** (**-oedd**) *nf* woof
**anwedd** *nm* vapour, steam
**anweddaidd** *adj* unseemly, indecent
**anweddus** *adj* improper, indecent
**anweledig** *adj* unseen, invisible
**anwes** *nm* indulgence; caress
**anwesog** *adj* pampered, affectionate
**anwesu** *vb* fondle, caress, pamper, indulge
**anwir** *adj* untrue, lying, false; wicked
**anwiredd** (**-au**) *nm* untruth; iniquity

**anwireddu** *vb* falsify
**anwireddus** *adj* untruthful, false, lying
**anwr** (**-wyr**) *nm* wretch, coward
**anwybod** *nm* ignorance
**anwybodaeth** *nf* ignorance
**anwybodus** *adj* ignorant
**anwybyddu** *vb* ignore
**anwydog** *adj* cold, chilly; having a cold
**anwydwst** *nf* influenza
**anwyldeb** *nm* belovedness, dearness
**anwyliaid** *npl* beloved ones, favourites
**anwylo** *vb* cherish, fondle, caress
**anwylyd** (**-liaid**) *nm* beloved
**anwylyn** *nm* favourite
**anwythiad** *nm* induction
**anwytho** *vb* induce
**anwythol** *adj* inductive
**anymarferol** *adj* impractical, impracticable
**anymddiried** *vb, nm* mistrust, distrust
**anymwybodol** *adj* unconscious
**anymwybyddiaeth** *nf* unconsciousness
**anynad** *adj* peevish, petulant; brawling
**anysgrifenedig** *adj* unwritten
**anysgrythurol** *adj* unscriptural
**anystwyth** *adj* stiff, rigid
**anystwytho** *vb* stiffen
**anystyriaeth** *nf* heedlessness, rashness
**anystyriol** *adj* heedless, reckless, rash
**anystywallt, -ell** *adj* unmanageable
**apêl** (**apelion**) *nm/f*, **apeliad** (**-au**) *nm* appeal
**apelio** *vb* appeal
**apostol** (**-ion**) *nm* apostle
**apostolaidd, -ig** *adj* apostolic
**apostoliaeth** *nf* apostleship
**apwyntiad** (**-au**) *nm* appointment

**apwyntio** *vb* appoint
**âr** *nm* ploughed land, tilth; ground
**ar** *prep* on, upon, over
**arab** *adj* facetious, merry, pleasant
**arabedd** *nm* facetiousness, wit
**arabus** *adj* witty
**aradr** (**erydr**) *nm* plough
**araf** *adj* slow, soft, gentle, still
**arafu** *vb* slow; quiet; moderate
**arafwch** *nm* slowness; moderation
**arail** *vb* guard, care for, foster ♦ *adj* attending, careful
**araith** (**areithiau**) *nf* speech
**arall** (**eraill**) *adj, pron* another, other; else
**aralleg** (**-au**) *nf/m* allegory
**aralleiriad** (**-au**) *nm* paraphrase
**aralleirio** *vb* paraphrase
**araul** *adj* sunny, sunlit; serene
**arawd** *nf* speech, oration
**arbed** *vb* spare, save
**arbediad** (**-au**) *nm* save, salvage
**arbedol** *adj* sparing, saving
**arbenigaeth** *nf* expertise; specialisation
**arbenigo** *vb* specialise
**arbenigrwydd** *nm* speciality, prominence
**arbenigwr** (**-wyr**) *nm* specialist
**arbennig** *adj* special
**arbrawf** (**arbrofion**) *nm* experiment
**arbrofi** *vb* experiment
**arbrofol** *adj* experimental
**arch** (**eirchion**) *nf* request, petition; bidding
**arch** (**eirch**) *nf* ark, coffin; trunk, waist
**archaeoleg** *nf* archaeology
**archangel** (**-ylion**) *nm* archangel
**archddiacon** (**-iaid**) *nm* archdeacon
**archeb** (**-ion**) *nf* order
**archebu** *vb* order
**archen** *nf*, **-ad** *nm* shoe; clothing
**archesgob** (**-ion**) *nm* archbishop
**archesgobaeth** (**-au**) *nf* archbishopric
**archfarchnad** (**-oedd**) *nf*

supermarket

**archiad** *nm* bidding

**archif** (**-au**) *nm* archive

**archifdy** (**-dai**) *nm* record office

**archifydd** (**-ion**) *nm* archivist

**archoffeiriad** (**-iaid**) *nm* high priest

**archoll** (**-ion**) *nf* wound

**archolli** *vb* wound

**archwaeth** *nm* taste, appetite

**archwaethu** *vb* taste, savour

**archwilio** *vb* examine, audit; explore

**archwiliwr** (**-wyr**) *nm* examiner, auditor; explorer

**ardal** (**-oedd**) *nf* region, district

**ardalydd** (**-ion**) *nm* marquis

**ardreth** (**-i**) *nf* rent

**ardrethu** *vb* rent

**ardystiad** (**-au**) *nm* pledge, attestation

**ardystio** *vb* pledge, attest

**arddangos** *vb* show, exhibit, indicate

**arddangosfa** (**-feydd**) *nf* show, exhibition

**arddegol** *adj* teenage

**arddel** *vb* avow, own

**arddeliad** *nm* claim, avowal; unction

**arddderchog** *adj* excellent, noble, splendid

**arddderchowgrwydd** *nm* excellency

**arddodi** *vb* prefix; impose

**arddodiad** (**-iaid**) *nm* preposition

**arddu** *vb* plough (*properly* **aredig**)

**arddull** (**-iau**) *nf* style

**arddulleg** *nf* stylistics

**ardduniant** *nm* sublimity

**arddunol** *adj* sublime

**arddwr** (**-wyr**) *nm* ploughman

**arddwrn** (**-ddyrnau**) *nm* wrist

**arddywediad** (**-au**) *nm* dictation

**aredig** *vb* plough

**areitheg** *nf* rhetoric

**areithio** *vb* speak, make a speech

**areithiwr** (**-wyr**) *nm* speaker,

orator

**areithyddiaeth** *nf* oratory; elocution

**arel** *nm* laurel

**aren** (**-nau**) *nf* kidney; (*pl.*) reins

**arestio** *vb* arrest

**arf** (**-au**) *nm/f* weapon, (*pl.*) arms; tool

**arfaeth** (**-au**) *nf* purpose; decree

**arfaethu** *vb* purpose, intend

**arfbais** (**-beisiau**) *nf* coat of arms

**arfdy** (**-dai**) *nm* armoury

**arfer** *vb* use, accustom ♦ (**-ion**) *nf/m* use, custom, habit

**arferiad** *nm/f* use, custom, habit

**arferol** *adj* usual, customary

**arfod** *nf* stroke of a weapon, fight; armour; opportunity

**arfog** *adj* armed

**arfogaeth** *nf* armour

**arfogi** *vb* arm

**arfoll** (**-au**) *nm* pledge, oath

**arfordir** (**-oedd**) *nm* coast

**arforol** *adj* maritime

**arffed** (**-au**) *nf* lap

**argae** (**-au**) *nm* dam, embankment; enclosed place

**argeisio** *vb* seek

**argel** *nm/f* concealment, refuge ♦ *adj* hidden, occult

**arglwydd** (**-i**) *nm* lord

**arglwyddaidd** *adj* lordly

**arglwyddes** (**-au**) *nf* lady

**arglwyddiaeth** (**-au**) *nf* lordship, dominion

**arglwyddiaethu** *vb* have dominion

**argoed** (**-ydd**) *nm* enclosure of trees

**argoel** (**-ion**) *nf* sign, token, omen

**argoeli** *vb* betoken, portend, augur

**argoelus** *adj* ominous

**argraff** (**-ion, -au**) *nf* print, impression

**argraffdy** (**-dai**) *nm* printing-house

**argraffiad** (**-au**) *nm* impression; edition

**argraffu** *vb* print, impress

**argraffwaith** *nm* print, typography
**argraffwasg** *nf* printing-press
**argraffwr** (**-wyr**), **-ydd** (**-ion**) *nm* printer
**argrwm, -wn** *adj* convex
**argyfwng** (**-yngau, -yngoedd**) *nm* crisis
**argyhoeddi** *vb* reprove; convince, convict
**argyhoeddiad** (**-au**) *nm* conviction
**argyhoeddiadol** *adj* convincing
**argymell** *vb* urge, recommend
**argymhelliad** *nm* recommendation
**arholi** *vb* examine
**arholiad** (**-au**) *nm* examination
**arholwr** (**-wyr**) *nm* examiner
**arhosfa** *nf* abode; stopping-place (*bus*)
**arhosiad** *nm* staying, stay
**arhosol** *adj* abiding, permanent
**arial** *nm/f* vigour, mettle
**arian** *nm* silver ◆ *coll n* money, cash. **a. breiniol** currency. **a. byw** mercury. **a. gleision** silver. **a. parod** cash. **a. pen** exact money. **a. treigl** current money
**ariandy** (**-dai**) *nm* bank
**ariangar** *adj* fond of money, avaricious
**ariangarwch** *nm* love of money, avarice
**ariannaid** *adj* silver, silvern
**ariannaidd** *adj* silvery
**arianneg** *nm/f* finance
**Ariannin** *nf* Argentina
**ariannog** *adj* moneyed, wealthy, rich
**ariannol** *adj* financial, monetary
**ariannu** *vb* silver; finance/fund
**ariannydd** (**arianyddion**) *nm* banker, investor, financier
**arlais** (**-leisiau**) *nf* temple
**arloesi** *vb* clear, prepare the way, pioneer
**arloesydd** (**-wyr**) *nm* pioneer
**arluniaeth** *nf* portraiture, painting
**arlunio** *vb* draw, paint, portray

**arlunydd** (**-wyr**) *nm* artist
**arlwy** (**-au, -on**) *nm/f* provision, feast, menu
**arlwyaeth** (**-au**) *nf* catering
**arlwyo** *vb* prepare, provide; cook
**arlywydd** (**-ion**) *nm* president
**arlywyddiaeth** *nf* presidency
**arlywyddol** *adj* presidential
**arlliw** (**-iau**) *nm* varnish, tint, shade, trace
**arlliwio** *vb* colour, tint, paint
**arllwys** *vb* pour out, empty
**arllwysfa** *nf* outfall, outlet, vent
**armel** *nm* second milk
**armes** *nf* prophecy; calamity
**arobryn** *adj* worthy, prize-winning
**arofun** *vb* intend, purpose
**arogl** (**-au**), **aroglau** (**-euon**) *nm* scent, smell
**arogl-darth** *nm* incense
**arogldarthu** *vb* burn incense
**arogli, arogleuo** *vb* scent; smell
**arogliad** *nm* smelling, sense of smell
**arolwg** *nm* survey
**arolygiaeth** *nf* superintendency
**arolygu** *vb* superintend
**arolygwr** (**-wyr**), **-ydd** (**-ion**) *nm* superintendent, inspector
**aros** *vb* wait, await, stay, stop, tarry, abide, remain
**arswyd** *nm* dread, terror, horror
**arswydo** *vb* dread; shudder
**arswydus** *adj* fearful, terrible, dreadful
**arsyllfa** (**-feydd**) *nf* observatory
**arsylwi** *vb* observe
**artaith** (**-teithiau**) *nf* torture, torment, pang
**arteithio** *vb* torture, rack
**arteithiol** *adj* racking, excruciating
**arth** (**eirth**) *nm/f* bear
**arthes** (**-au**) *nf* she-bear
**arthio, -u** *vb* bark, growl
**Artig:** **yr A.** *nf* the Arctic
**artistig** *adj* artistic
**aruchel** *adj* lofty, sublime

**arucheledd** *nm* loftiness, sublimity
**aruthr** *adj* marvellous, strange
**aruthredd** *nm* amazement, horror
**aruthrol** *adj* huge, prodigious
**arwahanrwydd** *nm* uniqueness, individuality
**arwain** *vb* conduct, lead, guide, carry
**arwedd** (**-au, -ion**) *nf* bearing, aspect
**arweddu** *vb* bear
**arweddwr** (**-wyr**) *nm* bearer
**arweiniad** *nm* guidance; introduction
**arweiniol** *adj* leading, introductory
**arweinydd** (**-ion**) *nm* guide, leader; conductor
**arweinyddiaeth** *nf* leadership
**arwerthiant** (**-iannau**) *nm* auction
**arwerthu** *vb* sell by auction
**arwerthwr** (**-wyr**) *nm* auctioneer
**arwisgiad** *nm* investiture
**arwisgo** *vb* enrobe, array, invest
**arwr** (**-wyr**) *nm* hero
**arwraidd** *adj* heroic, epic
**arwres** (**-au**) *nf* heroine
**arwrgerdd** (**-i**) *nf* epic poem
**arwriaeth** *nf* heroism
**arwrol** *adj* heroic, gallant
**arwybod** *nm* awareness
**arwydd** (**-ion**) *nm/f* sign, signal; ensign
**arwyddair** (**-eiriau**) *nm* motto
**arwyddlun** (**-iau**) *nm* emblem, symbol
**arwyddluniol** *adj* emblematic, symbolic
**arwyddnod** (**-au**) *nm* mark, token
**arwyddo** *vb* sign; signify
**arwyddocâd** *nm* signification, significance
**arwyddocaol** *adj* significant
**arwyddocáu** *vb* signify, denote
**arwyl** (**-ion**) *nf* funeral, funeral rites
**arwylo** *vb* mourn over the dead
**arwynebedd** *nm* surface, superficies
**arwynebol** *adj* superficial
**arwyrain** *nm/f* praise, panegyric ♦ *vb* rise, extol
**arwystlo** *vb* pledge, mortgage
**arysgrif** (**-au**), **-en** (**-nau**) *nf* inscription, epigraph
**asb** (**-iaid**) *nf* asp
**asbri** *nm* animation, vivacity, spirits
**asen** (**-nau**) *nf* rib
**asen** (**-nod**) *nf* she-ass
**asesu** *vb* assess
**aseth** *nf* stake, spar, lath
**asgell** (**esgyll**) *nf* wing, fin. **a. fraith** chaffinch
**asgellog** *adj* winged
**asgellwr** (**-wyr**) *nm* wing, outside-forward
**asglod, asglodion** *npl* (**asglodyn** *nm*) chips
**asgre** *nf* bosom, heart
**asgwrn** (**esgyrn**) *nm* bone
**asiad** (**-au**) *nm* joint, weld
**asiant** (**-au**) *nm* agent
**asio** *vb* join, weld; solder; cement
**astell** (**estyll, ystyllod**) *nf* plank, shelf
**astroleg** *nf* astrology
**astrus** *adj* abstruse, difficult
**astud** *adj* attentive
**astudiaeth** (**-au**) *nf* study
**astudio** *vb* study
**astudrwydd** *nm* attentiveness
**aswy** *adj* left
**asyn** (**-nod**) *nm* he-ass
**asynnaidd** *adj* asinine
**at** *prep* to, towards; for; at; by
**atafaeliad** *nm* confiscation, distraint
**atafaelu** *vb* distrain, confiscate
**atal** *vb* stop, hinder, withhold ♦ (**-ion**) *nm* hindrance, impediment. **a. dweud** stammering
**ataleb** (**-au**) *nf* injunction
**atalfa** (**-feydd**) *nf* check; stoppage
**ataliad** (**-au**) *nm* stoppage

**ataliol** *adj* preventive
**atalnod** (-au) *nf* stop, point
**atalnodi** *vb* point, punctuate
**atblygol** *adj* reflexive
**ateb** *vb* answer, reply ♦ (-ion) *nm* answer
**atebol** *adj* answerable, responsible
**ateg** (-ion) *nf* prop, stay, support
**ategiad** (-au) *nm* affirmation
**ategol** *adj* confirming; auxiliary
**ategu** *vb* support
**atgas** *adj* odious, hateful
**atgasedd** *nm* hatred
**atgasrwydd** *nm* odiousness, hatefulness
**atgenhedliad** *nm* regeneration
**atgenhedlu** *vb* regenerate
**atgno** (-oeau, -oeon) *nm* remorse
**atgof** (-ion) *nm* remembrance, reminiscence
**atgofio** *vb* recollect, remember, remind
**atgofus** *adj* reminiscent
**atgoffa** *vb* recall, remind
**atgyfnerthion** *npl* reinforcements
**atgyfnerthu** *vb* reinforce
**atgyfodi** *vb* rise, raise again
**atgyfodiad** *nm* resurrection
**atgynhyrchu** *vb* reproduce
**atgyweiriad** (-au) *nm* repair
**atgyweirio** *vb* repair, mend
**atgyweiriwr** (-wyr) *nm* repairer, mender
**Athen** *nf* Athens
**atig** (-au) *nm/f* attic
**atodi** *vb* add, append, affix
**atodiad** (-au) *nm* addition, appendix
**atodlen** (-ni) *nf* supplement; schedule
**atodol** *adj* supplementary
**atolwg, atolygu** *vb* pray, beseech
**atom** (-au) *nm/f* atom
**atomfa** (-feydd) *nf* nuclear power station
**atomig** *adj* atomic
**atsain** (-seiniau) *nf* echo

**atseinio** *vb* resound, echo
**atwf** (atyfion) *nm* second growth
**atyniad** (-au) *nm* attraction
**atyniadol** *adj* attractive
**atynnu** *vb* attract
**athletau** *npl* athletics
**athrawes** (-au) *nf* teacher, governess
**athrawiaeth** (-au) *nf* doctrine
**athrawiaethol** *adj* doctrinal
**athrist** *adj* very sad, pensive, sorrowful
**athro** (-athrawon) *nm* teacher, master
**athrod** (-ion) *nm* slander, libel
**athrodwr** (-wyr) *nm* slanderer, libeller
**athrofa** (-feydd) *nf* college, academy, institute
**athrofaol** *adj* academic
**athroniaeth** *nf* philosophy
**athronydd** (-ion, -wyr) *nm* philosopher
**athronyddol** *adj* philosophical
**athronyddu** *vb* philosophize
**athrylith** (-oedd) *nf* genius
**athrylithgar** *adj* of genius, talented
**athrywyn** *nm* mediation, intervention ♦ *vb* mediate, arbitrate
**aur** *nm* gold
**awch** *nm* edge; ardour, zest; relish, appetite
**awchlym** *adj* sharp, keen, acute
**awchlymu** *vb* sharpen, whet
**awchus** *adj* sharp, keen; eager; greedy
**awdl** (-au, odlau) *nf* ode
**awdur** (-on, -iaid) *nm* author
**awdurdod** (-au) *nm/f* authority
**awdurdodedig** *adj* authorised
**awdurdodi** *vb* authorize
**awdurdodol** *adj* authoritative
**awdures** (-au) *nf* authoress
**awduriaeth** *nf* authorship
**awel** (-on) *nf* breeze, wind
**awelog** *adj* breezy, windy

**awen** (-au) *nf* muse
**awen** (-au) *nf* rein
**awenydd** (-ion) *nm* poet
**awenyddiaeth** *nf* poetry, poesy
**awenyddol** *adj* poetical
**awenyddu** *vb* poetize
**awgrym** (-au, -iadau) *nm* hint, suggestion
**awgrymiadol** *adj* suggestive
**awgrymog** *adj* suggestive
**awgrymu** *vb* hint, suggest
**awr** (oriau) *nf* hour
**Awst** *nm* August
**Awstralia** *nf* Australia
**Awstria** *nf* Austria
**awtistig** *adj* autistic
**awydd** (-au) *nf* desire, eagerness
**awyddfryd** *nm* vehement desire, zeal
**awyddu** *vb* desire
**awyddus** *adj* desirous, eager, zealous
**awyr** *nf* air, sky
**awyrdrom** (-au) *nf* aerodrome
**awyren** (-nau, -ni) *nf* balloon, aeroplane
**awyrendy** (-dai) *nm* hangar
**awyrgylch** (-au, -oedd) *nm/f* atmosphere
**awyriad** *nm* ventilation
**awyrlong** (-au) *nf* airship
**awyro, -u** *vb* air, ventilate

# B

**baban** (-od) *adj* baby
**babanaidd** *adj* babyish
**babandod** *nm* babyhood, infancy
**babi** *nm/f* baby
**bacas** (bacs(i)au) *nf* footless stocking; hair on horse's fetlocks
**baco** *nm* tobacco
**bacwn** *nm* bacon
**bach** (-au) *nm* hook. **bachau petryal** square brackets
**bach** *adj* little, small

**bachell** (-au, -ion) *nf* nook, corner; snare
**bachgen** (bechgyn) *nm* boy
**bachgendod** *nm* boyhood
**bachgennaidd** *adj* boyish
**bachgennyn** (bechgynnos) *nm* little boy
**bachigyn** (bachigion) *nm* little bit, diminutive
**bachog** *adj* hooked
**bachu** *vb* hook, grapple
**bachwr** (-wyr) *nm* hooker (*rugby*)
**bad** (-au) *nm* boat. **b. achub** lifeboat
**badwr** (-wyr) *nm* boatman
**badd** (-au), **baddon** (-au) *nm* bath
**bae** (-au) *nm* bay
**baedd** (-od) *nm* boar
**baeddu** *vb* beat, buffet; soil
**baetio** *vb* bait, maltreat
**bag** (-iau) *nm* bag
**bagad** (-au) *nm* cluster; troop, multitude
**bagl** (-au) *nf* crook; crutch; leg
**baglor** (-ion) *nf* bachelor
**bagloriaeth** *nf* bachelorship
**baglu** *vb* entangle, ensnare, trip
**bai** (beiau) *nm* fault, vice; defect; blame
**baich** (beichiau) *nm* burden, load
**bais** *nm* bottom, ford; walking
**bala** *nm* efflux of river from lake
**balch** *adj* proud; glad
**balchder** *nm* pride
**balchdra** *nm* joy, gladness
**balchïo** *vb* pride
**baldordd** *nm* babble, balderdash
**baldorddi** *vb* babble
**bale** *nm* ballet
**baled** (-i) *nf* ballad
**baledwr** (-wyr) *nm* ballad-monger
**balm** *nm* balm
**balmaidd** *adj* balmy
**balog** (-au, -ion) *nf* fly, cod-piece; flap
**balleg** *nf* hamper, net, purse
**ballegrwyd** (-au) *nf* drag-net

**ban** (-nau) *nm/f* peak; horn; corner; stanza

**banadl** *npl* (-badlen *nf*) broom

**banc** (-iau) *nm* bank

**banc** (bencydd) *nm* bank, mound, hill

**bancaw** (-iau) *nm* band, tuft

**baner** (-au, -i) *nf* banner, flag

**banerog** *adj* with banners, bannered

**banerwr** (-wyr) *nm* standard-bearer; ensign

**banffagl** (-au) *nf* bonfire, blaze

**bangaw** *adj* eloquent, melodious, skilful

**bangor** (-au, bangyr) *nf/m* upper row of rods in wattle fence; monastery

**baniar** (-ieri) *nm/f* shout; banner

**banllawr** (-lloriau) *nm* platform

**banllef** (-au) *nf* loud shout

**bannod** (banodau) *nf* article

**bannog** *adj* elevated, conspicuous; horned

**bar** (-rau) *nm* bar

**bâr** *nm* fury, greed

**bara** *nm* bread

**barbaraidd** *adj* barbarous

**barbareidd-dra** *nm* barbarity

**barbareiddio** *vb* barbarize

**barbariad** (-iaid) *nm* barbarian

**barbariaeth** *nm* barbarism

**barbwr** (-wyr) *nm* barber

**barcer** (-iaid) *nm* tanner

**barclod** (-iau) *nm* apron

**barcud** (-iaid), **barcutan** (-od) *nm* kite

**bardd** (beirdd) *nm* bard, poet

**barddas** *nm/f* bardism

**barddol** *adj* bardic

**barddoni** *vb* compose poetry, poetize

**barddoniaeth** *nf* poetry, verse

**barddonol** *adj* poetic, poetical

**barf** (-au) *nf* beard, whiskers

**barfog** *adj* bearded

**bargeinio, bargenna** *vb* bargain

**bargen** (-einion) *nf* bargain

**bargod** (-ion) *nm* eaves

**bargyfreithiwr** (-wyr) *nm* barrister

**bariaeth** *nf/m* evil, grief, wrath; greed

**baril** (-au) *nf* barrel

**barilaid** (-eidiau) *nf* barrelful

**bario** *vb* bar, bolt

**barlad** *nm* drake

**barlys** *nm* barley

**barn** (-au) *nf* judgment; opinion; sentence

**barnais** *nf* varnish

**barnedigaeth** (-au) *nf* judgment

**barneisio** *vb* varnish

**barnol** *adj* judicial, condemnatory, annoying

**barnu** *vb* judge

**barnwr** (-wyr) *nm* judge

**baromedr** *nm* barometer

**barrug** *nm* hoar-frost

**barugo** *vb* cast hoar-frost

**barugog** *adj* white with hoar-frost

**barus** *adj* voracious, greedy

**barwn** (-iaid) *nm* baron

**barwnes** (-au) *nf* baroness

**barwniaeth** (-au) *nf* barony

**barwnig** (-iaid) *nm* baronet

**bas** *adj* shallow ♦ (bais, beis) *npl* shallows

**bas** *adj*, *nm* bass

**basged** (-i, -au) *nf* basket

**basgedaid** (-eidiau) *nf* basketful

**basgedwr** (-wyr) *nm* basket-maker

**basn** (-au, -ys) *nm* basin

**bastard** (-iaid) *nm* bastard

**bastardiaeth** *nf* bastardy

**batri** *nm* battery

**bath** (-au) *nm* kind, sort; stamp; coin

**bathdy** (-dai) *nm* mint

**bathodyn** (-odau) *nm* medal, badge

**bathol** *adj* coin, coined

**bathu** *vb* coin

**baw** *nm* dirt, mire, dung, filth

**bawaidd** *adj* dirty, vile; sordid,

mean
**bawd** (bodiau) *nf* thumb, toe
**bechan** *adj* f. of **bychan**
**bechgynnos** *npl* little boys,
youngsters
**bedw** *npl* (-en *nf*) birch
**bedydd** *nm* baptism
**bedyddfa** (-fâu, -feydd) *nf*
baptistry
**bedyddfaen** (-feini) *nm* font
**bedyddio** *vb* baptize
**bedyddiol** *adj* baptismal; baptized
**Bedyddiwr** (-wyr) *nm* Baptist
**bedd** (-au) *nm* grave, tomb,
sepulchre
**beddargraff** (-iadau) *nm* epitaph
**beddfaen** (-feini) *nm* tombstone
**beddgell** (-oedd) *nf* vault,
catacomb
**beddrod** (-au) *nm* tomb, sepulchre
**Beibl** (-au) *nm* Bible
**Beiblaidd** *adj* Biblical
**beichio** *vb* burden; low; sob
**beichiog** *adj* pregnant
**beichiogi** *vb* conceive
**beichus** *adj* burdensome,
oppressive
**beicio** *vb* cycle
**beiddgar** *adj* daring, audacious
**beiddgarwch** *nm* daring, audacity
**beiddio** *vb* dare, presume
**beili** (beiliaid) *nm* bailiff
**beio** *vb* blame, censure
**beirniad** (-iaid) *nm* adjudicator;
critic
**beirniadaeth** (-au) *nf* adjudication;
criticism
**beirniadol** *adj* critical
**beirniadu** *vb* adjudicate; criticize
**beisgawn** (-au) *nf* stack, heap of
corn sheaves
**beiston** *nf* sea-shore, beach; surf
**beius** *adj* faulty; blameworthy
**bellach** *adv* now, at length
**bendigaid, bendigedig** *adj*
blessed
**bendigedigrwydd** *nm* blessedness

**bendith** (-ion) *nf* blessing,
benediction
**bendithio** *vb* bless
**bendithiol** *adj* conferring blessings
**benthyca, -io** *vb* borrow, lend
**benthyciwr** (-wyr) *nm* borrower,
lender
**benthyg** *nm* loan
**benyw** *adj* female ♦ (-od) *nf*
female, woman
**benywaidd** *adj* feminine;
effeminate
**benywol** *adj* feminine, female
**ber** *adj* f. of **byr**
**bêr** (berau, -i) *nm* spear; roasting-
spit
**bera** *nf/m* rick; pyramid
**berdys** *npl* (-yn *nm*, -en *nf*)
shrimps
**berf** (-au) *nf* verb. **b. anghyflawn**
transitive verb. **b. gyflawn**
intransitive verb
**berfa** (-fâu, -feydd) *nf* barrow
**Berlin** *nf* Berlin
**berth** *adj* beautiful, valuable
**berthog** *adj* wealthy, fair
**berw** *nm, adj* boiling, seething,
ebullition
**berwedig** *adj* boiling
**berwedydd** (-ion) *nm* boiler
**berwedd-dy** (-dai) *nm* brewery
**berweddu** *vb* brew
**berwi** *vb* boil, seethe, effervesce
**berwr** *coll n* cress
**betgwn** *nm/f* bedgown
**betws** *nm* oratory, chapel; birch
grove
**beudy** (-dai) *nm* cow-house, byre
**beunoeth, beunos** *adv* nightly,
every night
**beunydd** *adv* daily, every day,
always
**beunyddiol** *adj* daily, quotidian
**bidog** (-au) *nf* dagger; bayonet
**bil** (-iau) *nm* bill
**bilidowcar** *nm* cormorant
**bilwg** (-ygau) *nm* billhook

**bing** (**-oedd**) *nm* alley, bin
**biocemeg** *nm/f* biochemistry
**bir** (**-oedd**) *nm* beer
**biswail** *nm* dung
**blaen** *adj* fore, foremost, first; front ♦ (**-au**, **-ion**) *nm* point, end, top, tip; front, van, priority, precedence; edge
**blaenasgellwr** (**-wyr**) *nm* wing-forward
**blaenbrawf** (**-brofion**) *nm* foretaste
**blaendal** *nm* prepayment, deposit
**blaendarddu** *vb* sprout
**blaenddalen** (**-nau**) *nf* title page
**blaenddodi** *vb* prefix
**blaenddodiad** (**-iaid**) *nm* prefix
**blaenffrwyth** *nm* first-fruits
**blaengar** *adj* prominent, progressive
**blaengroen** (**-grwyn**) *nm* foreskin
**blaenllaw** *adj* forward, prominent
**blaenllym** *adj* sharp, keen
**blaenllymu** *adj* sharpen, whet
**blaenor** (**-iaid**) *nm* leader; elder
**blaenori** *vb* lead, precede
**blaenoriaeth** *nf* preference; precedence
**blaenorol** *adj* previous, antecedent
**blaenu** *vb* point; outrun; precede
**blaenwr** (**-wyr**) *nm* leader; forward
**blagur** *coll n* sprouts, buds, shoots
**blaguro** *vb* sprout, bud; flourish
**blaguryn** *nm* sprout, bud, shoot
**blaidd** (**bleiddiaid**, **bleiddiau**) *nm* wolf
**blas** *nm* taste, savour, relish
**blasio**, **-u** *vb* taste
**blasus** *adj* tasty, savoury, delicious
**blawd** (**blodion**, **-iau**) *nm* flour, meal
**blêr** *adj* untidy, slovenly
**blerwm** *nm* blabberer; blab-blab
**blew** *npl* (**-yn** *nm*) hairs; hair; fur
**blewog** *adj* hairy, shaggy
**bliant** *nm* lawn, fine linen
**blif** (**-iau**) *nm* catapult

**blingo** *vb* skin, flay
**blin** *adj* tired, weary; peevish, irritable
**blinder** (**-au**) *nm* weariness; trouble
**blinderog**, **-derus** *adj* wearisome
**blinfyd** *nm* tribulation
**blino** *vb* tire, weary; trouble, vex
**blith** (**-ion**) *nm* milk ♦ *adj* milch
**blith draphlith** *adv* helter-skelter
**blodeugerdd** (**-i**) *nf* anthology
**blodeuglwm** *nm* bunch, nosegay
**blodeuo** *vb* flower, bloom, flourish
**blodeuog** *adj* flowery; flourishing
**blodeuyn**, **blodyn** (**blodau**) *nm* flower
**blodiog** *adj* floury, mealy
**bloddest** *nf* rejoicing, acclamation
**bloedd** (**-iau**, **-iadau**) *nf* shout
**bloeddio**, **-ian** *vb* shout, cry
**bloeddiwr** (**-wyr**) *nm* shouter
**bloesg** *adj* lisping, faltering, indistinct
**bloesgi** *vb* lisp, falter, speak indistinctly
**bloneg** *nm*, **-en** *nf* lard, grease
**blwch** (**blychau**) *nm* box
**blwng** *adj* angry, sullen, cheerless ♦ *nm* anger
**blwydd** (**-au**, **-i**) *nf*, *adj* year of age; year-old
**blwydd-dal** *nm* annuity, pension
**blwyddiad** (**-iaid**) *nm* yearling, annual
**blwyddiadur** (**-on**) *nm* yearbook, annual
**blwyddyn** (**blynyddoedd**) *nf* year
**blychaid** (**-eidiau**) *nm* boxful
**blynedd** *nplf* years (*after numerals*)
**blynyddol** *adj* annual, yearly
**blys** (**-iau**) *nm* craving, lust
**blysig** *adj* greedy, lustful
**blysigrwydd** *nm* greediness
**blysio** *vb* crave, lust
**bocs** (**-ys**) *nm* box
**bocsach** *nm* vaunt, boast, brag
**boch** (**-au**) *nf* check

**bochgoch** *adj* rosy-cheeked
**bod** *vb* be, exist ♦ (**-au**) *nm* being, existence. **Y Bod Mawr** *nm* God
**boda** *nm/f* buzzard
**bodio** *vb* thumb, finger
**bodlon** *adj* content, willing
**bodloni** *vb* satisfy, content; be content
**bodlonrwydd** *nm* contentment
**bodolaeth** *nf* existence
**bodoli** *vb* exist
**bodd** *nm* pleasure, will, consent
**boddfa** *nf* flood, drenching
**boddhad** *nm* pleasure, satisfaction
**boddhaol** *adj* pleasing, satisfactory
**boddhau** *vb* please, satisfy
**boddhaus** *adj* pleased
**boddi** *vb* drown; flood
**boddio** *vb* please, satisfy
**boddlon** *etc* see **bodlon**
**bogail** (**-eiliau**) *nm/f* navel; boss, hub
**boglwm** (**-lymau**), **-lyn** (**-lynnau**) *nm* boss, knob, stud, bud, bubble
**bol, bola** (**boliau**) *nm* belly
**bolaid** (**-eidiau**) *nm* bellyful
**bolera** *vb* gorge, guzzle; sponge (*fig*)
**bolerwr** (**-wyr**) *nm* sponge, parasite
**bolgi** (**-gwn**) *nm* gourmand, glutton
**bolgno** *nm*, **-fa** *nf* gripes, colic
**bolheulo** *vb* bask in the sun
**bolio** *vb* belly, gorge
**boliog** *adj* big-bellied, corpulent
**boloch** *nm* pain, anxiety, destruction
**bolrwth** *adj* gluttonous, greedy
**bolrwym** *adj* costive, constipated
**bollt** (**-au, -ydd, byllt**) *nf* bolt
**bolwst** *nf/m* gripes, colic
**bol(y)sothach** *nm* hotchpotch; jargon
**bom** (**-iau**) *nm/f* bomb
**bomio** *vb* bomb
**bôn** (**bonau, bonion**) *nm* bottom; stump

**boncath** (**-od**) *nm* buzzard
**bonclust** (**-iau**) *nm* box on the ear
**boncyff** (**-ion**) *nm* stump, trunk, stock
**bondigrybwyll** *adv* forsooth ♦ *adj* hardly mentionable
**bondo** *nm* eaves
**bonedd** *nm* gentility, nobility
**boneddigaidd** *adj* noble; gentlemanly
**boneddigeiddrwydd** *nm* gentlemanliness
**boneddiges** (**-au**) *nf* lady
**bonesig** *nf* lady; Miss
**bonet** (**-i**) *nf* bonnet
**bongam** *adj* bandy-legged
**bonheddig** *adj* noble, gentle, gentlemanly ♦ (**boneddigion**) *nmpl* gentlemen
**bonheddwr** (**-wyr**) *nm* gentleman
**bonllef** (**-au**) *nf* shout
**bonllwm** *adj* bare-bottomed, breechless; bare-backed
**Bonn** *nf* Bonn
**bonyn** (**bonion**) *nm* stump
**bord** (**-ydd, -au**) *nf* table, board
**bore** (**-au**) *nm* morning ♦ *adj* early
**boreddydd** *nm* day-break, morning
**borefwyd** *nm* breakfast
**boreol** *adj* morning
**bors** *nf* hernia
**bos** *nf* palm of the hand, fist
**bost** (**-iau**) *nm* boast, brag
**bostio** *vb* boast, brag
**botas, en** (**-asau**) *nf* boot
**botwm** (**-ymau**) *nm* button
**botymog** *adj* buttoned
**botymu** *vb* button
**both** (**-au**) *nf* nave of wheel; boss
**brac** *adj* free, frank, talkative
**bracso** *vb* wade, paddle
**bracty** (**-tai**) *nm* malt-house, brewery
**brad** (**-au**) *nm* treason; plot
**bradfwriadu** *vb* plot, conspire
**bradlofrudd** (**-ion**) *nm* assassin

**bradlofruddiaeth** (**-au**) *nf*
assassination

**bradlofruddio** *vb* assassinate

**bradwr** (**-wyr**) *nm* traitor

**bradwriaeth** (**-au**) *nf* treason,
treachery

**bradwrus** *adj* traitorous,
treacherous

**bradychu** *vb* betray

**braen** *adj* rotten, corrupt

**braenar** (**-au**) *nm* fallow

**braenaru** *vb* fallow, pioneer

**braenu** *vb* rot, putrify

**braf** *adj* fine

**brag** *nm* malt

**bragad** *nf* army, battle; offspring

**bragaldian** *vb* jabber, gabble,
prate

**bragio** *vb* brag, boast

**bragiwr** (**-wyr**) *nm* bragger,
boaster

**bragod** (**-au**, **-ydd**) *nm* bragget

**bragu** *vb* malt, brew

**bragwair** *nm* moorland hay, coarse
grass

**bragwr** (**-wyr**) *nm* maltster,
brewer

**braich** (**breichiau**) *nf* arm; branch,
handle; headland

**braidd** *adv* rather, somewhat

**braint** (**breintiau**) *nf* privilege

**braisg** *adj* gross, thick, large;
pregnant

**braith** *adj* f. of **brith**

**brân** (**brain**) *nf* crow, rook, raven

**bras** (**breision**) *adj* fat; coarse;
rich; luxuriant

**brasáu** *vb* grow fat or gross

**brasbwytho** *vb* baste, tack

**brasgamu** *vb* stride

**Brasil** *nf* Brazil

**braslun** (**-iau**) *nm* sketch, outline

**braslunio** *vb* sketch, outline

**brasnaddu** *vb* rough-hew

**braster** *nm* fat

**brasterog** *adj* fat, greasy

**brat** (**-iau**) *nm* rag, clout; pinafore

**bratiaith** *nf* debased language

**bratiog** *adj* ragged, tattered

**brath** (**-au**) *nm* stab, wound; sting;
bite

**brathog** *adj* that bites; biting

**brathu** *vb* stab, wound; sting; bite

**brau** *adj* brittle, frail, fragile;
kindly; prompt

**braw** (**-iau**) *nm* terror, dread,
fright

**brawd** (**brodyr**) *nm* brother; friar

**brawd** (**brodiau**) *nf* judgment

**brawdgarwch** *nm* brotherly love

**brawdle** (**-oedd**) *nf/m* judgement-
seat

**brawdlys** (**-oedd**) *nf/m* assize-court

**brawdmaeth** *nm* foster-brother

**brawdol** *adj* brotherly, fraternal

**brawdoliaeth** (**-au**) *nf*
brotherhood, fraternity

**brawddeg** (**-au**) *nf* sentence

**brawddegu** *vb* construct sentences

**brawl** *nm* boast, brag; gabble,
tattle

**brawychu** *vb* frighten, terrify

**brawychus** *adj* frightful, terrible

**bre** (**-on**, **-oedd**) *nf* hill, highland

**brebwl** (**-yliaid**) *nm* blockhead;
prattler

**breci** *nm* wort; spree

**brecwast** (**-au**) *nm/f* breakfast

**brecwasta** *vb* breakfast

**brech** *nf* eruption, pox

**brech** *adj* f. of **brych**

**brechdan** (**-au**) *nf* slice of bread
and butter

**brechiad** (**-au**) *nm* inoculation,
vaccination

**brechu** *vb* vaccinate, inoculate

**bredych** (**-au**, **-ion**) *nm* betrayal;
fear; rascal

**bref** (**-iadau**) *nf* lowing; bleat; bray

**breferad** (**-au**) *nm* bellowing

**brefiad** (**-au**) *nm* lowing; bleating

**brefu** *vb* low; bleat; bray

**breg** *nm* guile, blemish, breach ♦
*adj* fragile, faulty

**bregliach** *vb* jabber
**bregus** *adj* frail, brittle, rickety
**breichled** (**-au**) *nf* bracelet
**breichrwy(f)** (**-au**) *nm/f* bracelet
**breinio** *vb* privilege, enfranchise
**breiniol** *adj* privileged, free
**breinlen** (**-ni**) *nf* charter
**breintal** *nm* bonus; royalty
**breintiedig** *adj* patented, patent
**breintio** *vb* privilege, favour
**brenhinaidd** *adj* kingly, regal
**brenhindod** *nm* royalty
**brenhindref** (**-i**) *nf* royal city
**brenhindy** (**-dai**) *nm* royal palace
**brenhines** (**breninesau**) *nf* queen
**brenhinfainc** *nf* throne
**brenhiniaeth** (**breniniaethau**) *nf* kingdom
**brenhinol** *adj* royal, regal
**brenin** (**-hinoedd**) *nm* king
**brest** (**-iau**) *nf* breast, chest
**bresych** *npl* (**-en** *nf*) cabbages
**brethyn** (**-nau**) *nm* cloth
**brethynnwr** (**-ynwyr**) *nm* clothier; cloth-worker
**breuan** (**-au**) *nf* quern; print of butter
**breuder** *nm* brittleness, frailty
**breuddwyd** (**-ion**) *nm/f* dream. **b. gwrach** wishful thinking
**breuddwydio** *vb* dream
**breuddwydiol** *adj* dreaming, dreamy
**breuddwydiwr** (**-wyr**) *nm* dreamer
**brëyr, brehyr** (**brehyrion, -iaid**) *nm* nobleman, chief, baron
**bri** *nm* honour, renown, distinction
**briallu** *npl* (**briallen** *nf*) primroses
**bribys** *npl* fragments, scraps
**brifo** *vb* hurt
**brig** (**-au**) *nm* top; (*pl*) twigs
**brigâd** (**-au**) *nf* brigade. **b. dân** fire-brigade
**briger** (**-au**) *nm* hair of head; top
**brigo** *vb* top; branch
**brigog** *adj* branching; flourishing
**brigwyn** *adj* white-topped, white-crested
**brigyn** (**brigau**) *nm* twig
**brith** *adj* mottled, speckled; *f* **braith**
**britho** *vb* mottle, speckle; dazzle
**Brithwr** (**-wyr**) *nm* Pict
**brithyll** (**-od, -iaid**) *nm* trout
**briw** *adj* broken, bruised, sore ♦ (**-iau**) *nm* wound, sore
**briwfwyd** *nm* crumbs, mince
**briwlaw** *nm* drizzling rain
**briwlio** *vb* broil
**briwo** *vb* wound, hurt
**briwsion** *npl* (**-yn** *nm*) crumbs, fragments.
**briwsioni** *vb* crumble
**briwsyn** (**briwsion**) *nm* crumb, morsel
**bro** (**-ydd**) *nf* land; region; vale
**broch** *nm* badger
**broch** *nm* froth, anger, tumult
**brochi** *vb* chafe, fume; bluster
**brochus** *adj* fuming; blustering
**brodio** *vb* embroider; darn
**brodor** (**-ion**) *nm* native; fellow countryman
**brodorol** *adj* native, indigenous
**broga** (**-od**) *nm* frog
**brol** *nf* boast, brag
**brolio** *vb* boast, brag, vaunt
**broliwr** (**-wyr**) *nm* boaster, braggart
**bron** (**-nau, -nydd**) *nf* breast; hillside
**bron** *adv* almost, nearly. **o'r b.** completely, in succession
**bronfraith** (**-freithod**) *nf* thrush
**brongoch** (**-iaid**) *nf/m* robin redbreast
**bronwen** *nf* weasel
**bru** *nm* womb
**brud** (**-iau**) *nm* chronicle; divination
**brudio** *vb* prognosticate, divine
**brudiwr** (**-wyr**) *nm* wizard, soothsayer
**brwd** *adj* hot, fervent ♦ *nm* boil,

heat
**brwdfrydedd** *nm* ardour,
enthusiasm
**brwdfrydig** *adj* ardent,
enthusiastic
**brwmstan** *nm* brimstone, sulphur
**brwmstanaidd** *adj* brimstony,
sulphury
**brwnt** *adj* foul, nasty, dirty;
harsh; *f* **bront**
**brwyd** (**-au**) *nm* embroidering
frame; skewer
**brwyd** *adj* variegated;
bloodstained; shattered
**brwydo** *vb* embroider; tear,
consume
**brwydr** (**-au**) *nf* battle, combat
**brwydro** *vb* battle, combat
**brwydrwr** (**-wyr**) *nm* fighter,
combatant
**brwydwaith** *nm* embroidery
**brwylio** *vb* broil
**brwyn** *nm* grief, sadness
**brwynen** (**brwyn**) *nf* rush
**brwynog** *adj* rushy
**brwysg** *adj* drunk; vigorous
**brycan, brecan** (**-au**) *nf/m* blanket,
rug
**brych** *adj* mottled, brindled,
freckled; *f* **brech** ♦ *nm* the after-
birth of a cow
**brychau** *npl* (**-euyn** *nm*) spots,
freckles
**brycheulyd** *adj* spotted, brindled
**brychni** *nm* spots, freckles
**brychu** *vb* spot, freckle
**bryd** *nm* mind, heart, will
**brydio** *vb* burn, inflame, boil, throb
**brygawthan** *vb* jabber, prate, rant
**bryn** (**-iau**) *nm* hill
**bryncyn** (**-nau**) *nm* hillock
**bryniog** *adj* hilly
**brynti, bryntni** *nm* filthiness, filth
**brys** *nm* haste, hurry
**brysio** *vb* hasten, hurry
**brysiog** *adj* hurried, hasty
**bryslythyr** (**-au**) *nm* dispatch

**brysneges** (**-au**) *nf* telegram
**brytheirio** *vb* belch; utter oaths,
threats *etc*
**Brython** (**-iaid**) *nm* Briton,
Welshman
**Brythoneg** *nf* British language,
Welsh
**brythwch** *nm* storm, tumult;
groan
**bryweddu** *vb* brew
**brywes** *nm* brewis
**bual** (**buail**) *nm* buffalo, drinking
horn
**buan** *adj* fast, quick, swift, fleet;
soon
**buander, -dra** *nm* swiftness, speed
**buandroed** *adj* swift-footed
**buarth** (**-au**) *nm* yard
**buchdraeth** (**-au**) *nf* biography,
memoir
**buchedd** (**-au**) *nf* life, conduct
**bucheddol** *adj* right-living,
virtuous
**bucheddu** *vb* live, flourish
**buches** (**-au**) *nf* herd of cows
**buchfrechu** *vb* vaccinate
**budr** *adj* dirty, filthy, foul, vile
**budreddi** *nm* filthiness, filth
**budro** *vb* dirty, soil, foul
**budd** (**-ion**) *nm* benefit, profit, gain
**buddai** (**-eiau**) *nf* churn
**buddel** (**-wydd**) *nm/f* cow-house
post, pillar
**buddiant** (**-iannau**) *nm* interest
**buddio** *vb* profit, avail
**buddiol** *adj* profitable, beneficial,
useful
**buddioldeb** *nm* profitableness,
expediency
**buddsodd** (**-ion**), **-iad** (**-au**) *nm*
investment
**buddsoddi** *vb* invest
**buddugol** *adj* winning, victorious
**buddugoliaeth** (**-au**) *nf* victory
**buddugoliaethus** *adj* victorious,
triumphant
**buddugwr** (**-wyr**) *nm* winner,

victor
**bugail** (-eiliaid) *nm* shepherd; pastor
**bugeiles** (-au) *nf* shepherdess
**bugeiliaeth** (-au) *nf* pastorate
**bugeilio, -a** *vb* watch, shepherd
**bugeiliol** *adj* pastoral
**bugunad** *nm* bellowing, roar
**bun** *nf* maid, maiden
**burgyn** (-nod, iaid) *nm* carcass, carrion
**burman, burum** *nm* barm, yeast
**busnes** (-ion) *nm/f* business
**busnesa** *vb* interfere, meddle
**busnesgar, busneslyd** *adj* meddlesome
**bustach** (-tych) *nm* bullock, steer
**bustachu** *vb* buffet about, bungle
**bustl** *nm* gall, bile
**bustlaidd** *adj* like gall; bitter as gall
**buwch** (buchod) *nf* cow. **b. goch gota** ladybird
**bwa** (bwâu) *nm* bow; arch
**bwaog** *adj* arched, vaulted
**bwbach** (-od) *nm* bugbear, bogey, scarecrow
**bwced** (-i) *nm/f* bucket
**bwci** (-ïod) *nm* bugbear, bogey, ghost
**bwcl** (byclau) *nm* buckle
**bwcled** (-au) *nf* buckler
**bwch** (bychod) *nm* buck. **b. dihangol** scapegoat. **b. gafr** he-goat
**bwgan** (-od) *nm* bogey, ghost, scarecrow
**bwgwl** (bygylau) *nm* threat, menace
**bwgwth** see bygwth, bygythio
**bwhwman** *vb* beat about; vacillate
**bŵl** (bylau) *nm* globe, ball, knob
**bwlch** (bylchau) *nm* gap; pass; notch
**bwled** (-i) *nf* bullet
**bwn** (bynnoedd, byniaid) *nm*

bittern
**bwndel** (-i) *nm* bundle
**bwngler** (-iaid) *nm* bungler
**bwnglera** *vb* bungle
**bwngleraidd** *adj* bungling, clumsy
**bwnglerwaith** *nm* bungle, botch
**bwnglerwch** *nm* clumsiness
**bwr** (byr) *adj* fat, big, strong
**bwrdais** (-deisiaid) *nm* burgess
**bwrdeistref** (-i) *nm* borough
**bwrdd** (byrddau) *nm* table; deck; board. **b. du** black-board
**bwriad** (-au) *nm* purpose, intention
**bwriadol** *adj* intentional
**bwriadu** *vb* purpose, intend
**bwrlwm** (byrlymau) *nm* bubble; gurgling
**bwrn** (byrnau) *nm* burden, incubus; bale
**bwrw** *vb* cast, shed; strike; imagine, suppose; spend ♦ *nm* cast, throw; woof
**bwtler** (-iaid) *nm* butler
**bwtri** *nm* buttery, pantry, dairy
**bwth** (bythod) *nm* hut, booth, cot
**bwthyn** (bythynnod) *nm* cottage, cabin, hut
**bwyall, -ell** (-eill, -yll) *nf* axe
**bwyd** (-ydd) *nm* food
**bwyda, bwydo** *vb* feed
**bwyd-offrwm** (-ymau) *nm* meat-offering
**bwydwr** (-wyr) *nm* feeder
**bwygilydd** *adv* (from one) to the other
**bwylltid** (-au) *nm* swivel
**bwyllwr(w)** (-yriau) *nm* provisions for journey
**bwysel** (-au, -i) *nm* bushel
**bwystfil** (-od) *nm* (wild) beast
**bwystfilaidd** *adj* beastly, brutish
**bwystfiles** (-au) *nf* beast
**bwyta** *vb* eat; corrode
**bwytadwy** *adj* eatable, edible
**bwytawr** (-wyr) *nm* eater
**bwyteig** *adj* greedy, voracious
**bwyty** (-tai, -tyau) *nm* restaurant

**bychan** adj little, small; f **bechan**
**bychander, -dra** nm littleness, smallness
**bychanu** vb belittle, minimize
**bychanus** adj derogatory
**byd (-oedd)** nm world; state; life
**bydaf (-au)** nm/f beehive
**bydio** vb live, fare
**bydol** adj worldly, secular
**bydolddyn (-ion)** nm worldling
**bydolrwydd** nm worldliness
**bydwraig (-wragedd)** nf midwife
**bydwreigiaeth** nf midwifery
**bydysawd** nm universe
**byddag (-au)** nf running knot, noose
**byddar** adj deaf ♦ **(-iaid, byddair)** nm deaf person
**byddardod** nm deafness
**byddarol** adj deafening
**byddaru** vb deafen, stun
**byddin (-oedd)** nf army, host
**byddino** vb set army in array, embattle
**byddinog** adj with armies
**bygwth** vb threaten, menace ♦ **(-ythion, -ythiau)** nm threat, menace
**bygythiad (-au)** nm threat
**bygythio** vb threaten, menace
**bygythiol** adj threatening, menacing
**byl (-au)** nm/f edge, brim (of vessel). **hyd y f.** to the brim
**bylb (-au)** nm bulb
**bylchog** adj gapped, gappy; notched
**bylchu** vb make a gap, breach; notch
**byngalo (-s, -au)** nm bungalow
**bynnag** pron -ever, -soever
**byr** adj short, brief; f **ber**
**byrbryd (-iau)** nm luncheon, snack
**byrbwyll** adj impulsive, rash
**byrbwylltra** nm impulsiveness
**byrder, -dra** nm shortness, brevity
**byrdwn** nm burden, refrain, chorus

**byrddaid (-eidiau)** nm tableful
**byrddio** vb board
**byrddiwr (-wyr)** nm boarder
**byrfyfyr** adj impromptu
**byrgorn** adj shorthorn
**byrhau** vb shorten, abridge
**byrhoedlog** adj short-lived
**byrlymu** vb bubble, gurgle
**byrllysg (-au)** nm/f mace
**byrnio (-u)** vb bale, bundle
**byrnwr (-wyr)** nm baler
**bys (-edd)** nm finger; toe; hand of dial, latch
**bysaid (-eidiau)** nm pinch
**byseddu** vb finger
**bysled(r) (-au)** nm finger-stall
**byth** adv ever, for ever ♦ nm eternity
**bytheiad (-aid)** nm hound
**bytheirio** vb belch, threaten
**bythfywiol** adj everliving
**bythgofiadwy** adj memorable
**bythol** adj everlasting, eternal, perpetual
**bytholi** vb perpetuate
**bytholwyrdd (-ion)** adj, nm evergreen
**bythynnwr (-ynwyr)** nm cottager
**byw** vb live ♦ adj alive, living, quick ♦ nm life
**bywgraffiad (-au)** nm biography
**bywgraffiadol** adj biographical
**bywgraffiadur (-on)** nm biographical dictionary
**bywgraffydd (-ion)** nm biographer
**bywgraffyddol** adj biographical
**bywhau, bywiocáu** vb animate, vivify, quicken
**byw(i)ad** nm soft part of bread
**bywiog** adj lively, animated, vivacious
**bywiogi** vb enliven, animate
**bywiol** adj living, animate
**bywoliaeth (-iolaethau)** nf living
**bywyd (-au)** nm life
**bywydeg** nf biology

**bywydegwr** (**-wyr**) *nm* biologist
**bywydfad** (**-au**) *nm* lifeboat
**bywydol** *adj* of life, vital
**bywyn** (**-nau**) *nm* pith, core

# C

**cabaets** *npl* (**cabaetsen** *nf*) cabbage
**caban** (**-au**) *nm* cabin
**cabidwl** *nm* consistory, chapter
**cabl** (**-au**) *nm* blasphemy, reviling
**cabledd** (**-au**) *nm* blasphemy
**cableddus** *adj* blasphemous
**cablu** *vb* blaspheme, revile
**cablwr** (**-wyr**), **-ydd** (**-ion**) *nm* blasphemer
**caboli** *vb* polish
**cacamwci** *nm* burdock
**cacen** (**-nau, -ni**) *nf* cake
**cacwn** *npl* (**cacynen** *nf*) wasps; wild bees
**cachfa** (**-feydd**) *nf* excretion; closet
**cachgi** (**-gwn**) *nm* coward; sneak
**cachiad** *nm* excretion, jiffy; coward
**cachlyd** *adj* befouled, dirty
**cachu** *vb* defecate
**cachwr** (**-wyr**) *nm* coward; sneak; one who excretes
**cad** (**-au, -oedd**) *nf* battle; army, host
**cadach** (**-au**) *nm* cloth, kerchief, clout
**cadair** (**-eiriau**) *nf* chair, seat; cradle; udder
**cadarn** (**cedyrn**) *adj* strong, mighty; firm
**cadarnhad** *nm* affirmation, confirmation
**cadarnhaol** *adj* affirmative
**cadarnhau** *vb* strengthen, confirm
**cadeirfardd** (**-feirdd**) *nm* chaired bard
**cadeirio** *vb* chair
**cadeiriog** *adj* chaired
**cadeiriol** *adj* pertaining to a chair, cathedral

**cadeirydd** (**-ion**) *nm* chairman
**cadernid** *nm* strength; stability
**cadfarch** (**-feirch**) *nm* war-horse
**cadfridog** (**-ion**) *nm* general
**cadfwyall** (**-eill, -yll**) *nf* battleaxe
**cadlas** (**-lesydd**) *nf* close, enclosure
**cadlong** (**-au**) *nf* warship, battleship
**cadlys** (**-oedd**) *nf* camp, headquarters
**cadno** (**cadnoid, cadnawon**) *nm* fox
**cadnöes, cadnawes** (**-au**) *nf* vixen
**cadoediad** (**-au**) *nm* armistice, truce
**cadofydd** (**-ion**) *nm* tactician, strategist
**cadofyddiaeth** *nf* tactics, strategy
**cadofyddol** *adj* tactical, strategic
**cadw** *vb* keep, preserve, save; hold
**cadwedig** *adj* saved
**cadwedigaeth** *nf* salvation
**cadw-mi-gei** *nm* money-box
**cadwraeth** *nf* keeping; observance; conservation
**cadwyn** (**-au, -i**) *nf* chain
**cadwyno** *vb* chain
**cadwynog** *adj* chained, in chains
**caddug** *nm* darkness; mist, fog
**caddugo** *vb* darken, obscure
**cae** (**-au**) *nm* field; fence, hedge; brooch
**caead** (**-au**) *nm* cover, lid ♦ *adj* shut, closed
**caeadle** (**-oedd**) *nm* enclosure
**caeëdig** *adj* closed, fenced
**cael** *vb* have; get; find
**caen** (**-au**) *nf* surface; peel; coating
**caenen** (**-nau**) *nf* layer, film, flake
**caentach** (**-au**) *nf* wrangle, grumbling ♦ *vb* wrangle, grumble
**caenu** *vb* coat, finish
**caer** (**-au, ceyrydd**) *nf* wall; castle; city
**Caerdydd** *nf* Cardiff

**Caeredin** *nf* Edinburgh
**caeriwrch** *nm* roebuck
**caerog** *adj* walled, fortified; brocaded
**Caersalem** *nf* Jerusalem
**caeth** *adj* bound, captive, confined
♦ **(-ion)** *nm* bondman, slave
**caethder** *nm* strictness; restraint; asthma
**caethfab (-feibion)** *nm* slave
**caethfasnach** *nf* slave-trade
**caethferch (-ed)** *nf* slave
**caethforwyn (-forynion)** *nf* slave
**caethglud** *nf* captivity
**caethgludiad (-au)** *nm* captivity
**caethgludo** *vb* lead captive
**caethiwed** *nm* slavery, bondage, captivity, detention
**caethiwo** *vb* bind, confine, enslave
**caethiwus** *adj* confining; confined, tied
**caethlong (-au)** *nf* slave-ship
**caethwas (-weision)** *nm* slave
**caethwasanaeth, -wasiaeth** *nm* slavery
**cafell (-au)** *nf* cell; sanctuary, oracle
**cafn (-au)** *nm* trough, gutter
**cafnedd** *nm* concavity
**cafnio, -u** *vb* hollow out, scoop, gouge
**cafod** see **cawod**
**caffael** *vb* get, obtain
**caffaeledd** *nm* availability; acquisitiveness
**caffaeliad (-au)** *nm* acquisition, asset; prey, spoil
**caffe, -i (-s)** *nm* café, restaurant
**caffio** *vb* snatch, grapple
**cafflo** *vb* cheat; entangle
**cagl** *nm* clotted dirt
**caglu** *vb* befoul, bedraggle
**cangell (-hellau)** *nf* chancel
**cangelloriaeth** *nf* chancellorship
**cangen (-hennau)** *nf* branch, bough
**canghellor (cangellorion)** *nm* chancellor

**canghennog** *adj* branching
**canghennu** *vb* branch, ramify
**caib (ceibiau)** *nf* pickaxe, mattock
**cail (ceiliau)** *nf* sheepfold, flock of sheep
**caill (ceilliau)** *nf* testicle
**cain** *adj* fair, fine, elegant
**cainc (cangau, ceinciau)** *nf* branch; strand; strain
**cais (ceisiadau)** *nm* application; attempt; try
**cal(a) (-iau)** *nf* penis
**calan (-nau)** *nm* first day of month. **Dydd C.** New Year's Day
**calch** *nm* lime
**calchaidd** *adj* calcareous
**calchbibonwy** *nm* stalactite
**calchbost (-byst)** *nm* stalagmite
**calchen** *nf* limestone; lump of lime
**calchfaen (-feini)** *nm* limestone
**calcho, calchu** *vb* lime
**calcwlws (calcwli)** *nm* calculus
**caled** *adj* hard; severe; harsh; dry
**caledfwrdd** *nm* hardboard
**caledi** *nm* hardness; hardship
**caledu** *vb* harden, dry
**caledwch** *nm* hardness
**calen (-nau, -ni)** *nf* whetstone; bar
**calendr** *nm* calendar
**calennig** *nm/f* New Year's gift
**calon (-nau)** *nf* heart
**calondid** *nm* encouragment
**calon-dyner** *adj* tender-hearted
**calon-galed** *adj* hard-hearted
**calon-galedwch** *nm* hard-heartedness
**calonnog** *adj* hearty; high-spirited
**calonogi** *vb* hearten, encourage
**calori (-iau)** *nm* calorie
**call** *adj* wise, sensible, rational
**callestr (cellystr)** *nf* flint
**callineb** *nm* wisdom, sense
**calsiwm** *nm* calcium
**cam (-au)** *nm* step
**cam** *adj* crooked, wry; wrong ♦
**(-au)** *nm* injury, wrong
**cam-** *prefix* wrong, mis-

**camarfer** vb misuse, abuse ♦
(**-ion**) nm/f misuse, malpractice
**camargraff** nf/m wrong impression
**camarwain** vb mislead
**camarweiniol** adj misleading
**Cambodia** nf Cambodia
**cambren** (**-ni**) nm swingletree
**camchwarae** nm foul play
**camdafliad** (**-au**) nm foul throw
**camdaflu** vb foul throw
**camder, -dra** nm crookedness
**cam-drefn** nf disorder
**camdreuliad** nm indigestion
**camdreulio** vb mis-spend
**cam-drin** vb ill-treat, abuse
**camdriniaeth** (**-au**) nf ill-treatment
**camdystiolaeth** (**-au**) nf false
witness
**camdystiolaethu** vb bear false
witness
**camddeall** vb misunderstand
**camddealltwriaeth** nm
misunderstanding
**camddefnydd** nm misuse
**camddefnyddio** vb misuse
**camedd** nm bend, curvature. **c. y
droed** instep. **c. y gar** knee-joint
**cameg** (**-au, cemyg**) nf felloe
**camel** (**-od**) nm camel
**camenw** (**-au**) nm misnomer
**camenwi** vb misname
**camfa** (**-feydd**) nf stile
**camfarnu** vb misjudge
**camgred** (**-oau, -au**) nf misbelief,
heresy
**camgredu** vb misbelieve
**camgredwr** (**-wyr**) nm heretic
**camgwl** nm penalty, fine; blame
**camgyfrif** vb miscalculate
**camgyhuddiad** (**-au**) nm false
accusation
**camgyhuddo** vb accuse falsely
**camgymeriad** (**-au**) nm mistake
**camgymryd** vb mistake, err
**camlas** (**-lesi, -lesydd**) nf/m canal
**camliwio** vb misrepresent
**camochri** vb be offside

**camog** (**-au**) nf felloe
**camp** (**-au**) nf feat, exploit; game;
prize
**campfa** (**-feydd**) nf gymnasium
**campus** adj excellent, splendid,
grand
**campwaith** (**-weithiau**) nm
masterpiece, feat
**campwr** (**-wyr**) nm champion
**camre** nm walk, footstep(s)
**camsyniad** (**-au**) nm mistake
**camsynied** vb mistake
**camsyniol** adj mistaken
**camu** vb bow, bend, stoop
**camu** vb step, stride
**camwedd** (**-au**) nm iniquity,
transgression
**camweddu** vb transgress
**camwri** nm injury, wrong
**camymddwyn** vb misbehave
**camymddygiad** (**-au**) nm
misconduct
**cân** (**caniadau, caneuon**) nf song
**can** adj white ♦ nm flour
**Canada** nf Canada
**cancr** nm canker; cancer
**cancro** vb canker, corrode
**candryll** adj shattered, wrecked
**canfasio** vb canvass
**canfed** adj hundredth
**canfod** vb see, perceive, behold
**canfyddadwy** adj perceptible
**canfyddiad** nm perception
**canhwyllbren** (**canwyllbrenni, -au**)
nm/f candlestick
**canhwyllwr** (**canhwyllwyr**) nm
chandler
**caniad** nm singing; ringing;
crowing
**caniad** (**-au**) nf song, poem
**caniadaeth** nf singing, psalmody
**caniatâd** nm leave, permission,
consent
**caniataol** adj permissive; granted
**caniatáu** vb permit, allow
**caniedydd** (**-ion**) nm singer,
songster; song-book

**canlyn** *vb* follow, pursue
**canlyniad** (**-au**) *nm* consequence, result
**canlynol** *adj* following, consequent
**canlynwr** (**-wyr**) *nm* follower
**canllaw** (**-iau**) *nf/m* hand-rail, parapet, aid
**canmlwyddiant** *nm* centenary
**canmol** *vb* praise, commend
**canmoladwy** *adj* praiseworthy
**canmoliaeth** (**-au**) *nf* praise, commendation
**canmoliaethus** *adj* eulogistic, complimentary
**cannaid** *adj* white, bright, luminous
**cannu** *vb* whiten, bleach
**cannwr** (**canwyr**) *nm* bleacher
**cannwyll** (**canhwyllau**) *nf* candle
**canol** *adj* ♦ (**-au**) *nm* middle, centre, midst
**canolbarth** (**-au**) *nm* middle part, midland
**canolbwynt** (**-iau**) *nm* centre, focus
**canolbwyntio** *vb* centre, concentrate
**canoldir** (**-oedd**) *nm* inland region
**canolddydd** *nm* mid-day, noon
**canolfan** (**-nau**) *nm/f* centre
**canoli** *vb* centre; arbitrate; centralize
**canolig** *adj* middling
**canoloesol** *adj* mediaeval
**canolog** *adj* central
**canolradd** (**-ol**) *adj* intermediate
**canolwr** (**-wyr**) *nm* mediator, referee; centrehalf, centre. **c. blaen** centreforward
**canon** (**-au**) *nf/m*, (**-iaid**) *nm* canon
**canonaidd** *adj* canonical
**canoneiddio** *vb* canonize
**canoniaeth** (**-au**) *nf* canonry
**canonwr** (**-wyr**) *nm* canon, canonist
**canradd** (**-au**) *adj*, *nf* centigrade, percentile

**canran** (**-nau**) *nm* percentage
**canrif** (**-oedd**) *nf* century
**cansen** (**-ni**) *nf* cane
**canser** *nm* cancer
**canslo** *vb* cancel
**cant** (**-au**) *nm* circle, ring, rim; tyre
**cant** (**cannoedd**) *nm* hundred
**cantel** (**-au**) *nm* rim, brim
**cantîn** (**cantinoedd**) *nf* canteen
**cantor** (**-ion**) *nm* singer
**cantores** (**-au**) *nf* songstress, singer
**cantref** (**-i, -ydd**) *nm* hundred
**cantwr** (**-orion**) *nm* singer, songster
**cantwraig** *nf* songstress, singer
**canu** *vb* sing, chant; play; crow; ring. **c. gwlad** country music
**canŵ** (**-od**) *nm* canoe
**canŵo** *vb* canoe
**canwr** (**-wyr**) *nm* singer
**canwriad** (**-iaid**) *nm* centurion
**canwyr** (**-au, -ion**) *nm* plane (*in carpentry*)
**canys** *conj* because, for
**cap** (**-iau**) *nm* cap
**capan** (**-au**) *nm* cap; lintel
**capel** (**-i, -ydd, -au**) *nm* chapel
**capelwr** (**-wyr**) *nm* chapel-goer
**caplan** (**-iaid**) *nm* chaplain
**caplaniaeth** (**-au**) *nf* chaplaincy
**capteiniaeth** *nf* captaincy
**capten** (**-einiaid**) *nm* captain
**car** (**ceir**) *nm* car. **c. campau** sports car
**câr** (**ceraint**) *nm* friend; relation
**carafán** (**-au**) *nf* caravan
**carbohydrad** (**-au**) *nm* carbohydrate
**carbon** (**-au**) *adj*, *nm* carbon
**carbwl** *adj* clumsy, awkward
**carco** *vb* take care
**carcus** *adj* solicitous, anxious, careful
**carchar** (**-au**) *nm* prison; restraint
**carchardy** (**-dai**) *nm* prison-house

**carchariad** *nm* imprisonment
**carcharor** (-ion) *nm* prisoner
**carcharu** *vb* imprison
**carden** (**cardiau**) *nf* card
**cardigan** (-au) *nf* cardigan
**cardod** (-au) *nf* charity, alms, dole
**cardota** *vb* beg
**cardotyn** (-wyr) *nm* beggar
**cardydwyn, -odwyn** *nm*, **-wen** *nf* weakest of brood or litter
**caredig** *adj* kind
**caredigrwydd** *nm* kindness
**caregog** *adj* stony
**caregu** *vb* stone; petrify; gather stones
**carennydd** *nm* friendship; kinship
**caretsen** (**carets**) *nf* carrot
**carfaglog** *adj* clumsy
**carfan** (-au) *nf* beam; swath; party, faction
**cariad** (-au) *nm* love
**cariad** (-au, -on) *nm/f* lover, sweetheart
**cariadfab** *nm* lover, sweetheart
**cariadferch** *nf* sweetheart, mistress
**cariadlawn** *adj* full of love, loving
**cariadus** *adj* loving, beloved, dear
**caridým** (-s) *nm* ragamuffin
**cario** *vb* carry, bear
**carismatig** *adj* charismatic
**carlam** (-au) *nm* prance, gallop
**carlamu** *vb* prance, gallop
**carlwm** (-lymod) *nm* ermine, stoat
**carn** (-au) *nm* hoof; hilt, haft, handle
**carn** (-au), **carnedd** (-au) *nf* cairn
**cárnifal** *nm* carnival
**carniforus** *adj* carnivorous
**carnog, -ol** *adj* hoofed
**carol** *nm/f* carol
**carp** (-iau) *nm* clout, rag
**carped** (-au, -i) *nm* carpet
**carpiog** *adj* ragged, tattered
**carrai** (**careiau**) *nf* lace, thong
**carreg** (**cerrig**) *nf* stone
**cart** (**ceirt**) *nm/f* cart

**cartaid, certaid** (-eidiau) *nm* cartful
**cartilag** (-au) *nm* cartilage
**cartref** (-i, -ydd) *nm* home, abode
**cartrefle** (-oedd) *nm* abode
**cartreflu** *nm* militia
**cartrefol** *adj* homely, domestic, home; civil
**cartrefu** *vb* make one's home, settle
**cartŵn** (**cartwnau**) *nm* cartoon
**cartwnydd** (-ion) *nm* cartoonist
**carth** (-ion) *nm* tow, oakum; offscouring
**carthen** (-ni, -nau) *nf* Welsh blanket, coverlet
**carthffos** (-ydd) *nf* sewer
**carthffosaeth** *nf* sewage
**carthu** *vb* cleanse, purge, scavenge
**caru** *vb* love; like; court
**caruaidd** *adj* loving, kind
**carw** (**ceirw**) *nm* stag, deer
**carwden** (-ni) *nf* back-chain; tall awkward fellow
**carwr** (-wyr) *nm* lover, wooer
**carwriaeth** (-au) *nf* courtship
**cas** *adj* hateful, odious; nasty, disagreeable ♦ *nm* hatred, aversion
**cas** (**caseion**) *nm* hater, foe, enemy
**casáu** *vb* hate, detest, abhor
**casbeth** (-au) *nm* aversion, nuisance
**caseg** (**cesig**) *nf* mare
**casét** (-iau) *nm* cassette
**casgen** (-ni, **casgiau**) *nf* cask
**casgl** *nf/m* collection
**casgliad** (-au) *nm* collection; gathering
**casglu** *vb* collect, gather; infer
**casglwr** (-wyr), **-ydd** (-ion) *nm* collector
**casineb** *nm* hatred
**cast** (-iau) *nm* vice, knack
**castan** (-au) *nf* chestnut
**castanwydd** *npl* (**-en** *nf*) chestnut-trees

**castell** (**cestyll**) *nm* castle
**castellog** *adj* castled, castellated
**castellu** *vb* castle, encamp
**castio** *vb* trick, cheat; cast, calculate
**castiog** *adj* full of tricks, tricky
**casul** (**-(l)au**) *nm/f* chasuble, cassock
**caswir** *nm* unpalatable truth
**casyn** (**casiau**) *nm* case, casing
**cat** (**-iau**) *nm* bit, piece, fragment; pipe
**catalog** (**-au**) *nm* catalogue
**catalogio** *vb* catalogue
**catalydd** (**-ion**) *nm* catalyst
**categori** (**-ïau**) *nm* category
**catel** *coll n* chattels; cattle
**catgor** (**-(i)au**) *nm* ember day(s)
**catrawd** (**-rodau**) *nf* regiment
**cath** (**-od, -au**) *nf* cat
**cathl** (**-au**) *nf* melody, hymn, lay
**cathlu** *vb* sing, hymn
**cathod** (**-au**) *nf* cathode
**catholig** *adj* catholic
**Catholigiaeth** *nf* Catholicism
**catholigrwydd** *nm* catholicity
**cau** *adj* hollow, concave
**cau** *vb* shut, close, enclose
**caul** (**ceulion**) *nm* maw; rennet; curd
**caw** (**-(i)au**) *nm* band, swaddling-clothes
**cawdel** *nm* hotchpotch, mess
**cawell** (**cewyll**) *nm* hamper, basket, cradle
**cawellaid** (**-eidiau**) *nm* hamperful
**cawellwr** (**-wyr**) *nm* basket-maker
**cawg** (**-iau**) *nm* basin, bowl, pitcher
**cawl** *nm* broth, soup; hotchpotch
**cawn** *npl* (**-en** *nf*) reeds
**cawod** (**-ydd**) *nf* shower
**cawodi** *vb* shower
**cawodog** *adj* showery
**cawr** (**cewri**) *nm* giant
**cawraidd** *adj* gigantic
**cawres** (**-au**) *nf* giantess

**caws** *nm* cheese; curd
**cawsai, cawsi** *nf/m* causeway
**cawsaidd** *adj* cheesy, caseous
**cawsellt** (**-ydd, -i, -au**) *nm* cheese-vat
**cawsio** *vb* curd, curdle
**cawsiog** *adj* curdled
**cecian** *vb* stammer
**cecren** (**-nod**) *nf* shrew, scold, cantankerous woman
**cecru** *vb* wrangle, bicker
**cecrus** *adj* cantankerous, quarrelsome
**cecryn** (**-nod**) *nm* wrangler, brawler
**cedor** *nm/f* pubic hair
**cedrwydd** *npl* (**-en** *nf*) cedars
**cefn** (**-au**) *nm* back; support
**cefndedyn** *nm* mesentery; diaphragm, pancreas
**cefnder** (**-dyr**) *nm* first cousin
**cefndir** (**-oedd**) *nm* background
**cefnen** (**-nau**) *nf* ridge
**cefnfor** (**-oedd**) *nm* main sea, ocean
**cefngrwm** *adj* hump-backed
**cefnog** *adj* well-off, well-to-do
**cefnogaeth** *nf* encouragement, support
**cefnogi** *vb* encourage, support
**cefnogol** *adj* encouraging
**cefnu** *vb* back, turn the back, forsake
**cefnwlad** (**-wledydd**) *nf* hinterland
**cefnwr** (**-wyr**) *nm* back, full-back
**ceffyl** (**-au**) *nm* horse
**ceg** (**-au**) *nf* mouth
**cega** *vb* mouth, prate
**cegaid** (**-eidiau**) *nf* mouthful
**cegen** (**-nau**) *nf* gullet, windpipe
**cegid, -en** (**-au**) *nf* green woodpecker, jay
**cegin** (**-au**) *nf* kitchen
**cegrwth** *adj* gaping
**cegyr** *npl* hemlock
**cengl** (**-au**) *nf* band; girth; hank
**cenglu** *vb* hank; girth; wind

**cei** (-au) *nm* quay
**ceibio** *vb* pick with pickaxe
**ceidwad** (-aid) *nm* keeper, saviour
**ceidwadaeth** *nf* conservatism; conservancy
**ceidwadol** *adj* conservative
**Ceidwadwr** (-wyr) *nm* Conservative
**ceiliagwydd** (-au) *nm* gander
**ceiliog** (-od) *nm* cock. **c. rhedyn** grasshopper
**ceinach** (-od) *nf* hare
**ceincio** *vb* branch out, ramify
**ceinciog** *adj* branched, branching
**ceinder** *nm* elegance, beauty
**ceiniog** (-au) *nf* penny
**ceiniogwerth** (-au, -i) *nf* pennyworth
**ceinion** *npl* beauties, gems
**ceintach** *vb* grumble, croak
**ceintachlyd** *adj* querulous
**ceintachwr** (-wyr) *nm* grumbler, croaker
**ceirch** (-en *nf*) *coll n* oats
**ceirios** *npl* (-en *nf*) cherries
**ceisbwl** (-byliaid) *nm* catchpole, bailiff
**ceisio** *vb* seek; ask; try, attempt, endeavour; fetch, get
**cêl** *adj* hidden, concealed ♦ *nm* concealment ♦ *npl* kale
**celain** (celanedd) *nf* dead body
**celanedd** *coll nf* carnage, slaughter
**celc** *nm/f* concealment; hoard
**celf** (-au) *nf* art, craft
**celfi** *npl* (-cyn *nm*) tools, gear; furniture
**celfydd** *adj* skilled, skilful
**celfyddgar** *adj* ingenious; artistic
**celfyddwr** (-wyr) *nm* artificer, artist
**celfyddyd** (-au) *nf* art, craft; skill. **celfyddydau graffig** graphic arts
**celfyddydol** *adj* relating to art/the Arts
**celu** *vb* hide, conceal
**celwrn** (-yrnau) *nm* tub, bucket,

pail
**celwydd** (-au) *nm* lie, falsehood, untruth
**celwyddog** *adj* lying, mendacious; false
**celwyddwr** (-wyr) *nm* liar
**celyn** *npl* (-nen *nf*) holly
**cell** (-oedd, -au) *nf* cell, chamber. **celloedd cenhedlu** germ cells. **enyniad y celloedd** cellulitis
**celli** (celliau, -ïoedd) *nf* grove
**cellog** *adj* cellular
**cellwair** *vb* jest, trifle ♦ *nm* fun
**cellweiriwr** (-wyr) *nm* jester, trifler
**cellweirus** *adj* playful, jocular
**cemeg** *nm* chemistry
**cemegol** *adj* chemical
**cemegwr, -ydd** (-wyr) *nm* chemist
**cemegyn** (cemegau) *nm* chemical
**cen** *coll n* skin, peel, scales, scurf, film, lichen
**cenadwri** *nf* message
**cenau** (cenawon) *nm* cub, whelp; rascal
**cenedl** (-hedloedd) *nf* nation; gender
**cenedlaethol** *adj* national
**cenedlaetholdeb** *nm* nationalism
**cenedlaetholi** *vb* nationalize
**cenedlaetholwr** (-wyr) *nm* nationalist
**cenedl-ddyn** (-ion) *nm* gentile
**cenfaint** (-feiniau) *nf* herd
**cenfigen** (-nau) *nf* envy, jealousy
**cenfigennu** *vb* envy
**cenfigennus, -enllyd** *adj* envious, jealous
**cenhadaeth** (cenadaethau) *nf* mission
**cenhadol** *adj* missionary
**cenhadu** *vb* permit; propagate, conduct a mission
**cenhadwr** (-hadon) *nm* missionary
**cenhedlaeth** (cenedlaethau) *nf* generation
**cenhedlig** *adj* gentile, pagan

**cenhedlu** *vb* beget, generate
**cenllif** *nm* flood, torrent, deluge
**cenllysg** *coll nm* hailstones, hail
**cennad (-hadau, -hadon)** *nf* leave; messenger
**cennin** *npl* (**-hinen** *nf*) leeks
**cennog** *adj* scaly, scurfy
**cennu** *vb* scale, scurf
**cêr** *nf* gear, tools, trappings
**cerameg** *nm/f* ceramics
**ceramig** *adj* ceramic
**cerbyd (-au)** *nm* chariot, coach, car
**cerbydwr (-wyr)** *nm* coachman
**cerdyn (cardiau)** *nm* card
**cerdd (-i)** *nf* song, poem; music, poetry
**cerddbrenni** *npl* woodwinds
**cerddbresi** *npl* brass section (orchestra)
**cerdded** *vb* walk; go; travel
**cerddediad** *nm* walking, going; pace
**cerddgar** *adj* harmonious, musical
**cerddin, cerdin** *npl* (**-en** *nf*) rowan
**cerddor (-ion)** *nm* singer, musician
**cerddorfa (-feydd)** *nf* orchestra
**cerddorfaol** *adj* orchestral
**cerddoriaeth** *nf* music
**cerddorol** *adj* musical
**cerddwr (-wyr)** *nm* walker
**cerfddelw (-au)** *nf* graven image, statue
**cerfio** *vb* carve
**cerflun (-iau)** *nm* statue; engraving
**cerfluniaeth** *nf* sculpture
**cerflunydd (-lunwyr)** *nm* sculptor
**cerfwaith** *nm* carving, sculpture
**cern (-au)** *nf* cheek, jaw
**cernod (-iau)** *nf* buffet
**cernodio** *vb* buffet, clout
**cerpyn (carpiau)** *nm* clout, rag
**cerrynt** *nm/f* course, road; current
**cert (-i)** *nf* cart
**certiwr (-wyr)** *nm* carter
**certh** *adj* right; awful
**cerub, ceriwb (-iaid)** *nm* cherub

**cerwyn (-i)** *nf* tub; vat; winepress
**cerydd (-on)** *nm* correction, chastisement; rebuke, reproof, censure
**ceryddol** *adj* chastising, chastening
**ceryddu** *vb* correct, chastise; rebuke
**ceryddwr (-wyr)** *nm* chastiser; rebuker
**cesail (-eiliau)** *nf* arm-pit; bosom
**cesair** *npl, coll n* hailstones, hail
**cest (-au)** *nf* belly, paunch
**cestog** *adj* corpulent
**cetyn (catiau)** *nm* piece, bit; pipe
**cethin** *adj* dark, fierce, ugly
**ceubren (-nau)** *nm* hollow tree
**ceubwll (-byllau)** *nm* pit
**ceudod** *nm* cavity; abdomen; thought, heart
**ceuffordd (-ffyrdd)** *nf* tunnel
**ceuffos (-ydd)** *nf* drain, ditch
**ceugrwm** *adj* concave
**ceulan (-nau, -lennydd)** *nf* bank, brink
**ceulo** *vb* curdle, coagulate
**ceunant (-nentydd)** *nm* ravine, gorge
**cewyn (-nau, cawiau)** *nm* napkin
**ci (cŵn)** *nm* dog, hound
**ciaidd** *adj* dog-like, houndish; brutal
**cib (-au)** *nm* pod, husk
**cibddall** *adj* purblind
**cibo** *vb* frown, scowl
**cibog** *adj* scowling
**cibws, cibwst** *nf* kibes, chilblains
**cibwts (-au)** *nm* kibbutz
**cibyn (-nau)** *nm* shell; husk; half a bushel
**cic (-iau)** *nm/f* kick
**cicio** *vb* kick
**ciciwr (-wyr)** *nm* kicker
**cidwm (-ymiaid, -ymod)** *nm* wolf; rascal
**cieidd-dra** *nm* houndishness, brutality
**cig (-oedd)** *nm* flesh, meat

**cigfran** (-frain) *nf* raven
**cignoeth** *adj* touching to the quick, caustic
**cigog** *adj* fleshy
**cigwain** (-weiniau) *nf* flesh-hook
**cigydd** (-ion) *nm* butcher
**cigyddiaeth** *nf* butchery
**cigysol** *adj* carnivorous
**cigysydd** (-ion) *nm* carnivore
**cil** (-iau, -ion) *nm* back; retreat; corner
**cilagor** *vb* open partly
**cilagored** *adj* ajar
**cilbost** (cilbyst) *nm* gate-post
**cilchwyrn** *npl* (-en *nf*), (-au, -od *nm*) glands
**cildrem** (-iau) *nf* leer
**cildremio** *vb* leer
**cildroi** *vb* reverse
**cildwrn** *nm* tip, bribe
**cildyn** *adj* obstinate, stubborn
**cildynnu** *vb* be obstinate
**cildynnus** *adj* obstinate, stubborn
**cildynrwydd** *nm* obstinacy
**cilddant** (-ddannedd) *nm* molar
**cilfach** (-au) *nf* nook; creek, bay
**cilfilyn** (-filod) *nm* ruminant
**cilgnoi** *vb* chew the cud, ruminate
**cilgwthio** *vb* push, shove, jostle
**cilgynnyrch** (-gynhyrchion) *nm* by-product
**cilio** *vb* retreat, recede, swerve
**cilocalori** (-ïau) *nm* kilocalorie
**cilogram** (-au) *nm* kilogram
**cilomedr** (-au) *nm* kilometre
**cilwen** (-au) *nf* half smile
**cilwenu** *vb* simper, smile, leer
**cilwg** (-ygon) *nm* frown, scowl
**cilydd** (-ion) *nm* fellow, companion
**cilyddol** *adj* reciprocal
**cimwch** (-ychiaid) *nm* lobster
**cingroen** *nf* stink-horn
**ciniawa** *vb* dine
**cinio** (ciniawau) *nm* dinner
**cip** (-ion) *nm* pluck, snatch; glimpse
**cipdrem** (-iau) *nf/m* glance, glimpse

**cipedrych** *vb* glance, glimpse
**cipio** *vb* snatch
**cipiwr** (-wyr) *nm* snatcher
**cipolwg** *nm/f* glance, glimpse
**ciprys** *vb, nm* scramble
**cis** (-iau) *nm/f* buffet; slap, touch
**cist** (-iau) *nf* chest, coffer, box; bin
**ciw** (-iau) *nm* cue, queue
**ciwb** *nm* cube
**ciwed** *coll nf* rabble, mob, crew
**ciwrad** (-iaid) *nm* curate
**ciwt** *adj* cute, clever, ingenious
**claddedigaeth** (-au) *nf/m* burial
**claddfa** (-feydd) *nf* burial-ground, cemetery
**claddu** *vb* bury
**claear** *adj* lukewarm, tepid; mild; cool
**claearineb** *nm* lukewarmness
**claearu** *vb* make mild or tepid; soothe
**claer** *adj* clear, bright, shining
**claerder** *nm* clearness, brightness
**claf** (cleifion) *adj* sick, ill ♦ *nm* sick person, patient
**clafdy** (-dai) *nm* hospital, infirmary
**clafr** *nm* itch, mange
**clafrllyd** *adj* mangy
**clafychu** *vb* sicken, fall ill
**clai** (cleiau) *nm* clay
**clais** (cleisiau) *nm* stripe; bruise
**clamp** (-iau) *nm* mass, lump; monster
**clap** (-iau) *nm* lump
**clapgi** (-gwn) *nm* telltale
**clapio** *vb* lump; strike; gossip
**clapiog** *adj* lumpy
**clas** *nm* monastic community, cloister, college
**clasur** (-on) *nm* classic
**clasurol** *adj* classical
**clau** *adj* quick, swift, soon; true; audible
**clawdd** (cloddiau) *nm* hedge; dyke, embankment
**clawr** (cloriau) *nm* face, surface;

cover, lid; board

**clebar, cleber** *nf/m* idle talk, gossip, tattle

**clebran** *vb* chatter, gossip, tattle

**clebryn** *nm*, **clebren** *nf* tattler

**clec** (-iau, -s) *nf* click; clack; crack; gossip

**cleci** (-cwn) *nm* telltale

**clecian** *vb* click; clack; crack, snap

**clecyn** *nm*, **clecen** *nf* gossip, telltale

**cledr** (-au) *nf* pole; rail; palm (of hand)

**cledren** (-nau, -ni) *nf* pale, pole, rail

**cleddyf, cleddau, cledd** (cleddyfau) *nm* sword; brace

**cleddyfwr** (-wyr) *nm* swordsman

**clefyd** (-au) *nm* disease; fever. **c. melys** diabetes

**clegar** *vb* clack, cluck, cackle

**clegyr, clegr** *nm* rock; cairn, stony place

**cleiog** *adj* clayey

**cleiriach** *nm* decrepit one

**cleisio** *vb* bruise

**cleisiog** *adj* bruised

**clem** (-iau) *nf* notion, idea; look, gaze; *pl* grimaces

**clep** (-iau) *nf* clack, clap; gossip

**clepgi** (-gwn) *nm* babbler; telltale

**clepian** *vb* clap; slam; blab

**clêr** *coll nf* itinerant minstrels; bards

**clêr** *npl* (**cleren** *nf*) flies

**clera** *vb* stroll as minstrels

**clerc** (-od) *nm* clerk

**clercio** *vb* serve as clerk

**clerigol** *adj* clerical

**clerigwr** (-wyr) *nm* clergyman

**clerwr** (-wyr) *nm* itinerant minstrel

**clerwriaeth** *nf* minstrelsy

**clewt** (-iau) *nm* clout

**clewtian** *vb* clout

**clic** (**cliciau**) *nm* clique

**clicied** (-au) *nf* clicket; trigger

**cliciedu** *vb* latch, fasten

**clindarddach** *vb* crackle ♦ *nm* crackling

**clinig** (-au) *nm* clinic

**clir** *adj* clear

**clirio** *vb* clear

**clo** (**cloeau, cloeon**) *nm* lock, conclusion

**clobyn** *nm*, **cloben** *nf* monster

**cloc** (-iau) *nm* clock

**clocian** *vb* cluck

**clocsiau** *npl* (**clocsen** *nf*) clog

**cloch** (**clych, clychau**) *nf* bell. **o'r/ar gloch** o'clock

**clochaidd** *adj* sonorous, noisy

**clochdar** *vb* cluck, cackle

**clochdy** (-dai) *nm* belfry, steeple

**clochydd** (-ion) *nm* bell-man; sexton

**clod** (-ydd) *nm/f* praise, fame, renown

**clodfori** *vb* praise, extol

**clodwiw** *adj* commendable, praiseworthy

**cloddfa** (-feydd) *nf* quarry, mine

**cloddio** *vb* dig, delve; quarry, mine

**cloddiwr** (-wyr) *nm* digger, navvy

**cloëdig** *adj* locked, closed

**cloer** (-(i)au) *nm/f* locker; niche, embrasure; pigeon-hole

**cloff** *adj* lame

**cloffi** *vb* lame, halt ♦ *nm* lameness

**cloffni** *nm* lameness

**cloffrwym** (-au) *nm* fetter, hobble. **c. y cythraul, c. y mwci** great bindweed

**clog** (-au) *nm/f* cloak

**clog** (-au) *nf* rock, precipice

**clogfaen** (-feini) *nm* boulder

**clogwyn** (-i) *nm* cliff, crag, precipice

**clogwynog** *adj* craggy, precipitous

**clogyn** (-nau) *nm* cloak, cape

**clogyrnaidd** *adj* rough, rugged, clumsy

**cloi** *vb* lock
**clonc** *nf* clank; gossip ♦ *adj* addled
**clopa** (**-âu**) *nf/m* noddle; knob; club
**cloren** (**-nau**) *nf* rump, tail
**clorian** (**-nau**) *nm/f* pair of scales
**cloriannu** *vb* weigh, balance
**clorin** *nm* chlorine
**clorinio, -adu** *vb* chlorinate
**clos** (**-ydd**) *nm* yard
**clos** (**closau**) *nm* pair of breeches
**clòs** *adj* close
**closio** *vb* close, near
**cludadwy** *adj* portable
**cludair** (**-eiriau**) *nf* heap, load, wood-pile
**cludiad** *nm* carriage
**cludiant** (**-nnau**) *nm* transport, haulage
**cludo** *vb* carry, convey
**cludwr** (**-wyr**), **-ydd** (**-ion**) *nm* porter
**clul** (**-iau**) *nm* knell
**clun** (**-iau**) *nf* hip, haunch, thigh, leg; moor
**cluro** *vb* rub, smear
**clust** (**-iau**) *nf/m* ear; handle
**clustfeinio** *vb* prick up the ears; eavesdrop
**clustfys** *nm* little finger
**clustffôn** (**-ffonau**) *nm* earphone
**clustlws** (**-lysau**) *nm* earring
**clustnod** (**-au**) *nm* earmark
**clustog** (**-au**) *nf/m* cushion, pillow
**clwb** (**clybiau**) *nm* club
**clwc** *adj* addled
**clwcian** *vb* cluck
**clwm** (**clymau**) *nm* knot, tie
**clwpa** (**-od**) *nm* knob, boss; club; dolt
**clws** *adj* pretty, nice; *f* **clos**
**clwstwr** (**clystyrau**) *nm* cluster
**clwt** (**clytiau**) *nm* patch, clout, rag
**clwyd** (**-au, -i, -ydd**) *nf* hurdle; gate; roost
**clwydo** *vb* roost
**clwyf** (**-au**) *nm* wound; disease

**clwyfo** *vb* wound
**clwyfus** *adj* wounded; sore; sick
**clybodeg** *nf* acoustics
**clybodig** *adj* acoustic
**clyd** *adj* warm, sheltered, snug, cosy
**clydwch, clydwr** *nm* warmth, shelter
**clyfar** *adj* clever; pleasant, agreeable
**clymblaid** (**-bleidiau**) *nf* clique, cabal
**clymog** *adj* knotty, entangled
**clymu** *vb* knot, tie
**clytio** *vb* patch, piece
**clytiog** *adj* patched; ragged
**clytwaith** (**-weithiau**) *nm* patchwork
**clyw** *nm* sense of hearing
**clywadwy** *adj* audible
**clywed** *vb* hear; feel; taste; smell
**clywedigaeth** *nf* hearing
**clywedol** *adj* aural
**clywedydd** (**-ion**) *nm* hearer, auditor
**clyweled** *adj* audio-visual
**cnaf** (**-on, -iaid**) *nm* knave, rascal
**cnafaidd** *adj* knavish, rascally
**cnaif** (**cneifion**) *nm* shearing, fleece
**cnap** (**-iau**) *nm* lump, knob, boss
**cnapan** (**-au**) *nm* ball, bowl, kind of ball game
**cnapiog** *adj* lumpy
**cnau** *npl* (**cneuen** *nf*) nuts
**cnawd** *nm* flesh
**cnawdol** *adj* carnal, fleshly, fleshy
**cneifio** *vb* shear, fleece
**cneifiwr** (**-wyr**) *nm* shearer
**cneua** *vb* nut
**cneuen** (**cnau**) *nf* nut
**cnewyllyn** (**cnewyll**) *nm* kernel, nucleus
**cnith** (**-iau, -ion**) *nm* slight touch, blow; pluck
**cno** *nm* bite, chewing, gnawing
**cnoc** (**-iau**) *nm/f* knock
**cnocio** *vb* knock

**cnofa** (**-feydd**) *nf* gnawing, pang
**cnofil** (**-od**) *nm* rodent
**cnoi** *vb* gnaw, chew, bite; ache
**cnot** (**-iau**) *nm* knot, bunch
**cnu** (**-au**), **cnuf** (**-iau**) *nm* fleece
**cnud** (**-oedd**) *nf* pack (*of wolves, etc.*)
**cnùl, cnul** (**-iau**) *nm* knell
**cnwd** (**cnydau**) *nm* crop; covering
**cnydfawr** *adj* fruitful, productive
**cnydio** *vb* crop, yield increase
**cnydiog** *adj* fruitful, productive
**cob** (**cobau**) *nf* coat, cloak, robe
**còb** (**-iau**) *nm* embankment; miser; wag; cob
**coban** (**-au**) *nf*: **c. nos** nightshirt
**coblyn** (**-nod**) *nm* sprite, goblin, imp
**cocos** *npl* cogs. **olwyn g.** cog-wheel
**cocos, cocs** *npl* (**cocsen** *nf*) cockles
**coch** *adj*, *nm* red
**coch-gam** *nf* robin
**cochi** *vb* redden, blush
**cochi, cochder** *nm* redness
**cochl** (**-au**) *nm/f* mantle, cloak
**cod** (**-au**) *nf* bag, pouch
**codaid** (**-eidiau**) *nf* bagful
**codi** *vb* rise, raise, lift, erect
**codiad** (**-au**) *nm* rise, rising; erection
**codog** *adj* baggy ♦ (**-ion**) *nm/f* rich man; miser
**codwm** (**codymau**) *nm* fall, tumble
**codwr** (**-wyr**) *nm* riser; raiser, lifter. **c. canu** precentor
**codymu** *vb* wrestle
**codymur** (**-wyr**) *nm* wrestler
**codded** *nm* anger; grief
**coddi** *vb* anger, offend
**coed** (**-ydd**) *coll nm* wood, timber, trees
**coeden** (**coed**) *nf* tree
**coedio** *vb* timber
**coediog** *adj* wooded, woody
**coedwig** (**-oedd**) *nf* wood, forest
**coedwigaeth** *nf* forestry

**coedwigwr** (**-wyr**) *nm* woodman, forester
**coedd** *adj* public
**coeg** *adj* empty, vain; one-eyed, blind
**coegddyn** (**-ion**) *nm* fop, coxcomb, fool
**coegedd** *nm* emptiness, silliness
**coegen** (**-nod**) *nf* minx, coquette
**coegennaidd** *adj* coquettish
**coegfalch** *adj* vain, foppish
**coegi** *vb* jeer at, mock
**coeglyd** *adj* vain, sarcastic
**coegni** *nm* vanity; spite; sarcasm
**coegwr** (**-wyr**) *nm* fool
**coegwych** *adj* gaudy, garish, tawdry
**coegyn** (**-nod**) *nm* coxcomb
**coel** (**-ion**) *nf* belief, trust, credit
**coelbren** (**-nau, -ni**) *nm* lot
**coelcerth** (**-i**) *nf* bonfire, blaze
**coelgrefydd** (**-au**) *nf* superstition
**coelgrefyddol** *adj* superstitious
**coelio** *vb* believe, credit, trust
**coes** (**-au**) *nf* leg, shank ♦ *nm/f* handle; stem, stalk
**coetgae** *nm* hedge; enclosure
**coetmon** (**-myn**) *nm* lumberjack
**coetref** *nf* woodland, homestead
**coeth** *adj* fine, refined; elegant
**coethder** *nm* refinement, elegance
**coethi** *vb* refine; chastise; babble
**coethwr** (**-wyr**) *nm* refiner
**cof** (**-ion**) *nm* memory; remembrance
**cofadail** (**-eiladau**) *nf* monument
**cofeb** (**-ion**) *nf* memorandum; memorial
**cofgolofn** (**-au**) *nf* monument
**cofiadur** (**-on, -iaid**) *nm* recorder
**cofiadwy** *adj* memorable
**cofiannydd** (**-anyddion**) *nm* biographer
**cofiant** (**-iannau**) *nm* memoir, biography
**cofio** *vb* remember, recollect
**cofl** (**-au**) *nf* embrace; bosom

**coflaid** (-eidiau) *nf* armful; bundle
**coflech** (-au) *nf* memorial tablet
**cofleidio** *vb* embrace, hug
**coflyfr** (-au) *nm* record, chronicle
**cofnod** (-ion) *nm* memorandum, minute
**cofnodi** *vb* record, register
**cofrestr** (-au) *nf* register, roll
**cofrestrfa** *nf* registry
**cofrestru** *vb* register
**cofrestrydd** (-ion) *nm* registrar
**cofus** *adj* mindful
**cofweini** *vb* prompt
**cofweinydd** (-ion) *nm* prompter
**coffa** *vb* remember ♦ *nm* remembrance
**coffâd** *nm* remembrance
**coffadwriaeth** *nf* remembrance, memory
**coffadwriaethol** *adj* memorial
**coffáu** *vb* remember; remind; commemorate
**coffi** *nm* coffee
**coffr** (-au) *nm* coffer, trunk, chest
**cog** (-au) *nf* cuckoo
**cog** (-au) *nm* cook
**coginiaeth** *nf* cookery
**coginio** *vb* cook
**cogio** *vb* cog; sham, feign, pretend
**cogiwr** (-wyr) *nm* pretender, swindler
**cogor** *vb* chatter, caw, croak ♦ *nm* chattering
**cogwrn** (-yrnau, cegyrn) *nm* knob, cone; cock (of corn); shell
**cogydd** (-ion) *nm*, **cogyddes** (-au) *nf* cook
**cogyddiaeth** *nf* cookery
**congl** (-au) *nf* corner
**côl** *nf* bosom, embrace
**col** (-ion) *nm* awn, beard
**coladu** *vb* collate
**coledd, -u** *vb* cherish, foster
**coleddwr** (-wyr) *nm* cherisher, fosterer, patron, supporter
**coleg** (-au) *nm* college
**colegol** *adj* collegiate

**colegwr** (-wyr) *nm* collegian
**coler** (-i) *nf/m* collar
**colfen** (-nau, -ni) *nf* bough, branch; tree
**colofn** (-au) *nf* column, pillar
**colomen** (-nod) *nf* dove, pigeon
**colomendy** (-dai) *nm* dove-cot
**colomennaidd** *adj* dove-like
**coluddion** *npl* (-yn *nm*) bowels
**colur** (-au) *nm* make-up, colour
**coluro** *vb* make-up, paint; conceal
**colwyn** (-od) *nm* puppy
**colyn** (-nau) *nm* pivot; sting; tail
**colynnog** *adj* stinging; hinged
**colynnu** *vb* sting
**coll** (-iadau) *nm* loss; failing, defect
**colladwy** *adj* perishable
**collddail** *adj* deciduous
**colled** (-ion) *nm/f* loss
**colledig** *adj* lost, damned
**colledigaeth** *nf* perdition
**colledu** *vb* occasion loss
**colledus** *adj* fraught with loss
**colledwr** (-wyr) *nm* loser
**collen** (cyll) *nf* hazel
**collfarn** (-au) *nf* doom, condemnation
**collfarnu** *vb* condemn
**colli** *vb* lose; be lost, perish; spill, shed
**collnod** (-au) *nm* apostrophe
**collwr** (-wyr) *nm* loser
**côma** (comâu) *nm* coma
**coma** (-s) *nm* comma
**comed** (-au) *nf* comet
**comedi** (-ïau) *nf/m* comedy
**comig** *adj* comic, comical ♦ *nm* comic (paper)
**comisiwn** (-iynau) *nm* commission
**comisiynu** *vb* commission
**comiwnydd** (-ion) *nm* communist
**comiwnyddiaeth** *nf* communism
**comiwnyddol** *adj* communist
**conach** *vb* grumble
**conclaf** *nm* conclave
**concro** *vb* conquer

**concwerwr** (**-wyr**) *nm* conqueror
**concwest** (**-au**) *nf* conquest, victory
**condemniad** *nm* condemnation
**condemnio** *vb* condemn
**confensiwn** (**-iynau**) *nm* convention
**conffederasiwn** (**-asiynau**) *nm* confederation
**conffirmasiwn** *nm* confirmation
**conffirmio** *vb* confirm
**conifferaidd** *adj* coniferous
**cono** *nm* rascal; wag; old fogey
**consesiwn** (**-iynau**) *nm* concession
**consuriaeth** *nf* conjuring
**consurio** *vb* conjure
**consuriwr** (**-wyr**) *nm* conjurer
**conwydd** *npl* (**-en** *nf*) coniferous trees
**cop, copyn** (**-nod, -nau**) *nm* spider
**copa** (**-âu**) *nf* top, crest; head
**copi** (**-ïau**) *nm* copy; copy-book
**copïo** *vb* copy, transcribe
**copïwr** (**-wyr**) *nm* copyist, transcriber
**copr** *nm* copper
**côr** (**corau**) *nm* choir; stall, pew. **c. feistr** choirmaster
**cor** (**-rod**) *nm* dwarf; spider
**corachaidd** *adj* dwarfish, stunted
**corawl** *adj* choral
**corbwll** (**-byllau**) *nm* whirlpool; puddle
**corcyn** (**cyrc**) *nm* cork
**cord** (**-iau**) *nm* cord; chord
**cordeddu** *vb* twist, twine
**corddi** *vb* churn; turn; agitate
**corddiad** (**-au**) *nm* churning
**corddwr** (**-wyr**) *nm* churner
**cored** (**-au**) *nf* weir, dam
**coreograffiaeth** *nf* choreography
**corfan** (**-nau**) *nm* metrical foot
**corff** (**cyrff**) *nm* body
**corfflu** (**-oedd**) *nm* corps
**corffol** *adj* corpulent; physical
**corffolaeth** *nf* bodily form; stature
**corfforaeth** (**-au**) *nf* corporation

**corffori** *vb* embody, incorporate
**corfforiad** (**-au**) *nm* embodiment
**corfforol** *adj* bodily, corporeal, corporal
**corgan, côr-gân** (**-au**) *nf* chant
**corganu** *vb* chant
**corgi** (**-gwn**) *nm* cur, corgi
**corgimwch** (**-ychiaid**) *nm* prawn
**corhwyad** (**-aid**) *nf* teal; moorhen
**corlan** (**-nau**) *nf* fold
**corlannu** *vb* fold
**corn** (**cyrn**) *nm* horn; pipe, tube; roll; corn; stethoscope. **c. gwddw(f), c. gwynt** windpipe. **c. siarad** loudspeaker
**cornant** (**-nentydd**) *nm* brook, rill
**cornboer** *nm* phlegm
**cornchwiglen** (**-chwiglod**) *nf* lapwing
**cornel** (**-i, -au**) *nf/m* corner
**cornelu** *vb* corner
**cornicyll** (**-od**) *nm* lapwing, plover, peewit
**cornio** *vb* horn, butt; examine with a stethoscope
**corniog** *adj* horned
**cornwyd** (**-ydd**) *nm* boil, abscess, sore
**coron** (**-au**) *nf* crown
**coroni** *vb* crown ♦ *nm* coronation
**coroniad** *nm* coronation
**coronog** *adj* crowned
**corpws** *nm* body (*facetious*)
**corrach** (**corachod**) *nm* dwarf, pygmy
**corryn** (**corynnod**) *nm* spider
**cors** (**-ydd**) *nf* bog, swamp
**corsen** (**-nau, cyrs**) *nf* reed; stem, stalk; cane
**cortyn** (**-nau**) *nm* cord, rope
**corun** (**-au**) *nm* crown of the head; tonsure
**corwg(l)** (**-yg(l)au**) *nm* coracle
**corws** *nm* chorus
**corwynt** (**-oedd**) *nm* whirlwind
**cosb** (**-au**) *nf* punishment, penalty. **c. ddihenydd** capital punishment

**cosbadwy** *adj* punishable
**cosbedigaeth** *nf* punishment
**cosbi** *vb* punish
**cosbol** *adj* punitive, penal
**cosbwr** (-wyr) *nm* punisher
**cosfa** (-feydd) *nf* itch, itching; thrashing
**cosi** *vb* scratch, itch ♦ *nm* itching
**cosmetigau** *npl* cosmetics
**cosmig** *adj* cosmic
**cost** (-au) *nf* cost, expense
**costiad** (-au) *nm* costing
**costio** *vb* cost
**costiwm** (-tiymau) *nm/f* costume
**costog** (-ion) *nm* mastiff; cur ♦ *adj* surly
**costowci** (-cwn) *nm* mastiff, mongrel
**costrel** (-au, -i) *nf* bottle
**costrelaid** (-eidiau) *nf* bottleful
**costrelu** *vb* bottle
**costus** *adj* costly, expensive
**cosyn** (-nau, -nod) *nm* a cheese
**côt, cot** (cotiau) *nf* coat
**cotwm** *nm* cotton
**cowlas** (-au) *nm/f* bay of building; hay-mow
**cownter** (-au, -i) *nm* counter
**cowntio** *vb* count, account, esteem
**crac** (-iau) *nm* crack
**cracio** *vb* crack
**craciog** *adj* cracked
**crach** *npl* (-en *nf*) scabs ♦ *adj* scabby; petty ♦ **-ach** *npl* snobs
**crachboer** *nm* phlegm
**crachfardd** (-feirdd) *nm* poetaster
**crachfeddyg** (-on) *nm* quack doctor
**crachfonheddwr** (-wyr) *nm* snob
**crafangio, -u** *vb* claw, grab
**crafanc** (-angau) *nf* claw; talon; clutch
**crafiad** (-au) *nm* scratch
**crafog** *adj* cutting, sarcastic
**crafu** *vb* scrape; scratch ♦ *nm* itch
**crafwr** (-wyr) *nm* scraper
**craff** *adj* close; keen; sagacious ♦

*nm* hold, grip
**craffter** *nm* keenness, sagacity
**craffu** *vb* look closely, observe intently
**craffus** *adj* keen, sagacious
**cragen** (cregyn) *nf* shell
**crai** *adj* new, fresh, raw
**craidd** (creiddiau) *nm* middle, centre
**craig** (creigiau) *nf* rock
**crair** (creiriau) *nm* relic
**craith** (creithiau) *nf* scar
**cramen** (-nau) *nf* crust, scab
**cranc** (-od) *nm* crab
**crand** *adj* grand
**crandrwydd** *nm* grandeur, finery
**crap** (-iau) *nm* hold; smattering
**crapio** *vb* grapple; pick up
**cras** (creision) *adj* parched, dry; harsh
**crasiad** *nm* baking
**craslyd** *adj* harsh, grating
**craster** *nm* dryness; harshness
**crasu** *vb* parch, scorch; bake
**crau** (creuau) *nm* hole, eye, socket
**crau** *nm/f* blood, gore
**crau** (creuau) *nm* sty; stockade
**crawcian, crawcio** *vb* croak, caw
**crawen** (-nau) *nf* crust
**crawn** *nm* matter, pus
**crawni** *vb* gather, suppurate
**crawnllyd** *adj* purulent
**cread** *nm* creation
**creadigaeth** (-au) *nf* creation
**creadigol** *adj* creative
**creadur** (-iaid) *nm* creature; animal
**creadures** (-au) *nf* female creature
**creawdwr** (-wyr) *nm* creator
**crebach** *adj* shrunk, withered
**crebachlyd** *adj* crabbed, wrinkled
**crebachu** *vb* shrink, shrivel, wrinkle, pucker
**crebwyll** (-ion) *nm* invention, understanding, fancy
**crecian** *vb* cluck; crackle
**crechwen** *nf* loud laughter, guffaw

**crechwenu** vb laugh loud, guffaw
**cred** (**-au**) nf belief; trust; pledge, troth
**credadun** (**credinwyr**) nm believer
**credadwy** adj credible
**crediniaeth** nf belief
**crediniol** adj believing
**credo** (**-au**) nm/f creed, belief
**credu** vb believe
**credwr** (**-wyr**) nm believer
**credyd** (**-on**) nm credit
**credydu** vb credit
**cref** adj f. of **cryf**
**crefu** vb crave, beg, implore
**crefydd** (**-au**) nf religion
**crefydda** vb profess or practise religion
**crefyddol** adj religious, pious
**crefyddolder** nm religiousness, piety
**crefyddwr** (**-wyr**) nm religioner, religionist
**crefft** (**-au**) nf handicraft, trade
**crefftus** adj skilled, workmanlike
**crefftwaith** nm craftwork
**crefftwr** (**-wyr**) nm craftsman
**cregyn** npl (**cragen** nf) shells
**creider** nm freshness
**creifion** npl scrapings
**creigiog** adj rocky
**creigiwr** (**-wyr**) nm quarryman
**creigle** (**-oedd**) nm rocky place
**creinio** vb wallow, lie or fall down; cringe
**creision** npl flakes, crisps
**crempog** (**-au**) nf pancake
**crensio** vb grind (the teeth)
**crepach** adj numb ♦ nf numbness
**crest** nm crust, scurf
**Creta** nf Crete
**creu** vb create
**creulon** adj cruel
**creulondeb** (**-derau**) nm cruelty
**crëwr** (**crewyr**) nm creator
**crëyr** (**crehyrod**) nm heron
**cri** (**-au**) nm cry, clamour
**cri** adj new, fresh, raw; unleavened

**criafol, -en** nf mountain ash
**crib** (**-au**) nf/m comb, crest; ridge
**cribddeilio** vb grab, extort
**cribddeiliwr** (**-wyr**) nm extortioner; speculator
**cribin** (**-iau**) nf/m rake; skinflint
**cribinio** vb rake
**cribo** vb comb; card
**criced** nm cricket
**cricedwr** (**-wyr**) nm cricketer
**crimog** (**-au**) nf, **crimp** (**-(i)au**) nm shin
**crin** adj withered, sear, dry
**crino** vb wither, dry up
**crintach, -lyd** adj niggardly, stingy
**crintachrwydd** nm niggardliness
**crintachu** vb scrimp, skimp, stint
**crio** vb cry, weep
**cripio** vb scratch; climb, creep
**cris-groes** nf criss-cross
**crisial** (**-au**) nm, adj crystal
**crisialu** vb crystallise
**Cristion** (**-ogion, Cristnogion**) nm Christian
**Cristionogaeth** nf Christianity
**Cristionogol** adj Christian
**criw** (**-iau**) nm crew
**criwr** (**-wyr**) nm crier
**crocbont** (**-ydd**) nf suspension bridge
**crocbren** (**-ni**) nm/f gallows, gibbet
**crocbris** (**-iau**) nm exorbitant price
**croch** adj loud, vehement
**crochan** (**-au**) nm pot, cauldron
**crochanaid** (**-eidiau**) nm potful
**crochenydd** (**-ion**) nm potter
**crochenwaith** (**-weithiau**) nm pottery
**croen** (**crwyn**) nm skin; hide; peel, rind
**croendenau** adj thin-skinned
**croeni, -io** vb form skin, skin over
**croes** (**-au**) nf cross ♦ nm transept
**croes** (**-ion**) adj cross, contrary
**croesair** (**-eiriau**) nm crossword
**croesawgar** adj hospitable
**croesawiad** nm welcome,

reception
**croesawu** *vb* welcome
**croesawus** *adj* hospitable
**croesbren** (-nau) *nm/f* cross
**croesddweud** *vb* contradict
**croesfan** (-nau) *nf* crossing
**croesffordd** (-ffyrdd) *nf* crossroad
**croesgad** (-au) *nf* crusade
**croesgadwr** (-wyr) *nm* crusader
**croeshoeliad** *nm* crucifixion
**croeshoelio** *vb* crucify
**croesholi** *vb* cross-examine
**croesholiad** (-au) *nm* cross-
examination
**croesi** *vb* cross
**croeso** *nm* welcome
**croesymgroes** *adj* criss-cross;
vice-versa
**crofen** (-nau, -ni) *nf* rind, crust
**crog** (-au) *nf* cross, rood ♦ *adj*
hanging
**crogi** *vb* hang, suspend
**croglath** (-au) *nf* springe, snare,
gibbet
**Croglith** *nm/f*: **Dydd Gwener y G.**
Good Friday
**croglofft** (-ydd, -au) *nf* garret;
rood-loft
**crogwr** (-wyr) *nm* hangman
**cronglwyd** (-ydd) *nf*: **tan fy ngh.**
under my roof
**crombil** (-iau) *nf* crop; gizzard;
bowels
**cromen** (-ni, -nau) *nf* dome
**cromfach** (-au) *nf* bracket,
parenthesis
**cromlech** (-au, -i) *nf* cromlech
**cromosom** (-au) *nm* chromosome
**cron** *adj* f. of **crwn**
**cronfa** (-feydd) *nf* reservoir; fund
**cronicl** (-au) *nm* chronicle
**croniclo** *vb* chronicle
**cronnell** (cronellau) *nf* sphere,
globe
**cronni** *vb* collect, hoard; dam
**cronolegol** *adj* chronological
**cropian** *vb* creep, crawl, grope

**crosiet** (-au, -i) *nm* crotchet
**croth** (-au) *nf* womb; calf (*of leg*)
**croyw** *adj* clear, plain, distinct;
fresh
**croywder** *nm* clearness; freshness
**croywi** *vb* clear; freshen
**crud** (-au) *nm* cradle
**crug** (-iau) *nm* hillock; tumulus;
heap; multitude; abscess, blister
**cruglwyth** (-i) *nm* heap, pile
**cruglwytho** *vb* heap, pile up;
overload
**crugo** *vb* fester, vex, plague
**crwban** (-od) *nm* tortoise, turtle
**crwca** *adj* crooked, bowed, bent
**crwm** *adj* convex, curved, bowed;
*f* **crom**
**crwn** *adj* round; complete; *f* **cron**
**crwner** (-iaid) *nm* coroner
**crwsâd** (-adau) *nm/f* crusade
**crwst** (crystiau) *nm* crust
**crwt** (cryts) *nm* boy, lad
**crwth** (crythau) *nm* crowd, fiddle;
purring; hump
**crwybr** *nm* honeycomb; mist;
hoarfrost
**crwydr** *nm* wandering. **ar g.** astray
**crwydro** *vb* wander, stray, roam
**crwydrol, crwydrus** *adj*
wandering
**crwydrwr** (-wyr) *nm* wanderer,
rover
**crwydryn** (-riaid) *nm* vagrant,
tramp
**crwys** *nf, npl* cross, crucifix. **dan ei**
**g.** laid out for burial
**crybwyll** *vb* mention ♦ (-ion) *nm*
mention
**crybwylliad** *nm* mention, notice
**crych** *adj* rippling; curly;
quavering ♦ (-au) *nm* crease,
ripple, wrinkle
**crychlais** (-leisiau) *nm* trill,
tremolo
**crychlyd** *adj* wrinkled, puckered
**crychnaid** (-neidiau) *nf* leap,
gambol

**crychneidio** vb skip, frisk
**crychni** nm curliness; wrinkle
**crychu** vb wrinkle, pucker; ruffle, ripple
**cryd** (-iau) nm shivering; fever; ague
**crydd** (-ion) nm cobbler, shoemaker
**crydda** vb cobble
**cryf** adj strong; f **cref**
**cryfder, -dwr** nm strength
**cryfhaol** adj strengthening
**cryfhau** vb strengthen; grow strong
**cryg** adj hoarse; f **creg**
**cryglyd** adj hoarse, raucous
**crygni** nm hoarseness
**crygu** vb hoarsen
**cryman** (-au) nm reaping-hook, sickle
**crymanwr** (-wyr) nm reaper
**crymu** vb bow, bend, stoop
**cryn** adj considerable, much
**crŷn, cryn** nm, adj shivering
**crynder** nm roundness
**cryndod** nm trembling, shivering
**crynedig** adj trembling, tremulous
**crynfa** (-feydd) nf tremble, tremor
**crynhoad** (-noadau) nm collection, digest
**crynhoi** vb gather together, collect
**cryno** adj compact; neat, tidy
**crynodeb** (-au) nm summary
**crynswth** nm mass, bulk, whole
**crynu** vb shiver, tremble, quake
**Crynwr** (-wyr) nm Quaker
**crys** (-au) nm shirt
**crysbaid** (-beisiau) nf jacket, jerkin
**crystyn** (crystiau) nm crust
**crythor** (-ion) nm fiddler, violinist
**cryw** (-iau) nm creel; weir
**cu** adj dear, fond, kind
**cuchio** vb scowl, frown
**cuchiog** adj scowling, frowning
**cudyll** (-od) nm hawk
**cudyn** (-nau) nm lock (of hair), tuft
**cudd** adj hidden, concealed
**cuddfa** (-feydd) nf hiding-place; hoard
**cuddiad** nm hiding
**cuddiedig** adj hidden, concealed
**cuddio** vb hide, conceal
**cufydd** (-au) nm cubit
**cul** (-ion) adj narrow, lean
**culfor** (-oedd) nm strait
**culhau** vb narrow; grow lean
**culni** nm narrowness
**cun** adj dear, beloved; lovely
**cunnog** (cunogau) nf pail
**cur** nm throb, ache, pain; care, trouble
**curad** (-iaid) nm curate
**curadiaeth** (-au) nf curacy
**curfa** (-feydd) nf beating, flogging
**curiad** (-au) nm beat, throb, pulse
**curio** vb pine, waste
**curlaw** nm pelting rain
**curn** (-au), **curnen** (-nau) nf mound, core, rick
**curnennu** vb heap, stack
**curo** vb beat, strike, knock; throb; clap
**curwr** (-wyr) nm beater
**curyll** (-od) nm hawk
**cusan** (-au) nf/m kiss
**cusanu** vb kiss
**cut** (-iau) nm hovel, shed, sty
**cuwch** (cuchiau) nm scowl, frown
**cwafrio** vb quaver, trill
**cwar** (-rau) nm quarry
**cwb** (cybiau) nm kennel, coop, sty
**cwbl** adj, nm all, whole, total
**cwblhad** nm fulfilment
**cwblhau** vb fulfil, complete, finish
**cwcer** (-au) nm cooker
**cwcw** nf cuckoo
**cwcwallt** (-iaid) nm cuckold
**cwcwalltu** vb cuckold
**cwcwll** (cycyllau) nm hood, cowl
**cwch** (cychod) nm boat; hive. **c. gwyllt** speed boat
**cwd** (cydau) nm pouch, bag

**cweir** (-iau) *nm* thrashing, hiding
**cweryl** (-on) *nm* quarrel
**cweryla** *vb* quarrel
**cwerylgar** *adj* quarrelsome
**cwest** (-au) *nm* inquest
**cwestiwn** (-iynau) *nm* question
**cwestiynu** *vb* question
**cwffio** *vb* fight, box
**cwgn** (cygnau) *nm* knot; knuckle; joint
**cwilt** (-iau) *nm* quilt
**cwlbren** (-ni) *nm* bludgeon
**cwlff, -yn** (cylffiau) *nm* chunk
**cwlwm** see **clwm**
**cwlltwr** (cylltyrau) *nm* coulter
**cwm** (cymau, cymoedd) *nm* valley
**cwman** *nm* rump; stoop; churn
**cwmanu** *vb* stoop
**cwmni** (-iau, -ïoedd) *nm* company
**cwmnïaeth** *nf* companionship
**cwmpas** (-oedd) *nm* round. **o.g.** about
**cwmpasog** *adj* round about, circuitous
**cwmpasu** *vb* round, wind, surround
**cwmpawd** (-odau) *nm* compass
**cwmpeini, cwmpni** *nm* company
**cwmwd** (cymydau) *nm* commot
**cwmwl** (cymylau) *nm* cloud
**cŵn** see **ci**
**cwndid** (-au) *nm* song, carol
**cwningen** (-ingod) *nf* rabbit
**cwnsel** (-au, -oedd, -i) *nm* council; counsel, advice, secret
**cwnsela** *vb* counsel
**cwnsler** (-iaid) *nm* counsellor
**cwnstabl** (-iaid) *nm* constable
**cworwm** *nm* quorum
**cwota** (-au) *nm* quota
**cwpan** (-au) *nm/f* cup, goblet; chalice
**cwpanaid** (-eidiau) *nm/f* cupful
**cwpl** (cyplau) *nm* couple; tie beam
**cwplâd, cwpláu** see **cwblhad, cwblhau**
**cwpled** (-i, -au) *nm* couplet

**cwplws** (cyplysau) *nm* coupling; brace
**cwpwrdd** (cypyrddau) *nm* cupboard
**cwr** (cyrrau) *nm* edge, border, skirt
**cwrcwd** *nm* stooping; squatting
**cwrdd** (cyrddau) *nm* meeting
**cwrdd, cwrddyd** *vb* meet, touch
**cwrel** *nm* coral
**cwricwlwm** (cwricwla) *nm* curriculum
**cwrlid** (-au) *nm* coverlet
**cwrs** (cyrsiau) *nm* course; fit
**cwrt** (cyrtiau) *nm* court
**cwrtais** *adj* courteous
**cwrteisi, cwrteisrwydd** *nm* courtesy
**cwrw** (cyrfau) *nm* ale, beer
**cwrwg(l)** see **corwg(l)**
**cwsg** *nm* sleep
**cwsmer** (-iaid) *nm* customer
**cwsmeriaeth** *nf* custom
**cwstard** (-iau) *nm* custard
**cwstwm** (cystymau) *nm* custom, patronage
**cwt** (cytiau) *nf/m* tail, skirt, queue
**cwt** (cytiau) *nm* hut, sty
**cwta** *adj* short, curt
**cwter** (-i, -ydd) *nf* gutter, channel
**cwtogi** *vb* shorten, curtail
**cwthr** (cythrau) *nm* anus, rectum
**cwthwm** (cythymau) *nm* puff of wind, storm
**cwymp** (-au) *nm* fall, tumble
**cwympo** *vb* fall; fell
**cwyn** (-ion) *nm/f* complaint, plaint
**cwynfan** *vb* complain, lament
**cwynfanllyd** *adj* querulous
**cwynfanus** *adj* plaintive, mournful
**cwyno** *vb* complain, lament
**cwyr** *nm* wax
**cwyro** *vb* wax
**cwys** (-au, -i) *nf* furrow-slice, furrow
**cybôl** *nm* nonsense, rubbish
**cybolfa** *nf* hotchpotch, medley
**cyboli** *vb* muddle; talk nonsense;

mess, bother
**cybydd** (**-ion**) *nm* miser, niggard
**cybydda** *vb* stint, hoard
**cybydd-dod, -dra** *nm* miserliness
**cybyddlyd** *adj* miserly
**cycyllog** *adj* hooded, cowled
**cychaid** (**-eidiau**) *nm* boatful;
hiveful
**cychwr** (**-wyr**) *nm* boatman
**cychwyn** *vb* rise, stir, start
**cychwynfa** *nf* start, starting-point
**cychwyniad** (**-au**) *nm* start,
beginning
**cyd** *adj* joint, united, common;
fellow ♦ *prefix* together
**cydadrodd** *vb* to recite together
**cydaid** (**-eidiau**) *nm* bagful
**cydbwysedd** *nm* balance
**cyd-destun** (**-au**) *nm* content
**cydfod** *nm* agreement, concord
**cydfodolaeth** *nf* coexistence
**cydfyned** *vb* go with, concur,
agree
**cydfyw** *vb* cohabit
**cydffurfio** *vb* conform
**cydgordio** *vb* agree, harmonize
**cydgwmni** (**-ïau**) *nm* consortium
**cydiedig** *adj* adjoined
**cydio** *vb* join; bite; take hold
**cydnabod** *vb* acknowledge ♦ *nm*
acquaintance
**cydnabyddiaeth** *nf* acquaintance;
recognition
**cydnabyddus** *adj* acquainted;
familiar
**cydnaws** *adj* congenial
**cydnerth** *adj* well set
**cydol** *nf/m, adj* whole
**cydradd** *adj* equal
**cydraddoldeb** *nm* equality
**cyd-rhwng** *prep* between
**cydsyniad** *nm* consent
**cydsynio** *vb* consent
**cydwastad** *adj* level (with), even
**cydweddog** *adj* conjugal
**cydweddu** *vb* accord, agree
**cydweithfa** (**-feydd**) *nf* co-

operative
**cydweithrediad** *nm* co-operation
**cydweithredol** *adj* co-operative
**cydweithredu** *vb* co-operate
**cydweled** *vb* agree
**cydwladol** *adj* international
**cyd-wladwr** (**-wyr**) *nm* compatriot
**cydwybod** (**-au**) *nf* conscience
**cydwybodol** *adj* conscientious
**cydwybodolrwydd** *nm*
conscientiousness
**cydymaith** (**cymdeithion**) *nm*
companion
**cydymdeimlad** *nm* sympathy
**cydymdeimlo** *vb* sympathize
**cydymffurfiad** *nm* conformity
**cydymffurfio** *vb* conform
**cydymgais** *nm* competition,
rivalry, joint effort
**cydymgeisydd** (**-wyr**) *nm* rival
**cyddwysiad** (**-au**) *nm* condensation
**cyfadran** (**-nau**) *nf* faculty (*in
college*); period (*in music*)
**cyfaddas** *adj* fit, suitable,
convenient
**cyfaddasiad** (**-au**) *nm* adaptation
**cyfaddaster** *nm* fitness, suitability
**cyfaddasu** *vb* fit, adapt
**cyfaddawd** (**-odau**) *nm*
compromise
**cyfaddawdu** *vb* compromise
**cyfaddef** *vb* confess, own, admit
**cyfaddefiad** (**-au**) *nm* confession,
admission
**cyfaenad** *nm, adj* harmonious song
**cyfagos** *adj* near, adjacent,
neighbouring
**cyfaill** (**-eillion**) *nm* friend
**cyfair** (**-eiriau**) *nm* acre
**cyfair, -er** *nm* direction. **ar g.** for;
opposite
**cyfalaf** *nm* capital
**cyfalafiaeth** *nf* capitalism
**cyfalafol** *adj* capitalistic
**cyfalafwr** (**-wyr**) *nm* capitalist
**cyfamod** (**-au**) *nm* covenant
**cyfamodi** *vb* covenant

**cyfamodol** *adj* federal; covenanted
**cyfamodwr** (**-wyr**) *nm* covenanter
**cyfamser** *nm* meantime
**cyfamserol** *adj* timely;
synchronous
**cyfan** *adj, nm* whole
**cyfandir** (**-oedd**) *nm* continent
**cyfandirol** *adj* continental
**cyfanfor** (**-oedd**) *nm* main sea,
ocean
**cyfanfyd** *nm* whole world, universe
**cyfangorff** *nm* whole, bulk, mass
**cyfan gwbl** *adj:* **yn g.** altogether,
complete
**cyfanheddol** *adj* habitable,
inhabited
**cyfanheddu** *vb* dwell, inhabit
**cyfannedd** *adj* inhabited ♦
(**-anheddau**) *nf* inhabited place,
habitation
**cyfannol** *adj* integrated, integral
**cyfannu** *vb* make whole, complete
**cyfanrwydd** *nm* wholeness,
entirety
**cyfansawdd** *adj* composite,
compound
**cyfansoddi** *vb* compose, constitute
**cyfansoddiad** (**-au**) *nm*
composition; constitution
**cyfansoddiadol** *adj* constitutional
**cyfansoddwr** (**-wyr**) *nm* composer
**cyfansoddyn** (**-ion**) *nm*
constituent, compound
**cyfanswm** (**-symiau**) *nm* total
**cyfantoledd** (**-au**) *nm* equilibrium
**cyfanwaith** (**-weithiau**) *nm*
complete composition, whole
**cyfarch** *vb* greet, salute, address
**cyfarchiad** (**-au**) *nm* greeting,
salutation
**cyfaredd** (**-ion**) *nf* charm, spell
**cyfareddol** *adj* enchanting
**cyfareddu** *vb* charm, enchant
**cyfarfod** *vb* meet ♦ (**-ydd**) *nm*
meeting
**cyfarfyddiad** (**-au**) *nm* meeting
**cyfarpar** *nm* provision, equipment;

diet. **c. rhyfel** munitions of war
**cyfarparu** *vb* equip
**cyfartal** *adj* equal, even
**cyfartaledd** *nm* proportion,
average
**cyfartalu** *vb* proportion, equalize
**cyfarth** *vb, nm* bark
**cyfarwydd** *adj* skilled; familiar ♦
(**-iaid**) *nm* storyteller
**cyfarwyddo** *vb* direct; become
familiar
**cyfarwyddwr** (**-wyr**) *nm* director
**cyfarwyddyd** (**-iadau**) *nm*
direction, instruction
**cyfatal** *adj* unsettled, hindering
**cyfateb** *vb* correspond, agree, tally
**cyfatebiaeth** (**-au**) *nf*
correspondence, analogy
**cyfatebol** *adj* corresponding,
proportionate
**cyfathrach** (**-au**) *nf* affinity;
intercourse
**cyfathrachu** *vb* have intercourse
**cyfathrachwr** (**-wyr**) *nm* kinsman
**cyfathreb** (**-au**) *nm* communication
**cyfathrebu** *vb* communicate
**cyfddydd** *nm* day-break, dawn
**cyfeb, cyfebr** *adj* pregnant (*of
mare, ewe*)
**cyfebol** *adj* in foal
**cyfeddach** (**-au**) *nf* carousal
**cyfeddachwr** (**-wyr**) *nm* carouser
**cyfeiliant** *nm* musical
accompaniment
**cyfeilio** *vb* accompany
**cyfeiliorn** *nm* error; wandering,
lost (*person etc*). **ar g.** astray
**cyfeiliornad** (**-au**) *nm* error,
heresy
**cyfeiliorni** *vb* err, stray
**cyfeiliornus** *adj* erroneous,
mistaken
**cyfeilydd** (**-ion**) *nm* accompanist
**cyfeillach** (**-au**) *nf* fellowship;
fellowship-meeting
**cyfeillachu** *vb* associate
**cyfeilles** (**-au**) *nf* female friend

**cyfeillgar** *adj* friendly
**cyfeillgarwch** *nm* friendship
**cyfeiriad** (**-au**) *nm* direction; reference; (postal) address
**cyfeiriannu** *nm* orienteering
**cyfeirio** *vb* point; direct; refer; address (*letter*)
**cyfeirnod** (**-au**) *nm* mark of reference; aim; direct (*in music*)
**cyfeirydd** (**-ion**) *nm* indicator, guide
**cyfenw** (**-au**) *nm* surname; namesake
**cyfenwi** *vb* surname
**cyfer** *nm*: **ar g.** for; opposite
**cyferbyn** *adj* opposite
**cyferbyniad** (**-au**) *nm* contrast
**cyferbyniol** *adj* opposing, opposite, contrasting
**cyferbynnu** *vb* contrast, compare
**cyfethol** *vb* co-opt
**cyfiaith** *adj* of the same language
**cyfiawn** *adj* just, righteous
**cyfiawnder** (**-au**) *nm* justice, righteousness
**cyfiawnhad** *nm* justification
**cyfiawnhau** *vb* justify
**cyfieithiad** (**-au**) *nm* translation, version
**cyfieithu** *vb* translate, interpret
**cyfieithydd** (**-wyr**) *nm* translator, interpreter
**cyfisol** *adj* of the present month, instant
**cyflafan** (**-au**) *nf* outrage; massacre
**cyflafareddiad** *nm* arbitration
**cyflafareddu** *vb* arbitrate
**cyflafareddwr** (**-wyr**) *nm* arbitrator
**cyflaith** *nm* toffee
**cyflawn** *adj* full, complete
**cyflawnder** *nm* fullness; abundance
**cyflawni** *vb* fulfil, perform, commit
**cyflawniad** (**-au**) *nm* fulfilment, performance

**cyfle** (**-oedd**) *nm* place; chance, opportunity
**cyfled** *adj* as broad as
**cyflegr** (**-au**) *nm* gun, cannon, battery
**cyflegru** *vb* bombard
**cyflenwad** (**-au**) *nm* supply
**cyflenwi** *vb* supply
**cyfleu** *vb* place, set; convey
**cyfleus** *adj* convenient
**cyfleustra** (**-terau**) *nm* opportunity, convenience
**cyflin** *adj* parallel
**cyfliw** *adj* of the same colour
**cyflo** *adj* in calf
**cyflog** (**-au**) *nm/f* hire, wage, wages
**cyflogaeth** *nf* employment
**cyflogedig** (**-ion**) *nm* employee
**cyflogi** *vb* hire; engage in service
**cyflogwr** (**-wyr**) *nm* hirer, employer
**cyflwr** (**-lyrau**) *nm* condition; case
**cyflwyniad** *nm* presentation; dedication
**cyflwyno** *vb* present; dedicate
**cyflwynydd** (**-ion**) *nm* compère, presenter
**cyflychwr**, **-wyr** *nm* evening twilight, dusk
**cyflym** *adj* quick, fast, swift
**cyflymder**, **-dra** *nm* swiftness, speed
**cyflymu** *vb* speed, accelerate
**cyflynu** *vb* stick together
**cyflyru** *vb* condition
**cyflythreniad** (**-au**) *nm* alliteration
**cyfnerthu** *vb* confirm; aid, help
**cyfnerthydd** (**-ion**, **-wyr**) *nm* strengthener, booster
**cyfnesaf** (**-iaid**, **-eifiaid**) *nm/f* next of kin, kinsman ♦ *adj* next, nearest
**cyfnewid** *vb* change, exchange
**cyfnewidfa** (**-oedd**, **-feydd**) *nf* exchange
**cyfnewidiad** (**-au**) *nm* change,

alteration

**cyfnewidiol** adj changeable

**cyfnewidiwr** (-wyr) nm changer, trader

**cyfnither** (-oedd) nf female cousin

**cyfnod** (-au) nm period

**cyfnodol** adj periodic(al) ♦ **-yn** (-ion) nm periodical publication

**cyfnos** nm evening twilight, dusk

**cyfochredd** nm parallelism

**cyfochrog** adj parallel

**cyfodi** vb rise, arise; raise

**cyfodiad** nm rise, rising

**cyfoed** adj contemporary, of the same age ♦ (-ion) nm contemporaries

**cyfoes** adj contemporary

**cyfoesi** vb be contemporary

**cyfoeswr** (-wyr) nm contemporary

**cyfoeth** nm power; riches, wealth

**cyfoethog** adj powerful; rich, wealthy

**cyfoethogi** vb make or grow rich

**cyfog** nm sickness

**cyfogi** vb vomit

**cyfor** nm flood, abundance; rim, brim, edge ♦ adj entire, brim-full

**cyforiog** adj brim-full, overflowing

**cyfosodiad** nm apposition

**cyfradd** (-au) nf rate. **c. llog** rate of interest ♦ adj of equal rank

**cyfraid** (-reidiau) nm necessity

**cyfraith** (-reithiau) nf law

**cyfran** (-nau) nf part, portion, share

**cyfranc** (-rangau) nf/m meeting; combat; incident; story, tale

**cyfranddaliad** (-au) nm share

**cyfranddaliwr** (-wyr) nm shareholder

**cyfraniad** (-au) nm contribution

**cyfrannog** adj participating, partaking

**cyfrannol** adj contributing

**cyfrannu** vb contribute; impart

**cyfrannwr** (-anwyr) nm contributor

**cyfranogi** vb participate, partake

**cyfranogwr** (-wyr) nm partaker

**cyfredol** adj current, concurrent

**cyfreithio** vb go to law, litigate

**cyfreithiol** adj legal

**cyfreithiwr** (-wyr) nm lawyer

**cyfreithlon** adj lawful, legitimate

**cyfreithlondeb** nm lawfulness

**cyfreithloni** vb legalize; justify

**cyfreithus** adj legitimate

**cyfres** (-i) nf series

**cyfresol** adj serial

**cyfresu** vb serialise

**cyfresymiad** (-au) nm syllogism

**cyfresymu** vb syllogise

**cyfrgolli** vb lose utterly; damn

**cyfrif** vb count, reckon; account; impute ♦ (-on) nm account, reckoning

**cyfrifeg** nm/f accountancy

**cyfrifiad** (-au) nm counting; census

**cyfrifiadur** (-on) nm computer

**cyfrifiadureg** nf computer science

**cyfrifianell** nf calculator

**cyfrifol** adj of repute; responsible

**cyfrifoldeb** (-au) nm responsibility

**cyfrifydd** (-ion) nm statistician, accountant

**cyfrin** adj secret, subtle

**cyfrinach** (-au) nf secret

**cyfrinachol** adj secret, private, confidential

**cyfrinfa** nf lodge of friendly society or trade union

**cyfrin-gyngor** (-nghorau) nm privy council

**cyfriniaeth** nf mystery; mysticism

**cyfriniol** adj mysterious, mystic

**cyfriniwr** (-wyr) nm mystic

**cyfrodedd** adj twisted, twined

**cyfrodeddu** vb twist, twine

**cyfrol** (-au) nf volume

**cyfrwng** (-ryngau) nm medium, means

**cyfrwy** (-au) nm saddle

**cyfrwyo** vb saddle

**cyfrwys** adj cunning

**cyfrwystra** nm cunning

**cyfrwywr** (-wyr) *nm* saddler
**cyfryngdod** *nm* mediation,
intercession; mediatorship
**cyfryngiad** *nm* mediation;
intervention
**cyfryngol** *adj* mediatorial
**cyfryngu** *vb* mediate; intervene
**cyfryngwr** (-wyr) *nm* mediator
**cyfryngwriaeth** *nf* mediatorship
**cyfryw** *adj* like, such
**cyfuchlinedd** (-au) *nm* contour
**cyfuchliniau** *npl* contours
**cyfundeb** (-au) *nm* union;
connexion
**cyfundebol** *adj* connexional;
denominational
**cyfundrefn** (-au) *nf* system
**cyfundrefnol** *adj* systematic
**cyfundrefnu** *vb* systematize
**cyfuniad** (-au) *nm* combination
**cyfuno** *vb* unite, combine
**cyfunol** *adj* united
**cyfunrywiol** *adj* homosexual
**cyfuwch** *adj* as high
**cyfweld** *vb* interview
**cyfweliad** (-au) *nm* interview
**cyfwerth** *adj* equivalent
**cyfwng** (-yngau) *nm* space;
interval
**cyfwrdd** *vb* meet
**cyfyng** *adj* narrow, confined
**cyfyngder** (-au) *nm* trouble,
distress
**cyfyngdra** *nm* narrowness;
distress
**cyfyngedig** *adj* confined,
restricted, limited
**cyfyng-gyngor** *nm* perplexity
**cyfyngu** *vb* narrow, confine, limit
**cyfyl** *nm* neighbourhood. **ar ei g.**
near him
**cyfyrder** (-dyr) *nm* second cousin
**cyfystlys** *adj* side by side
**cyfystyr** *adj* synonymous
**cyfystyron** *npl* synonyms
**cyff** (-ion) *nm* stock
**cyffaith** (-ffeithiau) *nm* confection

**cyffelyb** *adj* like, similar
**cyffelybiaeth** (-au) *nf* likeness,
similitude
**cyffelybiaethol** *adj* figurative
**cyffelybrwydd** *nm* likeness,
similarity
**cyffelybu** *vb* liken, compare
**cyffes** (-ion) *nf* confession
**cyffesgell** (-oedd) *nf* confessional
**cyffesu** *vb* confess
**cyffeswr** (-wyr), **-ydd** (-ion) *nm*
confessor
**cyffin** (-iau, -ydd) *nf/m* border,
confine
**cyffindir** (-oedd) *nm* frontier,
march
**cyffio** *vb* stiffen; fetter, shackle;
beat
**cyffion** *npl* stocks
**cyffordd** (-ffyrdd) *nf* junction
**cyffredin** *adj* common; general
**cyffredinedd** *nm* mediocrity,
banality
**cyffredinol** *adj* general, universal
**cyffredinoli** *vb* universalize,
generalize
**cyffredinolrwydd** *nm* universality
**cyffredinwch** *nm* commonness
**cyffro** (-adau) *nm* motion, stir;
excitement
**cyffroi** *vb* move, excite; provoke
**cyffrous** *adj* exciting; excited
**cyffur** (-iau) *nm/f* ingredient, drug
**cyffuriwr** (-wyr) *nm* apothecary,
druggist
**cyffwrdd** *vb* meet, touch
**cyffylog** (-od) *nm* woodcock
**cyffyrddiad** (-au) *nm* touch,
contact
**cyffyrddus** *adj* comfortable
**cygnog** *adj* knotted, gnarled
**cyngaf, cyngaw** *nm* burdock; burs
**cyngan** *adj* suitable, harmonious
**cynganeddol** *adj* in *cynghanedd*
**cynganeddu** *vb* form *cynghanedd*;
harmonize
**cynganeddwr** (-wyr) *nm* writer of

*cynghanedd*

**cyngaws (cynghawsau, -ion)** *nm*
lawsuit, action; trial; battle

**cyngerdd (-ngherddau)** *nm/f*
concert

**cynghanedd (cynganeddion)** *nf*
music, harmony; Welsh metrical
alliteration

**cynghori** *vb* counsel, advise;
exhort

**cynghorwr (-wyr)** *nm* councillor;
counsellor; exhorter

**cynghrair (-eiriau)** *nm/f* alliance,
league

**cynghreiriad (-iaid)** *nm*
confederate, ally

**cynghreirio** *vb* league, confederate

**cynghreiriwr (-wyr)** *nm*
confederate, ally

**cyngor (-nghorion)** *nm* counsel,
advice ♦ **(-nghorau)** *nm* council.
**C. Bro** Community Council. **C.
Tref** Town Council. **C. Sir** County
Council

**cyngres (-au, -i)** *nf* congress

**cyngresydd (-wyr)** *nm*
congressman

**cyngwystl (-(i)on)** *nm/f* wager,
pledge

**cyhoedd** *adj*, *nm* public

**cyhoeddi** *vb* publish, announce

**cyhoeddiad (-au)** *nm* publication;
announcement; (preaching)
engagement

**cyhoeddus** *adj* public

**cyhoeddusrwydd** *nm* publicity

**cyhoeddwr (-wyr)** *nm* publisher

**cyhuddiad (-au)** *nm* accusation,
charge

**cyhuddo** *vb* accuse, charge

**cyhuddwr (-wyr)** *nm* accuser

**cyhwfan** *vb* wave, heave

**cyhyd** *adj* as long, so long

**cyhydedd** *nm* equator

**cyhydeddol** *adj* equatorial,
equinoctial

**cyhyr (-au)** *nm* flesh, muscle

**cyhyrog** *adj* muscular

**cylch (-au, oedd)** *nm* round, circle,
sphere, hoop

**cylchdaith (-deithiau)** *nf* circuit

**cylchdro (-eon, -adau)** *nm* orbit

**cylchdroi** *vb* rotate, revolve

**cylched (-au)** *nm* coverlet, blanket

**cylchedd (-au)** *nm/f* compass,
circle, circuit

**cylchgrawn (-gronau)** *nm*
magazine

**cylchlythyr (-au)** *nm* circular

**cylchredeg** *vb* circulate

**cylchrediad** *nm* circulation

**cylchres (-i)** *nf* round, rota

**cylchwyl (-iau)** *nf* anniversary,
festival

**cylchynol** *adj* surrounding

**cylchynu** *vb* surround, encompass

**cylion** *npl* **(-yn** *nm*, **-en** *nf*) flies,
gnats

**cylymu** *vb* knot, tie

**cyll** *npl* **(collen** *nf*) hazel-trees

**cylla (-on)** *nm* stomach

**cyllell (-yll)** *nf* knife

**cyllid (-au)** *nm* revenue, income

**cyllideb (-au)** *nf* budget

**cyllidol** *adj* financial, fiscal

**cyllidwr (-wyr)**, **cyllidydd (-ion)**
*nm* taxgatherer, revenue or
excise officer, financier

**cymaint** *adj* as big, as much, as
many; so big, *etc*

**cymal (-au)** *nm* joint; clause
(*gram.*)

**cymalwst** *nf* rheumatism

**cymanfa (-oedd)** *nf* assembly;
festival

**cymantoledd (-au)** *nm* equilibrium

**cymanwlad** *nf* commonwealth

**cymar (-heiriaid)** *nm* fellow,
partner

**cymathiad** *nm* assimilation

**cymathu** *vb* assimilate

**cymdeithas (-au)** *nf* society,
association. **C. yr Iaith Gymraeg**
The Welsh Language Society

**cymdeithaseg** *nf/m* sociology
**cymdeithasegol** *adj* sociological
**cymdeithasgar** *adj* sociable
**cymdeithasol** *adj* social
**cymdeithasu** *vb* associate
**cymdogaeth** (**-au**) *nf* neighbourhood
**cymdogol** *adj* neighbourly
**cymedr** (**-au**) *nm* mean (*maths*), average
**cymedrol** *adj* moderate, temperate
**cymedroldeb** *nm* moderation, temperance
**cymedroli** *vb* moderate
**cymedrolwr** (**-wyr**) *nm* moderator; moderate drinker
**cymell** *vb* urge, press, persuade, induce
**cymen** *adj* wise, skilful, neat, becoming
**cymer** (**-au**) *nm* confluence
**cymeradwy** *adj* acceptable, approved, commendable
**cymeradwyaeth** *nf* approval; applause
**cymeradwyo** *vb* approve; recommend
**cymeradwyol** *adj* commendatory
**cymeriad** (**-au**) *nm* character, reputation
**cymesur** *adj* proportionate, symmetrical
**cymesuredd** *nm* proportion, symmetry
**cymesurol** *adj* commensurate, proportionate
**cymhareb** (**cymarebau**) *nf* ratio
**cymhariaeth** (**cymariaethau**) *nf* comparison
**cymharol** *adj* comparative
**cymharu** *vb* pair; compare
**cymhathu** *vb* assimilate
**cymhelliad** (**-hellion**) *nm* motive, inducement
**cymhelliant** (**-nnau**) *nm* motivation
**cymhendod** *nm* knowledge; proficiency; tidiness; eloquence;
affection
**cymhennu** *vb* put in order, trim; scold, reprove
**cymhercyn** *adj* limping, infirm ♦ *nm* valetudinarian
**cymhleth** (**-au**) *adj* complex, complicated
**cymhlethdod** (**-au**) *nm* complexity
**cymhlethu** *vb* complicate
**cymhorthdal** (**cymorthdaloedd**) *nm* subsidy, grant
**cymhwysiad** *nm* application, adjustment
**cymhwyso** *vb* apply, adjust
**cymhwyster** (**cymwysterau**) *nm* fitness, suitability; (*pl*) qualifications
**cymod** *nm* reconciliation
**cymodi** *vb* reconcile; be reconciled
**cymodol** *adj* reconciliatory, propitiatory
**cymodwr** (**-wyr**) *nm* reconciler
**cymon** *adj* orderly, tidy; seemly
**cymorth** *vb* assist, aid, help ♦ *nm* assistance, aid, help
**Cymraeg** *nf/m, adj* Welsh
**Cymraes** *nf* Welshwoman
**cymrawd** (**-odyr**) *nm* comrade, fellow
**Cymreictod** *nm* Welshness
**Cymreig** *adj* Welsh
**Cymreigaidd** *adj* Welshy
**Cymreiges** (**-au**) *nf* Welshwoman
**Cymreigio** *vb* translate into Welsh
**Cymreigiwr** (**-wyr**) *nm* one versed or skilled in Welsh; Welsh-speaking Welshman
**Cymro** (**Cymry**) *nm* Welshman
**cymrodedd** *nm* arbitration; compromise
**cymrodeddu** *vb* compromise, reconcile
**cymrodor** (**-ion**) *nm* consociate, fellow
**cymrodoriaeth** *nf* fellowship
**Cymru** *nf* Wales
**cymrwd** *nm* mortar, plaster

**Cymry** see **Cymro**
**cymryd** vb take, accept. **c. ar** pretend
**cymun, -deb** nm communion, fellowship
**cymuned** nf community
**cymunedol** adj community
**cymuno** vb commune
**cymunwr** (-wyr) nm communicant
**cymwy** (-au) nm affliction
**cymwynas** (-au) nf kindness, favour
**cymwynasgar** adj obliging, kind
**cymwynasgarwch** nm obligingness, kindness
**cymwynaswr** (-wyr) nm benefactor
**cymwys** adj fit, proper, suitable; exact
**cymwysedig** adj applied
**cymwysiadol** adj applicable
**cymydog** (cymdogion) nm neighbour; f **cymdoges**
**cymylog** adj cloudy, clouded
**cymylu** vb cloud, dim, obscure
**cymyndod** nm committal
**cymynnu** vb bequeath
**cymynrodd** (-ion) nf legacy, bequest
**cymynroddi** vb bequeath
**cymynu** vb hew, fell
**cymynwr** (-wyr) nm hewer, feller
**cymysg** adj mixed
**cymysgedd** nm/f mixture
**cymysgfa** nf mixture, medley, hotchpotch
**cymysgliw** adj motley
**cymysglyd** adj muddled, confused
**cymysgryw** adj mongrel; heterogeneous
**cymysgu** vb mix, blend; confuse
**cymysgwch** nm mixture, jumble
**cymysgwr** (-wyr) nm mixer, blender
**cyn** prefix before, previous, first, former, pre-, ex-
**cyn** adv: **cyn wynned â** as white as

**cŷn** (cynion) nm wedge, chisel
**cynadledda** vb meet in conference
**cynaeafu** vb harvest
**cynamserol** adj premature, untimely
**cynaniad** nm pronunciation
**cynanu** vb pronounce
**cyndad** (-au) nm forefather, ancestor
**cynderfynol** adj semi-final
**cyndyn** adj stubborn, obstinate
**cyndynnu** vb be obstinate
**cyndynrwydd** nm stubborness, obstinacy
**cynddaredd** nf madness; rabies
**cynddeiriog** adj mad, rabid
**cynddeiriogi** vb madden, enrage
**cynddeiriogrwydd** nm rage, fury
**cynddrwg** adj as bad
**cynddydd** nm day-break, dawn
**cynefin** adj acquainted, accustomed, familiar ♦ nm haunt, habitat
**cynefindra** nm use, familarity
**cynefino** vb get used, become accustomed
**cynefinol** adj usual, accustomed
**cynfas** (-au) nf/m (bed) sheet; canvas
**cynfyd** nm primitive world, antiquity
**cynffon** (-nau) nf tail; tang
**cynffonna** vb fawn, toady, cringe
**cynffonnwr** (-onwyr) nm toady, sycophant; sneak
**cyn-geni** adj antenatal
**cynhadledd** (cynadleddau) nf conference
**cynhaeaf** (cynaeafau) nm harvest
**cyn(h)aeafa** vb dry in the sun
**cyn(h)aeafu** vb harvest
**cyn(h)aeafwr** (-wyr) nm harvester
**cynhaliaeth** nf maintenance, support
**cynhaliol** adj sustaining
**cynhaliwr** (-wyr) nm supporter, sustainer

**cynhanesiol** *adj* prehistoric
**cynhebrwng** (**-yngau**) *nm* funeral
**cynhenid** *adj* innate
**cynhennu** *vb* contend, quarrel
**cynhennus** *adj* contentious, quarrelsome
**cynhennwr** (**-henwyr**) *nm* wrangler
**cynhesol** *adj* agreeable, amiable
**cynhesrwydd** *nm* warmth
**cynhesu** *vb* warm, get warm
**cynhorthwy** (**cynorthwyon**) *nm* help, aid
**cynhwynol** *adj* natural, congenital, innate
**cynhwysedd** (**cynwyseddau**) *nm* capacity, capacitance
**cynhwysfawr** *adj* comprehensive
**cynhwysiad** *nm* contents
**cynhyrchiad** (**-au**) *nm* production
**cynhyrchiol** *adj* productive
**cynhyrchu** *vb* produce
**cynhyrchydd** (**-ion, cynhyrchwyr**) *nm* producer, generator
**cynhyrfiad** (**cynyrfiadau**) *nm* stirring, agitation
**cynhyrfiol** *adj* stirring, thrilling
**cynhyrfu** *vb* stir, agitate
**cynhyrfus** *adj* agitated; exciting
**cynhyrfwr** (**-wyr**) *nm* agitator, disturber
**cynhysgaeth** *nf* dower, portion, fortune
**cyni** *nm* anguish, distress, adversity
**cynifer** *adj, nm* as many, so many
**cynigiad** (**-au**) *nm* proposal, motion
**cynigiwr** (**-wyr**), **-ydd** (**-ion**) *nm* proposer, mover
**cynildeb** *nm* frugality, economy
**cynilion** *npl* savings
**cynilo** *vb* save, economise
**cynio** *vb* chisel, gouge
**cyniwair** *vb* go to and fro, frequent
**cyniweirfa** (**-feydd**) *nf* resort, haunt

**cyniweirydd** *nm* wayfarer
**cynllun** (**-iau**) *nm* pattern; plan
**cynllunio** *vb* plan, design
**cynllunydd** (**-ion, -wyr**) *nm* designer
**cynllwyn** *vb* plot, conspire ♦ (**-ion**) *nm* plot
**cynllwynio** *vb* conspire, plot
**cynllwynwr** (**-wyr**) *nm* conspirator
**cynnal** *vb* hold, uphold, support, sustain
**cynnar** *adj* early
**cynnau** *vb* kindle, light
**cynneddf** (**cyneddfau**) *nf* quality, faculty
**cynnen** (**cynhennau**) *nf* contention, strife. **asgwrn y g.** bone of contention
**cynnes** *adj* warm
**cynnig** *vb* offer; attempt; propose, move; bid; apply ♦ (**cynigion**) *nm* offer; attempt; motion
**cynnil** *adj* economical; delicate
**cynnor** (**cynhorau**) *nf* door-post
**cynnud** *nm* firewood, fuel
**cynnull** *vb* collect, gather, assemble
**cynnwrf** *nm* stir, commotion, agitation
**cynnwys** *vb* contain, include, comprise, comprehend ♦ *nm* content(s)
**cynnydd** *nm* increase, growth, progress
**cynnyrch** (**cynhyrchion**) *nm* produce, product; (*pl*) productions
**cynoesol** *adj* primeval
**cynorthwyo** *vb* help, assist
**cynorthwyol** *adj* auxiliary; assistant
**cynorthwywr** (**-wyr**) *nm* helper, assistant
**cynradd** *adj* primary
**cynrhon** *npl* (**-yn** *nm*) maggots
**cynrhoni** *vb* breed maggots
**cynrhonllyd** *adj* maggoty

**cynrychioladol** *adj* representative
**cynrychiolaeth** *nf* representation
**cynrychioli** *vb* represent
**cynrychiolwr (-wyr), -ydd (-ion)** *nm* representative, delegate
**cynt** *adj* earlier, sooner, quicker ♦ *adv* see **gynt**
**cyntaf** *adj, adv* first
**cyntedd (-au)** *nm* court; porch, foyer
**cyntefig** *adj* prime, primitive
**cyntun** *nm* nap
**cynulleidfa (-oedd)** *nf* congregation
**cynulleidfaol** *adj* congregational
**cynulliad (-au)** *nm* gathering
**cynuta** *vb* gather fuel
**cynyddol** *adj* increasing, growing
**cynyddu** *vb* increase
**cynysgaeddu** *vb* endow, endue
**cyplad** *nm* copula
**cypladu** *vb* copulate
**cyplu, cyplysu** *vb* couple
**cyraeddadwy** *adj* attainable
**cyraeddiadau** *npl* attainments
**cyrbibion** *npl* atoms, smithereens
**cyrcydu** *vb* squat, cower
**cyrch (-au)** *nm* attack
**cyrchfa (-feydd)** *nf* resort
**cyrchu** *vb* go, resort, repair
**cyrhaeddgar** *adj* telling, incisive
**cyrhaeddiad (cyraeddiadau)** *nm* reach, attainment
**cyrliog** *adj* curly
**cyrraedd** *vb* reach, attain; arrive
**cyrren** *npl* (**cyrensen** *nf*) currants
**cyrydiad** *nm* corrosion
**cyrydu** *vb* corrode
**cysawd (-odau)** *nm* system; constellation
**cysefin** *adj* original, primordial
**cysegr (-au, -oedd)** *nm* sanctuary
**cysegredig** *adj* consecrated, sacred
**cysegredigrwydd** *nm* sacredness
**cysegriad (-au)** *nm* consecration
**cysegr-ladrad** *nm* sacrilege

**cysegr-lân** *adj* holy
**cysegru** *vb* consecrate, dedicate, devote
**cyseinedd** *nm* alliteration
**cysetlyd** *adj* fastidious
**cysgadrwydd** *nm* sleepiness, drowsiness
**cysgadur (-iaid)** *nm* sleeper
**cysglyd** *adj* sleepy
**cysgod (-au, -ion)** *nm* shade, shadow; shelter; type
**cysgodi** *vb* shadow, shade; shelter
**cysgodol** *adj* shady, sheltered
**cysgu** *vb* sleep
**cysgwr (-wyr)** *nm* sleeper
**cysidro** *vb* consider
**cysodi** *vb* set type, compose
**cysodydd (-ion, -wyr)** *nm* compositor
**cyson** *adj* consistent, constant
**cysondeb** *nm* consistency; regularity
**cysoni** *vb* harmonize; reconcile
**cysonwr (-wyr), -ydd (-ion)** *nm* harmonist
**cystadleuaeth (-au)** *nf* competition
**cystadleuol** *adj* competitive
**cystadleuwr, -ydd (-wyr)** *nm* competitor
**cystadlu** *vb* compete; compare
**cystal** *adj* as good, so good ♦ *adv* as well, so well
**cystrawen (-nau)** *nf* construction, syntax
**cystudd (-iau)** *nm* affliction; illness
**cystuddiedig** *adj* afflicted, contrite
**cystuddio** *vb* afflict, trouble
**cystuddiol** *adj* afflicted
**cystuddiwr (-wyr)** *nm* afflicter, oppressor
**cystwyo** *vb* chastise, castigate, trounce
**cysur (-on)** *nm* comfort, consolation
**cysuro** *vb* comfort, console
**cysurus** *adj* comfortable

**cysurwr** (-wyr) *nm* comforter
**cyswllt** (-ylltiadau) *nm* joint, junction
**cysylltiad** (-au) *nm* conjunction; joining, connexion
**cysylltiol** *adj* connecting; connected
**cysylltnod** (-au) *nm* ligature, hyphen
**cysylltu** *vb* join, connect
**cysylltydd** (-ion) *nm* connector, contact
**cysyniad** (-au) *nm* concept
**cytbell** *adj* equidistant
**cytbwys** *adj* of equal weight
**cytbwysedd** *nm* balance
**cytew** *nm* batter
**cytgan** (-au) *nm/f* chorus
**cytgord** *nm* concord
**cytir** (-oedd) *nm* common
**cytras** *adj* allied, related; cognate
**cytsain** (-seiniaid) *nf* consonant
**cytûn** *adj* agreed, of one accord, unanimous
**cytundeb** (-au) *nm* agreement, consent
**cytuno** *vb* agree, consent
**cythlwng** *nm* fasting, fast, hunger
**cythraul** (-euliaid) *nm* devil, demon
**cythreuldeb** *nm* devilment
**cythreulig** *adj* devilish, fiendish
**cythru** *vb* snatch, rush
**cythruddo** *vb* annoy, provoke, irritate
**cythrwfl** *nm* uproar, tumult
**cythryblu** *vb* trouble, agitate
**cythryblus** *adj* troubled, agitated
**cyw** (-ion) *nm* young bird, chick, chicken; baby
**cywain** *vb* convey, carry; garner
**cywair** (-eiriau) *nm* order; key; tune
**cywaith** (-weithiau) *nm* collective work, project
**cywarch** *nm* hemp
**cywasg, -edig** *adj* compressor, diminished

**cywasgiad** (-au) *nm* contraction, compression
**cywasgu** *vb* contract, compress
**cywasgydd** (-ion) *nm* compressor
**cyweiriad** (-au) *nm* repair
**cyweiriadur** (-on) *nm* modulator
**cyweirio** *vb* set in order; prepare, dress
**cyweirnod** (-au) *nm* key-note
**cywen** (-nod) *nf* pullet, young hen
**cywerth** *adj* equivalent
**cywilydd** *nm* shame; shyness
**cywilydd-dra** *nm* shamefulness
**cywilyddgar** *adj* bashful, shy
**cywilyddio** *vb* shame; be ashamed
**cywilyddus** *adj* shameful, disgraceful
**cywir** *adj* correct, accurate, true, faithful
**cywirdeb** *nm* correctness; integrity
**cywiriad** (-au) *nm* correction
**cywiro** *vb* correct; make good; perform
**cywirwr** (-wyr) *nm* corrector
**cywladu** *vb* naturalize
**cywrain** *adj* skilful; curious
**cywreinbeth** (-au, -einion) *nm* curiosity
**cywreindeb** *nm* skill, ingenuity
**cywreinrwydd** *nm* skill; curiosity
**cywydd** (-au) *nm* alliterative Welsh poem
**cywyddwr** (-wyr) *nm* composer of *cywyddau*

# CH

**Chile** *nf* Chile
**China** *nf* China
**chwa** (-on) *nf* puff, gust, breeze
**chwaer** (chwiorydd) *nf* sister
**chwaeroliaeth** *nf* sisterhood
**chwaeth** (-au, -oedd) *nf* taste
**chwaethu** *vb* taste
**chwaethus** *adj* tasteful; decent

**chwaith** adv nor either, neither
**chwâl** adj scattered, loose
**chwalfa** (-feydd) nf upset, rout
**chwalu** vb scatter, spread
**chwalwr** (-wyr) nm scatterer, demolisher
**chwaneg** adj, nm more
**chwanegiad** (-au) nm addition
**chwanegol** adj additional
**chwanegu** vb add, augment, increase
**chwannen** (chwain) nf flea
**chwannog** adj desirous; addicted; prone
**chwant** (-au) nm desire, craving, lust
**chwantu** vb desire, lust
**chwap** nm sudden blow, moment ♦ adv instantly
**chwarae, chware** vb play ♦ (-on) nm play
**chwaraedy** (-dai) nm playhouse, theatre
**chwaraefa** (-feydd) nf pitch, playground
**chwaraegar** adj playful, sportive
**chwaraewr** (-wyr) nm player, actor, performer
**chwaraeydd** (-ion) nm actor
**chwarddiad** (-au) nm laugh
**chwarel** (-au, -i, -ydd) nf quarry
**chwarelwr** (-wyr) nm quarryman
**chwareus** adj playful
**chwarren** (-arennau) nf gland; kernel
**chwart** (-iau) nm quart
**chwarter** (-i, -au) nm quarter
**chwarterol** adj quarterly
**chwarterolyn** (-olion) nm quarterly (magazine)
**chwarteru** vb quarter
**chwe** adj six (before a noun)
**chweban** (-nau) nm sestet, sextain
**chwech** adj six ♦ (-au) nm six; sixpence
**chwechawd** (-au) nm sextet
**chwedl** (-au) nf story, tale

**chwedleua** vb talk, gossip
**chwedleuwr** (-wyr) nm story-teller
**chwedloniaeth** nf mythology
**chwedlonol** adj mythical, mythological
**chwedlonydd** (-wyr) nm mythologist
**chwedyn** adv: **na chynt na ch.** neither before nor after
**Chwefror, Chwefrol** nm February
**chwennych, chwenychu** vb covet, desire
**chwenychiad** (-au) nm desire
**chweongl** (-au) nm hexagon
**chwephlyg** adj sixfold
**chwerthin** vb laugh ♦ nm laughter
**chwerthiniad** (-au) nm laugh
**chwerthinllyd** adj laughable, ridiculous
**chwerthinog** adj laughing, merry
**chwerw** adj bitter
**chwerwder, -dod** nm bitterness
**chwerwedd** nm bitterness
**chwerwi** vb grow bitter, embitter
**chwi** pron you
**chwib** (-iau) nm whistle
**chwiban** vb, nm whistle
**chwibaniad** nm whistling, whistle
**chwibanogl** (-au) nf whistle, flute
**chwibanu** vb whistle
**chwibon** (-iaid) nm curlew, stork
**chwifio** vb wave, flourish, brandish
**chwiff** (-iau) nf whiff, puff
**chwiffiad** nm whiff, jiffy
**chwil** (-od) nm/f beetle, chafer
**chwil** adj whirling, reeling
**chwilboeth** adj scorching, piping hot
**chwildroi** vb whirl, spin
**chwilen** (chwilod) nf beetle
**chwilenna** vb rummage; pry; pilfer
**chwiler** (-od) nm chrysalis, pupa
**chwilfriw** adj smashed to atoms
**chwilfriwio** vb smash, shatter
**chwilfrydedd** nm curiosity
**chwilfrydig** adj curious, inquisitive

**chwilgar** *adj* curious, inquisitive
**chwilgarwch** *nm* inquisitiveness
**chwiliad** (-au) *nm* search, scrutiny
**chwilibawa(n)** *vb* dawdle, trifle
**chwilio** *vb* search; examine
**chwiliwr** (-wyr) *nm* searcher
**chwil-lys** *nm* inquisition
**chwilmantan** *vb* pry, rummage
**chwilolau** (-oleuadau) *nm* searchlight
**chwilota** *vb* rummage, pry
**chwilotwr** (-wyr) *nm* searcher, rummager
**chwim** *adj* nimble, quick, agile
**chwimder, -dra** *nm* nimbleness
**chwimio** *vb* move, stir, accelerate
**chwimwth** *adj* nimble, brisk
**chwinc** *nm* wink
**chwinciad** *nm* twinkling, trice
**chwiorydd** see **chwaer**
**chwip** (-iau) *nf* whip; whipping
**chwipiad** (-au) *nm* whipping
**chwipio** *vb* whip
**chwipyn** *adv* instantly
**chwirligwgan** *nf* whirligig
**chwisgi** *nm* whisky
**chwisl** (-au) *nm* whistle
**chwistrell** (-au, -i) *nf* squirt, syringe
**chwistrelliad** (-au) *nm* injection
**chwistrellu** *vb* squirt, syringe, inject
**chwit-chwat** *adj* fickle, inconstant
**chwith** *adj* left; wrong; sad; strange
**chwithau** *pron conj* you (on your part), you also
**chwithdod, -dra** *nm* strangeness
**chwithig** *adj* strange, wrong, awkward
**chwithigrwydd** *nm* awkwardness
**chwiw** (-iau) *nf* fit, attack, malady
**chwiwgar** *adj* fickle
**chwychwi** *pron* you yourselves
**chwŷd, chwydiad** *nm* vomit
**chwydu** *vb* vomit, spew
**chwydd, chwyddi** *nm* swelling

**chwyddiant** (-nnau) *nm* inflation; inflammation
**chwyddo** *vb* swell, increase, magnify
**chwyddwydr** (-au) *nm* microscope
**chwŷl** (chwylion) *nm/f* turn, rotation
**chwyldro** (-ion) *nm* rotation; orbit
**chwyldroad** (-au) *nm* revolution
**chwyldroadol** *adj* revolutionary
**chwyldroadwr** (-wyr) *nm* revolutionary
**chwyldroi** *vb* whirl, revolve, rotate
**chwyldrowr** see **chwyldroadwr**
**chwylolwyn** (-ion) *nf* flywheel
**chwyn** (chwynnyn *nm*) *coll n, npl* weeds
**chwynladdwr** *nm* weed-killer
**chwynnu** *vb* weed
**chwyrligwgan** (-od) *nm* spinning top, whirligig
**chwyrlïo** *vb* whirl, spin, speed
**chwyrlwynt** (-oedd) *nm* whirlwind
**chwyrn** *adj* rapid, swift
**chwyrnellu** *vb* whirl, whiz
**chwyrnu** *vb* hum; snore; snarl
**chwyrnwr** (-wyr) *nm* snorer; snarler
**chwys** *nm* sweat, perspiration
**chwysfa** (-feydd) *nf* sweating
**chwysiant** *nm* exudation
**chwysigen** (-igod) *nf* blister, vesicle
**chwyslyd** *adj* sweaty
**chwystyllau** *npl* pores
**chwysu** *vb* sweat, perspire; exude
**chwyswr** (-wyr) *nm* sweater
**chwyth, chwythad** *nm* breath
**chwythbib** (-au) *nf* blowpipe
**chwythbrenni** *npl* woodwinds
**chwythell** (-i) *nf* jet
**chwythiad** (-au) *nm* blow, blast
**chwythu** *vb* blow, blast; breathe; hiss
**chwythwr** (-wyr) *nm* blower

# D

**da** *adj* good, well ♦ (**-oedd**) *nm* good; goods; stock, cattle

**da-da** *nm* sweets

**dacw** *adv* there is, are; behold there

**dad-, dat-** *prefix* un-, dis- re-, back

**dadansoddi** *vb* analyse

**dadansoddiad** (**-au**) *nm* analysis

**dadansoddol** *adj* analytic(al)

**dadansoddwr** (**-wyr**) *nm* analyst

**dadansoddydd** (**-wyr**) *nm* analyser

**dadchwyddiant** (**-nnau**) *nm* deflation

**dad-ddyfrio** *vb* dehydrate

**dadebriad** *nm* resuscitation

**dadebru** *vb* resuscitate, revive

**dadelfeniad** (**-au**) *nm* decomposition

**dadelfennu** *vb* decompose; refine

**dadeni** *vb* regenerate, reanimate ♦ *nm* rebirth, renascence, renaissance

**dadfachu** *vb* unhook

**dadfathiad** *nm* dissimulation

**dadfeiliad** *nm* decay

**dadfeilio** *vb* fall to ruin, decay

**dadflino** *vb* rest (after exertion)

**dadl** (**-euon**) *nf* debate; doubt; plea

**dadlaith** *vb* thaw; dissolve

**dadlau** *vb* argue, debate; plead

**dadleniad** (**-au**) *nm* disclosure, exposure

**dadlennol** *adj* revealing, disclosing, exposing

**dadlennu** *vb* disclose, expose

**dadleoli** *vb* dislocate

**dadleoliad** (**-au**) *nm* dislocation

**dadleuaeth** *nf* polemics, controversy

**dadleugar** *adj* argumentative

**dadleuol** *adj* controversial, polemical

**dadleuwr** (**-wyr**), **-ydd** (**-ion**) *nm* debater, controversialist; advocate

**dadluddedu** *vb* rest (after exertion)

**dadlwytho** *vb* unload, unburden

**dadlygru** *vb* decontaminate

**dadmer** *vb* thaw; dissolve

**dadnitreiddiad** *nm* denitrification

**dadolwch** *nm* propitiation ♦ *vb* worship, seek forgiveness

**dadorchuddio** *vb* unveil, uncover

**dadreolaeth** *nf* decontrol

**dadrewlifiant** *nm* deglaciation

**dadrithiad** (**-au**) *nm* disillusionment

**dadrithio** *vb* disillusion

**dadsefydlu** *vb* disestablish

**dadwaddoli** *vb* disendow

**dadwaddoliad** *nm* disendowment

**dadwneuthur, dadwneud** *vb* undo, unmake

**dadwrdd** *nm* noise, uproar, hubbub

**dadymchwel, -yd** *vb* overturn, overthrow

**daear** (**-oedd**) *nf* earth, ground, soil

**daeardy** (**-dai**) *nm* dungeon

**daeareg** *nf* geology

**daearegol** *adj* geological

**daearegwr** (**-wyr**), **-ydd** (**-ion**) *nm* geologist

**daearen** *nf* the earth; land, country

**daearfochyn** (**-foch**) *nm* badger

**daeargell** (**-oedd**) *nf* dungeon, vault

**daeargi** (**-gwn**) *nm* terrier

**daeargryd** (**-iau**) *nm* earth tremor

**daeargryn** (**-fâu**) *nm/f* earthquake

**daearol** *adj* terrestrial, earthly, earthy

**daearu** *vb* earth; inter

**daearyddiaeth** *nf* geography

**daearyddol** *adj* geographical

**daearyddwr** (-wyr) *nm* geographer

**dafad** (**defaid**) *nf* sheep; wart

**dafaden** (-ennau) *nf* wart

**dafn** (-au) *nm* drop

**dafnu** *vb* trickle

**dagr** (-au) *nm* dagger, bayonet, dirk

**dagrau** *npl* (**deigryn** *nm*) tears

**dagreuol** *adj* tearful, sad

**dangos** see **dan-**

**dail** *npl* (**dalen, deilen** *nf*) leaves

**daioni** *nm* goodness, good

**daionus** *adj* good; beneficial; beneficent

**dal, -a** *vb* hold; catch; arrest; last

**dalen** (-nau, **dail**) *nf* leaf

**dalfa** (-feydd) *nf* hold; arrest, custody; prison

**dalgylch** (-oedd) *nm* catchment area

**daliad** (-au) *nm* holding; tenet; spell

**daliwr** (-wyr) *nm* jig, catcher

**dall** (**deillion**) *adj* blind

**dallbleidiaeth** *nf* bigotry

**dallbleidiol** *adj* bigoted

**dallbleidiwr** (-wyr) *nm* bigot

**dallineb** *nm* blindness

**dallu** *vb* blind; dazzle

**damcaniaeth** (-au) *nf* theory

**damcaniaethol** *adj* theoretical

**damcaniaethwr** (-wyr) *nm* theorist

**damcanu** *vb* theorize, speculate

**dameg** (-hegion) *nf* parable

**damhegol** *adj* parabolic(al), allegorical

**damhegwr** (-wyr) *nm* allegorist

**damnedig** *adj* damned, damnable

**damnedigaeth** *nf* damnation, condemnation

**damnio** *vb* damn

**damniol** *adj* damning, damnatory

**damsang** *vb* tread, trample

**damwain** (-weiniau) *nf* accident, chance, fate

**damweinio** *vb* befall, happen

**damweiniol** *adj* accidental, casual

**dan** see **tan**

**danadl** *npl* (**danhadlen** *nf*) nettles

**danas** *coll n* deer. **bwch d.** buck

**danfon** *vb* send, convey; escort

**dangos** *vb* show

**dangoseg** (-ion) *nf* index; indication

**dangosol** *adj* indicative, demonstrative

**danheddog** *adj* jagged, serrated, toothed

**dannod** *vb* reproach, upbraid, taunt, twit

**dannoedd** *nf* toothache

**dansoddol** *adj* abstract

**dant** (**dannedd**) *nm* tooth

**danteithfwyd** (-teithion) *nm* dainty

**danteithiol** *adj* dainty, delicious

**danteithion** *npl* delicacies

**darbodus** *adj* provident, thrifty

**darbwyllo** *vb* persuade, convince

**darfod** *vb* finish, end; perish; happen

**darfodadwy** *adj* transitory, perishable

**darfodedig** *adj* perishable, transient

**darfodedigaeth** *nm* consumption

**darfudiad** (-au) *nm* convection

**darfudol** *adj* convectional

**darganfod** *vb* discover

**darganfyddiad** (-au) *nm* discovery

**darganfyddwr** (-wyr) *nm* discoverer

**dargludedd** *nm* conductivity

**dargludo** *vb* conduct

**dargludydd** (-ion) *nm* conductor

**dargyfeiredd** *nm* divergence

**dargyfeirio** *vb* diverge, divert

**darlith** (-iau, -oedd) *nf* lecture

**darlithfa** (-feydd) *nf* lecture room

**darlithio** *vb* lecture

**darlithiwr** (-wyr), **-ydd** (-ion) *nm* lecturer

**darlun** (-iau) *nm* picture

**darluniad** (-au) *nm* portrayal, description

**darluniadol** adj pictorial, illustrated

**darluniaeth** nf imagery

**darlunio** vb portray, depict, describe

**darluniol** adj pictorial

**darllediad** (-au) nm broadcast

**darlledu** vb broadcast

**darlledwr** (-wyr) nm broadcaster

**darllen** vb read

**darllenadwy** adj readable, legible

**darllenfa** (-feydd) nf reading room; reading-desk; lectern

**darllengar** adj fond of reading, studious

**darlleniad** (-au) nm reading

**darllenwr** (-wyr), **-ydd** (-ion) nm reader

**darn** (-au) nm piece, fragment, part

**darnguddio** vb conceal or withhold a part

**darniad** (-au) nm fragmentation

**darnio** vb cut up, hack

**darn-ladd** vb beat mercilessly

**darogan** vb predict, foretell, forebode ♦ (-au) nf prediction, foreboding

**daroganu** vb predict, foretell

**daroganwr** (-wyr) nm predictor, prophet, soothsayer, forecaster

**darostwng** vb lower; subdue; subject, humiliate

**darostyngiad** nm humiliation; subjection

**darpar** (-ion, -iadau) nm preparation, provision ♦ adj intended, elect

**darpariaeth** (-au) nf preparation, provision

**darparu** vb prepare, provide

**darparwr** (-wyr) nm provider

**darwden** nf ringworm

**das** (-au, deisi) nf rick, stack

**dat-** prefix see **dad-**

**data** nm data

**datblygiad** (-au) nm development, evolution

**datblygol** adj nascent, developing

**datblygu** vb develop, evolve

**datblygus** adj developmental

**datblygydd** (-ion) nm developer

**datchwyddiant** nm deflation

**datgan** vb declare; recount; render

**datganiad** (-au) nm declaration; rendering

**datganoli** vb devolve, decentralize

**datganoli(ad)** nm devolution

**datganu** vb declare; sing, render

**datgeliad** (-au) nm detection; revelation

**datgelu** vb detect; reveal

**datgloi** vb unlock

**datglymu** vb unhitch, undo

**datgorffori** vb dissolve (parliament)

**datgorfforiad** nm dissolution

**datguddiad** (-au) nm revelation, disclosure

**datguddio** vb reveal, disclose

**datgyffesiad** nm recantation

**datgyffesu** vb recant

**datgymalu** vb dislocate, dismember

**datgysylltiad** nm disestablishment

**datgysylltu** vb disconnect; disestablish

**datod** vb undo, untie, dissolve

**datrannu** vb dissect

**datro** vb change; undo

**datru** vb de-code

**datrys** vb solve

**datrysiad** (-au) nm solution, resolution

**datseinio** vb resound, reverberate

**datsgwar** (-au) nm square root

**datysen** (datys) nf date

**dathliad** (-au) nm celebration

**dathlu** vb celebrate

**dau** adj, nm two; f **dwy**

**dau-, deu-** prefix two, bi-

**dauddyblyg** adj twofold, double

**daufiniog** adj double-edged

**dauwynebog** *adj* two-faced
**dawn** (**doniau**) *nm/f* gift, talent
**dawns** (**-iau**) *nf* dance
**dawnsio** *vb* dance
**dawnsiwr** (**-wyr**) *nm* dancer
**dawnus** *adj* gifted, talented
**de** see **deau**
**De Affrica** *nf* South Africa
**deall** *vb* understand ♦ *nm* understanding, intellect, intelligence
**dealladwy** *adj* intelligible
**deallgar** *adj* intelligent
**deallol** *adj* intellectual
**dealltwriaeth** (**-au**) *nf* understanding, intelligence
**deallus** *adj* understanding, intelligent
**deallusion** *npl* intelligentsia
**deallusrwydd** *nm* intelligence
**deau** *adj*, *nm* right; south
**debentur** (**-on**) *nm* debenture
**debyd** (**-au**) *nm* debit
**debydu** *vb* debit
**dec** (**-iau, -s**) *nm* deck
**decilitr** (**-au**) *nm* decilitre
**decimetr** (**-au**) *nm* decimetre
**decstros** *nm* dextrose
**dectant** *nm* ten-stringed instrument, psaltery
**dechrau** *vb* begin ♦ *nm* beginning
**dechreuad** (**-au**) *nm* beginning
**dechreunos** *nf* nightfall, dusk
**dechreuol** *adj* initial
**dechreuwr** (**-wyr**) *nm* beginner
**dedfryd** (**-au**) *nf* verdict; sentence
**dedfrydu** *vb* sentence
**dedwydd** *adj* happy, blessed
**dedwyddwch, -yd** *nm* happiness, bliss
**deddf** (**-au**) *nf* law, statute, act
**deddfeg** *nf* jurisprudence
**deddfegwr** (**-wyr**) *nm* jurist
**deddfol** *adj* legal, lawful
**deddfu** *vb* legislate, enact
**deddfwr** (**-wyr**) *nm* legislator
**deddfwriaeth** *nf* legislation,
legislature
**deddfwriaethol** *adj* legislative
**deddlyfr** (**-au**) *nm* statute book
**defni** *vb* drip, trickle
**defnydd** (**-iau**) *nm* material, stuff; use
**defnyddio** *vb* use, utilize, employ
**defnyddiol** *adj* useful
**defnyddioldeb** *nm* usefulness, utility
**defnyddiwr** (**-wyr**) *nm* user, consumer
**defnyn** (**-nau**) *nm* drop
**defnynnu** *vb* drop, drip, dribble, distil
**defod** (**-au**) *nf* custom; rite, ceremony
**defodaeth** *nf* ritualism
**defodol** *adj* ritualistic
**defosiwn** (**-ynau**) *nm* devotion
**defosiynol** *adj* devotional, devout
**deffiniad, -io** see **diff-**
**deffro, deffroi** *vb* rouse; wake
**deffroad** (**-au**) *nm* awakening
**deg** *adj* ten ♦ (**-au**) *nm* ten
**degawd** (**-au**) *nm* decade
**degaidd** *adj* denary
**degiad** (**-au**) *nm* decimal
**degol** (**-ion**) *nm*, *adj* decimal
**degoli** *vb* decimalise
**degoliad** *nm* decimalisation
**degolyn** (**degolion**) *nm* decimal
**degwm** (**-ymau**) *nm* tenth, tithe
**degymu** *vb* tithe
**deng** *adj* ten (*before certain words*)
**dehau, deheu** see **deau**
**deheubarth, -dir** *nm* southern region, south
**deheuig** *adj* dexterous, skilful
**deheulaw** *nf* right hand
**deheuol** *adj* southern
**deheurwydd** *nm* dexterity, skill
**deheuwr** (**-wyr**) *nm* southerner, southman
**deheuwynt** *nm* south wind
**dehongli** *vb* interpret
**dehongliad** (**-au**) *nm* interpretation

**dehonglwr** (-wyr), **-ydd** (-ion) *nm* interpreter

**dehydrad** (-au) *nm* dehydration

**dehydru** *vb* dehydrate

**deial** (-au) *nm* dial

**deialog** (-au) *nm/f* dialogue

**deialu** *vb* dial

**deifio** *vb* singe, scorch; blast; dive

**deifiol** *adj* scorching, scathing

**deifiwr** (-wyr) *nm* diver

**deigryn** (**dagrau**) *nm* tear

**deilbridd** *nm* humus

**deildy** (-dai) *nm* bower, arbour

**deilen** (**dail**) *nf* leaf

**deilgoll** *adj* deciduous

**deiliad** (-on, **deiliaid**) *nm* tenant; subject

**deiliant** (-nnau) *nm* foliage

**deilio** *vb* leaf

**deiliog** *adj* leafy

**deillio** *vb* proceed, emanate, issue

**deinameg** *nf/m* dynamics

**deinamig** *adj* dynamic

**deinamo** (-s, -au) *nm* dynamo

**deincod** *nm* teeth on edge

**deincryd** *nm* chattering or gnashing of teeth

**deintio** *vb* nibble

**deintrod** (-au) *nf* cog

**deintydd** (-ion) *nm* dentist

**deintyddiaeth** *nf* dentistry

**deintyddol** *adj* dental

**deiseb** (-au) *nf* petition

**deisebu** *vb* petition

**deisebwr**, **-ydd** (-wyr) *nm* petitioner

**deisyf**, **deisyfu** *vb* desire, wish; beseech, entreat

**deisyfiad** (-au) *nm* request, petition

**del** *adj* pretty, neat

**delfryd** (-au) *nm* ideal

**delfrydiaeth** *nf* idealism

**delfrydol** *adj* ideal

**delfrydwr** (-wyr) *nm* idealist

**delff** *nm* churl, oaf, dolt, rascal

**delio** *vb* deal

**delw** (-au) *nf* image; form, mode, manner

**delwedd** (-au) *nf* image

**delweddaeth** *nf* imagery

**delweddu** *vb* portray

**delwi** *vb* be wool-gathering; pale, be paralysed with fright.

**dellni** *nm* blindness

**dellt** *npl* (-en *nf*) laths, lattice, splinters

**democratiaeth** (-au) *nf* democracy

**democratig** *adj* democratic

**demograffeg** *nf* demography

**demograffig** *adj* demographic

**dengar** *adj* attractive

**dengarwch** *nm* attractiveness

**deniadau** *npl* attractions, allurements

**deniadol** *adj* attractive

**Denmarc** *nf* Denmark

**denu** *vb* attract, allure, entice

**deon** (-iaid) *nm* dean

**deondy** (-dai) *nm* deanery

**deoniaeth** (-au) *nf* deanery

**deor** *vb* brood, hatch, incubate

**deorfa** (-fâu, -feydd) *nf* hatchery

**deorydd** (-ion) *nf* incubator

**derbyn** *vb* receive; accept; admit

**derbyniad** (-au) *nm* receipt; reception

**derbyniadwy** *adj* admissible

**derbyniol** *adj* acceptable

**derbyniwr** (-wyr), **-nnydd** (-ynyddion) *nm* receiver, acceptor

**derbynneb** (-ynebau, -ynebion) *nf* receipt, voucher

**derbynnydd** (-ynyddion) *nm* receiver

**deri** *npl* (**dâr** *nf*) oak-trees, oak

**dernyn** (-nau) *nm* piece, scrap

**derwen** (**derw**, **deri**) *nf* oak-tree, oak

**derwydd** (-on) *nm* druid

**derwyddiaeth** *nf* druidism

**derwyddol** *adj* druidic(al)

**desg** (-iau) *nf* desk

**desgant** (-au) *nm* descant

**desibel** (-au) *nm* decibel
**destlus** *adj* neat
**destlusrwydd** *nm* neatness
**detector** (-au) *nm* detector
**dethol** *vb* select, pick, choose ♦ *adj* select
**detholedd** *nm* selectivity
**detholiad** (-au, detholion) *nm* selection, anthology
**deu-** see **dau-**
**deuawd** (-au) *nm/f* duet
**deublyg** *adj* double, twofold
**deuddeg** *adj, nm* twelve
**deufin** *adj* two-edged
**deuffocal** *adj* bifocal
**deugain** *adj, nm* forty
**deugraff** *nm* digraph
**deunaw** *adj, nm* eighteen
**deunydd** (-iau) *nm* stuff, material
**deuocsid** *nm* dioxide
**deuod** (-au) *nm* diode, binary
**deuol** *adj* dual
**deuoliaeth** *nf* dualism, duality
**deuparth** *nd* two-thirds
**deuris** *adj* two-tier
**deurudd** *nd* the cheeks
**deuryw** *adj* bisexual
**deusain** *nd* diphthong
**deutu** *nd:* o dd. about
**dewin** (-iaid) *nm* diviner, magician, wizard
**dewines** (-au) *nf* witch, sorceress
**dewiniaeth** *nf* divination, witchcraft
**dewinio** *vb* divine
**dewin(i)ol** *adj* prophetic, divinatory
**dewis** *vb* choose, select ♦ *nm* choice
**dewisiad** *nm* choice, option
**dewisol** *adj* choice, desirable
**dewr** *adj* brave ♦ (-ion) *nm* brave man, hero
**dewrder** *nm* bravery, valour
**di-** *neg prefix* without, not, un-, non-, -less
**diabetig** *adj, nm/f* diabetic

**diacon** (-iaid) *nm* deacon
**diacones** (-au) *nf* deaconess
**diaconiaeth** *nf* diaconate
**diadell** (-au, -oedd) *nf* flock
**diaddurn** *adj* unadorned, plain, rude
**diaelodi** *vb* dismember; expel a member
**diafael** *adj* slippery, careless
**diafol** (diefyl, dieifl) *nm* devil
**diaffram** (-au) *nm* diaphragm
**diagnosis** *nm* diagnosis
**diangen** *adj* unnecessary, free from want
**dianghenraid** *adj* unnecessary, needless
**di-ail** *adj* unequalled, unrivalled
**dial** *vb* avenge, revenge ♦ *nm* vengeance, revenge
**dialedd** (-au) *nm* vengeance, nemesis
**dialgar** *adj* revengeful, vindictive
**dialgarwch** *nm* vindictiveness
**di-alw-amdano** *adj* redundant, uncalled for
**dialwr** (-wyr), **-ydd** (-ion) *nm* avenger
**diamau** *adj* doubtless
**diamcan** *adj* aimless, purposeless
**diamedr** (-au) *nm* diameter
**diamedral** *adj* diametral
**diamheuol** *adj* undoubted, indisputable
**diamod** *adj* unconditional, absolute
**diamodol** *adj* unconditional, unqualified
**diamwys** *adj* unambiguous
**diamynedd** *adj* impatient
**dianc** *vb* escape
**dianwadal** *adj* unwavering, immutable
**dianwadalwch** *nm* immutability
**diarddel** *vb* expel, excommunicate
**diarddeliad** *nm* expulsion, excommunication
**diarfogi** *vb* disarm
**diarfogiad** *nm* disarmament

**diarffordd** adj out of the way, inaccessible

**diargyhoedd** adj blameless

**diarhebol** adj proverbial

**diaroglydd** (-ion) nm deodorant

**diarwybod** adj unawares

**diasbad** nf cry, scream

**diasbedain** vb resound, ring

**diatreg** adj immediate

**diau** adj true, certain; doubtless

**diawl** (-iaid) nm devil

**diawledig** adj devilish

**di-baid, dibaid** adj unceasing, ceaseless

**di-ball, diball** adj unfailing, infallible, sure

**diben** (-ion) nm end, purpose, aim

**di-ben-draw** adj endless

**dibeniad** (-au) nm ending, conclusion, predicate

**di-benllanw** adj off-peak

**dibennu** vb end, conclude, finish

**diberfeddu** vb disembowel, eviscerate

**dibetrus** adj unhesitating

**dibl** (-au) nm border, edge

**diboblogaeth** nf depopulation

**diboblogi** vb depopulate

**dibrin** adj abundant, plentiful

**dibriod** adj unmarried, single

**dibris** adj reckless, contemptuous

**dibrisio** vb depreciate, despise

**dibristod** nm depreciation, contempt

**dibwys** adj trivial, unimportant

**dibwysiant** (-nnau) nm depression

**dibyn** (-nau) nm steep, precipice

**dibynadwy** adj reliable

**dibynadwyedd** nm reliability

**dibyniad** nm dependence

**dibyniant** nm dependence

**dibynnedd** nm reliability

**dibynnol** adj depending; subjunctive

**dibynnu** vb depend, rely

**dibynnydd** (dibynyddion) nm dependant

**dicllon** adj wrathful, angry

**dicllonrwydd** nm wrath, indignation

**dicotomi** (-iau) nm dichotomy

**dicra** adj squeamish, fastidious, slow

**dicter** nm anger, wrath, displeasure

**dichell** (-ion) nf wile, craft, guile

**dichellgar** adj wily, crafty, cunning

**dichlyn** vb choose, pick ♦ adj careful, circumspect, exact

**dichon** vb be able; it may be

**di-dact** adj tactless

**didactig** adj didactic

**didaro** adj unaffected, unconcerned, cool

**di-daw** adj ceaseless, clamant

**diden** (-nau) nf nipple, teat

**diderfyn** adj unlimited

**didoli** vb separate, segregate

**didoliad** nm separation, segregation

**didolnod** (-au) nm/f diæresis

**di-dor, didor** adj unbroken, uninterrupted

**didoreth** adj shiftless, silly, fickle

**didoriad** adj unbroken, untamed, rough

**di-drais, didrais** adj non-violent, meek

**diduedd** adj impartial, unbiassed

**didwyll** adj guileless, sincere

**didwylledd** nm guilelessness, sincerity

**di-ddadl** adj unquestionable, indisputable

**diddan** adj amusing, diverting, pleasant

**diddanion** npl pleasantries, jokes

**diddanu** vb amuse, divert; comfort

**diddanwch** nm comfort, consolation

**diddanwr** (-wyr), **-ydd** (-ion) nm comforter

**diddarbod** adj shiftless

**di-dderbyn-wyneb** *adj* outspoken
**diddig** *adj* contented, pleased
**diddigrwydd** *nm* contentment,
placidity
**diddim** *adj, nm* void
**diddordeb** *nm* interest
**diddori** *vb* interest
**diddorol** *adj* interesting
**diddos** *adj* watertight, sheltered;
snug
**diddosi** *vb* shelter
**diddosrwydd** *nm* shelter, safety
**di-dduw, didduw** *adj* ungodly ♦
*nm* atheist
**di-ddweud** *adj* taciturn, stubborn
**diddwythiad** *nm* deduction
**diddwytho** *vb* deduce
**diddyfnu** *vb* wean
**diddymdra** *nm* nothingness, void
**diddymiad** (**-iant**) *nm* annihilation
**diddymu** *vb* annihilate, abolish
**dieflig** *adj* devilish, diabolical,
fiendish
**diegwyddor** *adj* unprincipled
**dieisiau** *adj* unnecessary, needless
**dieithr** *adj* strange, alien, foreign ♦
(**-iaid**) *nm* stranger
**dieithrio** *vb* estrange, alienate
**dieithrwch** *nm* strangeness
**dienaid** *adj* soulless, senseless
**dienyddiad** (**-au**) *nm* execution
**dienyddio** *vb* put to death, execute
**dienyddiwr** (**-wyr**) *nm* executioner
**dieuog** *adj* guiltless, innocent
**difa** *vb* consume, destroy, devour
**di-fai, difai** *adj* blameless, faultless
**difalch** *adj* humble
**difancoll** *nf* total loss, perdition
**difaol** *adj* consuming, devouring
**difater** *adj* indifferent, unconcerned
**difaterwch** *nm* indifference,
apathy
**difeddiannu** *vb* dispossess, deprive
**di-feind** *adj* heedless
**difenwad** (**-au**) *nm* defamation
**difenwi** *vb* revile, abuse, belittle
**diferlif** *nm* stream, issue

**diferol** *adj* dripping, dropping
**diferu** *vb* drip, drop, dribble, distil
**diferyn** (**-nau, diferion**) *nm* drop
**difesur** *adj* huge, immeasurable,
unstinted
**di-feth, difeth** *adj* infallible,
certain
**difetha** *vb* destroy, spoil, waste
**difethwr** (**-wyr**) *nm* destroyer
**Difiau** *nm* Thursday
**difidend** (**-au**) *nm* dividend
**diflanbwynt** *nm* vanishing point
**diflanedig** *adj* evanescent, fleeting
**diflannu** *vb* vanish, disappear
**di-flas** *adj* tasteless
**diflas** *adj* insipid, dull, wearisome
**diflastod** *nm* disgust
**diflasu** *vb* disgust; weary, surfeit
**diflin, -o** *adj* untiring, indefatigable
**difodi** *vb* annihilate, exterminate
**difodiad, -iant** *nm* annihilation
**di-foes, difoes** *adj* rude,
unmannerly
**difreiniad** *nm* disfranchisement
**difreinio** *vb* disfranchise, deprive
**difriaeth** *nf* abuse, calumny
**difrif** *nm* seriousness, earnestness
**difrifddwys** *adj* solemn
**difrifol** *adj* serious, earnest,
solemn, grave
**difrifoldeb** see **difrifwch**
**difrifoli** *vb* sober, solemnize
**difrifwch** *nm* seriousness,
earnestness, solemnity
**difrio** *vb* scold, abuse, malign
**difrod** *nm* waste, havoc, damage
**difrodi** *vb* waste, spoil, ravage
**difrodol** *adj* destructive
**difrodwr** (**-wyr**) *nm* spoiler,
devastator
**difrycheulyd** *adj* spotless,
immaculate
**di-fudd, difudd** *adj* unprofitable,
useless, futile
**di-fwlch, difwlch** *adj* without a
break, continuous
**difwyniad** (**-au**) *nm* adulteration,

pollution

**difwyniant** *nm* defilement

**difwyno** *vb* mar, soil, sully, defile

**difyfyr** *adj* impromptu

**difynio** *vb* dissect, vivisect

**difyr** *adj* pleasant, diverting, amusing

**difyrion** *npl* diversions, amusements

**difyrru** *vb* divert, amuse, beguile

**difyrrus** *adj* diverting, amusing

**difyrrwch** *nm* diversion, amusement, fun

**difyrrwr** (-**yrwyr**) *nm* entertainer

**difyrwaith** (-**weithiau**) *nm* hobby

**difywyd** *adj* inert

**diffaith** *adj* waste, desert; base, mean ♦ (-**ffeithydd**) *nm* wilderness, desert

**diffeithdra** *nm* dereliction

**diffeithio** *vb* lay waste

**diffeithwch** (-**ychau**) *nm* desert, wilderness

**diffiniad** (-**au**) *nm* definition

**diffinio** *vb* define

**diffodd, -i** *vb* quench, extinguish

**diffoddiad** *nm* quenching, extinction

**diffoddwr** (-**wyr**), -**ydd** (-**ion**) *nm* quencher

**diffrwyth** *adj* barren; numb, paralysed

**diffrwythder, -dra** *nm* barrenness; numbness

**diffrwytho** *vb* make barren; paralyse

**diffuant** *adj* unfeigned, sincere, genuine

**diffuantrwydd** *nm* genuineness

**di-ffurf** *adj* amorphous

**diffwys** *adj* wild, waste; high, steep; huge, awful

**diffyg** (-**ion**) *nm* defect, want, lack; eclipse

**diffygiant** *nm* deficiency

**diffygio** *vb* fail; faint, weary

**diffygiol** *adj* defective; faint,

weary

**diffyndoll** (-**au**) *nf* tariff

**diffyndollaeth** *nf* protectionism

**diffynnydd** (-**ynyddion**) *nm* defendant

**dig** *adj* angry, wrathful ♦ *nm* anger, wrath

**digalon** *adj* disheartened, depressed, dejected, sad

**digalondid** *nm* depression, dejection

**digalonni** *vb* dishearten, discourage

**digamsyniol** *adj* unmistakable

**digasedd** *nm* hatred, enmity

**digid** (-**au**) *nm* digit

**digidiad** (-**au**) *nm* digitation

**digidol** *adj* digital

**digio** *vb* anger, offend; take offence

**di-glem** *adj* inept

**digllon** see **dicllon**

**digofaint** *nm* anger, wrath, indignation

**digofus** *adj* angry, indignant

**digolledu** *vb* indemnify, compensate

**digon** *nm, adj, adv* enough; done (*of cooking*)

**digonedd** *nm* abundance, plenty

**digoni** *vb* suffice; satisfy; cook

**digonol** *adj* satisfying; sufficient, adequate; satisfied

**digonolrwydd** *nm* sufficiency, abundance

**digornio** *vb* dehorn

**di-gred** *adj* infidel

**di-grefft, digrefft** *adj* unskilled

**digrif, -ol** *adj* mirthful, funny

**digriflun** (-**iau**) *nm* caricature, cartoon

**digrifwas** (-**weision**) *nm* clown, buffoon

**digrifwch** *nm* mirth, fun

**digroeso** *adj* inhospitable

**digwydd** *vb* befall, happen, occur

**digwyddiad** (-**au**) *nm* happening,

occurrence, event
**digyfnewid** *adj* unchangeable
**digyffelyb** *adj* incomparable
**digymysg** *adj* unmixed
**digyswllt** *adj* incoherent
**digywilydd** *adj* impudent
**digywilydd-dra** *nm* impudence
**dihafal** *adj* unequalled, peerless
**dihangfa** (**diangfâu**) *nf* escape
**dihangol** *adj* escaped, safe
**dihareb** (**diarhebion**) *nf* proverb
**dihatru** *vb* strip, undress
**dihefelydd** *adj* unequalled
**diheintio** *vb* disinfect
**diheintydd** (**-ion**) *nm* disinfectant,
   sterilizer
**di-hid(io)** *adj* heedless, indifferent,
   reckless
**dihidlo** *vb* drop, distil; shed
**dihidrwydd** *nm* indifference,
   recklessness
**dihiryn** (**-hirod**) *nm* rascal,
   scoundrel
**dihoeni** *vb* languish, pine
**dihuno** *vb* wake, rouse
**di-hwyl** *adj* out of sorts
**dihyder** *adj* lacking confidence
**dihydradu** *vb* dehydrate
**dihysbydd** *adj* inexhaustible
**dihysbyddu** *vb* empty, exhaust
**dil** (**-iau**) *nm*: **d. mêl** honeycomb
**dilead** *nm* abolition, deletion
**dilechdid** *nm* dialectic
**diledryw** *adj* pure, genuine
**dileu** *vb* blot out, delete; abolish
**dilewyrch** *adj* dismal;
   unprosperous
**dilorni** *vb* abuse, revile
**di-lun** *adj* slovenly
**diluw** see **dilyw**
**dilyffethair** *adj* unencumbered,
   unfettered
**dilyn** *vb* follow, pursue; imitate
**dilyniad** *nm* following; imitation
**dilyniant** (**-nnau**) *nm* sequence,
   progression
**dilynol** *adj* following; consequent

**dilynwr** (**-wyr**) *nm* follower;
   imitator
**dilys** *adj* sure, certain; genuine
**dilysiant** (**-nnau**) *nm* validation
**dilysnod** (**-au**) *nm* hallmark
**dilysrwydd** *nm* genuineness
**dilysu** *vb* certify, warrant,
   guarantee
**dilyw** *nm* flood, deluge
**dillad** (**dilledyn** *nm*) *npl* clothes,
   clothing
**dilladu** *vb* clothe
**dilledydd** *nm* clothier
**dilledyn** *nm* garment
**dim** *adj* any; (*with negative*
   *understood*) no ♦ *nm* anything;
   none, nothing
**dimensiwn** (**-iynau**) *nm* dimension
**dimensiynol** *adj* dimensional
**di-nam, dinam** *adj* faultless
**dinas** (**-oedd**) *nf* city
**dinasol** *adj* municipal
**dinasyddiaeth** *nf* citizenship
**dincod** see **deincod**
**dinesig** *adj* civil, civic
**dinesydd** (**dinasyddion**) *nm* citizen
**dinistr** *nm* destruction
**dinistrio** *vb* destroy
**dinistriol** *adj* destroying,
   destructive
**dinistriwr** (**-wyr**) *nm* destroyer
**dinistrydd** (**-ion**) *nm* destroyer
**diniwed** *adj* harmless, innocent
**diniweidrwydd** *nm* innocence
**di-nod, dinod,** *adj* insignificant,
   obscure
**dinodedd** *nm* insignificance,
   obscurity
**dinoethi** *vb* bare, denude, expose
**diod** (**-ydd**) *nf* drink, beverage
**diodi** *vb* give drink
**dioddef** *vb* suffer, bear; wait ♦
   (**-iadau**) *nm* suffering
**dioddefaint** *nm* suffering, passion
**dioddefgar, -efus** *adj* patient
**dioddefgarwch** *nm* patience
**dioddefwr, -ydd** (**-wyr**) *nm*

sufferer, patient
**di-oed, dioed** *adj* without delay, immediate
**diofal** *adj* careless
**diofalwch** *nm* carelessness
**diog** *adj* slothful, indolent, lazy
**diogel** *adj* safe, secure; sure, certain
**diogelu** *vb* make safe, secure
**diogelwch** *nm* safety, security
**diogi** *vb* be lazy, idle ♦ *nm* laziness
**dioglyd** *adj* lazy, sluggish, indolent
**diogyn** *nm* lazy one, idler, sluggard
**diolch** *vb* thank, give thanks ♦ (**-iadau**) *nm* thanks, thanksgiving
**diolchgar** *adj* thankful, grateful
**diolchgarwch** *nm* thankfulness, gratitude, thanksgiving
**diolwg** *adj* ugly
**diorseddu** *vb* dethrone, depose
**di-os** *adj* without doubt
**diosg** *vb* undress, put off, strip, divest
**diota** *vb* tipple
**diotwr** (**-wyr**) *nm* boozer, drunkard
**dioty** (**-tai**) *nm* ale-house, public-house
**diploma** (**-âu**) *nm/f* diploma
**diplomateg** *nf* diplomacy
**diplomydd** (**-ion**) *nm* diplomat
**diplomyddol** *adj* diplomatic
**dipton** (**-au**) *nf* diphthong
**dir** *adj* certain, necessary
**diraddiad** (**-au**) *nm* degradation
**diraddio** *vb* degrade
**diraddiol** *adj* degrading
**di-raen** *adj* shabby, dull
**dirboeni** *vb* torture, excruciate
**dirdyniad** (**-au**) *nm* convulsion
**dirdynnol** *adj* excruciating
**dirdynnu** *vb* rack, torture
**direidi** *nm* mischievousness, mischief
**direidus** *adj* mischievous
**direol** *adj* unruly, disorderly

**direwydd** *nm* defroster
**direwyn** *nm* antifreeze
**dirfawr** *adj* vast, huge, immense, enormous
**dirgel** *adj* secret ♦ (**-ion**) *nm* secret
**dirgeledig** *adj* hidden, secret; mystical
**dirgeledigaeth** (**-au**) *nm/f* mystery
**dirgelu** *vb* secrete, conceal, hide
**dirgelwch** *nm* secrecy, mystery, secret
**dirgryniad** (**-au**) *nm* tremor, vibration
**dirgrynol** *adj* vibrating
**dirgrynu** *vb* tremble, vibrate
**diriaethol** *adj* concrete
**dirlawn** *adj* saturated
**dirmyg** *nm* contempt, scorn
**dirmygu** *vb* despise, scorn
**dirmygus** *adj* contemptuous; contemptible
**dirnad** *vb* discern, comprehend
**dirnadaeth** *nf* discernment, comprehension
**dirnadwy** *adj* discernible
**dirprwy** (**-on**) *nm* deputy; delegate
**dirprwyaeth** (**-au**) *nf* commission; deputation
**dirprwyo** *vb* deputise, delegate
**dirprwyol** *adj* vicarious
**dirprwywr** (**-wyr**) *nm* commissioner
**dirwasgiad** (**-au**) *nm* depression
**dirwest** *nm/f* abstinence, temperance
**dirwestol** *adj* temperate
**dirwestwr** (**-wyr**) *nm* abstainer
**dirwy** (**-on**) *nf* fine
**dirwyn** *vb* wind, twist, twine
**dirwynwr** (**-wyr**) *nm* winder
**dirwyo** *vb* fine
**di-rym** *adj* powerless, void
**dirymu** *vb* nullify, annul, cancel
**diryw** *adj* neuter
**dirywiad** *nm* degeneration, deterioration
**dirywiaeth** *nf* degeneracy

**dirywiedig** *adj* degenerate
**dirywio** *vb* degenerate, deteriorate
**dirywiol** *adj* decadent, retrograde
**dis** (**-iau**) *nm* die, dice
**di-sail** *adj* groundless, baseless
**disbaddu** *vb* castrate, geld, spay
**disbaddwr** (**-wyr**) *nm* castrator
**disberod** *nm*: **ar dd.** wandering,
  astray
**disbyddedig** *adj* exhausted
**disbyddu** *vb* empty, exhaust
**disbyddwr** *nm* exhaust
**disco** (**-au**) *nm* disco
**diserch** *adj* sullen, sulky, loveless
**disg** (**-iau**) *nm* disk, record
**disgen** (**disgiau**) *nf* discus
**disglair** *adj* bright, brilliant
**disgleirdeb, -der** *nm* brightness,
  brilliance
**disgleirio** *vb* shine, glitter
**disgloff** *adj* free from lameness
**disgownt** (**-iau, -s**) *nm* discount
**disgrifiad** (**-au**) *nm* description
**disgrifiadol** *adj* descriptive
**disgrifio** *vb* describe
**disgwyl** *vb* look, expect, wait
**disgwylfa** (**-feydd**) *nf* watch-tower
**disgwylgar** *adj* watchful,
  expectant
**disgwyliad** (**-au**) *nm* expectation
**disgybl** (**-ion**) *nm* disciple, pupil
**disgyblaeth** *nf* discipline
**disgyblu** *vb* discipline
**disgyblwr** (**-wyr**) *nm* disciplinarian
**disgyn** *vb* descend; fall, drop; let
  down
**disgynfa** (**-feydd**) *nf* descent,
  declivity; landing place
**disgyniad** (**-au**) *nm* descent
**disgynnol** *adj* descending
**disgynnydd** (**-ynyddion**) *nm*
  descendant
**disgyrchedd** *nm* gravitation
**disgyrchiad, -iant** *nm* gravity.
  **craidd d.** centre of gravity
**disgyrchu** *vb* gravitate
**di-sigl** *adj* unshaken, steadfast,

firm
**disiog** *adj* diced
**disodli** *vb* trip up, supplant
**dist** (**-iau**) *nm* joist, beam
**distadl** *adj* insignificant, low, base,
  mean
**distadledd** *nm* insignificance,
  obscurity
**distain** (**-einiaid**) *nm* steward
**distaw** *adj* silent, quiet
**distawrwydd** *nm* silence, quiet
**distewi** *vb* silence; calm, quiet
**distryw** *nm* destruction
**distrywgar** *adj* destructive,
  wasteful
**distrywio** *vb* destroy
**distrywiwr** (**-wyr**) *nm* destroyer
**distyll** *nm* ebb; **-iad** distillation
**distyllio** *vb* distil
**di-sut** *adj* unwell; small
**diswta** *adj* sudden, abrupt
**diswyddiad** (**-au**) *nm* dismissal
**diswyddo** *vb* dismiss from office,
  discharge
**disychedu** *vb* quench thirst
**di-syfl** *adj* immovable, impregnable
**disyfyd** *adj* sudden, instantaneous
**disyml** *adj* simple, artless,
  ingenuous
**disymwth** *adj* sudden,
  instantaneous
**disynnwyr** *adj* senseless
**ditectif** (**-s**) *nm* detective
**diwahân** *adj* inseparable,
  indiscriminate
**diwair** *adj* chaste
**di-waith, diwaith** *adj* unemployed,
  idle
**diwall** *adj* satisfied, full, perfect
**diwallu** *vb* satisfy, supply
**diwarafun** *adj* unforbidden,
  ungrudging
**diwasgedd** (**-au**) *nm* depression
  (*weather*)
**diwedydd** (**-iau**) *nm* evening,
  eventide
**diwedd** *nm* end, conclusion

**diweddar** *adj* late, modern
**diweddaru** *vb* modernize
**diweddarwch** *nm* lateness
**diweddeb** *nf* cadence
**diweddglo** *nm* conclusion
**diweddu** *vb* end, finish, conclude
**diweirdeb** *nm* chastity
**diweithdra** *nm* unemployment
**diwelfa** (-feydd) *nf* watershed
**diwethaf** *adj* last
**diwinydd** (-ion) *nm* divine,
theologian
**diwinyddiaeth** *nf* divinity,
theology
**diwinyddol** *adj* theological
**diwreiddio** *vb* uproot, eradicate
**diwrnod** (-iau) *nm* day
**diwrthdro** *adj* inexorable
**diwyd** *adj* diligent, industrious
**diwydianfa** *nf* industrial estate
**diwydiannaeth** *nf*
industrialization, industrialism
**diwydiannol** *adj* industrial
**diwydiannwr** (-ianwyr) *nm*
industrialist
**diwydiant** (-iannau) *nm* industry
**diwydrwydd** *nm* diligence,
industry
**diwyg** *nm* form, dress, garb
**diwygiad** (-au) *nm* reform,
reformation; revival
**diwygiadol** *adj* reformatory;
revivalistic
**diwygiedig** *adj* reformed; revised
**diwygio** *vb* amend, reform, revise
**diwygiol** *adj* reformatory
**diwygiwr** (-wyr) *nm* reformer;
revivalist
**diwylliadol** *adj* cultural
**diwylliannol** *adj* cultural
**diwylliant** (-nnau) *nm* culture
**diwylliedig** *adj* cultured
**diwyllio** *vb* cultivate
**diymadferth** *adj* helpless
**diymadferthedd** *nm* helplessness
**diymdroi** *adj* without delay
**diymhongar** *adj* unassuming

**diymod** *adj* steadfast, immovable
**diymwad** *adj* undeniable,
indisputable
**diysgog** *adj* steadfast, firm, stable
**diystyr** *adj* contemptuous;
contemptible; meaningless
**diystyrllyd** *adj* contemptuous,
disdainful
**diystyru** *vb* disregard, despise
**diystyrwch** *nm* contempt, disdain,
scorn
**do** *adv* yes (*to questions in preterite
tense*)
**doc** (-iau) *nm* dock
**docfa** (-feydd) *nf* berth
**docio** *vb* shorten; dock, berth
**doctor** (-iaid) *nm* doctor
**doctora** *vb* doctor
**dod** see **dyfod**
**dodi** *vb* put, place; give
**dodrefn** *npl* (-yn *nm*) furniture
**dodrefnu** *vb* furnish
**dodrefnwr** (-wyr) *nm* furnisher
**dodwy** *vb* lay eggs
**doe** *adv* yesterday
**doeth** (-ion) *adj* wise
**doethineb** *nm/f* wisdom
**doethinebu** *vb* discourse wisely,
pontificate
**doethor** (-iaid) *nm* doctor (*of
university*)
**doethur** (-iaid) *nm* doctor (*of
university*)
**doethuriaeth** (-au) *nf* doctorate
**dof** *adj* tame, domesticated;
garden
**dofednod** *npl* fowls, poultry
**dofi** *vb* tame, domesticate;
assuage
**dofn** *adj f* of **dwfn**
**Dofydd** *nm* God
**dogfen** (-ni, -nau) *nf* document
**dogfennaeth** *nf* documentation
**dogfennen** (-ennau) *nf*
documentary
**dogfennol** *adj* documentary
**dogn** (-au) *nm* share, portion; dose

**dogni** *vb* ration
**doili** *nm* doyley
**dol** (**-iau**) *nf* doll
**dôl** *nm* dole
**dôl** (**dolydd, dolau**) *nf* meadow
**dolbridd** (**-oedd**) *nm* alluvium, meadow soil
**doldir** (**-oedd**) *nm* meadow-land
**dolef** (**-au**) *nf* cry
**dolefain** *vb* cry out
**dolefus** *adj* wailing, plaintive
**dolen** (**-nau**) *nf* loop, link, ring, bow
**dolennog** *adj* ringed, looped; winding
**dolennu** *vb* loop; wind, meander
**doler** (**-i**) *nf* dollar
**dolffin** *nm* dolphin
**dolur** (**-iau**) *nm* sore; ailment; grief
**dolurio** *vb* hurt, wound; grieve
**dolurus** *adj* sore
**dominyddu** *vb* dominate
**donio** *vb* endow, gift
**doniol** *adj* gifted; witty, humorous
**donioldeb, -wch** *nm* wit, humour
**dôr** (**dorau**) *nf* door
**dos** (**-ys, -au**) *nf* dose
**dosbarth** (**au, -iadau**) *nm* reason; class; district
**dosbarthiad** *nm* distribution
**dosbarthu** *vb* class, classify; distribute
**dosbarthwr** (**-wyr**) *nm* distributor
**dosio** *vb* dose
**dosran** (**-nau**) *nf* division, section
**dosrannu** *vb* separate, analyse
**dot** (**-iau**) *nm/f* dot
**dot** *nf* giddiness, vertigo
**dotio** *vb* dote
**drachefn** *adv* again
**dracht** (**-iau**) *nm* draught (*of liquor*)
**drachtio** *vb* drink deep
**draen** (**-iau**) *nf* drain
**draen** (**drain**) *nf* prickle, thorn
**draen, -en** (**drain**) *nf* thorn

**draeniad** (**-au**) *nm* drainage
**draenio** *vb* drain
**draenog** (**-od**) *nm* hedgehog
**drafft** (**-iau**) *nm* draft, draught
**draffts** *npl* draughts
**dragio** *vb* drag, tear, mangle
**draig** (**dreigiau**) *nf* dragon
**drain** see **draen, draenen**
**drama** (**dramâu**) *nf* drama
**dramateiddio** *vb* dramatize
**dramatig** *adj* dramatic
**dramodiad** (**-au**) *nm* dramatization
**dramodwr** (**-wyr**) *nm* dramatist
**draw** *adv* yonder, away
**dreflan** *vb* dribble
**dreng** *adj* morose, surly, sullen, harsh
**dresel, -er** (**-i, -ydd**) *nm* dresser
**drewdod** *nm* stink, stench
**drewi** *vb, nm* stink
**drewllyd** *adj* stinking
**driblo** *vb* dribble
**drifft** (**-iau**) *nm* drift
**dril** (**-iau**) *nm* drill
**drilio** *vb* drill
**dringad** *vb, nm* climb
**dringfa** (**-feydd**) *nf* climb, ascent
**dringo** *vb* climb
**dringwr** (**-wyr**) *nm* climber
**dripsych** *adj* dripdry
**drôr** (**drors**) *nm* drawer
**dros** see **tros**
**drud** *adj* dear, precious, costly; reckless
**drudfawr** *adj* costly, expensive
**drudwen** *nf*, **drudwy** *nm* starling
**drwg** *adj* evil, bad, naughty, wicked ♦ (**drygau**) *nm* evil, harm, hurt
**drwgdybiaeth** (**-au**) *nf* suspicion
**drwgdybio** *vb* suspect
**drwgdybus** *adj* suspicious
**drwglosgiad** *nm* arson
**drwgweithredwr** (**-wyr**) *nm* evildoer
**drwm** (**drymiau**) *nm* drum
**drws** (**drysau**) *nm* door

**drwy** see **trwy**

**drycin** (-oedd) *nf* foul weather

**drycinog** *adj* stormy

**drych** (-au) *nm* spectacle; mirror; object, pattern

**drychfeddwl** (-yliau) *nm* idea

**drychiolaeth** (-au) *nf* apparition, phantom

**drygair** *nm* ill report; scandal

**dryganadl** *nm* halitosis

**drygfyd** *nm* adversity

**drygioni** *nm* badness, wickedness

**drygionus** *adj* bad, wicked

**drygu** *vb* hurt, harm, injure

**dryll** (-iau) *nm* piece; part ♦ *nm/f* gun, rifle

**drylliad** (-au) *nm* breaking; wreck

**drylliedig** *adj* broken

**dryllio** *vb* break in pieces, shatter

**drylliog** *adj* broken, contrite

**drysi** *npl* (-ien *nf*) thorns, briers

**dryslwyn** (-i) *nm* thicket

**dryslyd** *adj* perplexing; confused

**drysu** *vb* tangle; perplex; be confused

**dryswch** *nm* tangle; perplexity; confusion

**dryw** (-od) *nm/f* wren

**du** *adj, nm* black

**duc, dug** (-iaid) *nm* duke

**dugiaeth** *nf* duchy

**dull** (-iau) *nm* form, manner, mode

**dullwedd** (-au) *nm* mannerism

**Dulyn** *nf* Dublin

**duo** *vb* black, blacken

**dur** *nm* steel

**duw** (-iau) *nm* god. **Duw** God

**duwch** *nm* blackness

**duwdod** *nm* godhead, divinity, deity

**duwies** (-au) *nf* goddess

**duwiol** (-ion) *adj* godly, pious

**duwioldeb** *nm* godliness, piety

**duwiolfrydedd** *nm* godliness, piety

**duwiolfrydig** *adj* god-fearing, pious

**dwbio** *vb* daub, plaster

**dwbl** *adj* double

**dweud, dweyd** see **dywedyd**

**dwfn** *adj* deep, profound; *f* **dofn**

**dwfr, dŵr** (dyfroedd) *nm* water

**dwl** *adj* dull, stupid, foolish

**dwlu** *vb* dote

**dwmbwr-dambar** *adv* helter-skelter

**dwndwr** *nm* din, babble, hubbub

**dwnsiwn** (-iynau) *nm* dungeon

**dŵr** see **dwfr**

**dwrdio** *vb* scold

**dwrn** (dyrnau) *nm* fist; knob, handle, hilt

**dwsin** (-inau) *nm* dozen

**dwst** *nm* dust, powder

**dwster** (-i) *nm* duster

**dwthwn** *nm* day

**dwy** see **dau**

**dwyfol** *adj* divine

**dwyfoldeb** *nm* divinity, deity

**dwyfoli** *vb* deify

**dwyfron** (-nau) *nf* breast, chest

**dwyfronneg** *nf* breastplate

**dwyieithedd** *nm* bilingualism

**dwyieitheg** *nf* study of bilingualism

**dwyieithog** *adj* bilingual, duoglot

**dwyieithrwydd** *nm* bilingualism

**dwylaw, -lo** *nd, pl* two hands, hands

**dwyn** *vb* bear; bring; steal

**dwyochredd** *nm* bilateralism

**dwyochrol** *adj* bilateral

**dwyradd** *adj* quadratic, two-tier

**dwyrain** *nm, adj* east. **D. yr Almaen** East Germany

**dwyraniad** *nm* dichotomy

**dwyrannu** *vb* bisect

**dwyreiniol** *adj* easterly, eastern, oriental

**dwyreiniwr** (-wyr) *nm* easterner, oriental

**dwys** *adj* dense, grave, deep, intense

**dwysáu** *vb* deepen, intensify

**dwysbigo** *vb* prick, sting

**dwysedd** (-au) *nm* density
**dwyster** *nm* gravity, solemnity
**dwythell** (-au) *nf* duct
**dwywaith** *adv* twice
**dy** *pron* thy, thine
**dyblu** *vb* double; repeat
**dyblyg** *adj* twofold, double
**dyblygiad** (-au) *nm* duplication, duplicate
**dyblygu** *vb* double, fold
**dyblygydd** (-ion) *nm* duplicator
**dybryd** *adj* sore, dire; flagrant
**dychan** (-au) *nf* lampoon, satire
**dychangerdd** (-i) *nf* satirical poem, satire
**dychanol** *adj* satirical
**dychanu** *vb* lampoon, satirize, revile
**dychanwr** (-wyr) *nm* satirist
**dychmygadwy** *adj* imaginable
**dychmygol** *adj* imaginary
**dychmygu** *vb* imagine
**dychmygus** *adj* imaginative, inventive
**dychryn** (-iadau) *nm* fright, terror
♦ *vb* frighten
**dychrynllyd** *adj* frightful, terrible
**dychrynu** *vb* frighten, be frightened
**dychweledig** *adj* returned
**dychweliad** (-au) *nm* return; conversion
**dychwelyd** *vb* return
**dychymyg** (dychmygion) *nm* imagination, fancy; riddle, device
**dydd** (-iau) *nm* day. dyddiau cŵn silly season
**dyddfu** *vb* flag, pine, faint
**dyddiad** (-au) *nm* date
**dyddiadur** (-on) *nm* diary, journal
**dyddiedig** *adj* dated
**dyddio** *vb* become day, dawn; date
**dyddiol** *adj* daily
**dyddlyfr** (-au) *nm* diary, journal
**dyddodyn** (-odion) *nm* deposit
**dyfais** (-feisiau) *nf* device, invention
**dyfal** *adj* diligent
**dyfalbarhad** *nm* perseverance
**dyfalbarhau** *vb* persevere
**dyfaliad** (-au) *nm* guess, conjecture
**dyfalu** *vb* guess, conjecture
**dyfalwch** *nm* diligence, assiduity
**dyfarniad** (-au) *nm* decision, verdict
**dyfarnu** *vb* adjudge
**dyfarnwr** (-wyr) *nm* judge, umpire
**dyfeisio** *vb* devise, invent, imagine; guess
**dyfeisiwr** (-wyr) *nm* inventor
**dyfnant** (-nentydd) *nf* ravine
**dyfnder** (-au, -oedd) *nm* deep, depth
**dyfnhau** *vb* deepen
**dyfod, dod** *vb* come, become
**dyfodfa** *nf* access, entrance
**dyfodiad** *nm* coming, arrival, advent
**dyfodiad** (-iaid) *nm* incomer, stranger
**dyfodol** *adj* coming, future ♦ *nm* future
**dyfradwy** *adj* watered; watering
**dyfredig** *adj* irrigated
**dyfrffos** (-ydd) *nm* canal, watercourse
**dyfrgi** (-gwn) *nm* otter
**dyfrhad** *nm* irrigation
**dyfrhau, dyfrio** *vb* water
**dyfrllyd** *adj* watery
**dyfyniad** (-au) *nm* citation, quotation
**dyfynnod** (-ynodau) *nm* quotation mark
**dyfynnol** *adj* citatory, summoned
**dyfynnu** *vb* cite, quote; summon
**dyffryn** (-noedd) *nm* valley
**dyffryndir** (-oedd) *nm* low country; vale
**dygn** *adj* hard, severe, grievous, dire
**dygnu** *vb* strive, persevere

**dygnwch** *nm* perseverance, assiduity

**dygwyl** *nm* holiday, feast day

**dygymod** *vb* agree (with), put up (with)

**dyhead** (-au) *nm* aspiration

**dyheu** *vb* pant; long, yearn, aspire

**dyhiryn** see **dihiryn**

**dyladwy** *adj* due

**dylanwad** (-au) *nm* influence

**dylanwadol** *adj* influential

**dylanwadu** *vb* influence

**dyled** (-ion) *nf* debt, obligation

**dyledog** *adj* in debt, indebted

**dyledus** *adj* due

**dyledwr** (-wyr) *nm* debtor

**dyletswydd** (-au) *nf* duty, obligation

**dylif** *nm* flood, deluge ♦ *nf* warp

**dylifo** *vb* flow, stream, pour

**dylni** *nm* stupidity, dullness

**dyluniad** (-au) *nm* design, drawing

**dylunio** *vb* design

**dylunydd** (-ion) *nm* designer

**dylyfu gên** *vb* yawn, gape

**dylluan** see **tylluan**

**dyma** *adv* here is, here are; this is, these are

**dymchweliad** *nm* overthrow

**dymchwelyd** *vb* overthrow, upset, subvert

**dymuniad** (-au) *nm* wish, desire

**dymuno** *vb* wish, desire

**dymunol** *adj* desirable, agreeable, pleasant

**dyn** (-ion) *nm* man, person

**dyna** *adv* there is, there are; that is, those are

**dynad** *npl* nettles

**dyndod** *nm* manhood, humanity

**dyneiddiaeth** *nf* humanism

**dyneiddiol** *adj* humanistic

**dyneiddiwr** (-wyr) *nm* humanist

**dynes** *nf* woman

**dynesiad** *nm* approach

**dynesu** *vb* draw near, approach

**dyngar** *adj* humane

**dyngarol** *adj* philanthropic

**dyngarwch** *nm* philanthropy

**dyngarwr** (-wyr) *nm* philanthropist

**dyniawed** (-iewaid) *nm* yearling, steer

**dyn-laddiad** *nm* manslaughter

**dynodi** *vb* denote, signify

**dynodiad** (-au) *nm* denotation

**dynol** *adj* human; man-like; manly

**dynoliaeth** *nf* humanity

**dynoliaethau** *npl* humanities

**dynolryw** *coll n* mankind

**dynwared** *vb* imitate, mimic

**dynwarededd** *nm* mimicry

**dynwarediad** (-au) *nm* imitation, mimicry

**dynwaredol** *adj* imitative

**dynwaredwr** (-wyr) *nm* imitator, mimic

**dyraddiant** *nm* degradation

**dyraniad** (-au) *nm* allocation

**dyrchafael** *vb* rise, ascend ♦ *nm* ascension

**dyrchafedig** *adj* exalted

**dyrchafiad** *nm* elevation, promotion

**dyrchafol** *adj* elevating

**dyrchafu** *vb* raise, elevate; rise, ascend

**dyri** (-iau), **dyrif** (-au) *nf* ballad, lyric

**dyrnaid** (-eidiau) *nm* handful

**dyrnio** *vb* punch

**dyrnod** (-iau) *nm/f* blow, stroke

**dyrnu** *vb* thump; thresh

**dyrnwr** (-wyr) *nm* thresher

**dyrnwr medi** *nm* combine harvester

**dyrys** *adj* tangled; difficult; perplexing

**dyryslyd, dyrysu, dyryswch** see **dryslyd, drysu, dryswch**

**dysg** *nm/f* learning

**dysgedig** (-ion) *adj* learned

**dysgeidiaeth** *nf* teaching, doctrine

**dysgl** (-au) *nf* dish

**dysglaid** (-eidiau) *nf* dishful, dish

**dysgu** *vb* learn, teach
**dysgwr** (-**wyr**) *nm* learner, teacher
**dywalgi** (-**gwn**) *nm* tiger
**dywediad** (-**au**) *nm* saying
**dywedwst** *adj* taciturn ♦ *nm* taciturnity
**dywedyd** *vb* say, speak, tell
**dyweddi** (-**iau**) *nf* betrothal, fiancé(e) ♦ *n coll* betrothed
**dyweddïad** *nm* betrothal
**dyweddïo** *vb* betroth

# E

**eang** *adj* wide, broad, immense
**eangder, eangu** see **ehangder, ehangu**
**eangfrydedd** *nm* magnanimity
**eangfrydig** *adj* broad-minded, magnanimous
**eb, ebe, ebr** *vb* said, quoth
**ebargofiant** *nm* oblivion
**ebill** (-**ion**) *nm* auger, borer; peg
**ebillio** *vb* bore
**ebol** (-**ion**) *nm* colt, foal
**eboles** (-**au**) *nf* foal, filly
**eboni** *nm* ebony
**ebran** (-**nau**) *nm* provender, fodder
**Ebrill** *nm* April
**ebrwydd** *adj* quick, swift, soon
**ebwch** (-**ychau**) *nm* gasp
**ebychiad** (-**au**) *nm* interjection, ejaculation
**ebychu** *vb* gasp, interject, ejaculate
**eciwmenaidd** *adj* ecumenical
**ecliptig** *adj, nm* ecliptic
**ecoleg** (-**au**) *nf/m* ecology
**ecolegol** *adj* ecological
**ecolegwr** (-**wyr**) *nm* ecologist
**economaidd** *adj* economic
**economeg** *nf* economics
**economegol** *adj* economic
**economegwr** (-**wyr**) *nm* economist
**economegydd** (-**ion**) *nm* economist

**economi** (-**ïau**) *nm* economy
**economydd** *nm* economist
**ecsbloetio** *vb* exploit
**ecsbloetiwr** (-**wyr**) *nm* exploiter
**ecseis** *nm* excise
**ecseismon** (-**myn**) *nm* exciseman
**ecsema** *nm* eczema
**ecsentredd** (-**au**) *nm* eccentricity
**ecsentrig** *adj* eccentric (*maths*)
**ecstasi** *nm* ecstasy
**ecstatig** *adj* ecstatic
**echblyg** *adj* explicit, outward
**echblygol** *adj* extrovert
**echdoe** *adv* day before yesterday
**echdoriad** (-**au**) *nm* eruption
**echel** (-**au**) *nf* axle, axletree; axis
**echelin** (-**au**) *nm* axis
**echnos** *adv* night before last
**echrydus** *adj* fearful, frightful, shocking
**echwyn** (-**ion**) *nm* loan
**echwynna** *vb* borrow, lend
**echwynnwr** (-**wynwyr**) *nm* lender, creditor
**edau** (**edafedd**) *nf* thread; (*pl*) yarn, wool
**edfryd** *vb* restore
**edifar** *adj* penitent, sorry
**edifarhau, -faru** *vb* repent, be sorry
**edifarus, -feiriol** *adj* repentant, penitent
**edifeirwch** *nm* repentance, penitence
**edliw** *vb* upbraid, reproach, taunt
**edmygedd** *nm* admiration
**edmygol** *adj* admiring
**edmygu** *vb* admire
**edmygwr, -ydd** (-**wyr**) *nm* admirer
**edrych** *vb* look, examine
**edrychiad** *nm* look
**edrychwr** (-**wyr**) *nm* beholder, spectator
**edwi, edwino** *vb* fade, wither, decay
**eddi** *npl* thrums; fringe, nap

**ef, efe** *pron* he, him; it
**efallai** *adv* perhaps, peradventure
**efengyl** (-au) *nf* gospel
**efengylaidd** *adj* evangelical
**efengyleiddio** *vb* evangelize
**efengyles** (-au) *nf* female
evangelist
**efengylu** *vb* evangelize
**efengylwr, -ydd** (-wyr) *nm*
evangelist
**efelychiad** (-au) *nm* imitation
**efelychiadol** *adj* imitative
**efelychu** *vb* imitate
**efelychwr** (-wyr) *nm* imitator
**efelychydd** (-ion) *nm* simulator
**eferw** *adj* effervescent
**eferwad** (-au) *nm* effervescence
**eferwi** *vb* effervesce
**efo** *prep* with
**efô** *pron* he, him; it
**efrau** *npl* tares
**Efrog Newydd** *nf* New York
**efrydiaeth** (-au) *nf* study
**efrydu** *vb* study
**efrydydd** (-ion, -wyr) *nm* student
**efydd** *nm* bronze, copper, brass
**effaith** (-eithiau) *nf* effect
**effeithio** *vb* effect, affect
**effeithiol** *adj* effectual, effective,
efficient
**effeithioli** *vb* render effectual
**effeithiolrwydd** *nm* efficacy
**effeithlon** *adj* efficient
**effeithlonedd** *nm* efficiency (*of
machines etc*)
**effeithlonrwydd** *nm* efficiency
**effro** *adj* awake, vigilant
**eger** (-au) *nm* bore, eagre
**egin** *npl* (-yn *nm*) germs, sprouts
**eginhad, eginiad** (-au) *nm*
germination, sprouting
**egino** *vb* germinate, shoot, sprout
**eginol** *adj* germinal, shooting
**eginyn** (egin) *nm* sprout
**eglur** *adj* clear, plain, evident
**eglurdeb, -der** *nm* clearness
**eglureb** (-au) *nf* illustration

**eglurhad** *nm* explanation,
demonstration
**eglurhaol** *adj* explanatory
**egluro** *vb* make clear, explain
**eglwys** (-i, -ydd) *nf* church
**eglwysig** *adj* church, ecclesiastical
**eglwyswr** (-wyr) *nm* churchman
**eglwyswraig** (-wragedd) *nf*
churchwoman
**egni** (-ïon) *nm* effort, might,
energy
**egnïo** *vb* endeavour, make an
effort
**egniol** *adj* energetic
**egnioli** *vb* energise
**ego** *nm* ego
**egoistiaeth** *nm* egoism
**egosentrig** *adj* egocentric
**egöydd** *nm* egoist
**egr** *adj* sharp; sour; severe;
savage; cheeky
**egroes** *npl* (-en *nf*) hips
**egwan** *adj* weak, feeble
**egwyd** (-ydd) *nf* fetlock; fetter
**egwyddor** (-ion, -au) *nf* rudiment;
principle; alphabet
**egwyddorol** *adj* high-principled
**egwyl** *nf* lull, respite; opportunity
**enghraifft** (-eifftiau) *nf* example,
instance
**enghreifftiol** *adj* exemplary,
illustrative
**englyn** (-ion) *nm* Welsh alliterative
stanza
**englyna, -u** *vb* compose *englynion*
**englynwr** (-wyr) *nm* composer of
*englynion*
**engyl** see **angel**
**ehangder** (eangderau) *nm* breadth,
immensity
**ehangu** *vb* enlarge, extend
**ehedeg** *vb* fly; run to seed
**ehedfa** (-feydd) *nf* flight
**ehedfan** *vb* hover, fly
**ehediad** (-au) *nm* flight
**ehediad** (-iaid) *nm* fowl, bird
**ehedog** *adj* flying

**ehedydd** (-ion) *nm* lark
**ehofndra** *nm* fearlessness,
  boldness
**ei** *pron* his, hers; its
**eich** *pron* your
**Eidal: yr E.** Italy
**eidion** (-nau) *nm* ox
**eiddew** *coll n* ivy
**eiddgar** *adj* zealous, ardent
**eiddgarwch** *nm* zeal, ardour
**eiddigedd** *nm* jealousy; zeal
**eiddigeddu** *vb* be jealous, envy;
  have zeal
**eiddigeddus** *adj* jealous, envious
**eiddigus** *adj* jealous; zealous
**eiddil** *adj* slender, feeble
**eiddilwch** *nm* slenderness,
  feebleness
**eiddiorwg** *coll n* ivy
**eiddo** *nm* property, possessions ♦
  *pron* his, *etc*
**eidduno** *vb* desire, wish, pray
**Eifftaidd** *adj* Egyptian
**Eifftiwr** (-wyr), **Eifftiad** (-iaid) *nm*
  Egyptian
**eigion** *nm* depth, ocean
**eigioneg** *nf/m* oceanography
**eigionol** *adj* pelagic
**eingion** (-au) *nf* anvil
**Eingl** *npl* Angles, Englishmen
**Eingl-Gymro** (-Gymry) *nm* Anglo-
  Welshman
**Eingl-Sais** (-Saeson) *nm* Anglo-
  Saxon
**Eingl-Seisnig** *adj* Anglo-Saxon
**eil-** *prefix* second (**ail**)
**eiladur** (-on) *nm* alternator
**eilchwyl** *adv* again
**eiliad** (-au) *nm/f* second, moment
**eilio** *vb* weave, plait; sing; second
**eiliwr** (-wyr) *nm* seconder
**eilradd** (-ol) *adj* secondary,
  inferior
**eilrif** (-au) *nm* even number
**eilun** (-od) *nm* image, idol
**eilunaddolgar** *adj* idolatrous
**eilunaddoli** *vb* worship idols

**eilunaddolwr** (-wyr) *nm* idolator
**eilwaith** *adv* again
**eilydd** (-ion) *nm* seconder, reserve
**eillio** *vb* shave
**eilliwr** (-wyr) *nm* shaver, barber
**ein** *pron adj* our
**einioes** *nf* life, lifetime
**einion** (-au) *nf* anvil
**eira** *nm* snow
**eirchion** see **arch**
**eirias** *adj* burning, glowing, fiery
**eirin** *npl* (-en *nf*) plums. **e. gwlanog**
  peaches. **e. duon** damsons. **e.
  duon bach** sloes. **e. Mair**
  gooseberries
**eiriol** *vb* plead, pray, intercede
**eiriolaeth** *nf* intercession
**eiriolwr** (-wyr) *nm* intercessor,
  mediator
**eirlaw** *nm* sleet
**eirlin** (-iau) *nm* snowline
**eirlithrad** (-au) *nm* avalanche
**eirlys** (-iau) *nm* snowdrop
**eironi** *nm* irony
**eisen** (ais) *nf* rib; lath
**eisglwyf** *nm* pleurisy
**eisiau** *nm* want, need, lack
**eisin** *coll n* bran, husk
**eising** *nm* icing
**eisio** *vb* ice
**eisoes** *adv* already
**eistedd** *vb* sit, seat
**eisteddfa** (-oedd, -fâu) *nf* seat
**eisteddfod** (-au) *nf* session;
  eisteddfod
**eisteddfodol** *adj* eisteddfodic
**eisteddfodwr** (-wyr) *nm*
  frequenter of *eisteddfodau*
**eisteddfota** *vb* frequent
  *eisteddfodau*
**eisteddiad** (-au) *nm* sitting,
  session
**eisteddle** (-oedd) *nm* seat, sitting,
  pew
**eitem** (-au) *nf* item
**eithaf** (-ion) *adj, nm* extreme;
  superlative ♦ *adv* very, quite

**eithafbwynt** (-iau) *nm* extremity;
  apogee
**eithafiaeth** *nf* extremism
**eithafion** *npl* extremes, extremities
**eithafol** *adj* extreme
**eithafwr** (-wyr) *nm* extremist
**eithin** *npl* (-en *nf*) furze, gorse
**eithinog** *adj* furzy
**eithr** *prep* except; besides ♦ *conj*
  but
**eithriad** (-au) *nm* exception
**eithriadol** *adj* exceptional
**eithrio** *vb* except, exclude
**elastig** *adj*, *nm* elastic
**elastigedd** *nm* elasticity
**electromagneteg** *nf/m*
  electromagnetism
**electromedr** (-au) *nm*
  electrometer
**electron** (-au) *nm* electron
**electroneg** *nf/m* electronics
**electronig** *adj* electronic
**elegeiog** *adj* elegiac, mournful
**eleni** *adv* this year
**elfen** (-nau) *nf* element
**elfennig** *adj* elemental
**elfennol** *adj* elementary
**eli** (elïoedd) *nm* ointment, salve
**elifiant** (-nnau) *nm* effluence
**elifyn** (elifion) *nm* effluent
**eliffant** (-od, -iaid) *nm* elephant
**eliffantaidd** *adj* elephantine
**elin** (-au, -oedd) *nf* elbow; angle,
  bend
**elips** (-au) *nm* ellipse
**eliptig** *adj* elliptical
**elor** (-au) *nf* bier
**elusen** (-nau) *nf* alms
**elusendy** (-dai) *nm* almshouse
**elusengar** *adj* charitable,
  benevolent
**elusengarwch** *nm* charity,
  benevolence
**elusennol** *adj* eleemosynary
**elusennwr** (-enwyr) *nm* almoner
**elw** *nm* possession, gain, profit
**elwa** *vb* gain, profit

**elwlen** (-wlod) *nf* kidney
**ellyll** (-on) *nm* fiend; goblin
**ellyllaidd** *adj* fiendish; elfish
**ellylles** (-au) *nf* fury, she-goblin
**ellyn** (-au, -od) *nm* razor
**embryo** *nm* embryo
**embryoleg** *nf* embryology
**emosiwn** (-iynau) *nm* emotion
**emosiynol** *adj* emotional
**empeiraeth** *nf* empiricism
**empeiraidd** *adj* empirical
**empirig** *adj* empirical
**emrallt** *nm* emerald
**emyn** (-au) *nm* hymn
**emyn-dôn** (-au) *nf* hymn-tune
**emyniadur** (-on) *nm* hymnal
**emynwr** (-wyr) *nm* hymnist
**emynydd** (-ion, -wyr) *nm* hymnist
**emynyddiaeth** *nf* hymnody,
  hymnology
**enaid** (eneidiau) *nm* life, soul
**enamel** (-au) *nm* enamel
**enamlio** *vb* enamel
**enbyd, -us** *adj* dangerous, perilous
**enbydrwydd** *nm* peril, danger,
  jeopardy
**encil** (-ion) *nm* retreat, flight
**encilfa** (-feydd) *nf* retreat
**enciliad** (-au) *nm* retreat;
  desertion
**encilio** *vb* retreat; desert
**enciliwr** (-wyr) *nm* retreater;
  deserter
**enclitig** *adj* enclitic
**encôr** *nm* encore
**encyd** *nm* space; while
**enchwythu** *vb* inflate
**endemig** *adj* endemic
**endid** *nm* entity, existence
**endothermig** *adj* endothermic
**eneidiog** *adj* animate
**eneidiol** *adj* animate, living
**eneiniad** (-au) *nm* anointing,
  unction
**eneinio** *vb* anoint
**Eneiniog** *nm* The Messiah, Christ
**eneiniog** *adj*, *nm* anointed

**enfawr** adj enormous, huge, immense

**enfys** (-au) nf rainbow

**engiriol** adj nefarious, cruel, terrible

**engrafiad** (-au) nm engraving

**engrafu** vb engrave

**enhuddo** see **anhuddo**

**enigma** nm enigma

**enigmatig** adj enigmatic

**enillfawr** adj lucrative, remunerative

**enillgar** adj gainful; winsome

**enillion** npl profits, earnings

**enillwr, -ydd** (-wyr) nm gainer, winner

**enllib** (-ion, -iau) nm slander, libel

**enllibaidd** adj slanderous, libellous

**enllibio** vb slander, libel

**enllibiwr** (-wyr) nm slanderer, libeller

**enllibus** adj slanderous, libellous

**enllyn** nm relish eaten with bread

**ennaint** (eneiniau) nm ointment

**ennill** vb gain, win, earn ♦ (enillion) nm gain, profit; (pl) earnings

**ennyd** nm/f while, moment

**ennyn** vb kindle, burn, inflame; excite

**ensyniad** (-au) nm insinuation

**ensynio** vb insinuate

**entrych** (-ion) nm firmament, height, zenith

**enw** (-au) nm name; noun

**enwad** (-au) nm denomination, sect

**enwadaeth** nf sectarianism

**enwadol** adj sectarian; nominative

**enwadwr** (-wyr) nm sectarian, sectary

**enwaediad** nm circumcision

**enwaedu** vb circumcise

**enwebai** (-eion) nm nominee

**enwebiad** (-au) nm nomination

**enwebu** vb nominate

**enwedig** adj: yn e. particularly, especially

**enwi** vb name

**enwog** (-ion) adj famous, renowned, noted

**enwogi** vb make famous

**enwogrwydd** nm fame, renown

**enwol** adj nominal, nominative

**enwyn** nm: llaeth e. buttermilk

**enynfa** nf inflammation; itching

**enyniad** (-au) nm inflammation

**enynnol** adj inflammatory; inflamed

**eofn** adj fearless, bold

**eog** (-iaid) nm salmon

**eos** (-au) nf nightingale

**eosaidd** adj like a nightingale

**epa** (-od) nm ape, monkey

**epidemig** adj, nm epidemic

**epig** nf epic

**epiglotis** (-au) nm epiglottis

**epigram** (-au) nm epigram

**epil** nm offspring, brood

**epilepsi** nm epilepsy

**epilgar** adj prolific, teeming

**epiliad** (-au) nm reproduction

**epilio** vb bring forth, teem, breed

**epilog** nm epilogue

**episeicloid** (-au) nm epicycloid

**epistol** (-au) nm epistle

**eples** nm leaven, ferment

**eplesiad** nm fermentation

**eplesu** vb leaven, ferment

**er** prep for, in order to; since ♦ conj though

**eraill** see **arall**

**erbyn** vb receive, meet ♦ prep against, by

**erch** adj speckled; frightful

**erchi** vb ask, pray, command, demand

**erchwyn** (-ion) nm side, bed-side

**erchyll** adj hideous, horrible

**erchyllter** (-au) nm atrocity

**erchylltod, -tra** nm hideousness, horror

**eres** adj wonderful, strange

**erestyn** nm minstrel, buffoon

**erfin** *npl* (**-en** *nf*) turnips

**erfyn** *vb* beg, pray, implore, expect

**erfyniad** (**-au**) *nm* prayer, petition

**ergyd** (**-ion**) *nm/f* blow, stroke; shot; cast

**ergydio** *vb* strike; throw, cast

**ergydiwr** (**-wyr**) *nm* striker

**erial** (**-au**) *nm* aerial

**erioed** *adv* ever

**erledigaeth** (**-au**) *nf* persecution

**erlid** *vb* persecute ♦ (**-iau**) *nm* persecution

**erlidiwr** (**-wyr**) *nm* persecutor

**erlyn** *vb* pursue, prosecute

**erlyniad** *nm* prosecution

**erlynydd** (**-ion**) *nm* prosecutor

**ern, ernes** (**-au**) *nf* earnest, pledge, deposit

**ers** *prep* since (**er ys**)

**erthwch** *nm* grunt, pant

**erthygl** (**-au**) *nf* article

**erthyl** (**-od**) *nm* abortion

**erthylaidd** *adj* abortive

**erthyliad** (**-au**) *nm* abortion, miscarriage

**erthylu** *vb* abort, miscarry

**erw** (**-au**) *nf* acre

**erwain** *npl* meadow-sweet

**erwydd** *npl* stave (*in music*)

**erydiad** (**-au**) *nm* erosion

**erydol** *adj* erosive

**erydu** *vb* erode

**erydydd** (**-ion**) *nm* erosive agent

**eryr** (**-od**) *nm* eagle; shingles

**eryraidd** *adj* eagle-like, aquiline

**esblygiad** (**-au**) *nm* evolution

**esblygiadaeth** *nf* evolutionism

**esboniad** (**-au**) *nm* explanation; commentary

**esboniadaeth** *nf* exposition, exegesis

**esboniadol** *adj* expository, explanatory

**esbonio** *vb* explain, expound

**esboniwr** (**-wyr**) *nm* expositor, commentator

**esbonydd** (**-ion**) *nm* exponent

**esbonyddol** *adj* exponential

**escaladur** (**-on**) *nm* escalator

**esgair** (**-eiriau**) *nf* shank, leg; ridge

**esgeirlwm** *adj* exposed, wind-swept

**esgeulus** *adj* neglectful, negligent

**esgeuluso** *vb* neglect

**esgeulustod, -tra** *nm* negligence

**esgid** (**-iau**) *nf* boot, shoe

**esgob** (**-ion**) *nm* bishop

**esgobaeth** (**-au**) *nf* bishopric, see, diocese

**esgobyddiaeth** *nf* episcopalianism

**esgoli** *vb* escalate

**esgor** *vb* bring forth, bear

**esgud** *adj* quick, swift, active

**esgus** (**-ion, -odion**) *nm* excuse, pretext

**esgusodi** *vb* excuse

**esgusodol** *adj* excusable, excused

**esgymun** *adj* execrable, excommunicate

**esgymuno** *vb* excommunicate

**esgyn** *vb* ascend, rise

**esgynbren** (**-nau**) *nm* perch

**esgynfa** (**-feydd**) *nf* ascent, rise

**esgynfaen** *nm* horse-block

**esgyniad** *nm* ascension

**esgynneb** (**esgynebau**) *nf* climax

**esgynnol** *adj* ascending

**esgyrn** see **asgwrn**

**esgyrnog** *adj* bony

**esiampl** (**-au**) *nf* example

**esmwyth** *adj* soft, smooth; easy

**esmwythâd** *nm* ease, relief

**esmwythau** *vb* soothe, ease

**esmwythder, -dra** *nm* ease

**esmwytho, -áu** *vb* ease, soothe, soften

**esmwythyd** *nm* ease, luxury

**estron** (**-iaid**) *nm* foreigner, alien

**estron** *adj* foreign, strange, alien

**estrones** (**-au**) *nf* alien woman

**estronol** *adj* strange, foreign, alien

**estrys** (**-od**) *nm/f* ostrich

**estyll** *npl* (**-en** *nf*) planks, boards

**estyn** *vb* extend, reach; stretch, prolong
**estynadwy** *adj* extensible
**estyniad** *nm* extension, prolongation
**estheteg** *nm/f* aesthetics
**esthetig** *adj* aesthetic
**etifedd** (-ion) *nm* heir, inheritor
**etifeddeg** *nm/f* heredity
**etifeddes** (-au) *nf* heiress
**etifeddiaeth** (-au) *nf* inheritance
**etifeddol** *adj* hereditary
**etifeddu** *vb* inherit
**eto** *conj* yet, still ♦ *adv* again; yet, still
**ether** *nm* ether
**ethnig** *nm* ethnic
**ethnoleg** *nf* ethnology
**ethol** *vb* elect
**etholaeth** (-au) *nf* constituency
**etholedig** (-ion) *adj* elect
**etholedigaeth** *nf* election (*theol.*)
**etholiad** (-au) *nm* election
**etholiadol** *adj* electoral, elective
**etholwr** (-wyr) *nm* elector, voter
**ethos** *nm* ethos
**eu** *pron* their
**euog** *adj* guilty
**euogrwydd** *nm* guiltiness, guilt
**euraid, -aidd** *adj* golden, (of) gold
**euro** *vb* apply or bestow gold; gild
**eurych** (-od) *nm* goldsmith
**ewig** (-od) *nf* hind
**ewin** (-edd) *nm/f* nail, talon, claw; hoof
**ewino** *vb* claw
**ewinog** *adj* having nails or claws
**ewinrhew** *nf* frost-bite
**Ewrop** *nf* Europe
**Ewropead** (-aid) *nm* European
**Ewropeaidd** *adj* European
**ewyllys** (-iau) *nf* will
**ewyllysio** *vb* will, wish
**ewyn** *nm* foam, froth, surf
**ewynnog** *adj* foaming, foamy, frothy
**ewynnu** *vb* foam, froth

**ewythr** (-edd) *nm* uncle

# F

**fagddu** *nf*: **y f.** gross darkness
**falf** (-iau) *nf* valve
**fan** (-iau) *nf* van
**fandal** (-iaid) *nm* vandal
**fandaleiddio** *vb* vandalise
**fandaliaeth** *nf* vandalism
**farnais** (-eisiau) *nm* varnish
**farneisio** *vb* varnish
**fe** *pron* he, him ♦ *preverbal particle*
**feallai** *adv* perhaps, peradventure
**fel** *adv, conj, prep* so, as, that, thus, like; how
**felly** *adv* so, thus
**festri** (-ïoedd) *nf* vestry
**ficer** (-iaid) *nm* vicar
**ficerdy** (-dai) *nm* vicarage
**finegr** *nm* vinegar
**fiola** (-s) *nf* viola
**firws** (-au, fira) *nm* virus
**fitamin** (-au) *nm* vitamin
**folt** (-iau) *nf* volt
**foltamedr** (-au) *nm* voltameter
**foltedd** (-au) *nm* voltage
**foltmedr** (-au) *nm* voltmeter
**fortais** (-eisiau) *nm* vortex
**fory** *adv* tomorrow (**yfory**)
**fry** *adv* above, aloft
**fwltur** (-iaid) *nm* vulture
**fy** *pron* my
**fyny** *adv* up, upwards

# FF

**ffa** *npl* (**ffäen, ffeuen** *nf*) beans. **ffa'r gors** buckbeans. **ffa pob** baked beans
**ffabrigo** *vb* fabricate
**ffacbys** *npl* fitches, vetches
**ffactor** (-au) *nm/f* factor. **ff. cyffredin mwyaf** highest common factor. **ff. cysefin** prime factor

**ffactori, -o** *vb* factorize
**ffactri** (**-ïoedd**) *nf* factory, mill
**ffaeledig** *adj* fallible, ailing
**ffaeledigrwydd** *nm* fallibility
**ffaeledd** (**-au**) *nm* failing, defect, fault.
**ffaelu** *vb* fail
**ffafr** (**-au**) *nf* favour
**ffafraeth** *nf* favouritism
**ffafrio** *vb* favour
**ffafriol** *adj* favourable
**ffagl** (**-au**) *nf* blaze, flame; torch
**ffagotsen** (**ffagots**) *nf* faggot
**ffair** (**ffeiriau**) *nf* fair, exchange.
  **ffair sborion** jumble sale
**ffaith** (**ffeithiau**) *nf* fact
**ffald** (**-au**) *nf* fold; pound
**ffals** (**ffeilsion**) *adj* false, deceitful
**ffalsedd** *nm* falsehood, deceit
**ffalster** *nm* deceitfulness, cunning
**ffalwm** *nm* whitlow
**ffan** (**-nau**) *nf* fan
**ffanatig** *nm* fanatic
**ffansi** *nf* fancy
**ffansïo** *vb* fancy
**ffansïol** *adj* fanciful, pleasing to the fancy
**ffanatigiaeth** *nf* fanaticism
**ffantasi(a)** (**-ïau**) *nf/m* fantasy
**ffarm** (**ffermydd**) *nf* farm
**ffarmio** *vb* farm
**ffarmwr** (**ffermwyr**) *nm* farmer
**ffarmwraig** (**-wragedd**) *nf* farmwoman
**ffârs** (**-iau**) *nf* farce
**ffarwél** *nf* farewell
**ffarwelio** *vb* bid farewell
**ffaryncs** (**-au**) *nm* pharynx
**ffas** (**-ys, -au**) *nf* face, coal-face
**ffasâd** (**ffasadau**) *nm* facade
**ffasiwn** (**-iynau**) *nm* fashion
**ffasiynol** *adj* fashionable
**ffasner** (**-i**) *nm* fastener
**ffasnin** (**-au**) *nm* fastening
**ffasno** *vb* fasten
**ffasnydd** (**-ion**) *nm* fastener
**ffatri** (**-ïoedd**) *nf* factory, mill

**ffatrïaeth** *nf* manufacturing
**ffau** (**ffeuau**) *nf* den
**ffawd** (**ffodion**) *nf* fortune, fate
**ffawdheglu** *vb* hitch-hike
**ffawdheglwr** (**-wyr**) *nm* hitch-hiker
**ffawna** *nf* fauna
**ffawydd** *npl* (**-en** *nf*) beech trees
**ffederal** *adj* federal
**ffederaliaeth** *nf* federalism
**ffederasiwn** (**-iynau**) *nm* federation
**ffed(e)reiddio** *vb* federate
**ffefryn** (**-nau**) *nm* favourite
**ffeil** *nf* file
**ffein, ffeind** *adj* fine
**ffeirio** *vb* barter, exchange
**ffelt** *nm* felt
**ffelwm** *nm* whitlow
**ffemwr** (**ffemora**) *nm* femur
**ffendir** *nm* fenland
**ffenestr** (**-i**) *nf* window
**ffenigl** *nm* fennel
**ffenomen** (**-au**) *nf* phenomenon
**ffens** (**-ys**) *nf* fence
**ffensio** *vb* fence
**ffêr** (**fferau**) *nf* ankle
**fferdod** *nm* numbness
**fferi** (**-ïau**) *nf* ferry
**fferins** *npl* sweets
**fferm** (**-ydd**) *nf* farm
**ffermdy** (**-dai**) *nm* farm-house
**ffermio** *vb* farm
**ffermwr** (**-wyr**) *nm* farmer
**fferru** *vb* congeal, freeze; perish with cold
**fferyllfa** (**-feydd**) *nf* dispensary
**fferylliaeth** *nf* pharmacy
**fferyllol** *adj* chemical, pharmaceutical
**fferyllydd** (**-wyr**) *nm* chemist, pharmacist
**ffesant** (**-s, -au**) *nm* pheasant
**ffest** *adj* fast
**ffest** *nf* feast
**ffetan** (**-au**) *nf* sack, bag
**ffi** (**-oedd**) *nf* fee
**ffiaidd** *adj* loathsome, abominable
**ffibr** (**-au**) *nm* fibre

**ffibrog, -us** *adj* fibrous
**Ffichtiad (-iaid)** *nm* Pict
**ffidil (ffidlau)** *nf* fiddle
**ffidlan** *vb* fiddle, dawdle
**ffidler (-iaid)** *nm* fiddler
**ffidlo** *vb* fiddle
**ffieiddbeth (-au)** *nm* abomination
**ffieidd-dra** *nm* abomination
**ffieiddio** *vb* loathe, abominate, abhor
**ffigur (-au)** *nf* figure, type
**ffigurol** *adj* figurative
**ffigys** *npl* (**-en** *nf*) figs
**ffigysbren (-nau)** *nm* fig-tree
**ffiled (-au, -i)** *nf* fillet
**ffilharmonig** *adj* philharmonic
**ffilm (-iau)** *nf* film
**ffilmio** *vb* film
**ffiloreg** *nf* rigmarole, nonsense
**ffilter (-au, -i)** *nm* filter
**ffin (-iau)** *nf* boundary, limit
**Ffindir: y F.** *nf* Finland
**ffindir (-oedd)** *nm* borderland
**ffinedig** *adj* bounded
**ffinio** *vb* border (upon), abut
**ffiniol** *adj* bordering
**ffiol (-au)** *nf* vial; cup
**ffiseg** *nm* physics
**ffisegol** *adj* physical
**ffisegwr (-wyr)** *nm* physicist
**ffisig** *nm* physic, medicine
**ffisigwr (-wyr)** *nm* physician
**ffisigwriaeth** *nm* physic, medicine
**ffisioleg** *nf/m* physiology
**ffit** *adj* fit ♦ **(-iau)** *nf* fit, paroxysm
**ffit-ffatio** *vb* flip-flop
**ffitrwydd** *nm* fitness
**ffiwdal** *adj* feudal
**ffiwg (-iau)** *nf* fugue
**ffiws (-iau)** *nm* fuse
**ffiwsio** *vb* fuse
**fflach (-iau)** *nf*, **fflachiad (-au)** *nm* flash
**fflachio** *vb* flash
**fflachiog** *adj* flashing
**fflag (-iau)** *nf* flag
**fflagen (-ni)** *nf* flagon, flag-stone

**fflangell (-au)** *nf* scourge
**fflangelliad (-au)** *nm* flagellation
**fflangellu** *vb* scourge, whip, flog
**fflam (-au)** *nf* flame
**fflamadwy** *adj* (in)flammable
**fflamio** *vb* flame, blaze
**fflamllyd** *adj* flaming, blazing
**fflan (-iau)** *nm* flan
**fflap (-iau)** *nm* flap
**fflasg (-iau)** *nf* flask, basket
**fflat** *adj* flat ♦ **(-iau)** *nm* flat-iron ♦ **(-au, -iau)** *nf* a flat
**fflatio** *vb* flat, flatten
**fflatwadn** *adj* flatfooted
**fflecs (-ys)** *nm* flex
**fflêm, fflem** *nf* phlegm
**fflint** *nm* flint
**ffliwt (-iau)** *nf* flute
**ffloch (-au)** *nm* floe. **ffloch iâ** ice floe
**fflodiad, -iart** *nf* floodgate
**ffo** *nm* flight
**ffoadur (-iaid)** *nm* fugitive, refugee
**ffodus** *adj* fortunate, lucky
**ffôedigaeth** *nf* flight
**ffoi** *vb* flee
**ffôl** *adj* foolish, silly ♦ **(ffols)** *nf* fall (in a slate quarry)
**ffoledd** *nm* foolishness, folly, fatuity
**ffolen (-nau)** *nf* buttock
**ffoli** *vb* infatuate, dote; fool
**ffolineb** *nm* foolishness, folly
**ffon (ffyn)** *nf* stick, staff
**ffonnod (ffonodiau)** *nf* stroke, blow, stripe
**ffonodio** *vb* cudgel, beat
**fforc (ffyrc)** *nf* (table) fork
**fforch (-au, ffyrch)** *nf* fork
**fforchi** *vb* fork
**fforchog** *adj* forked, cleft, cloven
**ffordd (ffyrdd)** *nf* way, road; distance
**fforddio** *vb* afford
**fforddol (-ion)** *nm* wayfarer, passer-by
**fforest (-ydd, -au)** *nf* forest

**fforffedu** *vb* forfeit
**ffortiwn** (**-iynau**), **-un** (**-au**) *nf* fortune
**fforwm** (**-ymau**) *nm* forum
**ffos** (**-ydd**) *nf* ditch, trench
**ffosffad** (**-au**) *nm* phosphate
**ffosil** (**-au**) *nm* fossil
**ffracsiwn** (**-iynau**) *nm* fraction
**ffrae** (**-au**) *nf* quarrel
**ffraeo** *vb* quarrel
**ffraeth** *adj* fluent; witty, facetious
**ffraetheb** (**-ion**) *nf* joke, witticism
**ffraethineb** *nm* wit, facetiousness
**Ffrangeg** *nf* French (language)
**Ffrainc** *nf* France
**ffrâm** (**fframiau**) *nf* frame
**fframio** *vb* frame
**fframwaith** *nm* framework
**Ffrances** (**-au**) *nf* Frenchwoman
**Ffrancwr** (**-wyr, Ffrancod**) *nm* Frenchman
**Ffrengig** *adj* French. **llygod ff.** rats
**ffrenoleg** *nm/f* phrenology
**ffres** *adj* fresh
**ffresgo** (**-au**) *nm* fresco
**ffresni** *nm* freshness
**ffretwaith** *nm* fretwork
**ffreutur** *nf* refectory
**ffrewyll** (**-au**) *nf* whip, scourge
**ffridd** (**-oedd**) *nf* mountain pasture, sheep-walk
**ffrimpan** (**-au**) *nf* frying pan
**ffrind** (**-iau**) *nm* friend
**ffrio** *vb* fry; hiss
**ffris** (**-iau**) *nf* frieze
**ffrit** (**-iau**) *nm* frit, flop ♦ *adj* worthless, unsubstantial
**ffrith** (**-oedd**) *nf* mountain pasture, sheep-walk
**ffrithiant** (**-nnau**) *nm* friction
**ffroch, ffrochwyllt** *adj* furious
**ffroen** (**-au**) *nf* nostril; muzzle (of gun)
**ffroenell** (**-au**) *nf* nozzle
**ffroeni** *vb* snort, snuff, sniff
**ffroenuchel** *adj* haughty, disdainful
**ffroes** *npl* (**-en** *nf*) pancakes

**ffrog** (**-iau**) *nf* frock
**ffrom** *adj* angry, irascible, testy, touchy
**ffromi** *vb* fume, chafe, rage
**ffrostgar** *adj* boastful
**ffrwd** (**ffrydiau**) *nf* stream, torrent
**ffrwgwd** (**ffrygydau**) *nm* squabble
**ffrwst** *nm* hurry, haste, bustle
**ffrwtian** *vb* splutter
**ffrwydriad** (**-au**) *nm* explosion
**ffrwydro** *vb* explode
**ffrwydrol** *adj* explosive
**ffrwydryn** (**-nau, ffrwydron**) *nm* mine, explosive
**ffrwyn** (**-au**) *nf* bridle
**ffrwyno** *vb* bridle, curb
**ffrwyth** (**-au, -ydd**) *nm* fruit; vigour, use
**ffrwythlon** *adj* fruitful, fertile
**ffrwythlondeb, -der** *nm* fruitfulness, fertility
**ffrwythlonedd** *nm* fecundity
**ffrwythloni** *vb* become fruitful; fertilize
**ffrwytho** *vb* bear fruit
**ffrydio** *vb* stream, gush
**ffrydlif** *nm/f* stream, flood, torrent
**ffug** *adj* fictitious, false, sham ♦ (**-ion**) *nm* fiction, sham
**ffug-bas** (**-ys**) *nf* dummy (pass)
**ffugbasio** *vb* dummy
**ffugenw** (**-au**) *nm* pseudonym
**ffugiad** (**-au**) *nm* forgery
**ffugio** *vb* feign; forge
**ffugiwr** (**-wyr**) *nm* impostor; forger
**ffuglen** *nf* fiction
**ffugliw** (**-iau**) *nm* camouflage
**ffugliwio** *vb* camouflage
**ffunud** *nm* form, manner. **yr un ffunud â** exactly like
**ffured** (**-au**) *nf* ferret
**ffureta** *vb* ferret
**ffurf** (**-iau**) *nf* form, shape
**ffurfafen** *nf* firmament, sky
**ffurfdro** (**-eon**) *nm* inflection
**ffurfeb** (**-au**) *nf* formula

**ffurfiad** (**-au**) *nm* formation
**ffurfiant** (**-nnau**) *nm* accidence; formation
**ffurfio** *vb* form
**ffurfiol** *adj* formal
**ffurfiolaeth** *nf* formalism
**ffurfioldeb** *nm* formality, formalism
**ffurflen** (**-ni**) *nf* form (*to fill*)
**ffurflin** (**-iau**) *nm* formline
**ffurfwasanaeth** (**-au**) *nm* liturgy
**ffurfwedd** (**-au**) *nf* configuration
**ffust** (**-iau**) *nf* flail
**ffustio, -o** *vb* beat
**ffwdan** *nf* fuss, bustle, flurry
**ffwdanllyd** *adj* fussy, bustling
**ffwdanu** *vb* fuss, bustle
**ffwdanus** *adj* fussy, fidgety, flurried
**ffwng** (**ffyngoedd, ffyngau**) *nm* fungus
**ffwngleiddiad** (**-au**) *nm* fungicide
**ffŵl** (**ffyliaid**) *nm* fool
**ffwlbart** (**-iaid**) *nm* polecat
**ffwlbri** *nm* fudge, nonsense, tomfoolery
**ffwlcyn** *nm* fool, ninny, nincompoop
**ffwndro** *vb* founder, become confused
**ffwndrus** *adj* confused, bewildered
**ffwndwr** *nm* confusion, hurly-burly
**ffwr** *nm* fur
**ffwrdd** *nm* way. **I ff.** away
**ffwrn** (**ffyrnau**) *nf* furnace, oven
**ffwrnais** (**-eisiau**) *nf* furnace
**ffwrwm** (**ffyrymau**) *nf* form, bench
**ffydd** *nf* faith
**ffyddiog** *adj* strong in faith, trustful
**ffyddlon** *adj* faithful
**ffyddlondeb** *nm* faithfulness, fidelity
**ffyddloniaid** *npl* faithful ones
**ffynhonnell** (**ffynonellau**) *nf* fount, source
**ffyniannus** *adj* prosperous

**ffyniant** *nm* prosperity
**ffynidwydd** *npl* (**-en** *nf*) fir-trees, pine-trees
**ffynnon** (**ffynhonnau**) *nf* fountain, well, spring
**ffynnu** *vb* prosper, thrive
**ffyrf** *adj* thick, stout; *f* **fferf**
**ffyrfder** *nm* thickness, stoutness
**ffyrling** (**-au, -od**) *nf* farthing
**ffyrnig** *adj* fierce, savage, ferocious
**ffyrnigo** *vb* grow fierce; enrage
**ffyrnigrwydd** *nm* fierceness, ferocity

# G

**gadael, gadu** *vb* leave, forsake; let, allow
**gaeaf** (**-au, -oedd**) *nm* winter
**gaeafaidd, -ol** *adj* wintry
**gaeafu** *vb* winter, hibernate
**gafael, -yd** *vb* hold, grasp ♦ (**-ion**) *nf* hold, grasp
**gafaelgar** *adj* gripping, tenacious
**gafl** (**-au, geifl**) *nf* fork, groin
**gafr** (**geifr**) *nf* goat
**gafrewig** (**-od**) *nf* gazelle, antelope
**gagendor** see **agendor**
**gaing** (**geingau**) *nf* chisel. **g. gau** gouge
**gair** (**geiriau**) *nm* word
**galanas** (**-au**) *nf* murder, massacre
**galanastra** *nm* slaughter; mess
**galar** *nm* mourning, grief, sorrow
**galarnad** (**-au**) *nf* lamentation
**galarnadu** *vb* bewail, lament
**galaru** *vb* mourn, grieve, lament
**galarus** *adj* mournful, lamentable, sad
**galarwr** (**-wyr**) *nm* mourner
**galw** *vb* call ♦ *nm* call, demand
**galwad** (**-au**) *nm/f* call, demand
**galwedigaeth** (**-au**) *nf* occupation, vocation, calling
**galwyn** (**-i**) *nm* gallon
**gallt** (**gelltydd**) *nf* wooded slope;

hill, rise

**gallu** *vb* be able ♦ (**-oedd**) *nm* power, ability

**galluog** *adj* able, powerful, mighty

**galluogi** *vb* enable, empower

**gan** *prep* with, by; of, from

**gar** (**-rau**) *nf/m* thigh, shank

**garan** (**-od**) *nf* heron, crane

**Garawys** *nm* Lent

**gardas, -ys** (**-ysau**) *nm/f* garter

**gardd** (**gerddi**) *nf* garden; garth, yard

**garddio** *vb* garden ♦ *nm* gardening

**garddwr** (**-wyr**) *nm* gardener

**garddwriaeth** *nf* horticulture

**gargam** *adj* knock-kneed

**garlant** (**-au**) *nm* garland

**garlleg** *npl* (**-en** *nf*) garlic

**gartref** *adv* at home (*mut. of* **cartref**)

**garth** *nm* hill; enclosure

**garw** (**geirwon**) *adj* coarse, rough, harsh

**garwedd** *nm* roughness

**garwhau** *vb* roughen; ruffle

**gast** (**geist**) *nf* bitch

**gau** *adj* false; hollow

**gefail** (**-eiliau**) *nf* smithy

**gefel** (**-eiliau**) *nf* tongs, pincers

**gefell** (**-eilliaid**) *n coll* twin

**gefelldref** (**-i**) *nf* twinned town

**gefyn** (**-nau**) *nm* fetter, shackle

**gefynnu** *vb* fetter, shackle

**geingio** *vb* chisel, gouge

**geilwad** (**-waid**) *nm* caller

**geirfa** (**-oedd**) *nf* vocabulary, glossary

**geiriad** *nm* wording, phraseology

**geiriadur** (**-on**) *nm* dictionary, lexicon

**geiriadurol** *adj* lexicographical

**geiriadurwr** (**-wyr**) *nm* lexicographer

**geirio** *vb* word, phrase

**geirlyfr** (**-au**) *nm* word-book, dictionary

**geirwir** *adj* truthful, truth-speaking

**geirwiredd** *nm* truthfulness

**gelau, gelen** (**gelod**) *nf* leech

**gelyn** (**-ion**) *nm* foe, enemy

**gelyniaeth** *nf* enmity, hostility

**gelyniaethus** *adj* hostile, inimical

**gelynol** *adj* hostile, adverse

**gellyg** *npl* (**-en** *nf*) pears

**gem** (**-au**) *nf* gem, jewel

**gêm** (**gemau**) *nf* game

**gemog** *adj* gemmed, jewelled

**gemydd** (**-ion**) *nm* jeweller

**gên** *nf* jaw, chin

**genau** (**-euau**) *nm* mouth, orifice

**genau-goeg, genauoeg** (**-ion**) *nf* lizard; newt

**genedigaeth** (**-au**) *nf* birth

**genedigol** *adj* native

**Genefa** *nf* Geneva

**geneth** (**-od**) *nf* girl

**genethaidd** *adj* girlish

**genethig** *nf* little girl, maiden

**geni** *vb* be born

**genni** *vb* be contained

**genwair** (**-eiriau**) *nf* fishing-rod

**genweirio** *vb* angle, fish

**genweiriwr** (**-wyr**) *nm* angler

**ger** *prep* by, near

**gêr** *coll n* gear, tackle

**gerbron** *prep* before (*place*); in the presence of

**gerfydd** *prep* by

**geri** *nm* bile, gall. **g. marwol** cholera morbus

**geriach** *coll n* gear, odds and ends

**gerllaw** *prep* near ♦ *adv* at hand

**gerwin** *adj* rough, severe, harsh

**gerwindeb, -der** *nm* roughness, severity

**gerwino** *vb* roughen

**gewyn** (**-nau, giau**) *nm* sinew, tendon

**gewynnog** *adj* sinewy

**Ghana** *nf* Ghana

**gïach** (**-od**) *nm* snipe

**Gibralter** *n* Gibraltar

**gieuwst** *nf* neuralgia

**gildio** *vb* yield; gild

**gilydd** *nm*: **ei g.** each other. **gyda'i
  g.** together
**gimbill** *nf* gimlet
**glafoerio** *vb* drivel, slobber
**glafoerion** *npl* drivel, slobber
**glaif, gleifiau** *nm* lance, sword,
  glaive
**glain** (**gleiniau**) *nm* gem, jewel;
  bead
**glan** (**-nau, glennydd**) *nf* bank,
  shore
**glân** *adj* clean; holy; fair,
  beautiful
**glanhad** *nm* cleansing, purification
**glanhaol** *adj* cleansing, purging
**glanhau** *vb* cleanse, purify
**glaniad** *nm* landing,
  disembarkation
**glanio** *vb* land, disembark
**glanwaith** *adj* clean, tidy
**glanweithdra** *nm* cleanliness
**glas** (**gleision**) *adj* blue, green,
  grey, silver ♦ *nm* blue
**glasgoch** *adj, nm* purple
**glaslanc** (**-iau**) *nm* youth, stripling
**glasog** (**-au**) *nf* crop, gizzard
**glastwr** *nm* milk and water
**glastwraidd** *adj* watered down,
  feeble; muddled
**glasu** *vb* become blue, green or
  grey; turn pale
**glaswellt** *coll n* grass
**glaswelltyn** *nm* blade of grass;
  tigridia
**glaw** (**-ogydd**) *nm* rain
**glawiad** (**-au**) *nm* rainfall
**glawio** *vb* rain
**glawlen** (**-ni**) *nf* umbrella
**glawog** *adj* rainy
**gleisiad** (**-iaid**) *nm* sewin
**gleision** *npl* whey
**glendid** *nm* cleanness; fairness,
  beauty
**glesni** *nm* blueness, verdure
**glew** (**-ion**) *adj* brave, daring;
  astute
**glewdra, -der** *nm* courage,

resource
**glin** (**-iau**) *nm* knee
**glo** *nm* coal
**gloddest** (**-au**) *nm* carousal,
  revelling
**gloddesta** *vb* carouse, revel
**gloddestwr** (**-wyr**) *nm* reveller
**gloes** (**-au, -ion**) *nf* pang; qualm
**glofa** (**-feydd**) *nf* colliery
**glöwr** (**-wyr**) *nm* collier
**glowty** (**-tai**) *nm* cow-house,
  shippon
**glöyn** *nm* coal. **g. byw** butterfly
**gloyw** (**-on**) *adj* bright, clear;
  shiny, glossy
**gloywder** *nm* brightness, clearness
**gloywi** *vb* brighten, polish
**glud** (**-ion**) *nm* glue; bird-lime
**gludio** *vb* glue
**gludiog** *adj* sticky
**glwth** (**glythau**) *nm* couch
**glwth** (**glythion**) *adj* gluttonous ♦
  *nm* glutton
**glwys** *adj* fair; holy
**glyn** (**-noedd**) *nm* glen, valley
**glynu** *vb* stick, adhere, cleave
**glythineb, glythni** *nm* gluttony
**glythinebu, glythu** *vb* glut,
  gormandize
**go** *adv* rather, somewhat
**goachul** *adj* lean; puny; sickly,
  poorly
**gobaith** (**-eithion**) *nm* hope
**gobeithio** *vb* hope
**gobeithiol** *adj* hopeful
**gobeithlu** (**-oedd**) *nm* Band of
  Hope
**gobennydd** (**-enyddiau**) *nm*
  bolster, pillow
**goblygu** *vb* fold, wrap
**gochel** see **gochelyd**
**gocheladwy** *adj* avoidable
**gochelgar** *adj* wary, cautious
**gocheliad** *nm* avoidance. **ar ei o.**
  on his guard
**gochelyd** *vb* avoid, shun
**godidog** *adj* excellent, splendid

**godidowgrwydd** *nm* excellence
**godineb** *nm* adultery
**godinebu** *vb* commit adultery
**godinebus** *adj* adulterous
**godinebwr (-wyr)** *nm* adulterer
**godre (-on)** *nm* skirt, border, edge
**godriad (-au)** *nm* milking
**godro** *vb* milk
**goddaith (-eithiau)** *nf* fire, bonfire
**goddef** *vb* bear, suffer, allow, permit
**goddefgar** *adj* forbearing, tolerant
**goddefgarwch** *nm* forbearance, tolerance
**goddefiad (-au)** *nm* licence; toleration
**goddefol** *adj* tolerable; passive
**goddiweddyd, goddiwes** *vb* over-take
**goddrych** *nm* subject (*in grammar*)
**goddrychol** *adj* subjective
**gof (-aint)** *nm* smith
**gofal (-on)** *nm* care, charge
**gofalu** *vb* care, mind, take care
**gofalus** *adj* careful
**gofaniaeth** *nf* smith's craft
**gofer (-oedd, -ydd)** *nm* overflow of well; rill
**gofid (-iau)** *nm* grief, sorrow, trouble
**gofidio** *vb* afflict, grieve, vex
**gofidus** *adj* grievous, sad
**gofod** *nm* space. **llong o.** *nf* spaceship
**gofodwr (-wyr)** *nm* astronaut
**gofyn** *vb* ask, demand, require ♦ **(-ion)** *nm* demand, requirement
**gofyniad (-au)** *nm* question, query
**gofynnod (-ynodau)** *nm* note of interrogation, question-mark
**gofynnol** *adj* necessary, requisite; interrogative (*pronoun etc*)
**gogan** *nf* defamation, satire
**goganu** *vb* defame, satirize, lampoon
**goganwr (-wyr)** *nm* satirist
**goglais** *vb, nm* tickle

**gogledd** *nm, adj* north
**Gogledd Iwerddon** *nf* Northern Ireland
**gogleddol** *adj* northern
**gogleddwynt** *nm* north wind
**gogleddwr (-wyr)** *nm* northman; North Walian
**gogleisio** *vb* tickle
**gogleisiol** *adj* tickling, titillating, amusing
**gogoneddu** *vb* glorify
**gogoneddus** *adj* glorious
**gogoniant** *nm* glory
**gogor (-ion)** *nf* fodder, provender
**gogr (-au)** *nm* sieve, riddle
**gogri, gogrwn, gogryn** *vb* sift, riddle
**gogwydd** *nm* slant, inclination, bent
**gogwyddiad (-au)** *nm* inclination
**gogwyddo** *vb* incline, slope, lean
**gogyfer** *adj* opposite; for, by
**gogyfuwch** *adj, prep* of equal height
**gogyhyd** *adj* of equal length
**gogymaint** *adj* equal in size
**gohebiaeth (-au)** *nf* correspondence
**gohebol** *adj* corresponding
**gohebu** *vb* correspond (*by letter etc*); reply
**gohebydd (-wyr)** *nm* correspondent, reporter
**gohiriad (-au)** *nm* postponement
**gohirio** *vb* delay, postpone, defer
**golau** *adj, nm, vb* light
**golau-leuad** *nm* moonlight
**golch (-ion)** *nm* wash; coating; lye
**golchdy (-dai)** *nm* wash-house, laundry
**golchfa** *nf* wash; lathering
**golchi** *vb* wash; coat
**golchiad (-au)** *nm* washing; plating, coating
**golchion** *npl* slops; suds
**golchwr (-wyr), -ydd (-ion)** *nm* washer

**golchwraig** (**-wragedd**) *nf* washerwoman

**golchyddes** (**-au**) *nf* laundress

**goledd(f)** *nm* slant, slope

**goledd(f)u** *vb* slant, slope

**goleuad** (**-au**) *nm* light, luminary

**goleudy** (**-dai**) *nm* lighthouse

**goleuni** *nm* light

**goleuo** *vb* light, enlighten, illuminate

**golosg** *nm* coke, charcoal

**golud** (**-oedd**) *nm* wealth, riches

**goludog** *adj* wealthy, rich

**golwg** (**-ygon**) *nf/m* sight, look; (*pl*) eyes

**golwr** (**-wyr**) *nm* goalkeeper

**golwyth** (**-ion**) *nm* chop, slice, cut

**golygfa** (**-feydd**) *nf* scene, view; (*pl*) scenery

**golygiad** (**-au**) *nm* view

**golygu** *vb* view; mean; edit

**golygus** *adj* slightly, comely, handsome

**golygwedd** (**-au**) *nf* feature, aspect

**golygydd** (**-ion, -wyr**) *nm* editor

**golygyddiaeth** *nf* editorship

**golygyddol** *adj* editorial

**gollwng** *vb* drop, release, let go; discharge; dismiss; leak

**gollyngdod** *nm* release; absolution

**gomedd** *vb* refuse

**gomeddiad** *nm* refusal, omission

**gonest, onest** *adj* honest

**gonestrwydd** *nm* honesty

**gôr** *nm* pus

**gor-** *prefix* over-, super-

**gorau** (**-euon**) *adj* best. **o'r g.** very well

**gorawen** *nf* joy, ecstasy

**gorblu** *npl* immature feathers

**gorboblogi** *vb* overpopulate

**gorbwyso** *vb* outweigh, overweigh

**gorchest** (**-ion**) *nf* feat, exploit

**gorchestol** *adj* excellent, masterly

**gorchfygu** *vb* overcome, conquer

**gorchfygwr** (**-wyr**) *nm* victor; conqueror

**gorchudd** (**-ion**) *nm* cover, covering, veil

**gorchuddio** *vb* cover

**gorchwyl** (**-ion**) *nm* task, undertaking

**gorchymyn** *vb* command ♦ (**gorchmynion**) *nm* command, commandment

**gordoi** *vb* overspread, cover

**gordyfu** *vb* overgrow

**gordd** (**gyrdd**) *nf* sledge-hammer, mallet

**gordderch** (**-adon**) *nf* concubine; lover; bastard

**goresgyn** *vb* overrun, invade; conquer

**goresgyniad** *nm* invasion; conquest

**goresgynnydd** *nm* invader; conqueror

**goreuro** *vb* gild

**gorfod** *vb* be obliged ♦ *nm* obligation, necessity

**gorfodaeth** *nf* obligation, compulsion

**gorfodi** *vb* oblige, compel

**gorfodol** *adj* obligatory, compulsory

**gorfoledd** *nm* joy, rejoicing, triumph

**gorfoleddu** *vb* rejoice, triumph

**gorfoleddus** *adj* jubilant, triumphant

**gorffen** *vb* finish, complete, conclude

**gorffeniad** *nm* finishing, finish

**Gorffennaf** *nm* July

**gorffennol** *adj*, *nm* past

**gorffwyll** *adj* mad, frenzied

**gorffwyllo** *vb* rave

**gorffwyllog** *adj* mad, insane

**gorffwylltra** *nm* madness, insanity

**gorffwys** *vb*, *nm* rest, repose

**gorffwysfa** (**-oedd**) *nf* resting-place, rest

**gorffwysiad** (**-au**) *nm* rest, pause

**gorffwyso, gorffwystra** see
  **gorffwys**
**gorhendaid** *nm* great-great-
  grandfather
**gorhennain** *nf* great-great-
  grandmother
**gori** *vb* hatch
**gorifyny** *nm* ascent, hill, steep
  climb
**goris** *prep* below, beneath, under
**goriwaered** *nm* descent, declivity
**gorlawn** *adj* superabundant
**gorlenwi** *vb* overfill
**gorliwio** *vb* colour too highly,
  exaggerate
**gorllewin** *nm* west. **G. yr Almaen**
  West Germany
**gorllewinol** *adj* westerly, western
**gorllewinwr (-wyr)** *nm* westerner
**gormes** *nm* oppression, tyranny
**gormesol** *adj* oppressive,
  tyrannical
**gormesu** *vb* oppress, tyrannize
**gormeswr (-wyr), -ydd (-ion)** *nm*
  oppressor, tyrant
**gormod (-ion)** *nm* too much,
  excess
**gormodedd** *nm* excess, superfluity
**gormodiaith** *nf* hyperbole,
  exaggeration
**gormodol** *adj* excessive
**gormwyth** *nm* catarrh
**gornest, ornest (-au)** *nf* contest,
  match
**goroesi** *vb* outlive, survive
**goroesiad (-au)** *nm* survival
**goroeswr (-wyr)** *nm* survivor
**goror (-au)** *nm* border, coast,
  frontier
**gorsaf (-oedd)** *nf* station
**gorsedd (-au)** *nf*, **gorseddfa
  (-oedd)** *nf*, **gorseddfainc
  (-feinciau)** *nf* throne
**gorseddu** *vb* throne, enthrone,
  install
**gorsin, gorsing (-au)** *nf* door-post
**gorthrech** *nm* oppression; coercion

**gorthrechu** *vb* oppress; coerce
**gorthrwm** *nm* oppression
**gorthrymder** *nm* oppression,
  tribulation
**gorthrymedig** *adj* oppressed
**gorthrymu** *vb* oppress
**gorthrymus** *adj* oppressive
**gorthrymwr, -ydd (-wyr)** *nm*
  oppressor
**goruchaf** *adj* most high, supreme
**goruchafiaeth** *nf* supremacy;
  triumph
**goruchel** *adj* high, exalted
**goruchwyliaeth (-au)** *nf* oversight, supervision; dispensation
**goruchwylio** *vb* oversee, supervise
**goruchwyliwr (-wyr)** *nm*
  supervisor, steward
**goruwch** *prep* above, over
**goruwchnaturiol** *adj* supernatural
**goruwchreoli** *vb* overrule
**gorwedd** *vb* lie
**gorweddfa (-oedd), -fan (-nau)** *nf*
  bed, couch
**gorweddian** *vb* lounge, loll
**gorweiddiog** *adj* bedridden
**gorwel (-ion)** *nm* horizon
**gorwych** *adj* gorgeous
**gorwyr (-ion)** *nm* great-grandson
**gorwyres (-au)** *nf* great-grand-
  daughter
**gorymdaith (-deithiau)** *nf*
  procession
**gorymdeithio** *vb* walk in
  procession
**gorynys (-oedd)** *nf* peninsula
**gosber (-au)** *nm* vespers
**gosgedd (-au)** *nm* form, figure
**gosgeiddig** *adj* comely, graceful
**gosgordd (-ion)** *nf* retinue, train,
  escort
**gosgorddlu (-oedd)** *nm* body-
  guard
**goslef (-au)** *nf* tone, intonation
  (**oslef**)
**gosod** *vb* put, place, set; let ♦ *adj*
  false, artificial

**gosodiad** (**-au**) *nm* proposition, statement

**gosteg** (**-ion**) *nf* silence; (*pl*) banns

**gostegu** *vb* silence, still, quell

**gostwng** *vb* lower, reduce; bow; put down, humble

**gostyngedig** *adj* humble

**gostyngeiddrwydd** *nm* humility

**gostyngiad** *nm* reduction; humiliation

**gowt** *nm* gout

**gradell** (**-gredyll**) *nf* griddle

**gradd** (**-au**) *nm/f* grade, degree, stage

**graddedigion** *npl* graduates

**graddfa** (**-feydd**) *nf* scale

**graddio** *vb* graduate

**graddol** *adj* gradual

**graddoli** *vb* grade, graduate

**graean** *coll n* (**greyenyn** *nm*) gravel

**graeanu** *vb* granulate

**graeanwst** *nf* gravel (*complaint*)

**graen** *nm* grain, gloss, lustre

**graenus** *adj* of good grain, glossy, sleek

**graff** (**-iau**) *nm* graph

**gramadeg** (**-au**) *nm* grammar

**gramadegol** *adj* grammatical

**gramadegwr, -ydd** (**-wyr**) *nm* grammarian

**gran** (**-nau**) *nm* cheek

**gras** (**-au, -usau**) *nm* grace

**graslawn, -lon** *adj* full of grace, gracious

**graslonrwydd** *nm* graciousness, grace

**grasol, grasusol** *adj* gracious

**grât** (**gratiau**) *nm* grate

**grawn** *npl* (**gronyn** *nm*) grain; grapes; roe

**grawnfwyd** (**-ydd**) *coll n* cereal

**grawnwin** *npl* grapes

**Grawys** *nm* Lent

**gre** (**-oedd**) *nf* stud, flock

**greddf** (**-au**) *nf* instinct, intuition

**greddfol** *adj* instinctive, intuitive, rooted

**greddfu** *vb* become ingrained

**grefi** *nm* gravy

**gresyn** *nm* pity

**gresyni, -dod** *nm* misery, wretchedness

**gresynu** *vb* commiserate, pity

**gresynus** *adj* miserable, wretched

**gridyll** (**-au**) *nm/f* griddle

**griddfan** *vb* groan, moan ♦ (**-nau**) *nm* groan

**grillian, -io** *vb* squeak, creak; chirp; crunch

**gris** (**-iau**) *nm* step, stair

**grisial** *nm* crystal

**grisialaidd** *adj* crystal, crystalline

**gro** *coll n* (**gröyn** *nm*) gravel, pebbles

**Groeg** *nf* Greek language; Greece ♦ *adj* Greek

**Groegaidd** *adj* Grecian, Greek

**Groeges** (**-au**) *nf* Greek woman

**Groegwr** (**-wyr, -iaid**) *nm* Greek

**gronell** (**-au**) *nf* roe

**Grønland** *nf* Greenland

**gronyn** (**-nau**) *nm* grain, particle; while

**grot** (**-iau**) *nm* groat, fourpence

**grual** *nm* gruel

**grud** *nm* grit

**grudd** (**-iau**) *nf* cheek

**gruddfan** see **griddfan**

**grug** *nm* heather

**grugiar** (**-ieir**) *nf* moor-hen, grouse

**grugog** *adj* heathery

**grwgnach** *vb* grumble, murmur

**grwgnachlyd** *adj* given to grumbling

**grwgnachwr** (**-wyr**) *nm* grumbler

**grwn** (**grynnau**) *nm* ridge (*in ploughing*)

**grŵn, grwndi** *nm* purr

**grwnan** *vb* croon, purr

**grwndwal** (**-au**) *nm* foundation

**grydian** *vb* murmur; grunt

**grym** (**-oedd**) *nm* force, power, might

**grymial** *vb* mutter, murmur, grumble

**grymus** *adj* strong, powerful, mighty

**grymuso** *vb* strengthen

**grymuster, -tra** *nm* power, might

**gwacáu** *vb* empty

**gwacsaw** *adj* trivial, frivolous

**gwacsawrwydd** *nm* levity, vanity

**gwacter** *nm* emptiness, vacuity

**gwachul** see **goachul**

**gwad, gwadiad** *nm* denial, disavowal

**gwadn (-au)** *nm* sole

**gwadnu** *vb* sole; foot it

**gwadu** *vb* deny, disown; renounce, forsake

**gwadwr (-wyr)** *nm* denier

**gwadd (-od)** *nf* mole

**gwadd** see **gwahodd**

**gwaddod (-ion)** *nm* sediment, lees, dregs

**gwaddodi** *vb* deposit sediment

**gwaddol (-ion, -iadau)** *nm* endowment; dowry

**gwaddoli** *vb* endow

**gwae (-au)** *nm/f* woe

**gwaed** *nm* blood

**gwaedlif, gwaedlyn** *nm* hæmorrhage, dysentery

**gwaedlyd** *adj* bloody, sanguinary

**gwaedoliaeth** *nf* blood, consanguinity

**gwaedu** *vb* bleed

**gwaedd (-au)** *nf* cry, shout

**gwaeddi** see **gweiddi**

**gwaeg (gwaegau)** *nf* buckle, clasp

**gwael** *adj* poor, vile; poorly, ill

**gwaelder, -dra** *nm* poorness, vileness

**gwaeledd** *nm* illness

**gwaelod (-ion)** *nm* bottom; (*pl*) sediment

**gwaelodi** *vb* settle, deposit sediment

**gwaelu** *vb* sicken

**gwaell (gwëyll, gweill)** *nf* knitting-needle

**gwaered** *nm* descent. **I w.** down

**gwaeth** *adj* worse

**gwaethwaeth** *adj* worse and worse

**gwaethygu** *vb* worsen

**gwaew** see **gwayw**

**gwag (gweigion)** *adj* empty, vacant, vain

**gwagedd** *nm* vanity

**gwagelog** *adj* wary, circumspect

**gwagen (-i)** *nf* waggon

**gwagenwr (-wyr)** *nm* waggoner

**gwagfa (-feydd)** *nf* vacuum

**gwagle (-oedd)** *nm* space, void

**gwagu** *vb* empty

**gwahadden (gwahaddod)** *nf* mole

**gwahan, gwahân** *nm*: **ar w.** apart, separately

**gwahangleifion** *npl* lepers

**gwahanglwyf** *nm* leprosy

**gwahanglwyfus** *adj* leprous ♦ *nm* leper

**gwahaniaeth (-au)** *nm* difference

**gwahaniaethol** *adj* distinguishing

**gwahaniaethu** *vb* differ; distinguish

**gwahanol** *adj* different

**gwahanu** *vb* divide, part, separate

**gwahardd** *vb* forbid, prohibit

**gwaharddiad (-au)** *nm* prohibition, veto

**gwahodd** *vb* invite

**gwahoddedigion** *npl* guests

**gwahoddiad (-au)** *nm* invitation

**gwahoddwr (-wyr)** *nm* inviter, host

**gwain (gweiniau)** *nf* sheath, scabbard

**gwair (gweiriau)** *nm* hay

**gwaith (gweithiau)** *nm* work

**gwaith (gweithiau)** *nf* time, turn

**gwal (-iau, gwelydd)** *nf* wall

**gwâl (gwalau)** *nf* couch, bed; lair

**gwala** *nf* enough, plenty

**gwalch (gweilch)** *nm* hawk; rogue, rascal

**gwaled** (-au) *nf* wallet
**gwalio** *vb* wall, fence
**gwall** (-au) *nm* defect, want; mistake, error
**gwallgof** *adj* mad, insane
**gwallgofdy** (-dai) *nm* madhouse, lunatic asylum
**gwallgofddyn** (-gofiaid) *nm* madman
**gwallgofi** *vb* go mad, rave
**gwallgofrwydd** *nm* madness, insanity
**gwallt** (-iau) *nm, coll n* hair of the head
**gwalltog** *adj* hairy
**gwallus** *adj* faulty, incorrect, inaccurate
**gwamal** *adj* fickle, frivolous
**gwamalio, -u** *vb* waver; behave frivolously
**gwamalrwydd** *nm* frivolity, levity
**gwan** (gweiniaid, gweinion) *adj* weak, feeble
**gwanaf** (-au) *nf* layer; row, swath
**gwanc** *nm* greed, voracity
**gwancus** *adj* greedy, voracious
**gwaneg** (-au, gwenyg) *nf* wave, billow
**gwangalon** *adj* faint-hearted
**gwangalonni** *vb* lose heart
**gwanhau** *vb* weaken, enfeeble
**gwanllyd, gwannaidd** *adj* weakly, delicate
**gwant** *nm* caesura; division
**gwantan** *adj* unsteady, fickle; feeble, poor
**gwanu** *vb* pierce, stab
**gwanwyn** (-au) *nm* spring
**gwanwynol** *adj* vernal, spring-like
**gwanychu** *vb* weaken, enfeeble
**gwar** (-rau) *nm/f* (nape of) neck
**gwâr** *adj* civilised, tame, gentle
**gwaradwydd** (-iadau) *nm* shame, disgrace
**gwaradwyddo** *vb* shame, disgrace
**gwaradwyddus** *adj* shameful, disgraceful

**gwarafun** *vb* forbid, refuse, grudge
**gwaraidd** *adj* gentle, civilized
**gwarant** (-au) *nf* warrant
**gwarantu** *vb* warrant, guarantee
**gwarchae** *vb* besiege ♦ *nm* siege
**gwarcheidiol** *adj* guardian, tutelary
**gwarcheidwad** (-waid) *nm* guardian
**gwarchod** *vb* watch, ward, mind
**gwarchodaeth** *nf* ward, custody
**gwarchodlu** (-oedd) *nm* garrison, guards
**gward** (-iau) *nm/f* ward
**gwarden** (-deiniaid) *nm* warden
**gwared** *vb* rid; deliver, redeem
**gwaredigaeth** (-au) *nf* deliverance
**gwaredigion** *npl* redeemed, ransomed
**gwaredu** *vb* save, deliver, redeem; rid
**gwaredwr** (-wyr), **-ydd** (-ion) *nm* saviour
**gwaredd** *nm* mildness, gentleness
**gwareiddiad** *nm* civilization
**gwareiddiedig** *adj* civilized
**gwareiddio** *vb* civilize
**gwargaled** *adj* stiffnecked, stubborn
**gwargaledwch** *nm* stubbornness
**gwargam** *adj* stooping
**gwargamu** *vb* stoop
**gwarged** *nm* remains
**gwargrwm** *adj* round-shouldered
**gwargrymu** *vb* stoop
**gwario** *vb* spend
**gwarogaeth** see **gwrogaeth**
**gwarth** *nm* shame, disgrace
**gwarthaf** *nm* top, summit. **ar w.** on top of, upon
**gwarthafl** (-au) *nf* stirrup
**gwartheg** *npl* cows, cattle
**gwarthnod** (-au) *nm* stigma
**gwarthnodi** *vb* stigmatize
**gwarthol** (-ion) *nf* stirrup
**gwarthrudd** *nm* shame, disgrace

**gwarthruddo** *vb* shame, disgrace
**gwarthus** *adj* shameful,
disgraceful
**gwas (gweision)** *nm* lad; servant
**gwasaidd** *adj* servile, slavish
**gwasanaeth (-au)** *nm* service
**gwasanaethferch (-ed)** *nf*
handmaid
**gwasanaethgar** *adj* serviceable;
obliging
**gwasanaethu** *vb* serve, minister
**gwasanaethwr (-wyr)** *nm*
manservant, servant
**gwasanaethwraig (-wragedd)** *nf*
maidservant
**gwasanaethydd (-ion)** *nm* servant
**gwasanaethyddes (-au)** *nf*
handmaid
**gwaseidd-dra** *nm* servility
**gwasg (-au, -oedd, gweisg)** *nf*
press ♦ *nm* waist; bodice
**gwasgar** *nm* dispersion. **ar w.**
scattered, dispersed
**gwasgaredig (-ion)** *adj* scattered
**gwasgarog** *adj* scattered; divided
**gwasgaru** *vb* scatter, disperse;
spread
**gwasgarwr (-wyr)** *nm* scatterer;
spreader
**gwasgfa (-feydd, -feuon)** *nf*
squeeze; fit
**gwasgod (-au)** *nf* waistcoat
**gwasgu** *vb* press, squeeze, crush,
wring
**gwasod** *adj* in heat (*of a cow*)
**gwastad** *adj* level, flat; even;
constant, continual
**gwastadedd (-au)** *nm* plain
**gwastadol** *adj* continual, perpetual
**gwastadrwydd** *nm* evenness
**gwastatáu** *vb* make even, level;
settle
**gwastatir (-oedd)** *nm* level
ground, plain
**gwastraff** *nm* waste, extravagance
**gwastraffu** *vb* waste, squander
**gwastraffus** *adj* wasteful,

extravagant
**gwastrawd (-odion)** *nm* groom,
ostler
**gwastrodaeth, -odi** *vb* grooming;
discipline
**gwatwar** *vb* mock; mimic ♦ *nm*
mockery
**gwatwareg** *nf* sarcasm, satire,
irony
**gwatwarus** *adj* mocking, scoffing
**gwatwarwr (-wyr)** *nm* mocker,
scoffer
**gwau** *vb* knit, weave
**gwaun (gweunydd)** *nf* moor,
meadow
**gwawch (-iau)** *nf*, **-io** *vb* scream,
yell
**gwawd** *nm* scoff, scorn, ridicule
**gwawdiaeth** *nf* ridicule
**gwawdio** *vb* mock, scoff, jeer,
ridicule
**gwawdiwr (-wyr)** *nm* mocker,
scoffer
**gwawdlyd** *adj* mocking, jeering,
sneering
**gwawl** *nm* light
**gwawn** *nm* gossamer
**gwawr** *nf* dawn, day-break; hue,
nuance
**gwawrio** *vb* dawn
**gwayw (gwewyr)** *nm* pang, pain,
stitch
**gwaywffon (-ffyn)** *nf* spear
**gwden (-ni, gwdyn)** *nf* withe
**gwdihŵ** *nm* owl
**gwddf (gyddfau)** *nm* neck, throat
**gwe (-oedd)** *nf* web; texture
**gwead** *nm* weaving, knitting;
texture
**gwedd (-au)** *nf* aspect, form;
appearance
**gwedd (-oedd)** *nf* yoke; team
**gweddaidd** *adj* seemly, decent
**gweddeidd-dra** *nm* seemliness,
decency
**gwedder (gweddrod)** *nm* wether.
**cig g.** mutton

**gweddgar** *adj* plump, sleek

**gweddi** (**-ïau**) *nm* prayer

**gweddigar** *adj* prayerful

**gweddill** (**-ion**) *nm* remnant, remainder, rest; (*pl*) remains

**gweddillio** *vb* leave spare, leave a remnant

**gweddïo** *vb* pray

**gweddïwr** (**-ïwyr**) *nm* one who prays

**gweddol** *adj* fair, fairly

**gweddu** *vb* suit, become, befit

**gweddus** *adj* seemly, decent, proper

**gweddustra** *nm* decency, propriety

**gweddw** *adj* single; widow, widowed. **gŵr g.** widower ♦ (**-on**) *nf* widow

**gweddwdod** *nm* widowhood

**gweddwi** *vb* widow

**gwefl** (**-au**) *nf* lip (*usu. of animal*)

**gwefr** *nm* thrill, excitement; charge

**gwefreiddio** *vb* electrify, thrill

**gwefreiddiol** *adj* thrilling

**gwefus** (**-au**) *nf* (human) lip

**gwefusol** *adj* of the lip, labial

**gwegi** *nm* vanity, levity

**gwegian** *vb* sway, totter

**gwegil** *nm* back of head

**gwehelyth** *nm/f* lineage, pedigree

**gwehilion** *npl* refuse, trash, riffraff

**gwehydd** (**-ion**) *nm* weaver

**gwehynnu** *vb* draw, pour, empty

**gweiddi** *vb* cry, shout

**gweilgi** *nf* sea, torrent

**gweili** *adj* empty, idle

**gweini** *vb* serve, minister; be in service

**gweinidog** (**-ion**) *nm* minister, servant

**gweinidogaeth** (**-au**) *nf* ministry, service

**gweinidogaethol** *adj* ministerial

**gweinidogaethu** *vb* minister

**gweinio** *vb* sheathe

**gweinyddes** (**-au**) *nf* attendant, nurse; waitress

**gweinyddiaeth** (**-au**) *nf* administration

**gweinyddol** *adj* administrative

**gweinyddu** *vb* administer, officiate

**gweirglodd** (**iau**) *nf* meadow

**gweitied, -io** *vb* wait

**gweithdy** (**-dai**) *nm* workshop

**gweithfa** (**-oedd, -feydd**) *nf* works

**gweithfaol** *adj* industrial

**gweithgar** *adj* hard-working, industrious

**gweithgaredd** (**-au**), **-garwch** *nm* activity

**gweithio** *vb* work; ferment; purge

**gweithiwr** (**-wyr**) *nm* workman, worker

**gweithred** (**-oedd**) *nf* act, deed, work

**gweithrediad** (**-au**) *nm* action, operation

**gweithredol** *adj* active, actual, virtual

**gweithredu** *vb* act, work, operate

**gweithredwr** (**-wyr**) *nm* doer

**gweithredydd** (**-ion**) *nm* doer, factor, agent

**gweladwy** *adj* perceptible, visible

**gweled, gweld** *vb* see, perceive

**gwelediad** *nm* sight, appearance

**gweledig** *adj* seen, visible

**gweledigaeth** (**-au**) *nf* vision

**gweledydd** (**-ion**) *nm* seer

**gwelw** *adj* pale

**gwelwi** *vb* pale

**gwely** (**-au, gwelâu**) *nm* bed; river basin; sea bed; stratum; flat surface

**gwell** *adj* better, superior

**gwella** *vb* better, mend, improve, recover

**gwellau, gwellaif** (**-eifiau**) *nm* shears

**gwellen** (**gweill**) *nf* knitting-needle

**gwellhad** *nm* recovery,

improvement
**gwellhau** vb better, improve
**gwelliant** (-iannau) nm amendment, improvement
**gwellt** coll n grass; sward; straw
**gwelltglas** nm grass, greensward
**gwelltog** adj grassy, green
**gwelltyn** nm blade of grass; a straw
**gwellwell** adv better and better
**gwen** adj f. of **gwyn**
**gwên** (gwenau) nf smile
**gwenci** (-iod) nf stoat, weasel
**gwendid** (-au) nm weakness, frailty
**Gwener** nf Venus. **Dydd G.** Friday
**gwenerol** adj venereal
**gwenfflam** adj blazing, ablaze
**gweniaith** nf flattery
**gwenieithio** vb flatter
**gwenieithiwr** (-wyr) nm flatterer
**gwenieithus** adj flattering
**gwenith** npl (-en nf) wheat
**gwenithfaen** nm granite
**gwennol** (gwenoliaid) nf swallow, martin; shuttle
**gwenu** vb smile
**gwenwisg** (-oedd) nf surplice
**gwenwyn** nm poison, venom; jealousy
**gwenwynig, -wynol** adj poisonous, venomous
**gwenwynllyd** adj peevish; jealous
**gwenwyno** vb poison; fret; be jealous
**gwenyn** npl (-en nf) bees
**gwep** nf visage, grimace
**gwêr** nm tallow, suet etc
**gwer** nm shade
**gwerchyr** nm cover, lid, valve
**gwerdd** adj f. of **gwyrdd**
**gwerin** coll nf men, people; democracy; crew
**gweriniaeth** (-au) nf democracy; republic
**Gweriniaeth Iwerddon** nf Eire
**gwerinlywodraeth** (-au) nf

republic
**gwerinol** adj plebian, vulgar
**gwerinos** coll nf the rabble, the mob
**gwerinwr** (-wyr) nm democrat
**gwern** (-i, -ydd) nf swamp, meadow; alder-grove
**gwern** npl (-en nf) alder-trees
**gwerog** adj tallowy, suety
**gwers** (-i) nf verse; lesson
**gwersyll** (-oedd) nm camp, encampment
**gwersyllu, -a** vb encamp
**gwerth** nm worth, value. **ar w.** for sale
**gwerthfawr** adj valuable, precious
**gwerthfawredd** nm preciousness
**gwerthfawrogi** vb appreciate
**gwerthfawrogiad** nm appreciation
**gwerthu** vb sell
**gwerthwr** (-wyr) nm seller
**gwerthyd** (-au) nf spindle, axle
**gweryd** (-au) nm earth, soil; sward ♦ nf groin
**gweryriad** nm neighing
**gweryru** vb neigh
**gwestai** (-eion) nm guest
**gwesty** (-au, -tai) nm inn, hotel
**gweu** vb weave, knit
**gwewyr** nm anguish
**gwg** nm frown, scowl; disapproval
**gwgu** vb frown, scowl, lower
**gwialen** (gwiail) nf rod, switch
**gwialennod** (-enodiau) nf stroke, stripe
**gwialenodio** vb beat with a rod
**gwib** nf wandering, jaunt ♦ adj wandering
**gwibdaith** (-deithiau) nf excursion
**gwiber** (-od) nf viper
**gwibio** vb flash, flit, dart, wander
**gwibiog** adj flitting, darting, wandering
**gwiblong** (-au) nf cruiser
**gwich** nf squeak; creak; wheeze, wheezing
**gwichiad** (-iaid) nm periwinkle

**gwichian** *vb* squeak, squeal; creak; wheeze

**gwichlyd** *adj* creaking; wheezy

**gwiddon** (-od) *nf* witch

**gwiddon** *npl* mites

**gwif** (-iau) *nm* lever, crowbar

**gwig** (-oedd) *nf* wood

**gwingo** *vb* wriggle, fidget; writhe; kick, struggle

**gwin** (-oedd) *nm* wine

**gwinau** *adj* bay, brown, auburn

**gwinc** (-od) *nf* chaffinch

**gwinegr** *nm* vinegar

**gwinllan** (-noedd, -nau) *nf* vine-yard

**gwinllannwr, -nydd** *nm* vine-dresser

**gwinwryf** (-oedd) *nm* wine-press

**gwinwydd** *npl* (-en *nf*) vines

**gwir** *adj* true ♦ *nm* truth

**gwireb** (-au, -ion) *nf* truism, axiom

**gwireddu** *vb* verify, substantiate

**gwirfodd** *nm* goodwill; own accord

**gwirfoddol** *adj* voluntary, spontaneous

**gwirfoddolwr** (-wyr) *nm* volunteer

**gwirio** *vb* verify

**gwirion** (-iaid) *adj* innocent; silly

**gwiriondeb** *nm* innocence; silliness

**gwirionedd** (-au) *nm* truth, verity, reality

**gwirioneddol** *adj* true, real, genuine

**gwirioni** *vb* infatuate, dote

**gwirionyn** *nm* simpleton

**gwirod** (-ydd) *nm* liquor, spirits

**gwisg** (-oedd) *nf* dress, garment, robe

**gwisgi** *adj* brisk, lively, nimble; ripe

**gwisgo** *vb* dress; wear

**gwisgwr** (-wyr) *nm* wearer

**gwiw** *adj* fit, meet; worthy

**gwiwer** (-od) *nf* squirrel

**gwlad** (gwledydd) *nf* country, land

**gwladaidd** *adj* countrified, rustic

**Gwlad Belg** *nf* Belgium

**Gwlad yr Iâ** *nf* Iceland

**Gwlad Thai** *nf* Thailand

**gwladfa** (-oedd) *nf* colony, settlement

**gwladgar** see **gwlatgar**

**gwladgarol** *adj* patriotic

**gwladgarwch** *nm* patriotism

**gwladgarwr** (-wyr) *nm* patriot

**gwladol** *adj* of a country, civil, state

**gwladoli** *vb* nationalize

**gwladweiniaeth** *nf* statesmanship

**gwladweinydd** (-ion, -wyr) *nm* statesman

**gwladwr** (-wyr) *nm* countryman, peasant

**gwladwriaeth** (-au) *nf* state

**gwladwriaethol** *adj* state, political

**gwladychfa** (-oedd) *nf* settlement, colony

**gwladychu** *vb* inhabit, settle, colonize; rule

**gwladychwr** (-wyr) *nm* settler, colonist

**gwlân** (gwlanoedd) *nm* wool

**gwlana** *vb* gather wool

**gwlanen** (-ni) *nf* flannel

**gwlanog** *adj* woolly

**gwlatgar** *adj* patriotic

**gwlaw** see **glaw**

**gwledig** *adj* countrified, country, rural

**gwledd** (-oedd) *nf* feast, banquet

**gwledda** *vb* feast

**gwleddwr** (-wyr) *nm* feaster

**gwleidydd** (-ion) *nm* politician, statesman

**gwleidyddiaeth** *nf* politics

**gwleidyddol** *adj* political

**gwleidyddwr** (-wyr) *nm* politician

**gwlith** (-oedd) *nm* dew

**gwlitho** *vb* dew, bedew

**gwlithog** *adj* dewy; inspiring

**gwlithyn** *nm* dewdrop

**gwlyb** (-ion) *adj* wet, fluid, liquid ♦ *nm* fluid, liquid

**gwlybaniaeth** *nm* wet, moisture
**gwlybwr** *nm* wet, moisture, liquid, fluid
**gwlybyrog** *adj* wet, damp, rainy
**gwlych** *nm* wet. **rhoi yng ng.** steep
**gwlychu** *vb* wet, moisten; get wet; dip
**gwlydd** *npl*, *coll n* (**-yn** *nm*) haulm
**gwn** (**gynnau**) *nm* gun
**gŵn** (**gynau**) *nm* gown
**gwndwn** *see* **gwyndwn**
**gwneud, gwneuthur** *vb* do, make
**gwneuthuriad** *nm* make, making
**gwneuthurwr** (**-wyr**) *nm* maker, doer, manufacturer
**gwniad** *nm* sewing, stitching, seam
**gwniadur** (**-iau, on**) *nm/f* thimble
**gwniadwraig** *nf* stitcher, seamstress
**gwniadyddes** (**-au**) *nf* seamstress
**gwnïo** *vb* sew, stitch
**gwnïyddes** (**-au**) *nf* seamstress
**gwobr** (**-au**) *nf/m*, **gwobrwy** (**-au, -on**) *nm* reward, prize
**gwobrwyo** *vb* reward
**gwobrwywr** (**-wyr**) *nm* rewarder
**gŵr** (**gwŷr**) *nm* man; husband
**gwra** *vb* seek *or* marry a husband
**gwrach** (**-iod, -od**) *nf* hag, witch. **breuddwyd g.** wishful thinking
**gwrachïaidd** *adj* old-womanish
**gwraidd** (**gwreiddiau**) *coll n* roots
**gwraig** (**gwragedd**) *nf* woman; wife
**gwrandaw** *see* **gwrando**
**gwrandawiad** *nm* listening, hearing
**gwrandawr** (**-wyr**) *nm* listener, hearer
**gwrando** *vb* listen, hearken
**gwrcath** (**-od**) *nm* tom-cat
**gwregys** (**-au**) *nm* girdle, belt, truss; zone
**gwregysu** *vb* girdle, gird
**gwrêng** *nm*, *coll n* (one of the) common people

**gwreica** *vb* seek *or* marry a wife
**gwreichion** *npl* (**-en** *nf*) sparks
**gwreichioni** *vb* emit sparks, sparkle
**gwreiddio** *vb* root
**gwreiddiol** *adj* radical, rooted; original
**gwreiddioldeb** *nm* originality
**gwreiddyn** (**gwreiddiau**) *nm* root
**gwres** *nm* heat, warmth
**gwresfesurydd** (**-ion**) *nm* thermometer
**gwresog** *adj* warm, hot; fervent
**gwresogi** *vb* warm, heat
**gwrhyd** (**-oedd**), **gwryd** *nm* fathom
**gwrhydri** *nm* exploit; valour
**gwrid** *nm* blush, flush
**gwrido** *vb* blush, flush
**gwridog, gwritgoch** *adj* rosy-cheeked, ruddy
**gwrogaeth** *nf* homage
**gwrogi** *vb* do homage
**gwrol** *adj* brave, courageous
**gwroldeb** *nm* bravery, courage
**gwroli** *vb* hearten
**gwron** (**-iaid**) *nm* hero
**gwroniaeth** *nf* heroism
**gwrtaith** (**-teithiau**) *nm* manure, fertiliser
**gwrteithiad** *nm* cultivation, culture
**gwrteithio** *vb* manure; cultivate, culture
**gwrth-** *prefix* counter-, contra-, anti-
**gwrthban** (**-au**) *nm* blanket
**gwrthblaid** *nf* (party in) opposition
**gwrthbrofi** *vb* disprove, refute
**gwrthbwynt** *nm* counterpoint
**gwrthdaro** *vb* clash, collide
**gwrthdrawiad** (**-au**) *nm* collision
**gwrthdystiad** (**-au**) *nm* protest
**gwrthdystio** *vb* protest
**gwrthddadl** (**-euon**) *nf* objection
**gwrthddadlau** *vb* object,

controvert
**gwrthddywediad** (-au) *nm*
contradiction
**gwrthddywedyd** *vb* contradict
**gwrthgiliad** (-au) *nm* backsliding
**gwrthgilio** *vb* backslide, secede
**gwrthgiliwr** (-wr) *nm* backslider,
seceder
**gwrthglawdd** (-gloddiau) *nm*
rampart
**gwrthgyferbyniad** (-au) *nm*
contrast, antithesis
**gwrthgyferbynnu** *vb* contrast
**gwrthnaws** *nm* antipathy ♦ *adj*
repugnant
**gwrthnysig** *adj* obstinate, stubborn
**gwrthod** *vb* refuse, reject
**gwrthodedig** *adj* rejected,
reprobate
**gwrthodiad** *nm* refusal, rejection
**gwrthodwr** (-wyr) *nm* refuser,
rejecter
**gwrthol** *nm, adv* back. ôl a g. to
and fro
**gwrthrych** (-au) *nm* object;
subject (*of biography*)
**gwrthrychol** *adj* objective
**gwrthryfel** (-oedd) *nm* rebellion,
mutiny
**gwrthryfela** *vb* rebel
**gwrthryfelgar** *adj* rebellious,
mutinous
**gwrthryfelwr** (-wyr) *nm* rebel,
mutineer
**gwrthsafiad** *nm* resistance
**gwrthsefyll** *vb* withstand, resist
**gwrthun** *adj* repugnant, odious,
absurd
**gwrthuni** *nm* odiousness, absurdity
**gwrthuno** *vb* mar, deform,
disfigure
**gwrthweithio** *vb* counteract
**gwrthwyneb** *nm* opposite,
contrary
**gwrthwynebiad** (-au) *nm*
objection
**gwrthwynebol** *adj* opposed

**gwrthwynebu** *vb* resist, oppose
**gwrthwynebus** *adj* repugnant;
antagonistic
**gwrthwynebwr, -ydd** (-wyr) *nm*
opponent, adversary
**gwrych** (-oedd) *nm* hedge
**gwrych** *npl, coll n* (-yn *nm*) bristles
**gwryd** see **gwrhyd**
**gwryf** (-oedd) *nm* press
**gwrym** (-iau) *nm* seam; wale
**gwrysg** *npl* (-en *nf*) stalks, haulm
**gwryw** *adj* male ♦ (-od) *nm* male
**gwrywaidd, -ol** *adj* masculine
**gwrywgydiaeth** *nm* homosexuality
**gwrywgydiol** *adj* homosexual
**gwrywgydiwr** (-wyr) *nm*
homosexual
**gwth** *nm* push, thrust, shove; gust
**gwthio** *vb* push, thrust, shove
**gwthiwr** (-wyr) *nm* pusher
**gwyar** *nm* gore, blood
**gwybed** *npl* (-yn *nm*) flies
**gwybod** *vb* know ♦ (-au) *nm*
knowledge. **gwybodau** studies
**gwybodaeth** (-au) *nf* knowledge
**gwybodeg** *nm* epistemology
**gwybodus** *adj* knowing, well-
informed
**gwybyddus** *adj* known, aware of
**gwych** *adj* fine, splendid, brilliant
**gwychder** *nm* splendour, pomp
**gwŷd** (gwydiau) *nm* vice
**gwydn** *adj* tough
**gwydnwch** *nm* toughness
**gwydr** (-au) *nm* glass
**gwydraid** (-eidiau) *nm* glassful,
glass
**gwydro** *vb* glaze
**gwydrwr** (-wyr) *nm* glazier
**gwydryn** (gwydrau) *nm* drinking-
glass
**gwŷdd** *nm* presence
**gwŷdd** (gwyddau) *nm* goose
**gwŷdd** (gwehyddion, gwyddion)
*nm* loom; plough
**gwŷdd** *npl* (gwydden *nf*) trees
**gwyddbwyll** *nf* chess

**Gwyddel** (-od, Gwyddyl) *nm* Irishman

**Gwyddeleg** *nf* Irish language

**Gwyddeles** (-au) *nf* Irishwoman

**Gwyddelig** *adj* Irish

**gwyddfa** *nf* tumulus, grave

**gwyddfid** *nm* honeysuckle

**gwyddfod** *nm* presence

**gwyddoniadur** (-on) *nm* encyclopædia

**gwyddoniaeth** *nf* science

**gwyddonol** *adj* scientific

**gwyddonydd** (-wyr) *nm* scientist

**gwyddor** (-ion) *nf* rudiment; science. **yr w.** the alphabet

**gwyddori** *vb* instruct, ground

**gwyfyn** (-od) *nm* moth

**gwŷg** *coll n* vetch

**gŵyl** *adj* bashful, modest

**gŵyl** (-iau) *nf* holiday, feast, festival

**gwylaidd** *adj* bashful, modest

**gwylan** (-od) *nf* sea-gull

**gwylder** *nm* bashfulness, modesty

**gwyleidd-dra** *nm* bashfulness, modesty

**gwylfa** (-fâu, -feydd) *nf* watch; lookout

**gwyliadwriaeth** *nm* watchfulness, caution ♦ (-au) *nf* watch; guard

**gwyliadwrus** *adj* watchful, cautious

**gwyliedydd** (-ion) *nm* watchman, sentinel

**gwylio** *vb* watch, mind, beware

**gwyliwr** (-wyr) *nm* watchman, sentinel

**gwylmabsant** (-au) *nf* wake

**gwylnos** (-au) *nf* watch-night, wake, vigil

**gwyll** *nm* darkness, gloom

**gwylliad** (-iaid) *nm* robber, bandit

**gwyllt** *adj* wild, savage, mad; rapid ♦ (-oedd) *nm* wild

**gwylltineb** *nm* wildness; rage, fury

**gwylltio, -u** *vb* frighten; fly into a passion

**gwymon** *nm* seaweed

**gwyn** *adj* white; blessed; *f* **gwen**

**gwŷn** (gwyniau) *nm/f* ache, smart; lust

**gwynder, -dra** *nm* whiteness

**gwyndwn** *nm* unploughed land

**gwyneb** see **wyneb**

**gwynegon** *nm* rheumatism

**gwynegu** *vb* throb, ache

**gwynfa** *nf* paradise

**gwynfyd** (-au) *nm* blessedness, bliss; (*pl*) beatitudes

**gwynfydedig** *adj* blessed, happy, beatific

**gwyngalch** *nm* whitewash

**gwyngalchog** *adj* whitewashed

**gwyngalchu** *vb* whitewash

**gwyniad** (-iaid) *nm* whiting

**gwynias** *adj* white-hot

**gwyniedyn** *nm* sewin

**gwynio** *vb* throb, ache

**gwynnu** *vb* whiten, bleach

**gwynnwy** *nm* white of egg

**gwynt** (-oedd) *nm* wind; breath; smell

**gwyntell** (-i) *nf* round basket without handle

**gwyntio** *vb* smell

**gwyntog** *adj* windy

**gwyntyll** (-au) *nf* fan

**gwyntylliad** *nm* ventilation

**gwyntyllio, -u** *vb* ventilate, winnow

**gŵyr** *adj* crooked, oblique, sloping

**gwŷr** see **gŵr**

**gwyrdraws** *adj* perverse

**gwyrdro** (-ion) *nm* perversion

**gwyrdoi** *vb* pervert, distort

**gwyrdd** (-ion) *adj, nm* green

**gwyrddlas** *adj* green, verdant

**gwyrddlesni** *nm* verdure

**gwrddni** *nm* greenness, verdure

**gwyrgam** *adj* crooked

**gwyrni** *nm* crookedness, perverseness

**gwyro** *vb* swerve; slope; stoop;

tilt; deviate

**gwyrth** (**-iau**) *nf* miracle

**gwyrthiol** *adj* miraculous

**gwyry, gwyryf** (**gwyryfon**) *nf* virgin

**gwyryfdod** *nm* virginity

**gwyryfol** *adj* virgin

**gwŷs** (**gwysion**) *nf* summons

**gwysio** *vb* summon

**gwystl** (**-on**) *nm* pledge; hostage

**gwystlo** *vb* pledge, pawn

**gwystno** *vb* dry, wither, flag

**gwythïen** (**gwythi, gwythiennau**) *nf* vein, blood vessel, artery. **cwlwm gwythi** cramp

**gwyw** *adj* withered, faded, sere

**gwywo** *vb* wither, fade

**gyda, -g** *prefix* with

**gyddfol** *adj* guttural

**gyferbyn** *prefix* over against, opposite

**gylfin** (**-od**) *nm* bill, beak

**gylfinir** *nm* curlew

**gynfad** (**-au**) *nm* gunboat

**gynnau** *adv* a little while ago, just now

**gynt** *adv* formerly, of yore

**gyr** (**-roedd**) *nm* drove

**gyrfa** (**-oedd, -feydd**) *nf* race; course; career

**gyriedydd** (**-ion**) *nm* driver

**gyrru** *vb* drive; send; work, forge

**gyrrwr** (**gyrwyr**) *nm* driver; sender

**gyrwynt** (**-oedd**) *nm* hurricane, tornado

**gysb** *nm* staggers

# H

**ha** *excl* ha

**hac** (**-iau**) *nf* cut, notch, hack

**hacio** *vb* hack

**had** (**-au**) *nm, coll n* (**hedyn** *nm*) seed

**hadlif** *nm* seminal fluid

**hadog** *nm* haddock

**hadu** *vb* seed

**hadyd** *coll n* seed-corn

**haearn** (**heyrn**) *nm* iron. **h. bwrw** cast iron. **h. gyr** wrought iron

**haearnaidd** *adj* like iron

**haeddiannol** *adj* meritorious; merited

**haeddiant** (**-iannau**) *nm* merit, desert

**haeddu** *vb* deserve, merit

**hael** *adj* generous, liberal

**haelfrydedd** *nm* liberality

**haelfrydig** *adj* generous, free

**haelioni** *nm* generosity

**haelionus** *adj* generous, liberal

**haen** (**-au**) *nf* layer, stratum; seam

**haenen** (**-nau**) *nf* layer, film

**haenu** *vb* stratify

**haeriad** (**-au**) *nm* assertion

**haerllug** *adj* importunate; impudent

**haerllugrwydd** *nm* importunity; impudence

**haeru** *vb* affirm, assert

**haf** (**-au**) *nm* summer

**hafaidd** *adj* summer-like, summery

**hafal** *adj* like, equal

**hafaliad** *nm* equation

**hafan** *nf* haven

**hafn** (**-au**) *nf* hollow, gorge, ravine

**hafod** (**-ydd**) *nf* summer dwelling, upland farm

**hafog** *nm* havoc

**hafoty** (**-tai**) *nm* summer residence

**hagr** *adj* ugly

**hagru** *vb* mar, disfigure

**hagrwch** *nm* ugliness

**haid** (**heidiau**) *nf* swarm, drove, horde

**haidd** (**heiddiau**) *nm, coll n* (**heidden** *nf*) barley

**haig** (**heigiau**) *nf* shoal

**haint** (**heintiau**) *nm/f* pestilence; faint

**hala** *vb* send, spend

**halen** *nm* salt, brine

**halog, -edig** adj defiled, polluted
**halogi** vb defile, profane, pollute
**halogrwydd** nm defilement, pollution
**halogwr (-wyr)** nm defiler, profaner
**hallt** adj salt, salty; severe
**halltedd, -rwydd** nm saltness, saltiness
**halltu** vb salt
**halltwr (-wyr)** nm salter
**hambwrdd (-byrddau)** nm tray
**hamdden** nf leisure, respite
**hamddenol** adj leisurely
**hanerob (-au)** nf flitch of bacon
**haneru** vb halve
**hanes (-ion)** nm history, story, account
**hanesydd (-wyr)** nm historian
**hanesyddol** adj historical
**hanesyn (-nau)** nm anecdote
**hanfod** vb descend from, issue ♦ nm essence
**hanfodol** adj essential
**haniad** nm derivation, descent
**haniaeth** nf abstraction
**haniaethol** adj abstract
**hanner (hanerau, haneri)** nm, adj, adv half
**hanu** vb proceed, be derived, be descended
**hapus** adj happy
**hapusrwydd** nm happiness
**hardd** adj beautiful, handsome
**harddu** vb beautify, embellish, adorn
**harddwch** nm beauty
**harnais (-eisiau)** nm harness
**harneisio** vb harness
**hatling (-au, -od)** nf mite, half a farthing
**hau** vb sow, disseminate
**haul (heuliau)** nm sun
**hawdd** adj easy
**hawddamor** nm, excl good luck, welcome
**hawddfyd** nm ease, prosperity

**hawddgar** adj amiable; comely
**hawddgarwch** nm amiability
**hawl (-iau)** nf claim; right. **h. ac ateb** question and answer
**hawlio** vb claim, demand
**hawlydd (-ion)** nm claimant, plaintiff
**haws** adj easier
**heb** prep without
**heblaw** prep beside(s)
**hebog (-au)** nm hawk, falcon
**Hebraeg** nf, adj Hebrew (language)
**Hebreaidd, Hebreig** adj Hebrew, Hebraic
**Hebrees (-au)** nf Hebrew woman
**Hebreigydd (-ion)** nm Hebraist
**Hebrëwr (-wyr)** nm a Hebrew
**hebrwng** vb accompany, conduct, convey, escort
**hebryngydd (-ion)** nm conductor, guide
**hedeg** vb fly; run to seed
**hedegog** adj flying; high-flown
**hedfa (-feydd)** nf flight
**hedfan** vb fly, hover
**hedydd (-ion)** nm lark
**hedyn (hadau)** nm seed, germ
**hedd** nm peace, tranquillity
**heddgeidwad (-waid)** nm policeman
**heddiw** adv today
**heddlu** nm police force
**heddwas (-weision)** nm policeman
**heddwch** nm peace, quiet, tranquillity
**heddychiaeth** nf pacifism
**heddychlon** adj peaceful, peaceable
**heddychol** adj peaceable, pacific
**heddychu** vb pacify, appease
**heddychwr (-wyr)** nm pacifist, peace-maker
**heddyw** see **heddiw**
**hefelydd** adj similar
**hefyd** adv also, besides
**heffer (heffrod)** nf heifer
**hegl (-au)** nf leg, shank

**heglog** adj leggy, long-legged
**heglu** vb foot it, 'hook it'
**heibio** adv past
**heidio** vb swarm, throng, flock
**heidden** nf grain of barley
**heigio** vb shoal, team
**heini** adj active, lively, nimble, brisk
**heintio** vb infect
**heintus** adj infectious, contagious
**heislan** (-od) nf hackle, hatchel
**heislanu** vb hackle flax
**hel** vb gather, collect; drive, chase
**hela** vb hunt, spend (money, time). cŵn h. hounds
**helaeth** adj ample, abundant, extensive
**helaethrwydd** nm abundance
**helaethu** vb enlarge, extend, amplify
**helaethwych** adj sumptuous
**helbul** (-on) nm trouble
**helbulus** adj troubled, troublous
**helcyd** vb hunt ♦ nm worry, trouble
**helfa** (-fâu, -feydd) nf hunt, catch
**helfarch** (-feirch) nm hunter (horse)
**helgi** (-gwn) nm hound
**heli** nm salt water, brine
**heliwr** (-wyr) nm hunter, huntsman
**helm** (-au) nf helm, helmet, stack
**help** nm help, aid, assistance
**helpio, -u** vb help, aid, assist
**helwriaeth** nf game, hunting; chase
**helyg** npl (-en nf), willows
**helynt** (-ion) nf trouble, fuss, bother
**helltni** nm saltiness, saltness
**hem** nm rivet
**hem** (-iau) nf hem, border
**hen** adj old, aged, ancient, of old
**henadur** (-iaid) nm alderman
**henaduriad** (-iaid) nm Presbyterian, elder

**henaduriaeth** (-au) nf presbytery
**henafgwr, henafol** see **hy-**
**henaint** nm old age
**hendaid** (-deidiau) nm great-grandfather
**hender** nm oldness
**hendref** (-i, -ydd) nf winter dwelling, lowland farm
**heneb** (-ion) nf ancient monument
**heneiddio** vb grow old, age
**henfam** nf grandmother
**henffassiwn** adj old-fashioned
**hennain** (heneiniau) nf great-grandmother
**heno** adv tonight
**henoed** coll n elderly people, the aged
**henuriad** (-iaid) nm elder, presbyter
**heol** (-ydd) nf road
**hepgor** vb spare, dispense with ♦ (-ion) nm what may be dispensed with
**hepian** vb slumber, doze
**her** (-iau) nf challenge
**herc** (-iau) nf hop; limp
**hercian** vb hop, hobble, limp
**heresi** (-iau) nf heresy
**heretic** (-iaid) nm heretic
**hereticaidd** adj heretical
**herfeiddio** vb dare, brave, defy
**herfeiddiol** adj daring, defiant
**hergwd** nm push, thrust, shove
**herio** vb challenge, dare, brave, defy
**herw** nm raid; outlawry
**herwa** vb scout, prowl, raid
**herwgipio** vb kidnap
**herwgipiwr** (-wyr) nm kidnapper
**herwhela** vb poach (game)
**herwr** (-wyr) nm scout, raider; outlaw
**herwydd** see **oherwydd**
**hesb** adj f. of **hysb**
**hesben** (-nau) nf hasp
**hesbin** (-od) nf yearling ewe
**hesbio** vb dry up

**hesbwrn** (**-yrniaid**) *nm* young ram
**hesg** *npl* (**-en** *nf*), sedge, rushes
**het** (**-iau**) *nf* hat
**heulo** *vb* shine (*as the sun*); sun
**heulog** *adj* sunny
**heulwen** *nf* sunshine
**heuwr** (**-wyr**) *nm* sower
**hi** *pron* she, her; it
**hidio** *vb* heed
**hidl** *adj*: **wylo yn h.** weep
abundantly
**hidl** (**-au**) *nf* strainer, sieve
**hidlen** (**-ni**) *nf* strainer, sieve
**hidlo** *vb* distil, run; strain, filter
**hil** *nf* race, lineage, posterity
**hilio** *vb* bring forth, teem, breed
**hiliogaeth** *nf* offspring, issue,
posterity
**hilydd** (**-ion**) *nm* racist
**hilyddiaeth** *nf* racism
**hin** *nf* weather
**hinfynegydd** (**-ion**) *nm* barometer
**hiniog** (**-au**) *nf* threshold, door-
frame
**hinon** *nf* fair weather
**hinsawdd** (**-soddau**) *nf* climate
**hinsoddol** *adj* climatic
**hir** (**hirion**) *adj*, *prefix* long
**hiraeth** *nm* longing, nostalgia,
grief; homesickness
**hiraethu** *vb* long, yearn, sorrow
**hiraethus** *adj* longing; homesick
**hirbell** *adj*: **o h.** from afar
**hirben** *adj* long-headed, shrewd
**hirhoedledd** *nm* longevity
**hirhoedlog** *adj* long-lived
**hirymarhous** *adj* longsuffering
**hirymaros** *nm* longsuffering
**hithau** *pron conj* she (on her part),
she also
**hobaid** (**-eidiau**) *nf* peck
**hobi** (**hobïau**) *nm* hobby
**hoced** (**-ion**) *nf* deceit, fraud
**hocedu** *vb* cheat, deceive, defraud
**hocedwr** (**-wyr**) *nm* cheat, fraud
**hoci** *nm* hockey
**hocys** *npl* mallows

**hodi** *vb* shoot, ear, run to seed
**hoe** *nf* spell, rest
**hoeden** (**-nau**) *nf* hoyden
**hoedl** (**-au**) *nf* lifetime, life
**hoel, -en** (**-ion**) *nf* nail
**hoelio** *vb* nail
**hoeliwr** (**-wyr**) *nm* nailer
**hoen** *nf* joy, gladness; vigour
**hoenus** *adj* joyous, blithesome,
gay
**hoenusrwydd** *nm* liveliness,
sprightliness
**hoenyn** (**-nau**) *nm* snare
**hoew** see **hoyw**
**hofran** *vb* hover
**hoff** *adj* dear, fond; favourite
**hoffi** *vb* like, love
**hoffter** *nm* fondness; delight
**hoffus** *adj* lovable, amiable,
affectionate
**hogen** (**-nod**) *nf* girl; **-naidd** *adj*
girlish
**hogfaen** (**-feini**) *nm* whetstone,
hone
**hogi** *vb* sharpen, whet
**hogyn** (**hogiau**) *nm* boy, lad
**hongiad** (**-au**) *nm* suspension
**hongian** *vb* hang, dangle
**holgar** *adj* inquisitive, curious
**holi** *vb* ask, question, inquire
**holiad** (**-au**) *nm* interrogation,
question
**holiadur** (**-on**) *nm* questionnaire
**holwr** (**-wyr**) *nm* questioner,
interrogator; catechist, question-
master
**holwyddoreg** (**-au**) *nf* catechism
**holwyddori** *vb* catechize
**holl** *adj* all, whole
**hollalluog** *adj* almighty,
omnipotent
**hollalluowgrwydd** *nm*
omnipotence
**hollbresennol** *adj* omnipresent
**hollbresenoldeb** *nm* omnipresence
**hollfyd** *nm* universe
**hollgyfoethog** *adj* almighty

**holliach** adj whole, sound
**hollol** adj quite
**hollt** (-au) nf split, slit, cleft
**hollti** vb split, cleave, slit
**hollwybodaeth** nf omniscience
**hollwybodol** adj omniscient
**homili** (-iau) nf homily
**hon** pron f. of **hwn**
**honcian** vb waggle; jolt; limp
**honedig** adj alleged
**honiad** (-au) nm claim, assertion, allegation
**honni** vb assert, allege, profess, pretend
**honno** pron f. of **hwnnw**
**hopran** (-au) nf mill-hopper; mouth
**hosan** (-au) nf stocking
**hoyw** adj alert, sprightly, lively, gay
**hoywdeb, -der** nm sprightliness
**hoywi** vb brighten, smarten
**hual** (-au) nm fetter, shackle
**hualu** vb fetter, shackle
**huan** nf the sun
**huawdl** adj eloquent
**hud** nm magic, illusion, charm, enchantment
**hudlath** (-au) nf magic wand
**hudo** vb charm, allure, beguile
**hudol** adj enchanting ♦ (-ion) nm enchanter
**hudoles** (-au) nf enchantress, sorceress
**hudoliaeth** (-au) nf enchantment, allurement
**hudolus** adj enchanting, alluring
**hudwr** (-wyr) nm enticer, allurer
**huddygl** nm soot
**hufen** nm cream
**hugan** (-au) nf cloak, covering; rug
**hulio** vb cover, spread
**hun** (-au) nf sleep, slumber
**hun** pron self. **yn ei dŷ ei h.** his own house
**hunan** (-ain) pron self ♦ prefix self-

**hunan-dyb** nm self-conceit
**hunangar** adj self-loving, selfish
**hunaniaeth** nf identity
**hunanladdiad** nm self-murder, suicide
**hunanol** adj selfish, conceited
**hunanoldeb** nm selfishness; conceit
**hunanymwadiad** nm self-denial
**hunanymwadu** vb deny oneself
**hunell** (-au) nf wink (of sleep)
**hunllef** (-au) nf nightmare
**huno** vb sleep
**huodledd** nm eloquence
**hur** (-iau) nm hire, wage
**hurio** vb hire
**huriwr** (-wyr) nm hirer; hireling
**hurt** adj stunned, stupid
**hurtio** vb stun, stupefy
**hurtrwydd** nm stupidity
**hurtyn** (-nod) nm stupid, blockhead
**hwb** (hybiau) nm push; effort; lift
**hwde** (hwdiwch) vb imper take, accept
**Hwngari** nf Hungary
**hwn** adj, pron this (one); f **hon**
**hwnnw** adj, pron that one (absent); f **honno**
**hwnt** adv beyond, away, aside. **tu h.** beyond
**hwp** nm push; -io, -o vb push
**hwrdd** (hyrddod) nm ram
**hwrdd** (hyrddiau) nm impulse, stroke
**hwre** vb see **hwde**
**hwsmon** (-myn) nm farm-bailiff
**hwtio** vb hoot, hiss
**hwy** pron they, them
**hwyad, -en** (hwyaid) nf duck
**hwyhau** vb lengthen, elongate
**hwyl** (-iau) nf sail; humour; religious fervour
**hwylbren** (-nau, -ni) nm mast
**hwylio** vb sail; prepare, order
**hwyliog** adj fervent, eloquent
**hwylus** adj easy, convenient,

comfortable
**hwyluso** *vb* facilitate
**hwylustod** *nm* ease, facility,
convenience
**hwynt** *pron* them, they
**hwynt-hwy** *pron* they, they
themselves
**hwyr** *adj* late ♦ *nm* evening
**hwyrach** *adv* perhaps ♦ *adj* later
**hwyrdrwm** *adj* sluggish, drowsy,
dull
**hwyrfrydig** *adj* slow, tardy,
reluctant
**hwyrfrydigrwydd** *nm* tardiness,
reluctance
**hwyrhau** *vb* get late
**hwyrol** *adj* evening
**hwythau** *pron conj* they (on their
part), they also
**hy** *adj* bold
**hybarch** *adj* venerable
**hyblyg** *adj* flexible, pliant, pliable
**hyblygrwydd** *nm* flexibility,
pliancy
**hybu** *vb* improve in health;
promote
**hyd** (**-au, -oedd**) *nm* length ♦ *prep*
to, till, as far as
**hyder** *nm* confidence, trust
**hyderu** *vb* confide, rely, trust
**hyderus** *adj* confident
**hydred** (**-ion**) *nm* longitude
**hydredol** *adj* longitudinal
**hydref** (**-au**) *nm* autumn. **H.**
October
**hydrefol** *adj* autumnal
**hydrin** *adj* tractable, docile
**hydwyll** *adj* gullible
**hydwylledd** *nm* gullibility
**hydwyth** *adj* supple, elastic
**hydwythedd** *nm* elasticity
**hydyn** *adj* tractable, docile
**hydd** (**-od**) *nm* stag
**hyddysg** *adj* well versed, learned
**hyf** see **hy**
**hyfder, -dra** *nm* boldness
**hyfedr** *adj* expert, skilful, clever

**hyfryd** *adj* pleasant, delightful,
agreeable
**hyfrydu** *vb* delight
**hyfrydwch** *nm* delight, pleasure
**hyfwyn** *adj* kindly, genial
**hyfforddi** *vb* direct, instruct, train
**hyfforddiadol** *adj* training
**hyfforddiant** *nm* instruction,
training
**hyfforddwr** (**-wyr**) *nm* guide,
instructor
**hygar** *adj* amiable
**hygarwch** *nm* amiability
**hyglod** *adj* celebrated, renowned,
famous
**hyglyw** *adj* audible
**hygoel** *adj* credible
**hygoeledd** *nm* credibility;
credulity
**hygoelus** *adj* credulous, gullible
**hygyrch** *adj* accessible
**hyhi** *pron f emphat. of* **hi**
**hylaw** *adj* handy, convenient;
dexterous
**hylif** (**-au**) *nm, adj* fluid, liquid
**hylithr** *adj* slippery, fluent
**hylosg** *adj* combustible,
inflammable
**hylwydd** *adj* prosperous
**hyll** *adj* ugly, hideous
**hylltra** *nm* ugliness
**hyllu** *vb* mar, disfigure
**hyn** *adj, pron* this; these; that
**hynafgwr** (**-gwyr**) *nm* old man,
elder
**hynafiad** (**-iaid**) *nm* ancestor
**hynafiaeth** (**-au**) *nf* antiquity
**hynafiaethol** *adj* antiquarian
**hynafiaethwr, -ydd** (**-wyr**) *nm*
antiquary
**hynafol** *adj* ancient
**hynaws** *adj* kind, genial
**hynawsedd** *nm* kindness, geniality
**hynny** *adj, pron* that; those
**hynod** *adj* noted, notable,
remarkable
**hynodi** *vb* distinguish, characterize

**hynodion** *npl* peculiarities
**hynodrwydd** *nm* peculiarity
**hynt** (**-iau, -oedd**) *nf* way, course
**hyrddio, -u** *vb* hurl, impel
**hyrddwynt** (**-oedd**) *nm* hurricane
**hyrwyddo** *vb* facilitate, promote
**hyrwyddwr** (**-wyr**) *nm* sponsor, promoter
**hysb** *adj* dry, barren; *f* **hesb**
**hysbio** *vb* dry
**hysbyddu** *vb* exhaust, drain
**hysbys** *adj* known, evident. **dyn h.** *nm* wise man, sorcerer
**hysbyseb** (**-ion**) *nf* advertisement
**hysbysebu** *vb* advertise
**hysbysebwr** (**-wyr**) *nm* advertiser
**hysbysiad** (**-au**) *nm* announcement, advertisement
**hysbysrwydd** *nm* information
**hysbysu** *vb* inform, announce
**hysbyswr** (**-wyr**) *nm* informant, informer
**hysian, -io** *vb* hiss; set on, incite
**hytrach** *adv* rather
**hywaith** *adj* industrious, dexterous
**hywedd** *adj* trained, tractable

# I

**i** *prep* to, into
**i** *pron* I, me
**iâ** *nm* ice
**iach** *adj* healthy, well
**iachâd** *nm* healing
**iacháu** *vb* heal; save
**iachawdwr** (**-wyr**) *nm* saviour
**iachawdwriaeth** *nf* salvation
**iachawr** (**-wyr**) *nm* healer
**iachus, -ol** *adj* healthy, healthful, wholesome
**iad** (**-au**) *nf* pate, cranium
**iaith** (**ieithoedd**) *nf* language. **yr i. fain** English
**iâr** (**ieir**) *nf* hen
**iard** (**ierdydd**) *nf* yard
**iarll** (**ieirll**) *nm* earl

**iarllaeth** (**-au**) *nf* earldom
**iarlles** (**-au**) *nf* countess
**ias** (**-au**) *nf* shiver; thrill
**Iau** *nm* Jupiter. **Dydd I.** Thursday
**iau** (**ieuau**) *nm* liver
**iau** (**ieuau, ieuoedd**) *nf* yoke
**iawn** *adj* right ♦ *nm* right; atonement ♦ *adv* very
**iawndal** *nm* compensation
**iawnder** (**-au**) *nm* right, equity
**iawnol** *adj* atoning, expiatory
**idealaeth** *nf* idealism
**ideoleg** (**-au**) *nf* ideology
**idiom** (**-au**) *nm* idiom
**Iddew** (**-on**) *nm* Jew
**Iddewiaeth** *nf* Judaism
**Iddewes** (**-au**) *nf* Jewess
**Iddewig** *adj* Jewish
**iddwf** *nm:* **tân i.** erysipelas
**ie** *adv* yes, yea
**iechyd** *nm* health
**iechydaeth** *nf* hygiene, sanitation
**iechydol** *adj* hygienic, sanitary
**iechydwriaeth** *nf* salvation
**ieitheg** *nf* philology
**ieithegydd** (**-ion, -wyr**) *nm* philologist
**ieithwedd** (**-au, -ion**) *nf* diction, (literary) style
**ieithydd** (**-ion**) *nm* linguist
**ieithyddiaeth** *nf* linguistics, philology
**ieithyddol** *adj* linguistic, philological
**iet** (**-au, -iau**) *nf* gate
**ieuanc** (**-ainc**) *adj* young
**ieuenctid** *nm* youth
**ieuo** *vb* yoke
**ifanc** (**-ainc**) *adj* young
**ifori** *nm* ivory
**ig** (**-ion**) *nm* hiccup
**igam-ogam** *adj* zigzag
**igian** *vb* hiccup
**ing** (**-oedd**) *nm* agony, anguish
**ingol** *adj* agonizing, agonized
**ill** *pron* they. **i. dau** they both
**impio** *vb* sprout, shoot; bud, graft

**impyn** *nm* graft; scion
**inc** *nm* ink
**incil** (**-iau**) *nm* tape
**incwm** *nm* income
**India** *nf* India
**India'r Gorllewin** *npl* West Indies
**iod** *nm* iota, jot
**lôn** *nm* the Lord
**lonawr** *nm* January
**lôr** *nm* the Lord
**lorddonen** *nf* Jordan
**iorwg** *nm* ivy
**ir** *adj* fresh, green, raw
**irai** *nm* ox-goad
**iraid** (**ireidiau**) *nm* grease
**iraidd** *adj* fresh, succulent,
  luxuriant
**Iran** *nf* Iran
**Iraq** *nf* Iraq
**irder** *nm* freshness, greenness
**ireidd-dra** *nm* freshness, vigour
**ireiddio** *vb* freshen
**iriad** (**-au**) *nm* lubrication, greasing
**iro** *vb* grease, smear, rub, anoint
**irwr** (**-wyr**) *nm* greaser
**is** *adj* inferior, lower ♦ *prep* below,
  under ♦ *prefix* under-, sub-, vice-
**isadran** (**-nau**) *nf* subsection
**Isalmaen** *nf* Holland
**isel** *adj* low; base; humble;
  depressed
**iselder** (**-au**) *nm* lowness, depth;
  depression
**iseldir** (**-oedd**) *nm* lowland
**Iseldiroedd: Yr I.** *npl* Netherlands
**iselfryd** *adj* humble-minded
**iselfrydedd** *nm* humility,
  condescension
**iselhau** *vb* lower, abase, degrade
**isetholiad** (**-au**) *nm* by-election
**is-gadeirydd** *nm* vice-chairman
**is-ganghellor** *nm* vice-chancellor
**is-gapten** (**-iaid, -einiaid**) *nm*
  lieutenant
**isgell** *nm* broth, stock
**isiarll** (**-ieirll**) *nm* viscount
**islaw** *prep* below, beneath

**isod** *adv* below, beneath
**isop** *nm* hyssop
**isosod** *vb* sublet
**isradd** (**-iaid**) *nm* inferior,
  subordinate
**israddol** *adj* inferior
**israddoldeb** *nm* inferiority
**Israel** *nf* Israel
**iswasanaethgar** *adj* subservient
**isymwybod** *nm* subconscious
**isymwybyddiaeth** *nf*
  subconsciousness
**ithfaen** *nm* granite
**Iwerddon** *nf* Ireland
**Iwerddon Rydd** *nf* Eire
**Iwerydd** *nm* the Atlantic
**Iwgoslavia** *nf* Yugoslavia
**iwrch** (**iyrchod**) *nm* roebuck

# J

**jac codi baw** *nm* JCB
**jac-y-do** *nm* jackdaw
**jam** *nm* jam ♦ **-io** *vb* preserve
**Jamaica** *nf* Jamaica
**jar** (**-iau**) *nf* jar, hot water bottle
**jersi** (**-s**) *nf* jersey
**jest** *adv* just, almost
**jeti** (**-iau**) *nm* jetty
**jetlif** *nm* jet stream
**ji-binc** (**-od**) *nf* chaffinch
**jîns** *npl* jeans
**job** (**-sys**) *nf* job
**jobyn** *nm* job
**jôc** *nf* joke
**jocan** *vb* joke
**joci** (**-s**) *nm* jockey
**jwg** (**jygiau**) *nf* jug
**jyngl** (**-oedd**) *nm* jungle

# L

**label** (**-i**) *nf* label
**labelu** *vb* label
**labordy** (**-dai**) *nm* laboratory

**labro** *vb* labour
**labrwr** (-**wyr**) *nm* labourer
**lafant** *nm* lavender
**lamp** (-**au**) *nf* lamp
**lamplen** (-**ni**) *nf* lampshade
**lapio** *vb* lap, wrap
**larwm** *nm* alarm
**lawnt** (-**iau**) *nf* lawn
**lefain** *nm* leaven
**lefeinio** *vb* leaven
**lefeinllyd** *adj* leavened
**lefel** (-**au**) *nf* level
**leicio** *vb* like
**lein** (-**iau**) *nf* clothes line, line-out
  (*rugby*)
**lesbiad** (-**iaid**) *nf* lesbian
**letys** *npl* (-**en** *nm*) lettuce
**Libanus** *nf* Lebanon
**libart** *nm* back-yard
**Libya** *nf* Libya
**lifft** (-**iau**) *nm* lift
**lifrai** *nm/f* livery
**lili** *nf* lily
**lindys** *npl* (-**yn** *nm*) caterpillars
**locust** (-**iaid**) *nm* locust
**lodes** see **herlodes**
**loetran** *vb* loiter
**lol** *nf* nonsense
**lolfa** (-**feydd**) *nf* lounge
**lolian** *vb* talk nonsense
**lôn** (**lonydd**) *nf* lane
**loncian** *vb* jog
**lonciwr** (-**wyr**) *nm* jogger
**lori** (-**ïau**) *nf* lorry
**losin** *npl* (-**en** *nf*) sweets
**lot** (-**iau**) *nf* lot
**Luxembourg** *nf* Luxembourg
**lŵans, lwfans** *nm* allowance
**lwc** *nf* luck
**lwcus** *adj* lucky
**lwmp** (**lympiau**) *nm* lump

# LL

**llabed** (-**au**) *nf* lappet, lapel, flap
**llabwst** (-**ystiau**) *nm* lubber, lout

**llabyddio** *vb* stone
**llac** *adj* slack, loose, lax
**llacio** *vb* slacken, loosen, relax
**llacrwydd** *nm* slackness, laxity
**llacs** *nm* mud, dirt
**llacsog** *adj* muddy, dirty
**llach** (-**iau**) *nf* lash, slash
**llachar** *adj* bright, brilliant,
  flashing
**llachio** *vb* lash, slash
**Lladin** *nf* Latin
**lladmerydd** (-**ion**) *nm* interpreter
**lladrad** (-**au**) *nm* theft, robbery
**lladradaidd** *adj* stealthy, furtive
**lladrata** *vb* thieve, steal
**lladron** see **lleidr**
**lladrones** (-**au**) *nf* female thief
**lladronllyd** *adj* thievish, pilfering
**lladd** *vb* cut; kill, slay, slaughter
**lladd-dy** (-**dai**) *nm* slaughter-house
**lladdedig** (-**ion**) *adj* killed, slain
**lladdedigaeth** (-**au**), **lladdfa**,
  (-**fâu, -feydd**) *nf* slaughter, a
  tiring job
**lladdwr** (-**wyr**) *nm* killer, slayer
**llaes** *adj* long, loose. **Y treigliad ll.**
  spirant mutation
**llaesod(r)** *nf* litter (*for animals*)
**llaesu** *vb* slacken, loosen, relax,
  droop, flag
**llaeth** *nm* milk
**llaetha** *vb* yield milk
**llaethdy** (-**dai**) *nm* milk-house,
  dairy
**llaethog** *adj* rich in milk; milky
**llafar** *nm* utterance, speech ♦ *adj*
  vocal; loud
**llafariad** (-**iaid**) *nf* vowel
**llafn** (-**au**) *nm* blade
**llafrwyn** *npl* (-**en** *nf*) bulrushes
**llafur** (-**iau**) *nm* labour; corn
**llafurfawr** *adj* elaborate; laborious
**llafurio** *vb* labour, toil; till
**llafurlu** (-**oedd**) *nm* manpower,
  labour force, workforce
**llafurus** *adj* laborious, toilsome,
  painstaking

**llafurwr (-wyr)** *nm* labourer, husbandman

**llai** *adj* smaller

**llaid** *nm* mud, mire

**llain (lleiniau)** *nf* patch, piece, narrow strip

**llais (lleisiau)** *nm* voice, vote

**llaith** *adj* damp, moist

**llall (lleill)** *pron* other, another

**llam (-au)** *nm* stride, leap, jump, bound

**llamhidydd (llamidyddion)** *nm* porpoise

**llamsachus** *adj* prancing, frisky

**llamu** *vb* stride, leap, bound

**llan (-nau)** *nf* church; village

**llanast(r)** *nm* confusion, mess

**llanc (-iau)** *nm* young man, youth, lad

**llances (-au, -i)** *nf* young woman, lass

**llannerch (llennyrch), llanerchau (-i, -ydd)** *nf* spot, patch, glade

**llanw** *nm* flow (of tide) ♦ *vb* flow, fill

**llaprwth** *nm* lout

**llariaidd** *adj* mild, meek, gentle

**llarieidd-dra** *nm* meekness, gentleness

**llarieiddio** *vb* soothe, mollify

**llarp (-iau)** *nm* shred, clout

**llarpio** *vb* rend, tear, mangle, maul

**llarpiog** *adj* tattered, ragged

**llaswyr (-au)** *nm* psalter

**llatai (-eion)** *n coll* love-messenger

**llath (-au)** *nf* yard, wand

**llathen (-ni)** *nf* yard

**llathr** *adj* bright, glossy, smooth

**llathraidd** *adj* smooth; of fine growth

**llathru** *vb* polish

**llau** *npl* (**lleuen** *nf*) lice

**llaw (dwylaw, dwylo)** *nf* hand

**llawcio** *vb* gulp, gorge, gobble

**llawchwith** *adj* left-handed

**llawdde** *adj* dexterous

**llawddryll (-iau)** *nm* pistol, revolver

**llawen** *adj* merry, joyful, glad, cheerful

**llawenhau** *vb* rejoice, gladden

**llawenychu** *vb* rejoice

**llawenydd** *nm* joy, gladness, mirth

**llawer (-oedd)** *nm, adj, adv* many, much

**llawes (llewys)** *nf* sleeve

**llawfaeth** *adj* reared by hand

**llawfeddyg (-on)** *nm* surgeon

**llawfeddygaeth** *nf* surgery

**llawfeddygol** *adj* surgical

**llaw-fer** *nf* shorthand

**llawfom (-iau)** *nf* grenade

**llawforwyn (-forynion)** *nf* handmaid

**llawn** *adj* full ♦ *adv* quite

**llawnder, -dra** *nm* fullness, abundance

**llawr (lloriau)** *nm* floor, ground, earth

**llawryf (-oedd)** *nm* laurel, bay

**llawryfog, -ol** *adj* laureate

**llawysgrif (-au)** *nf* manuscript

**llawysgrifen** *nf* handwriting

**lle (-oedd, llefydd)** *nm* place

**llecyn (-nau)** *nm* place, spot

**llech (-au, -i)** *nf* slab, flag, slate

**llechgi (-gwn)** *nm* sneak

**llechres (-i)** *nf* table, catalogue, list

**llechu** *vb* hide, shelter; lurk, skulk

**llechwedd (-au, -i)** *nf* slope, hillside

**llechwraidd** *adj* stealthy, underhand, insidious

**lled (-au)** *nm* breadth, width

**lled** *adv* partly, rather

**lledaenu** *vb* spread, disseminate, circulate

**lleden (lledod)** *nf* flat-fish

**llediaith** *nf/m* foreign accent

**llednais** *adj* modest, delicate; meek

**llednant (-nentydd)** *nf* tributary

**lledneisrwydd** *nm* modesty,

delicacy

**lled-orwedd** vb recline, lounge, loll

**lledr** (-au) nm leather. **ll. y gwefusau** gums

**lledred** (-ion) nm latitude

**lledrith** nm magic, illusion, phantasm

**lledrithio** vb appear, haunt

**lledrithiol** adj illusory, illusive

**lledrwr** (-wyr) nm leather-merchant

**lledryw** adj degenerate

**lledu** vb widen, broaden, expand, spread

**lleddf** adj slanting; flat, minor; plaintive

**lleddfolyn** (-olion) nm sedative

**lleddfu** vb flatten; soften, soothe, allay

**llef** (-au) nf voice, cry

**llefain** vb cry

**llefareg** nf speech training

**llefaru** vb speak, utter

**llefarwr** (-wyr), **-ydd** (-ion) nm speaker

**lleferydd** nm/f utterance, voice, speech

**llefn** adj f. of **llyfn**

**llefrith** nm sweet milk, new milk, milk

**llegach** adj weak, feeble, infirm, decrepit

**lleng** (-oedd) nf legion

**lleiaf** adj least, smallest

**lleiafrif** (-au) nm minority

**lleian** (-od) nf nun

**lleiandy** (-dai) nm nunnery, convent

**lleibio** vb lap, lick

**lleidiog** adj miry

**lleidr** (lladron) nm thief, robber

**lleiddiad** (-iaid) nm assassin

**lleihad** nm diminution, decrease

**lleihau** vb lessen, diminish, decrease

**lleill** see **llall**

**lleisio** vb sound, utter, voice

**lleisiol** adj vocal

**lleisiwr** (-wyr) nm vocalist

**lleithder, -dra** nm damp, moisture

**lleithig** nf couch; footstool

**lleitho** vb damp, moisten

**llem** adj f. of **llym**

**llen** (-ni) nf sheet; veil, curtain

**llên** nf literature, lore, learning

**llencyn** nm stripling, lad

**llencynnod** nm adolescence

**llengar** adj literary, learned

**llengig** nf diaphragm, midriff. **tor ll.** rupture

**llên-ladrad** (-au) nm plagiarism

**llenor** (-ion) nm literary man

**llenwi** vb fill; flow in

**llenydda** vb practise literature

**llenyddiaeth** (-au) nf literature

**llenyddol** adj literary

**lleol** adj local

**lleoli** vb locate; localize

**lleoliad** nm location; localization

**llercian** vb lurk, loiter

**lles** nm benefit, profit, good, advantage. **y wladwriaeth les** the welfare state

**llesâd** nm advantage, profit, benefit

**llesáu** vb benefit, advantage

**llesg** adj feeble, faint; languid, sluggish

**llesgáu** vb weaken, languish, faint

**llesgedd** nm weakness, languor, debility

**llesmair** (-meiriau) nm faint, swoon

**llesmeirio** vb faint, swoon

**llesol** adj advantageous, profitable, beneficial

**llestair, llesteirio** vb hinder, impede, baulk

**llestr** (-i) nm vessel

**llesyddiaeth** nf utilitarianism

**lletbai** adj askew, awry; oblique

**lletchwith** adj awkward, clumsy

**lletem** (-au) nf wedge, stud, rivet

**lletraws** adj diagonal

**lletwad** (-au) nf ladle

**llety** (**-au**) *nm* lodging(s)
**lletya** *vb* lodge
**lletygar** *adj* hospitable
**lletygarwch** *nm* hospitality
**lletywr** (**-wyr**) *nm* lodger; host
**lletywraig** (**-wragedd**) *nf* landlady
**llethol** *adj* oppressive,
 overpowering
**llethr** (**-au**) *nf* slope, declivity
**llethrog** *adj* sloping, steep,
 declining
**llethu** *vb* overlie; smother;
 oppress, overpower, overwhelm
**lleuad** (**-au**) *nf* moon
**lleuog** *adj* lousy
**llew** (**-od**) *nm* lion. **dant y ll.**
 dandelion
**llewaidd** *adj* lionlike, leonine
**llewes** (**-au**) *nf* lioness
**llewpart** (**-pardiaid**) *nm* leopard
**llewych** *nm* light, brightness
**llewyg** (**-on**) *nm* faint, swoon
**llewygu** *vb* faint, swoon
**llewyrch** *nm* brightness, radiance,
 gleam
**llewyrchu** *vb* shine
**llewyrchus** *adj* flourishing,
 prosperous
**lleyg** (**-ion**) *adj* lay
**lleygwr** (**-wyr**) *nm* layman
**lliain** (**-einiau**) *nm* linen; cloth;
 towel
**lliaws** *nm* host, multitude
**llibin** *adj* limp, feeble; awkward,
 clumsy
**llid** *nm* wrath; irritation,
 inflammation
**llidiart** (**-ardau**) *nm* gate
**llidio** *vb* be angry, chafe, inflame
**llidiog** *adj* angry, wrathful;
 inflamed
**llidiowgrwydd** *nm* wrath,
 indignation
**llidus** *adj* inflamed
**llieiniwr** (**-wyr**) *nm* linen-draper
**llif** (**-iau**) *nf* saw
**llif** (**-ogydd**) *nm* stream, flood,
 current
**llifbridd** *nm* alluvium
**llifddor** (**-au**) *nf* floodgate
**llifddwfr** (**-ddyfroedd**) *nm* flood,
 torrent
**llifeiriant** (**-iaint**) *nm* flood
**llifeirio** *vb* flow, stream
**llifeiriol** *adj* streaming, overflowing
**llifio** *vb* saw
**llifiwr** (**-wyr**) *nm* sawyer
**llifo** *vb* flow, stream
**llifo** *vb* grind (*tool*)
**llifo** *vb* dye
**llifolau** (**-euadau**) *nm* floodlight
**llifwr** (**-wyr**) *nm* dyer
**llifyn** (**-nau, -ion**) *nm* dye
**llilinio** *vb* streamline
**llin** *nm* flax. **had ll.** linseed
**llinach** (**-au**) *nf* lineage, pedigree
**llindagu** *vb* strangle, throttle,
 choke
**llinell** (**-au**) *nf* line. **ll. gais** try line.
 **ll. gwsg** touch-in goal
**llinelliad** (**-au**) *nm* lineation,
 drawing
**llinellog** *adj* lined, ruled
**llinellol** *adj* lineal
**llinglwm** *nm*: **cwlwm ll.** tight knot
**lliniaru** *vb* ease, soothe, allay
**llinorog** *adj* eruptive; purulent,
 suppurating
**llinos** (**-od**) *nf* linnet
**llinyn** (**-nau**) *nm* line, string, twine
**llinynnu** *vb* string
**llipa** *adj* limp, weak
**llipryn** (**-nod**) *nm* hobbledehoy,
 weakling
**lliprynnaidd** *adj* limp, flabby
**llith** (**-iau, -oedd**) *nf* lesson, lecture;
 bait, mash
**llithio** *vb* entice, allure, seduce;
 feed
**llithriad** (**-au**) *nm* slip, glide
**llithren** (**-nau**) *nf* chute
**llithrig** *adj* slippery, glib, fluent
**llithrigrwydd** *nm* slipperiness,
 glibness

**llithro** vb slip, glide, slide
**lliw** (-iau) nm colour, hue, dye
**lliwio** vb colour, dye
**lliwiog** adj coloured
**llo** (lloi) nm calf
**lloc** (-iau) nm fold, pen
**lloches** (-au) nf refuge, shelter, den
**llochesu** vb harbour, shelter
**llochi** vb stroke, caress, fondle
**llodig** adj in heat (of a sow)
**llodrau** npl trousers, breeches
**Lloegr** nf England
**lloer** (-au) nf moon
**lloeren** (-ni, -nau) nf satellite
**lloerig** adj, nm lunatic
**llofnod, -iad** (-au) nm signature
**llofnodi** vb sign
**llofrudd** (-ion) nm murderer
**llofruddiaeth** (-au) nf murder
**llofruddio** vb murder
**llofruddiog** adj guilty of murder
**lloffa** vb glean
**lloffion** npl gleanings
**llofft** (-ydd) nf loft, bedroom, gallery
**lloffwr** (-wyr) nm gleaner
**lloffyn** nm bundle of gleanings
**llog** (-au) nm interest
**llogi** vb hire
**llogwr** (-wyr) nm hirer
**llong** (-au) nf ship
**llongddrylliad** (-au) nm shipwreck
**llongwr** (-wyr) nm sailor
**llongwriaeth** nf seamanship
**llom** adj f. of llwm
**llon** adj glad, merry
**llonaid, llond** nm full
**llonder** nm gladness, joy
**llongyfarch** vb congratulate
**llongyfarchiad** (-au, -archion) nm congratulation
**lloniant** nm joy, cheer
**llonni** vb cheer, gladden
**llonydd** adj quiet, still ♦ nm quiet, calm
**llonyddu** vb quiet, still, calm

**llonyddwch** nm quietness, quiet
**llorgynllun** (-iau) nm ground plan
**llorio** vb floor, ground (rugby)
**llorwedd** adj horizontal
**llosg** nm, adj burning
**llosgach** nm incest
**llosgadwy** adj combustible
**llosgfa** (-fâu, -feydd) nf burning, inflammation
**llosgfynydd** (-oedd) nm volcano
**llosgi** vb burn, scorch; smart
**llosgwrn** (-yrnau) nm tail
**llosgydd** (-ion) nm incinerator
**llu** (-oedd) nm host
**lluched** npl (-en nf) lightning
**lluchfa** (-feydd) nf snowdrift
**lluchio** vb throw, fling, pelt
**lluchiwr** (-wyr) nm thrower
**lludlyd** adj ashy
**lludu, lludw** nm ashes, ash
**lludded** nm weariness, fatigue
**lluddedig** adj wearied, tired, fatigued
**lluddedu** vb tire, weary
**lluddias, -io** vb hinder; forbid
**lluest** (-au) nm tent, booth
**lluestfa** (-feydd) nf encampment
**lluestu** vb encamp
**lluesty** (-tai) nm tent, booth
**llugoer** adj lukewarm
**lluman** (-au) nm banner, standard, ensign
**llumanwr** (-wyr) nm linesman
**llumon** nm chimney stack, peak
**llun** (-iau) nm form, image, picture
**Llun, Dydd Llun** nm Monday
**Llundain** nf London
**lluniad** (-au) nm drawing
**lluniadaeth** (-au) nf draughtsmanship
**lluniaeth** nm food, nourishment
**lluniaethu** vb order, ordain, decree
**lluniedydd** nm draughtsman
**lluniaidd** adj shapely
**llunio** vb form, shape, fashion
**lluniwr** (-wyr) nm former, maker
**llun-recordydd** (-ion) nm video-

tape recorder
**lluosflwydd** *adj* perennial
**lluosi** *vb* multiply
**lluosiad** *nm* multiplication
**lluosill, -afog** *adj* polysyllabic
**lluosog** *adj* numerous; plural
**lluosogi** *vb* multiply
**lluosogiad** *nm* multiplication
**lluoswm** *nm* product (*maths*)
**lluosydd** *nm* multiplier
**llurgunio** *vb* mangle, mutilate
**llurguniwr (-wyr)** *nm* mangler,
  mutilator
**llurig (-au)** *nf* coat of mail, cuirass
**llurigog** *adj* mail-clad
**llus** *npl* (**-en** *nf*) bilberries,
  whinberries
**llusern (-au)** *nf* lantern, lamp
**llusg (-ion)** *nm* draught; drag
**llusgfad (-au)** *nm* tugboat
**llusgo** *vb* drag; trail; crawl; drawl
**llusgwr (-wyr)** *nm* dragger,
  slowcoach
**llutrod** *nm* mire, ashes, debris
**lluwch** *nm* dust; spray; snowdrift
**lluydd** *nm* host, army
**lluyddu** *vb* mobilise
**llw (-on)** *nm* oath
**llwch** *nm* dust, powder
**llwdn (llydnod)** *nm* young of
  animals
**llwfr** *adj* timid, cowardly
**llwfrdra** *nm* cowardice
**llwfrddyn, -gi** *nm* coward
**llwfrhau** *vb* faint
**llwglyd** *adj* hungry, famished
**llwgr** *nm* corruption ♦ *adj* corrupt
**llwgrwobrwy (-on)** *nm* bribe
**llwgrwobrwyo** *vb* bribe
**llwgu** *vb* starve, famish
**llwm** *adj* bare; destitute; poor; *f*
  **llom**
**llwnc** *nm* gulp, swallow; gullet
**llwncdestun** *nm* toast (*health*)
**llwr, llwrw** *nm* track. II. **ei ben**
  headlong. II. **ei gefn** backwards
**llwy (-au)** *nf* spoon, ladle

**llwyaid (-eidiau)** *nf* spoonful
**llwybr (-au)** *nm* path, track
**llwybreiddio** *vb* direct, forward
**llwybro** *vb* walk
**llwyd** *adj* brown; grey; pale;
  hoary
**llwydaidd** *adj* greyish, palish
**llwydi, llwydni** *nm* greyness;
  mould, mildew
**llwydnos** *nf* dusk, twilight
**llwydo** *vb* turn grey; become
  mouldy
**llwydrew** *nm* hoar-frost
**llwydrewi** *vb* cast hoar-frost
**llwydd, -iant** *nm* success,
  prosperity
**llwyddiannus** *adj* successful,
  prosperous
**llwyddo** *vb* succeed, prosper
**llwyfan (-nau)** *nm/f* platform, stage
**llwyfandir (-oedd)** *nm* plateau
**llwyfannu** *vb* stage
**llwyfen (llwyf)** *nf* elm
**llwyn (-i)** *nm* grove; bush
**llwyn (-au)** *nf* loin
**llwynog (-od)** *nm* fox
**llwynoges (-au)** *nf* vixen
**llwynwst** *nf* lumbago
**llwyo** *vb* use a spoon; ladle
**llwyr** *adj* entire, complete, total ♦
  *adv* entirely, altogether ♦ *prefix*
  total
**llwyredd** *nm* entireness,
  completeness
**llwyrymatal, -ymwrthod** *vb*
  abstain totally
**llwyrymwrthodwr (-wyr)** *nm*
  teetotaller
**llwyth (-au)** *nm* tribe, clan
**llwyth (-i)** *nm* load, burden
**llwytho** *vb* load, burden
**llwythog** *adj* laden, burdened
**llychlyd** *adj* dusty
**Llychlyn** *nf* Scandinavia
**llychwino** *vb* spot, tarnish, soil,
  sully
**llychyn** *nm* particle of dust, mote

**llydan** adj broad, wide
**Llydaw** nf Brittany
**llydnu** vb bring forth, foal
**llyfn** adj smooth, sleek; f **llefn**
**llyfnder, -dra** nm smoothness, sleekness
**llyfndew** adj plump, sleek
**llyfnhau** vb smooth, level
**llyfnu** vb smooth, level; harrow
**llyfr (-au)** nm book
**llyfrbryf (-ed)** nm bookworm
**llyfrgell (-oedd)** nf library
**llyfrgellydd (-ion)** nm librarian
**llyfrifeg** nm/f book-keeping
**llyfrnod (-au)** nm bookmark
**llyfrwerthwr (-wyr)** nm bookseller
**llyfrydd (-ion)** nm bibliographer, transcriber of books
**llyfryddiaeth** nf bibliography
**llyfrfa** nf (-feydd) library; bookroom; official publishing house of religious denomination, government etc
**llyfryn (-nau)** nm booklet, pamphlet
**llyfu** vb lick
**llyffant (-od, llyffaint)** nm frog, toad
**llyffethair (-eiriau)** nf fetter, shackle
**llyffetheirio** vb fetter, shackle
**llyg (-od)** nm/f shrew(-mouse)
**llygad (llygaid)** nm eye. **ll. y dydd** daisy
**llygad-dynnu** vb bewitch
**llygadog** adj eyed, sharp-eyed
**llygadrwth** adj wide-eyed, staring
**llygadrythu** vb stare
**llygadu** vb eye
**llygatgraff** adj keen-eyed, sharp-sighted
**llygedyn** nm ray of light
**llygeidiog** adj eyed
**llygoden (llygod)** nf mouse. **ll. fawr, ll. ffrengig** rat
**llygota** vb catch mice
**llygotwr (-wyr)** nm mouser,

ratter; f **llygotwraig**
**llygradwy** adj corruptible
**llygredig** adj corrupt, depraved, degraded
**llygredigaeth (-au)** nf corruption
**llygredd** nm corruptness, depravity
**llygriad (-au)** nm corruption, adulteration
**llygru** vb corrupt, adulterate
**llygrwr (-wyr)** nm corrupter, adulterator
**llynges (-au)** nf fleet, navy
**llyngeswr (-wyr)** nm navy-man
**llyngesydd (-ion)** nm admiral
**llyngyr** npl (-en nf) (intestinal) worms
**llym** adj sharp, keen, severe; f **llem**
**llymaid (-eidiau)** nm sip, drink
**llymarch (llymeirch)** nm oyster
**llymder** nm sharpness, keenness, severity
**llymder, -dra** nm bareness, poverty
**llymeitian, -io** vb sip, tipple
**llymeitiwr (-wyr)** nm tippler, sot
**llymhau** vb make bare (from **llwm**)
**llymhau** vb sharpen (from **llym**)
**llymrïaid** npl (-ien nf) sand-eels
**llymru** nm flummery
**llymsur** adj acrid
**llymu** vb sharpen, whet
**llyn (-noedd)** nm lake, pond, pool
**llynciad (-au)** nm draught, gulp
**llyncu** vb swallow, gulp, absorb
**llyncwr (-wyr)** nm swallower, guzzler
**llynedd** nf last year
**llyo** vb lick
**llys (-oedd)** nm court, hall, palace
**llysaidd** adj courtly, polite
**llysblant** npl step-children
**llyschwaer** nf step-sister
**llysenw (-au)** nm nickname
**llysenwi** vb nickname
**llysfab** nm step-son
**llysfam** nf step-mother

**llysferch** *nf* step-daughter
**llysfrawd** *nm* step-brother
**llysgenhadaeth** *nf* embassy, legation
**llysgenhadol** *adj* ambassadorial
**llysgenhadwr, llysgennad** (**-genhadon**) *nm* ambassador
**llysiau** *npl* (**-ieuyn** *nm*) herbs, vegetables
**llysieuol** *adj* herbal, vegetable
**llysieuydd** (**-ion, -wyr**) *nm* botanist; vegetarian
**llysnafedd** *nm* snivel, slime
**llystad** *nm* step-father
**llyswenwyn** *nm* herbicide
**llysysol** *adj* herbivorous
**llysywen** (**llysywod**) *nf* eel
**llysywenna** *vb* catch eels
**llythrennol** *adj* literal
**llythyr** (**-au**) *nm* letter, epistle
**llythyrdy** (**-dai**) *nm* post-office
**llythyren** (**llythrennau**) *nf* letter, type
**llythyrwr** (**-wyr**) *nm* letter-writer
**llyw** (**-iau**) *nm* ruler; rudder, helm
**llywaeth** *adj* hand-fed, tame, pet
**llywiawdwr** (**-wyr**) *nm* ruler, governor
**llywio** *vb* rule, govern, direct, steer
**llywiwr** (**-wyr**) *nm* steersman, helmsman
**llywodraeth** (**-au**) *nf* government
**llywodraethol** *adj* governing, dominant
**llywodraethu** *vb* govern, rule
**llywodraethwr** (**-wyr**) *nm* governor, ruler
**llywydd** (**-ion**) *nm* president
**llywyddiaeth** (**-au**) *nf* presidency
**llywyddol** *adj* presidential
**llywyddu** *vb* preside

# M

**mab** (**meibion**) *nm* boy, son; man, male
**mabaidd** *adj* filial
**maban** (**-od**) *nm* babe, baby
**mabandod** *nm* childhood, infancy
**mabinogi** *nm* tale, story
**mablygad** *nm* eyeball
**mabmaeth** (**-au, -od**) *nm* foster-son
**maboed** *nm* childhood, infancy, youth
**mabolaeth** *nf* sonship; boyhood, youth
**mabolaidd** *adj* youthful, boyish
**mabolgamp** (**-au**) *nf* game, sport, feat
**mabsant** *nm* patron saint
**mabwysiad** *nm* adoption
**mabwysiadol** *adj* adoptive; adopted
**mabwysiadu** *vb* adopt
**macrell** (**mecryll**) *nf/m* mackerel
**macsu** *vb* to brew
**macwy** (**-aid**) *nm* youth, page
**machlud, -o** *vb* set, go down. **m. haul** sunset
**machludiad** *nm* setting, going down
**machnïydd** *nm* mediator
**madarch** *npl* (**-en** *nf*) mushrooms
**madfall** (**-od**) *nm* lizard
**madrondod** *nm* giddiness, stupefaction
**madroni** *vb* make or become giddy
**madru** *vb* putrefy, fester, rot
**madruddyn** *nm* cartilage. **m. y cefn** spinal cord
**maddau** *vb* pardon, forgive, remit
**maddeuant** *nm* pardon, forgiveness
**maddeugar** *adj* of a forgiving disposition
**maddeuol** *adj* pardoning, forgiving
**maddeuwr** (**-wyr**) *nm* pardoner

**mae** *vb* is, are; there is, there are
**maeden** *nf* slut, jade
**maeddu** see **baeddu**
**maen** (**meini**) *nm* stone
**maenol, maenor** (**-au**) *nf* manor
**maentumio** *vb* maintain
**maer** (**-od, meiri**) *nm* mayor
**maeres** (**-au**) *nf* mayoress
**maerol** *adj* mayoral
**maeryddiaeth** *nf* mayoralty
**maes** (**meysydd**) *nm* field. **i m.** out.
**m. glanio** airport
**maesglaf** (**-gleifion**) *nm* outpatient
**maeslywydd** (**-ion**) *nm* field-
marshal
**maestir** (**-oedd**) *nm* open country,
plain
**maestref** (**-i, -ydd**) *nf* suburb
**maeth** *nm* nourishment, nutriment
**maethlon** *adj* nourishing,
nutritious
**maethu** *vb* nourish, nurture
**maethydd** (**-ion**) *nm* nourisher
**maethyn** (**-nau**) *nm* nutrient;
suckling
**mafon** *npl* (**-en** *nf*) raspberries
**magl** (**-au**) *nf* snare; mesh
**maglu** *vb* snare, mesh, trip
**magnel** (**-au**) *nf* gun, cannon
**magnelaeth** *nf* artillery
**magnelwr** (**-wyr**) *nm* gunner
**magnesiwm** *nm* magnesium
**magnetedd** *nmf* magnetism
**magneteiddio** *vb* magnetise
**magu** *vb* breed, rear, nurse; gain,
acquire
**magwraeth** *nf* nourishment,
nurture
**magwyr** (**-ydd**) *nf* wall
**maharen** (**meheryn**) *nm* ram;
wether
**Mai** *nm* May
**mai** *conj* that it is
**maidd** *nm* whey
**main** (**meinion**) *adj* fine, slender,
thin. **m. y cefn** small of the back
**mainc** (**meinciau**) *nf* bench, form,
seat

**maint** *nm* size, quantity, number
**maintioli** *nm* size, stature
**maip** *npl* (**meipen** *nf*) turnips
**maith** (**meithion**) *adj* long, tedious
**mâl** *adj* ground
**malais** *nm* malice
**maldod** *nm* dalliance, affection
**maldodi** *vb* pet, pamper, indulge
**maleisus** *adj* malicious
**maleithiau** *npl* chilblains
**malio** *vb* care, mind, heed
**Malta** *nf* Malta
**malu** *vb* grind, mince, chop, smash
**malurio** *vb* pound; crumble,
moulder
**malurion** *npl* fragments, debris
**malwod** *npl* (**-en, malwen** *nf*)
snails
**malwr** (**-wyr**) *nm* grinder
**mall** *nf* blight. **y f.** Belial, perdition
**malltod** *nm* rot, blight, blast
**mallu** *vb* rot, blast
**mam** (**-au**) *nf* mother. **mam-gu**
grandmother
**mamaeth** (**-od**) *nf* nurse
**mamal** (**-iaid**) *nm* mammal
**mamiaith** (**-ieithoedd**) *nf* mother-
tongue
**mamog** (**-iaid**) *nf* dam, sheep with
young
**mamolaeth** (**-au**) *nf* maternity
**mamwlad** (**-wledydd**) *nf*
motherland
**man** (**-nau**) *nmf* place, spot;
blemish
**mân** *adj* small, fine, petty
**mandyllog** *adj* porous
**maneg** (**menig**) *nf* glove, gauntlet
**mangre** *nf* place, spot
**manion** *npl* scraps, trifles, minutiæ
**mantais** (**-eision**) *nf* advantage
**manteisio** *vb* take advantage,
profit
**manteisiol** *adj* advantageous
**mantell** (**-oedd, mentyll**) *nf* mantle
**mantellog** *adj* mantled

**mantol** (-ion) *nf* balance
**mantolen** (-ni) *nf* balance-sheet
**mantoli** *vb* turn scale, balance, weigh
**manŵaidd** *adj* delicate, fine
**mân-werthu** *vb* retail
**manwl** *adj* exact, precise, strict, particular
**manwl-gywir** *adj* precise
**manylion** *npl* particulars, details
**manylrwydd** *nm* exactness, precision
**manylu** *vb* go into detail, particularize
**manylwch** *nm* exactness, precision
**map** (-iau) *nm* map
**mapio** *vb* map
**mapiwr** (-wyr) *nm* cartographer
**marblen** (marblys) *nf* marble
**marc** (-iau) *nm* mark
**marcio** *vb* mark
**march** (meirch) *nm* horse, stallion
**marchlu** (-oedd) *nm* cavalry
**marchnad** (-oedd) *nf* market
**marchnadfa** (-oedd) *nf* marketplace
**marchnata** *vb* market, trade
**marchnatwr** (-wyr) *nm* merchant
**marchnerth** (-oedd) *nm* horsepower
**marchocáu** *vb* ride a horse
**marchog** (-ion) *nm* horseman, rider; knight
**marchogaeth** *vb* ride
**marchogwr** (-wyr) *nm* rider, horseman
**marchredyn** *npl* (-en *nf*) polypody fern
**marchwellt** *nm* tall, coarse grass
**marian** *nm* holm, strand, moraine
**marlad** *nm* drake
**marmaléd** (-au) *nm* marmalade
**marmor** *nm* marble
**marsialydd** (-ion) *nm* marshal
**marsiandïaeth** *nf* merchandise
**marsiandïwr** (-wyr) *nm* merchant
**marsipan** *nm* marzipan

**marw** *vb* die
**marw** (meirw, meirwon) *n, adj* dead
**marwaidd** *adj* lifeless, sluggish, moribund
**marwdon** *nf* dandruff
**marweidd-dra** *nm* deadness, sluggishness
**marweiddio** *vb* deaden, mortify
**marwhad** *nm* mortification
**marwhau** *vb* deaden, mortify
**marwnad** (-au) *nf* lament, elegy
**marwol** *adj* deadly, mortal, fatal
**marwolaeth** (-au) *nf* death
**marwoldeb** *nm* mortality
**marwolion** *npl* mortals
**marwor** *npl* (-yn *nm*) embers; charcoal
**marwydos** *npl* embers
**masarnen** (masarn) *nf* sycamore
**masgl** (-au) *nf* shell, pod
**masglo, -u** *vb* shell; interlace
**masnach** (-au) *nf* trade, traffic, commerce
**masnachol** *adj* commercial, business
**masnachu** *vb* do business, trade, traffic
**masnachwr** (-wyr) *nm* dealer, merchant
**masw** *adj* wanton
**maswedd** *nm* wantoness, ribaldry
**masweddol** *adj* wanton, ribald
**maswr** (-wyr) *nm* outside half
**mat** (-iau) *nm* mat
**mater** (-ion) *nm* matter
**materol** *adj* material; materialistic
**materoliaeth** *nf* materialism
**matog** (-au) *nf* mattock
**matras** (-resi) *nm* mattress
**matrics** (-au) *nm* matrix
**matsien** (matsys) *nf* match
**math** (-au) *nm* sort, kind
**mathemateg** *nm* mathematics
**mathru** *vb* trample, tread
**mathrwr** (-wyr) *nm* trampler
**mawl** *nm* praise

**mawn** *coll n* (**-en** *nf*) peat
**mawnog** *adj* peaty ♦ *nf* peat-bog
**mawr** (**-ion**) *adj* big, great, large
**mawredd** *nm* greatness, grandeur, majesty
**mawreddog** *adj* grand, majestic; grandiose
**mawrfrydig** *adj* magnanimous
**mawrfrydigrwydd** *nm* magnanimity
**mawrhau** *vb* magnify, enlarge
**mawrhydi** *nm* majesty
**Mawrth** *nm* Mars; March. **Dydd M.** Tuesday
**mawrygu** *vb* magnify, extol
**mebyd** *nm* childhood, infancy, youth
**mecaneg** *nf* mechanics
**mecanwaith** (**-weithiau**) *nm* mechanism
**mecanyddol** *adj* mechanical
**mechnïaeth** *nf* surety, bail
**mechnïo** *vb* go bail, become surety
**mechnïol** *adj* vicarious
**mechnïydd** (**-ion**) *nm* surety, bail
**medel** (**-au**) *nf* reaping; reaping party
**medelwr** (**-wyr**) *nm* reaper
**medi** *vb* reap
**Medi** *nm* September
**medr** *nm* skill, ability
**medru** *vb* know, be able
**medrus** *adj* clever, skilful
**medrusrwydd** *nm* cleverness, skilfulness, skill
**medrydd** (**-ion**) *nm* gauge
**medd** *nm* mead
**medd** *vb* says
**meddal** *adj* soft, tender
**meddalhau, meddalu** *vb* soften
**meddalwch** *nm* softness
**meddalwedd** *nm* softwear
**meddiannol** *adj* possessing, possessive
**meddiannu** *vb* possess, occupy
**meddiant** (**-iannau**) *nm* possession

**meddu** *vb* possess, own
**meddw** (**-on**) *adj* drunk, intoxicated
**meddwdod** *nm* drunkenness, intoxication
**meddwi** *vb* get drunk, intoxicate, inebriate
**meddwl** *vb* think; mean ♦ (**-yliau**) *nm* thought; meaning; opinion
**meddwol** *adj* intoxicating
**meddwyn** (**-won**) *nm* drunkard, inebriate
**meddyg** (**-on**) *nm* physician, doctor
**meddygaeth** *nf* medicine
**meddygfa** (**-feydd**) *nf* surgery
**meddyginiaeth** (**-au**) *nf* medicine, remedy
**meddyginiaethol** *adj* medicinal, remedial
**meddyginiaethu** *vb* cure, remedy, heal
**meddygol** *adj* medicinal; medical
**meddylfryd** *nm* mind, affection, bent
**meddylgar** *adj* thoughtful
**meddylgarwch** *nm* thoughtfulness
**meddyliol** *adj* mental, intellectual
**meddyliwr** (**-wyr**) *nm* thinker
**mefus** *npl* (**-en** *nf*) strawberries
**megin** (**-au**) *nf* bellows
**megino** *vb* work bellows, blow
**megis** *conj, prep* as, so as, like a
**Mehefin** *nm* June
**meicrobioleg** *nm/f* microbiology
**meicro-brosesydd** *nm* microprocessor
**meicroffon** (**-au**) *nm* microphone
**meicro-sglodyn** (**-ion**) *nm* microchip
**meicrosgop** (**-au**) *nm* microscope
**meichiad** (**-iaid**) *nm* swineherd
**meichiau** (**-iafon**) *nm* surety, bail
**meidrol** *adj* finite
**meidroldeb** *nm* finiteness
**meiddio** *vb* dare, venture
**meiddion** *npl* curds and whey

**meiddlyd** *adj* wheyey, curdled
**meilart** *nm* drake
**meillion** *npl* (-en *nf*) clover
**meim** (-iau) *nm/f* mime
**meimio** *vb* mime
**meinder** *nm* fineness, slenderness
**meindio** *vb* mind, care
**meinedd** *nm* slender part, small
**meingefn** *nm* small of the back
**meinhau** *vb* grow slender, taper
**meini** see **maen**
**meinllais** *nm* shrill voice, treble
**meintoli** *vb* quantify
**meintoliad** *nm* quantification
**meinwe** (-bledd) *nf* tissue
**meipen** (maip) *nf* turnip
**meirch** see **march**
**meirioli** *vb* thaw
**meirw** see **marw**
**meistr** (-iaid, -i, -adoedd) *nm* master
**meistres** (-i) *nf* mistress
**meistrolaeth** *nf* mastery
**meistrolgar** *adj* masterful, masterly
**meistroli** *vb* master
**meitin** *nm:* **ers m.** some time since
**meitr** (-au) *nm* mitre
**meithder** *nm* length
**meithrin** *vb* nurture, rear, foster
**meithrinfa** (-oedd) *nf* nursery
**mêl** *nm* honey
**mela** *vb* gather honey
**melan** *nf* melancholy
**melen** *adj* f. of **melyn**
**melfaréd** *nm* corduroy
**melfed** *nm* velvet
**melin** (-au) *nf* mill
**melinydd** (-ion) *nm* miller
**melodaidd** *adj* melodious
**melodi** *nm* melody
**melyn** *adj* yellow; *f* **melen** ♦ *nm* yellow. **m. wy** yolk of egg. **Y clefyd m.** jaundice
**melynaidd** *adj* yellowish, tawny
**melynder, -dra** *nm* yellowness
**melynddu** *adj* tawny, swarthy

**melyngoch** *adj* yellowish red, orange
**melyni** *nm* yellowness; jaundice
**melynu** *vb* yellow
**melynwyn** *adj* yellowish white, cream
**melys** *adj* sweet ♦ (-ion) *npl* sweets
**melyster, -tra** *nm* sweetness
**melysu** *vb* sweeten
**mellt** *npl* (-en *nf*) lightning
**melltennu** *vb* flash lightning
**melltigaid, -edig** *adj* accursed, cursed
**melltith** (-ion) *nf* curse
**melltithio** *vb* curse
**memorandwm** (-anda) *nm* memorandum
**memrwn** (-rynau) *nm* parchment, vellum
**men** (-ni) *nf* wain, waggon, cart
**mên** *adj* mean
**mendio** *vb* mend, heal, recover
**menestr** *nm* cup-bearer
**menig** see **maneg**
**mentr** *nf* venture, hazard
**mentro** *vb* venture, hazard
**mentrus** *adj* adventurous
**mentrwr** (-wyr) *nm* entrepreneur
**menyw** (-od) *nf* woman
**mêr** (merion) *nm* marrow
**mercwri** *nm* mercury
**merch** (-ed) *nf* daughter, woman
**Mercher** *nm* Mercury. **Dydd M.** Wednesday
**mercheta** *vb* womanise
**merchetaidd** *adj* effeminate
**merddwr** (-ddyfroedd) *nm* stagnant water
**merf, -aidd** *adj* insipid, tasteless, flat
**merfdra, merfeidd-dra** *nm* insipidity
**merlota** *vb* pony-trek
**merlyn** (-nod, merlod) *nm* pony; *f* **merlen**
**merllyd** *adj* insipid
**merthyr** (-on, -i) *nm* martyr

**merthyrdod** *nm* martyrdom
**merthyru** *vb* martyr
**merwindod** *nm* numbness, tingling
**merwino** *vb* benumb, tingle, smart
**meryw** *npl* (**-en** *nf*) juniper trees
**mes** *npl* (**-en** *nf*) acorns
**mesa** *vb* gather acorns
**mesur** (**-au**) *nm* measure; metre; tune; bill
**mesur, mesuro** *vb* measure, mete
**mesureg** *nf* mensuration
**mesuriad** (**-au**) *nm* measurement
**mesurwr** (**-wyr**) *nm* measurer; surveyor
**mesurydd** (**-ion**) *nm* measurer, meter
**metamorffedd** *nm* metamorphism
**metel** (**-oedd**) *nm* metal; mettle
**metelaidd** *adj* metallic
**metelydd** (**-ion**) *nm* metallurgist
**metelyddiaeth** *nf* metallurgy
**metr** (**-au**) *nm* metre
**metrig** *adj* metric
**metrigeiddio** *vb* metricate
**meth** (**-ion**) *nm* miss, failure
**methdaliad** (**-au**) *nm* bankruptcy
**methdalwr** (**-wyr**) *nm* bankrupt
**methedig** (**-ion**) *adj* decrepit, infirm, disabled
**methiannus** *adj* failing, decayed
**methiant** *nm* failure
**methodoleg** *nf* methodology
**methu** *vb* fail, miss
**meudwy** (**-aid, -od**) *nm* hermit, recluse
**meudwyaidd** *adj* hermit-like, retiring
**meudwyol** *adj* eremitic
**mewian** *vb* mew
**mewn** *prep* in, within
**mewnadlu** *vb* inhale
**mewnforio** *vb* import ♦ (**-ion**) *npl* imports
**mewnfudwr** (**-wyr**) *nm* immigrant
**mewnol** *adj* inward, internal; subjective
**mewnwr** (**-wyr**) *nm* scrum-half

**mewnyn** (**mewnion**) *nm* filling
**México** *nf* Mexico
**mi** *pron* I, me
**mieri** *npl* (**miaren** *nf*) brambles
**mig** *nf*: **chwarae m.** play bo-peep
**mign, -en** *nf* bog, quagmire
**migwrn** (**-yrnau**) *nm* knuckle; ankle
**mil** (**-od**) *nm* animal
**mil** (**-oedd**) *nf* thousand
**milain** *adj* angry, fierce, savage, cruel
**mileindra** *nm* savageness, ferocity
**mileinig** *adj* savage, ferocious, malignant
**milfed** *adj* thousandth
**milfeddyg** (**-on**) *nm* veterinary surgeon
**milfil** *nf* million, an indefinite number
**milflwyddiant** *nm* millennium
**milgi** (**-gwn**) *nm* greyhound
**miliast** (**-ieist**) *nf* greyhound bitch
**militariaeth** *nf* militarism
**militarydd** *nm* militarist
**miliwn** (**-iynau**) *nf* million
**miliynydd** (**-ion**) *nm* millionaire
**milodfa** (**-oedd, -feydd**) *nf* menagerie
**milwr** (**-wyr**) *nm* soldier
**milwraidd** *adj* soldierly
**milwriad** (**-iaid**) *nm* colonel
**milwriaeth** *nf* warfare
**milwriaethus** *adj* militant
**milwrio** *vb* militate
**milwrol** *adj* military
**milltir** (**-oedd**) *nf* mile
**min** (**-ion**) *nm* edge; brink; lip
**mindlws** *adj* simpering, affected, precious
**mingamu** *vb* grimace
**minio** *vb* edge, sharpen; make impression
**miniog** *adj* sharp, keen, cutting
**minlliw** (**-iau**) *nm* lipstick
**minnau** *pron conj* I (on my part), I also

**mintai** (-eioedd) nf band, troop
**mintys** nm mint
**mirain** adj fair, beautiful, comely
**mireinder** nm beauty, comeliness
**miri** nm merriment, fun, festivity
**mis** (-oedd) nm month
**misio** vb miss, fail
**misol** (-ion) adj monthly
**misolyn** (-olion) nm monthly (magazine)
**mitsio** vb mitch, play truant
**miwsig** nm music
**mo** contr. of dim o: nid oes mo'i debyg there is none like him
**moch** npl (-yn nm) swine, pigs, hogs
**mocha** adj pig, litter
**mochaidd** adj swinish, hoggish
**mochynnaidd** adj piggish, swinish
**modfedd** (-i) nf inch
**modrwy** (-au) nf ring
**modrwyo** vb ring
**modrwyog** adj ringed
**modryb** (-edd) nf aunt
**modur** (-on) nm motor
**modurdy** (-dai) nm garage
**modurwr** (-wyr) nm motorist
**modylu** vb modulate
**modylydd** (-ion) nm modulator
**modd** (-ion, -au) nm mode, manner; means; mood
**moddion** npl means; medicine
**moddol** adj modal
**moel** (-ion) adj bare, bald; hornless, polled
**moel** (-ydd) nf hill
**moeli** vb make or become bald; hang (ears)
**moelni** nm bareness, baldness
**moelyn** nm bald-head
**moes** vb imper give, bring hither
**moes** (-au) nf morality; (pl) manners, morals
**moeseg** nf ethics
**Moesenaidd** adj Mosaic
**moesgar** adj mannerly, polite
**moesgarwch** nm politeness

**moesol** adj moral, ethical
**moesoldeb** nm morality
**moesoli** vb moralize
**moesolwr** (-wyr) nm moralist
**moeswers** (-i) nf moral
**moesymgrymu** vb bow
**moeth** (-au) nm luxury, indulgence
**moethi** vb pamper, indulge
**moethlyd** adj pampered, spoilt
**moethus** adj luxurious, pampered
**moethusrwydd** nm luxuriousness, luxury
**molawd** nm/f eulogy, panegyric
**molecwl** (-cylau) nm molecule
**molecwlar** adj molecular
**moled** (-au) nf kerchief; muffler
**moli, moliannu** vb praise, laud
**moliannus** adj praised, praiseworthy
**moliant** (-iannau) nm praise
**mollt** (myllt) nm wether
**molltgig** nm mutton
**moment** (-au) nf moment
**momentwm** (momenta) nm momentum
**monarchiaeth** nf monarchy
**monarchydd** (-ion) nm monarchist
**monni** vb sulk, pout
**monocsid** (-au) nm monoxide
**monópoli** (-ïau) nm monopoly
**môr** (moroedd) nm sea, ocean
**Môr: Y M. Canoldir** nm Mediterranean Sea. **Y M. Coch** nm Red Sea. **Y M. Tawel** nm Pacific Ocean. **M. Udd** nm English Channel. **M. y Gogledd** nm North Sea
**mor** adv how, so, as
**moratoriwm** (-atoria) nm moratorium
**mordaith** (-deithiau) nf voyage
**mordeithiwr** (-wyr) nm voyager
**mordwyaeth** nf navigation
**mordwyo** vb go by sea, voyage, sail
**mordwywr** (-wyr) nm mariner, sailor

**morddwyd** (-ydd) *nf/m* thigh
**morfa** (-feydd) *nm* moor, fen, marsh
**morfil** (-od) *nm* whale
**môr-forwyn** (-forynion) *nf* mermaid
**morfran** (-frain) *nf* cormorant
**morffoleg** *nm/f* morphology
**morffolegol** *adj* morphological
**morgainc** (-geinciau) *nf* gulf
**morgais** (-geisiau) *nm* mortgage
**morgeisi** *nm* mortgagee
**morgeisio** *vb* mortgage
**môr-gerwyn** *nf* whirlpool, vortex, abyss
**morglawdd** (-gloddiau) *nm* embankment, mole
**morgrug** *npl* (-yn *nm*) ants
**morio** *vb* voyage, sail
**môr-ladrad** (-au) *nm* piracy
**môr-leidr** (-ladron) *nm* pirate
**morlen** (-ni) *nm* chart
**morlo** (-loi) *nm* sea-calf, seal
**morllyn** (-noedd) *nf/m* lagoon
**Morocco** *nf* Morocco
**morol** *adj* maritime
**moron** *npl* (-en *nf*) carrots
**mortais** (-eisiau) *nf* mortise
**morteisio** *vb* mortise
**morter** (-au) *nm* mortar
**morthwyl** (-ion) *nm* hammer
**morthwylio** *vb* hammer
**morthwyliwr** (-wyr) *nm* hammerer
**morwr** (-wyr) *nm* seaman, sailor, mariner
**morwriaeth** *nf* seamanship, navigation
**morwydd** *npl* (-en *nf*) mulberry-trees
**morwyn** (-ynion) *nf* maid, virgin
**morwyndod** *nm* virginity
**morwynol** *adj* virgin, maiden
**moryd** (-iau) *nf* estuary
**moryn** (-nau) *nm* billow, breaker
**mosaig** (-au) *nm*, *adj* mosaic
**Moscow** *nf* Moscow

**motif** (-au) *nm* motive
**motiff** (-au) *nm* motif
**muchudd** *nm* jet
**mud** *adj* dumb, mute; dull
**mudan** (-od) *nm* mute
**mudandod** *nm* muteness
**mudanes** (-au) *nf* dumb woman
**mudferwi** *vb* simmer
**mudiad** (-au) *nm* removal; movement
**mudo** *vb* move, remove
**mudol** *adj* mobile, moving, migratory
**mudwr** (-wyr) *nm* remover
**mul** (-od) *nm* mule; donkey
**mulaidd** *adj* mulish, asinine
**mules** (-au) *nf* she-mule, she-ass
**mulfran** (-frain) *nf* cormorant
**mun** see **bun**
**munud** (-au) *nm/f* minute, moment
**munud** (-iau) *nm* sign, gesture; nod
**munudio** *vb* make gestures, gesticulate
**mur** (-iau) *nm* wall
**murddun** (-od) *nm* ruin, ruins
**murio** *vb* wall
**murlun** (-iau) *nm* mural
**murmur** *vb* murmur ♦ (-on) *nm* murmur
**mursen** (-nod) *nf* coquette; prude
**mursendod** *nm* prudery, affectation
**mursennaidd** *adj* prudish, affected
**mursennu** *vb* coquette, mince
**musgrell** *adj* feeble, decrepit
**musgrellni** *nm* feebleness, debility
**mwd** *nm* mud
**mwdwl** (mydylau) *nm* cock (of hay)
**mwg** *nm* smoke
**mwgwd** (mygydau) *nm* blind mask
**mwng** (myngau) *nm* mane
**mwngial** *vb* mumble
**mwlsyn** *nm* nincompoop; mule
**mwlwg** *nm* refuse, sweepings,

chaff

**mwll** *adj* close, warm, sultry

**mwmian** *vb* hum, mumble

**mŵn** see **mwyn**

**mwnci (-iod)** *nm* monkey

**mwnciaidd** *adj* monkeyish, apish

**mwnglawdd** see **mwyn-**

**mwnwgl (mynyglau)** *nm* neck

**mwnws** *coll n* small particles, dust, debris

**mwrdro** *vb* murder

**mwrllwch** *nm* fog, mist, vapour

**mwrn** *adj* sultry, close, warm

**mwrndra** *nm* sultriness

**mwrthwl (myrthylau)** *nm* hammer

**mws** *adj* stale, rank, stinking

**mwsg** *nm* musk

**mwsged (-i)** *nm/f* musket

**mwsogl, -wgl** *nm* moss

**mwstard, -tart** *nm* mustard

**mwstro** *vb* fidget, hurry

**mwstwr** *nm* muster; bustle, commotion

**mwy** *adj* more, bigger ♦ *adv* more, again

**mwyach** *adv* any more, henceforth

**mwyafrif (-au)** *nm* majority

**mwyalch, -en (-od)** *nf* blackbird

**mwyar** *npl* (**-en** *nf*) blackberries

**mwyara** *vb* gather blackberries

**mwydion** *npl* crumb; pith, pulp

**mwydo** *vb* moisten, soak, steep

**mwydro** *vb* moider, bewilder

**mwydyn (mwydod)** *nm* worm

**mwyfwy** *adv* more and more

**mwyhau** *vb* increase, enlarge, magnify

**mwyn** *nm* sake

**mwyn, mŵn (-au)** *nm* ore, mineral

**mwyn** *adj* kind, gentle, mild; dear

**mwynder (-au)** *nm* gentleness; (*pl*) delights

**mwyndoddi** *vb* refine

**mwyneidd-dra** *nm* kindness, gentleness

**mwynglawdd (-gloddiau)** *nm* mine

**mwyngloddio** *vb* mine

**mwynhad** *nm* enjoyment, pleasure

**mwynhau** *vb* enjoy

**mwyniant (-iannau)** *nm* pleasure

**mwynofydd (-ion)** *nm* mineralogist

**mwynoleg** *nf* mineralogy

**mwynwr (-wyr)** *nm* miner

**mwys** *adj* ambiguous, equivocal

**mwythau** *npl* indulgence, caresses

**mwytho** *vb* pet, fondle, pamper

**mwythus** *adj* pampered

**myctod** *nm* asphyxia

**mydr (-au)** *nm* metre, verse

**mydryddiaeth** *nf* versification

**mydryddol** *adj* metrical

**mydryddu, mydru** *vb* versify

**mydylu** *vb* cock

**myfi** *pron* I, me, myself

**myfiaeth** *nf* egotism

**myfiol** *adj* egotistic

**myfyrdod (-au)** *nm* meditation

**myfyrgar** *adj* studious, contemplative

**myfyrgell (-oedd)** *nf* study

**myfyrio** *vb* meditate, study

**myfyriol** *adj* meditative

**myfyriwr (-wyr)** *nm* student

**mygedol** *adj* honorary

**mygfa (-feydd)** *nf* suffocation

**myglyd** *adj* smoky; close; asthmatic

**myglys** *nm* tobacco

**mygu** *vb* smoke; suffocate, stifle, smother

**mygydu** *vb* blindfold

**mygyn** *nm* a smoke

**myngial** *vb* mumble, mutter

**myngog** *adj* maned

**myngus** *adj* indistinct, mumbling

**myllni** *nm* sultriness

**mympwy (-on)** *nm* whim, caprice, fad

**mympwyol** *adj* arbitrary, capricious

**mymryn (-nau)** *nm* particle, bit, mite

**myn** *prep* by (*in swearing*)
**myn** (-nod) *nm* kid
**mynach** (-aich, -od) *nm* monk
**mynachaeth** *nf* monasticism
**mynachdy** (-dai) *nm* monastery, convent
**mynachlog** (-ydd) *nf* monastery, abbey
**mynawyd** (-au) *nm* awl
**mynci** (-ïau) *nm* hame(s)
**myned, mynd** *vb* go, proceed
**mynedfa** (-oedd, -feydd) *nf* entrance, passage
**mynediad** *nm* going; access, admission
**mynegai** (-eion) *nm* index, exponent
**mynegair** (-eiriau) *nm* concordance
**mynegfys** (-edd) *nm* forefinger, index
**mynegi** *vb* tell, express, relate, declare
**mynegiad** (-au) *nm* statement, declaration
**mynegiant** *nm* expression
**mynnu** *vb* will; wish; insist; get, obtain
**mynor** (-ion) *nm* marble
**mynwent** (-au, -ydd) *nf* churchyard, graveyard
**mynwes** (-au) *nf* breast, bosom
**mynwesol** *adj* bosom
**mynwesu** *vb* cherish
**mynych** *adj* frequent, often
**mynychiad** *nm* frequenting; repetition
**mynychu** *vb* frequent, attend; repeat
**mynydd** (-oedd) *nm* mountain
**mynydda** *vb* mountaineer
**mynydd-dir** *nm* hill-country
**mynyddig** *adj* mountainous, hilly
**mynyddwr** (-wyr) *nm* mountaineer
**myrdd, -iwn** (-iynau) *nm* myriad
**myrllyd** *adj* myrrhy
**myrndra** *nm* sultriness
**myrr** *nm* myrrh

**myrtwydd** *npl* (-en *nf*) myrtles
**mysg** *nm* middle, midst. **ymysg** among
**mysgu** *vb* loose, undo
**myswynog** (-ydd) *nf* barren cow
**mysyglog** *adj* mossy
**mytholeg** *nf* mythology
**mytholegol** *adj* mythological

# N

**na** *conj* nor, neither; than ♦ *adv* no, not
**nac** *adv* no, not ♦ *conj* nor, neither
**nacâd** *nm* refusal, denial
**nacaol** *adj* negative
**nacáu** *vb* refuse, deny
**nad** *adv* not
**nâd** (nadau) *nf* cry, howl; clamour
**Nadolig** *nm* Christmas
**Nadoligaidd** *adj* Christmassy
**nadu** *vb* cry (out), howl
**nadu** *vb* stop, hinder
**nadd** *adj* hewn, wrought
**naddion** *npl* chips; shreds; lint
**naddo** *adv* no (*to questions in preterite tense*)
**naddu** *vb* hew, chip, whittle
**Naf** *nm* Lord
**nag** *conj* than
**nage** *adv* not so, no
**nai** (neiaint) *nm* nephew
**naid** (neidiau) *nf* jump, leap, bound
**naïf** *adj* naïve
**naïfder** *nm* naïveté
**naill** *dem pron* the one ♦ *conj* either
**nain** (neiniau) *nf* grandmother
**nam** (-au) *nm* mark, blemish, flaw
**namyn** *pron* except, but, save
**nant** (nentydd) *nf* brook; gorge, ravine
**napcyn** (-au) *nm* napkin
**narcotig** *nm*, *adj* narcotic
**natur** *nf* nature; temper
**naturiaeth** (-au) *nf* nature
**naturiaethwr** (-wyr) *nm* naturalist

**naturiol** *adj* natural
**naturioldeb** *nm* naturalness
**naturus** *adj* angry, quick-tempered
**naw** *adj, nm* nine
**nawdd** *nm* protection; patronage
**nawddogaeth** *nf* patronage, protection
**nawfed** *adj* ninth
**nawn** *nm* noon
**naws** *nf* nature, disposition; essence, tincture
**nawseiddio** *vb* temper, soften
**neb** *nm* any one; (*with negative understood*) no one
**nedd** *npl* (**-en** *nf*) nits
**neddau, neddyf** (**neddyfau**) *nf* adze
**nef** (**-oedd**) *nf* heaven
**nefol, -aidd** *adj* heavenly, celestial
**nefoli** *vb* make or become heavenly
**nefrosis** *nm* neurosis
**neges** (**-au, -euau**) *nf* errand, message
**negesa, -eua** *vb* run errands; trade
**negeseuwr** (**-wyr**) *nm* messenger
**negodi** *vb* negotiate
**negyddiaeth** *nf* negativism
**negyddol** *adj* negative
**neidio** *vb* leap, jump; throb
**neidiwr** (**-wyr**) *nm* leaper, jumper
**neidr** (**nadroedd, nadredd**) *nf* snake
**neiedd** *nm* nepotism
**neillog** (**-ion**) *nm* alternative
**neilltu** *nm* one side. **o'r n.** aside, apart
**neilltuad** *nm* separation
**neilltuaeth** *nf* separation, privacy, seclusion
**neilltuedig** *adj* separated, secluded
**neilltuo** *vb* set apart, separate
**neilltuol** *adj* particular, peculiar, special
**neilltuolion** *npl* peculiarities
**neilltuolrwydd** *nm* peculiarity, distinction

**neis** *adj* nice
**neisied** (**-i**) *nf* kerchief
**neithdar** *nm* nectar
**neithior** (**-au**) *nf* marriage feast
**neithiwr** *adv* last night
**nemor** *adj* few. **nid n.** hardly any
**nen** (**-nau, -noedd**) *nf* ceiling; heaven. **n. tŷ** house-top
**nenbren** *nm* roof-tree
**nenfwd** (**-fydau**) *nm* ceiling
**nepell** *adv* far. **nid n.** not far
**nerf** (**-au**) *nf* nerve
**nerfwst** *nm* neurasthenia
**nerth** (**-oedd**) *nm* might, power, strength
**nerthol** *adj* strong, powerful, mighty
**nerthu** *vb* strengthen
**nes** *adj* nearer. **yn n. ymlaen** further on
**nes** *adv* till, until
**nesaf** *adj* nearest, next
**nesáu** *vb* draw near, approach
**nesnes** *adv* nearer and nearer
**nesu** *vb* draw near. **n draw** move away
**neu** *conj* or
**neuadd** (**-au**) *nf* hall
**newid** *vb* change, alter ♦ *nm* change
**newidiant** *nm* variability
**newidiol** *adj* changeable, variable
**newidydd** (**-ion**) *nm* transformer
**newidyn** (**-nau**) *nm* variable
**newydd** *adj* new, novel; fresh ♦ (**-ion**) *nm* news
**newyddbeth** (**-au**) *nm* novelty
**newydd-deb, -der** *nm* newness, novelty
**newyddiadur** (**-on**) *nm* newspaper
**newyddiaduriaeth** *nf* journalism
**newyddiadurwr** (**-wyr**) *nm* journalist
**newyddian** (**-od**) *n coll* novice, neophyte
**newyn** *nm* hunger, famine
**newynog** *adj* hungry, starving

**newynu** *vb* starve, famish
**ni** *pron* we, us
**ni, nid** *adv* not
**nifer** (-oedd, -i) *nm/f* number
**nifwl** *nm* mist, fog; nebula
**Nigeria** *nf* Nigeria
**Nihon** *nf* Japan
**ninnau** *pron conj* we (on our part),
  we also
**nionyn** (nionod) *nm* onion
**nis** *adv* not ... it. **n. cafodd** he did
  not find it
**nitrad** (-au) *nm* nitrate
**nith** (-oedd) *nf* niece
**nithio** *vb* sift, winnow
**nithiwr** (-wyr) *nm* sifter, winnower
**nithlen** (-ni) *nf* winnowing-sheet
**niwed** (-eidiau) *nm* harm, injury
**niwclear** *adj* nuclear
**niweidio** *vb* harm, hurt, injure,
  damage
**niweidiol** *adj* harmful, injurious
**niwl** (-oedd) *nm*, **-en** *nf* mist, fog,
  haze
**niwliog, niwlog** *adj* misty, foggy,
  hazy
**niwmatig** *adj* pneumatic
**niwmonia** *nm* pneumonia
**niwtral** *adj* neutral
**niwtraleiddio** *vb* neutralise
**niwtraliaeth** *nf* neutrality
**nobyn** (nobiau) *nm* knob
**nod** (-au) *nm/f* note; mark, token
**nodachfa** (-feydd) *nf* bazaar
**nodedig** *adj* appointed, set;
  remarkable
**nodi** *vb* mark, note, appoint, state
**nodiad** (-au) *nm* note
**nodiadur** (-on) *nm* notebook
**nodiant** *nm* notation
**nodwedd** (-ion) *nf* character,
  characteristic, feature
**nodweddiadol** *adj* characteristic
**nodweddu** *vb* characterize
**nodwydd** (-au) *nf* needle
**nodyn** (-nau, nodau, nodion) *nm*
  note

**nodd** (-ion) *nm* moisture; juice,
  sap
**nodded** *nm* refuge, protection
**noddfa** (-fâu, -feydd) *nf* refuge
**noddi** *vb* protect
**noddlyd** *adj* juicy, sappy
**noddwr** (-wyr) *nm* protector;
  patron
**noe** (-au) *nf* dish; kneading-trough
**noeth** *adj* naked, bare, exposed,
  raw
**noethder** *nm* bareness, nakedness
**noethi** *vb* bare, denude
**noethlymun** *adj* nude
**noethlymunwr** (-wyr) *nm* streaker
**noethlymunwraig** *nf* stripper
**noethni** *nm* nakedness, nudity
**noethwr** (-wyr) *nm* nudist
**nofel** (-au) *nf* novel
**nofelwr, -ydd** (-wyr) *nm* novelist
**nofiadwy** *adj* swimmable
**nofiedydd** (-ion) *nm* swimmer
**nofio** *vb* swim; float
**nofiwr** (-wyr) *nm* swimmer
**nogio** *vb* jib
**noglyd** *adj* jibbing
**nôl** *vb* fetch, bring
**Norwy** *nf* Norway
**nos** (-au, nosweithiau) *nf* night
**nosi** *vb* become night
**noson, noswaith** (nosweithiau) *nf*
  a night, an evening
**noswyl** (-iau) *nf* eve of festival,
  vigil
**noswylio** *vb* cease work at eve
**nudden** *nf* fog, mist, haze
**nwy** (-on) *nm* gas
**nwyd** (-au) *nm* passion; emotion
**nwydd** (-au) *nm* substance,
  article; (*pl*) goods
**nwyf** *nm* vivacity, energy, vigour
**nwyfiant** *nm* vivacity, vigour
**nwyfus** *adj* sprightly, spirited,
  lively
**nwyol** *adj* gaseous
**nychdod** *nm* feebleness, infirmity
**nychlyd** *adj* sickly, feeble

**nychu** *vb* sicken, pine, languish
**nydd-dro** (**-droeau, -droeon**) *nm* twist
**nydd-droi** *vb* twist, screw
**nyddu** *vb* spin, twist
**nyddwr** (**-wyr**) *nm* spinner
**nyf** *coll n* snow
**nyni** *pron* we, us
**nyrs** (**-ys**) *nm/f* nurse
**nyrsio** *adj* nurse
**nytmeg** *nm* nutmeg
**nyth** (**-od**) *nm/f* nest
**nythu** *vb* nest, nestle

# O

**o** *prep* from; of, out of; by
**o** *excl* oh!, O!
**oblegid** *conj, prep* because, for
**obry** *adv* beneath, below
**obstetreg** *nm* obstetrics
**obstetregydd** (**-wyr**) *nm* obstetrician
**ocsid** (**-iau**) *nm* oxide
**ocsidiad** *nm* oxidisation
**ocsidio** *vb* oxidise
**ocsidydd** (**-ion**) *nm* oxidising agent
**ocsigen** *nm* oxygen
**och** *excl* oh, alas, woe
**ochenaid** (**-eidiau**) *nf* sigh
**ocheneidio, ochneidio** *vb* sigh
**ochr** (**-au**) *nf* side
**ochrgamu** *vb* sidestep
**ochri** *vb* side
**ôd** *nm* snow
**od** *adj* odd, remarkable
**odiaeth** *adj* excellent, exquisite ♦ *adv* very, most, extremely
**odid** *adv* perchance, peradventure
**odl** (**-au**) *nf* rhyme; ode, song
**odli** *vb* rhyme
**odrif** (**-au**) *nm* odd number
**odrwydd** *nm* oddity
**odyn** (**-au**) *nf* kiln
**oddeutu** *prep* about
**oddi** *prep* out of, from

**oddieithr, oddigerth** *prep* except, unless
**oed** (**-au**) *nm* age; time
**oed-dâl** (**-iadau**) *nm* superannuation
**oedfa** (**-on, -feuon**) *nf* meeting, service
**oedi** *vb* delay; postpone, defer
**oediad** (**-au**) *nm* delay
**oedran** *nm* age, full age
**oedrannus** *adj* aged
**oedd** *vb* was, were
**oen** (**ŵyn**) *nm* lamb
**oena** *vb* lamb, yean
**oenig** *nf* ewe-lamb
**oer** *adj* cold, chill, frigid; sad
**oeraidd** *adj* coldish, cool, chilly
**oerddrws** (**-ddrysau**) *nm* wind gap
**oerfel** *nm* cold
**oergell** (**-oedd**) *nf* refrigerator
**oeri** *vb* cool, chill
**oerllyd** *adj* chilly, frigid; cool
**oernad** (**-au**) *nf* howl, wail, lamentation
**oernadu** *vb* howl, wail, lament
**oerni** *nm* cold, coldness, chillness
**oes** (**-oedd, -au**) *nf* age, lifetime.
  **yn o. oesoedd** for ever and ever
**oes** *vb* there is, there are; is there?
**oesoffagws** *nm* oesophagus
**oesol** *adj* age-long, perpetual
**ofer** *adj* vain, idle; prodigal, dissipated; waste
**ofera** *vb* waste, squander, idle
**oferedd** *nm* vanity, dissipation
**ofergoel** (**-ion**) *nf* superstition
**ofergoeledd, -iaeth** *nm* superstition
**ofergoelus** *adj* superstitious
**oferwr** (**-wyr**) *nm* idler, waster
**ofn** (**-au**) *nm* fear, dread
**ofnadwy** *adj* awful, terrible, dreadful
**ofnadwyaeth** *nf* awe, terror, dread
**ofni** *vb* fear, dread

**ofnog** *adj* fearful, timorous
**ofnus** *adj* timid, nervous
**ofnusrwydd** *nm* timidity, nervousness
**ofwl** (-au) *nm* ovule
**ofydd** (-ion) *nm* ovate
**offeiriad** (-iaid) *nm* priest, clergyman
**offeiriadaeth** *nf* priesthood
**offeiriades** (-au) *nf* priestess
**offeiriadol** *adj* priestly, sacerdotal
**offeiriadu** *vb* officiate, minister
**offer** *npl* implements, tools, gear
**offeren** (-nau) *nf* mass
**offeryn** (-nau, offer) *nm* instrument, tool
**offerynnol** *adj* instrumental
**offerynoliaeth** *nf* instrumentality
**offrwm** (-ymau) *nm* offering, oblation
**offrymu** *vb* offer, sacrifice
**offrymwr** (-wyr) *nm* offerer, sacrificer
**offthalmia** *nm* ophthalmia
**offthalmosgop** (-au) *nm* ophthalmoscope
**og** (-au), **oged** (-au, -i) *nf* harrow
**ogof** (-au, -fâu, -feydd) *nf* cave, cavern; den
**ogylch** *prep* about
**ongl** (-au) *nf* angle, corner
**onglog** *adj* angled, angular
**oherwydd** *conj*, *prep* because, for
**ôl** *adj* back, hind, hindmost ♦ (olion) *nm* mark, print, trace, track. **Yn ôl** according to; ago
**ôl-dâl** (-oedd) *nm* back-pay
**ôl-ddodiad** (-iaid) *nm* suffix
**ôl-ddyddio** *vb* post-date
**ôl-ddyled** (-ion) *nf* arrears
**olew** (-au) *nm* oil
**olewydd** *npl* (-en *nf*) olive-trees
**olifaid** *npl* olive-berries
**olrhain** *vb* trace
**olwr** (-wyr) *nm* back (*rugby*)
**olwyn** (-ion) *nf* wheel
**olwyno** *vb* wheel, cycle

**olwynog** *adj* wheeled
**olyniaeth** *nf* succession, sequence
**olynol** *adj* successive, consecutive
**olynu** *vb* succeed (to)
**olynwr** (-wyr), **-ydd** (-ion) *nm* successor
**ôlysgrif** (-au) *nf* postscript
**oll** *adv* all, wholly; ever, at all
**ombwdsman** (-myn) *nm* ombudsman
**omlet** (-i) *nm* omelette
**ond** *conj* but, only ♦ *prep* except, save, but
**onest** *adj* honest
**onestrwydd** *nm* honesty
**oni, onid** *adv* not?, is it not? ♦ *conj* if not, unless ♦ *prep* except, save, but
**onid e** *adv* otherwise, else; is it not?
**onis** *conj* if it is not. **o. caiff** if he does not get it
**onnen** (onn, ynn) *nf* ash
**opiniwn** (-ynau) *nm* opinion
**opiniynllyd, -iynus** *adj* opinionated
**optimistaeth** *nf* optimism
**optimistaidd** *adj* optimistic
**optimwm** (-tima) *nm* optimum
**oracl** (-au) *nm* oracle
**oraclaidd** *adj* oracular
**oraens** *nm* orange
**ordeiniad** (-au) *nm* ordination, ordinance
**ordeinio** *vb* ordain
**ordinhad** (-au) *nf* ordinance, sacrament
**oren** (-nau) *nm/f* orange
**organ** (-au) *nf/m* organ
**organaidd** *adj* organic
**organeb** (-au) *nf* organism
**organig** *adj* organic
**organydd** (-ion) *nm* organist
**orgraff** (-au) *nf* orthography
**orgraffyddol** *adj* orthographical
**oriawr** (oriorau) *nf* watch
**oriel** (-au) *nf* gallery
**orig** *nf* little while

**oriog** adj fickle, changeable, inconstant
**os** conj if
**osgo** nm slant, slope, inclination
**osgoi** vb swerve, avoid, evade, shirk
**oslef** nf tone, voice
**ow** excl oh!, alas!

# P

**pa** adj what, which
**pab** (-au) nm pope
**pabaeth** nf papacy
**pabaidd** adj papal, popish
**pabell** (pebyll) nf tent, tabernacle
**pabellu** vb tent, tabernacle, encamp
**pabi** nm poppy
**pabwyr** npl (-en nf, -yn nm) rushes
**pabwyr** nm wick, candle-wick
**pabydd** (-ion) nm Roman Catholic
**pabyddiaeth** nf Roman Catholicism
**pabyddol** adj Roman Catholic
**pac** (-iau) nm pack, bundle
**pacio** vb pack
**padell** (-au, -i, pedyll) nf pan, bowl
**padellaid** (-eidiau) nf panful
**pader** (-au) nm paternoster, Lord's Prayer
**padera** vb repeat prayers, patter
**pae** nm pay, wage
**paediatreg** nm paediatrics
**paediatregydd** nm paediatrician
**paent** nm paint
**paentiad** (-au) nm painting
**pafiliwn** nm pavilion
**paffio** vb box, fight
**paffiwr** (-wyr) nm boxer
**pagan** (-iaid) nm pagan, heathen
**paganaidd** adj pagan, heathen
**paganiaeth** nf paganism, heathenism
**pang** (-au) nm, **pangfa** (-feydd) nf pang, fit

**paham** adv why, wherefore
**paill** nm flour; pollen
**pair** (peiriau) nm cauldron, furnace
**pais** (peisiau) nf coat, petticoat
**paith** (peithiau) nm prairie
**Pacistan** nf Pakistan
**pâl** (palau) nf spade
**paladr** (pelydr) nm ray, beam; staff; stem
**palaeolithig** adj palaeolithic
**palas** (-au) nm palace
**Palestina** nf Palestine
**palf** (-au) nf palm, hand; paw
**palfais** (-eisiau) nf shoulder
**palfalu** vb feel, grope
**palfod** (-au) nf smack, slap, buffet
**palff** nm fine, well-built man
**pali** nm silk brocade
**palis** (-au) nm pale, partition, wainscot
**palmant** (-mentydd) nm pavement
**palmantu** vb pave
**palmwydd** npl (-en nf) palm-trees
**palu** vb dig, delve
**palwr** (-wyr) nm digger
**pall** (-au) nm mantle; tent
**pall** nm fail, failing; lack; lapse
**pallu** vb fail, cease; neglect; refuse
**pam** adv why, wherefore (**paham**)
**pamffled** (-i, -au), -yn nm pamphlet
**pan** conj when
**pandy** (-dai) nm fulling-mill
**pannas** npl (panasen nf) parsnips
**pannu** vb full cloth
**pannwl** (panylau) nm dimple, hollow
**pannwr** (panwyr) nm fuller
**pant** (-iau) nm hollow, valley
**pantio** vb depress, dent, sink
**pantiog** adj hollow, sunken; dimpled
**papur** (-au) nm paper
**papuro** vb paper
**papurwr** (-wyr) nm paperer, paperhanger

**papuryn** *nm* scrap of paper
**pâr** (**parau**) *nm* pair; suit
**pâr** (**peri**) *nm* spear, lance
**para** *vb* last, endure, continue
**parabl** (**-au**) *nm* speech, discourse
**parablu** *vb* speak
**paradeim** (**-au**) *nm* paradigm
**paradwys** *nf* paradise
**paradwysaidd** *adj* paradisean
**paragraff** (**-au**) *nm* paragraph
**paratoad** (**-au**) *nm* preparation
**paratoawl** *adj* preparatory
**paratoi** *vb* prepare, get ready
**parc** (**-iau**) *nm* park, field
**parch** *nm* respect, reverence
**parchedig** (**-ion**) *adj* reverend;
  reverent
**parchedigaeth** *nf* reverence
**parchu** *vb* respect, revere,
  reverence
**parchus** *adj* respectful;
  respectable
**parchusrwydd** *nm* respectability
**pardwn** (**-ynau**) *nm* pardon
**pardynu** *vb* pardon
**parddu** *nm* fire-black, smut; soot
**pardduo** *vb* blacken, vilify, defame
**pared** (**parwydydd**) *nm* partition
  wall, wall
**paredd** *nm* parity
**parhad** *nm* continuance,
  continuation
**parhaol** *adj* lasting, perpetual
**parhau** *vb* last, continue;
  persevere
**parhaus** *adj* lasting; continual,
  perpetual
**Paris** *nf* Paris
**parlwr** (**-yrau**) *nm* parlour
**parlys** *nm* paralysis, palsy
**parlysu** *vb* paralyse
**parod** *adj* ready, prepared; prompt
**parodrwydd** *nm* readiness,
  willingness
**parôl** (**-au**) *nm* parole
**parsel** (**-i, -ydd**) *nm* parcel
**parti** (**-ion**) *nm* party

**partïaeth** *nf* partisanship
**partïol** *adj* partial, biassed,
  partisan
**parth** (**-au**) *nm* part, region; floor
**parthed** *prefix* about, concerning
**parthu** *vb* part, divide
**parwyden** (**-nau**) *nf* wall, side;
  breast
**pas** *nm* whooping-cough
**Pasg** *nm* Passover, Easter
**pasgedig** (**-ion**) *adj* fatted,
  fattened, fat
**pasiant** (**-iannau**) *nm* pageant
**pasio** *vb* pass
**past** *nm* paste
**pastai** (**-eiod**) *nf* pasty, pie
**pastio** *vb* paste
**pasturedig** *adj* pasteurised
**pasturo** *vb* pasteurise
**pastwn** (**-ynau**) *nm* baton, club,
  cudgel
**pastynu** *vb* club, cudgel, bludgeon
**patriarch** (**-iaid, patrieirch**) *nm*
  patriarch
**patriarchaeth** (**-au**) *nf* patriarchate
**patriarchaidd** *adj* patriarchal
**patrwm** (**-ymau**) *nm* pattern
**patrymlun** (**-iau**) *nm* template
**pathew** (**-od**) *nm* dormouse
**patholeg** *nf* pathology
**patholegol** *adj* pathological
**patholegydd** (**-egwyr**) *nm*
  pathologist
**pau** *nf* country
**paun** (**peunod**) *nm* peacock
**pawb** *pron* everybody, all
**pawen** (**-nau**) *nf* paw
**pawl** (**polion**) *nm* pole, stake
**pe** *conj* if
**pebyll** see **pabell**
**pecyn** (**-nau**) *nm* packet, package
**pech-aberth** (**-au**) *nm* sin-offering
**pechadur** (**-iaid**) *nm* sinner,
  offender
**pechadures** (**-au**) *nf* woman sinner
**pechadurus** *adj* sinful, wicked
**pechadurusrwydd** *nm* sinfulness

**pechod** (-au) *nm* sin, offence
**pechu** *vb* sin, offend
**ped** *conj* if
**pedair** *adj* f. of **pedwar**
**pedeirongl** *adj* foursquare
**pedi** *vb* worry, grieve
**pedol** (-au) *nf* horseshoe
**pedoli** *vb* shoe
**pedrain** *nf* haunches, crupper
**pedrongl** *adj* square ♦ (-au) *nf* square
**pedronglog** *adj* quadrangular
**pedryfan** *adj* four-cornered ♦ -noedd *nm* four quarters
**pedryfwrdd** (-fyrddau) *nm* quarter-deck
**pedwar** *adj* four; *f* **pedair**
**pedwarawd** *nm* quartette
**pedwarcarnol** (-ion) *adj* four-footed, quadruped
**pedwaredd** *adj* f. of **pedwerydd**
**pedwarplyg** *adj* fourfold, quarto
**pedwerydd** *adj* fourth; *f* **pedwaredd**
**peddestr** *nm* pedestrian
**peddestrig** *nm* walking; pedestrian
**pefr** *adj* radiant, bright, beautiful
**pefrio** *vb* radiate, sparkle
**peg** (-iau) *nm* peg
**pegio** *vb* peg
**pegor** (-au) *nm* manikin; dwarf; imp
**pegwn** (-ynau) *nm* pivot, pole, axis
**Pegwn y Gogledd** *nm* North Pole
**pegynol** *adj* axial, polar
**peidio** *vb* cease, stop, desist
**peilon** (-au) *nm* pylon
**peilot** (-iaid) *nm* pilot
**peillio** *vb* bolt, sift
**peint** (-iau) *nm* pint
**peintiad** (-au) *nm* painting
**peintio** *vb* paint
**peintiwr** (-wyr) *nm* painter
**peipen** (peipiau) *nf* pipe
**peirianneg** *nm* engineering
**peiriannol** *adj* mechanical
**peiriannydd** (-ianyddion) *nm* engineer
**peiriant** (-iannau) *nm* machine, engine. **p. golchi** washing machine
**peirianwaith** *nm* mechanism
**peiswyn** *nm* chaff
**peithyn** (-au) *nm* ridge-tile
**Pecing** *nf* Peking
**pêl** (pelau, peli) *nf* ball
**pelawd** (-au) *nf* over (*cricket*)
**pêl-droed** *nf* football
**pêl-fasged** *nf* basket-ball
**pelferyn** (-nau) *nm* ball-bearing
**pêl-foli** *nf* volley-ball
**pêl-rwyd** *nf* netball
**pelten** (pelts) *nf* blow
**pelydr** (-au) *nm* ray, beam
**pelydru** *vb* beam, gleam, radiate
**pelydryn** *nm* ray, beam
**pell** *adj* far, distant, remote, long
**pellen** (-nau, -ni) *nf* ball (of yarn)
**pellennig** *adj* far, distant, remote
**pellhau** *vb* put or remove far off
**pellter** (-au, -oedd) *nm* distance
**pen** (-nau) *nm* head; chief; end; top
**pen** *adj* head, chief, supreme
**penadur** (-iaid) *nm* sovereign
**penaduriaeth** *nf* sovereignty
**penagored** *adj* open, indefinite, undecided
**penarglwyddiaeth** *nf* sovereignty
**penbaladr** *adj* general, universal
**penben** *adv* at loggerheads
**penbleth** *nf* perplexity, quandary
**pen-blwydd** (-i) *nm* birthday
**penboeth** *adj* hot-headed, fanatical
**penboethni** *nm* fanaticism
**penboethyn** (-boethiaid) *nm* fanatic
**penbwl** (-byliaid) *nm* blockhead; tadpole
**pencadlys** *nm* head-quarters
**pencampwr** (-wyr) *nm* champion
**pencampwriaeth** (-au) *nf* championship
**pencerdd** (-ceirddiaid) *nm* chief musician

**penchwiban** adj giddy, flighty
**pendant** adj positive, emphatic
**pendantrwydd** nm positiveness
**pendefig** (-ion) nm prince, peer, noble
**pendefigaeth** nf aristocracy, peerage
**pendefigaidd** adj noble, aristocratic
**pendefiges** (-au) nf peeress
**penderfyniad** (-au) nm determination, resolution
**penderfynol** adj determined, resolute
**penderfynu** vb determine, resolve
**pendew** adj thick-headed, stupid
**pendifaddau** adj: **yn b.** especially
**pendil** (-iau) nm pendulum
**pendramwnwgl** adj topsyturvy; headlong
**pendraphen** adj helter-skelter, confused
**pendro** nf giddiness, vertigo; staggers
**pendroni** vb perplex oneself, worry over
**pendrwm** adj top-heavy; drowsy
**pendrymu** vb drowse, droop
**pendwmpian** vb nod, doze, slumber
**penddaredd** nm giddiness
**penddaru** vb make or become giddy
**pendduyn** (-nod) nm botch, boil
**penelin** (-oedd) nm/f elbow
**penelino** vb elbow
**penffest** (-au) nm headgear
**penffol** adj silly, idiotic
**penffrwyn** (-au) nm/f head-stall, halter
**pengaled** adj headstrong ♦ nf knapweed
**pengaledwch** nm stubbornness
**pengam** adj wrong-headed, perverse
**pen-glin** (-iau) nf knee
**penglog** (-au) nf skull

**pengryf** adj headstrong, stubborn
**pengryniad** (-iaid) nm roundhead
**peniad** (-au) nm header
**penigamp** adj excellent, splendid
**penisel** adj downcast, crestfallen
**penlinio** vb kneel
**penllwyd** adj grey-headed
**penllwydni** nm grey hair, white hair
**penllywydd** (-ion) nm sovereign
**penllywyddiaeth** nf sovereignty
**pennaeth** (penaethiaid) nm chief
**pennaf** adj chief, principal
**pennawd** (penawdau) nm heading; headline
**pennill** (penillion) nm verse, stanza
**pennod** (penodau) nf chapter
**pennoeth** adj bare-headed
**pennog** (penwaig) nm herring
**pennu** vb specify, appoint, determine
**penodi** vb appoint
**penodiad** (-au) nm appointment
**penodol** adj particular, specific
**penrhydd** adj unbridled, loose
**penrhyddid** nm licence, licentiousness
**penrhyn** (-noedd, -nau) nm cape, foreland
**pensaer** (-seiri) nm architect
**pensaernïaeth** nf architecture
**pensil** (-iau) nm pencil
**pensiwn** (-iynau) nm pension
**pen-swyddog** (-ion) nm chief officer
**pensyfrdan** adj stunned, dazed
**pensyfrdandod** nm giddiness, dizziness
**pensyfrdanu** vb stun, daze
**pensyth** adj perpendicular
**pentan** (-au) nm hob
**penteulu** (pennau teuluoedd) nm head of family
**pentewyn** (-ion) nm firebrand
**pentir** (-oedd) nm headland
**pentis** nm pentice, penthouse
**pentref** (-i, -ydd) nm village;

homestead
**pentrefan** (-nau) *nm* hamlet
**pentrefol** *adj* village
**pentrefwr** (-wyr) *nm* villager
**pentwr** (-tyrrau) *nm* heap, pile
**penty** (-tai) *nm* cottage, shed
**pentyrru** *vb* heap, pile, accumulate
**penuchel** *adj* proud, haughty
**penwan** *adj* weak-minded
**penwyn** *adj* white-headed
**penwynni** *nm* white hair, grey hair
**penyd** (-iau) *nm* penance, punishment
**penyd-wasanaeth** *nm* penal servitude
**penysgafn** *adj* light-headed, giddy, dizzy
**penysgafnder** *nm* giddiness, dizziness
**pêr** *adj* sweet, delicious, luscious
**peraidd** *adj* sweet, mellow
**perarogl** (-au) *nm* perfume, fragrance
**perarogli** *vb* perfume; embalm
**peraroglus** *adj* fragrant, scented
**percoladur** (-on) *nm* percolator
**perchen, -nog** (**perchenogion**) *nm* owner
**perchenogaeth** *nf* ownership
**perchenogi** *vb* possess, own
**perchentywr** (-wyr) *nm* householder
**pereidd-dra** *nm* sweetness
**pereiddio** *vb* sweeten
**pererin** (-ion) *nm* pilgrim
**pererindod** (-au) *nm/f* pilgrimage
**pererinol** *adj* pilgrim
**perfedd** (-ion) *nm* guts, bowels
**perfeddwlad** (-wledydd) *nf* interior, heartland
**perffaith** *adj* perfect
**perffeithio** *vb* perfect
**perffeithrwydd** *nm* perfection
**perffeithydd** (-ion) *nm* perfecter
**perfformiad** (-au) *nm* performance
**perfformio** *vb* perform

**perfformiwr** (-wyr) *nm* performer
**peri** *vb* cause, bid
**perl** (-au) *nm* pearl
**perlewyg** (-on) *nm* ecstasy, trance
**perlysiau** *npl* aromatic herbs; spices
**perllan** (-nau) *nf* orchard
**perocsid** (-au) *nm* peroxide
**peroriaeth** *nf* melody, music
**persain** *adj* euphonious, melodious
♦ (-seiniau) *nf* euphony
**persawr** (-au) *nm* fragrance
**perseiniol** *adj* melodious
**persli** *nm* parsley
**person** (-au) *nm* person
**person** (-iaid) *nm* parson, clergyman
**personadu** *vb* impersonate
**personadwr** (-wyr) *nm* impersonator
**persondy** (-dai) *nm* parsonage
**personol** *adj* personal
**personoli** *vb* personify
**personoliad** (-au) *nm* personification
**personoliaeth** (-au) *nf* personality
**perswâd** *nm* persuasion
**perswadio** *vb* persuade
**pert** *adj* quaint, pretty; pert
**perth** (-i) *nf* bush, hedge
**perthnasedd** (-au) *nm* relativity, relevance
**perthnasiad** (-au) *nm* affiliation
**perthnasol** *adj* relevant
**perthyn** *vb* belong, pertain, be related
**perthynas** (-au) *nf* relation; relationship
**perthynol** *adj* relative
**perwyl** *nm* purpose, effect
**perygl** (-on) *nm* danger, peril, risk
**peryglu** *vb* endanger, imperil
**peryglus** *adj* dangerous, perilous
**pes** *conj* if … it. **p. adwaenasent** had they known him
**pesgi** *vb* feed, fatten
**pesimist** (-iaid) *nm* pessimist

**pesimistaidd** *adj* pessimistic
**pesimistiaeth** *nf* pessimism
**pestl** (**-au**) *nm* pestle
**peswch** *nm* cough
**pesychiad** (**-au**) *nm* cough
**pesychu** *vb* cough
**petris** *npl* (**-en** *nf*) partridges
**petrocemegolau** (**petrocemogolyn** *nf*) *npl* petrochemicals
**petrol** (**-au**) *nm* petrol
**petroleg** *nm/f* petrology
**petrus** *adj* hesitating; doubtful
**petruso** *vb* hesitate, doubt
**petruster** *nm* hesitation, doubt
**petryal** *nm, adj* square
**peth** (**-au**) *nm* thing; part, some
**petheuach** *npl* odds and ends, trifles
**peunes** (**-od**) *nf* peahen
**pianydd** (**-ion**) *nm* pianist
**piau** *vb* own, possess
**pib** (**-au**) *nf* pipe, tube; diarrhœa
**pibell** (**-au, -i**) *nf* pipe, tube
**pibgorn** (**-gyrn**) *nm* recorder (music)
**pibo** *vb* pipe; squirt
**pibonwy** (**-en** *nf*) *npl* icicles
**pibydd** (**-ion**) *nm* piper
**picell** (**-au**) *nf* dart, javelin, spear
**picellu** *vb* spear, stab
**picfforch** (**-ffyrch**) *nf* pitchfork
**picil** *nm* pickle, trouble
**picio** *vb* dart, hie
**piclo** *vb* pickle
**pictiwr** (**-tiyrau**) *nm* picture
**picwns** (**-nen** *nf*) *npl* wasps
**piff** (**-iau**) *nm* puff, sudden blast
**piffian** *vb* snigger, giggle
**pig** (**-au**) *nf* point, spike; beak; spout
**pigan** *vb* drizzle
**pigdwr** (**-dyrau**) *nm* spire, steeple
**pigiad** (**-au**) *nm* prick, sting; injection
**pigion** *npl* pickings, selections
**pigo** *vb* pick; peck; prick; sting
**pigog** *adj* prickly

**pigyn** *nm* thorn, prickle
**pilcod** *npl* (**-yn** *nm*) minnows
**pilen** (**-nau**) *nf* membrane, film; cataract
**piler** (**-au, -i**) *nm* pillar
**pilio** *vb* peel, pare
**pili-pala** *nm* butterfly
**Pilipinas** *npl* the Philippines
**pilsen** (**pils**) *nf* pill
**pilyn** *nm* garment, rag, clout
**pîn** *nm* pine, fir
**pin** (**-nau**) *nm/f* pin ♦ *nm* pen
**pinacl** (**-au**) *nm* pinnacle
**pinaclog** *adj* pinnacled
**pinafal** (**-au**) *nf* pineapple
**pinbwyntio** *vb* pinpoint
**pinc** (**-od**) *nm* finch, chaffinch
**pincio** *vb* pink. **parlwr p.** beauty parlour
**pincws** (**-cysau**) *nm* pincushion
**pindwll** (**-dyllau**) *nm* pinhole
**pinsiad** (**-au**) *nm* pinch
**pinsio** *vb* pinch
**pioden** (**piod**) *nf* magpie
**piser** (**-au, -i**) *nm* pitcher, jug, can
**pistyll** (**-oedd**) *nm* spout; cataract
**pistyllio** *vb* spout, gush
**pisyn** (**-nau, pisiau**) *nm* piece
**piti** *nm* pity
**pitw** *adj* petty, puny, paltry
**piw** (**-od**) *nm* dug, udder
**Piwritan** (**-iaid**) *nm* Puritan
**piwritanaidd** *adj* puritan, puritanical
**piwritaniaeth** *nf* puritanism
**pla** (**plâu**) *nm/f* plague, pestilence; nuisance
**pladur** (**-iau**) *nf* scythe
**pladurwr** (**-wyr**) *nm* mower
**plaen** *adj* plain, clear
**plaen** (**-au**) *nm* plane
**plaenio** *vb* plane
**plagio** *vb* plague, tease, torment
**plagus** *adj* annoying, troublesome
**plaid** (**pleidiau**) *nf* side, party. **P. Cymru** The Welsh National Party
**planced** (**-i**) *nf* blanket

**planed** (-au) *nf* planet
**planhigfa** (-feydd) *nf* plantation
**planhigyn** (-higion) *nm* plant
**plannu** *vb* plant; dive
**plannwr** (planwyr) *nm* planter
**plant** *npl* (plentyn *nm*) children
**planta** *vb* beget or bear children
**plantos** *npl* (little) children
**plas** (-au) *nm* hall, mansion, palace
**plasaidd** *adj* palatial
**plastr** (-au) *nm* plaster
**plastro** *vb* plaster
**plastrwr** (-wyr) *nm* plasterer
**plât, plat** (-iau) *nm* plate
**platŵn** (-tynau) *nm* platoon
**platwydr** *nm* plate-glass
**ple** *nm* plea
**pledio** *vb* plead, argue
**pledren** (-nau, -ni) *nf* bladder
**pleidgarwch** *nm* partisanship
**pleidio** *vb* side with, support
**pleidiol** *adj* favourable, partial
**pleidiwr** (-wyr) *nm* partisan, supporter
**pleidlais** (-leisiau) *nf* vote, suffrage
**pleidleisio** *vb* vote
**pleidleisiwr** (-wyr) *nm* voter
**plencyn** (planciau) *nm* plank
**plentyn** (plant) *nm* child, infant
**plentyndod** *nm* childhood, infancy
**plentyneiddiwch** *nm* childishness
**plentynnaidd** *adj* childish, puerile
**plentynrwydd** *nm* childishness
**pleser** (-au) *nm* pleasure
**pleserdaith** (-deithiau) *nf* trip, excursion
**pleserus** *adj* pleasurable, pleasant
**plesio** *vb* please
**plet, pleten** (pletiau) *nf* pleat
**pletio** *vb* pleat
**pletiog** *adj* pleated
**pleth** (-au) *nf* plait
**plethdorch** (-au) *nf* wreath
**plethu** *vb* plait, weave, fold
**plewra** (-e) *nm* pleura
**plicio** *vb* pluck, peel, strip

**plisg** *coll n* (-yn *nm*) shells, husks, pods
**plisgo** *vb* shell, husk
**plisman, -mon** (-myn) *nm* policeman
**plismones** (-au) *nf* policewoman
**plith** *nm* midst
**pliwrisi** *nm* pleurisy
**plocyn** (plociau) *nm* block
**plod** *adj, nm* plaid, tartan
**ploryn** (-nod) *nm* pimple
**plu** *npl* (-en *nf*), **pluf** *npl* (-yn *nm*) feathers. p. eira snow-flakes
**pluo, plufio** *vb* pluck, deplume; plume
**pluog** *adj* feathered, fledged
**plwc** (plyciau) *nm* pluck; space, while
**plwg** (plygiau) *nm* plug
**plwm** *nm* lead
**plws** *nm* plus
**plwtonium** *nm* plutonium
**plwyf** (-i, -ydd) *nm* parish
**plwyfol** *adj* parochial
**plwyfolion** *npl* parishioners
**plycio** *vb* pluck
**plyg** (-ion) *nm* fold, double; hollow
**plygain** *nm* cock-crow, dawn; matins
**plygeiniol** *adj* dawning; very early
**plygell** (-au) *nf* folder
**plygiad** (-au) *nm* folding, fold
**plygu** *vb* fold; bend, stoop; bow
**plymen** *nf* plummet
**plymio** *vb* plumb, sound
**plymwr** (-wyr) *nm* plumber
**po** *particle used before superlative.* gorau po gyntaf the sooner the better
**pob** *adj* each, every; all
**pobi** *vb* bake; roast; toast
**pobiad** (-au) *nm* baking, batch
**pobl** (-oedd) *nf* people
**poblog** *adj* populous
**poblogaeth** (-au) *nf* population
**poblogaidd** *adj* popular
**poblogeiddio** *vb* popularize

**poblogi** *vb* people, populate
**poblogrwydd** *nm* popularity
**pobwr** (**-wyr**), **-ydd** (**-ion**) *nm* baker
**poced** (**-i**) *nf* pocket
**pocedu** *vb* pocket
**pocer** (**-i, -au**) *nm* poker
**poen** (**-au**) *nm/f* pain, torment
**poenedigaeth** *nf* torment
**poeni** *vb* pain, torment; worry, grieve
**poenus** *adj* painful
**poenwr** (**-wyr**) *nm* tormentor, torturer
**poenydio** *vb* torment, torture; fret, vex
**poenydiwr** (**-wyr**) *nm* tormentor
**poer** (**-ion**) *nm* spittle, saliva
**poeri** *vb* spit, expectorate
**poeryn** *nm* spittle
**poeth** *adj* hot; burning. **dŵr p.** heart-burn
**poethder, -ni** *nm* hotness, heat
**poethdon** (**-nau**) *nf* heatwave
**poethi** *vb* heat
**pôl** (**polau**) *nm* poll
**polaredd** *nm* polarity
**polareiddiad** *nm* polarisation
**polareiddio** *vb* polarise
**polymorff** *nm* polymorph
**polymorffedd** *nm* polymorphism
**polyn** (**polion**) *nm* pole
**pomgranad** (**-au**) *nm* pomegranate
**pompiwn** (**-iynau**) *nm* pumpkin, gourd
**pompren** *nf* plank bridge, footbridge
**ponc** (**-iau**), **-en** *nf*, **-yn** *nm* hillock, tump; bank
**pont** (**-ydd**) *nf* bridge, arch
**pontffordd** (**-ffyrdd**) *nf* fly-over, viaduct
**pontio** *vb* bridge
**popeth** *nm* everything
**poplys** *npl* (**-en** *nf*) poplar-trees
**popty** (**-tai**) *nm* bakehouse; oven
**porc** *nm* pork

**porchell** (**perchyll**) *nm* little pig
**porfa** (**-feydd**) *nf* pasture, grass
**porffor** *adj, nm* purple
**pori** *vb* graze, browse; eat
**pornograffiaeth** *nf* pornography
**Portiwgal** *nf* Portugal
**portread** (**-au**) *nm* portrayal, pattern
**portreadu** *vb* portray
**porth** *nm* aid, help, succour
**porth** (**pyrth**) *nm* gate, gateway; porch door. **p. awyr** airport
**porthfa** (**-feydd**) *nf* port, harbour; ferry
**porthi** *vb* feed
**porthiannus** *adj* well-fed, high-spirited
**porthiant** *nm* food, sustenance, support
**porthladd** (**-oedd**) *nm* port, harbour, haven
**porthmon** (**-myn**) *nm* cattle-dealer
**porthor** (**-ion**) *nm* porter, door-keeper, commissionaire
**pôs** (**-au**) *nm* riddle, conundrum, puzzle
**posibilrwydd** *nm* possibility
**posib(l)** *adj* possible
**positif** *adj* positive
**positifiaeth** *nf* positivism
**post** (**pyst**) *nm* post; pillar
**poster** (**-i**) *nm* poster
**postfarc** (**-iau**) *nm* postmark
**postio** *vb* post
**postman, -mon** (**-myn**) *nm* postman
**postyn** (**pyst**) *nm* post
**pot** (**-iau**) *nm* pot
**potel** (**-i**) *nf* bottle
**potelaid** (**-eidiau**) *nf* bottleful
**potelu** *vb* bottle
**poten** (**-ni**) *nf* paunch; pudding
**potensial** (**-au**) *nm, adj* potential
**potes** *nm* pottage, broth, soup
**potio** *vb* pot; tipple
**potsiar** (**-s**) *nm* poacher
**potsio** *vb* poach

**pothell** (**-au, -i**) *nf* blister
**powdr** (**-au**) *nm* powder
**powl, -en** (**powliau**) *nf* bowl, basin
**powlio** *vb* roll; wheel, trundle
**powltis** (**-au**) *nm* poultice
**practis** *nm* practice
**praff** *adj* thick, stout
**praffter** *nm* thickness, stoutness, girth
**pragmatiaeth** *nf* pragmatism
**praidd** (**preiddiau**) *nm* flock
**pranc** (**-iau**) *nm* frolic, prank
**prancio** *vb* caper, prance
**pratio** *vb* pat, stroke, caress
**praw, prawf** (**profion**) *nm* test, trial, proof
**preblan** *vb* chatter, babble
**pregeth** (**-au**) *nf* sermon, discourse
**pregethu** *vb* preach
**pregethwr** (**-wyr**) *nm* preacher
**pregethwrol** *adj* preacher-like
**pregowtha** *vb* jabber, rant
**preifat** *adj* private
**preifatrwydd** *nm* privacy
**preimin** *nm* ploughing match
**prelad** (**-iaid**) *nm* prelate
**preladiaeth** *nf* prelacy
**preliwd** (**-au**) *nf* prelude
**premiwm** (**-iymau**) *nm* premium
**pren** (**-nau**) *nm* tree, timber; wood
**prentis** (**-iaid**) *nm* apprentice
**prentisiaeth** *nf* apprenticeship
**prentisio** *vb* apprentice
**prepian** *vb* babble, blab
**pres** *nm* brass; bronze; copper; money
**preseb** (**-au**) *nm* crib, stall
**presennol** *adj, nm* present
**presenoldeb** *nm* presence; attendance
**presenoli** *vb* be present (*reflexive*)
**presgripsiwn** (**-iynau**) *nm* prescription
**preswyl** *nm*, **-fa** (**-feydd**) *nf*, **-fod** *nm* abode, dwelling
**preswylio** *vb* dwell, reside, inhabit
**preswylydd** (**-ion, -wyr**) *nm* dweller, inhabitant
**pric** (**-iau**) *nm* stick, chip
**prid** *adj* dear, costly ♦ *nm* price, value
**pridwerth** *nm* ransom
**pridd** *nm* mould, earth, soil, ground
**priddell** (**-au, -i**) *nf* clod
**priddglai** *nm* loam
**priddlech** (**-au, -i**) *nf* tile
**priddlestr** (**-i**) *nm* earthenware vessel
**priddlyd** *adj* earthy
**pridd(i)o** *vb* earth
**priddyn** *nm* earth, soil, mould
**prif** *adj* prime, principal, chief
**prifardd** (**-feirdd**) *nm* chief bard
**prifathro** (**-athrawon**) *nm* headmaster, principal
**prifddinas** (**-oedd**) *nf* metropolis, capital
**prifiant** *nm* growth
**prifio** *vb* grow
**prifodl** (**-au**) *nf* chief rhyme
**prifysgol** (**-ion**) *nf* university
**priffordd** (**-ffyrdd**) *nf* highway
**prin** *adj* scarce, rare ♦ *adv* scarcely
**prinder, -dra** *nm* scarceness, scarcity
**prinhau** *vb* make or grow scarce, diminish
**print** (**-iau**) *nm* print
**printiedig** *adj* printed
**printio** *vb* print
**printiwr** (**-wyr**) *nm* printer
**priod** *adj* own; proper; married ♦ *n coll* husband or wife
**priodas** (**-au**) *nf* marriage, wedding
**priodasfab** (**-feibion**) *nm* bridegroom
**priodasferch** (**-ed**) *nf* bride
**priodasol** *adj* matrimonial
**priod-ddull** (**-iau**) *nm* idiom
**priodfab** (**-feibion**) *nm* bridegroom
**priodferch** (**-ed**) *nf* bride

**priodi** *vb* marry
**priodol** *adj* proper, appropriate
**priodoldeb** (-au) *nm* propriety
**priodoledd** (-au) *nf* attribute
**priodoli** *vb* attribute
**prior** (-iaid) *nm* prior
**priordy** (-dai) *nm* priory
**pris** (-iau) *nm* price, value
**prisiad, -iant** *nm* valuation
**prisio** *vb* price, value; prize
**prisiwr** (-wyr) *nm* valuer
**problem** (-au) *nm/f* problem
**proc** (-iau) *nm* poke
**procer** (-au, -i) *nm* poker
**procio** *vb* poke; throb
**procsi** *nm* proxy
**prodin** (-au) *nm* protein
**profedig** *adj* approved, tried
**profedigaeth** (-au) *nf* trouble, tribulation
**profedigaethus** *adj* beset with trials
**profi** *vb* prove; taste; try; experience
**profiad** (-au) *nm* experience
**profiadol** *adj* experienced
**profiannaeth** (-au) *nf* probation
**proflen** (-ni) *nf* proof-sheet
**profocio** *vb* provoke, tease
**profoclyd** *adj* provoking, provocative
**profwr** (-wyr) *nm* taster, tester
**proffes** (-au) *nf* profession
**proffesiwn** (-iynau) *nm* profession
**proffesu** *vb* profess
**proffid** *nf* profit
**proffidio** *vb* profit, benefit
**proffidiol** *adj* profitable
**proffwyd** (-i) *nm* prophet
**proffwydes** (-au) *nf* prophetess
**proffwydo** *vb* prophesy
**proffwydol** *adj* prophetic
**proffwydoliaeth** (-au) *nf* prophecy
**project** (-au) *nm* project
**proses** (-au) *nm/f* process
**prosesu** *vb* process
**prosesydd** *nm* processor. **p. geiriau**

word processor
**protest** (-au) *nf* protest
**Protestannaidd** *adj* Protestant
**Protestant** (-aniaid) *nm* Protestant
**protestio** *vb* protest
**protestiwr** (-wyr) *nm* protestor
**prudd** *adj* grave, serious, sad; wise
**pruddaidd** *adj* sad, gloomy, mournful
**prudd-der** *nm* sadness, gloom
**pruddglwyf** *nm* depression, melancholy
**pruddglwyfus** *adj* depressed, melancholy
**pruddhau** *vb* sadden, depress
**Prwsia** *nf* Prussia
**pryd** (-iau) *nm* time; season ♦ (-au) *nm* meal
**pryd** *adv* while, when, since
**pryd** *nm* form, aspect; complexion
**Prydain** *nf* Britain
**Prydeindod** *nm* Britishness
**Prydeinig** *adj* British
**Prydeiniwr** (-wyr) *nm* Britisher
**pryder** (-on) *nm* anxiety, solicitude
**pryderu** *vb* be anxious
**pryderus** *adj* anxious, solicitous
**prydferth** *adj* beautiful, handsome
**prydferthu** *vb* beautify
**prydferthwch** *nm* beauty
**prydles** (-au, -i) *nf* lease
**prydlon** *adj* timely, punctual
**prydlondeb** *nm* punctuality
**prydydd** (-ion) *nm* poet
**prydyddu** *vb* compose poetry, poetize
**pryddest** (-au) *nf* poem in free metre
**pryf** (-ed) *nm* insect; worm; vermin
**pryfedog** *adj* verminous
**pryfleiddiad** (-au) *nm* insecticide
**pryfyn** *nm* worm
**pryn** *adj* bought, purchased
**prynedigaeth** *nf/m* redemption
**prynhawn** (-au) *nm* afternoon

**prynhawnol** *adj* afternoon, evening
**pryniad** *nm* purchase
**prynu** *vb* buy, purchase; redeem
**prynwr (-wyr)** *nm* buyer; redeemer
**prysg** *nm* bush, wood
**prysgwydd** *npl* brushwood
**prysur** *adj* busy, hasty; diligent; serious
**prysurdeb** *nm* haste, hurry; busyness
**prysuro** *vb* hurry, hasten
**publican (-od)** *nm* publican (New Test.)
**pulpud (-au)** *nm* pulpit
**pulsau** *npl* pulses
**pum, pump** *adj* five
**pumawd (-au)** *nm* quintet
**pumed** *adj* fifth
**pumongl (-au)** *nm* pentagon
**punt (punnoedd, punnau)** *nf* pound (money)
**pupur** *nm* pepper
**pur** *adj* pure, sincere ♦ *adv* very, fairly
**purdan** *nm* purgatory
**purdeb** *nm* purity, sincerity
**puredigaeth** *nf* purification
**puredd** *nm* purity, innocence
**purfa (-feydd)** *nf* refinery
**purion** *adj* very well; right enough
**puro** *vb* purify, cleanse
**puror** *nm* harpist
**purwr (-wyr)** *nm* purifier, refiner
**purydd (-ion)** *nm* purist
**putain (-einiaid)** *nf* prostitute
**puteindra** *nm* prostitution
**puteinio** *vb* commit fornication
**puteiniwr (-wyr)** *nm* fornicator
**pw** *excl* pooh
**pwbig** *adj* pubic
**pwdin** *nm* pudding, dessert
**pwdlyd** *adj* sulking
**pwdr** *adj* rotten, corrupt, putrid
**pwdu** *vb* pout, sulk
**pŵer (-au)** *nm* power
**pwerus** *adj* powerful

**pwff (pyffiau)** *nm* puff, blast
**pwffian** *vb* puff
**pŵl** *adj* blunt, obtuse; dull, dim
**pwl (pyliau)** *nm* fit, attack, paroxysm
**pwll (pyllau)** *nm* pit, pool, pond. **p. glo** coal pit. **p. tro** whirlpool
**pwmp (pympiau)** *nm* pump
**pwn (pynnau)** *nm* pack, burden
**pwnc (pynciau)** *nm* point, subject, question
**pwniad (-au)** *nm* nudge, dig
**pwnio** *vb* nudge; beat, thump, wallop
**pwrcas (-au)** *nm* purchase
**pwrcasu** *vb* purchase
**pwrffil** *nm* purfle, train
**pwrpas (-au)** *nm* purpose
**pwrpasol** *adj* suitable
**pwrpasu** *vb* purpose, intend
**pwrs (pyrsau)** *nm* purse, bag; udder; scrotum
**pwt (pytiau)** *nm* anything short; stump
**pwt, -ian** *vb* prod, poke
**pwti** *nm* putty
**pwy** *pron* who
**Pŵyl** *nf* Poland
**pwyll** *nm* sense, discretion
**pwyllgor (-au)** *nm* committee
**pwyllgorwr (-wyr)** *nm* committee-man
**pwyllo** *vb* pause, consider, reflect
**pwyllog** *adj* discreet, prudent, deliberate
**pwynt (-iau)** *nm* point
**pwyntil** *nm* tab, tag; pencil
**pwyntio** *vb* point; fatten
**pwyo** *vb* beat, batter, pound
**pwys (-au, -i)** *nm* weight, burden, pressure; pound (lb.); importance
**pwysau** *nm* weight
**pwysedd** *nm* pressure
**pwysi (-iau)** *nm* posy
**pwysig** *adj* important
**pwysigrwydd** *nm* importance

**pwyslais** (-leisiau) *nm* emphasis
**pwysleisio** *vb* emphasize
**pwyso** *vb* weigh, press; lean, rest; rely
**pwyswr** (-wyr) *nm* weigher
**pwyth** (-au) *nm* stitch. **talu'r p.** requite
**pwytho** *vb* stitch
**pwythwr** (-wyr) *nm* stitcher
**pybyr** *adj* strong, stout, staunch, valiant
**pybyrwch** *nm* stoutness, vigour, valour
**pydew** (-au) *nm* well, pit
**pydredig** *adj* rotten, putrid
**pydredd** *nm* rottenness, putridity, rot
**pydru** *vb* rot, putrefy
**pyg** *nm* pitch, bitumen
**pygddu** *adj* pitch-black
**pygu** *vb* pitch
**pyngad, pyngu** *vb* cluster
**pylni** *nm* bluntness, dullness
**pylor** *nm* dust, powder
**pylu** *vb* blunt, dull
**pyllog** *adj* full of pits
**pyllu** *vb* pit
**pymtheg** *adj, nm* fifteen
**pymthegfed** *adj* fifteenth
**pyncio** *vb* sing, play, make melody
**pynfarch** (-feirch) *nm* pack-horse; mill-race
**pynio** *vb* burden, load
**pys** *npl* (-en *nf*) peas
**pysgod** *npl* (-yn *nm*) fishes, fish. **p. a sglodion** fish and chips
**pysgodfa** (-feydd) *nf* fishery
**pysgota** *vb* fish
**pysgotwr** (-wyr) *nm* fisherman
**pystylad** *vb* stamp with the feet
**pytaten** (-tws) *nf* potato
**pythefnos** (-au) *nm/f* fortnight

## PH

**Pharisead** (-aid) *nm* Pharisee
**Phariseaeth** *nf* Pharisaism
**Phariseaidd** *adj* Pharisaic(al)
**Philistiad** (-iaid) *nm* Philistine
**Philistiaeth** *nf* Philistinism

## R

**rabi** (-niaid) *nm* rabbi
**rabinaidd** *adj* rabbinical
**radio** *nm* radio
**radioleg** *nf* radiology
**radiws** *nm* radius
**ras** (-ys) *nf* race
**rasal, raser** (-elydd, -erydd) *nf* razor
**record** (-iau) *nf/m* record
**recordiad** (-au) *nm* recording
**reiat** *nf* row, riot
**reis** *nm* rice
**reit** *adv* right, very, quite
**ridens** *nf* fringe, nap
**riwl** *nf* ruler
**robin goch** *nm* robin
**robin y gyrrwr** *nm* gadfly
**roced** (-i) *nf* rocket
**România** *nf* Romania
**ruban** (-au) *nm* ribbon
**rŵan** *adv* now
**rwbel** *nm* rubble, rubbish
**rwber** *nm* rubber
**rwdins** *npl* (rwden *nf*) swedes
**Rwsiad** (Rwsiaid) *nm* Russian (citizen)
**Rwsieg** *nm* Russian (language)

## RH

**rhaca** (-nau) *nf*, **-nu** *vb* rake
**rhacs** (rhecsyn *nm*) *npl* rags
**rhad** *adj* free; cheap

**rhad** (-au) *nm* grace, favour, blessing

**rhadlon** *adj* gracious, kind; genial

**rhadlondeb, -rwydd** *nm* graciousness, cheapness

**rhadus** *adj* economical

**rhaeadr** (-au) *nf* cataract, waterfall

**rhaeadru** *vb* pour, gush

**rhaff** (-au) *nf* rope, cord

**rhaffo, -u** *vb* rope

**rhag** *prep* before, against; from; lest ♦ *prefix* pre-, fore-, ante-

**rhagafon** (-ydd) *nf* tributary

**rhagair** (-au) *nm* preface

**rhagarfaethiad** *nm* predestination

**rhagarfaethu** *vb* predestine

**rhagarweiniad** *nm* introduction

**rhagarweiniol** *adj* introductory, preliminary

**rhagarwyddo** *vb* foretoken, portend

**rhagbaratoawl** *adj* preparatory

**rhagbrawf** (-brofion) *nm* foretaste; preliminary test

**rhagdraeth** (-au) *nm* preface, introduction

**rhag-dyb** (-ion) *nm* presupposition

**rhagdybied, -io** *vb* presuppose

**rhagddodiad** (-iaid) *nm* prefix

**rhagddywedyd, rhagddweud** *vb* foretell

**rhagenw** (-au) *nm* pronoun

**rhagenwol** *adj* pronominal

**rhagfarn** (-au) *nf* prejudice

**rhagfarnllyd** *adj* prejudiced

**rhagferf** (-au) *nf* adverb

**rhagflaenor** (-iaid) *nm* forerunner

**rhagflaenu** *vb* precede, anticipate, forestall

**rhagflaenydd** (-ion, -wyr) *nm* predecessor, precursor

**rhagflas** *nm* foretaste

**rhagfur** (-iau) *nm* bulwark

**rhagfyfyrio** *vb* premeditate

**rhagfynegi** *vb* foretell

**Rhagfyr** *nm* December

**rhaglaw** (-iaid, -lofiaid) *nm* prefect, viceroy, governor

**rhaglawiaeth** *nf* prefecture, governorship

**rhaglen** (-ni) *nf* programme

**rhagluniaeth** (-au) *nf* providence

**rhagluniaethol** *adj* providential

**rhaglunio** *vb* predestine, predestinate

**rhagod** *vb* ambush, hinder, waylay

**rhagofnau** *npl* forebodings

**rhagolwg** (-ygon) *nm* prospect, outlook

**rhagor** (-au, -ion) *nm* difference; more

**rhagorfraint** (-freintiau) *nf* privilege

**rhagori** *vb* exceed, excel, surpass

**rhagoriaeth** (-au) *nf* superiority; excellence

**rhagorol** *adj* excellent, splendid

**rhagoroldeb** *nm* excellence

**rhagorsaf** (-oedd) *nf* out-station; outpost

**rhagredegydd** (-ion) *nm* forerunner

**rhagrith** (-ion) *nm* hypocrisy

**rhagrithio** *vb* practise hypocrisy

**rhagrithiol** *adj* hypocritical

**rhagrithiwr** (-wyr) *nm* hypocrite

**rhagrybuddio** *vb* forewarn

**rhagweld** *vb* foresee

**rhagwelediad** *nm* foresight, prescience

**rhagwybod** *vb* foreknow

**rhagwybodaeth** *nf* foreknowledge

**rhagymadrodd** (-ion) *nm* introduction

**rhai** *pron* ones ♦ *adj* some

**rhaib** *nm* rapacity, greed; spell

**rhaid** (rheidiau) *nm* need, necessity

**rhaidd** (rheiddiau) *nf* antler

**rhain** *pron* these

**rhamant** (-au) *nf* romance

**rhamantus** *adj* romantic

**rhan** (-nau) *nf* part, portion; fate

**rhanbarth** (-au) *nm* division,

district

**rhandir** (-oedd) *nm/f* division, district

**rhangymeriad** (-iaid) *nm* participle

**rhaniad** (-au) *nm* division

**rhannu** *vb* divide, share, distribute

**rhannwr** (rhanwyr) *nm* divider, sharer

**rhanrif** *nm* fraction

**rhathell** (-au) *nf* rasp

**rhathiad** *nm* friction, chafing

**rhathu** *vb* rub, rasp, file

**rhaw** (-iau, rhofiau) *nf* spade, shovel

**rhawd** *nf* course, career

**rhawg** *adv* for a long time (to come)

**rhawio, rhofio** *vb* shovel

**rhawn** *coll n* coarse long hair, horse-hair

**rhech** *nf* fart

**rhechain** *vb* fart

**rhedeg** *vb* run; flow

**rhedegfa** (-feydd) *nf* racecourse, race

**rhedegog** *adj* running, flowing

**rhedegydd** (-ion, -wyr) *nm* runner

**rhedfa** *nf* running, course, race

**rhediad** *nm* running, trend; slope

**rhedweli** (-iau) *nf* artery

**rhedyn** *npl* (-en *nf*) fern

**rheffyn** (-nau) *nm* cord; string, rigmarole

**rheg** (-au, -feydd) *nf* curse

**rhegen yr ŷd, rhegen ryg** *nf* corncrake

**rhegi** *vb* curse

**rheglyd** *adj* given to cursing, profane

**rheng** (-au, -oedd) *nf* row, rank

**rheibio** *vb* raven, ravage, ravish

**rheibus** *adj* rapacious, of prey

**rheidiol** *adj* necessary, needful

**rheidrwydd** *nm* necessity, need

**rheidus** *adj* necessitous, needy

**rheilffordd** (-ffyrdd) *nf* railway

**rheini** *pron* those

**rheitheg** *nf* rhetoric

**rheithfarn** (-au) *nf* verdict

**rheithgor** (rheithwyr) *nm* jury

**rheithiwr** (-wyr) *nm* juryman, juror

**rheithor** (-ion, -iad) *nm* rector

**rhelyw** *nm* residue, rest, remainder

**rhemp** *nf* excess; defect

**rhent** (-i) *nm* rent

**rhentu** *vb* rent

**rheol** (-au) *nf* rule, regulation

**rheolaeth** *nf* rule, management, control

**rheolaidd** *adj* regular

**rheoleiddio** *vb* regulate; regularize

**rheoli** *vb* rule, govern, control

**rheolwr** (-wyr) *nm* ruler, controller

**rhes** (-i) *nf* line, stripe; row, rank

**rhesen** (rhesi) *nf* line, parting, streak, stripe

**rhesin** (-au, -ingau) *nm* raisin

**rhesog** *adj* striped; ribbed

**rhestl** (-au) *nf* rack

**rhestr** (-au, -i) *nf* list; row

**rhestru** *vb* list

**rheswm** (-ymau) *nm* reason

**rhesymeg** *nf* logic

**rhesymegol** *adj* logical

**rhesymol** *adj* reasonable, rational

**rhesymoldeb** *nm* reasonableness

**rhesymolwr** (-wyr) *nm* rationalist

**rhesymu** *vb* reason

**rhetoreg, rhethreg** *nf* rhetoric

**rhew** (-oedd, -ogydd) *nm* frost, ice

**rhewfryn** (-iau) *nm* iceberg

**rhewgell** (-oedd) *nf* freezer

**rhewi** *vb* freeze

**rhewllyd** *adj* icy, frosty, frigid

**rhewyn** (-au) *nm* ditch, stream

**rhewynt** (-oedd) *nm* freezing wind

**rhi** *nm* king, lord

**rhiain** (rhianedd) *nf* maiden

**rhialtwch** *nm* pomp; festivity, jollity

**rhibidirês** *nf* rigmarole
**rhibin** *nm* streak
**rhic** (**-iau**) *nm* notch, nick; groove
**rhiciog** *adj* notched; grooved; ribbed
**rhidyll** (**-iau**) *nm* riddle, sieve
**rhidyllio, -u** *vb* riddle, sift
**rhieingerdd** (**-i**) *nf* love-poem
**rhieni** *npl* parents
**rhif** (**-au**) *nm*, **rhifedi** *nm* number
**rhifo** *vb* number, count, reckon
**rhifol** (**-ion**) *nm* numeral
**rhifyddeg, -yddiaeth** *nf* arithmetic
**rhifyddwr** (**-wyr**) *nm* arithmetician
**rhifyn** (**-nau**) *nm* number
**rhigol** (**-au, -ydd**) *nf* rut, groove
**rhigwm** (**-ymau**) *nm* rigmarole; rhyme
**rhigymu** *vb* rhyme, versify
**rhigymwr** (**-wyr**) *nm* rhymester
**rhingyll** (**-iaid**) *nm* sergeant, bailiff
**rhimyn** (**-nau**) *nm* strip, string
**rhin** (**-iau**) *nf* virtue, essence
**rhincian** *vb* creak; gnash
**rhiniog** (**-au**) *nm* threshold
**rhinwedd** (**-au**) *nm/f* virtue
**rhinweddol** *adj* virtuous
**rhip** *nm* strickle
**rhisgl** *nm* bark
**rhith** (**-iau**) *nm* form, guise, appearance, image; foetus
**rhithio** *vb* appear
**rhithyn** *nm* atom, particle, scintilla
**rhiw** (**-iau**) *nf* hill, acclivity
**rhoch** *nf* grunt, groan; deathrattle
**rhochain, -ian** *vb* grunt
**rhod** (**-au**) *nf* wheel, orb; ecliptic
**rhodfa** (**-feydd**) *nf* walk, promenade, avenue
**rhodiad** *nm* walk
**rhodianna** *vb* stroll
**rhodio** *vb* walk, stroll
**rhodres** *nm* ostentation, affectation
**rhodresa** *vb* behave ostentatiously
**rhodresgar** *adj* ostentatious, affected
**rhodreswr** (**-wyr**) *nm* swaggerer

**rhodd** (**-ion**) *nf* gift, present
**rhoddi** *vb* give, bestow, yield; put
**rhoddwr** (**-wyr**) *nm* giver, donor
**rhoi** *vb* give, bestow, yield; put
**rhôl** (**-iau**) *nf*, **rholyn** *nm* roll
**rholbren** (**-ni**) *nm* rolling-pin
**rholio** *vb* roll
**rhombws** (**rhombi**) *nm* rhombus
**rhonc** *adj* rank, stark, out-and-out
**rhos** (**-ydd**) *nf* moor, heath; plain
**rhos** *npl* (**-yn** *nm*) roses
**rhost** *adj* roast, roasted
**rhostio** *vb* roast
**rhosyn** (**-nau**) *nm* rose
**rhuad** (**-au**) *nm* roaring, roar
**rhuadwy** *adj* roaring
**rhuchen** (**rhuchion**) *nf* husk; film, pellicle
**rhudd** *adj* red, crimson
**rhuddell** *nf* rubric
**rhuddem** (**-au**) *nf* ruby
**rhuddin** *nm* heart of timber
**rhuddion** *npl* bran
**rhuddygl** *nm* radish
**Rhufain** *nf* Rome
**Rhufeinaidd** *adj* Roman
**Rhufeiniad** (**-iaid**), **-iwr** (**-wyr**) *nm* Roman
**Rhufeinig** *adj* Roman
**rhugl** *adj* free, fluent, glib
**rhuglen** (**-ni**) *nf* rattle
**rhuglo** *vb* rattle
**rhuo** *vb* roar, bellow, bluster
**rhusio** *vb* start, scare, take fright
**rhuthr** (**-au**) *nm* rush; attack; sally
**rhuthro** *vb* rush; attack, assault
**rhwbio** *vb* rub, chafe
**rhwd** *nm* rust
**rhwng** *prep* between, among
**rhwnc** *nm* snort, snore; death-rattle
**rhwth** *adj* gaping, distended
**rhwyd** (**-au, -i**) *nf* net, snare
**rhwydo** *vb* net, ensnare
**rhwydog** *adj* reticulated, netted
**rhwydwaith** (**-weithiau**) *nm*

network

**rhwydd** *adj* easy, expeditious, prosperous

**rhwyddhau** *vb* facilitate

**rhwyddineb** *nm* ease, facility

**rhwyf** (-au) *nf* oar

**rhwyflong** (-au) *nf* galley

**rhwyfo** *vb* row; sway; toss about

**rhwyfus** *adj* restless

**rhwyfwr** (-wyr) *nm* rower, oarsman

**rhwyg** (-iadau) *nf* rent, rupture; schism

**rhwygo** *vb* rend, tear

**rhwyll** (-au) *nf*, **-yn** *nm* buttonhole, aperture; lattice

**rhwyllwaith** *nm* fretwork, lattice-work

**rhwym** *adj* bound ♦ (-au) *nm* bond, tie; obligation

**rhwymedig** *adj* bound, obliged

**rhwymedigaeth** (-au) *nf* bond, obligation

**rhwymedd** *nm* constipation

**rhwymiad** (-au) *nm* binding

**rhwymo** *vb* bind, tie; constipate

**rhwymwr** (-wyr) *nm* binder

**rhwymyn** (-nau) *nm* band, bond, bandage

**rhwysg** (-au) *nm* sway; pomp

**rhwysgfawr** *adj* pompous, ostentatious

**rhwystr** (-au) *nm* hindrance, obstacle

**rhwystro** *vb* hinder, prevent, obstruct

**rhwystrus** *adj* embarrassed, confused

**rhy** *adv* too

**rhybedio** *vb* rivet

**rhybudd** (-ion) *nm* notice, warning

**rhybuddio** *vb* warn, admonish, caution

**rhybuddiwr** (-wyr) *nm* warner

**rhych** (-au) *nm/f* furrow, rut, groove

**rhychog** *adj* furrowed, seamed

**rhychwant** (-au) *nm* span

**rhychwantu** *vb* span

**rhyd** (-au, -iau) *nf* ford

**rhydio** *vb* ford

**rhydlyd** *adj* rusty

**rhydu** *vb* rust

**rhydd** *adj* free; loose; liberal

**Rhyddfrydiaeth** *nf* Liberalism

**rhyddfrydig** *adj* liberal, generous

**Rhyddfrydol** *adj* liberal (*in politics*)

**Rhyddfrydwr** (-wyr) *nm* Liberal, Radical

**rhyddhad** *nm* liberation, emancipation

**rhyddhau** *vb* free, release, liberate

**rhyddhawr** (-wyr) *nm* liberator

**rhyddiaith** *nf* prose

**rhyddid** *nm* freedom, liberty

**rhyddieithol** *adj* prose, prosaic

**rhyddni** *nm* looseness, diarrhœa

**rhyfedd** *adj* strange, queer, wonderful

**rhyfeddnod** (-au) *nm* note of exclamation

**rhyfeddod** (-au) *nm/f* wonder, marvel

**rhyfeddol** *adj* wonderful, marvellous

**rhyfeddu** *vb* wonder, marvel

**rhyfel** (-oedd) *nm/f* war, warfare

**rhyfela** *vb* wage war, war

**rhyfelgar** *adj* warlike, bellicose

**rhyfelgri** *nm* war-cry, battle-cry

**rhyfelgyrch** (-oedd) *nm* campaign

**rhyfelwr** (-wyr) *nm* warrior

**rhyferthwy** *nm* torrent, inundation

**rhyfon** *npl* currants

**rhyfyg** *nm* presumption, foolhardiness

**rhyfygu** *vb* presume, dare

**rhyfygus** *adj* presumptuous; foolhardy

**rhyg** *nm* rye

**rhyglyddu** *vb* deserve, merit

**rhygnu** *vb* rub, grate, jar; harp

**rhygyngu** *vb* amble; caper; mince

**rhyngu** *vb:* **rh. bodd** please
**rhyngwladol** *adj* international
**rhyndod** *nm* shivering, chill
**rhynion** *npl* grits, groats
**rhynllyd** *adj* shivering, chilly
**rhynnu** *vb* starve with cold
**rhysedd** *nm* abundance, excess
**rhython** *npl* cockles
**rhythu** *vb* gape; stare
**rhyw** *adj* some, certain ♦ (**-iau**) *nf/m* sort; sex
**rhywbeth** *nm* something
**rhywfaint** *nm* some amount
**rhywfodd, rhywsut** *adv* somehow
**rhywiog** *adj* kindly, genial; fine; tender
**rhywiol** *adj* sexual
**rhywle** *adv* somewhere, anywhere
**rhywogaeth** (**-au**) *nf* species, sort, kind
**rhywun** (**rhywrai**) *nm* someone, anyone
**Rwsia** *nf* Russia

# S

**Sabath, -oth** (**-au**) *nm* Sabbath
**Sabothol** *adj* Sabbath, sabbatic(al)
**sacrament** (**-au**) *nm/f* sacrament
**sacramentaidd** *adj* sacramental
**sach** (**-au**) *nf/m* sack
**sachaid** (**-eidiau**) *nf* sackful
**sachlen** *nf,* **sachliain** *nm* sack-cloth
**sachu** *vb* sack, bag
**sad** *adj* firm, steady, solid; sober
**sadio** *vb* firm, steady
**sadistiaeth** *nf* sadism
**sadrwydd** *nm* firmness, steadiness
**Sadwrn** (**-yrnau**) *nm* Saturn; Saturday
**saer** (**seiri**) *nm* wright, mason, carpenter
**saernïaeth** *nf* workmanship, construction
**saernïo** *vb* fashion, construct

**Saesneg** *nf, adj* English
**Saesnes** (**-au**) *nf* Englishwoman
**saets** *nm* sage
**saeth** (**-au**) *nf* arrow, dart
**saethiad** (**-au**) *nm* shooting
**saethu** *vb* shoot, dart; blast
**saethwr** (**-wyr**) *nm* shooter, shot
**saethydd** (**-ion**) *nm* shooter, archer
**saethyddiaeth** *nf* archery
**saethyn** (**-nau**) *nm* projectile
**safadwy** *adj* stable
**safanna** *nm* savannah
**safbwynt** (**-iau**) *nm* standpoint
**safiad** *nm* standing; stature; stand
**safio** *vb* save
**safle** (**-oedd**) *nm* position, station, situation
**safn** (**-au**) *nf* mouth, jaws
**safnrhwth** *adj* open-mouthed, gaping
**safnrhythu** *vb* gape, stare
**safon** (**-au**) *nf* standard, criterion
**safoni** *vb* standardise
**safonol** *adj* standard
**saffir** *nm* sapphire
**saffrwm, saffron** *nm* crocus
**sagrafen** (**-nau**) *nf* sacrament
**sang** (**-au**) *nf* pressure, tread
**sangu, sengi** *vb* tread, trample
**saib** (**seibiau**) *nm* leisure; pause, rest
**saig** (**seigiau**) *nf* meal, dish
**sail** (**seiliau**) *nf* base, foundation
**saim** (**seimiau**) *nf* grease
**sain** (**seiniau**) *nf* sound, tone
**Sais** (**Saeson**) *nm* Saxon, Englishman
**saith** *adj, nm* seven
**sâl** *adj* poor; poorly, ill
**saldra** *nm* poorness; illness
**salm** (**-au**) *nf* psalm
**salmydd** (**-ion**) *nm* psalmist
**salw** *adj* poor, mean, vile; ugly
**salwch** *nm* illness
**Sallwyr** *nm* Psalter
**sampl** (**-au**) *nf* sample

**samplu** *vb* sample
**Sanct** *nm* the Holy One
**sanctaidd** *adj* holy
**sancteiddio** *vb* sanctify, hallow
**sancteiddrwydd** *nm* holiness, sanctity
**sandal** (-au) *nm* sandal
**sant** (saint, seintiau) *nm* saint
**santes** (-au) *nf* female saint
**sarff** (seirff) *nf* serpent
**sarhad** (-au) *nm* insult, disgrace, injury
**sarhau** *vb* insult, affront, injure
**sarhaus** *adj* insulting, offensive, insolent
**sarn** (-au) *nf* causeway ♦ *nm* litter, ruin, destruction
**sarnu** *vb* trample; litter; spoil, ruin
**sarrug** *adj* gruff, surly, morose
**sarugrwydd** *nm* gruffness, surliness
**sasiwn** (-iynau) *nm* C.M. Association
**satan** (-iaid) *nm* satan
**sathredig** *adj* common, vulgar
**sathru** *vb* tread, trample
**Saudi Arabia** *nf* Saudi Arabia
**sawdl** (sodlau) *nm/f* heel
**sawl** *pron* whoso, he that. **Pa s.** how many
**sawr, sawyr** *nm* savour
**sawrio, -u** *vb* savour
**sawrus** *adj* savoury
**saws** *nm* sauce
**sba** (-on) *nm* spa
**Sbaen** *nf* Spain
**sbageti** *nm* spaghetti
**sbaner** (-i) *nf* spanner
**sbâr** (sbarion) *nm* spare; (*pl*) leavings
**sbario** *vb* spare, save
**sbectol** *nf* spectacle(s)
**sbeit** *nf* spite
**sbeitio** *vb* spite
**sbeitlyd** *adj* spiteful
**sbel** (-iau) *nf* spell

**sbon** *adv*: **newydd s.** brand-new
**sbonc** (-iau) *nm* leap, jerk
**sboncen** *nf* squash
**sbort** *nf* sport, fun, game
**sbri** *nm* spree, fun
**sbring** *nm* spring
**sbwylio** *vb* spoil
**sebon** (-au) *nm* soap
**seboni** *vb* soap, lather; soft-soap, flatter
**sebonwr** (-wyr) *nm* flatterer
**sect** (-au) *nf* sect
**sectyddiaeth** *nf* sectarianism
**sectyddol** *adj* sectarian
**sech** *adj* f. of **sych**
**sedd** (-au) *nf* seat, pew
**sef** *conj* that is to say, namely, to wit
**sefnig** *nm* pharynx
**sefydledig** *adj* established
**sefydliad** (-au) *nm* establishment, institution
**sefydlog** *adj* fixed, settled, stationary, stable
**sefydlo(w)grwydd** *nm* stability
**sefydlu** *vb* establish, found, settle
**sefyll** *vb* stand; stop; stay
**sefyllfa** (-oedd) *nf* situation, position
**sefyllian** *vb* stand about, loiter
**sefyllwyr** *npl* bystanders
**segur** *adj* idle
**segura** *vb* idle
**segurdod** *nm* idleness
**segurwr** (-wyr) *nm* idler
**seguryd** *nm* idleness
**seguryn, segurwr** (-wyr) *nm* idler
**sengi** *vb* tread, trample
**sengl** *adj* single
**seiat** (-adau) *nf* fellowship meeting, 'society'
**seibiant** *nm* leisure, respite
**seibio** *vb* pause
**seiciatreg** *nm* psychiatry
**seiciatrydd** *nm* psychiatrist
**seicoleg** *nf* psychology
**seidin** *nm* sidings

**seilio** *vb* ground, found
**seimio** *vb* grease
**seimllyd** *adj* greasy
**seinber** *adj* melodious, euphonious
**seindorf** (**-dyrf**) *nf* band
**seineg** *nf* phonetics
**seinfawr** *adj* loud
**seinfforch** (**-ffyrch**) *nf* tuning-fork
**seinio** *vb* sound, resound; pronounce
**seintio** *vb* saint, canonize
**seintwar** *nf* sanctuary
**seinyddol** *adj* phonetic
**Seisnig** *adj* English
**Seisnigaidd** *adj* English, Anglicized
**Seisnigeiddio, -igo** *vb* Anglicize
**seithblyg** *adj* sevenfold
**seithfed** *adj* seventh
**seithongl** (**-au**) *nf* septangle, heptagon
**seithug** *adj* futile, fruitless, bootless
**sêl** *nf* zeal
**sêl** (**seliau**) *nf* seal
**Seland Newydd** *nf* New Zealand
**seld** (**-au**) *nf* dresser, sideboard, bookcase
**seler** (**-au, -i, -ydd**) *nf* cellar
**selio** *vb* seal
**selni** *nm* illness
**selog** *adj* zealous, ardent
**selsig** (**-od**) *nf* black-pudding, sausage
**semanteg** *nf* semantics
**seml** *adj* f. of **syml**
**sen** (**-nau**) *nf* reproof, rebuke, censure, snub
**senedd** (**-au**) *nf* senate; parliament
**seneddol** *adj* senatorial, parliamentary
**seneddwr** (**-wyr**) *nm* senator
**sennu** *vb* rebuke, censure
**sentimentaleiddiwch** *nm* sentimentality
**sêr** see **seren**

**seraff** (**-iaid**) *nm* seraph
**serch** *conj, prep* although, notwithstanding
**serch** (**-iadau**) *nm* affection, love
**serchog** *adj* affectionate, loving
**serchowgrwydd** *nm* affectionateness, love
**serchu** *vb* love
**serchus** *adj* loving, affectionate, pleasant
**sêr-ddewin** (**-iaid**) *nm* astrologer
**sêr-ddewiniaeth** *nf* astrology
**seremoni** (**-ïau**) *nf* ceremony
**seremonïol** *adj* ceremonial
**seren** (**sêr**) *nf* star; asterisk
**serennog** *adj* starry
**serennu** *vb* sparkle, scintillate
**serfyll** *adj* unsteady
**seri** *nm* causeway, pavement
**serio** *vb* sear
**sero** (**-au**) *nm* zero
**serth** *adj* steep, precipitous; obscene
**serthedd** *nm* ribaldry, obscenity
**serwm** *nm* serum
**seryddiaeth** *nf* astronomy
**seryddol** *adj* astronomical
**seryddwr** (**-wyr**) *nm* astronomer
**sesbin** *nm* shoehorn
**set** (**-iau**) *nf* set
**sêt** (**seti**) *nf* seat, pew. **s. fawr** deacons' pew
**setl** (**-au**) *nf* settle
**setlo** *vb* settle
**sethrydd** (**-ion**) *nm* treader, trampler
**sew** (**-ion**) *nm* juice; pottage; delicacy
**sffêr** *nf* sphere
**sg-** see also **ysg-**
**sgâm** (**sgamiau**) *nf* scheme, dodge
**sgamio** *vb* scheme, dodge
**sgarff** (**-iau**) *nf* scarf
**sgaprwth** *adj* uncouth, rough
**sgil** *nm* pillion. **s. effaith** side effect
**sgiw** *nf* settle. **ar y s.** askew
**sglefren** *nf* slide

**sglefrio** *vb* skate, slide
**sgolor** (-ion) *nm* scholar
**sgôr** *nm* score
**sgrafell** (-i) *nf* scraper
**sgrech y coed** *nf* jay
**sgrechian** *vb* shriek
**sgrîn** (-au) *nf* screen
**sgriw** (-iau) *nf* screw
**sgwâr** (-iau) *nm* square
**sgwyd** (sgydiau) *nf* cataract, waterfall
**sgwrs** (sgyrsiau) *nf* talk, chat, conversation
**sgwrsio** *vb* talk, chat
**si** *nm* whiz, buzz; rumour, murmur
**siaced** (-i) *nf* jacket, coat
**siâd** (sidau) *nf* pate
**sialc** *nm* chalk
**sialens** *nf* challenge
**sialensio** *vb* challenge
**siambr** *nf* chamber
**sianel** (-i, -ydd) *nf* channel
**siant** (-au) *nf* chant
**siâr** *nf* share
**siarad** *vb* talk, speak ♦ *nm* talk
**siaradus** *adj* talkative, garrulous
**siaradwr** (-wyr) *nm* talker, speaker
**siario** *vb* share
**siars** *nf* charge, command
**siarsio** *vb* charge, enjoin, warn
**siart** (-iau) *nm* chart
**siartr** (-au) *nf* charter
**siasbi** *nm* shoehorn
**siawns** *nf* chance
**siawnsio** *vb* chance
**sibrwd** *vb* whisper, murmur ♦ (-ydion) *nm* whisper, murmur
**sicr** *adj* sure, certain; secure
**sicrhau** *vb* assure, affirm, confirm; secure
**sicrwydd** *nm* certainty, assurance
**sidan** (-au) *nm* silk
**sidanaidd** *adj* silky
**sidanbryf** (-ed) *nm* silkworm
**siêd** *nm* escheat, forfeit
**sied** (-au) *nf* shed

**siesbin** *nm* shoehorn
**siew** *nf* show
**siffrwd** *vb* rustle, shuffle
**sigâr** *nf* cigar
**sigaret** (sigaretau) *nf* cigarette
**sigledig** *adj* shaky, rickety, unstable
**siglen** (-nydd) *nf* swing; bog, swamp
**siglo** *vb* shake, quake, rock, swing, wag
**sil** (-od) *nm* spawn, fry
**silff** (-oedd) *nf* shelf
**silwair** *nm* silage
**sill** (-iau), -af (-au) *nf* syllable
**sillafiaeth** *nf* spelling
**sillafu** *vb* spell
**sillgoll** (-au) *nf* apostrophe
**simnai** (-neiau) *nf* chimney
**simsan** *adj* unsteady, tottering, rickety
**simsanu** *vb* totter
**sinach** (-od) *nf* balk, waste ground; skinflint
**sinc** *nm* zinc
**sinema** (sinemâu) *nf* cinema
**sinig** *nm* cynic
**sinigaidd** *adj* cynical
**sinsir** *nm* ginger
**sïo** *vb* hiss, whiz; murmur, purl
**sioe** (-au) *nf* show
**siòl** (-au) *nf* skull, pate
**siôl** (siolau) *nf* shawl
**siom** (-au) *nm* disappointment
**siomedig** *adj* disappointed, disappointing
**siomedigaeth** (-au) *nf* disappointment
**siomi** *vb* disappoint; balk, thwart; deceive
**siomiant** *nm* disappointment
**sionc** *adj* brisk, nimble, agile, active
**sioncio** *vb* brisk
**sioncrwydd** *nm* briskness, agility
**sioncyn y gwair** *nm* grasshopper
**siop** (-au) *nf* shop

**siopwr** (**-wyr**) *nm* shopman, shopkeeper
**sipian** *vb* sip, sup, suck
**siprys** *nm* mixed corn (oats and barley)
**sipsiwn** *npl* gipsies
**sir** (**-oedd**) *nf* shire, county
**siriol** *adj* cheerful, bright, pleasant
**sirioldeb** *nm* cheerfulness
**sirioli** *vb* cheer, brighten
**sirydd, -yf** (**-ion**) *nm* sheriff
**siryddiaeth** *nf* shrievalty
**sisial** *vb* whisper
**siswrn** (**-yrnau**) *nm* scissors
**siwgr** *nm* sugar
**siwmper** (**-i**) *nf* jumper
**siwr, siŵr** *adj* sure, certain
**siwrnai** (**-eiau**) *nf* journey ♦ *adv* once
**siwt** (**-iau**) *nf* suit
**slaf** (**slafiaid**) *nm* slave, drudge
**slei** *adj* sly
**sleifio** *vb* slink
**sleisen** *nf* slice
**slic** *adj* slick
**slotian** *vb* paddle, dabble; tipple
**slumyn** see **ystlum**
**slwt** *nf* slut
**smala** *adj* droll
**smalio** *vb* joke
**sment** *nm* cement
**smocio** *vb* smoke (tobacco)
**smociwr** (**-wyr**) *nm* smoker
**smotyn** (**smotiau**) *nm* spot
**smygu** see **smocio**
**snisin** *nm* snuff
**snwffian** *vb* snuff, sniff; snuffle; whimper
**sobr** *adj* sober, serious
**sobreiddio, sobri** *vb* sober
**sobrwydd** *nm* sobriety, soberness
**socas** (**-au**) *nf* gaiter, legging
**sodomiaeth** *nf* sodomy
**sodr** *nm* solder
**soddi** *vb* submerge
**soeg** *nm* brewers' grains, draff
**sofl** *npl* (**-yn** *nm*) stubble

**sofliar** (**-ieir**) *nf* quail
**sofraniaeth** *nf* sovereignty
**sofren** (**sofrod**) *nf* sovereign (coin)
**solas** *nm* solace, joy
**sol-ffa** *nm*, **solffaeo** *vb* sol-fa
**sôn** *vb, nm* talk, mention, rumour
**soned** (**-au**) *nf* sonnet
**sonedwr** (**-wyr**) *nm* composer of sonnets
**soniarus** *adj* melodious, tuneful; loud
**soriant** *nm* indignation, displeasure
**sorod** *npl* dross, dregs, refuse
**sorri** *vb* chafe, sulk, be displeased
**sosban** (**-nau, -benni**) *nf* saucepan
**sosej** (**-ys**) *nf* sausage
**soser** (**-i**) *nf* saucer
**sosialaeth** *nf* socialism
**sothach** *coll n* refuse, rubbish, trash
**st-** see also **yst-**
**stac** (**-iau**) *nf* stack
**staen** (**-au**) *nm*, **-io** *vb* stain
**stâl** (**-au**) *nf* stall
**stamp** (**-iau**) *nm/f* stamp
**stampio** *vb* stamp
**starts** *nm* starch
**stên** (**stenau**) *nf* pitcher
**stesion** (**-au**) *nf* station
**sticil, -ill** *nf* stile
**stilio** *vb* question
**stiward** (**-iaid**) *nm* steward
**stiwdio** *nf* studio
**stoc** (**-au**) *nf* stock
**stomp** *nf* bungle, mess, muddle
**stompio** *vb* beat, pound; bungle, mess
**stompiwr** (**-wyr**) *nm* bungler
**stori** (**-iau, -iâu, straeon**) *nf* story, tale
**stormus** *adj* stormy
**stor(o)m** (**stormydd**) *nf* storm
**straegar** *adj* gossiping, gossipy
**strancio** *vb* play tricks
**strategaeth** *nf* strategy
**strategol** *adj* strategic
**strategydd** (**-ion**) *nm* strategist

**streik** (**-iau**) *nf* strike
**strwythur** *nm* structure
**stryd** (**-oedd**) *nf* street
**stwc** (**stycau**) *nm* pail, bucket
**stwff** (**styffiau**) *nm* stuff
**stwffio** *vb* stuff, thrust
**stwffwl** (**styffylau**) *nm* post; staple
**styffylydd** (**-ion**) *nm* stapler
**su** *nm* buzz, murmur, hum
**suad** *nm* buzzing, lulling; hum
**sucan** *nm* gruel
**sudd** (**-ion**) *nm* juice, sap
**suddgloch** (**-glychau**) *nf* diving-bell
**suddlong** (**-au**) *nf* submarine
**suddo** *vb* sink, dive; invest (money)
**sug** (**-ion**) *nm* juice, sap
**sugn** *nm* suck; suction; sap
**sugno** *vb* suck, imbibe, absorb
**Sul** (**-iau**) *nm* Sunday
**Sulgwyn** *nm* Whitsunday
**suo** *vb* buzz, hum; lull, hush
**sur** (**-ion**) *adj* sour, acid
**surdoes** *nm* leaven
**surni** *nm* sourness, staleness, tartness
**suro** *vb* sour
**suryn** *nm* acid
**sut** *nm* manner; plight. **pa sut? sut?** how? what sort of?
**swalpio** *vb* flounder, jump, bounce
**swci** *adj* tame, pet
**swcro** *vb* succour
**swcwr** *nm* succour
**swch** (**sychau**) *nf* ploughshare; tip, grimble; lips
**Sweden** *nf* Sweden
**swil** *adj* shy, bashful
**swilder** *nm* shyness, bashfulness
**swllt** (**sylltau**) *nm* shilling
**Swistir: y S.** *nf* Switzerland
**swm** (**symiau**) *nm* sum, bulk
**swmbwl** (**symbylau**) *nm* goad
**swmer** (**-au**) *nm* beam; pack
**swmp** *nm* bulk
**swmpus** *adj* bulky
**swn** *nm* noise, sound

**swnian** *vb* murmur, grumble, nag
**swnio** *vb* sound, pronounce
**swnllyd** *adj* peevish, querulous
**swnt** *nm* sound, strait
**swoleg** *nf* zoology
**swp** (**sypiau**) *nm* mass, heap; cluster
**swper** (**-au**) *nm/f* supper
**swpera, -u** *vb* give or take supper
**swrn** (**syrnau**) *nf* fetlock, ankle ♦ *nm* good number
**swrth** *adj* heavy, sluggish; sullen
**sws** (**-ys**) *nf* kiss
**swta** *adj* abrupt, curt
**swydd** (**-au, -i**) *nf* office; county
**swyddfa** (**-feydd**) *nf* office
**swyddog** (**-ion**) *nm* officer, official
**swyddogaeth** *nf* office, function
**swyddogol** *adj* official
**swyn** (**-ion**) *nm* charm, fascination, spell, magic
**swyngyfaredd** (**-ion**) *nf* sorcery, witchcraft
**swyngyfareddwr** (**-wyr**) *nm* sorcerer
**swyno** *vb* charm, enchant, bewitch
**swynol** *adj* charming, fascinating
**swynwr** (**-wyr**) *nm* magician, wizard
**swynwraig** (**-wragedd**) *nf* sorceress
**sy** see **sydd**
**syber** *adj* sober, decent; clean, tidy
**sych** *adj* dry; *f* **sech**
**sychder** *nm* dryness, drought
**sychdir** (**-oedd**) *nm* dry land
**syched** *nm* thirst
**sychedig** *adj* thirsty, parched, dry
**sychedu** *vb* thirst
**sychin** *nf* drought
**sychlyd** *adj* dry
**sychu** *vb* dry, dry up; wipe dry, wipe
**sychydd** *nm* dryer
**sydyn** *adj* sudden, abrupt
**sydynrwydd** *nm* suddenness

**sydd** *vb* is, are
**syfi** *npl* (**syfien** *nf*) strawberries
**syflyd** *vb* stir, move, budge
**syfrdan** *adj* giddy, dazed, stunned
**syfrdandod** *nm* giddiness, stupor
**syfrdanol** *adj* stunning
**syfrdanu** *vb* daze, bewilder, stupefy, stun
**sylfaen** (**-feini**) *nf* foundation
**sylfaenol** *adj* basic
**sylfaenu** *vb* found
**sylfaenwr** (**-wyr**), **-ydd** (**-ion**) *nm* founder
**sylw** (**-adau**) *nm* notice, attention, remark
**sylwadaeth** *nf* observation
**sylwebaeth** *nf* commentary
**sylwedydd** (**-ion**) *nm* observer
**sylwedd** (**-au**) *nm* substance, reality
**sylweddol** *adj* substantial, real
**sylweddoli** *vb* realize
**sylweddoliad** *nm* realization
**sylwi** *vb* observe, regard, notice
**syllu** *vb* gaze
**symbal** (**-au**) *nm* cymbal
**symbol** *nm* symbol
**symboliaeth** *nf* symbolism
**symbyliad** *nm* stimulus, encouragement
**symbylu** *vb* goad, spur, stimulate
**symbylydd** (**-ion**) *nm* stimulant
**symio** *vb* sum
**syml** *adj* simple; *f* **seml**
**symledd** *nm* simplicity
**symleiddiad** *nm* simplification
**symleiddio** *vb* simplify
**symlrwydd** *nm* simplicity
**symol** *adj* middling, fair
**symud** *vb* move, remove
**symudiad** (**-au**) *nm* movement, removal
**symudol** *adj* moving, movable, mobile
**syn** *adj* amazed; astonishing, surprising
**synagog** (**-au**) *nm* synagogue

**synamon** *nm* cinnamon
**syndod** *nm* marvel, amazement, surprise
**synfyfyrdod** *nm* reverie
**synfyfyrio** *vb* muse
**synhwyro** *vb* sense
**synhwyrol** *adj* sensible
**syniad** (**-au**) *nm* notion, idea, view
**syniadaeth** *nf* conception
**synied, -io** *vb* think, believe, feel
**synnu** *vb* marvel, be amazed, surprise, be surprised
**synnwyr** (**synhwyrau**) *nm* sense
**synwyroldeb** *nm* sensibleness
**synwyrusrwydd** *nm* sensuousness
**sypio** *vb* pack, heap, bundle
**sypyn** (**-nau**) *nm* package, packet
**syr** *nm* sir
**syrcas** *nf* circus
**syrffed** *nm* surfeit
**syrffedu** *vb* surfeit
**Syria** *nf* Syria
**syrthiedig** *adj* fallen
**syrthio** *vb* fall, tumble
**syrthni** *nm* listlessness, sloth; inertia
**system** *nm/f* system
**systematig** *adj* systematic
**syth** *adj* stiff; straight
**sythu** *vb* stiffen, straighten; starve with cold
**sythwelediad** *nm* intuition

# T

**tabernacl** (**-au**) *nm* tabernacle
**tabl** (**-au**) *nm* table
**tablen** *nf* ale, beer
**tabŵ** *nm* taboo
**tabwrdd** (**-yrddau**) *nm* drum
**tabyrddu** *vb* drum, thrum
**taclau** *npl* (**teclyn** *nm*) tackle, gear
**taclo** *vb* tackle
**taclu** *vb* put in order, trim
**taclus** *adj* neat, trim, tidy
**tacluso** *vb* trim, tidy

**taclusrwydd** *nm* tidiness
**Tachwedd** *nm* November
**tacteg** (-au) *nf* tactic
**tad** (-au) *nm* father. **tad-cu** grandfather
**tadmaeth** (-au, -od) *nm* fosterfather
**tadogaeth** *nf* paternity; derivation
**tadogi** *vb* father
**tadol** *adj* fatherly, paternal
**taenelliad** *nm* sprinkling, affusion
**taenellu** *vb* sprinkle
**taenellwr** (-wyr) *nm* sprinkler
**taenu** *vb* spread, expand, stretch
**taenwr** (-wyr) *nm* spreader, disseminator
**taeog** *adj* churlish, blunt ♦ (-au, -ion) *nm* churl
**taeogaidd** *adj* churlish, rude
**taer** *adj* earnest, importunate, urgent
**taerineb, taerni** *nm* earnestness, importunity
**taeru** *vb* insist, maintain; contend, wrangle
**tafarn** (-au) *nf/m* tavern, inn, public-house
**tafarndy** (-dai) *nm* public-house
**tafarnwr** (-wyr) *nm* inn-keeper, publican
**tafell** (-au, -i, tefyll) *nf* slice
**tafl** (-au) *nf* cast; scale. **ffon d.** sling
**tafledigion** *npl* projectiles
**taflegryn** (taflegrau) *nm* missile
**tafleisiaeth** *nf* ventriloquism
**tafleisydd** (-ion, -wyr) *nm* ventriloquist
**taflen** (-nau, -ni) *nf* table, list, leaflet
**taflennu** *vb* tabulate
**tafliad** (-au) *nm* throw; set-back
**taflod** (-ydd) *nf* loft. **t. y genau** palate
**taflodol** *adj* palatal
**taflu** *vb* throw, fling, cast, hurl
**tafluniad** *nm* projection

**taflunio** *vb* project
**taflunydd** *nm* projector
**tafod** (-au) *nm* tongue
**tafodi** *vb* berate, scold
**tafodiaith** (-ieithoedd) *nf* speech, language, dialect
**tafod-leferydd** *nm* speech, utterance, **ar d.** by rote
**tafol** *nf* scales, balance
**tafol** *coll n* dock
**tafoli** *vb* weigh up, assess
**tafotrwg** *adj* foul-mouthed, abusive
**tafotrydd** *adj* garrulous, flippant
**tagell** (-au, tegyll) *nf* gill; wattle; dewlap; double chin
**tagellog** *adj* wattled; doublechinned
**tagfa** (-feydd) *nf* choking, strangling
**tagu** *vb* choke, stifle; strangle
**tangnefedd** *nm/f* peace
**tangnefeddu** *vb* make peace; appease
**tangnefeddus** *adj* peaceable, peaceful
**tangnefeddwr** (-wyr) *nm* peacemaker
**tai** see **tŷ**
**taid** (teidiau) *nm* grandfather
**tail** *nm* dung, manure
**tair** *adj* f. of **tri**
**taith** (teithiau) *nf* journey, voyage, progress
**tal** *adj* tall, high, lofty
**tâl** (talau, taloedd) *nm* end, forehead
**tâl** (taliadau) *nm* pay, payment. **taloedd** rates
**talaith** (-eithiau) *nf* diadem; province, state
**talar** (-au) *nf* headland in field
**talcen** (-nau, -ni) *nm* forehead; gable
**taldra** *nm* tallness, loftiness, stature
**taleb** (-au, -ion) *nf* receipt, voucher
**taledigaeth** *nf* payment,

recompense
**taleithiol** *adj* provincial
**talent** (**-au**) *nf* talent
**talentog** *adj* talented
**talfyriad** (**-au**) *nm* abbreviation, abridgement
**talfyrru** *vb* abbreviate, abridge
**talgryf** *adj* sturdy, robust; impudent
**taliad** (**-au**) *nm* payment
**talm** *nm* space, while; quantity, number. **er ys t.** long ago
**talog** *adj* jaunty
**talp** (**-au, -iau**) *nm* mass, lump
**talpiog** *adj* lumpy
**talu** *vb* pay, render; answer, suit; be worth
**talwr** (**-wyr**) *nm* payer
**talwrn** *nm* threshing floor; poetic contest
**tamaid** (**-eidiau**) *nm* morsel, bit, bite
**tan** *prep* to, till, until, as far; under
**tân** (**tanau**) *nm* fire
**tanbaid** *adj* fiery, hot, fervent; brilliant
**tanbeidrwydd** *nm* fierce heat, ardour
**tanchwa** (**-oedd**) *nf* fire-damp; explosion
**tanddaearol** *adj* underground, subterranean
**tanforol** *adj* submarine
**taniad** *nm* ignition, firing
**tanio** *vb* fire, stoke
**taniwr** (**-wyr**) *nm* firer, fireman, stoker
**tanlinellu** *vb* underline
**tanlwybr** *nm* subway
**tanlli** *adj*: **newydd sbon danlli** brand new
**tanllwyth** (**-i**) *nm* blazing fire
**tanllyd** *adj* fiery
**tannu** *vb* adjust, spread, make (bed)
**tanodd** *adv* below, beneath

**tant** (**tannau**) *nm* chord, string
**tanwent** *nm* fuel
**tanwydd** *coll n* firewood, fuel
**tanysgrifiad** (**-au**) *nm* subscription
**tanysgrifio** *vb* subscribe
**tanysgrifiwr** (**-wyr**) *nm* subscriber
**taradr** (**terydr**) *nm* auger. **t. y coed** woodpecker
**taran** (**-au**) *nf* (peal of) thunder
**taranfollt** (**-au**) *nf* thunderbolt
**taranu** *vb* thunder
**tarddell** *nf* source, spring
**tarddiad** (**-au**) *nm* source, derivation
**tarddle** (**-oedd**) *nm* source
**tarddu** *vb* sprout, spring; derive, be derived
**tarfu** *vb* scare, scatter
**targed** (**-au**) *nm* target
**tarian** (**-au**) *nf* shield
**tario** *vb* tarry
**taro** *vb* strike, smite, hit, knock; tap; stick; hot; suit
**tarren** (**tarenni, -ydd**) *nf* knoll, rock
**tarth** (**-oedd**) *nm* mist, vapour
**tarw** (**teirw**) *nm* bull
**tarwden** *nf* ringworm
**tas** (**teisi**) *nf* rick, stack
**tasel** *nm* tassel
**tasg** (**-au**) *nf* task
**tasgu** *vb* task; start, jump; splash, spirt
**tato, tatws** *npl* (**taten, tatysen** *nf*) potatoes
**taw** *nm* silence. **rhoi t. ar** silence
**taw** *conj* that
**tawch** *nm* vapour, haze, mist, fog
**tawdd** *adj* melted, molten, dissolved
**tawedog** *adj* silent, taciturn
**tawedogrwydd** *nm* taciturnity
**tawel** *adj* calm, quiet, still, tranquil
**tawelu** *vb* calm; grow calm
**tawelwch** *nm* calm, quiet, tranquillity
**tawelydd** *nm* silencer

**tawlbwrdd** nm draughtboard, backgammon
**tawtologiaeth** nf tautology
**te** nm tea
**tebot** (-au) nm teapot
**tebyg** adj similar, like, likely
**tebygol** adj likely, probable
**tebygolrwydd** nm likelihood, probability
**tebygrwydd** nm likeness, resemblance
**tebygu** vb liken, resemble; suppose
**tecáu** vb beautify, adorn, embellish
**teclyn** (**taclau**) nm tool, instrument
**techneg** nf technique ♦ **-ol** adj technical
**teg** adj fair, beautiful, fine
**tegan** (-au) nm plaything, toy, bauble
**tegell** (-au, -i) nm kettle, teakettle
**tegwch** nm fairness, beauty
**tei** nm/f tie
**teiar** nm tyre
**teigr** (-od) nm tiger
**teilchion** npl fragments, atoms, shivers
**teiliwr** (-eilwriaid) nm tailor
**teilo** vb dung, manure
**teilwng** adj worthy; deserved
**teilwra** vb tailor
**teilwres** (-au) nf tailoress
**teilwriaeth** nf tailoring
**teilyngdod** nm worthiness, merit
**teilyngu** vb deserve, merit; deign
**teim** nm thyme
**teimlad** (-au) nm feel, feeling, sensation, emotion ♦ **-ol** adj emotional
**teimladrwydd** nm feelingness, sensibility
**teimladwy** adj feeling; sensitive
**teimlo** vb feel, touch, handle, manipulate
**teimlydd** (-ion) nm feeler, antenna, tentacle
**teios** npl cottages

**teip** (-iau) nm type
**teipiadur** (-ion) nm typewriter
**teipio** vb type
**teipydd** (-ion) nm typist
**teisen** (-nau) nf cake
**teitl** (-au) nm title
**teithi** coll n traits, characteristics, qualities
**teithio** vb travel, journey
**teithiol** adj travelling, itinerant
**teithiwr** (-wyr) nm traveller, passenger
**telathrebiaeth** nf telecommunication
**teledu** nm television ♦ vb televise
**teleffon** (-au) nm telephone
**teler** (-au) nm term, condition
**teligraff** nm telegraph
**telm** (-au) nf snare
**telori** vb warble; quaver
**telyn** (-au) nf harp
**telyneg** (-ion) nf lyric
**telynegol** adj lyrical
**telynegwr** nm lyric poet
**telynor** (-ion) nm harpist
**telynores** nf female harpist
**teml** (-au) nf temple
**tempro** vb temper
**temtasiwn** (-iynau) nm/f temptation
**temtio** vb tempt
**temtiwr** (-wyr) nm tempter
**tenant** (-iaid) nm tenant
**tenantiaeth** nf tenancy
**tenau** adj thin, lean; slender; rarified; sensitive
**tendio** vb tend, mind
**teneuad** nm dilution
**teneuo** vb thin, become thin, dilute
**teneuwch** nm thinness, leanness; tenuity
**tenewyn** (-nau) nm flank
**tenis** nm tennis
**tenlli(f)** nm lining
**tennyn** (**tenynnau**) nm cord, rope, halter
**têr** adj clear, refined, pure, fine

**teras** (**-au**) *nm* terrace

**terfyn** (**-au**) *nm* end, extremity, bound

**terfyniad** (**-au**) *nm* ending, termination

**terfynol** *adj* final; conclusive

**terfynu** *vb* end, terminate, determine

**terfysg** (**-oedd**) *nm* tumult, riot

**terfysgaeth** *nf* terrorism

**terfysgaidd, -lyd** *adj* riotous, turbulent

**terfysgu** *vb* riot, rage, surge

**terfysgwr** (**-wyr**) *nm* rioter, insurgent

**term** (**-au**) *nm* term

**terminoleg** *nf* terminology

**tes** *nm* sunshine, warmth, heat; haze

**tesog** *adj* sunny, hot, close, sultry

**testament** (**-au**) *nm* testament

**testamentwr** (**-wyr**) *nm* testator

**testun** (**-au**) *nm* text, theme, subject

**testunio** *vb* taunt, deride

**tetanws** *nm* tetanus

**teth** (**-au**) *nf* teat

**teulu** (**-oedd**) *nm* family

**teuluaidd** *adj* family, domestic

**tew** *adj* thick, fat, plump

**tewdra, -dwr** *nm* thickness, fatness

**tewhau** *vb* thicken, fatten

**tewi** *vb* keep silence, be silent

**tewychu** *vb* thicken, fatten; condense

**tewychydd** *nm* condenser

**tewyn** (**-ion**) *nm* ember, brand

**teyrn** (**-edd, -oedd**) *nm* monarch, sovereign

**teyrnas** (**-oedd**) *nf* kingdom, realm. **y Deyrnas Gyfunol** the United Kingdom

**teyrnasiad** (**-au**) *nm* reign

**teyrnasu** *vb* reign

**teyrnfradwr** (**-wyr**) *nm* traitor

**teyrnfradwriaeth** *nf* (high) treason

**teyrngar** *adj* loyal

**teyrngarwch** *nm* loyalty

**teyrnged** (**-au**) *nf* tribute

**teyrnwialen** (**-wiail**) *nf* sceptre

**ti** *pron* you *(fam)*

**ticed** (**-i**) *nm/f* ticket

**tician** *vb* tick

**tid** (**-au**) *nf* chain

**tila** *adj* feeble, puny, insignificant

**tîm** (**timau**) *nm* team

**tin** (**-au**) *nf* bottom; rump; tail

**tinc** (**-iadau**) *nm* clang, tinkle

**tincian** *vb* tinkle, chink, clink, clank

**tip** (**-iadau**) *nm* tick (of clock)

**tipian** *vb* tick

**tipyn** (**-nau, tipiau**) *nm* bit

**tir** (**-oedd**) *nm* land, ground, territory

**tirio** *vb* land, ground

**tiriog** *adj* landed

**tiriogaeth** (**-au**) *nf* territory

**tiriogaethol** *adj* territorial

**tirion** *adj* kind, tender, gentle, gracious

**tiriondeb** *nm* kindness, tenderness

**tirlun** (**-iau**) *nm* landscape

**tirol** *adj* relating to land

**tirwedd** *nf* relief (*GEOG*)

**tisian** *vb* sneeze

**titw** *nf* puss, pussy

**tithau** *pron conj* thou (on thy part), thou also

**tiwmor** *nm* tumour

**tiwn** (**-iau**) *nf* tune

**tiwnio** *vb* tune

**tlawd** (**tlodion**) *adj* poor

**tlodaidd** *adj* poorish, mean, dowdy

**tlodi** *vb* impoverish ♦ *nm* poverty

**tlos** *adj* f. of **tlws**

**tloty** (**-ai**) *nm* poorhouse, workhouse

**tlotyn** (**tlodion**) *nm* pauper

**tlws** *adj* pretty; *f* **tlos**

**tlws** (**tlysau**) *nm* jewel, gem; medal

**tlysni** *nm* prettiness
**to** (**toeau**) *nm* roof; generation
**toc** *adv* shortly, presently, soon
**tocio** *vb* clip, dock, prune
**tocyn** (**tociau**) *nm* pack, heap,
  hillock; slice of bread
**tocyn** (**-nau**) *nm* ticket
**tocynnwr** (**-ynwyr**) *nm* bus
  conductor
**toddedig** *adj* molten; melting
**toddi** *vb* melt, dissolve, thaw
**toddiant** (**-nnau**) *nm* solution
**toddion** *npl* dripping
**toddwr** (**-wyr**), **-ydd** (**-ion**) *nm*
  melter
**toes** *nm* dough
**toi** *vb* cover; roof; thatch
**toili** *nm* spectral funeral
**tolach** *vb* fondle
**tolc** (**-iau**) *nm* dent, dinge
**tolchen** (**-au**) *nf* clot
**tolchennu** *vb* clot
**tolcio** *vb* dent, dinge
**tolciog** *adj* dented, dinged
**toll** (**-au**) *nf* toll, custom
**tolli** *vb* take toll
**tom** *nf* dirt, mire, dung
**tomen** (**-nydd**) *nf* heap; dunghill
**tomlyd** *adj* dirty, miry
**ton** (**-nau**) *nf* wave, billow, breaker
**ton** (**-nau**) *nm* lay-land
**tôn** (**tonau**) *nf* tone; tune
**tonc** (**-iau**) *nf* tinkle, ring, clash
**toncio, -ian** *vb* tinkle, ring
**tonfedd** (**-i**) *nf* wavelength
**tonig** (**-iau**) *adj* tonic (*MED*) tonic
  (*MUSIC*)
**tonnen** (**tonennydd, -au**) *nf* skin;
  sward; bog
**tonni** *vb* wave, undulate
**tonnog** *adj* wavy, billowy
**tonyddiaeth** *nf* tone, intonation
**topio** *vb* plug, stop up
**topyn** *nm* plug, stopper
**tor** (**-ion**) *nm* break, interruption
**tor** (**-rau**) *nf* belly; palm (of hand)
**torcalonnus** *adj* heartbreaking

**torch** (**-au**) *nf* wreath; coil
**torchi** *vb* wreathe; coil; roll, tuck
**torchog** *adj* wreathed; coiled
**tordyn** *adj* tight-bellied; hectoring
**toreithiog** *adj* abundant, teeming
**toreth** *nf* abundance
**torf** (**-eydd**) *nf* crowd, multitude
**torfynyglu** *vb* break neck of;
  behead
**torgoch** (**-ion**) *nm* roach
**torgwmwl** *nm* cloudburst
**torheulo** *vb* bask, sunbathe
**tori** (**-ïaid**) *nm* tory
**toriad** (**-au**) *nm* cut, break;
  fraction
**torïaeth** *nf* toryism
**torïaidd** *adj* tory, conservative
**torlan** (**-nau, -lennydd**) *nf* river
  bank
**torllengig** *nm* rupture
**torllwyth** (**-i**), **torraid** *nf* litter
**torogen** (**-ogod**) *nf* tick (in cattle)
**torri** *vb* break, cut; dig; write,
  trace
**torrwr** (**torwyr**) *nm* breaker, cutter
**tors** *nm/f* torch
**torsyth** *adj* swaggering
**torsythu** *vb* strut, swagger
**torth** (**-au**) *nf* loaf
**tost** *adj* severe, sharp, sore; ill
**tost** *nm* toast
**tosturi** (**-aethau**) *nm* compassion,
  pity
**tosturio** *vb* be compassionate, pity
**tosturiol** *adj* compassionate
**tosyn** (**tosau**) *nm* pimple
**töwr** (**towyr**) *nm* tiler
**tra** *adv* over; very ♦ *conj* while,
  whilst
**tra-arglwyddiaeth** (**-au**) *nf*
  tyranny
**tra-arglwyddiaethu** *vb* tyrannize
**tra-awdurdodi** *vb* lord it over,
  domineer
**trabludd** *nm* trouble, tumult,
  turmoil
**trac** (**-iau**) *nm* track

**trachefn** *adv* again

**trachwant** (**-au**) *nm* lust, covetousness

**trachwanta, -tu** *vb* lust, covet

**trachwantus** *adj* covetous

**tradwy** *adv* three days hence

**traddodi** *vb* deliver; commit

**traddodiad** (**-au**) *nm* tradition; delivery

**traddodiadol** *adj* traditional

**traddodwr** (**-wyr**) *nm* deliverer

**traean** *nm* one third, the third part

**traed** see **troed**

**traeth** (**-au**) *nm* strand, shore, beach

**traethawd** (**-odau**) *nm* treatise, essay; tract

**traethell** (**-au**) *nf* strand, sandbank

**traethiad** (**-au**) *nm* predicate

**traethodydd** (**-ion**) *nm* essayist

**traethu** *vb* utter, declare; treat

**trafael** (**-ion**) *nf* travail, trouble

**trafaelio** *vb* travel

**trafaeliwr** (**-wyr**) *nm* traveller

**trafaelu** *vb* travel; travail

**traflyncu** *vb* guzzle, gulp, devour

**trafnidiaeth** *nf* traffic

**trafod** *vb* handle; discuss; transact

**trafodaeth** (**-au**) *nf* discussion, transaction

**trafodion** *npl* transactions

**trafferth** (**-ion**) *nf/m* trouble

**trafferthu** *vb* trouble

**trafferthus** *adj* troublesome; troubled

**tragwyddol** *adj* everlasting, eternal

**tragwyddoldeb** *nm* eternity

**tragywydd** *adj* everlasting, eternal

**traha** *nm* arrogance, presumption

**trahaus** *adj* arrogant, haughty

**trahauster** *nm* arrogance, presumption

**trai** *nm* ebb

**trais** *nm* oppression, force, violence

**trallod** (**-ion, -au**) *nm* trouble, tribulation

**trallodi** *vb* afflict, vex, trouble

**trallodus** *adj* troubled; troublous

**trallodwr** (**-wyr**) *nm* troubler, afflicter

**tramgwydd** (**-iadau**) *nm* stumbling; offence

**tramgwyddo** *vb* stumble; offend; take offence

**tramgwyddus** *adj* scandalous; offensive

**tramor** *adj* foreign

**tramorwr** (**-wyr**) *nm* foreigner

**tramwy, -o** *vb* pass, traverse

**tramwyfa** (**-feydd**) *nf* passage, thoroughfare

**tranc** *nm* end, dissolution, death

**trancedig** *adj* deceased

**trancedigaeth** *nf* death, decease

**trannoeth** *adv* next day ♦ *nm* the morrow

**trapio** *vb* trap

**traphlith** *adv*: **blith d.** higgledy-piggledy

**tras** *nf* kindred, affinity

**traserch** *nm* great love, infatuation

**trasiedi** (**trasiediau**) *nf* tragedy

**traul** (**treuliau**) *nf* wear; cost, expense; digestion

**trawiad** (**-au**) *nm* stroke, beat, flash

**trawiadol** *adj* striking

**traws** *adj* cross; froward, perverse

**trawsblannu** *vb* transplant

**trawsdoriad** *nm* cross-section

**trawsenwad** *nm* metonymy

**trawsfeddiannu** *vb* usurp

**trawsfudo** *vb* transmigrate

**trawsffurfio** *vb* transform

**trawsgludo** *vb* transport, conduct

**trawsgyweiriad** *nm* transposition, modulation

**trawsgyweirio** *vb* transpose, change key

**trawslif** *nm* cross-saw

**trawslythrennu** *vb* transliterate

**traws-sylweddiad** *nm* transubstantiation

**trawst** (-iau) *nm* beam
**trebl** *nm, adj* treble
**treblu** *vb* treble
**trech** *adj* superior, stronger, mightier
**trechu** *vb* overpower, overcome, conquer
**tref** (-i, -ydd) *nf* home; town
**trefedigaeth** (-au) *nf* settlement, colony
**trefgordd** (-au) *nf* township
**treflan** (-nau) *nf* small town, townlet
**trefn** (-au) *nf* order, method, system
**trefniad** (-au) *nm* arrangement, ordering
**trefniant** *nm* arrangement, organization
**trefnlen** (-ni) *nf* schedule
**trefnu** *vb* order, arrange, dispose
**trefnus** *adj* orderly, methodical
**trefnusrwydd** *nm* orderliness
**trefnydd** (-ion) *nm* arranger; Methodist
**trefol** *adj* town, urban
**treftadaeth** *nf* patrimony, inheritance
**trengi** *vb* die, perish, expire
**treial** (-on) *nm* trial
**treiddgar** *adj* penetrating, keen
**treiddgarwch** *nm* penetration, acumen
**treiddio** *vb* pass, penetrate
**treiddiol** *adj* penetrating
**treigl** (-au) *nm* turn, revolution, course
**treigl(i)ad** (-au) *nm* mutation; inflection
**treiglo** *vb* roll; mutate; inflect; decline
**treio** *vb* ebb
**treio** *vb* try
**treisiad** (-iedi) *nf* heifer
**treisio** *vb* force, ravish, violate, oppress, rape
**treisiwr** (-wyr) *nm* violator,

oppressor; rapist
**trem** (-iau) *nf* sight, look, aspect
**tremio** *vb* look, gaze
**trên** (trenau) *nm* train
**trennydd** *adv* day after tomorrow
**tres** (-i) *nf* trace, chain; tress
**tresbasu, tresmasu** *vb* trespass
**tresglen** *nf* thrush
**treth** (-i) *nf* rate, tax, tribute. **t. y pen** community charge, poll tax
**trethadwy** *adj* rateable, taxable
**trethdalwr** (-wyr) *nm* ratepayer
**trethu** *vb* tax, rate, assess
**trethwr** (-wyr) *nm* taxer
**treuliad** *nm* digestion
**treulio** *vb* wear, consume; spend; digest
**tri** *adj, nm* three; *f* **tair**
**triagl** *nm* treacle, balsam, balm
**triawd** (-au) *nm* trio
**triban** (-nau) *nm* triplet (*metre*); Plaid Cymru badge
**tribiwnlys** (-oedd) *nm* tribunal
**tric** (-iau) *nm* trick
**tridiau** *npl* three days
**trigain** *adj, nm* sixty
**trigfa** (-feydd), **-fan** (-nau) *nf* dwelling-place, abode
**trigiannol** *adj* residentiary
**trigiannu** *vb* reside, dwell
**trigiannydd** (-ianwyr) *nm* resident
**trigo** *vb* stay, abide; dwell; die (*animals*)
**trigolion** *npl* inhabitants, dwellers
**trimio** *vb* trim
**trin** (-oedd) *nf* battle
**trin** *vb* handle; treat; dress; till; transact
**trindod** (-au) *nf* trinity
**tringar** *adj* skilful, tender
**triniaeth** (-au) *nf* treatment
**trioedd** *npl* triads
**triongl** (-au) *nm/f* triangle
**trionglog** *adj* triangular
**trist** *adj* sad, sorrowful
**tristáu** *vb* sadden, grieve
**tristwch** *nm* sadness, sorrow

**triw** *adj* loyal, faithful

**tro** (**troeau, troeon**) *nm* turn, twist; conversion

**troad** (**-au**) *nm* bend, turning; figure of speech

**trobwll** (**-byllau**) *nm* whirlpool

**trobwynt** (**-iau**) *nm* turning-point

**trochfa** (**-feydd**) *nf* plunge, immersion

**trochi** *vb* dip, plunge, immerse; soil

**trochion** *npl* lather, suds, foam

**trochioni** *vb* lather, foam

**trochwr** (**-wyr**) *nm* immerser, immersionist

**troed** (**traed**) *nm/f* foot, base; leg; handle

**troedfainc** (**-feinciau**) *nf* footstool

**troedfedd** (**-i**) *nf* foot (=12 inches)

**troëdig** *adj* turned, converted, perverse

**tröedigaeth** (**-au**) *nf* turning, conversion

**troedio** *vb* foot, tread, trudge

**troednodyn** *nm* footnote

**troednoeth** *adj* barefoot, barefooted

**troedwst** *nf* gout

**troell** (**-au**) *nf* wheel, spinning-wheel

**troelli** *vb* spin; twist, wind

**troellog** *adj* winding, tortuous

**troellwr** (**-wyr**) *nm* disc-jockey

**troetffordd** (**-ffyrdd**) *nf* footway, footpath

**trofa** (**-feydd**) *nf* turn; bend, turning

**trofan** (**-nau**) *nf* tropic

**trofannol** *adj* tropical

**trofaus** *adj* perverse

**trofwrdd** (**-fyrddau**) *nm* turntable

**trogen** see **torogen**

**trogylch** (**-au**) *nm* orbit

**troi** *vb* turn, revolve; convert; plough

**trol** (**-iau**) *nf* cart

**trolian, -io** *vb* roll

**troliwr** (**-wyr**) *nm* carter

**trom** *adj* f. of **trwm**

**tros** *prep* over, for, instead of, on behalf of

**trosedd** (**-au**) *nm* transgression, offence, crime

**troseddol** *adj* criminal

**troseddu** *vb* transgress, trespass, offend

**troseddwr** (**-wyr**) *nm* transgressor, trespasser, offender; criminal

**trosgais** (**trosgeisiau**) *nm* converted try

**trosglwyddiad** *nm* transference, transfer

**trosglwyddo** *vb* hand over, transfer

**trosgynnol** *adj* transcendental

**trosi** *vb* turn; translate; convert (a try)

**trosiad** (**-au**) *nm* translation; metaphor; conversion (*rugby*)

**trosodd** *adv* over, beyond

**trosol** (**-ion**) *nm* lever, crow-bar, bar; staff

**trostan** (**-au**) *nf* pole

**trotian** *vb* trot

**trothwy** (**-au**) *nm* threshold

**trowr** (**-wyr**) *nm* ploughman

**trowsus** (**-au**) *nm* trousers

**trowynt** (**-oedd**) *nm* whirlwind, tornado

**truan** (**truain**) *adj* poor, wretched, miserable ♦ (**trueiniaid**) *nm* wretch; *f* **truanes**

**trueni** *nm* wretchedness; misery; pity

**truenus** *adj* wretched, miserable

**trugaredd** (**-au**) *nf/m* mercy, compassion

**trugarhau** *vb* have mercy, take pity

**trugarog** *adj* merciful, compassionate

**trugarowgrwydd** *nm* mercifulness

**trulliad** (**-iaid**) *nm* butler, cupbearer

**trum** (-au, -iau) *nm* ridge

**truth** *nm* flattery; rigmarole

**trwbl** *nm*, **-o** *vb* trouble

**trwch** *nm* thickness. **t. y blewyn** hair's breadth

**trwch** *adj* broken; unfortunate; wicked

**trwchus** *adj* thick

**trwm** (**trymion**) *adj* heavy; *f* **trom**

**trwnc** (**trynciau**) *nm* trunk

**trwodd** *adv* through

**trwsgl** *adj* awkward, clumsy, bungling

**trwsiad** *nm* dress, attire

**trwsiadus** *adj* well-dressed, smart

**trwsio** *vb* dress, trim; mend, repair

**trwsiwr** (**-wyr**) *nm* mender, repairer

**trwst** *nm* noise, din, tumult

**trwstan** *adj* awkward, clumsy, untoward

**trwstaneiddiwch** *nm* awkwardness

**trwy** *prep* through, by, by means of

**trwyadl** *adj* thorough

**trwydded** (**-au**) *nf* leave, licence

**trwyddedu** *vb* license

**trwyn** (**-au**) *nm* nose, snout; point, cape

**trwyno** *vb* nose, nuzzle, sniff

**trwynol** *adj* nasal

**trwynsur** *adj* sour, morose

**trwyth** (**-i**) *nm* decoction, infusion, urine

**trwytho** *vb* steep, saturate, imbue

**trybedd, trybed** *nf* tripod, trivet

**trybelid** *adj* bright, brilliant

**trybestod** *nm* commotion, bustle, fuss

**trybini** *nm* trouble, misfortune, misery

**tryblith** *nm* muddle, chaos

**trychfil** (**-od**) *nm* insect, animalcule

**trychiad** (**-au**) *nm* cutting, fracture, section

**trychineb** (**-au**) *nm/f* disaster, calamity

**trychinebus** *adj* disastrous, calamitous

**trychu** *vb* cut, hew, pierce, lop

**trydan** *nm* electric fluid, electricity

**trydaneg** *nm/f* electrical engineering

**trydaniaeth** *nf* electricity; thrill

**trydanol** *adj* electric, electrical

**trydanu** *vb* electrify

**trydar** *nm, vb* chirp, chatter

**trydydd** *adj* third; *f* **trydedd**

**tryfer** (**-i**) *nf* harpoon, trident

**tryferu** *vb* spear, harpoon

**tryfesur** *nm* diameter

**tryfrith** *adj* speckled; swarming, teeming

**trylediad** (**-au**) *nm* diffusion

**tryledu** *vb* diffuse

**tryloyw** *adj* pellucid, transparent

**tryloywder** *nm* transparency

**trylwyr** *adj* thorough

**trylwyredd** *nm* thoroughness

**trymaidd** *adj* heavy, close, oppressive

**trymder** *nm* heaviness, drowsiness

**trymfryd** *nm* sadness, sorrow

**trymhau** *vb* make or grow heavy

**trymllyd** *adj* heavy, close, oppressive

**tryryw** *adj* thoroughbred

**trysor** (**-au**) *nm* treasure

**trysordy** (**-dai**) *nm* treasurehouse

**trysorfa** (**-feydd**) *nf* treasury, fund

**trysori** *vb* treasure

**trysorlys** *nm* treasury, exchequer

**trysorydd** (**-ion**) *nm* treasurer

**trystio** *vb* make a noise; trust

**trystiog** *adj* noisy, rowdy

**trythyll** *adj* wanton, lascivious

**trythyllwch** *nm* lasciviousness

**trywanu** *vb* transfix, stab, pierce

**trywel** *nm* trowel

**trywydd** (**-au**) *nm* scent, trail

**Tseina** *nf* China
**Tsiecoslofacia** *nf* Czechoslovakia
**tu** *nm* side, part, direction
**tua, tuag** *prep* towards; about
**tuchan** *vb* grumble, groan, murmur
**tudalen** (-nau) *nm/f* page
**tudded** (-i) *nf* covering; pillowcase
**tuedd** (-iadau) *nf* tendency, inclination
**tuedd** (-au) *nm* district, region
**tueddfryd** *nm* inclination, bent
**tueddol** *adj* inclined, apt
**tueddu** *vb* incline, tend, trend
**tufewnol** *adj* inward, internal
**tulath** (-au) *nf* beam, rafter
**Tunisia** *nf* Tunisia
**tunnell** (tunelli) *nf* ton; tun
**turio** *vb* root up, burrow, delve
**turn** *nm* lathe
**turniwr** (-wyr) *nm* turner
**turtur** (-od) *nf* turtle-dove
**tusw** (-au) *nm* wisp, bunch
**tuth** (-iau) *nm* trot
**tuthio** *vb* trot
**twb** (tybiau) *nm* tub
**twca** *nm* tuck-knife
**twffyn** (twffiau) *nm* tuft
**twlc** (tylciau) *nm* sty
**twlcio** *vb* horn, butt, gore
**twlciog** *adj* given to horning
**twll** (tyllau) *nm* hole
**twmpath** (-au) *nm* tump, hillock; bush; folk-dance
**twndis** (-au) *nm* funnel
**twndra** (-âu) *nm* tundra
**twnffed** (-i) *nm* funnel
**twnnel** (twnelau) *nm* tunnel
**twp** *adj* stupid, dull, obtuse
**twpdra** *nm* stupidity
**twpsyn** *nm* stupid person
**tŵr** (tyrau) *nm* tower
**twr** (tyrrau) *nm* heap; group, crowd
**Twrc** (Tyrciaid) *nm* Turk
**Twrci** *nf* Turkey
**twrci** (-îod) *nm* turkey

**twrch** (tyrchod) *nm* hog. **t. daear** mole
**twrf** (tyrfau) *nm* noise; (*pl.*) thunder
**twrnai** (-eiod) *nm* attorney, lawyer
**twrw** *nm* noise (**twrf**)
**twt** *excl* tut!
**twt** *adj* tidy, neat, smart
**twtio** *vb* tidy
**twyll** *nm* deceit, deception, fraud
**twyllo** *vb* deceive, cheat, swindle
**twyllodrus** *adj* deceitful, false
**twyllresymeg** *nf* sophism
**twyllresymiad** (-au) *nm* sophistry
**twyllwr** (-wyr) *nm* deceiver
**twym** *adj* warm, hot, sultry
**twymder, twymdra** *nm* warmness, warmth
**twymgalon** *adj* warm-hearted
**twymo, twymno** *vb* warm, heat
**twymyn** (-au) *nf* fever. **y dwymyn goch** scarlet fever. **y dwymyn doben** mumps
**twyn** (-i) *nm* hill, hillock, knoll; bush
**twysged** *nf* lot, quantity
**tŷ** (tai, teiau) *nm* house
**tyaid** (-eidiau) *nm* houseful
**tyb** (-iau) *nm/f* opinion, notion, surmise
**tybaco** *nm* tobacco
**tybed** *adv* I wonder; is that so?
**tybiaeth** (-au) *nf* supposition
**tybied, tybio** *vb* suppose, think, imagine
**tybiedig** *adj* supposed, putative
**tycio** *vb* prosper, succeed, avail
**tydi** *pron* thou, thyself
**tyddyn** (-nod) *nm* (small) farm, holding
**tyddynnwr** (-ynwyr) *nm* smallholder
**tyfadwy** *adj* growing
**tyfiant** *nm* growth
**tyfu** *vb* grow
**tyfwr** (-wyr) *nm* grower
**tynged** *nf* destiny, fate

**tyngedfennol** *adj* fateful, fatal
**tynghedu** *vb* destine, fate; adjure
**tyngu** *vb* swear, vow
**tyngwr** (-wyr) *nm* swearer
**tylath** see **tulath**
**tyle** *nm* slope, hill
**tylino** *vb* knead. **t. y corff** massage
**tylinwr** (-wyr) *nm* kneader, masseur
**tylwyth** (-au) *nm* household, family. **t. teg** fairies
**tyllog** *adj* holey
**tyllu** *vb* hole, bore, perforate, pierce
**tylluan** (-od) *nf* owl
**tyllwr** (-wyr) *nm* borer
**tymer** (-herau) *nf* temper
**tymestl** (-hestloedd) *nf* tempest, storm
**tymheredd** *nm* temperature
**tymherus** *adj* temperate
**tymhestlog** *adj* tempestuous, stormy
**tymhoraidd** *adj* seasonable
**tymhorol** *adj* temporal
**tymor** (-horau) *nm* season
**tymp** *nm* (appointed) time, season
**tympan** (-au) *nf* drum; timbrel
**tyn** *adj* tight
**tynder, -dra** *nm* tightness, tension
**tyndro** (tyndroeon) *nm* wrench
**tyner** *adj* tender, gentle
**tyneru** *vb* make tender, soften
**tynerwch** *nm* tenderness, gentleness
**tynfa** (-feydd) *nf* draw, attraction
**tynfaen** (-feini) *nm* loadstone, magnet
**tynhau** *vb* tighten, strain
**tynnu** *vb* draw, pull; take off, remove
**tyno** *nm* hollow; tenon
**tyrchu** *vb* root up, burrow
**tyrchwr** (-wyr) *nm* mole-catcher
**tyrfa** (-oedd) *nf* multitude, host, crowd
**tyrfau** *npl* thunder

**tyrfedd** (-au) *nm* turbulence, thunder
**tyrfo, tyrfu** *vb* make a noise or commotion
**tyrpant** *nm* turpentine
**tyrpeg** *nm* turnpike
**tyrru** *vb* heap, amass; crowd together
**tyst** (-ion) *nm* witness
**tysteb** (-au) *nf* testimonial
**tystio** *vb* testify, witness
**tystiolaeth** (-au) *nf* testimony, evidence
**tystiolaethu** *vb* bear witness, testify
**tystlythyr** (-au) *nm* testimonial
**tystysgrif** (-au) *nf* certificate
**tywallt** *vb* pour, shed, spill
**tywalltiad** (-au) *nm* outpouring
**tywarchen** (tywyrch) *nf* sod, turf
**tywel** (-ion) *nm* towel
**tywod** *nm* sand
**tywodfaen** *nm* sandstone
**tywodlyd, -odog** *adj* sandy
**tywodyn** *nm* grain of sand
**tywydd** *nm* weather
**tywyll** *adj* dark, obscure; blind
**tywyllu** *vb* darken, obscure
**tywyllwch** *nm* darkness
**tywyn** (-au) *nm* sea-shore, strand
**tywynnu** *vb* shine
**tywys** *vb* lead, guide
**tywysen** (-nau, tywys) *nf* ear of corn
**tywysog** (-ion) *nm* prince
**tywysogaeth** (-au) *nf* principality
**tywysogaidd** *adj* princely
**tywysoges** (-au) *nf* princess
**tywysydd** (-ion) *nm* leader, guide

# TH

**theatr** (-au) *nf* theatre
**thema** (themâu) *nf* theme
**theorem** (-au) *nf* theorem
**theori** (-iau) *nf* theory

**thermomedr** *nm* thermometer
**thesis** (**-au**) *nm* thesis
**thus** *nm* frankincense

# U

**ubain** *vb* howl, wail, moan; sob
**uchaf** *adj* uppermost, highest
**uchafbwynt** (**-iau**) *nm* climax; zenith
**uchafiaeth** *nf* supremacy; ascendancy
**uchafion** *npl* heights
**uchafrif** (**-au**) *nm* maximum
**uchder** *nm* height; top
**uchel** *adj* high, lofty; uppish; loud
**uchelder** (**-au**) *nm* highness, height
**ucheldir** (**-oedd**) *nm* highland
**uchelfryd** *adj* high-minded
**uchelgais** *nm/f* ambition
**uchelgeisiol** *adj* ambitious
**uchelion** *npl* heights
**uchelradd** *adj* of high degree, superior
**uchelseinydd** (**-ion**) *nm* loudspeaker
**uchelwr** (**-wyr**) *nm* gentleman, nobleman
**uchelwydd** *coll n* mistletoe
**uchgapten** (**-teiniaid**) *nm* major
**uchod** *adv* above
**udo** *vb* howl
**udd** *nm* lord
**ufudd** *adj* obedient, humble
**ufudd-dod** *nm* obedience, humility
**ufuddhau** *vb* obey
**uffern** *nf* hell
**uffernol** *adj* infernal, hellish
**ugain** (**ugeiniau**) *adj*, *nm* twenty, score
**Ulster** *nf* Ulster
**ulw** *coll n* ashes, powder ♦ *adv* utterly
**un** *adj* one, only; same ♦ (**-au**) *coll n* one, unit
**unawd** (**-au**) *nm/f* solo

**unawdydd** (**-wyr**) *nm* soloist
**unben** (**-iaid, unbyn**) *nm* sovereign lord, despot
**unbenaethol** *adj* despotic
**unbennaeth** *nf* sovereignty, despotism
**undeb** (**-au**) *nm* unity, union. **yr U. Sofietaidd** the Soviet Union
**undebaeth** *nf* unionism
**undebol** *adj* united, union
**undebwr** (**-wyr**) *nm* unionist
**undod** (**-au**) *nm* unity; unit
**Undodaidd** *adj* Unitarian
**Undodiaeth** *nf* Unitarianism
**Undodwr** (**-wyr, -iaid**) *nm* Unitarian
**undonedd** *nm* monotony
**undonog** *adj* monotonous
**uned** (**-au**) *nf* unit
**unfan** *nm* same place
**unfarn** *adj* unanimous
**unfryd, -ol** *adj* unanimous
**unfrydedd** *nm* unanimity
**unffurf** *adj* uniform
**unffurfiaeth** *nf* uniformity
**ungell** *adj* monocellular
**uniaith** *adj* monoglot
**uniawn** *adj* straight; right, upright; just
**unig** *adj* sole, only; alone, lonely
**unigedd** *nm* loneliness, solitude
**unigol** *adj* singular; individual ♦ (**-ion**) *nm* individual
**unigoliaeth** *nf*, **-rwydd** *nm* individuality
**unigrwydd** *nm* loneliness, solitude
**union** *adj* straight, direct; just, exact
**uniondeb** *nm* straightness; rectitude
**uniongred** *adj* orthodox
**uniongrededd** *nm/f* orthodoxy
**uniongyrch, -ol** *adj* immediate, direct
**unioni** *vb* straighten; rectify; make for
**unionsgwar** *adj* perpendicular

**unionsyth** *adj* straight, direct; erect
**unllygeidiog** *adj* one-eyed
**unman** *adv* anywhere
**unnos** *adj* of one night
**uno** *vb* join, unit, amalgamate
**unochrog** *adj* unilateral, biased
**unodl** *adj* of the same rhyme
**unol** *adj* united. **yr U. Daleithiau** *npl* the United States
**unoli** *vb* unify
**unoliaeth** *nf* unity, oneness, identity
**unplyg** *adj* of one fold; folio; simple, ingenuous
**unplygrwydd** *nm* sincerity
**unrhyw** *adj* same; any
**unrhywiol** *adj* unisexual
**unsain** *adj* unison. **yn u.** in unison
**unsill** *adj* monosyllabic
**unswydd** *adj* of one purpose
**unwaith** *adv* once
**unwedd** *adj* like ♦ *adv* likewise
**urdd** (-au) *nf* order; rank
**urddas** (-au) *nm* dignity, honour
**urddasol** *adj* dignified, noble
**urddo** *vb* ordain, confer degree or rank
**us** *coll n* chaff
**ust** *excl, nm* hush
**ustus** (-iaid) *nm* justice, magistrate
**usuriaeth** *nf* usury
**utganu** *vb* sound a trumpet
**utganwr** (-wyr) *nm* trumpeter
**utgorn** (-gyrn) *nm* trumpet
**uwch** *adj* higher ♦ *prep* above, over
**uwchbridd** (-oedd) *nm* topsoil
**uwchgapten** (-iaid) *nm* major
**uwchradd** *nm, adj* superior
**uwchsonig** *adj* ultrasonic, supersonic
**uwd** *nm* porridge

# W

**wadi** (-iaũ) *nm* wadi
**wagen** (-ni) *nf* truck, waggon
**waldio** *vb* wallop, beat
**warws** (warysau) *nm* warehouse
**wats** (-iau) *nm* watch
**wedi** *prep* after ♦ *adv* afterwards
**wedyn** *adv* afterwards, then
**weiren** *nf* wire
**weir(i)o** *vb* wire
**weithian, -ion** *adv* now, now at length
**weithiau** *adv* sometimes
**wel** *excl* well
**wele** *excl* behold, lo
**wermod** *nf* wormwood
**wfft** *excl* fie, for shame
**wfftio** *vb* cry fie, flout, scout
**whado** *vb* beat, thrash
**wiced** (-i) *nf* wicket
**wicedwr** (-wyr) *nm* wicket-keeper
**widw** *nf* widow
**Wien** *nf* Vienna
**wlser** (-au) *nm* ulcer
**wmbredd** *nm* abundance
**wraniwm** *nm* uranium
**wrth** *prep* by; with; to; because, since
**wy** (-au) *nm* egg
**wybr** (-au), **wybren** (-nau, -nydd) *nf* sky; cloud
**wybrol** *adj* ethereal
**wyf** *vb* I am
**wygell** (-oedd) *nf* ovary
**wylo** *vb* weep, cry
**wylofain** *vb* wail, weep ♦ *nm* wailing
**wylofus** *adj* wailing, doleful, tearful
**ŵyn** see **oen**
**ŵyna** *vb* lamb
**wyneb** (-au) *nm* face, surface; front
**wyneb-ddalen** *nf* title-page

**wynebgaled** *adj* barefaced, impudent

**wyneblun** (**-iau**) *nm* frontispiece

**wynebu** *vb* face, front

**wynepryd** *nm* countenance

**wynwyn** *npl* onions

**ŵyr** (**wyrion**) *n coll* grandchild, grandson

**wysg** *nm* track. **yn w. ei gefn** backwards

**wystrys** *npl, coll n* oysters

**wyth** (**-au**) *adj, nm* eight

**wythawd** (**-au, -odau**) *nf* octave

**wythblyg** *adj* octavo

**wythfed** *adj* eighth

**wythnos** (**-au**) *nf* week

**wythnosol** (**-ion**) *adj* weekly

**wythnosolyn** (**-olion**) *nm* weekly paper

**wythongl** (**-au**) *nf* octagon

**wythwr** (**-wyr**) *nm* number eight (*rugby*)

# Y

**y, yr, 'r** *adj* the

**y, yr** *preverbal and relative particle*

**ych** (**-en**) *nm* ox

**ychwaith** *adv* (nor) either, neither

**ychwaneg** *nm* more

**ychwanegiad** (**-au**) *nm* addition

**ychwanegol** *adj* additional

**ychwanegu** *vb* add, augment, increase

**ychydig** *adj, adv, nm* little, few

**ŷd** (**ydau**) *nm* corn

**ydlan** (**-nau**) *nf* stack-yard, rickyard

**ydwyf** *vb* I am

**ydys** *vb*: **yr ydys yn disgwyl** it is expected

**ydyw** *vb* is, are

**yfed** *vb* drink; absorb

**yfory** *adv* tomorrow

**yfwr** (**-wyr**) *nm* drinker

**yfflon** *npl* (**yfflyn** *nm*) shivers, pieces, bits ♦ *adj* highly annoyed

**yng** *prep* in (*mutation of* **yn**)

**yngan, -u** *vb* utter, speak

**ynghyd** *adv* together

**ynghylch** *prep* about, concerning

**ynglŷn â** *prep* in connection with

**ym** *prep* in (*mutation of* **yn**)

**ym-** *prefix* (*usu. reflexive or reciprocal*)

**yma** *adv* here, in this place; this

**ymadael, ymadaw** *vb* depart

**ymadawedig** *adj* departed, deceased

**ymadawiad** *nm* departure; decease

**ymadawol** *adj* farewell, valedictory

**ymado** *vb* depart

**ymadrodd** (**-ion**) *nm* speech, saying, expression

**ymadroddus** *adj* eloquent

**ymaddasu** *vb* adjust, adapt

**ymaelodi** *vb* become a member, join

**ymaelyd, ymafael, ymaflyd** *vb* take hold

**ymageru** *vb* evaporate

**ymagor** *vb* open, unfold, expand

**ymagweddiad** (**-au**) *nm* demeanour, attitude

**ymaith** *adv* away, hence

**ymarfer** *vb* practise, exercise ♦ (**-ion**) *nf* practice, exercise

**ymarferiad** (**-au**) *nm* exercise

**ymarhous** *adj* dilatory; long-suffering, patient

**ymaros** *vb* bear with, endure ♦ *nm* long-suffering, patience

**ymarweddiad** *nm* conduct, behaviour

**ymatal** *vb* forbear, refrain, abstain

**ymateb** *vb* answer, respond, correspond

**ymbalfalu** *vb* grope

**ymbaratoi** *vb* get oneself ready

**ymbarél** *nm* umbrella

**ymbelydredd** *nm* radiation

**ymbelydrol** *adj* radioactive
**ymbellhau** *vb* go further away
**ymbil** (**-iau**) *nm* supplication, entreaty
**ymbil, -io** *vb* implore, beseech, entreat
**ymboeni** *vb* take pains
**ymborth** *nm* food, sustenance
**ymbortheg** *nf/m* dietetics
**ymborthi** *vb* feed
**ymbriodi** *vb* marry; intermarry
**ymbwyllo** *vb* pause, reflect
**ymchwelyd** *vb* turn, return; overturn
**ymchwil** *nf* search, research, quest
**ymchwiliad** (**-au**) *nm* investigation
**ymchwydd** (**-iadau**) *nm* swelling, surge
**ymchwyddo** *vb* swell; surge
**ymdaith** *vb* journey, march ♦ (**-deithiau**) *nf* journey, march
**ymdebygu** *vb* grow like; resemble
**ymdeimlad** *nm* feeling, sense
**ymdeimlo** *vb* feel; be conscious of
**ymdeithio** *vb* travel, journey; sojourn
**ymdoddi** *vb* melt, become dissolved
**ymdopi** *vb* manage
**ymdrech** (**-ion**) *nm/f* effort, endeavour, struggle
**ymdrechgar** *adj* striving, energetic
**ymdrechu** *vb* wrestle; strive, endeavour
**ymdrin** *vb* treat, deal with
**ymdriniaeth** *nf* treatment; discussion
**ymdrochi** *vb* bathe
**ymdrochwr** (**-wyr**) *nm* bather
**ymdroi** *vb* linger, loiter, dawdle
**ymdrybaeddu** *vb* wallow
**ymdynghedu** *vb* vow
**ymddangos** *vb* appear, seem
**ymddangosiad** (**-au**) *nm* appearance
**ymddangosiadol** *adj* seeming, apparent
**ymddarostwng** *vb* submit
**ymddarostyngiad** *nm* humiliation, submission
**ymddatod** *vb* dissolve
**ymddeol** *vb* resign, retire
**ymddeoliad** (**-au**) *nm* retirement
**ymddiddan** *vb* talk, converse ♦ (**-ion**) *nm* talk, conversation
**ymddihatru** *vb* divest, undress
**ymddiheuriad** (**-au**) *nm* apology
**ymddiheuro** *vb* apologize
**ymddiosg** *vb* strip, undress
**ymddiried** *vb* trust ♦ *nm* trust, confidence
**ymddiriedaeth** *nf* trust, confidence
**ymddiriedolwr** (**-wyr**) *nm* trustee
**ymddiswyddo** *vb* resign
**ymddwyn** *vb* behave, act
**ymddygiad** (**-au**) *nm* behaviour, conduct; (*pl*) actions
**ymddyrchafu** *vb* exalt oneself; rise, ascend
**ymegnio** *vb* exert oneself
**ymehangu** *vb* become enlarged, expand
**ymennydd** (**ymenyddiau**) *nm* brain
**ymenyn** *nm* butter
**ymerawdwr** (**-wyr**) *nm* emperor
**ymerodraeth** (**-au**) *nf* empire
**ymerodres** (**-au**) *nf* empress
**ymerodrol** *adj* imperial
**ymesgusodi** *vb* excuse oneself, apologize
**ymestyn** *vb* stretch, extend, reach
**ymestyniad** (**-au**) *nm* extension
**ymfalchïo** *vb* pride oneself
**ymfodloni** *vb* acquiesce
**ymfudo** *vb* emigrate
**ymfudwr** (**-wyr**) *nm* emigrant
**ymffrost** *nm* boast
**ymffrostio** *vb* boast, vaunt
**ymffrostiwr** (**-wyr**) *nm* boaster
**ymgadw** *vb* keep oneself (from), forbear
**ymgais** *nm/f* effort, attempt
**ymgasglu** *vb* gather together

**ymgecru** *vb* quarrel, wrangle
**ymgeisio** *vb* try, apply; aim at
**ymgeisydd** (**-wyr**) *nm* applicant, candidate
**ymgeledd** *nm* succour, care
**ymgeleddu** *vb* cherish, succour
**ymgeleddwr** (**-wyr**) *nm* succourer; tutor, guardian
**ymgilio** *vb* retreat, recede
**ymgiprys** *vb, nm* scramble
**ymglymu** *vb* involve, bind together
**ymglywed** *vb* feel (oneself), be inclined
**ymgnawdoliad** *nm* incarnation
**ymgodymu** *vb* wrestle, fight
**ymgofleidio** *vb* mutually embrace
**ymgom** (**-ion**) *nf* chat, conversation
**ymgomio** *vb* chat, converse
**ymgorfforiad** *nm* embodiment
**ymgreinio** *vb* prostrate oneself; grovel
**ymgroesi** *vb* cross oneself; beware
**ymgryfhau** *vb* strengthen oneself, be strong
**ymgrymu** *vb* bow down, stoop
**ymguddfa** *nf* shelter, hiding-place
**ymguddio** *vb* hide (oneself)
**ymgydio** *vb* copulate
**ymgydnabod** *vb* acquaint oneself
**ymgyfathrachu** *vb* have dealings with
**ymgyfeillachu** *vb* associate
**ymgyfoethogi** *vb* get rich
**ymgynghori** *vb* consult, confer
**ymgynghoriad** *nm* consultation
**ymgymeriad** (**-au**) *nm* undertaking
**ymgymryd** *vb* undertake
**ymgynefino** *vb* become familiar, get used to
**ymgynnal** *vb* bear up; support oneself; control oneself
**ymgynnull** *vb* assemble, congregate
**ymgyrch** (**-oedd**) *nm/f* campaign, expedition
**ymgyrraedd** *vb* stretch, strive

after
**ymgysegriad** *nm* devotion, consecration
**ymgysegru** *vb* devote oneself
**ymhél** *vb* meddle
**ymhelaethu** *vb* abound; enlarge
**ymhell** *adv* far, afar
**ymhellach** *adv* further, furthermore
**ymherodr** *etc* see **ymerawdwr**
**ymhlith** *prep* among
**ymhlyg** *adj* implicit
**ymhoelyd** *vb* overturn, topple
**ymhoffi** *vb* take delight; boast
**ymholi** *vb* inquire
**ymholiad** (**-au**) *nm* inquiry
**ymhonni** *vb* lay claim to, pretend
**ymhonnwr** (**-honwyr**) *nm* pretender
**ymhŵedd** *vb* beseech, implore, crave
**ymhyfrydu** *vb* delight (oneself)
**ymiacháu** *vb* become healed, get well
**ymlacio** *vb* relax
**ymladd** *vb* fight ♦ (**-au**) *nm* fighting
**ymlâdd** *vb* kill oneself (with exertion), tire oneself out. **wedi y.** dead beat
**ymladdfa** (**-feydd**) *nf* fight
**ymladdgar** *adj* pugnacious, warlike
**ymladdwr** (**-wyr**) *nm* fighter, combatant
**ymlaen** *adv* on, onward
**ymlafnio** *vb* toil, strive, struggle
**ymlawenhau** *vb* rejoice
**ymledu** *vb* spread, expand
**ymlenwi** *vb* fill oneself
**ymlid** *vb* pursue, chase
**ymlidiwr** (**-wyr**) *nm* pursuer
**ymlonyddu** *vb* grow calm or still
**ymlosgiad** *nm* combustion
**ymlusgiad** (**-iaid**) *nm* reptile
**ymlusgo** *vb* creep, crawl
**ymlwybro** *vb* make one's way
**ymlyniad** *nm* attachment
**ymlynu** *vb* attach, adhere, cleave

(to)

**ymlynwr** (-wyr) *nm* adherent

**Ymneilltuaeth** *nf* Nonconformity

**ymneilltuo** *vb* retire

**Ymneilltuol** *adj* Nonconformist

**Ymneilltuwr** (-wyr) *nm* Nonconformist

**ymnesáu** *vb* approach, draw near

**ymochel, -yd** *vb* shelter; beware

**ymod, -i** *vb* move, stir

**ymofyn** *vb* ask, inquire, seek ♦ (-ion) *nm* inquiry

**ymofynnydd** (-ofynwyr) *nm* inquirer

**ymolchfa** (-feydd) *nf* wash; lavatory

**ymolchi** *vb* wash oneself, bathe

**ymollwng** *vb* sink, drop, give way, collapse

**ymorchestu** *vb* strive, labour

**ymorffwys** *vb* rest, repose

**ymorol** *vb* seek; take care, attend to, see to it

**ymosod** *vb* attack, assail, assault

**ymosodiad** (-au) *nm* attack, assault

**ymosodol** *adj* aggressive, offensive, forward

**ymosodwr** (-wyr) *nm* attacker, assailant

**ymostwng** *vb* stoop; humble oneself; submit

**ymostyngar** *adj* submissive

**ymostyngiad** *nm* submission

**ympryd** (-ion) *nm* fast

**ymprydio** *vb* fast

**ymprydiwr** (-wyr) *nm* faster

**ymrafael** (-ion) *nm* quarrel, contention

**ymrafaelgar** *adj* quarrelsome, contentious

**ymraniad** (-au) *nm* division, schism

**ymrannu** *vb* part, divide, separate

**ymrannwr** (-ranwyr) *nm* separatist

**ymreolaeth** *nf* self-government, Home Rule

**ymrestru** *vb* enlist

**ymresymiad** (-au) *nm* reasoning, argument

**ymresymu** *vb* reason, argue

**ymresymwr** (-wyr) *nm* reasoner

**ymrithio** *vb* appear

**ymroad** *nm* application, devotion

**ymroddedig** *adj* devoted

**ymroddgar** *adj* of great application

**ymroddi, ymroi** *vb* apply or devote oneself; yield or resign oneself, surrender, do one's best

**ymroddiad** *nm* application, devotion

**ymron** *adv* nearly, almost

**ymrous** *adj* assiduous

**ymrwyfo** *vb* struggle, toss about

**ymrwygo** *vb* tear, burst

**ymrwymiad** (-au) *nm* engagement

**ymrwymo** *vb* bind or engage oneself

**ymryson** *vb* contend, strive ♦ (-au) *nm* contention, strife, rivalry

**ymrysongar** *adj* contentious

**ymsefydlu** *vb* establish oneself, settle

**ymsefydlwr** (-wyr) *nm* settler

**ymserchu** *vb* cherish, dote

**ymson** *vb* soliloquize ♦ (-au) *nm* soliloquy

**ymsuddiant** *nm* subsidence

**ymswyno** *vb* cross oneself; beware

**ymsymud** *vb* move

**ymuno** *vb* join, unite

**ymwacâd** *nm* kenosis

**ymwacáu** *vb* empty oneself

**ymwadiad** *nm* denial, abnegation

**ymwadu** *vb* deny (oneself); renounce

**ymwahanu** *vb* part, divide, separate

**ymwahanwr** (-wyr) *nm* separatist

**ymwared** *nm* deliverance

**ymwasgu** *vb* embrace, hug

**ymweithydd** (-ion) *nm* reactor

**ymweld** *vb* visit
**ymweliad** (-au) *nm* visit, visitation
**ymwelwr, -ydd** (-wyr) *nm* visitor, visitant
**ymwrando** *vb* hearken
**ymwroli** *vb* take heart, be of good courage
**ymwrthod** *vb* abstain; renounce
**ymwrthodiad** *nm* abstinence
**ymwthgar** *adj* pushing, obtrusive
**ymwthio** *vb* push oneself, obtrude
**ymwthiol** *adj* obtrusive, intrusive
**ymwybodol** *adj* conscious
**ymwybyddiaeth** *nf* consciousness
**ymwylltio** *vb* fly into a passion
**ymyl** (-au, -on) *nm/f* edge, border, margin
**ymylu** *vb* border
**ymylwe** *nf* selvedge
**ymyrgar** *adj* meddlesome, officious
**ymyrraeth, ymyrru, -yd** *vb* meddle, interfere ♦ *nf* interference
**ymyrrwr** (-yrwyr) *nm* meddler
**ymysg** *prep* among, amid
**ymysgaroedd** *npl* bowels
**ymysgwyd** *vb* bestir oneself
**yn** *prep* in, at, into; for ♦ *also* introduces verb-nouns
**yn** *adj* particle
**yna** *adv* there; then; thereupon; that
**ynad** (-on) *nm* judge, justice, magistrate
**yn awr** *adv* now, at present
**yndeintiad** (-au) *nm* indentation
**ynfyd** (-ion) *adj* foolish, rash
**ynfydrwydd** *nm* foolishness, folly
**ynfydu** *vb* rave, be mad
**ynfytyn** (-fydion) *nm* fool, madman
**ynni** *nm* energy, vigour
**yno** *adv* there
**yntau** *pron conj* he (on his part), he also
**ynteu, ynte** *conj* or, or else, otherwise; then
**Ynyd** *nm* Shrovetide

**ynys** (-oedd) *nf* island, river meadow
**ynysfor** (-oedd) *nm* archipelago
**Ynysoedd Dedwydd**: yr Y. *npl* the Canary Islands
**ynysol** *adj* island, insular
**ynyswr** (-wyr) *nm* islander
**ynysydd** (-ion) *nm* insulator
**yr** see y
**yrhawg** *adv* for a long time (to come)
**yrŵan** *adv* now (N.W.)
**ys** *vb* it is ♦ *conj* as
**ysbaddu** *vb* castrate
**ysbaid** (-beidiau) *nm/f* space (of time)
**ysbail** (-beiliau) *nf* spoil, plunder
**ysbardun** *nm/f* spur
**ysbarduno** *vb* spur
**ysbeidiol** *adj* occasional, intermittent
**ysbeilio** *vb* spoil, plunder
**ysbeiliwr** (-wyr) *nm* spoiler, robber
**ysbienddrych** (-au) *nm* spying-glass
**ysbïo** *vb* spy, look
**ysbïwr** (-wyr) *nm* spy
**ysblander** *nm* splendour
**ysblennydd** *adj* splendid
**ysbonc** (-iau) *nf* jump, bound; spurt
**ysboncio** *vb* jump, bounce; spurt, splash
**ysborion** *npl* cast-offs
**ysbrigyn** *nm* sprig, twig
**ysbryd** (-ion, -oedd) *nm* spirit, ghost
**ysbrydegaeth** *nf* spiritualism
**ysbrydegol** *adj* spiritualistic
**ysbrydegydd** (-ion) *nm* spiritualist
**ysbrydiaeth** *nf* encouragement, inspiration
**ysbrydol** *adj* spiritual; high-spirited
**ysbrydoli** *vb* spiritualize; inspire; inspirit

**ysbrydoliaeth** *nf* inspiration
**ysbwng** *nm* sponge
**ysbwrial, -iel** *nm* rubbish, refuse
**ysbwylio** *vb* spoil
**ysbyty** (**-tai**) *nm* hospital; hospice
**ysfa** (**-feydd**) *nf* itching; hankering
**ysg-** see **sg-**
**ysgadan** *npl* (**-enyn** *nm*) herrings
**ysgafala** *adj* secure, careless, free
**ysgafn** *adj* light ♦ *nm* stack
**ysgafnder** *nm* lightness, levity
**ysgafnhau, ysgafnu** *vb* lighten
**ysgafnu** *vb* heap, pile
**ysgall** *npl* (**-en** *nf*) thistles
**ysgariad** *nm*, **-iaeth** *nf* separation, divorce
**ysgarlad** *nm* scarlet
**ysgarmes** (**-oedd, -au**) *nf* skirmish
**ysgaru** *vb* part, separate, divorce
**ysgatfydd** *adv* perhaps, peradventure
**ysgathru** *vb* spread, scatter
**ysgaw** *coll n* (**-en** *nf*) elder
**ysgeler** *adj* wicked, villainous, infamous
**ysgerbwd** (**-bydau**) *nm* skeleton, carcase
**ysgithr** (**-edd**) *nm* tusk, fang
**ysgithrog** *adj* fanged, tusked; craggy, rugged
**ysgiw** (**-ion**) *nf* settle
**ysglefrio** *vb* slide (on ice); skate
**ysglyfaeth** (**-au**) *nf* prey, spoil; carrion, filth
**ysglyfaethus** *adj* of prey; rapacious
**ysgogi** *vb* move, stir
**ysgogiad** (**-au**) *nm* movement, motion
**ysgol** (**-ion**) *nf* school; schooling
**ysgol** (**-ion**) *nf* ladder
**ysgoldy** (**-dai**) *nm* schoolhouse, schoolroom
**ysgolfeistr** (**-i, -iaid**) *nm* schoolmaster
**ysgolfeistres** (**-i**) *nf* schoolmistress
**ysgolhaig** (**-heigion**) *nm* scholar

**ysgolheictod** *nm* scholarship
**ysgolheigaidd** *adj* scholarly
**ysgolor** (**-ion**) *nm* scholar
**ysgoloriaeth** (**-au**) *nf* scholarship
**ysgorpion** (**-au**) *nm* scorpion
**Ysgotyn** (**-gotiaid**) *nm* Scot, Scotsman
**ysgrafell** (**-od, -i**) *nf* scraper; curry-comb
**ysgrafellu** *vb* scrape, curry
**ysgraff** (**-au**) *nf* boat, barge, ferry-boat
**ysgraffinio** *vb* scarify, graze, abrade
**ysgrech** (**-feydd**) *nf* scream, shriek
**ysgrechian, -in** *vb* scream, shriek
**ysgrepan** (**-au**) *nf* wallet, scrip
**ysgrif** (**-au**) *nf* writing, article, essay
**ysgrifbin** (**-nau**) *nm*, **-grifell** (**-au**) *nf* pen
**ysgrifen, -eniad** (**-iadau**) *nf* writing
**ysgrifennu** *vb* write
**ysgrifennwyr** (**-enwyr**) *nm* writer
**ysgrifennydd** (**-enyddion**) *nm* scribe, secretary
**ysgrifenyddiaeth** *nf* secretaryship
**ysgriw** (**-iau**) *nf* screw
**ysgriwio** *vb* screw
**ysgrwbio** *vb* scrub
**ysgryd** *nm* shiver
**ysgrythur** (**-au**) *nf* scripture
**ysgrythurol** *adj* scriptural
**ysgrythurwr** (**-wyr**) *nm* scripturist
**ysgub** (**-au**) *nf* sheaf; broom
**ysgubo** *vb* sweep
**ysgubol** *adj* sweeping
**ysgubor** (**-iau**) *nf* barn, granary
**ysgubwr** (**-wyr**) *nm* sweeper, sweep
**ysgutor** (**-ion**) *nm* executor
**ysguthan** (**-od**) *nf* wood-pigeon; jade
**ysgwâr** *adj*, *nf* square
**ysgwario** *vb* square
**ysgŵd** *nm* jerk, toss, fling, shove

**ysgwïer** (-iaid) *nm* squire
**ysgwrfa** *nf* scouring, lathering
**ysgwrio** *vb* scour, scrub; lather
**ysgwyd** *vb* shake; flutter; wag
**ysgwydd** (-au) *nf* shoulder
**ysgwyddo** *vb* shoulder, jostle
**ysgydwad** *nm* shaking, shake
**ysgyfaint** *npl* lungs, lights
**ysgyfarnog** (-od) *nf* hare
**ysgymun** *adj* excommunicate, accursed
**ysgymundod** *nm* excommunication, ban
**ysgymuno** *vb* excommunicate
**ysgyrion** *npl* staves, splinters, shivers
**ysgyrnygu** *vb* grind the teeth, snarl
**ysgytiad** (-au) *nm* shock
**ysgytio** *vb* shake violently, shock
**ysgythru** *vb* cut, carve; prune
**ysictod** *nm* contusion; sprain
**ysig** *adj* bruised, sore, sprained
**ysigo** *vb* bruise, crush; sprain
**yslotian** *vb* dabble, tipple
**ysmala** *adj* droll, funny, amusing
**ysmaldod** *nm* fun, drollery
**ysmalio** *vb* joke, jest
**ysmaliwr** (-wyr) *nm* joker, wit
**ysmotyn** (ysmotiau) *nm* spot
**ysmwddio** *vb* iron
**ysmygu** *vb* smoke (tobacco)
**ysmygwr** (-wyr) *nm* smoker
**ysol** *adj* consuming, devouring; corrosive
**yst-** see also **st-**
**ystabl** (-au) *nf* stable
**ystad** (-au) *nf* state; estate; furlong
**ystadegau** *npl* statistics
**ystadegol** *adj* statistical
**ystadegydd** (-ion) *nm* statistician
**ystafell** (-oedd) *nf* chamber, room
**ystalwyn** (-i) *nm* stallion
**ystanc** (-iau) *nm* stake, bracket
**ystarn** (-au) *nf* stern
**ystelcian** *vb* skulk, loaf, loiter

**ystelciwr** (-wyr) *nm* loafer, loiterer
**ystên** (-enau) *nf* pitcher, ewer, milk-can
**ystinos** *nm* asbestos
**ystiwart** (-wardiaid) *nm* steward
**ystlum** (-od) *nm* bat
**ystlys** (-au) *nf* side, flank
**ystlyswr** (-wyr) *nm* linesman
**ystod** (-ion) *nf* course; swath. **Yn y.** during
**ystof** *nm/f* warp
**ystofi** *vb* warp; weave, plan
**ystôl** (-olion) *nf* stool, chair
**ystôr** (-orau) *nm* store, abundance
**ystordy** (-dai) *nm* storehouse, warehouse
**ystorfa** (-feydd) *nf* store, storehouse
**ystorio** *vb* store
**ystorïwr** (-ïwyr) *nm* storyteller
**ystorm** (-ydd) *nf* storm
**ystormus** *adj* stormy
**ystrad** (-au) *nm/f* vale, flat
**ystranc** (-iau) *nf* trick
**ystrancio** *vb* play tricks; jib
**ystrodur** (-iau) *nf* cart-saddle
**ystryd** (ystrydoedd) *nf* street
**ystrydebol** *adj* stereotyped
**ystryw** (-iau) *nf* wile, craft, ruse
**ystrywgar** *adj* wily, crafty
**ystum** (-iau) *nm/f* bend; form; posture; (*pl*) grimaces
**ystumio** *vb* bend, distort; pose
**ystumog** (-au) *nf* stomach
**ystŵr** *nm* stir, noise, bustle, fuss
**Ystwyll** *nm* Epiphany
**ystwyrian** *vb* stretch and yawn, stir
**ystwyth** *adj* flexible, pliant, supple
**ystwythder** *nm* flexibility, pliancy
**ystwytho** *vb* make flexible; bend, soften
**ystyfnig** *adj* obstinate, stubborn
**ystyfnigo** *vb* behave obstinately
**ystyfnigrwydd** *nm* obstinacy
**ystyr** (-on) *nf/m* sense, meaning

**ystyrgar** *adj* thoughtful, meditative
**ystyriaeth** (**-au**) *nf* consideration, heed
**ystyried** *vb* consider, regard, heed
**ystyriol** *adj* mindful, heedful
**ysu** *vb* eat, consume; hanker; itch
**yswain** (**-weiniaid**) *nm* esquire

**yswil** *adj* shy, bashful, timid
**yswildod** *nm* shyness, bashfulness
**yswiriant** *nm* insurance
**yswirio** *vb* insure
**yswaeth** *adv* more's the pity
**yw** *vb* is, are
**yw** *npl, coll n* (**-en** *nf*) yew

# ENWAU PERSONAU  PERSONAL NAMES

**Adda** Adam
**Anghrist** Antichrist
**Andreas** Andrew
**Awstin** Augustine
**Bartholomeus** Bartholomew
**Beda** Bede
**Bedwyr** Bedivere
**Beti, Betsan, Betsi** Betty, Betsy
**Buddug** Boadicea; Victoria
**Bwda** Buddha
**Cadi** Catherine, Kate
**Cadog, Catwg** Cadoc
**Cai** Kay
**Caradog** Caratacos, Caractacus
**Caswallon** Cassivellaunus
**Catrin** Catherine
**Cesar** Caesar
**Crist** Christ
**Cystennin** Constantine
**Dafydd, Dewi** David
**Edmwnt, Emwnt** Edmund
**Efa** Eve
**Elen** Helen, Ellen
**Eleias** Elijah, Elias
**Eliseus** Elisha, Eliseus
**Emrys** Ambrose
**Ercwlff** Hercules
**Eseia, Esay** Isaiah
**Esyllt** Iseult
**Fychan** Vaughan
**Fyrsil, Fferyll** Virgil
**Ffowc** Foulkes
**Ffraid** Bride, Bridget
**Garmon** Germanus
**Geraint** Gerontius
**Gerallt** Gerald
**Glyndŵr** Glendower
**Gruffudd, Gruffydd** Griffith
**Gwallter** Walter
**Gwener** Venus
**Gwenffrewi, Gwenfrewi** Winifred
**Gwenhwyfar** Guinevere
**Gwilym** William

**Gwladus** Gladys
**Gwrtheyrn** Vortigern
**Harri** Harry, Henry
**Horas** Horace
**Hors** Horsa
**Hu, Huw** Hugh
**Iago** James
**Iau** Jove, Jupiter
**Iesu Grist** Jesus Christ
**Ieuan** Evan
**Ioan** John
**Iorwerth** Edward
**Iwan** John
**Lowri** Laura
**Luc** Luke
**Lleucu** Lucy
**Llwyd** Lloyd
**Llŷr** Lear
**Mabli** Mabel
**Mair** Mary
**Mali** Molly
**Mallt** Maud, Matilda
**Marc** Mark
**Marged, Margred** Margaret
**Mari** Mary
**Mawrth** Mars
**Mercher** Mercury
**Mererid** Margaret
**Meurig** Morris
**Mihangel** Michael
**Modlen, Magdalen** Magdalene
**Myrddin** Merlin
**Neifion** Neptune
**Ofydd** Ovid
**Oswallt** Oswald
**Owain** Owen
**Padrig** Patrick
**Pedr** Peter
**Peredur** Perceval
**Prys** Price, Preece
**Puw** Pugh
**Pyrs** Pierce
**Rheinallt** Reginald

**Rhisiart** Richard
**Rhobert** Robert
**Rhonwen** Rowena
**Rhydderch** Roderick
**Rhys** Rees, Rice
**Sadwrn** Saturn
**Sebedeus** Zebedee
**Selyf** Solomon
**Siân** Jane
**Siarl** Charles
**Siarlymaen** Charlemagne

**Sieffre** Geoffrey
**Siencyn** Jenkin
**Siôn** John
**Sioned** Janet
**Siôr, Siors** George
**Steffan** Stephen
**Timotheus** Timothy
**Tomos** Thomas
**Tudur** Tudor
**Twm** Tom
**Wmffre** Humphrey

# ENWAU LLEOEDD  PLACE NAMES

**Aberdâr** Aberdare
**Aberdaugleddyf** Milford Haven
**Aberddawan** Aberthaw
**Abergwaun** Fishguard
**Aberhonddu** Brecon
**Abermo, Bermo** Barmouth
**Aberpennar** Mountain Ash
**Abertawe** Swansea
**Aberteifi** Cardigan
**Afon Menai** Menai Straits
**Amwythig** Shrewsbury
**Arberth** Narberth
**Babilon** Babylon
**Breudeth** Brawdy
**Brycheiniog** Brecknock
**Brynbuga** Usk
**Bryste, Caerodor** Bristol
**Caer** Chester
**Caerdroea** Troy
**Caerdydd** Cardiff
**Caerefrog** York
**Caerfaddon** Bath
**Caerfyrddin** Carmarthen
**Caergaint** Canterbury
**Caergrawnt** Cambridge
**Caergybi** Holyhead
**Caergystennin** Constantinople
**Caerhirfryn** Lancaster, Lancashire
**Caerliwelydd** Carlisle
**Caerloyw** Gloucester
**Caerlŷr** Leicester(shire)
**Caerllion** Caerleon
**Caernarfon** Caernarvon
**Caersallog** Salisbury
**Caerwrangon** Worcester
**Caer-wynt** Winchester
**Caer-Wysg** Exeter
**Caint** Kent
**Calfaria** Calvary
**Casllwchwr** Loughor
**Cas-mael** Puncheston
**Casnewydd** Newport, Mon.
**Castell-Nedd** Neath

**Castellnewydd** Newcastle
**Ceinewydd** New Quay
**Ceredigion** Cardiganshire
**Cernyw** Cornwall
**Clawdd Offa** Offa's Dyke
**Clwydd** North East Wales
**Coed-duon** Blackwood
**Conwy** Conway
**Côr y Cewri** Stonehenge
**Croesoswallt** Oswestry
**Crucywel** Crickhowell
**Cydweli** Kidwelly
**Dinas Basing** Basingwerk
**Dinbych** Denbigh
**Dinbych-y-pysgod** Tenby
**Donaw** Danube
**Drenewydd** Newtown
**Dyfed** Demetia, South West Wales
**Dyfnaint** Devon
**Dyfrdwy** Dee
**Efrog** York
**Eryri** Snowdonia
**Fflandrys** Flanders
**Fflint** Flint
**Gâl** Gaul
**Glynebwy** Ebbw Vale
**Gwent** South East Wales
**Gwlad-yr-haf** Somerset
**Gwy** Wye
**Gwynedd** North West Wales
**Gŵyr** Gower
**Hafren** Severn
**Hendy-gwyn** Whitland
**Henffordd** Hereford
**Hwlffordd** Haverfordwest
**Iâl** Yale
**Lacharn, Talacharn** Laugharne
**Lerpwl** Liverpool
**Llanandras** Presteigne
**Llanbedr Pont Steffan** Lampeter
**Llandaf** Landaff
**Llandudoch** St Dogmaels
**Llaneirwg** St Mellons

**Llanelwy** St Asaph
**Llaneurgain** Northop
**Llanfair-ym-Muallt** Builth
**Llangatwg** Cadoxton
**Llangrallo** Coychurch
**Llanilltud Fawr** Llantwit Major
**Llanllieni** Leominster
**Llansawel** Briton Ferry
**Llanymddyfri** Llandovery
**Llwydlo** Ludlow
**Llyn Tegid** Bala Lake
**Maesyfed** Radnor
**Manaw** Isle of Man
**Manceinion** Manchester
**Meirionnydd** Merioneth
**Môn** Anglesey
**Morgannwg** Glamorgan
**Mynwy** Monmouth
**Mynyw** St David's
**Nanhyfer, Nyfer** Nevern
**Pennarlâg** Hawarden
**Pen-y-Fantach** Mumbles Head
**Penbedw** Birkenhead
**Pen-bre** Pembrey
**Penfro** Pembroke
**Penrhyn Gobaith Da** Cape of
  Good Hope
**Pen-y-bont ar Ogwr** Bridgend
**Pontarfynach** Devil's Bridge
**Pont-y-pŵl** Pontypool
**Porthaethwy** Menai Bridge
**Porthmadog** Portmadoc
**Powys** Mid Wales
**Rhuthun** Ruthin
**Rhydychen** Oxford
**Sain Ffagan** St Fagans
**Sili** Sully
**Solfach** Solva
**Tafwys** Thames

**Treamlod** Ambleston
**Trecelyn** Newbridge
**Trefaldwyn** Montgomery
**Trefdraeth** Newport, Pem
**Treforus** Morriston
**Trefyclo** Knighton
**Trefynwy** Monmouth
**Treffynnon** Holywell
**Tyddewi** St David's
**Tywi** Towy
**Wdig** Goodwick
**Wrecsam** Wrexham
**Wysg** the Usk
**Y Bont-faen** Cowbridge
**Y Fenni** Abergavenny
**Y Gelli (Gandryll)** Hay
**Y Gogarth** Great Orme
**Y Mot** New Moat
**Y Rhws** Rhoose
**Y Waun** Chirk
**Ynys Bŷr** Caldey Island
**Ynys Dewi** Ramsey Island
**Ynys Echni** Flat Holm
**Ynys Enlli** Bardsey Island
**Ynys Gybi** Holy Island
**Ynys Lawd** South Stack
**Ynys Seiriol** Puffin Island
**Ynysoedd Erch** Orkney Islands
**Ynysoedd Heledd** The Hebrides
**Ynysoedd y Moelrhoniaid** The
  Skerries
**Ynys y Garn** Guernsey
**Ynys Wyth** Isle of Wight
**Yr Wyddfa** Snowdon
**Yr Wyddgrug** Mold
**Ystrad-fflur** Strata Florida
**Ystrad Marchell** Strata Marcella
**Ystumllwynarth** Oystermouth
**Y Trallwng** Welshpool

# ENGLISH-WELSH DICTIONARY

## A

**a, an** *adj*: **a man** dyn. **an ass** asyn
**aback** *adv* yn ôl. **taken a.** wedi synnu
**abandon** *vt* rhoi'r gorau i, gadael
**abandoned** *adj* wedi ei adael, ofer, afradlon
**abase** *vt* darostwng, iselhau, gostwng
**abash** *vt* cywilyddio
**abate** *vb* gostwng, lleihau; gostegu
**abattoir** *n* lladd-dy
**abbess** *n* abades
**abbey** *n* abaty, mynachlog
**abbot** *n* abad
**abbreviate** *vt* byrhau, talfyrru
**abbreviation** *n* byrfodd
**abdicate** *vb* ymddeol, ymddiswyddo
**abdomen** *n* bol
**abdominal** *adj* perthynol i'r bol
**abduct** *vt* dwyn ymaith drwy drais, cipio
**aberration** *n* cyfeiliorn, gwyriad
**abet** *vt* cefnogi, cynorthwyo, ategu
**abeyance** *n* dirymedd dros dro, oediad
**abhor** *vt* ffieiddio, casáu
**abhorrence** *n* ffieidd-dod, atgasrwydd, atgasedd
**abide** *vb* aros, trigo; goddef
**abiding** *adj* arhosol, gwastadol
**ability** *n* gallu, medr
**abject** *adj* distadl, dirmygedig
**ablative** *n* abladol
**ablaze** *adv* ar ddân, yn wenfflam
**able** *adj* abl, galluog
**ablution** *n* golchiad; puredigaeth
**abnormal** *adj* anghyffredin, annormal
**aboard** *adv* ar fwrdd (llong)

**abode** *n* annedd, trigfa, cartrefle
**abolish** *vt* diddymu, dileu
**abominable** *adj* ffiaidd
**abomination** *n* ffieidd-dra
**aborigines** *npl* cyn-drigolion
**abort** *vb* erthylu, atal
**abortion** *n* erthyliad; erthyl
**abortive** *adj* seithug, ofer
**abound** *vi* amlhau, heigio; ymhelaethu
**about** *prep* am, oddeutu, tua ♦ *adv* oddeutu, o gwmpas
**above** *prep* uwch, uwchlaw ♦ *adv* fry
**abrasive** *adj* yn peri traul; annymunol
**abreast** *adj* ochr yn ochr, cyfystlys
**abridge** *vt* talfyrru, cwtogi
**abroad** *adv* allan, ar led, ar daen, dros y dŵr
**abrogate** *vt* diddymu, dileu
**abrupt** *adj* disymwth, sydyn, swta; serth
**abscess** *n* cornwyd, casgliad, crynhofa
**abscond** *vi* rhedeg i ffwrdd, dianc
**absence** *n* absenoldeb
**absent** *adj* absennol ♦ *vt* absenoli. **a.-minded** *adj* anghofus
**absenteeism** *n* absenoliaeth
**absolute** *adj* cwbl, hollol; diamodol ♦ *n* diamod, absolwt
**absolutely** *adv* yn hollol
**absolution** *n* gollyngdod; maddeuant
**absolve** *vt* rhyddhau, gollwng; maddau
**absorb** *vt* yfed, llyncu, sugno, sychu
**absorbent** *adj* amsugnol ♦ *n*

amsugnydd
**absorption** n llynciad, sychiad
**abstain** vb ymatal, ymgadw
**abstemious** adj cymedrol, sobr
**abstention** n ymataliad
**abstinence** n dirwest, ymataliad
**abstinent** adj cymedrol, sobr
**abstract** vt tynnu, haniaethu,
crynhoi ♦ adj haniaethol ♦ n
crynodeb
**abstraction** n haniaeth;
synfyfyrdod
**abstruse** adj tywyll, dyrys, astrus
**absurd** adj gwrthun, afresymol
**abundance** n digonedd,
helaethrwydd
**abundant** adj aml, helaeth, digonol
**abuse** vt camddefnyddio, cam-
drin; difrïo
**abuse** n camddefnydd; difrïaeth
**abusive** adj sarhaus, gwatwarus
**abysmal** adj diwaelod, dwys,
enbyd
**abyss** n y dyfnder, agendor
**academic, -al** adj athrofaol,
academig
**academy** n ysgol, athrofa,
academi
**accede** vi cytuno, cydsynio
**accelerate** vt cyflymu, chwimio
**accelerator** n ysbardun,
chwimiadur
**accent** n acen; llediaith ♦ vt
acennu
**accentuate** vt acennu; pwysleisio
**accept** vt derbyn (yn gymeradwy)
**acceptable** adj derbyniol,
cymeradwy
**acceptance** n derbyniad
**access** n dyfodfa, dyfodiad,
mynedfa, mynediad
**accessary** n cynorthwywr,
cefnogydd
**accessible** adj hygyrch; hawdd
dod ato
**accession** n esgyniad (i'r orsedd)
**accessory** adj cynorthwyol,

cyfranogol; atodol
**accidence** n ffurfiant
**accident** n damwain, anap
**accidental** adj damweiniol
**accidentally** adv yn ddamweiniol
**acclaim** vt datgan cymeradwyaeth
**acclamation** n bloddest,
cymeradwyaeth
**accommodate** vt cymhwyso;
lletya
**accommodating** adj cyfaddasol
**accommodation** n lle, llety
**accompaniment** n cyfeiliant
**accompanist** n cyfeilydd
**accompany** vb hebrwng; cyfeilio
**accomplice** n cynorthwywr mewn
trosedd
**accomplish** vt cyflawni, cwblhau
**accomplished** adj medrus
**accomplishment** n medr, dawn,
camp
**accord** vb cytuno; cyflwyno ♦ n
cydfod
**accordance** n : in a. with yn unol
â
**according** adv: a. to yn ôl
**accordingly** adv felly, gan hynny
**accordion** n acordion
**accost** vt cyfarch
**account** vb cyfrif ♦ n cyfrif; hanes
**accountable** adj cyfrifol, atebol
**accountant** n cyfrifydd
**accountancy** n cyfrifyddiaeth
**account number** n rhif cyfrif
**accredit** vt coelio, credu;
awdurdodi
**accrue** vt deillio, codi, digwydd
**accumulate** vb casglu, pentyrru,
cronni
**accumulator** n cronadur
**accuracy** n cywirdeb
**accurate** adj cywir
**accurately** adv yn gywir
**accursed** adj melltigedig,
melltigaid
**accusation** n cyhuddiad
**accusative** adj gwrthrychol

(*gram.*); cyhuddol
**accuse** *vt* cyhuddo
**accustom** *vt* arfer, ymarfer, cynefino
**accustomed** *adj* cyfarwydd, cyffredin
**ace** *n* as; mymryn
**ache** *vi* poeni, gwynio ♦ *n* poen, cur
**achieve** *vt* cyflawni, gorffen, cwpláu, cwblhau
**achievement** *n* cyflawniad, camp
**acid** *adj* siarp, sur ♦ *n* suryn, asid
**acidic** *adj* asidig
**acknowledge** *vt* cydnabod, cyfaddef
**acknowledgment** *n* cydnabyddiaeth
**acorn** *n* mesen
**acoustic** *adj* clybodig
**acoustics** *npl* acwsteg
**acquaint** *vt* hysbysu, ymgydnabod
**acquaintance** *n* cydnabod, cydnabyddiaeth, adnabyddiaeth
**acquainted** *adj* cydnabyddus, cynefin, cyfarwydd
**acquiesce** *vi* dygymod, cydsynio
**acquire** *vt* cael, ennill
**acquisition** *n* caffaeliad
**acquit** *vt* rhyddhau
**acre** *n* erw, cyfair, acer
**acrid** *adj* chwerw, llymsur
**acrimonious** *adj* chwerw, sarrug, cecrus
**acrobat** *n* acrobat
**across** *adv*, *prep* yn groes, ar draws; trosodd
**acrylic** *adj* acrylig
**act** *vb* gweithredu, actio ♦ *n* act, gweithred, deddf
**action** *n* gweithred, gweithrediad
**activate** *vb* gweithredoli
**active** *adj* bywiog; gweithredol
**activity** *n* gweithgarwch, gweithgaredd
**actor** *n* actor, actiwr
**actress** *n* actores

**actual** *adj* gwir, gwirioneddol
**actually** *adv* mewn gwirionedd
**actuary** *n* ystadegydd, cyfrifydd
**actuate** *vt* ysgogi, cymell, cyffroi
**acumen** *n* treiddgarwch, craffter
**acute** *adj* llym, tost; craff
**A.D.** *abbr* O.C.
**adage** *n* dihareb, dywediad
**adamant** *n* adamant, diemwnt
**adapt** *vt* cyfaddasu
**adapter** *n* adaptydd
**add** *vb* chwanegu, atodi; adio
**adder** *n* neidr, gwiber
**addict** *vt* ymroddi, gorddibynnu
**addiction** *n* ymroddiad, gorddibyniaeth, tueddiad
**addition** *n* ychwanegiad
**additional** *adj* ychwanegol
**additive** *n* adiolyn
**address** *vb* annerch; cyfeirio ♦ *n* anerchiad; cyfeiriad
**adduce** *vt* dwyn ymlaen; nodi
**adept** *n* un cyfarwydd; campwr
**adequate** *adj* digonol
**adhere** *vi* ymlynu, glynu wrth
**adhesion** *n* glyniad, ymlyniad
**adhesive** *adj* glynol, ymlynol ♦ *n* adlyn, glud
**adieu** *excl* bydd wych! ffarwel!
**adjacent** *adj* cyfagos, gerllaw
**adjective** *n* ansoddair
**adjoin** *vt* cydio, cyffwrdd â
**adjourn** *vt* gohirio, oedi
**adjudge** *vt* dyfarnu, barnu
**adjudicate** *vt* beirniadu, barnu
**adjudicator** *n* beirniad
**adjunct** *n* atodiad, ychwanegiad
**adjure** *vt* tynghedu, tyngu
**adjust** *vt* cymhwyso, addasu, unioni
**ad-lib** *adv* yn rhydd, difyfyr
**administer** *vt* gweinyddu
**administration** *n* gweinyddiaeth
**administrative** *adj* gweinyddol
**admirable** *adj* rhagorol, campus
**admiral** *n* llyngesydd
**admiralty** *n* morlys

**admiration** n edmygedd

**admire** vt edmygu

**admission** n derbyniad; addefiad

**admit** vt derbyn; addef, cyfaddef

**admittance** n derbyniad; trwydded

**admixture** n cymysgiad, cymysgedd

**admonish** vt rhybuddio, ceryddu

**admonition** n rhybudd, cerydd

**ad nauseam** adv hyd syrffed

**ado** n helynt, heldrin, ffwdan

**adolescence** n llencyndod, adolesens

**adolescent** n adolesent, llencyn, llances

**adopt** vb mabwysiadu

**adoption** n mabwysiad

**adore** vt addoli

**adorn** vt addurno

**adrift** adv yn rhydd, diangor

**adroit** adj medrus, deheuig, hyfedr

**adulation** n gweniaith, truth

**adult** n (un) mewn oed, oedolyn

**adulterate** vt llygru

**adulterer** n godinebwr

**adulteress** n godinebwraig

**adultery** n godineb

**advance** vb symud ymlaen; dyrchafu; rhoi benthyg ♦ n benthyg, echwyn

**advanced** adj ar y blaen

**advancement** n dyrchafiad; lles, budd

**advancing** adj cynyddol, ar gynnydd

**advantage** n mantais

**advantageous** adj manteisiol

**advent** n dyfodiad; yr Adfent

**adventure** n antur, anturiaeth

**adverb** n adferf

**adversary** n gwrthwynebydd

**adverse** adj adfydus, gwrthwynebus, croes

**adversity** n adfyd, drygfyd

**advert** n hysbyseb

**advertise** vt hysbysu, hysbysebu

**advertisement** n hysbysiad, hysbyseb

**advertiser** n hysbysydd

**advertising** adj hysbysebol

**advice** n cyngor, cyfarwyddyd

**advisable** adj doeth, buddiol

**advise** vt cynghori, annog; hysbysu

**advisedly** adv ar ôl ystyried, yn bwyllog

**advisory** adj ymgynghorol

**advocate** n eiriolwr, bargyfreithiwr ♦ vt eiriol, dadlau, cefnogi, pleidio

**adze** n neddau, neddyf

**aerial** adj awyrol, wybrol

**aeroplane** n awyren

**aerosol** n erosol

**aesthetic** adj esthetig

**aesthetics** n estheteg

**afar** adv pell, hirbell

**affable** adj hynaws, caruaidd, clên

**affair** n achos; mater; helynt

**affect** vt effeithio; cymryd arno, ffugio

**affectation** n mursendod, rhodres, ffug

**affection** n serch, cariad; clefyd, haint; affeithiad (gram.)

**affectionate** adj serchog, caruaidd

**affiliate** vt mabwysiadu, tadogi; uno

**affinity** n cyfathrach; tebygrwydd

**affirm** vb haeru, taeru; sicrhau, gwirio

**affirmation** n cadarnhad

**affirmative** adj cadarnhaol

**affix** vt sicrhau, gosod

**afflict** vt cystuddio

**affliction** n cystudd, adfyd

**affluence** n cyfoeth, digonedd

**affluent** adj goludog, cyfoethog, cefnog

**afford** vt rhoddi; fforddio

**afforestation** n coedwigaeth

**affray** n ymryson, ffrwgwd, ysgarmes

**affront** vt sarhau, tramgwyddo ♦ n

sarhad
**afield** adv: **far a.** ymhell i ffwrdd
**aflame** adv ar dân
**afloat** adv yn nofio; ar daen, ar led
**afoot** adv ar droed
**afraid** adj ag ofn arno, ofnus
**afresh** adv o'r newydd, eilwaith
**Africa** n Africa
**after** prep, conj wedi, ar ôl, yn ôl ♦
  adv wedyn
**after-care** n gofal wedyn, ôl-ofal
**after-effects** n ôl-effeithiau
**afterlife** n y byd a ddaw
**aftermath** n adladd, adlodd
**afternoon** n prynhawn
**afters** n y cwrs terfynol
**afterthought** n syniad diweddar
**afterwards** adv wedi hynny, wedyn
**again** adv eilwaith, drachefn, eto
**against** prep erbyn, yn erbyn
**age** n oed, oedran; oes; henaint ♦
  vb heneiddio
**aged** adj hen, oedrannus
**agency** n goruchwyliaeth, cyfrwng,
  asiantaeth
**agenda** n agenda
**agent** n goruchwyliwr;
  gweithredydd, cynrychiolydd
**aggravate** vt gwneuthur yn waeth
**aggregate** n cyfanswm, crynswth
**aggression** n ymosodiad, gormes
**aggressive** adj ymosodol,
  ymwthiol, gormesol
**aggrieve** vt blino, tramgwyddo
**aghast** adj syn, brawychedig
**agile** adj heini, sionc, gwisgi
**agitate** vt cynhyrfu, aflonyddu,
  cyffroi
**agnostic** n agnostig, anffyddiwr
**ago** adv yn ôl. **long a.** ers talm
**agog** adv yn awchus
**agonizing** adj mewn gwewyr
  meddwl
**agony** n ing, poen
**agrarian** adj tirol, gwledig
**agree** vi cytuno; dygymod; cyfateb
**agreeable** adj clên, dymunol,

hyfryd
**agreement** n cytundeb
**agricultural** adj amaethyddol
**agriculture** n amaethyddiaeth
**aground** adv ar lawr, ar dir, i dir
**ahead** adv ymlaen, o flaen
**aid** vt cynorthwyo, helpu ♦ n
  cymorth, cynhorthwy
**ail** vb clafychu; blino, poeni
**ailment** n dolur, afiechyd,
  anhwyldeb
**aim** vb anelu, amcanu ♦ n amcan,
  nod
**air** n awyr; osgo; cainc, alaw ♦ vt
  awyru
**aircraft** n awyren
**airforce** n llu awyr
**airline** n cwmni hedfan
**airlock** n aerglo
**airport** n maes glanio
**air mail** n post awyr
**airtight** adj aerglos, aerdyn
**aisle** n ystlys eglwys; llwybr; eil
**ajar** adv cilagored
**akin** adv, adj perthynol, perthnasol
**alack** excl och fi!
**alacrity** n bywiogrwydd,
  parodrwydd
**alarm** vt dychrynu ♦ n braw,
  dychryn; rhybudd; larwm
**alarm-clock** n cloc larwm
**alas** excl och!
**albeit** conj er, er hynny, eto
**album** n albwm; record hir
**alcohol** n alcohol
**alcoholic** adj, n alcoholig,
  meddwyn
**alcove** n cilfach wely; hafdy,
  deildy, alcof
**alder** n gwernen
**ale** n cwrw
**alert** adj esgud, effro, gwyliadwrus
**algebra** n algebra
**Algeria** n Algeria
**alias** adv mewn modd, dan enw
  arall
**alibi** n dadlau bod mewn man arall

**alien** *adj* estronol ♦ *n* estron
**alight** *vi* disgyn
**align** *vb* cyfunioni
**alike** *adj* yr un fath ♦ *adv* yn gyffelyb
**aliment** *n* maeth, ymborth
**alimony** *n* alimoni
**alive** *adv*, *adj* yn fyw, byw
**alkali** *n* alcali
**alkaline** *adj* alcaliaidd
**all** *adj* holl; oll, i gyd ♦ *adv* yn hollol ♦ *n* y cwbl, y cyfan; pawb
**allay** *vt* lleddfu, lliniaru; tawelu
**all clear** *adv* yn glir
**allege** *vt* honni, haeru
**allegedly** *adv* yn honedig
**allegiance** *n* teyrngarwch, gwrogaeth
**allegory** *n* alegori
**allergic** *adj* alergig
**allergy** *n* alergedd
**alleviate** *vt* ysgafnhau, esmwytho
**alley** *n* llwybr, ale
**alliance** *n* cyfathrach, cynghrair
**allied** *adj* cynghreiriol
**alliteration** *n* cyflythreniad, cyseinedd
**all-night** *adv* drwy'r nos
**allocate** *vt* cyfleu, rhannu, dosbarthu
**allot** *vb* gosod, penodi
**allotment** *n* cyfran; rhandir
**all-out** *adv* yn llwyr, a'i holl egni
**allow** *vt* caniatáu, goddef
**allowance** *n* goddefiad; dogn; lwfans
**alloy** *n* aloi
**allude** *vi* cyfeirio, sôn
**allure** *vb* hudo, denu, llithio
**allusion** *n* crybwylliad, cyfeiriad (at)
**alluvium** *n* llifbridd, dolbridd
**ally** *vt* cynghreirio ♦ *n* cynghreiriad
**almighty** *adj* hollalluog, hollgyfoethog
**almond** *n* almon
**almoner** *n* elusennwr

**almost** *adv* bron, agos, braidd
**alms** *n* elusen, cardod
**aloft** *adv* yn uchel, fry, i fyny
**alone** *adv*, *adj* unig, ar ei ben ei hun
**along** *adv* ymlaen; ar hyd. **all a.** o'r cychwyn
**aloof** *adv*, *adj* yn cadw draw; pell
**aloud** *adv* yn uchel, yn groch
**alphabet** *n* egwyddor, abiéc
**alphabetical** *adj* yn nhrefn yr wyddor
**Alps** *npl*: **the A.** yr Alpau
**already** *adv* eisoes, yn barod
**also** *adv* hefyd
**altar** *n* allor
**alter** *vb* newid, altro
**alteration** *n* newid, cyfnewidiad
**altercation** *n* ymryson, ffrae
**alternate** *adj* bob yn ail ♦ *vb* digwydd bob yn ail; eilio
**alternating** *adj* bob yn ail
**alternative** *n* dewis arall
**alternatively** *adv* ar yn ail
**although** *conj* er
**altitude** *n* uchder
**alto** *n* alto
**altogether** *adv* oll, i gyd, yn gyfan gwbl
**aluminium** *n* alwminiwm
**always** *adv* yn wastad(ol), bob amser
**a.m.** *abbr* a.m.
**amalgamate** *vb* cymysgu, cyfuno, uno
**amaneuensis** *n* ysgrifennydd dros arall
**amass** *vt* casglu, cronni, pentyrru
**amateur** *n* amatur
**amateurish** *adj* trwsgl, anfedrus, amaturaidd
**amatory** *adj* carwriaethol
**amaze** *vt* synnu, rhyfeddu, aruthro
**amazement** *n* syndod
**amazing** *adj* rhyfeddol
**ambassador** *n* llysgennad
**amber** *n* ambr

**ambidextrous** *adj* deheuig â'i ddwy law
**ambiguity** *n* amwysedd
**ambiguous** *adj* amwys
**ambition** *n* uchelgais
**ambitious** *adj* uchelgeisiol
**amble** *vi* rhygyngu ♦ *n* rhygyng
**ambulance** *n* ambiwlans
**ambush** *n*, *vb* cynllwyn, rhagod
**ameliorate** *vt* gwella, diwygio
**amenable** *adj* hydrin; atebol; cyfrifol
**amend** *vb* gwella, diwygio, cywiro
**amendment** *n* gwelliant
**amends** *n* iawn
**amenity** *n* hyfrydwch; hynawsedd
**America** *n* yr Amerig
**American** *adj* Americanaidd ♦ *n* Americanwr
**amiable** *adj* hawddgar, serchus
**amicable** *adj* cyfeillgar
**amid, -st** *prep* ynghanol, ymhlith, ymysg
**amiss** *adv* ar fai, o'i le
**amity** *n* cyfeillgarwch
**ammonia** *n* amonia
**ammunition** *n* arlwy rhyfel; pylor, *etc*
**amnesty** *n* maddeuant
**amok** *adv* yn wyllt, dilywodraeth
**among, -st** *prep* ymhlith, ymysg, rhwng
**amorous** *adj* hoff o garu, carwriaethus
**amorphous** *adj* di-ffurf, amorffus
**amount** *vi* cyrraedd; codi ♦ *n* swm
**amour** *n* carwriaeth
**ample** *adj* helaeth, eang; cyflawn, digon
**amplify** *vt* helaethu, ehangu
**amputate** *vt* torri aelod, trychu
**amulet** *n* peth a wisgir fel swyn
**amuse** *vt* difyrru, diddanu
**amusement** *n* difyrrwch, digrifwch
**an** Gwêl a
**anachronism** *n* camamseriad

**anaemia** *n* diffyg gwaed
**anaemic** *adj* di-waed, diwryg
**anaesthesia** *n* dideimladrwydd
**anaesthetic** *adj*, *n* anesthetig
**analogy** *n* cyfatebiaeth, cydweddiad
**analyse** *vt* dadansoddi, dadelfennu
**analysis (-yses)** *n* dadansoddiad
**analyst** *n* dadansoddwr
**analytical** *adj* dadansoddol
**anarchic, -al** *adj* anarchol
**anarchist** *n* anarchydd, terfysgwr
**anarchy** *n* anhrefn, aflywodraeth, anarchaeth
**anathema** *n* anathema
**anatomy** *n* anatomeg
**ancestor** *n* cyndad, (*pl*) hynafiaid
**ancestry** *n* ach, achau; hynafiaid
**anchor** *n* angor ♦ *vb* angori
**anchoress, -ite** *n* meudwy, ancr
**ancient** *adj* hen, hynafol; oesol
**ancillary** *adj* ategol, cynorthwyol
**and** *conj* a, ac
**anecdote** *n* hanesyn, chwedl
**anew** *adv* o'r newydd
**angel** *n* angel
**anger** *n* dicter, llid ♦ *vt* digio, llidio
**angle** *n* ongl ♦ *vi* genweirio, pysgota
**Anglican** *adj* perthynol i Eglwys Loegr, Anglicanaidd
**angling** *n* pysgota
**angry** *adj* dig, llidiog
**anguish** *n* ing
**angular** *adj* onglog
**animadvert** *vi* beirniadu, ceryddu, sennu
**animal** *n* anifail, mil ♦ *adj* anifeilaidd
**animate** *adj* byw ♦ *vt* bywhau; ysgogi
**animation** *n* bywiogrwydd
**animosity** *n* gelyniaeth, digasedd
**animus** *n* drwgdeimlad, gelyniaeth
**ankle** *n* migwrn, ffêr, swrn
**annals** *npl* cofnodion blynyddol
**annex** *vt* cysylltu, cydio;

meddiannu
**annihilate** vt diddymu, difodi
**annihilation** n diddymiant,
difodiant
**anniversary** n pen blwydd;
cylchwyl flynyddol
**annotate** vb gwneud nodiadau
**announce** vt datgan, cyhoeddi
**announcement** n cyhoeddiad,
hysbysiad
**announcer** n cyhoeddwr
**annoy** vt poeni, blino, cythruddo
**annoyance** n blinder, poendod
**annoying** adj trafferthus, blinderus
**annual** adj blynyddol
**annuity** n blwydd-dâl
**annul** vt diddymu, dileu, dirymu
**anoint** vt eneinio, iro
**anomaly** n peth croes i reol,
afreoleidd-dra
**anon** adv yn union, toc, yn y man
**anonymity** n cyflwr dienw
**anonymous** adj dienw, anhysbys
**anorak** n anorac
**another** pron, n arall
**answer** vb ateb ♦ n ateb, atebiad
**answerable** adj atebol, cyfrifol
**ant** n morgrugyn
**antagonism** n gelyniaeth,
gwrthwynebiaeth
**antagonist** n gwrthwynebydd
**Antarctic** n: the A. Antartica
**antarctic** adj o gylch y pegwn
deheuol
**ante-** prefix cyn, o flaen, rhag- ♦ n
rhagflaenydd
**antecedent** adj blaenorol
**antediluvian** adj cynddilywaidd
**antelope** n gafrewig, antelop
**antenatal** adj cyn-geni
**anterior** adj blaen, blaenorol, cyn-
**anthem** n anthem
**anthology** n blodeugerdd
**anthracite** n glo caled, glo carreg
**anthropology** n anthropoleg
**anti-, ant-** prefix gwrth-, yn erbyn
**antibiotic** n, adj gwrthfiotig

**antichrist** n anghrist
**anticipate** vt achub y blaen,
disgwyl
**anticlimax** n disgynneb
**antics** npl munudiau, ystumiau,
maldod, stranciau
**antidote** n gwrthwenwyn
**antifreeze** n, adj gwrthrew,
direwyn
**antipathy** n gwrthnaws; casineb
**antipodes** npl pellafoedd byd,
eithafoedd
**antiquarian** adj hynafiaethol ♦ n
hynafiaethydd
**antiquated** adj hen a di-les
**antique** adj hen, hynafol,
henffasiwn
**antique** n hen beth
**antique-shop** n siop hen bethau
**antiquity** n hynafiaeth; y
cynoesoedd
**anti-Semitism** n gwrth-Iddewiaeth
**antiseptic** adj, n antiseptig
**antisocial** adj gwrthgymdeithasol
**antithesis** (-es) n
gwrthgyferbyniad
**antler** n cainc o gorn carw, rhaidd
**anvil** n eingion, einion
**anxiety** n pryder
**anxious** adj pryderus, awyddus
**any** adj un, unrhyw, rhyw, peth,
dim
**anybody** pron unrhyw un, rhywun
**anyone** pron rhywun
**anything** pron dim, rhywbeth,
rhywfaint
**anywhere** adv rhywle
**apace** adv ar garlam, ar ffrwst, ar
frys
**apart** adv o'r neilltu, ar wahân
**apartheid** n aparteid
**apartment** n rhandy, llety
**apathetic** adj difraw, difater,
didaro
**apathy** n difrawder, difaterwch
**ape** n epa ♦ vt dynwared
**aperture** n bwlch, twll, agorfa

**apex** n blaen, brig, pen, copa
**aphis** (aphides) n pryf gwyrdd
**aphorism** n gwireb, dihareb
**apiece** adv yr un, ar wahân, un bob un
**apocalypse** n datguddiad
**apocryphal** adj anghanonaidd, apocryffaidd
**apologize** vi ymddiheuro, ymesgusodi
**apology** n ymddiheuriad, esgusawd
**apoplexy** n parlys mud, strôc
**apostasy** n gwrthgiliad
**apostate** n gwrthgiliwr
**apostle** n apostol
**apostolic, -al** adj apostolaidd
**apostrophe** n sillgoll, collnod (')
**apothecary** n apothecari, fferyllydd
**appal** vt brawychu, digalonni
**appalling** adj arswydus, gwarthus
**apparatus** n offer, aparatws
**apparel** n dillad, gwisg
**apparent** adj amlwg, eglur
**apparently** adv mae'n debyg
**apparition** n drychiolaeth, ysbryd
**appeal** vi apelio, erfyn ♦ n apêl
**appear** vi ymddangos, ymrithio
**appearance** n ymddangosiad
**appease** vt llonyddu, tawelu, dofi
**appellation** n enw, teitl
**append** vt atodi, ychwanegu
**appendicitis** n enyniad y coluddyn crog, apendiseitis
**appendix** n atodiad, ychwanegiad
**appertain** vi perthyn
**appetite** n archwaeth, chwant, awydd
**appetizer** n lluniaeth i greu blas, blasyn
**applaud** vt cymeradwyo, curo dwylo
**applause** n cymeradwyaeth
**apple** n afal. **a. of the eye** cannwyll llygad
**appliance** n offeryn, dyfais

**applicant** n ymgeisydd
**application** n cymhwysiad; cais; ymroddiad
**applied** adj cymwysedig
**apply** vb cymhwyso; ymroi; cynnig (am), ymgeisio
**appoint** vb gosod, penodi, pennu
**appointment** n cyhoeddiad; penodiad
**apportion** vt rhannu, dosbarthu
**apposite** adj addas, priodol
**appraise** vt prisio
**appreciate** vt prisio, gwerthfawrogi
**appreciation** n gwerthfawrogiad
**appreciative** adj gwerthfawrogol
**apprehend** vt ymaflyd mewn; dirnad; ofni
**apprehension** n dirnadaeth; ofn
**apprehensive** adj ofnus, pryderus
**apprentice** n prentis, dysgwr ♦ vt prentisio
**apprise** vb hysbysu; tafoli
**approach** vb nesáu, dynesu ♦ n dyfodfa
**approachable** adj hawdd mynd ato
**approbation** n cymeradwyaeth
**appropriate** vt meddiannu ♦ adj priodol, addas
**approval** n cymeradwyaeth
**approve** vt cymeradwyo; profi
**approximate** vi agosáu ♦ adj agos
**approximately** adv oddeutu, tua, yn agos i
**appurtenance** n peth perthynol
**apricot** n bricyllen
**April** n Ebrill
**apron** n (ar)ffedog, barclod
**apt** adj tueddol; cymwys, parod
**aquarium** n pysgodlyn, pysgoty
**aquatic** adj dyfrol, dyfriog
**aqueduct** n dyfrffos
**arable** adj: **a. land** tir âr
**arbiter** n dyddiwr, brawdwr, beirniad
**arbitrament** n rhaith, dedfryd
**arbitrary** adj gormesol, mympwyol

**arbitrate** *vb* cyflafareddu, athrywyn
**arbour** *n* deildy
**arc** *n* bwa, arc
**arcade** *n* arcêd
**arch** *n* bwa, pont; nen ♦ *vt* pontio
**arch-** *prefix* arch-, carn-, prif-
**archaeology** *n* archaeoleg
**archaic** *adj* hynafol, henaidd
**archangel** *n* archangel
**archbishop** *n* archesgob
**archdeacon** *n* archddiacon, archddiagon
**archdruid** *n* archddderwydd
**archer** *n* saethydd, saethwr
**archery** *n* saethyddiaeth
**archipelago** *n* twr ynysoedd, ynysfor
**architect** *n* pensaer
**architecture** *n* pensaernïaeth
**archive** *n* archif
**archway** *n* ffordd fŵaol
**Arctic** *n*: the A. yr Artig
**arctic** *adj* gogleddol
**ardent** *adj* gwresog, poeth, angerddol
**ardour** *n* angerdd, aidd
**arduous** *adj* llafurus, blin, caled
**area** *n* arwynebedd, wyneb
**Argentina** *n* Ariannin
**argue** *vb* dadlau, ymresymu
**argument** *n* dadl, ymresymiad
**arid** *adj* sych, crin, cras, gwyw
**aright** *adv* yn iawn, yn briodol
**arise** *vi* cyfodi, codi
**aristocracy** *n* pendefigaeth
**aristocrat** *n* pendefig, gŵr mawr
**aristocratic** *adj* pendefigaidd, bonheddig
**arithmetic** *n* rhifyddeg
**arithmetician** *n* rhifyddgwr
**ark** *n* arch
**arm** *n* braich; cainc
**arm** *n* arf ♦ *vb* arfogi
**armament** *n* offer rhyfel; arfogaeth
**armchair** *n* cadair freichiau

**armed** *adj* arfog
**armful** *adj* coflaid, ceseiliaid
**armistice** *n* cadoediad
**armour** *n* arfogaeth, arfwisg
**armoured** *adj* wedi ei amddiffyn
**armoury** *n* arfdy
**armpit** *n* cesail
**armrest** *n* man i orffwys braich
**army** *n* byddin
**aroma** *n* perarogl(au)
**aromatic** *adj* peraroglaidd, pêr, persawrus
**around** *adv, prep* am, o amgylch
**arouse** *vt* deffro(i), dihuno; cyffroi
**arraign** *vt* cyhuddo o flaen brawdle
**arrange** *vb* trefnu
**arrangement** *n* trefn, trefniad, trefniant
**arrant** *adj* dybryd, cywilyddus
**array** *vt* trefnu, cyfleu; gwisgo ♦ *n* trefn; gwisg
**arrears** *npl* ôl-ddyled
**arrest** *vt* atal; dal, dala, restio
**arrival** *n* dyfodiad, cyrhaeddiad
**arrive** *vi* cyrraedd, dyfod
**arrogance** *n* balchder, traha
**arrogant** *adj* balch, trahaus
**arrogate** *vt* hawlio, trawshawlio
**arrow** *n* saeth
**arsenal** *n* arfdy, ystordy neu ffatri arfau
**arson** *n* llosgiad, llosg
**art** *n* celfyddyd; ystryw
**artefact** *n* celfun
**artery** *n* rhedweli
**artful** *adj* ystrywgar, dichellgar, cyfrwys
**art gallery** *n* oriel gelf
**arthritis** *n* gwynegon, crydcymalau
**article** *n* erthygl; nwydd; bannod
**articulate** *vb* cymalu; cynanu ♦ *adj* â meddwl clir, trefnus
**artifice** *n* dyfais; ystryw, dichell
**artificer** *n* saer, crefftwr, celfyddydwr
**artificial** *adj* celfyddydol; gosod, dodi, ffug

**artillery** *n* offer rhyfel, magnelau
**artisan** *n* crefftwr
**artist** *n* celfyddydwr, arlunydd, artist
**artistic** *adj* celfydd, celfyddgar, artistig
**as** *conj, adv* megis, fel; cyn, mor; â, ag
**asbestos** *n* ystinos, asbestos
**ascend** *vb* esgyn, dringo, dyrchafu
**ascendancy** *n* goruchafiaeth, uchafiaeth
**ascension** *n* esgyniad, dyrchafael
**ascent** *n* esgynfa, rhiw, gorifyny
**ascertain** *vt* cael gwybod, mynnu gwybod
**ascetic** *n* meudwy ♦ *adj* meudwyaidd, ymgosbol, asgetig
**ascribe** *vt* cyfrif i, priodoli, rhoddi
**ash** *n* onnen, onn
**ash** (-es) *n* lludw, ulw
**ashamed** *adj* ag arno gywilydd
**ashore** *adv* i'r lan, ar y lan
**ashtray** *n* plat lludw
**aside** *adv* o'r neilltu
**ask** *vb* gofyn, holi; ceisio
**askance** *adv* yn llygatraws, yn gam
**askew** *adv* ar osgo, ar letraws
**aslant** *adv* ar ei ogwydd, ar oledd
**asleep** *adv* yng nghwsg, yn cysgu
**asparagus** *n* merllys, asbaragws
**aspect** *n* golwg, golygwedd, wyneb, agwedd
**aspen** *n* aethnen
**asperity** *n* gerwindeb, llymder
**asperse** *vt* taenellu; gwaradwyddo
**aspersion** *n* difrïad, enllib
**asphyxiate** *vt* mygu, tagu
**aspirate** *vt* seinio ag anadl ♦ *n* yr (*h*)
**aspiration** *n* dyhead
**aspire** *vi* dyheu
**aspirin** *n* asbrin
**ass** *n* asyn; asen
**assail** *vt* ymosod ar, rhuthro ar
**assailant** *n* ymosodwr

**assassin** *n* bradlofrudd, llofrudd
**assassinate** *vt* bradlofruddio
**assault** *n* ymosodiad ♦ *vt* ymosod
**assay** *n* praw(f) ♦ *vb* profi; cynnig, ceisio
**assemble** *vb* cynnull, ymgynnull
**assembly** *n* cynulliad, cymanfa
**assent** *vi* cydsynio ♦ *n* cydsyniad
**assert** *vt* haeru, honni, mynnu
**assess** *vt* trethu, prisio, asesu
**assessment** *n* asesiad
**assessor** *n* aseswr, cyfeisteddwr
**asset** *n* ased
**assets** *npl* eiddo, meddiannau
**assiduous** *adj* dyfal, diwyd
**assign** *vt* gosod, penodi; trosglwyddo
**assimilate** *vb* cymathu; tebygu
**assist** *vb* cynorthwyo, cymorth, helpu
**assistance** *n* cymorth
**assistant** *n* cynorthwyydd
**assize** *n* brawdlys
**associate** *vb* cymdeithasu, cyfeillachu, cysylltu ♦ *n* cydymaith
**association** *n* cymdeithas, cymdeithasfa
**assort** *vb* trefnu, dosbarthu
**assorted** *adj* amryfath
**assortment** *n* dosbarthiad, pigion
**assuage** *vt* llonyddu, lliniaru, lleddfu
**assume** *vt* cymryd ar; tybied; honni
**assumption** *n* tyb(iaeth), bwriant, honiad, dyrchafiad (Mair i'r nefoedd)
**assurance** *n* sicrwydd; hyder, hyfder
**assure** *vt* sicrhau; yswirio
**asterisk** *n* serennig, seren (*)
**asthma** *n* caethder, diffyg anadl, y fogfa
**asthmatic** *adj* byr ei wynt, caeth ei frest
**astonish** *vt* synnu

**astound** *vt* synnu, syfrdanu
**astral** *adj* serol
**astray** *adv* ar gyfeiliorn, ar grwydr
**astride** *adv* â'r traed ar led
**astrologer** *n* sêr-ddewin
**astrology** *n* sêr-ddewiniaeth
**astronaut** *n* gofodwr
**astronomer** *n* serydd, seryddwr
**astronomy** *n* seryddiaeth
**astute** *adj* craff, cyfrwys, call
**asunder** *adv* ar wahân, yn
  ddrylliau
**asylum** *n* noddfa. **lunatic a.**
  gwallgofdy
**at** *prep* yn, wrth, ger, ar
**atheist** *n* anffyddiwr
**Athens** *n* Athen
**athlete** *n* mabolgampwr
**athletics** *npl* mabolgampau
**atlantic** *adj* atlantaidd ♦ *n*: **the A.**
  **(Ocean)** Môr Iwerydd
**atlas** *n* llyfr mapiau, atlas
**atmosphere** *n* awyrgylch
**atom** *n* mymryn, gronyn, atom
**atomic** *adj* atomig
**atone** *vi* gwneuthur iawn
**atonement** *n* iawn, cymod
**atrocious** *adj* erchyll, anfad,
  ysgeler
**attach** *vb* gosod, glynu; atafaelu
**attachment** *n* ymlyniad, serch
**attack** *vt* ymosod ar ♦ *n* ymosodiad
**attain** *vt* ennill; cyrraedd; cael
  gafael
**attainment** *n* cyrhaeddiad
**attempt** *vt* ceisio, cynnig ♦ *n*
  cynnig, ymgais
**attend** *vb* gweini; ystyried; dilyn,
  mynychu
**attendance** *n* gwasanaeth;
  presenoldeb
**attendant** *n* gweinydd ♦ *adj* yn
  dilyn, ynghlwm wrth
**attention** *n* sylw, ystyriaeth
**attentive** *adj* astud, ystyriol
**attenuate** *vt* teneuo, lleihau
**attest** *vb* tystio, gwirio; ardystio

**attic** *n* nenlofft, nenlawr
**attire** *vt* gwisgo ♦ *n* gwisg, dillad
**attitude** *n* ystum, agwedd, osgo
**attorney** *n* twrnai
**attract** *vt* tynnu, atynnu, denu,
  hudo
**attraction** *n* atyniad
**attractive** *adj* atyniadol
**attribute** *n* priodoledd
**attribute** *vt* priodoli, cyfrif i
**attrition** *n* rhathiad, treuliad, traul
**attune** *vt* hwylio, cyweirio
**auburn** *adj* gwinau, browngoch
**auction** *n* arwerthiant, ocsiwn
**auctioneer** *n* arwerthwr
**audacious** *adj* hy, digywilydd,
  haerllug
**audacity** *n* hyfdra, ehofndra,
  beiddgarwch
**audible** *adj* hyglyw, clywadwy
**audience** *n* gwrandawyr,
  cynulleidfa
**audio-visual** *adj* clyweledol
**audit** *vt* archwilio cyfrifon ♦ *n*
  archwiliad
**audition** *n* clywelediad
**auditor** *n* gwrandawr; archwilydd
**auger** *n* taradr, ebill
**augment** *vt* ychwanegu, atodi
**augur** *n* dewin ♦ *vb* darogan;
  argoeli
**August** *n* Awst
**august** *adj* urddasol, mawreddog
**aunt** *n* modryb
**aura** *n* naws, awyrgylch
**aural** *adj* clywedol
**auspices** *npl* nawdd
**auspicious** *adj* yn argoeli'n dda,
  ffafriol
**austere** *adj* gerwin, llym, tost,
  caled
**austerity** *n* gerwindeb, llymder
**Australia** *n* Awstralia
**Australian** *n* Awstraliad ♦ *adj*
  Awstralaidd
**Austria** *n* Awstria
**Austrian** *n* Awstriad ♦ *adj*

Awstriaidd
**authentic** *adj* dilys, gwir
**author** *n* awdur, awdwr
**authoritarian** *adj* awdurdodus
**authoritative** *adj* awdurdodol
**authority** *n* awdurdod
**authorize** *vt* awdurdodi
**auto-** *prefix* hunan-, ym-
**autobiography** *n* hunangofiant
**autocracy** *n* unbennaeth
**autocrat** *n* unben; dyn awdurdodol
**autograph** *n* llofnod
**automatic** *adj* hunanysgogol, awtomatig
**automation** *n* awtomasiwn
**automobile** *n* cerbyd, modur
**autonomy** *n* ymreolaeth
**autumn** *n* hydref
**auxilliary** *adj* cynorthwyol, ategol ♦ *n* cynorthwywr
**avail** *vb* llesáu, tycio ♦ *n* lles, budd
**available** *adj* ar gael
**avalanche** *n* syrthfa, cwymp (eira, *etc*)
**avarice** *n* cybydd-dod, trachwant
**avaricious** *adj* cybyddlyd, ariangar
**avenge** *vt* dial cam
**avenue** *n* mynedfa, rhodfa
**aver** *vt* gwirio, haeru
**average** *n* canolbris; cyfartaledd; cyffredin
**averse** *adj* gwrthwynebol, gelynol; croesi
**aversion** *n* gwrthwynebiad; casbeth
**avert** *vt* troi heibio, gochel, osgoi
**aviary** *n* adardy
**avidity** *n* awydd, awch, gwanc
**avocation** *n* gorchwyl, galwedigaeth
**avoid** *vt* gochel, osgoi, arbed
**avouch** *vt* gwirio, haeru; arddelwi
**avow** *vt* addef; cydnabod
**await** *vt* disgwyl, aros
**awake** *vb* deffro, dihuno ♦ *adj* effro
**award** *vt* dyfarnu ♦ *n* dyfarniad

**aware** *adj* hysbys, ymwybodol
**awareness** *n* arwybod, ymwybyddiaeth
**awash** *adj* llawn, cyforiog
**away** *adv* ymaith, i ffwrdd
**awe** *n* (parchedig) ofn ♦ *vt* rhoi arswyd
**awful** *adj* ofnadwy, arswydus
**awhile** *adv* am ennyd, am dro
**awkward** *adj* trwsgl, lletchwith, anghyfleus
**awl** *n* mynawyd
**awning** *n* cysgodlen, adlen
**axe** *n* bwyall, bwyell
**axiom** *n* gwireb
**axis** (**axes**) *n* echel, pegwn
**axle** *n* echel
**ay** *adv* ie
**aye** *adv* yn wastad(ol), byth
**azure** *n* glas y ffurfafen, asur ♦ *adj* asur

# B

**babble** *vb* baldordd, clebran ♦ *n* baldordd
**babe** *n* baban, plentyn bach
**baby** *n* baban, maban, babi
**babysitter** *n* gwarchodwr babanod
**bachelor** *n* dyn dibriod, hen lanc; baglor
**back** *n* cefn ♦ *vb* cefnogi; bacio ♦ *adv* yn ôl
**background** *n* cefndir
**backhander** *n* tâl dirgel; ergyd â chefn y llaw
**backpack** *n* cefnbwn
**backslide** *vi* gwrthgilio
**backward** *adv* yn ôl, ar ôl ♦ *adj* hwyrfrydig; digynnydd; araf
**backwater** *n* dŵr disymud ar ymyl afon, lle o'r neilltu, dibwys, cwter gwsg
**bacon** *n* cig moch, bacwn
**bad** *adj* drwg, drygionus; gwael, sâl

**badge** n bathodyn
**badger** n mochyn daear, broch ♦ vt profocio, poeni
**badminton** n badminton
**bad-tempered** adj â thymer ddrwg
**baffle** vt drysu, siomi, trechu
**bag** n cwd, cod, bag
**baggage** n clud, celfi, pac
**bagpipe** n pibgod
**bah** excl pw!
**bail** n meichiau, gwystl ♦ vt mechnïo
**bail, bale** vt hysbyddu cwch
**bailiff** n beili; hwsmon, goruchwyliwr
**bait** vt abwydo; baeddu, eirthio ♦ n abwyd
**bake** vb pobi, crasu
**baker** n pobydd
**bakery** n popty
**balance** n clorian, mantol; gweddill ♦ vt mantoli; cydbwyso
**balanced** adj cytbwys, cymesur
**balcony** n oriel, balcon
**bald** adj moel, penfoel
**bale** n pwn, sypyn, bwrn
**baleful** adj alaethus, gresynol, galarus
**baler** n byrnwr
**balk, baulk** n balc; siom ♦ vt balcio; siomi
**ball** n pêl, pellen
**ball** n dawns, dawnsfa
**ballad** n baled
**ballast** n balast
**ball bearings** npl berynnau pêl, pelferynnau
**ballerina** n balerina
**ballet** n bale
**balloon** n balŵn
**ballot** n balot, tugel
**balm** n balm, triagl
**bamboozle** vb twyllo, llygaddynnu
**ban** vt gwahardd, ysgymuno
**banal** adj cyffredin, sathredig
**banana** n banana

**band** n band, rhwymyn; mintai; seindorf
**bandage** n rhwymyn ♦ vb rhwymo, rhwymynnu
**bandbox** n bocs hetiau
**bandit** n herwr, ysbeiliwr
**bandy** vt taflu (pêl, etc) yn ôl a blaen
**bandy-legged** adj coesgam
**bane** n dinistr, melltith
**baneful** adj dinistriol, andwyol
**bang** vb curo, dulio, clepian ♦ n ergyd, twrf
**bangle** n breichled
**banish** vt alltudio, deol
**bank** n mainc; rhes
**bank** n glan, torlan; traethell
**bank** n banc, ariandy ♦ vb bancio
**banker** n bancwr
**bankrupt** n methdalwr
**bankruptcy** n methdaliad
**bank statement** n datganiad banc, adroddiad banc
**banner** n baner, lluman
**banns** npl gostegion
**banquet** n gwledd ♦ vb gwledda
**bantam** n coriar, dandi
**banter** n ysmaldod, cellwair ♦ vb cellwair, profocio
**baptism** n bedydd
**Baptist** n Bedyddiwr
**baptize** vt bedyddio
**bar** n bar, bollt; rhwystr; traethell ♦ vt bario; eithrio
**barb** n barf; adfach
**barbarian** n barbariad, anwariad
**barbaric** adj barbaraidd
**barbecue** n rhostfa
**barbed wire** n weiar bigog
**barber** n barbwr
**bard** n bardd, prydydd
**bare** adj noeth, llwm, moel, prin ♦ vt dinoethi
**barefooted** adj troednoeth
**barely** adv prin, o'r braidd
**bargain** n bargen ♦ vb bargeinio
**barge** n bad mawr

**bark** *n* barc, llong, llestr
**bark** *vi* cyfarth, coethi ♦ *n* cyfarthiad
**bark** *n* rhisgl ♦ *vt* dirisglo, digroeni
**barley** *n* haidd, barlys
**barm** *n* burum, berem, berman
**barmaid** *n* barferch
**barman** *n* barmon
**barn** *n* ysgubor
**barometer** *n* hinfynegydd, baromedr
**baron** *n* barwn, arglwydd
**baronet** *n* barwnig
**barrack** *n* lluest, lluesty, gwersyllty
**barrage** *n* argae, clawdd
**barrel** *n* baril, casgen
**barren** *adj* diffrwyth; amhlantadwy
**barricade** *n* atalglawdd ♦ *vt* cau
**barrier** *n* atalfa, rhwystr, terfyn, ffin
**barrister** *n* bargyfreithiwr
**barrow** *n* berfa, whilber; crug
**barter** *vb* cyfnewid, ffeirio ♦ *n* cyfnewid
**base** *adj* isel, gwael, distadl, gau
**base** *n* sylfaen; bôn ♦ *vt* sylfaenu, seilio
**baseball** *n* pel-fâs
**basement** *n* islawr
**bashful** *adj* swil, gwylaidd
**basic** *adj* gwaelodol, sylfaenol
**basin** *n* basn, cawg, dysgl
**basis (bases)** *n* sail, sylfaen
**bask** *vi* ymheulo, torheulo
**basket** *n* basged, cawell
**basketful** *n* basgedaid
**bass** *n* bas, isalaw; bâs, draenogiad y môr
**bastard** *n* bastard, plentyn gordderch/siawns
**baste** *vt* iro, brasteru; ffusto, ffonodio
**bastinado** *n, vt* ffonodio gwadnau'r traed
**bat** *n* ystlum
**bat** *n* bat ♦ *vi* batio

**batch** *n* pobiad, ffyrnaid; swp, sypyn
**bath** *n* ymolchfa, badd, baddon; bath
**bathe** *vb* ymdrochi, ymolchi, golchi
**bathroom** *n* ystafell ymolchi
**baton** *n* llawffon, baton, arweinffon
**battalion** *n* byddin, mintai, bataliwn
**batter** *vt* curo, pwyo ♦ *n* defnydd crempog, cytew
**battery** *n* magnelfa; batri
**battle** *n* brwydr, cad ♦ *vi* brwydro
**battlefield** *n* maes y gad
**battlement** *n* canllaw, murganllaw.
**battleship** *n* llongryfel
**bauble** *n* ffril, tegan
**baulk** Gwêl **balk**
**bawdy** *adj* anllad, anweddus
**bawl** *vi* gweiddi, crochlefain, bloeddio
**bay** *n* bae
**bay** *vb, n* cyfarth. **to hold at b.** rhoi cyfarth
**bay** *n* llawryf
**bay** *adj* gwinau, gwineugoch
**bayonet** *n* bidog ♦ *vt* bidogi
**bazaar** *n* basâr
**be** *vi* bod
**beach** *n* traeth, traethell ♦ *vt* gyrru ar y traeth
**beacon** *n* gwylfa, goleudy; coelcerth
**bead** *n* glain. **beads** paderau
**beadle** *n* rhingyll
**beak** *n* pig, gylfin, duryn
**beaker** *n* cwpan, diodlestr â phig, bicer
**beam** *n* trawst, paladr; pelydryn ♦ *vi* pelydru
**bean** *n* ffäen, ffeuen
**bear** *n* arth; arthes
**bear** *vt* dwyn, cludo; geni; dioddef, goddef

**beard** n barf; col ŷd
**bearing** n ymddygiad; traul
**beast** n bwystfil, anifail
**beat** vt curo ♦ n cur, curiad
**beatitude** n gwynfyd
**beautiful** adj prydferth, hardd, teg
**beauty** n prydferthwch, harddwch, tegwch. **b. parlour** parlwr pincio
**beaver** n afanc, llostlydan
**becalm** vt tawelu, llonyddu
**because** adv, conj oherwydd, oblegid, o achos; gan, am
**beck** n amnaid, awgrym
**beckon** vb amneidio
**become** vb dyfod; gweddu
**becoming** adj gweddus
**bed** n gwely; cefn, pâm
**bedding** n dillad gwely
**bedeck** vt addurno, trwsio
**bedew** vt gwlitho, gwlychu
**bedfellow** n cywely
**bedlam** n bedlam
**bedraggled** adj wedi caglo, dwyno; aflêr
**bedrid(den)** adj gorweiddiog
**bedroom** n ystafell wely, llofft
**bedsitter** n ystafell un gwely, ceginlofft
**bedstead** n pren neu haearn gwely
**bee** n gwenynen
**beech** n ffawydden
**beef** (beeves) n eidion; cig eidion, biff
**beehive** n cwch gwenyn
**beeline** n llinell unionsyth, ddiwyro
**beer** n cwrw
**beestings** npl llaeth newydd, llaeth toro
**beet** n betys
**beetle** n chwilen
**beetroot** n betys
**befall** vb digwydd
**befit** vb gweddu
**before** prep o flaen, gerbron, cyn ♦ adv o'r blaen
**beforehand** adv ymlaen llaw
**befriend** vt ymgeleddu, bod yn gefn

**beg** vb erfyn, deisyf, ymbil; cardota
**beget** vb cenhedlu, creu, peri
**beggar** n cardotyn ♦ vt tlodi, llymhau
**begin** vb dechrau
**beginning** n dechreuad
**beguile** vt hudo, twyllo; swyno, diffyrru
**behalf** n plaid, rhan, achos, tu
**behave** vb ymddwyn
**behaviour** n ymddygiad
**behead** vt torri pen
**behest** n arch, archiad
**behind** adv, prep ar ôl, yn ôl, tu ôl, tu cefn
**behold** vt edrych, gweld ♦ vb imper wele
**behove** vt bod yn rhwymedig ar
**beige** adj beis
**being** n bod
**belated** adj diweddar; wedi ei ddal gan y nos
**belch** vb bytheirio
**beleaguer** vt gwarchae ar
**belfry** n clochdy
**Belgium** n Gwlad Belg
**belie** vt anwireddu, siomi
**belief** n cred, crediniaeth, coel
**believe** vb credu, coelio
**believer** n credwr, credadun
**belittle** vt bychanu
**bell** n cloch
**belle** n merch brydweddol, meinwen
**bellicose** adj rhyfelgar, ymladdgar
**belligerent** adj rhyfelog ♦ n rhyfelblaid
**bellow** vb rhuo, bugunad
**bellows** npl megin
**belly** n bol, bola; cest, tor ♦ vb bolio
**belong** vi perthyn
**belongings** n meddiannau, eiddo
**beloved** adj annwyl, cu ♦ n anwylyd

**below** *adv, prep* is, islaw, isod, obry, oddi tanodd

**belt** *n* gwregys

**bemoan** *vt* galaru am, arwylo

**bemused** *adj* syfrdan

**bench** *n* mainc

**bend** *vb* plygu, camu ♦ *n* tro, camedd

**beneath** *adv, prep* is, tan, oddi tanodd

**benediction** *n* bendith

**benefactor** *n* cymwynaswr, noddwr

**benefice** *n* bywoliaeth eglwysig

**beneficent** *adj* daionus, llesfawr

**beneficial** *adj* buddiol, llesol

**benefit** *n* budd, lles, elw ♦ *vb* llesáu, elwa

**benevolent** *adj* daionus, haelionus

**benighted** *adj* a ddaliwyd gan y nos; tywyll

**benign** *adj* tirion, mwyn

**bent** *n* tuedd, gogwydd

**benumb** *vt* merwino, fferru, diffrwytho

**bequeath** *vt* cymynnu, cymynroddi

**bequest** *n* cymynrodd

**bereave** *vt* difuddio, amddifadu

**beret** *n* bere

**Berlin** *n* Berlin

**berry** *n* aeronen, mwyaren

**berserk** *adj* gwyllt, aflywodraethus

**berth** *n* lle llong; gwely llongwr; swydd

**beseech** *vt* atolygu, deisyf, erfyn

**beseem** *vt* gweddu

**beset** *vt* cynllwyn; amgylchynu

**beside** *prep* gerllaw, wrth, yn ymyl. **to be b. oneself** o'i bwyll

**besides** *adv, prep* heblaw, gyda

**besiege** *vt* gwarchae ar

**besmirch** *vt* llychwino, pardduo

**bespeak** *vt* ymofyn ymlaen llaw

**best** *adj, adv* gorau

**bestial** *adj* bwystfilaidd

**bestir** *vt* cyffroi, ymysgwyd

**bestow** *vt* rhoddi, cyflwyno, anrhegu

**bestride** *vt* eistedd neu gamu yn groes i

**bet** *n* bet, cyngwystl ♦ *vb* betio, dal am

**betoken** *vt* arwyddo, argoeli

**betray** *vt* bradychu

**betrayal** *n* brad

**betroth** *vt* dyweddïo

**better** *adj* gwell, rhagorach ♦ *adv* yn well ♦ *vt* gwella

**between, betwixt** *prep* rhwng, cydrhwng

**beverage** *n* diod

**bewail** *vt* cwyno, cwynfan, galaru am

**beware** *vi* gochel, ymogelyd

**bewilder** *vt* drysu, mwydro, pensyfrdanu

**bewitch** *vt* rheibio

**beyond** *adv, prep* tu hwnt

**bi-** *prefix* dau-, deu-

**bias** *n* tuedd, gogwydd, rhagfarn ♦ *vt* tueddu

**Bible** *n* Beibl

**bibliography** *n* llyfryddiaeth

**bibulous** *adj* yfgar, llymeitgar

**bicker** *vi* ffraeo, ymrafaelio, ymgecru

**bicycle** *n* ceffyl haearn, deurod, beic

**bid** *vb* erchi; gwahodd; cynnig

**bide** *vb* aros, disgwyl

**biennial** *adj* dwyflynyddol

**bier** *n* elor

**bifocals** *npl* gwydrau deuffocal

**big** *adj* mawr; braisg

**bigamy** *n* dwywreigiaeth

**bigheaded** *adj* bras, mawreddog

**bigot** *n* penboethyn

**bikini** *n* bicini

**bilberries** *npl* llus

**bile** *n* bustl, geri

**bilingual** *adj* dwyieithog

**bilingualism** *n* dwyieithedd; dwyieitheg

**bill** *n* bil; mesur; rhaglen;

hysbyslen
**bill** *n* pig, gylfin, duryn
**billet** *n* lletty (milwr) ♦ *vt* lletya
**billiards** *n* biliards
**billion** *n* biliwn
**billow** *n* ton, gwaneg, moryn ♦ *vi* tonni
**billy-goat** *n* bwch gafr
**bin** *n* cist
**bind** *vt* rhwymo, caethiwo
**binge** *n* gloddest, sbri
**bingo** *n* bingo
**binoculars** *n* deulygadur
**biography** *n* bywgraffiad, cofiant
**biological** *adj* biolegol
**biology** *n* bywydeg, bioleg
**birch** *n* bedw, bedwen; gwialen fedw ♦ *vt* chwipio
**bird** *n* aderyn
**Biro** *n* biro
**birth** *n* genedigaeth
**birthday** *n* pen-blwydd. **b. card** *n* carden pen-blwydd
**birthmark** *n* man geni
**biscuit** *n* bisgeden
**bisect** *vt* dwyrannu, rhannu
**bisector** *n* dwyrannydd
**bisexual** *adj* deurywiol
**bishop** *n* esgob
**bishopric** *n* esgobaeth
**bison** *n* ych gwyllt, bual
**bit** *n* tamaid; tipyn, dernyn; genfa, bit
**bitch** *n* gast
**bite** *vb* cnoi, brathu ♦ *n* cnoad, brath; tamaid
**bitter** *adj* chwerw, bustlaidd, tost
**bittern** *n* aderyn y bwn, bwmp y gors
**bitterness** *n* chwerwedd, chwerwder
**bitumen** *n* pyg
**bituminous** *adj* pyglyd
**bizarre** *adj* rhyfedd, od, chwithig
**blab** *vb* prepian, clepian ♦ *n* clepgi
**black** *adj* du ♦ *n* du, dyn du ♦ *vt* duo. **b. ice** *n* iâ du

**blackberries** *npl* mwyar duon
**blackbird** *n* aderyn du, mwyalchen
**blackboard** *n* bwrdd du
**blackcurrant** *n* cyrensen ddu ♦ *adj* cwrens du
**blacken** *vt* duo, pardduo; tywyllu
**blackguard** *n* dihiryn ♦ *vt* difrïo
**blackleg** *n* bradwr
**blackmail** *n* arian bygwth, blacmel
**blacksmith** *n* gof
**bladder** *n* pledren, chwysigen
**blade** *n* llafn; eginyn, blewyn
**blame** *vt* beio ♦ *n* bai
**blameless** *adj* di-fai
**blanch** *vt* gwynnu, cannu
**bland** *adj* mwyn, tyner, tirion
**blandish** *vt* gwenieithio, truthio
**blank** *adj* gwag, syn. **b. verse** mesur di-odl. **b. cheque** *n* siec wag
**blanket** *n* blanced, gwrthban
**blare** *vb* canu utgorn ♦ *n* sain utgorn
**blarney** *n* gweniaith, truth
**blaspheme** *vb* cablu, difenwi
**blasphemy** *n* cabledd, cabl
**blast** *n* chwa, chwythiad, deifiad ♦ *vt* deifio; saethu. **b. furnace** *n* ffwrnais chwythu
**blatant** *adj* stwrllyd, digywilydd, haerllug
**blaze** *n* fflam, ffagl ♦ *vi* fflamio, ffaglu
**bleach** *vb* cannu, gwynnu
**bleak** *adj* oer, digysgod, noeth, noethlwm
**blear** *adj* pŵl, dolurus, dyfriog
**bleat** *vb* brefu ♦ *n* bref
**bleed** *vb* gwaedu
**blemish** *vt* anafu, anurddo ♦ *n* anaf, bai, mefl
**blend** *vb* cymysgu ♦ *n* cymysgedd
**bless** *vt* bendithio
**blessed** *adj* bendigedig, gwyn ei fyd
**blessing** *n* bendith
**blight** *n* malltod ♦ *vt* mallu, deifio

**blind** *adj* dall, tywyll ♦ *vt* dallu ♦ *n* llen, bleind
**blindness** *n* dallineb
**blink** *vb* cau'r llygaid, ysmicio, amrantu
**bliss** *n* gwynfyd, dedwyddyd
**blister** *n* chwysigen, pothell ♦ *vb* pothellu
**blithe** *adj* llawen, llon, hoenus
**blitz** *n* blits
**blizzard** *n* ystorm erwin o wynt ac eira
**bloat** *vb* chwyddo, chwythu
**blob** *n* ysmotyn, bwrlwm
**block** *n* plocyn, cyff ♦ *vt* cau, rhwystro
**blockade** *n* gwarchae ♦ *vb* gwarchae ar
**blockhead** *n* penbwl, hurtyn
**blonde** *adj* o bryd golau
**blood** *n* gwaed; gwaedoliaeth. **b. pressure** *n* pwysedd gwaed
**bloody** *adj* gwaedlyd
**bloom** *n* blodeuyn; gwawr, gwrid ♦ *vi* blodeuo
**blossom** *n* blodeuyn ♦ *vi* blodeuo
**blot** *n* ysmotyn du, blot, mefl ♦ *vb* blotio
**blotch** *n* ysmotyn, blotyn, ystremp
**blouse** *n* blows
**blow** *n* dyrnod, ergyd
**blow** *vb* chwythu
**blow-dry** *vb* chwythu'n sych
**bludgeon** *n* pastwn
**blue** *adj*, *n* glas ♦ *vt* glasu
**bluff** *adj* garw, brochus
**blunder** *n* amryfusedd ♦ *vb* amryfuso
**blunt** *adj* pŵl, di-fin; plaen ♦ *vt* pylu
**blur** *n* ysmotyn, ystaen
**blurb** *n* broliant
**blurt** *vt* rhuthro dywedyd
**blush** *vi* cochi, gwrido ♦ *n* gwrid
**bluster** *vi* trystio, brochi ♦ *n* brawl, broch
**blustery** *adj* stormus, rhuadus

**boar** *n* baedd
**board** *n* bwrdd, bord; ymborth ♦ *vb* byrddio
**boarding house** *n* llety
**boast** *n* ymffrost ♦ *vb* ymffrostio
**boat** *n* bad, cwch
**bobbin** *n* gwerthyd
**bobby** *n* plismon
**bode** *vt* darogan, argoeli
**body** *n* corff
**bog** *n* cors, mignen, siglen
**boggle** *vi* petruso; rhusio, ffwndro
**bogus** *adj* ffug, gau, ffuantus
**bogy, -ey** *n* bwbach, bwci, bwgan
**boil** *n* cornwyd, casgliad
**boil** *vb* berwi
**boiler** *n* pair, crochan
**boisterous** *adj* terfysglyd, trystiog, brochus
**bold** *adj* hy, eofn; hyderus; eglur
**bollard** *n* bolard
**bolster** *n* gobennydd ♦ *vt* ategu
**bolt** *n* bollt ♦ *vb* bolltio; dianc; traflyncu
**bomb** *n* bom
**bombast** *n* chwyddiaith
**bombastic** *n* chwyddedig
**bona fide** *adj* o'r iawn ryw, dilys, didwyll
**bond** *n* rhwymyn; ysgrifrwym ♦ *adj* caeth
**bondage** *n* caethiwed
**bone** *n* asgwrn
**bonfire** *n* coelcerth, banffagl
**Bonn** *n* Bonn
**bonnet** *n* bonet
**bonny** *adj* braf, nobl
**bonus** *n* bonws, ychwanegiad
**booby** *n* hurtyn, penbwl
**book** *n* llyfr
**boom** *n* bŵm
**boom** *vb* trystio, utganu ♦ *n* trwst, swae
**boon** *n* ffafr, bendith, caffaeliad
**boor** *n* taeog
**boost** *vb* gwthio, hybu
**boot** *n* botasen, esgid

**booth** n bwth, lluest, lluesty, caban

**booty** n ysglyfaeth, anrhaith, ysbail

**booze** vi diota, meddwi ♦ n diod feddwol

**border** n ffin, goror, ymyl ♦ vb ymylu

**bore** vb tyllu, ebillio ♦ n twll

**bore** n pla, dyn diflas ♦ vt blino, diflasu, llethu

**bored** adj wedi syrffedu ar beth, wedi alaru

**boring** adj diflas, annifyr, llethol

**born** adj wedi ei eni

**borough** n bwrdeistref

**borrow** vt benthyca

**bosom** n mynwes, côl

**boss** n meistr

**botany** n llysieueg

**botch** n ystomp ♦ vb ystompio, bwnglera

**both** adj, pron, adv y ddau, ill dau

**bother** vb blino, trafferthu ♦ n helynt, trafferth

**bottle** n potel, costrel ♦ vt potelu, costrelu. **b. opener** n agorwr poteli

**bottom** n gwaelod, godre, tin

**bough** n cainc, cangen

**boulder** n carreg fawr, clogfaen

**bounce** vb neidio, adlamu; bostio, ymffrostio

**bound** n terfyn, ffin, cyffin ♦ vt ffinio

**bound** vi llamu, neidio

**boundary** n ffin, terfyn

**bounty** n daioni, haelioni, ced

**bouquet** n blodeuglwm, pwysi

**bout** n sbel, term; ornest, ffrwgwd

**bow** n bwa; dolen

**bow** vb plygu, crymu, ymgrymu ♦ n moesymgrymiad

**bow** n pen blaen llong, bow

**bowels** npl ymysgaroedd, perfedd

**bower** n deildy

**bowl** n cawg, basn

**bowler** n het galed; bowliwr

**box** n bocs, pren bocs

**box** n bocs, blwch, cist; sedd, côr; bwth

**box** n bonclust ♦ vb taro bonclust; paffio. **b. office** n swyddfa docynnau

**boy** n bachgen, hogyn, mab, gwas

**boycott** n, vb ymwrthod â pherthynas a chydweithrediad, boicot(io)

**boyfriend** n cariadfab, anwylyd

**boyhood** n bachgendod, mebyd

**brace** n rhwymyn; pâr ♦ vt tynhau, cryfhau

**bracelet** n breichled

**bracket** n braced, cromfach

**bracken** n rhedyn ungoes

**brag** n brol, ymffrost, bocsach ♦ vb brolio, ymffrostio

**braid** n pleth, brwyd ♦ vt plethu, brwydo

**brain** n ymennydd

**brake** n dryslwyn, prysglwyn

**brake** n brêc ♦ vt brecio

**bramble** n miaren

**bran** n eisin, bran, rhuddion

**branch** n cangen, cainc ♦ vi canghennu

**brand** n pentewyn; nod ♦ vt gwarthnodi

**brandish** vb ysgwyd, chwifio

**brandy** n brandi

**brash** adj byrbwyll, ehud

**brass** n pres, efydd

**brassière** n bronglwm

**brat** n crwt, crwtyn; croten

**bravado** n gwag-ymffrost, bocsach, gorchest

**brave** adj dewr, gwrol, glew ♦ vt herio

**bravo** excl da iawn! campus!

**brawl** vi ffraeo, terfysgu ♦ n ffrae, ffrwgwd

**brawn** n cnawd

**bray** vt pwyo, briwio, malurio

**bray** vi brefu (megis asyn), nadu

**brazen** *adj* haerllug, hy
**Brazil** *n* Brasil
**breach** *n* adwy, rhwyg, tor; trosedd
**bread** *n* bara
**breadth** *n* lled
**break** *vb* torri ♦ *n* toriad, tor
**breakdown** *n* salwch, colli iechyd; (*car*) torri lawr
**breakfast** *n* brecwast ♦ *vb* brecwasta
**breakwater** *n* morglawdd
**breast** *n* bron, dwyfron, mynwes ♦ *vt* wynebu, ymladd â
**breath** *n* anadl, gwynt
**breathalyser** *n* anadlydd, anadliadur
**breathe** *vb* anadlu, chwythu
**breathing** *n* anadliad; anadlu
**breech** *n* tin, bôn
**breeches** *npl* llodrau, clos
**breed** *vb* magu; epilio; bridio ♦ *n* rhywogaeth, brid
**breeze** *n* awel, awelan, chwa
**brethren** *npl* brodyr (ffigurol yn bennaf)
**brevity** *n* byrder, byrdra
**brew** *vt* darllaw, bragu
**brewer** *n* darllawydd, bragwr
**bribe** *n* llwgrwobrwy ♦ *vt* llwgrwobrwyo
**brick** *n* bricsen, priddfaen ♦ *vt* bricio
**bride** *n* priodferch, priodasferch
**bridegroom** *n* priodfab
**bridesmaid** *n* morwyn briodas
**bridge** *n* pont ♦ *vt* pontio
**bridle** *n* ffrwyn ♦ *vt* ffrwyno
**brief** *adj* byr
**brier, briar** *n* miaren, drysïen
**brigade** *n* brigâd, mintai, torf
**brigand** *n* ysbeiliwr, carnleidr, herwr
**bright** *adj* disglair, claer, gloyw, hoyw
**brilliance** *n* disgleirdeb
**brilliant** *adj* disglair, llachar ♦ *n* gem

**brim** *n* ymyl, min, cyfor; cantel
**brimstone** *n* brwmstan
**brindled** *adj* brith, brych
**brine** *n* heli
**bring** *vt* dwyn, cyrchu, dyfod â, dod â
**brink** *n* min, ymyl, glan
**brisk** *adj* bywiog, heini, sionc
**bristle** *n* gwrychyn, gwrych ♦ *vi* codi gwrychyn
**Britain** *n* Prydain
**British** *adj* Prydeinig, Brytanaidd
**Briton** *n* Brython, Prydeiniwr
**Brittany** *n* Llydaw
**brittle** *adj* brau, bregus
**broach** *vt* agor baril, gollwng; agor ymddiddan
**broad** *adj* llydan; eang; bras
**broaden** *vb* lledu, ehangu
**broccoli** *n* brocoli, math o fresych
**brochure** *n* llyfryn
**brogue** *n* llediaith (Gwyddelod)
**broil** *vt* briwlio
**broken** *adj* toredig, briw, drylliedig
**broker** *n* brocer, dyn canol
**broil** *n* terfysg, ymrafael, ymryson
**bronchitis** *n* bronceitis
**bronze** *n* pres, efydd
**brooch** *n* tlws
**brood** *n* nythaid; hil, epil ♦ *vi* deor; synfyfyrio
**brook** *n* nant, cornant, afonig
**broom** *n* banadl; ysgub, ysgubell
**broth** *n* potes, cawl
**brothel** *n* puteindy
**brother** (**-s**, **brethren**) *n* brawd
**brotherly** *adj* brawdol. **b. love** brawdgarwch
**brow** *n* ael, talcen; crib
**brown** *adj* brown, llwyd, gwinau. **b. paper** *n* papur llwyd. **b. sugar** *n* siwgr coch
**browse** *vi* brigbori, pori, blewynna
**bruise** *vb* cleisio, ysigo ♦ *n* clais
**brunette** *n* gwineuferch

**brunt** *n* pwys a gwres, ergyd
**brush** *n* brws ♦ *vt* brwsio, ysgubo
**brushwood** *n* manwydd, prysgwydd
**brusque** *adj* cwta, anfoesgar, taeog
**Brussels sprouts** *npl* ysgewyll Brwsel
**brutal** *adj* creulon, bwysfilaidd
**brute** *n* anifail, creadur (direswm)
**bubble** *n* bwrlwm ♦ *vb* byrlymu
**buccaneer** *n* môr-leidr, môr-herwr
**buck** *n* bwch; coegyn ♦ *vb* llamsachu
**bucket** *n* bwced, ystwc
**buckle** *n* bwcl, gwäeg ♦ *vb* byclu, gwaëgu
**bud** *n* blaguryn, eginyn ♦ *vb* blaguro, egino
**budge** *vb* syflyd, chwimio
**budget** *n* cwd, coden; cyllideb
**buff** *adj* llwydfelyn
**buffalo** *n* bual
**buffet** *n* cernod ♦ *vt* cernodio, baeddu
**buffoon** *n* digrifwas, croesan, ysgentyn
**bug** *n* drewbryf, bwg
**bugbear** *n* bwgan, bwbach, bwci
**bugle** *n* corn, utgorn
**build** *vt* adeiladu ♦ *n* corffolaeth
**building** *n* adail, adeilad, adeiladaeth
**bulb** *n* bwlb
**bulge** *n* chwydd ♦ *vt* chwyddo
**bulk** *n* swm, crynswth
**bull** *n* tarw
**bulldozer** *n* peiriant clirio ffordd, tarw dur
**bullet** *n* bwled, bwleden
**bulletin** *n* bwletin
**bullfight** *n* ymladd teirw
**bullfinch** *n* coch y berllan
**bullion** *n* aur neu arian clamp, bwliwn
**bullock** *n* bustach, eidion, ych
**bull's eye** *n* trawiad union

**bully** *n* gormeswr, bwli ♦ *vt* gormesu, erlid
**bulrushes** *npl* llafrwyn, hesg
**bulwark** *n* gwrthglawdd; canllaw
**bumbailiff** *n* bwmbeili
**bumble-bee** *n* cacynen
**bump** *vb* bwmpio, hergydio ♦ *n* bwmp, hergwd
**bumper** *adj* llawn, helaeth
**bumpkin** *n* lleban, llabwst, llelo
**bumptious** *adj* hunandybus, rhodresgar
**bumpy** *adj* aflonydd, anwadal, garw
**bun** *n* bynsen, bynnen, teisen
**bunch** *n* swp; cwlwm, pwysi ♦ *vb* sypio
**bundle** *n* bwndel, coflaid ♦ *vt* bwndelu
**bungalow** *n* tŷ unllawr, byngalo
**bungle** *vb* bwnglera, ystompio ♦ *n* bwnglerwaith
**bunion** *n* corn ar fys troed
**bunker** *n* bwncer
**bunkum** *n* lol, ffiloreg, truth
**bunting** *n* (defnydd) banerau
**buoy** *n* bwi ♦ *vt* cynnal, cadw rhag suddo
**buoyant** *adj* hynawf; calonnog
**burden** *n* baich ♦ *vt* beichio, llwytho
**bureau** *n* ysgrifgist; swyddfa
**bureaucracy** *n* biwrocratiaeth
**burgess, burgher** *n* dinesydd, bwrdais
**burglar** *n* torrwr tŷ, bwrgler
**burial** *n* claddedigaeth, angladd
**burlesque** *n* digrifwawd, gwatwargerdd
**burly** *adj* corffol, praff, mawr
**burn** *vb* llosgi, ysu ♦ *n* llosg, llosgiad
**burnish** *vt* caboli, llathru, gloywi
**burrow** *n* twll cwningen ♦ *vb* tyllu, tyrchu
**bursar** *n* bwrser, swyddog ariannol
**bursary** *n* amneriaeth, ysgoloriaeth

**burst** vb byrstio, ymrwygo, ymddryllio, torri ♦ n rhwyg

**bury** vt claddu

**bus** n bws

**bush** n perth, llwyn; prysgwydd, drysi

**bushel** n bwysel, mesur wyth galwyn

**business** n busnes, masnach, gwaith. **b. trip** n taith fusnes

**businessman/woman** n gŵr busnes/gwraig fusnes

**bus-stop** n atalfa bws, arosfan

**bust** n penddelw; mynwes

**bustle** vi trafferthu, ffwdanu ♦ n ffwdan

**busy** adj prysur

**busybody** n ymyrrwr, dyn busneslyd, trwyn

**but** conj, prep ond, eithr

**butcher** n cigydd ♦ vt cigyddio, lladd

**butler** n trulliad, bwtler

**butt** n nod, targed; cyff clêr

**butt** vt cornio, hyrddu, twlcio, hwylio

**butt** n casgen, baril

**butter** n ymenyn ♦ vt rhoi ymenyn ar

**buttercup** n blodyn yr ymenyn

**butterfly** n glöyn byw, iâr fach yr haf, pili-pala

**buttermilk** n llaeth enwyn

**buttery** n bwtri

**buttock** n ffolen

**button** n botwm ♦ vt botymu

**buttress** n ateg, gwanas ♦ vt ategu

**buxom** adj glandeg, gweddgar, nwyfus

**buy** vt prynu

**buzz** vb suo, sisial, mwmian ♦ n su, sŵn gwenyn

**by** prep gan, wrth, trwy, ger, gerllaw ♦ adv heibio, yn agos ♦ prefix rhag-, is-

**by-election** n isetholiad

**by(e)-law** n is-ddeddf

**by-gone** n yr hyn a fu

**bypass** n ffordd osgoi

**by-product** n isgynnyrch

**bystander** n un yn sefyll gerllaw

**byword** n ymadrodd cynefin, cyffredin

# C

**cab** n cab

**cabal** n clymblaid, cabal ♦ vi clymbleidio

**cabaret** n cabare

**cabbage** n bresychen, bresych

**cabin** n caban ♦ vt cabanu, caethiwo

**cabinet** n cell, cist; cabinet

**cable** n rhaff fferf; cebl tanfor

**cackle** vi clegar

**cactus** n mwl ysgallen, cactws

**cad** n taeog, bryntyn, cenau

**caddie** n gwas golffwr

**cadence** n goslef, diweddeb

**cadet** n mab ieuengaf; cadlanc

**café** n tŷ bwyta, caffe

**cage** n cawell, caets ♦ vt cau, carcharu

**cairn** n carn, carnedd, crug

**cajole** vt twyllo drwy weniaith

**cake** n teisen, cacen ♦ vb torthi; caglu

**calamity** n adfyd, trallod, trychineb

**calcine** vb llosgi'n galch

**calculate** vb cyfrif, bwrw cyfrif, clandro

**calculation** n cyfrif

**calculator** n cyfrifiannell

**calendar** n calendr, almanac

**calf** (**calves**) n llo

**calf** n (of the leg) croth (coes)

**calibre** n calibr

**call** vb galw ♦ n galwad, galw; ymweliad

**calling** n galwedigaeth

**callous** adj croendew, dideimlad,

caled

**calm** *adj* tawel ♦ *n* tawelwch ♦ *vb* tawelu

**calorie** *n* calori, uned gwres

**calumny** *n* anair, enllib, athrod, cabl

**calve** *vi* bwrw llo

**Calvinism** *n* Calfiniaeth

**camber** *n* camber

**Cambodia** *n* Cambodia

**Cambrian** *adj* Cymreig

**camel** *n* camel

**cameo** *n* cameo

**camera** *n* ystafell; teclyn tynnu lluniau, camera

**camouflage** *n* cuddliw, dull o ddieithrio ♦ *vb* dieithrio, cuddio

**camp** *n* gwersyll ♦ *vi* gwersyllu

**campaign** *n* ymgyrch, rhyfelgyrch

**campbed** *n* gwely plyg

**campsite** *n* maes gwersylla

**campus** *n* campws

**can** *n* tyn, piser, stên ♦ *vb* gallu. **c. opener** *n* agorwr caniau

**Canada** *n* Canada

**Canadian** *adj* Canadaidd ♦ *n* Canadiad

**canal** *n* camlas; pibell

**canary** *n* caneri

**Canary Islands** *npl*: **the C.I.** yr Ynysoedd Dedwydd

**cancel** *vt* dileu, dirymu, diddymu

**cancer** *n* dafad wyllt, cancr, cranc

**candid** *adj* teg, onest, plaen

**candidate** *n* ymgeisydd

**candle** *n* cannwyll

**candlestick** *n* canhwyllbren

**candour** *n* onestrwydd, didwylledd

**candy** *n* candi

**cane** *n* corsen, cansen ♦ *vt* curo â chansen

**canine** *adj* perthynol i'r ci

**canister** *n* tyn cadw te, bocs (te)

**canker** *n* cancr ♦ *vb* cancro

**canned** *adj* ar gadw mewn can tun

**cannibal** *n* canibal

**cannon** *n* magnel

**canny** *adj* call, cyfrwys, ffel

**canoe** *n* ceufad, canŵ

**canon** *n* canon, rheol

**canopy** *n* gortho, nenlen

**cant** *n* ffugsancteiddrwydd, rhagrith ♦ *vi* rhagrithio

**cantankerous** *adj* cwerylgar, cynhennus

**cantata** *n* cantata, cantawd

**canteen** *n* cantîn

**canter** *vi* rhygyngu ♦ *n* rhygyng

**canticle** *n* cantigl, canig, cân, emyn

**canto** *n* cân, adran o gân

**canton** *n* rhandir, talaith

**canvas** *n* cynfas, lliain bras

**canvass** *vb* trafod; ymofyn pleidleisiau, canfasio

**canyon** *n* ceunant, canion

**cap** *n* cap, capan ♦ *vt* capio

**capable** *adj* galluog, cymwys, cyfaddas

**capacity** *n* gallu, cymhwyster; cynnwys

**cape** *n* penrhyn, pentir, trwyn

**cape** *n* mantell, cêp

**caper** *n* pranc ♦ *vi* prancio

**capital** *adj* prif, pen ♦ *n* priflythyren; prifddinas; cyfalaf

**capitalism** *n* cyfalafiaeth

**capital punishment** *n* y gosb eithaf

**capitulate** *vi* ymostwng ar amodau

**caprice** *n* mympwy, chwilen

**capsize** *vb* dymchwelyd, troi

**capsule** *n* capswl

**captain** *n* capten

**caption** *n* pennawd, teitl

**captivate** *vt* swyno, hudo, denu

**captive** *adj* caeth ♦ *n* carcharor

**captivity** *n* caethiwed; caethglud

**captor** *n* daliwr, deiliad

**capture** *n* daliad ♦ *vt* dal

**car** *n* car, cerbyd. **c. wash** golfcha geir

**caravan** *n* carafán; men. **c. site** *n* maes carafanau

**carbine** n dryll byr, byrddryll
**carbohydrate(s)** n carbohydrad(au)
**carbon** n carbon
**carbuncle** n carbwncl
**carburettor** n carburadur
**carcass, -ase** n celain, ysgerbwd
**card** n cerdyn, carden
**card** vt cribo gwlân
**cardiac** adj perthynol i'r galon
**Cardiff** n Caerdydd
**cardigan** n cardigan
**cardinal** adj prif, arbennig ♦ n cardinal
**care** n gofal, pryder ♦ vi gofalu, malio
**career** n gyrfa, hynt ♦ vi carlamu
**careful** adj gofalus, gwyliadwrus
**careless** adj diofal, esgeulus
**caress** n anwes, mwythau ♦ vt anwesu
**caret** n gwallnod, diffygnod (ˆ)
**caretaker** n gofalwr
**cargo** n llwyth (llong), cargo
**caricature** n gwawdlun, digriflun
**caring** adj gofalus
**carnage** n galanastra, lladdfa
**carnal** adj cnawdol
**carnation** n blodyn cigliw
**carnival** n carnifal
**carnivorous** adj cigysol, rheibus
**carol** n carol ♦ vi caroli, canu
**carouse** vi gloddesta, cyfeddach
**carp** vi pigo beiau, cecru, cadw sŵn
**car park** n maes parcio
**carpenter** n saer coed
**carpet** n carped ♦ vt carpedu
**carriage** n cerbyd; cludiad; ymarweddiad
**carrier** n cariwr, cludydd. **c. bag** n cludfag
**carrion** n burgyn, celain, ysgerbwd
**carrot** n moronen
**carry** vb cario, cludo, cywain
**cart** vb men, trol, cert, cart, car
**cartilage** n madruddyn

**carton** n carton
**cartoon** n digriflun, cartŵn
**cartridge** n cetrisen
**carve** vt cerfio, naddu; torri cig
**cascade** n rhaeadr
**case** n achos, cyflwr; dadl
**case** n cas, gwain; cist wydr
**casement** n ffenestr adeiniog, casment
**cash** n arian parod. **c. desk** n safle talu
**cashier** n ariannwr, trysorydd
**cashier** vt diswyddo
**casing** n plisgyn; casin
**casino** n casino
**cask** n casgen, baril
**casket** n cistan, prenfol, blwch
**casserole** n llestr coginio a dal bwyd
**cassette** n casét
**cassock** n llaeswisg ddu offeiriad, casog
**cast** vb bwrw, taflu ♦ n tafliad. **c. iron** haearn bwrw
**caste** n llwyth; gradd, braint; cast
**castigate** vt cystwyo
**casting-vote** n pleidlais y cadeirydd
**castle** n castell ♦ vi castellu
**castrate** vt disbaddu
**casual** adj damweiniol, achlysurol
**casualty** n un wedi ei anafu
**casuistry** n achosionaeth
**cat** n cath
**cataclysm** n dilyw, dylif, rhyferthwy
**catacomb** n claddgell, claddogof
**catalogue** n catalog
**catapult** n blif, catapwlt
**cataract** n rhaeadr, sgwd; pilen
**catarrh** n llif annwyd, gormwyth
**catastrophe** n trychineb
**catch** vt dal ♦ n bach, clicied; dalfa
**catching** adj heintus
**catchment area** n dalgylch
**catechism** n holwyddoreg,

catecism
**category** n trefn, dosbarth
**cater** vi arlwyo, darmerth, darparu
**caterpillar** n lindys
**cathartic** n carthlyn
**cathedral** n eglwys gadeiriol
**catholic** adj catholig; pabyddol ♦ n catholigydd; pabydd
**catkins** npl cenawon cyll, cywion gwyddau
**cattle** npl gwartheg, da
**caucus** n clymblaid
**caudle** n sucan
**cauldron** n crochan, pair, callor
**cauliflower** n blodfresychen
**causality** n achosiaeth
**cause** n achos ♦ vt achosi, peri
**causeway** n sarn, cawsai
**caustic** adj ysol, llosg, deifiol
**cauterize** vt serio
**caution** n pwyll, gwyliadwriaeth; rhybudd ♦ vt rhybuddio
**cautious** adj gwyliadwrus
**cavalcade** n mintai o farchogion
**cavalier** n marchog, marchfilwr
**cavalry** n gwŷr meirch
**cave** n ogof
**cavern** n ceudwll, ogof
**caviar(e)** n grawn pysgod, cafiâr
**cavil** vi cecru
**cavity** n ceudod, gwagle
**caw** vi crawcian
**cease** vb peidio, darfod
**cedar** n cedrwydden
**cede** vt rhoi i fyny, gildio, trosglwyddo
**ceiling** n nen, nenfwd
**celebrate** vt clodfori; dathlu; gweinyddu
**celebrated** adj clodfawr, enwog, hyglod
**celebrity** n bri, enwogrwydd; gŵr o fri
**celery** n seleri
**celestial** adj nefol, nefolaidd
**celibate** adj dibriod
**cell** n cell

**cellar** n seler
**cement** n sment ♦ vt smentio; cadarnhau
**cemetery** n mynwent, claddfa
**censer** n thuser
**censor** n beirniad; sensor
**censure** n cerydd, sen ♦ vt ceryddu
**census** n cyfrifiad
**cent** n y ganfed ran op ddoler
**centenarian** n canmlwyddiad
**centenary** n canmlwyddiant
**centigrade** adj canradd, sentigred
**central** adj canol, canolog. **c. heating** n gwres canolog
**centre** n canol, canolfan, canolbwynt ♦ vb canolbwyntio
**centre-forward** n canolwr blaen
**centre-threequarter** n canolwr
**centrifugal** adj allgyrchol
**centripetal** adj mewngyrchol
**centurion** n canwriad
**century** n canrif
**ceramic** adj perthynol i grefft y crochenydd, ceramig
**cereal** n grawn, ŷd
**cerebral** adj ymenyddol
**ceremony** n seremoni, defod
**certain** adj sicr; neilltuol; rhyw, rhai
**certainly** adv yn sicr, yn siwr
**certainty** n sicrwydd
**certificate** n tystysgrif
**certify** vt hysbysu, tystio
**cesspool** n carthbwll
**chafe** vb rhwbio; llidio ♦ n llid, cythrudd
**chaff** n us, manus, mân us
**chaffer** vi edwica, bargeinio, bargenna
**chaffinch** n pinc, asgell fraith
**chagrin** n cythrudd, siom
**chain** n cadwyn ♦ vt cadwyno
**chair** n cadair ♦ vt cadeirio
**chairman** n cadeirydd
**chalet** n bwthyn (haf)
**chalice** n cwpan cymun, caregl

**chalk** *n* sialc ♦ *vt* sialcio
**challenge** *n* her, sialens ♦ *vt* herio, sialensio
**chamber** *n* ystafell, siambr
**chamberlain** *n* gwas ystafell, siambrlen
**champ** *vt* cnoi, dygnoi
**champagne** *n* gwin Champagne
**champion** *n* pencampwr; pleidiwr ♦ *vt* cymryd plaid
**chance** *n* damwain, siawns ♦ *vt* digwydd
**chancel** *n* cangell
**chancellor** *n* canghellor
**chandelier** *n* canhwyllyr
**chandler** *n* canhwyllydd, masnachydd
**change** *vb* newid, cyfnewid ♦ *n* newid
**changing-room** *n* ystafell newid salmdon
**channel** *n* sianel, gwely; rhigol
**chant** *vt* corganu ♦ *n* corgan
**chaos** *n* tryblith, anhrefn
**chap** *vt* agennu, torri (am ddwylo)
**chapel** *n* capel
**chaplain** *n* caplan
**chapter** *n* pennod; cabidwl
**char** *vb* golosgi, deifio
**character** *n* cymeriad; nod, arwydd
**characteristic** *adj* nodweddiadol ♦ *n* nodwedd
**charcoal** *n* marwor, golosg, sercol
**charge** *vb* siarsio; cyhuddo; rhuthro; codi; llwytho ♦ *n* siars; gofal; cyhuddiad; rhuth; pris; ergyd
**charger** *n* march rhyfel, cadfarch
**chariot** *n* cerbyd
**charity** *n* cariad; cardod, elusen
**charlatan** *n* un yn honni gwybodaeth; cwac
**charm** *n* swyn, cyfaredd ♦ *vt* swyno
**charming** *adj* cyfareddol, swynol, cwrtais

**chart** *n* siart
**charter** *n* siarter, breinlen ♦ *vt* breinio; llogi. **c. flight** *n* hediad siartr
**charwoman** *n* morwyn wrth y dydd
**chary** *adj* gwagelog, gochelgar, gofalus
**chase** *vt* ymlid, erlid, hel ♦ *n* helwriaeth
**chasm** *n* hafn, ceunant, agendor
**chaste** *adj* diwair, pur, dillyn
**chasten** *vt* puro, coethi; ceryddu
**chastise** *vb* ceryddu, cosbi, cystwyo
**chastity** *n* diweirdeb, purdeb
**chat** *vi* sgwrsio, ymgomio ♦ *n* sgwrs, ymgom
**chattel** *n* catel
**chatter** *vi* trydar, cogor; clebran; rhincian
**chatterbox** *n* clebryn, clebren
**chatty** *adj* siaradus, parod am sgwrs
**chauffeur** *n* gyrrwr
**cheap** *adj* rhad, salw
**cheat** *n* twyll; twyllwr ♦ *vt* twyllo
**check** *n* rhwystr, atalfa ♦ *vt* atal, ffrwyno
**cheek** *n* grudd, boch; digywilydd-dra
**cheeky** *adj* digywilydd, haerllug, eg(e)r
**cheer** *n* calondid, cysur; arlwy ♦ *vb* llonni, sirioli, sirio
**cheerful** *adj* llon, siriol
**cheers!** *excl* iechyd da!
**cheese** *n* caws
**chef** *n* prif gogydd
**chemical** *adj* cemegol ♦ *n* cyffur
**chemise** *n* crys merch
**chemist** *n* fferyllydd; cemegwr
**chemistry** *n* cemeg
**cheque** *n* archeb (ar fanc), siec. **c. book** *n* llyfr siec; (*col*) llyfr main. **c. card** *n* carden siec
**chequer** *vt* amryliwio, britho

**chequered** adj brith, anwadal
**cherish** vt meithrin, coleddu, mynwesu
**cherry** n ceiriosen
**cherub** n ceriwb
**chess** n gwyddbwyll
**chest** n cist, coffr; brest
**chestnut** n castan
**chevalier** n marchog
**chew** vb cnoi. **c. the cud** cnoi cil
**chewing gum** n gwm cnoi
**chick, chicken** n cyw (iâr)
**chicken-pox** n brech yr ieir
**chide** vt ceryddu, dwrdio
**chief** adj pen, pennaf, prif ♦ n pennaeth
**chieftain** n blaenor, pennaeth
**chilblain** n llosg eira, cibwst, malaith
**child (-ren)** n plentyn
**childhood** n plentyndod, mebyd
**Chile** n Chile
**chill** n oerni, annwyd ♦ adj oer, anwydog ♦ vb oeri, fferru, rhynnu
**chime** n sain cloch neu gloc ♦ vb canu (clychau)
**chimera** n anghenfil; bwgan, bwbach
**chimney** n corn mwg, simnai
**chin** n gên
**China** n China, Tseina
**china** n llestri te (tsieni)
**chink** n agen, hollt
**chip** vb hacio, naddu ♦ n asglodyn, pric
**chips** npl sglodion
**chiropodist** n troedfeddyg
**chirp** vi yswitian, grillian, trydar
**chisel** n cŷn, gaing
**chit** n nodyn byr
**chivalry** n urddas marchog; sifalri
**chives** n cennin sifi
**chocolate** n siocled
**choice** n dewis, dewisiad ♦ adj dewisol, dethol
**choir** n côr; cafell
**choke** vb tagu; mygu; topio, cau

**choler** n geri, bustl; dicter, llid
**cholera** n y geri marwol, colera
**choose** vb dewis, dethol, ethol
**chop** vt torri ♦ n golwyth
**choral** adj corawl
**chord** n tant; cord
**chore** n y dwt
**chorus** n côr, cytgan, byrdwn, corws
**Christ** n Crist
**christen** vt bedyddio, enwi
**Christendom** n (gwledydd) Cred
**Christian** adj Cristnogol ♦ n Cristion
**Christianity** n Cristnogaeth
**Christmas** n Nadolig
**Christmassy** adj Nadoligaidd
**chrome** n crôm
**chronic** adj parhaol (am anhwyldeb)
**chronicle** n cronicl ♦ vt croniclo
**chronology** n amseryddiaeth
**chrysanthemum** n ffarwel haf
**chubby** adj wynepgrwn, tew
**chuck** vt taro dan yr ên; taflu, lluchio
**chuckle** vi chwerthin yn nwrn dyn
**chum** n cyfaill mebyd ♦ vi cyfrinachu
**chunk** n tafell dew, toc
**church** n eglwys, llan ♦ vt eglwysa
**churchyard** n mynwent
**churl** n taeog, costog, cerlyn
**churlish** adj afrywiog, taeogaidd
**churn** n buddai ♦ vb corddi
**chutney** n picl cymysg
**cider** n seidr
**cigar** n sigâr
**cigarette** n sigarét
**cincture** n gwregys, rhwymyn
**cinder** n marwor yn, colsyn
**cine-camera** n camera sine
**cinema** n sinema
**cinnamon** n sinamon
**cipher** n gwagnod (O); ysgrifen ddirgel ♦ vi cyfrif
**circle** n cylch ♦ vb cylchu

**circuit** *n* cylch; cylchdaith
**circular** *adj* crwn ♦ *n* cylchlythyr
**circulate** *vb* cylchredeg, lledaenu
**circum-** *prefix* cylch-, am-
**circumcise** *vt* enwaedu
**circumference** *n* cylchyn; cylchedd
**circumflex** *n* acen grom, to (ˆ)
**circumlocution** *n* cylchymadrodd
**circumscribe** *vt* cyfyngu
**circumspect** *adj* gwyliadwrus, gofalus
**circumstance** *n* amgylchiad
**circumstantial** *adj* amgylchus
**circumvent** *vb* twyllo
**circus** *n* syrcas
**cistern** *n* dyfrgist, pydew, sistern
**citadel** *n* castell, amddiffynfa, caer
**cite** *vt* gwysio; dyfynnu
**citizen** *n* dinesydd
**city** *n* dinas
**civic** *adj* dinesig
**civil** *adj* gwladol; moesgar
**civilian** *n* dinesydd (anfilwrol)
**civilization** *n* gwareiddiad
**civilize** *vt* gwareiddio
**civil service** *n* gwasanaeth sifil, gwasanaeth gwladol
**civil war** *n* rhyfel cartref
**clack** *vi* clecian, clepian, clegar
**claim** *vt* hawlio ♦ *n* hawl
**clamber** *vi* dringo, cribo
**clammy** *adj* gludiog, cleiog, toeslyd
**clamour** *n* gwaedd, dadwrdd ♦ *vi* crochlefain
**clamp** *n* ystyffwl, craff
**clan** *n* tylwyth, llwyth
**clandestine** *adj* lladradaidd
**clang, clank** *vb* cloncio ♦ *n* clonc
**clap** *n* twrf, trwst ♦ *vb* curo; taro; clepian
**claret** *n* claret
**clarify** *vt* gloywi, puro; egluro
**clarinet** *n* clarinet
**clarion** *n* utgorn
**clash** *vb* taro, gwrthdaro ♦ *n* gwrthdrawiad

**clasp** *n* gwäeg, bach, clesbyn ♦ *vt* gwaëgu; cofleidio
**class** *n* dosbarth ♦ *vt* dosbarthu
**classic** *n* clasur, campwaith, llên goeth ♦ *adj* clasurol
**classical** *adj* clasurol
**classics** *npl* clasuron
**classify** *vb* dosbarthu
**classroom** *n* ystafell ddosbarth
**clatter** *vb* clewtian, clepian, trystio ♦ *n* trwst
**clause** *n* adran, cymal
**claw** *n* crafanc, ewin ♦ *vt* crafangu, cripio
**clay** *n* clai
**clean** *adj* glân, glanwaith ♦ *vt* glanhau
**cleaner** *n* glanhawr, glanheydd
**cleaning** *n* glanhad, glanheuad
**cleanly** *adv* yn lân
**cleanse** *vt* glanhau
**cleanser** *n* glanhawr
**clear** *adj* clir, eglur, gloyw; croyw ♦ *vt* clirio
**cleave** *vi* glynu (wrth)
**cleave** *vt* hollti; fforchogi
**clef** *n* allwedd, cleff
**cleft** *n* hollt, agen
**clement** *adj* tyner, tirion, trugarog
**clench** *vt* cau yn dynn, clensio
**clergy** *n* offeiriaid
**clergyman** *n* clerigwr, offeiriad
**clerical** *adj* clerigol; perthynol i glerc
**clerk** *n* clerc
**clever** *adj* medrus, deheuig, clyfar
**cleverness** *n* medr, deheurwydd, clyfrwch
**click** *vi* clician, clepian ♦ *n* clic
**client** *n* cyflogydd cyfreithiwr, cwsmer
**cliff** *n* clogwyn, allt
**climate** *n* hinsawdd
**climax** *n* uchafbwynt
**climb** *vb* dringo
**climbing** *adj* dringol

**clinch** vt clensio; cau, cloi
**cling** vi glynu, cydio
**clinic** n meddygfa, clinig
**clinical** adj clinigol
**clink** vi tincian
**clip** vt cneifio, tocio, clipio
**clique** n clic, clymblaid
**cloak** n mantell, clogyn, clog ♦ vt cuddio, celu
**cloakroom** n ystafell ddillad
**clock** n cloc
**clod** n tywarchen
**clog** n clocsen ♦ vt llesteirio; tagu; clocsio
**cloister** n clwysty
**close** vb cau; terfynu ♦ n diwedd, diweddglo
**close** adj agos, clòs; caeth, tyn
**close** n clas, clos, buarth, clwt, cae
**closed shop** n gwaith cyfyngedig, gwaith i rai yn unig
**closet** n cell, ystafell; geudy
**close-up** n llun agos
**closure** n cau, gorffen, darfod
**clot** n tolchen ♦ vb tolchi, ceulo
**cloth** n brethyn, lliain
**clothe** vt dilladu, gwisgo
**clothes** npl dillad, gwisgoedd
**clothes peg** n bachyn dillad
**clothier** n brethynnwr, dilledydd
**clothing** n dillad
**cloud** n cwmwl ♦ vt cymylu
**clout** n cernod, clewt; clwt ♦ vt clewtian; clytio
**clover** n meillion, clofer
**clown** n lleban; croesan, clown
**club** n pastwn; clwb ♦ vb pastynu; clybio
**clue** n pen llinyn, arwydd
**clump** n clwmp, clamp, cyff
**clumsy** adj trwsgl, anfedrus, lletchwith
**cluster** n clwstwr, swp ♦ vb casglu, tyrru
**clutch** n crafanc; gafael, (pl). hafflau ♦ vb crafangu

**clutter** n dadwrdd, helynt
**co-** prefix cyd-
**coach** n cerbyd; hyfforddwr ♦ vb hyfforddi
**coagulate** vb ceulo
**coal** n glöyn, glo
**coalesce** vi cyfuno, cyd-doddi
**coalition** n cyfuniad; cynghrair, clymblaid
**coarse** adj garw, aflednais; bras
**coast** n arfordir, glan ♦ vi hwylio gyda'r lan
**coastal** adj arfordirol
**coastguard** n gwyliwr y glannau
**coastline** n morlin
**coat** n cot. **c. hanger** n cambren (dillad). **c. of arms** n arfbais
**coating** n caen, golchiad
**coax** vb hudo, denu, perswadio
**cobble, -stone** n carreg balmant
**cobbler** n crydd, cobler
**cobweb** n gwe pryf cop, gwe'r cor
**cock** n ceiliog; mwdwl; clicied (dryll) ♦ vb mydylu; codi clicied
**cockerel** n cyw ceiliog, ceiliogyn
**cock-eyed** adj â llygad tro
**cockles** npl cocos, cocs, rhython
**cockpit** n sedd peilot; ymladdfan ceiliogod
**cockroach** n chwilen ddu
**cock-sure** adj gorbendant, gorhyderus
**cocktail** n coctêl
**cocoa** n coco
**coconut** n cneuen goco, coconyt
**cod** n y penfras; cod
**code** n côd
**coerce** vb gorfodi, gorthrechu
**coercion** n gorfodaeth, gorthrech
**coffee** n coffi
**coffin** n arch, ysgrin
**cog** n dant olwyn, còg
**cogent** adj cryf, grymus, argyhoeddiadol
**cohabit** vi cyd-fyw
**cohere** vb cydlynu
**cohesion** n cydlyniad

**coil** vb torchi ♦ n torch
**coin** n arian bath ♦ vb bathu
**coincide** vi cyd-ddigwydd, cyd-daro
**coincidence** n cyd-ddigwyddiad
**coke** n golosg, côc
**colander** n hidl
**cold** adj oer ♦ n oerfel, oerni,
annwyd. **to catch a c.** dal annwyd
**colic** n bolwst, colig
**collapse** vb disgyn, cwympo ♦ n
cwymp, methiant
**collapsible** adj plygadwy
**collar** n coler ♦ vb coleru. **c. bone**
pont yr ysgwydd
**collateral** adj cyfochrog, cyfystlys
**colleague** n cydweithiwr
**collect** n colect ♦ vb crynhoi, hel,
ymgynnull, casglu
**collection** n casgliad
**collector** n casglwr
**college** n coleg
**collide** vb gwrthdaro
**collie** n ci defaid
**collier** n glöwr; llong lo
**colliery** n gwaith glo, pwll glo,
glofa
**collision** n gwrthdrawiad
**colloquial** adj llafar, tafodieithol
**colon** n gorwahannod, colon (:);
coluddyn mawr
**colonel** n cyrnol
**colonial** adj trefedigaethol
**colony** n trefedigaeth, gwladfa
**colosal** adj cawraidd, anferth
**colour** n lliw, baner ♦ vb lliwio;
cochi. **c. bar** gwahanfûr lliw. **c.
blind** lliwddall
**coloured** adj lliw
**colourful** adj lliwgar
**colouring** n lliwiad
**colourless** adj di-liw
**colt** n ebol
**column** n colofn
**columnist** n newyddiadurwr,
colofnydd
**coma** n hunglwyf, côma
**comb** n crib ♦ vb cribo

**combat** n brwydr, gornest ♦ vb
brwydro
**combination** n cyfuniad
**combine** vb cyfuno. **c. harvester**
cynaeafydd, combein
**come** vi dod, dyfod. **to c. across**
dod ar draws. **to c. to light** dod
i'r golwg. **to c. to an end** dod i
ben. **to c. by** meddiannu. **to c. to
pass** digwydd
**comedian** n comedïwr
**comedy** n comedi
**comfort** n cysur, diddanwch ♦ vt
cysuro, diddanu
**comfortable** adj cysurus,
cyffyrddus
**comfortably** adv yn gysurus, yn
gyffyrddus
**comic** adj comic, digrif, ysmala
**comma** n rhagwahannod, atalnod,
coma
**command** vb gorchymyn ♦ n
gorchymyn, awdurdod
**commandeer** vb meddiannu
**commander** n cadlywydd,
comander
**commandment** n gorchymyn
**commando** n mintai (o filwyr), un
o'r fintai
**commemorate** vt coffáu, dathlu
**commence** vb dechrau
**commend** vt cymeradwyo, canmol
**commensurate** adj cymesur
**comment** vi sylwi, esbonio ♦ n
sylw
**commentary** n sylwebaeth
**commentator** n esboniwr,
sylwebydd
**commerce** n masnach
**commercial** adj masnachol
**commiserate** vt cydymdeimlo â,
cyd-dosturio â
**commission** n comisiwn,
dirprwyaeth ♦ vb comisiynu
**commissionaire** n porthor
**commissioner** n comisiynydd
**commit** vt cyflawni; traddodi;

cyflwyno

**commitment** n ymrwymiad; traddodiad

**committee** n pwyllgor

**commodity** n nwydd (masnachol)

**common** adj cyffredin ♦ n tir cyffredin, cytir, comin. **the C. Market** y Farchnad Gyffredin

**commoner** n cominwr, gwerinwr

**commonplace** adj dibwys, cyffredin

**commons** npl y cyffredin. **House of C.** Tŷ'r Cyffredin

**common sense** n synnwyr cyffredin

**commonwealth** n cymanwlad

**commotion** n cyffro, terfysg

**communal** adj cymunol, cymunedol

**commune** vi ymddiddan; cymuno ♦ n cymundod; comun

**communicate** vb cyfathrebu; cymuno

**communication** n cyfathrebiad, cysylltiad, neges

**communion** n cymun, cymundeb

**communism** n comiwnyddiaeth

**communist** n comiwnydd

**community** n cymdeithas, cymuned. **c. centre** canolfan gymuned

**commute** vt cymudo, pendilio

**commuter** n cymudwr, pendiliwr

**compact** n cytundeb, cyfamod; bag bach, compact ♦ adj cryno ♦ vt crynhoi. **c. disc** cryno ddisg

**companion** n cydymaith

**companionship** n cwmnïaeth, cyfeillach

**company** n cymdeithas, cwmni. **keep c. with** cadw cwmni â

**comparative** adj cymharol

**comparatively** adv yn gymharol

**compare** vt cymharu, cyffelybu

**comparison** n cymhariaeth

**compartment** n adran, cerbydran

**compass** n cwmpawd; cwmpas ♦

vt amgylchu

**compassion** n tosturi

**compatible** adj cydweddol, cyson

**compatriot** n cydwladwr

**compel** vt cymell, gorfodi

**compendium** n crynodeb, talfyriad

**compensate** vt talu iawn, digolledu

**compensation** n iawndal

**compete** vi cystadlu

**competence** n cymhwysedd

**competent** adj cymwys, digonol

**competition** n cystadleuaeth

**competitive** adj cystadleuol

**competitor** n cystadleuydd

**complacency** n ymfoddhâd

**complacent** adj hunan-foddhaus, digonol

**complain** vi cwyno, achwyn, grwgnach

**complaint** n cwyn, achwyniad; anhwyldeb

**complement** n cyflawnder, cyflenwad

**complementary** adj cyflenwol

**complete** adj cyflawn ♦ vt cyflawni

**completely** adv yn llwyr

**completion** n cwblhad

**complex** adj cymhleth, dyrys

**complexion** n gwedd, pryd, gwawr

**compliance** n cydsyniad

**complicate** vt cymhlethu; drysu

**complicated** adj cymhleth, dyrys

**complication** n cymhlethdod

**compliment** n cyfarchiad; canmoliaeth

**comply** vi cydsynio, ufuddhau

**component** n cydran, cyfansoddyn

**compose** vt cyfansoddi; cysodi; tawelu

**composed** adj hunanfeddiannol

**composer** n cydsyniad

**composition** n cyfansoddiad, traethawd

**composure** n tawelwch, hunan-feddiant

**compound** *adj* cyfansawdd ♦ *n* cymysg ♦ *vb* cymysgu
**comprehend** *vt* amgyffred, dirnad
**comprehension** *n* amgyffred, dirnadaeth
**comprehensive** *adj* cynhwysfawr. **c. school** Ysgol Gyfun
**compress** *vt* gwasgu, crynhoi ♦ *n* plastr
**comprise** *vt* amgyffred, cynnwys
**compromise** *n* cymrodedd, cyfaddawd ♦ *vb* cymrodeddu, cyfaddawdu
**compulsion** *n* gorfodaeth
**compulsive** *adj* trwy orfod, o anfodd
**compulsory** *adj* gorfodol
**computer** *n* cyfrifiadur. **c. operator** cyfrifiadurwr. **c. science** cyfrifanneg, cyfrifiadureg
**comrade** *n* cydymaith
**concave** *adj* ceugrwm
**conceal** *vb* cuddio, celu, dirgelu
**concede** *vt* caniatáu, addef
**conceit** *n* tyb, mympwy; hunandyb, hunanoldeb, cysêt
**conceited** *adj* hunandybus, hunanol, balch
**conceive** *vb* dirnad; tybied, synied; beichiogi
**concentrate** *vt* crynodi, canolbwyntio
**concentration** *n* crynodiad, ymroddiad
**concept** *n* cysyniad
**conception** *n* syniad; beichiogiad
**concern** *vt* perthyn, ymwneud (â), gofalu (am), pryderu, bod a wnelo â ♦ *n* busnes, diddordeb; gofal, pryder
**concerned** *adj* yn teimlo pryder, pryderus, gofalus, yn ymboeni
**concerning** *prep* ynglŷn â, ynghylch
**concert** *n* cyngerdd ♦ *vt* cyd-drefnu
**concerted** *adj* cydunol, wedi ei gyd-drefnu

**concertina** *n* consertina
**conclude** *vb* diweddu; casglu, barnu
**conclusion** *n* diwedd; casgliad
**conclusive** *adj* terfynol
**concoct** *vt* llunio, dyfeisio
**concoction** *n* cymysgedd
**concourse** *n* tyrfa, torf
**concrete** *adj* diriaethol ♦ *n* concrit
**concur** *vi* cydredeg; cydgroesi; cytuno
**concurrently** *adv* yn gyfredol
**concussion** *n* cyd-drawiad, ysgytiad
**condemn** *vb* condemnio, collfarnu
**condensation** *n* cywasgiad, cyddwysedd
**condense** *vb* cywasgu, cyddwyso, cwtogi
**condensed** *adj* cyddwys
**condition** *n* cyflwr, ansawdd; amod ♦ *vb* cyflyru; amodi
**conditional** *adj* amodol
**conditionally** *adv* ar amod
**conditioner** *n* cyflyrydd
**condole** *vt* cydofidio, cydymdeimlo
**condolence** *n* cydymdeimlad
**condom** *n* condom. **condoms** *npl* (col) sachau dyrnu
**condominium** *n* cydlywodraeth, condominiwm
**condone** *vt* maddau, esgusodi, cymeradwyo
**conduce** *vi* arwain, tueddu
**conducive** *adj* tueddol i, â thuedd i
**conduct** *n* ymddygiad, ymarweddiad, tywys
**conduct** *vt* arwain
**conductor** *n* arweinydd; tocynnwr
**cone** *n* pigwrn, côn
**confection** *n* cyffaith
**confectioner** *n* cyffeithiwr
**confer** *vb* ymgynghori, cyflwyno
**conference** *n* cynhadledd
**confess** *vb* cyffesu, cyfaddef
**confession** *n* cyffesiad, cyffes
**confetti** *n* conffeti

**confide** vb ymddiried
**confidence** n ymddiried, hyder.
 **self-c.** hunanhyder
**confident** adj hyderus
**confidential** adj cyfrinachol
**confine** vt cyfyngu, carcharu,
 caethiwo
**confined** adj caeth, cyfyng
**confinement** n caethiwed, adeg
 geni
**confirm** vt cadarnhau; conffirmio
**confirmation** n cadarnhad; bedydd
 esgob, conffirmasiwn
**confirmed** adj cyson, arferol,
 gwastadol, wedi ei gadarnhau
**confiscate** vt atafaelu
**conflict** n gwrthdrawiad, ymryson
**conflict** vi anghytuno, gwrthdaro
**conflicting** adj anghyson
**conform** vb cydymffurfio;
 cydffurfio
**confound** vt cymysgu, drysu
**confront** vt wynebu
**confrontation** n gwrthdaro
**confuse** vt cymysgu, drysu
**confused** adj cymysg; didrefn;
 dyrys; tywyll
**confusion** n anhrefn
**confute** vt gwrthbrofi, dymchwelyd
**congeal** vb rhewi, fferru, tewychu,
 ceulo
**congenial** adj cydnaws, hynaws
**congest** vb cronni, gorlanw
**congested** adj gorlawn
**congestion** n gorlenwad, tagfa,
 crynhoad
**congratulate** vt llongyfarch
**congratulations** n
 llongyfarchiadau
**congregate** vb ymgynnull
**congregation** n cynulleidfa
**congress** n cyngres, cymanfa
**conjunction** n cysylltiad
**conjunctivitis** n llid yr amrant
**conjure** vb consurio
**conjurer** n consurwr
**connect** vb cysylltu, cydio

**connected** adj cysylltiedig,
 cysylltiol
**connection** n cysylltiad,
 perthynas. **in c.** with ynglŷn â
**connive** vi goddef, cau llygaid
 rhag
**conquer** vt gorchfygu, trechu
**conqueror** n gorchfygwr,
 concwerwr
**conquest** n buddugoliaeth,
 concwest
**conscience** n cydwybod
**conscientious** adj cydwybodol
**conscious** adj ymwybodol
**consciousness** n ymwybyddiaeth
**conscript** n gorfodog, gŵr rhif ♦
 vb gorfodi
**conscription** n gorfodaeth filwrol
**consecrate** vt cysegru
**consecutive** adj olynol
**consent** vi cydsynio ♦ n cydsyniad,
 caniatâd
**consequence** n canlyniad
**consequently** adv o ganlyniad
**conservation** n cadwraeth,
 gwarchodaeth
**conservative** adj ceidwadol ♦ n
 ceidwadwr
**conservatory** n tŷ gwydr
**conserve** vt cadw, diogelu,
 amddiffyn
**consider** vb ystyried
**considerable** adj cryn
**considerate** adj ystyriol, tosturiol
**consideration** n ystyriaeth
**considering** prep ag ystyried
**consign** vt traddodi, trosglwyddo
**consist** vt cynnwys
**consistency** n cysondeb
**consistent** n cyson
**consolation** n cysur, diddanwch
**console** vt cysuro, diddanu
**consonant** adj cysain; cyson ♦ n
 cytsain
**conspicuous** adj amlwg
**conspiracy** n bradwriaeth, brad,
 cynllwyn

**conspire** *vb* bradfwriadu, cynllwynio
**constable** *n* cwnstabl, heddgeidwad
**constant** *adj* cyson
**constantly** *adv* yn gyson
**constipate** *vt* rhwymo
**constipated** *adj* rhwym
**constipation** *n* rhwymedd
**constituency** *n* etholaeth
**constituent** *adj* cyfansoddol ♦ *n* etholwr; cyfansoddyn
**constitution** *n* cyfansoddiad
**constitutional** *adj* cyfansoddiadol
**constraint** *n* cyfyngydd, cyfyngiad
**construct** *vt* ffurfio, llunio, adeiladu, saernio
**construction** *n* adeiladwaith, lluniad; cystrawen
**constructive** *adj* ymarferol, adeiladol
**construe** *vt* cyfieithu; dehongli
**consul** *n* ynad, conswl; consul
**consulate** *n* consuliaeth
**consult** *vb* ymgynghori
**consultant** *n* ymgynghorwr
**consume** *vb* treulio, difa, ysu; nychu
**consumer** *n* prynwr, treuliwr, defnyddiwr
**consummate** *adj* perffaith, cyflawn
**consummate** *vt* perffeithio, cyflawni
**consumption** *n* traul; darfodedigaeth
**contact** *n* cyffyrddiad, cyswllt. **c. lenses** *npl* gwydrau cyffwrdd
**contagious** *adj* heintus
**contain** *vt* cynnwys, dal
**container** *n* cynhwysydd
**contaminate** *vt* halogi, llygru, heintio
**contemplate** *vb* ystyried, myfyrio; bwriadu
**contemporary** *adj* cyfoes(ol) ♦ *n* cyfoeswr

**contempt** *n* dirmyg, diystyrwch. **c. of court** dirmyg llys
**contemptuous** *adj* dirmygus
**contend** *vb* ymryson, cystadlu
**contender** *n* cystadleuydd
**content** *adj* bodlon ♦ *vt* bodloni
**content** *n* cynnwys
**contented** *adj* bodlon
**contention** *n* cynnen, ymryson
**contentment** *n* bodlonrwydd
**contents** *npl* cynnwys, cynhwysiad
**contest** *n* cystadleuaeth, ymryson
**contest** *vb* amau, ymryson, ymladd
**contestant** *n* cystadleuydd
**context** *n* cyd-destun
**continent** *adj* cymedrol; diwair
**continent** *n* cyfandir
**continental** *adj* cyfandirol
**contingency** *n* damwain, digwyddiad
**continual** *adj* parhaus, gwastadol
**continuation** *n* parhad
**continue** *vb* parhau, para, dal (i)
**continuous** *adj* parhaol, di-fwlch, di-dor
**contort** *vt* gwyrdroi, dirdynnu
**contour** *n* amlinell, cyfuchlinedd
**contra-** *prefix* gwrth-, croes-
**contraband** *adj*, *n* (nwyddau), gwaharddedig
**contraceptive** *n* cyfarpar gwrth-genhedlu
**contract** *n* cytundeb, cyfamod
**contract** *vb* byrhau; cytuno, cyfamodi
**contraction** *n* talfyriad, cywasgiad
**contractor** *n* contractwr, adeiladydd
**contradict** *vt* gwrth-ddweud
**contraption** *n* dyfais
**contrary** *adj* gwrthwyneb, croes. **on the c.** i'r gwrthwyneb
**contrast** *n* gwrthgyferbyniad ♦ *vb* gwrthgyferbynnu
**contribute** *vb* cyfrannu
**contribution** *n* cyfraniad

**contributor** n cyfrannwr
**contrive** vb dyfeisio, llwyddo, trefnu
**control** vt llywodraethu, rheoli ♦ n rheolaeth, awdurdod. **self c.** hunan-reolaeth
**controversial** adj dadleuol
**controversy** n dadl
**convalesce** vi ymadfer, gwella
**convene** vt galw, gwysio, cynnull
**convenience** n cyfleustra, hwylustod
**convenient** adj cyfleus, gweddus, hwylus
**convent** n cwfaint, lleiandy
**convention** n cnofensiwn, cynhadledd
**conventional** adj confensiynol
**conversant** adj cyfarwydd, cynefin
**conversation** n ymddiddan, sgwrs
**converse** vi ymddiddan, ymgomio
**converse** adj, n gwrthwyneb, cyferbyniol
**conversion** n trôedigaeth, tro
**convert** vt troi, newid, trosi. **converted try** trosgais gan
**convertible** adj trosadwy
**convex** adj crwm
**convey** vt cludo; trosi, trosglwyddo; cyfleu
**conveyor belt** n cludfelt
**convict** vt barnu'n euog, euogfarnu; argyhoeddi
**convict** n troseddwr
**conviction** n euogfarn; argyhoeddiad
**convince** vt argyhoeddi
**convincing** adj argyhoeddiadol
**convulse** vt dirgrynu, dirdynnu
**cook** n cogydd, cogyddes ♦ vb coginio, gwneud bwyd
**cooker** n cwcer. **pressure c.** gwascogydd, sosban wyllt
**cookery** n coginiaeth
**cooking** n coginiaeth
**cool** adj oeri, oeraidd; hunanfeddiannol ♦ vb oeri, claearu

**coop** n cawell, cut ieir ♦ vt cutio
**co-operate** vi cydweithio, cydweithredu
**co-operation** n cydweithrediad
**co-operative** n cydweithfa ♦ adj cydweithredol
**co-opt** vt cyfethol
**co-ordinate** n cyfesuryn ♦ vb cyfesur, cyd-drefnu
**cop** n plismon ♦ vt dal
**cope** n copa, crib
**cope** vi ymdaro â, ymdopi â
**copious** adj helaeth, dibrin
**copper** n copr, copor
**copse** n prysgwydd, prysglwyn
**copy** n copi ♦ vt copïo
**copyright** n hawlfraint
**coracle** n cwrwgl
**coral** n cwrel
**cord** n cortyn, rheffyn, tennyn ♦ vt rheffynnu
**cordial** adj o galon, calonnog ♦ n cordial, gwirod
**cordon** n rhes, cadwyn
**corduroy** n melfaréd, rib
**core** n calon, perfedd, craidd
**cork** n corc, corcyn ♦ vt corcio
**corkscrew** n corcsgriw
**cormorant** n mulfran, bilidowcar
**corn** n ŷd, llafur
**corn** n corn (ar droed)
**corned beef** n cornbiff
**corner** n congl, cornel, cil ♦ vt cornelu. **c. kick** cic gornel
**cornet** n corned
**cornflakes** npl creision ŷd
**cornflour** n blawd corn
**coronation** n coroniad
**coroner** n crwner
**coronet** n coronig
**corporal** adj corfforol
**corporate** adj yn un corff, corfforedig
**corporation** n corfforaeth; cest
**corporeal** adj corfforol; materol
**corps** n corfflu

**corpse** n corff (marw), celain
**corpuscle** n corffilyn
**correct** adj cywir ♦ vt cywiro,
ceryddu
**correction** n cywiriad; cerydd
**correspond** vi cyfateb; gohebu
**correspondence** n cyfatebiaeth;
gohebiaeth
**correspondent** n gohebydd
**corridor** n coridor
**corrode** vb cyrydu, ysu, rhydu,
treulio
**corrugated** adj rhychiog,
gwrymiog
**corrupt** adj llygredig, pwdr ♦ vb
llygru
**corruption** n llygredigaeth
**corset** n staes
**cosmetic** n cosmetig
**cost** vi costio ♦ n cost, traul
**costly** adj drudfawr, drud, prid
**costume** n gwisg, costiwm
**cosy** adj cysurus, clyd
**cot** n gwely bychan, cot
**cottage** n bwthyn
**cotton** n cotwm; edau. **c. wool**
gwlân cotwm
**couch** n glwth, soffa ♦ vb gorwedd
**cough** n peswch ♦ vb pesychu
**council** n cyngor. **c. house** tŷ
cyngor
**councillor** n cynghorwr
**counsel** n cyngor ♦ vt cynghori
**counsellor** n cynghorwr,
cyfarwyddwr
**count** n cyfrif ♦ vb rhifo, cyfrif. **c.
the cost** bwrw'r draul
**count** n iarll
**countenance** n wynepryd;
cefnogaeth ♦ vt cefnogi
**counter** n cownter
**counter-** prefix gwrth- ♦ adj croes
♦ adv yn erbyn, yn groes
**counteract** vt gwrthweithio
**counterfeit** n ffug, twyll ♦ adj gau,
ffug ♦ vt ffugio
**counterfoil** n gwrthddalen

**countermand** vt gwrthorchymyn
**counterpane** n cwrlid, cwilt gwely
**counterpart** n rhan gyfatebol,
cymar
**countess** n iarlles
**countless** adj aneirif, di-rif
**country** n gwlad, bro ♦ adj
gwladaidd, gwledig. **c. music** canu
gwlad
**countryman** n gwladwr
**countryside** n cefn gwlad
**county** n sir, swydd
**coup** n ergyd, trawiad, dymchwel,
llwyddiannus
**couple** n cwpl ♦ vt cyplu, cyplysu
**couplet** n cwpled
**coupon** n cwpon
**courage** n gwroldeb, dewrder
**courier** n cennad; tywyswr
**course** n cwrs, hynt ♦ vt hela,
ymlid. **of c.** wrth gwrs. **in the c.**
**of** yn ystod. **in due c.** yn ei bryd.
**crash c.** cwrs carlam
**court** n llys; cwrt; cyntedd ♦ vt
caru
**courteous** adj cwrtais
**courtesy** n cwrteisrwydd, cwrteisi
**courtier** n gŵr llys, llyswr
**courtly** adj llysaidd, boneddigaidd
**court-martial** n cwrt-marsial ♦ vb
dodi ar brawf
**courtship** n carwriaeth
**courtyard** n buarth, cwrt, clos,
iard
**cousin** n cefnder; cyfnither
**cove** n cil, cilfach
**covenant** n cyfamod ♦ vb
cyfamodi
**cover** vt gorchuddio, toi;
amddiffyn ♦ n gorchudd, clawr. **c.
charge** n tâl am wasanaeth. **book
c.** clawr llyfr. **to take c.** cuddio,
cysgodi
**covert** adj cêl, cudd, dirgel
**covert** n lloches; prysglwyn
**covet** vt chwennych, chwenychu
**cow** n buwch. **barren c.** myswynog.

milking **c.** buwch odro. **c. in calf** buwch gyflo

**coward** *n* llwfrddyn, llwfryn, llwfrgi

**cowardice** *n* llwfrdra

**cowardly** *adj* llwfr

**cowboy** *n* cowboi

**cower** *vi* swatio, cyrcydu

**cowl** *n* cwcwll, cwfl

**cowpox** *n* brech y fuwch

**cowslip** *n* briallu Mair

**coxwain** *n* llywydd cwch, cocs

**coy** *adj* swil, gwylaidd

**crab** *n* cranc

**crab (apple)** *n* afal sur, afal crabas

**crack** *vb* cracio, hollti ♦ *n* crac

**cracker** *n* cracer; bisgeden

**crackle** *vi* clindarddach

**cradle** *n* crud, cawell; cadair fagu

**craft** *n* crefft; cyfrwystra, dichell; llong, bad

**craftsman** *n* crefftwr

**craftsmanship** *n* crefftwriaeth

**crafty** *adj* cyfrwys, dichellgar

**crag** *n* craig, clegr, clogwyn

**cram** *vb* gorlenwi, stwffio, saco

**cramp** *n* cwlwm gwythi, cramp; creffyn ♦ *vt* caethiwo, gwasgu

**cramped** *adj* clòs

**cranberries** *npl* llugaeron

**crane** *n* garan, crëyr, crychydd, craen ♦ *vt* estyn (gwddf)

**cranium (-ia)** *n* penglog

**crank** *n* cranc; mympwywr ♦ *vi* cam-droi; troi

**crankshaft** *n* camwerthyd, crancsiafft

**cranny** *n* agen, hollt, agennig

**crape** *n* crêp

**crash** *vb* gwrthdaro, cwympo ♦ *n* gwrthdrawiad, cwymp. **c. helmet** *n* helmed ddiogelwch

**crate** *n* cawell

**crater** *n* safn llosgfynydd; ceudod, cawg

**cravat** *n* cadach gwddf, crafat

**crave** *vb* crefu, deisyf, chwennych, dyheu

**craving** *n* blys, chwant

**crawl** *vi* ymlusgo, cropian; crafu

**crayon** *n* creon

**craze** *n* ysfa

**crazy** *adj* penwan, gorffwyll, o'i gof

**creak** *vi* gwichian

**cream** *n* hufen

**creamery** *n* hufenfa

**creamy** *adj* hufennog

**crease** *n* ôl plygiad, plyg ♦ *vt* crychu

**create** *vt* creu

**creation** *n* cread, creadigaeth

**creative** *adj* creadigol

**creator** *n* crëwr, creawdwr

**creature** *n* creadur

**crêche** *n* meithrinfa

**credence** *n* cred, coel, ffydd

**credentials** *npl* credlythyrau

**credible** *adj* credadwy, hygoel, hygred

**credit** *n* coel, cred; clod, credyd ♦ *vt* coelio. **c. card** cerdyn credyd

**creditor** *n* credydwr

**credulous** *adj* hygoelus

**creed** *n* credo

**creek** *n* cilfach

**creep** *vi* ymlusgo, cropian

**creeper** *n* dringiedydd

**creepy** *adj* iasol

**cremate** *vt* amlosgi

**crematorium** *n* amlosgfa

**crêpe** *n* crêp

**crescent** *n* hanner lleuad; cilgant ♦ *adj* cynyddol

**cress** *n* berwr

**crest** *n* crib; mwng; arwydd ar arfbais

**Crete** *n* Creta

**crevice** *n* agen, hollt, rhigol

**crew** *n* criw, gwerin llong; haid

**crib** *n* preseb; caban; gwely plentyn ♦ *vt* copïo

**cricket** *n* criced; cricsyn

**crime** *n* trosedd

**criminal** adj troseddol ♦ n troseddwr
**crimson** adj, n rhuddgoch
**cringe** vi cynffonna, ymgreinio
**crinkle** vb crychu ♦ n crych, plyg
**cripple** n cloff, efrydd ♦ vt cloffi, efryddu
**crisis** (**crises**) n argyfwng
**crisp** adj cras, crych
**crisps** npl creision tatws
**criterion** (**-ia**) n maen prawf, safon
**critic** n beirniad
**critical** adj beirniadol; pryderus; peryglus
**criticism** n beirniadaeth
**criticize** vt beirniadu
**croak** vi crawcian ♦ n crawc
**crochet** vb crosio ♦ n crosiet, gwaith crosio
**crockery** n llestri
**crocodile** n crocodil
**crocus** n saffrwn, crocus
**croft** n tyddyn, crofft
**crony** n cyfaill agos, cydymaith
**crook** n crwca, bagl, ffon fugail; troseddwr
**crooked** adj crwca, cam
**crop** n cnwd, cynnyrch; crombil ♦ vt tocio, torri
**cross** n, adj croes ♦ vb croesi
**cross-cut** vb trawsdorri
**cross-examine** vb croesholi
**crossing** n croesfan
**cross-road** n croesffordd
**cross-section** n trawsdoriad
**crosswise** adv ar groes
**crossword** n croesair
**crotchet** n crosied
**crouch** vi cyrcydu ♦ n cwrcwd
**crow** n brân
**crow** vi canu fel ceiliog; ymffrostio
**crow-bar** n trosol, bar haearn
**crowd** n torf, tyrfa ♦ vb tyrru, heidio
**crowded** adj llawn o bobl
**crown** n coron; corun ♦ vt coroni

**crucial** adj hanfodol, terfynol
**crucifix** n croeslun
**crucifixion** n croeshoeliad
**crucify** vt croeshoelio
**crude** adj cri, crai; llymrig, amrwd
**cruel** adj creulon
**cruelty** n creulondeb
**cruet** n criwed
**cruise** vi morio ♦ n mordaith
**cruiser** n gwiblong
**crumb** n briwsionyn
**crumble** vb briwsioni, malurio ♦ n briwsiongrwst
**crumbly** adj briwsionllyd
**crumpet** n crymped; lefren
**crumple** vb crychu, gwasgu
**crunch** vb creinsio
**crupper** n pedrain, crwper, pen ôl
**crusade** n rhyfel y gròes, croesgad
**crush** vb gwasgu, llethu ♦ n gwasgiad, torf
**crust** n crawen, crofen, crystyn
**crutch** n bagl, ffon fagl
**crux** n craidd
**cry** vb llefain, wylo, crio ♦ n llef, sgrech, cri
**cryptic** adj dirgel, cyfrin
**crystal** n grisial ♦ adj grisialaidd
**crystallisation** n crisialiad
**cub** n cenau
**cube** n ciwb ♦ vb ciwbio
**cubic** adj ciwbig. **c. root** gwreiddyn ciwb
**cubicle** n cuddygl
**cuckoo** n cog, cwcw; gwirionyn
**cucumber** n cucumer
**cud** n cil
**cuddle** vb anwylo, anwesu, tolach
**cue** n awgrym; ciw
**cuff** n torch llawes
**cuff** vt cernodio ♦ n cernod, dyrnod
**cul-de-sac** n pen ffordd, heol hosan
**cull** vt dewis, pigo
**culminate** vi cyrraedd ei anterth, diweddu
**culmination** n anterth

**culpable** adj beius, camweddus
**culprit** n troseddwr, drwgweithredwr
**cult** n addoliad, cwlt
**cultivate** vt diwyllio, trin, meithrin
**cultural** adj diwylliannol
**culture** n diwylliant; gwrtaith
**cultured** adj diwylliedig, coeth
**cumbersome** adj afrosgo, beichus
**cunning** adj dichellgar, cyfrwys ♦ n cyfrwystra
**cup** n cwpan
**cupboard** n cwpwrdd
**cup-tie** n gornest gwpan
**curate** n curad
**curator** n curadur
**curb** n genfa, atalfa; cwrbyn ♦ vt ffrwyno
**curd** n caul, ceuled; caws
**curdle** vb ceulo, cawsio, cawsu
**cure** n iachâd, gwellhad; meddyginiaeth ♦ vb iacháu, gwella; halltu
**curfew** n hwyrgloch
**curiosity** n cywreinrwydd, chwilfrydedd
**curious** adj cywrain; chwilfrydig; hynod
**curl** n cwrl, cudyn ♦ vb cyrlio
**curlew** n gylfinir
**curly** adj cyrliog, crych
**currants** npl grawn Corinth, cwrens. **currant bread** bara brith
**currency** n arian breiniol
**current** adj rhedegol, cyfredol, cyfoes ♦ n ffrwd, llif. **c. account** cyfrif cyfredol. **c. affairs** materion cyfoes
**currently** adv ar hyn o bryd
**curriculum** n cwricwlwm. **National C.** Cwricwlwm Cenedlaethol
**curry** vt trin lledr ♦ n cyrri. **to c. favour** cynffonna, ceisio ffafr
**curse** n melltith, rheg ♦ vb melltithio, rhegi
**cursory** adj brysiog, diofal
**curt** adj cwta, byr, cryno

**curtail** vt cwtogi, talfyrru; prinhau
**curtain** n llen
**curtsy** n cyrtsi
**curve** vb camu, gŵyro, troi ♦ n tro; cromlin
**cushion** n clustog
**custard** n cwstard
**custodian** n ceidwad
**custody** n dalfa, cadwraeth
**custom** n defod; cwsmeriaeth; toll
**customary** adj arferol
**customer** n cwsmer
**customs** npl y tollau. **c. officer** n swyddog tollau
**cut** vb torri ♦ n toriad, archoll, briw. **c. back** torri yn ôl. **c. in** torri ar draws. **c. out** torri allan. **c. through** torri trwodd
**cute** adj ciwt, cyfrwys
**cuticle** n croen, pilen, cwticl
**cutlery** n cwtleri
**cutlet** n golwyth, cydled
**cycle** n cylch; cyfres; beic ♦ vb seiclo
**cycling** n beicio
**cyclist** n beiciwr
**cyclone** n trowynt
**cygnet** n cyw alarch, alarchen
**cylinder** n rhol; silindr
**cymbal** n symbal
**cynic** n gwawdiwr, sinig
**cynical** adj gwawdlyd, dirmygus
**cynicism** n coegni, gwawd
**cyst** n coden
**cystitis** n llid y bledren
**Czechoslovakia** n Tsiecoslofacia

# D

**dab** vt dabio ♦ n dab
**dabble** vb dablo
**dad, dada, daddy** n tad, tada, tyta, dada
**daffodil** n cenhinen Bedr
**daft** adj hurt, gwirion
**dagger** n dagr, bidog

**daily** adj dyddiol, beunyddiol ♦ adv beunydd, bob dydd

**dainty** n danteithfwyd, amheuthun ♦ adj danteithiol, dillyn, del

**dairy** n llaethdy. **d. products** cynhyrchion llaeth

**dais** n esgynlawr, llwyfan

**daisy** n llygad y dydd

**dale** n dyffryn, glyn, dôl, cwm, bro

**dam** n argae, cronfa ♦ vt argáu, cronni

**dam** n mamog, mam (anifail)

**damage** n niwed, difrod ♦ vt niweidio, difrodi. **damages** npl iawn

**damn** vb damnio, rhegi, melltithio

**damnation** n damnedigaeth

**damned** adj colledig

**damp** adj llaith ♦ n lleithder ♦ vb lleitho

**damson** n eirinen ddu

**dance** vb dawnsio ♦ n dawns. **folk d.** dawns werin. **public folk d.** twmpath dawns

**dancer** n dawnsiwr

**dandelion** n dant y llew

**dandruff** n marwdon, cen

**Dane** n brodor o Ddenmarc, Daniad

**danger** n perygl, enbydrwydd

**dangerous** adj peryglus, enbyd

**dangle** vb hongian; siglo

**dapper** adj del, twt, sionc, heini

**dare** vb beiddio, mentro

**dare-devil** n un byrbwyll, un mentrus

**daring** adj beiddgar, mentrus ♦ n beiddgarwch

**dark** adj tywyll ♦ n tywyllwch, nos

**darken** vb tywyllu

**darkness** n tywyllwch

**darling** n anwylyd, cariad ♦ adj annwyl

**darn** vt cyweirio, trwsio ♦ n cyweiriad, trwsiad

**dart** n dart, picell, saeth ♦ vb dartio, rhuthro

**dash** vb rhuthro, chwalu, chwilfriwio ♦ n rhuthr; llinell (—)

**dashboard** n dashfwrdd

**data** npl data

**date** n dyddiad, amseriad; datysen (ffrwyth) ♦ vb dyddio. **out of d.** henffasiwn, wedi dyddio. **up to d.** hyd yn hyn, cyfoes

**dated** adj dyddiedig

**daub** vb dwbio, iro

**daughter** n merch. **daughter-in-law** merch yng nghyfraith

**dawdle** vi ymdroi, swmera

**dawn** vi gwawrio, dyddio ♦ n gwawr

**day** n diwrnod, dydd. **by d.** liw dydd. **today** heddiw. **next d.** trannoeth. **the d. before yesterday** echdoe

**day-break** n gwawr, toriad dydd

**day-dream** vb pensynnu, synfyfyrio

**daylight** n golau dydd

**day-time** n y dydd

**daze** vt synnu, syfrdanu; dallu

**dazzle** vb disgleirio, pelydru; dallu

**dazzling** adj disglair, llachar

**deacon** n diacon, blaenor

**dead** adj marw; difywyd ♦ adv hollol. **the d.** y meirw. **d. centre** yn ei ganol. **d. tired** wedi blino 'n lân. **d. heat** cwbl gyfartal

**deaden** vb lleddfu, marweiddio

**deadlock** n methu symud mlaen na nôl

**deadly** adj marwol, angheuol

**Dead Sea** n: **the D. Sea** y Môr Marw

**deaf** adj byddar

**deafen** vb byddaru

**deafness** n byddardod

**deal** vb delio; trin ♦ n trafodaeth, dêl. **a great d.** llawer iawn. **to d. with** ymwneud â

**dealer** n masnachwr

**dean** n deon

**dear** adj annwyl, cu, hoff; drud ♦ n

anwylyd, cariad. **d. me** o'r
annwyl!
**death** *n* angau, marwolaeth, tranc.
**Black D.** y Pla Du
**deathly** *adj, adv* fel angau,
angheuol, marwol
**death rate** *n* cyfradd marw
**debar** *vt* atal, lluddias, cau allan
**debase** *vt* iselu, darostwng, llygru
**debate** *vb* dadlau, ymryson ♦ *n*
dadl
**debit** *n* debyd
**debt** *n* dyled
**debtor** *n* dyledwr
**decade** *n* degawd
**decadence** *n* dirywiad, adfeiliad
**decapitate** *vt* torri pen
**decay** *vi* dadfeilio, pydru ♦ *n*
dadfeiliad
**decease** *n* tranc, marwolaeth ♦ *vi*
marw, trengi
**deceased** *n* ymadawedig,
trancedig
**deceit** *n* twyll, dichell, hoced
**deceive** *vt* twyllo, hocedu, siomi
**December** *n* Rhagfyr
**decent** *adj* gweddus, gweddaidd
**deception** *n* twyll, ffug, dichell
**deceptive** *adj* twyllodrus,
dichellgar
**decide** *vb* penderfynu
**decided** *adj* pendant, penderfynol
**decidedly** *adv* yn siŵr, yn ddiau
**deciduous** *adj* collddail
**decimal** *adj* degol ♦ *n* degolyn. **d.
system** system ddegol. **d. point**
pwynt degol. **recurring d.** degolyn
cylchol
**decipher** *vt* datrys, dehongli
**decision** *n* penderfyniad
**decisive** *adj* penderfynol, pendant
**deck** *n* bwrdd llong, dec. **d. chair** *n*
cadair haul
**deck** *vt* trwsio, addurno
**declaration** *n* datganiad; cau
batiad
**declare** *vb* mynegi, datgan,

cyhoeddi
**decline** *vb* dadfeilio; gwrthod ♦ *n*
dadfeiliad; darfodedigaeth
**decompose** *vb* pydru, braenu;
dadelfennu
**decorate** *vt* addurno, arwisgo
**decoration** *n* addurn, tlws
**decorator** *n* addurnwr, peintiwr tai
**decoy** *n* hud, magl ♦ *vt* hudo,
llithio
**decrease** *vb* lleihau, gostwng ♦ *n*
lleihad
**decree** *n* gorchymyn, dyfarniad ♦
*vb* gorchymyn, dyfarnu
**dedicate** *vt* cysegru, cyflwyno
**dedication** *n* cysegriad, cyflwyniad
**deduce** *vt* tynnu, casglu,
diddwytho
**deduct** *vt* tynnu ymaith, didynnu
**deduction** *n* diddwythiad, didyniad
**deed** *n* gweithred
**deem** *vt* meddwl, ystyried, barnu
**deep** *adj* dwfn; dwys ♦ *n* dwfn,
dyfnder. **d. freeze** *n* rhewgell. **d.
litter** gwasarn
**deepen** *vb* dyfnhau, trymhau,
dwysáu
**deeply** *adv* yn ddwys
**deer** (**deer**) *n* carw, hydd
**deface** *vt* difwyno, anurddo, hagru
**default** *n* diffyg, gwall, pall, meth
♦ *vb* methu, torri
**defeat** *vt* gorchfygu, trechu ♦ *n*
gorchfygiad
**defect** *n* diffyg, nam
**defective** *adj* diffygiol
**defence** *n* amddiffyn, amddiffyniad
**defenceless** *adj* diamddiffyn
**defend** *vt* amddiffyn
**defendant** *n* diffynnydd
**defender** *n* amddiffynnwr
**defer** *vb* oedi, gohirio
**defiance** *n* her, herfeiddiad
**defiant** *adj* herfeiddiol
**deficient** *adj* diffygiol, prin, yn
eisiau
**deficit** *n* diffyg

**defile** *vi* symud yn rhes ♦ *n* culffordd, bwlch, ceunant
**defile** *vt* halogi, difwyno
**define** *vt* diffinio
**definite** *adj* penodol, pendant
**definitely** *adv* yn bendant, heb os
**definition** *n* diffiniad
**deflate** *vb* dadchwythu
**deflect** *vb* gwyro, osgoi
**deform** *vt* anffurfio, hagru, aflunieiddio
**deformed** *adj* afluniaidd, anffurf
**deformity** *n* anffurfiad
**defraud** *vt* twyllo, hocedu; ysbeilio
**defray** *vt* talu (treuliau)
**defrost** *vt* dadrewi (*fridge*)
**defroster** *n* dadrewydd
**deft** *adj* medrus, hylaw, deheuig
**defunct** *adj* marw, trancedig
**defy** *vt* beiddio, herfeiddio, herio
**degenerate** *vi* dirywio ♦ *adj* dirywiedig
**degrade** *vt* diraddio, difreinio
**degree** *n* gradd
**dehydrate** *vb* dihydradu
**dehydration** *n* dihydrad
**de-ice** *vb* toddi
**deign** *vb* ymostwng, teilyngu
**deity** *n* duwdod; duw
**deject** *vt* digalonni
**dejected** *adj* digalon
**delay** *vb* oedi, gohirio ♦ *n* oediad
**delectable** *adj* hyfryd, hyfrydlon
**delegate** *vt* dirprwyo ♦ *n* dirprwy, cynrychiolydd
**delete** *vt* dileu
**deliberate** *vb* ystyried yn bwyllog ♦ *adj* pwyllog, bwriadol
**deliberately** *adv* yn fwriadol
**delicacy** *n* amheuthun, danteithfwyd. **delicacies** danteithion
**delicate** *adj* tyner; cain; gwanllyd
**delicious** *adj* danteithiol, blasus
**delight** *vb* difyrru; ymhyfrydu ♦ *n* hyfrydwch
**delightful** *adj* hyfryd, braf

**delinquency** *n* bai, trosedd
**delinquent** *n* troseddwr, tramgwyddwr ♦ *adj* troseddol, tramgwyddus
**delirious** *adj* wedi drysu, yn drysu, gwallgof
**deliver** *vt* traddodi; gwaredu, danfon; cludo
**deliverance** *n* gwaredigaeth
**delivery** *n* traddodiad; danfoniad
**dell** *n* glyn, pant, ceunant, cwm
**delude** *vt* twyllo, hudo
**deluge** *n* dilyw, dylif ♦ *vt* gorlifo
**delusion** *n* twyll, cyfeiliornad; lledrith
**delve** *vb* cloddio, palu, ymchwilio
**demand** *vt* gofyn, hawlio, mynnu ♦ *n* gofyn, hawl
**demean** *vt* ymddwyn
**demeanour** *n* ymddygiad
**demented** *adj* gwallgof, gorffwyll
**demesne** *n* treftadaeth, tiriogaeth; bro
**demi-** *prefix* hanner
**demise** *n* marwolaeth
**democracy** *n* gweriniaeth, democrat, democratiaeth
**democrat** *n* gwerinydd, gweriniaethwr
**democratic** *adj* gwerinol, democratig
**demolish** *vt* dymchwelyd, distrywio
**demonstrate** *vb* arddangos, profi; gwrthdystio
**demonstration** *n* arddangosiad; gwrthdystiad
**demonstrator** *n* arddangoswr; gwrthdystiwr
**demote** *vb* darostwng
**demur** *vi* codi gwrthwynebiad, petruso
**demure** *adj* swil, gwylaidd
**den** *n* ffau, gwâl, lloches
**denial** *n* gwadiad; nacâd, gwrthodiad. **self-d.** hunanymwadiad

**Denmark** *n* Denmarc
**denomination** *n* enw, enwad
**denote** *vt* arwyddo, dynodi, hynodi
**denounce** *vt* lladd ar, cyhuddo, condemnio
**dense** *adj* tew, dwys; pendew, hurt
**density** *n* dwysedd, trwch
**dent** *n* tolc ♦ *vt* tolcio
**dental** *adj* deintiol
**dentist** *n* deintydd
**dentistry** *n* deintyddiaeth
**dentures** *npl* dannedd gosod/dodi
**deny** *vt* gwadu, gomedd, gwrthod
**deodorant** *n* diaroglydd
**depart** *vi* ymadael; cychwyn
**department** *n* adran, dosbarth. **d. store** *n* siop adrannol
**departure** *n* ymadawiad; cychwyniad
**depend** *vi* dibynnu
**dependable** *adj* dibynadwy
**dependant** *n* dibynnydd
**dependent** *adj* dibynnol
**depict** *vt* darlunio
**deplete** *vt* gwacáu, gwagu, hysbyddu
**depopulate** *vt* diboblogi
**deport** *vt* alltudio
**deportation** *n* alltudiaeth
**deportment** *n* ymddygiad, ymarweddiad
**deposit** *vt* dodi i lawr; adneuo; gwaddodi ♦ *n* adnau, blaendal; gwaddod. **d. account** cyfrif cadw
**depot** *n* storfa; gorsaf
**depreciate** *vb* dibrisio
**depredation** *n* anrheithiad
**depress** *vt* gostwng, iselu; digalonni
**depressed** *adj* digalon, iselfryd
**depression** *n* iseider (ysbryd); dibwysiant (tywydd); pant; dirwasgiad (diwydiant)
**deprivation** *n* enbydrwydd, amddifadedd, colled
**deprive** *vt* amddifadu
**deprived** *adj* amddifadus

**depth** *n* dyfnder
**deputation** *n* dirprwyaeth
**deputise** *vt* dirprwyo
**deputy** *n* dirprwy
**derail** *vb* taflu oddi ar gledrau
**derelict** *adj* wedi ei adael, diberchen, diffaith
**deride** *vt* gwatwar, gwawdio
**derision** *n* gwatwar, gwawd, dirmyg
**derive** *vb* derbyn, cael; tarddu, deillio
**derogatory** *adj* amharchus, difrïol, dilornus, gwawdus
**descant** *vi* desgant, cyfalaw
**descend** *vi* disgyn
**descent** *n* disgyniad, disgynfa; hil, ach
**describe** *vt* disgrifio, darlunio
**description** *n* disgrifiad, darluniad
**desecrate** *vt* digysegru, halogi
**desert** *n* haeddiant
**desert** *adj* diffaith, anial ♦ *n* diffeithwch
**desert** *vb* gadael, cefnu ar; encilio
**deserter** *n* enciliwr, ffoadur
**deserve** *vb* haeddu, teilyngu
**deserving** *adj* haeddiannol, teilwng
**design** *n* arfaeth; cynllun ♦ *vb* arfaethu; cynllunio
**designer** *n* cynllunydd, dylunydd
**desirable** *adj* dymunol, dewisol
**desire** *vb* dymuno ♦ *n* dymuniad, chwant
**desk** *n* desg
**desolate** *adj* anghyfannedd, diffaith ♦ *vt* anghyfanheddu
**despair** *n* anobaith ♦ *vi* anobeithio
**desperate** *adj* diobaith, anobeithiol; gorffwyll
**desperation** *n* anobaith, enbydrwydd, gorffwylltra
**despicable** *adj* dirmygedig, ffiaidd
**despise** *vt* dirmygu, diystyru
**despite** *prep* er, er gwaethaf
**despoil** *vt* anrheithio, ysbeilio
**despondent** *adj* digalon, isel-

ysbryd
**despot** n unben, gormeswr
**dessert** n pwdin, melysfwyd
**destination** n cyrchfan, pen y
daith
**destiny** n tynged, tynghedfen
**destitute** adj anghenus, amddifad
**destroy** vt distrywio, difetha,
dinistrio
**destroyer** n dinistrydd;
distrywlong
**destruction** n distryw, dinistr
**detach** vt datod, gwahanu,
dadgysylltu
**detached** adj ar wahân
**detachment** n adran; didoliad;
mintai (o filwyr)
**detail** n manylyn, (pl) manylion ♦
vb manylu, neilltuo. **in d.** yn
fanwl
**detain** vt cadw, atal, caethiwo
**detect** vt canfod, darganfod,
datgelu
**detection** n darganfyddiad,
datgeliad
**detective** n cuddswyddog, ditectif.
**d. story** stori dditectif
**detention** n carchariad, ataliad
**deter** vt cadw rhag, atal, rhwystro
**detergent** n golchydd
**deteriorate** vb dirywio, gwaethygu
**determination** n penderfyniad
**determine** vb penderfynu, pennu
**determined** adj penderfynol
**deterrent** vt atalrym, ataliad
**detest** vt ffieiddio, casáu, atgasu
**detour** n cylch
**detract** vt tynnu oddi wrth,
bychanu
**detriment** n colled, niwed,
anfantais
**detrimental** adj niweidiol,
colledus, o anfantais
**devaluation** n gwerthostyngiad,
datbrisiad
**devastate** vt diffeithio, difrodi
**devastating** adj difrodus

**develop** vb datblygu
**developing** adj datblygol, ar ei
brifiant
**development** n datblygiad
**device** n dyfais
**devil** n diafol, diawl, cythraul
**devilish** adj dieflig
**devious** adj diarffordd, troellog;
cyfeiliornus
**devise** vt dyfeisio
**devoid** adj amddifad
**devolution** n datganoli
**devote** vt cysegru, cyflwyno,
ymroddi
**devoted** adj ffyddlon, ymroddgar
**devotion** n defosiwn, ymroddiad
**devour** vt ysu, difa, traflyncu
**devout** adj duwiol, crefyddol,
defosiynol
**dew** n gwlith ♦ vb gwlitho
**diabetes** n clefyd melys/siwgr
**diabetic** adj, n diabetig
**diabolical** adj dieflig
**diagnosis** n diagnosis
**diagonal** n croeslin ♦ adj croeslinol
**diagram** n darlun eglurhaol,
diagram
**dial** n deial ♦ vb deialu
**dialect** n tafodiaith
**dialogue** n ymddiddan, deialog,
sgwrs
**diameter** n tryfesur, diamedr
**diamond** n diemwnt
**diaphragm** n llengig; diaffram
**diarrhoea** n rhyddni, dolur rhydd
**diary** n dyddiadur, dyddlyfr
**dice** n dis
**dictate** vb arddywedyd, gorchymyn
**dictate** n arch, galwad, gorchymyn
**dictation** n arddywediad
**dictatorship** n unbennaeth
**dictionary** n geiriadur
**diddle** vt twyllo, hocedu
**die** vi marw, trengi, trigo, darfod
**diehard** n un di-ildio
**diesel** n disel
**diet** n ymborth, lluniaeth, deiet

**dietetics** n deieteg
**differ** vi gwahaniaethu
**difference** n gwahaniaeth
**different** adj gwahanol
**differentiate** vb gwahaniaethu
**difficult** adj anodd, caled
**difficulty** n anhawster
**diffident** adj petrusgar, anhyderus
**dig** vb palu, cloddio, ceibio
**digest** vb treulio, toddi; cymathu
**digest** n crynhoad
**digestion** n treuliad, traul
**digit** n digid, bys
**digital** adj digidol
**dignified** adj urddasol
**dignify** vt anrhydeddu, urddasu
**dignity** n urddas, teilyngdod
**digress** vi gwyro, crwydro
**dike, dyke** n clawdd, ffos; argae
**dilapidate** vb adfeilio, malurio
**dilapidated** adj adfeiliedig
**dilemma** n dilema
**diligence** n diwydrwydd, dyfalwch
**diligent** adj diwyd, dyfal
**dilute** vt cymysgu â dwfr, teneuo, gwanhau
**dim** adj pŵl, aneglur ♦ vb tywyllu, cymylu
**dimension** n mesur, maintioli, dimensiwn
**diminish** vb lleihau, prinhau
**diminutive** adj bychan; bachigol; n bachigyn
**dimmer** n pylydd
**dimple** n pannwl, pant ♦ vb panylu
**din** n twrf, dadwrdd, mwstwr
**dine** vi ciniawa
**diner** n ciniäwr
**dinghy** n dingi
**dingle** n cwm, glyn, pant
**dingy** adj tywyll, dilewyrch; tlodaidd
**dining room** n ystafell fwyta
**dinner** n cinio. **d. jacket** n cot ginio, cot giniawa
**dint** n tolc; grym ♦ vt tolcio
**diocesan** adj esgobaethol ♦ n esgob

**diocese** n esgobaeth
**dioxide** n deuocsid
**dip** vb trochi, gwlychu; gostwng ♦ n trochfa
**diphthong** n deusain, dipton
**diploma** n tystysgrif, diploma
**diplomacy** n diplomyddiaeth
**diplomat** n diplomydd
**diplomatic** adj diplomyddol
**dire** adj dygn, arswydus, echryslon
**direct** adj union, uniongyrchol ♦ vt cyfarwyddo, cyfeirio
**direction** n cyfarwyddyd; cyfeiriad
**directly** adv yn union, yn ddi-oed
**director** n cyfarwyddwr
**directory** n cyfarwyddiadur
**dirge** n galarnad, marwnad
**dirt** n baw, llaid, llaca
**dirty** adj budr, brwnt ♦ vt budro, diwyno, maeddu
**disability** n anabledd
**disable** vt analluogi
**disabled** adj anabl
**disadvantage** n anfantais
**disagree** vi anghytuno
**disagreeable** adj annymunol, cas
**disappear** vi diflannu
**disappearance** n diflaniad
**disappoint** vt siomi
**disappointed** adj siomedig
**disappointment** n siom (edigaeth)
**disapprove** vb anghymeradwyo
**disarm** vb diarfogi
**disarmament** n diarfogiad
**disarray** n anhrefn ♦ vb anrhefnu
**disaster** n trychineb, aflwydd
**disband** vb dadfyddino; gwasgaru
**disbelief** n anghrediniaeth, angoel
**disc** n disg(en)
**discard** vt rhoi heibio, gwrthod
**discern** vt canfod, dirnad
**discerning** adj deallus, craff
**discharge** vb dadlwytho, rhyddhau ♦ n gollyngdod, rhyddhad, gollwng
**discipline** n disgyblaeth ♦ vt disgyblu

**disclaim** *vt* diarddel, gwadu
**disclose** *vt* dadlennu, datguddio
**disclosure** *n* datguddiad, dadleniad
**disco** *n* disgo
**discomfit** *vt* gorchfygu, dymchwelyd
**discomfort** *vt* anghysuro ♦ *n* anghysur
**discompose** *vt* aflonyddu, cyffroi
**disconcert** *vt* aflonyddu, cyffroi, tarfu
**disconnect** *vb* datgysylltu
**disconsolate** *adj* digysur, anniddan, galarus
**discontent** *n* anfodlonrwydd
**discontented** *adj* anfodlon
**discontinue** *vb* torri, atal
**discord** *n* anghytgord
**discount** *n* disgownt
**discourage** *vt* digalonni
**discourteous** *adj* anghwrtais
**discover** *vt* darganfod, canfod
**discovery** *n* darganfyddiad
**discredit** *n* anfri, anghlod, amarch ♦ *vt* anghoelio; amau, difrïo
**discreet** *adj* call, synhwyrol, pwyllog
**discrepancy** *n* anghysondeb
**discretion** *n* barn, pwyll, synnwyr
**discriminate** *vb* gwahaniaethu
**discrimination** *n* gwahaniaethu, rhagfarn, anffafriaeth
**discursive** *adj* crwydrol, anghysylltiol
**discuss** *vt* trin, trafod
**discussion** *n* trafodaeth, sgwrs
**disdain** *vb* diystyru, dirmygu, diystyrwch ♦ *n* dirmyg
**disease** *n* afiechyd, clefyd, clwyf
**disembark** *vb* glanio
**disengage** *vb* datgyweddu, rhyddhau
**disentangle** *vb* datod, datrys
**disestablish** *vt* datgysylltu
**disfigure** *vt* anffurfio, anharddu, hagru
**disgrace** *vt* gwaradwyddo ♦ *n* gwaradwydd, gwarth
**disgraceful** *adj* gwaradwyddus, gwarthus
**disguise** *vt* dieithrio, ffugio, lledrithio ♦ *n* rhith, dieithrwch
**disgust** *n* diflastod, ffieidd-dod ♦ *vt* diflasu, ffieiddio
**disgusting** *adj* ffiaidd, brwnt, gwrthun
**dish** *n* dysgl; dysglaid
**dishcloth** *n* cadach llestri
**dishearten** *vt* digalonni
**dishevelled** *adj* anhrefnus, aflêr, anniben
**dishonest** *adj* anonest
**dishonour** *n* amarch, gwarth ♦ *vb* amharchu
**dishwasher** *n* peiriant golchi llestri
**disillusion** *vb* dadrithio
**disincentive** *n* gwrthgymhelliant
**disinfect** *vb* diheintio
**disinfectant** *n* diheintydd
**disintegrate** *vb* datod, chwalu
**disinterested** *adj* heb ddiddordeb, diduedd
**disjointed** *adj* datgymalog
**disk** *n* disg(en)
**dislike** *vt* casáu ♦ *n* casineb
**dislocate** *vt* rhoi o'i le, datgymalu
**dislodge** *vt* symud, syflyd, gwared
**dismal** *adj* tywyll, dilewyrch, digalon
**dismay** *vt* brawychu, siomi, digalonni ♦ *n* braw, siom, chwithdod
**dismiss** *vt* gollwng; diswyddo
**dismount** *vb* disgyn, dymchwelyd
**disobedience** *n* anufudd-dod
**disobedient** *adj* anufudd
**disobey** *vb* anufuddhau
**disorder** *n* anhrefn; anhwyldeb ♦ *vt* anhrefnu
**disorderly** *adj* afreolus, anniben
**disown** *vt* gwadu, diarddel
**disparage** *vt* amharchu, bychanu, difrïo

**disparaging** adj amharchus, gwaradwyddus

**disparity** n anghyfartaledd, rhagor

**dispatch** vb anfon; diweddu ♦ n neges

**dispel** vt chwalu, gwasgaru

**dispensary** n fferyllfa

**dispense** vb rhannu; gweinyddu; hepgor

**disperse** vb gwasgaru, chwalu, taenu

**dispirit** vt digalonni, llwfrhau

**dispirited** adj digalon, gwangalon

**display** vt arddangos ♦ n arddangosiad

**displease** vt anfodloni, anfoddio, digio

**displeasure** n anfodlonrwydd, dicter

**disposable nappies** npl clytiau untro

**dispose** vt hepgor, gwaredu

**disposition** n anianawd

**disprove** vt gwrthbrofi

**dispute** vb dadlau, ymryson ♦ n dadl

**disqualify** vb difreinio, atal

**disquiet** vb anesmwytho

**disregard** vt diystyru, esgeuluso ♦ n diystyrwch, esgeulustra

**disreputable** adj gwarthus, amharchus

**disrespect** n amarch

**disrupt** vb rhwygo, amharu ar

**dissatisfaction** n anfodlonrwydd

**dissatisfy** vt anfodloni

**dissect** vb difynio, trychu; dadansoddi

**disseminate** vt hau, taenu, lledaenu

**dissent** vi anghytuno ♦ n anghytundeb; ymneilltuaeth

**dissertation** n traethawd

**dissimilar** adj annhebyg, gwahanol

**dissipate** vt chwalu, gwasgaru, afradloni

**dissociate** vt anghysylltu,

gwahanu, diaelodi

**dissolute** adj afradlon, ofer

**dissolution** n ymddatodiad, datodiad, diddymiad

**dissolve** vb toddi, datod; datgorffori, diddymu

**distance** n pellter

**distant** adj pell, pellennig, oeraidd

**distaste** n difiastod, cas

**distend** vt estyn, lledu, chwyddo

**distil** vb distyllu, dihidlo

**distillery** n distyllty

**distinct** adj gwahanol; eglur

**distinction** n arbenigrwydd, rhagoriaeth, gwahaniaeth

**distinctive** adj gwahanredol, arbennig

**distinguish** vb gwahaniaethu; hynodi

**distinguished** adj enwog, amlwg

**distort** vt ystumio, anffurfio, gwyrdroi

**distract** vb tynnu ymaith, drysu, mwydro

**distraction** n dryswch, diffyg sylw

**distress** n cyfyngder, ing, trallod

**distressing** adj trallodus, blin, poenus

**distribute** vt rhannu, dosbarthu

**distribution** n dosbarthiad, rhaniad

**distributor** n dosbarthydd, dosbarthwr

**district** n dosbarth, ardal, rhandir.
  **d. council** cyngor dosbarth

**distrust** n drwgdybiaeth ♦ vb drwgdybio

**disturb** vt aflonyddu, cyffroi

**disturbance** n aflonyddwch, cyffro, terfysg

**disturbed** adj blinderus, cynhyrfus

**ditch** n ffos

**ditto** adv eto, yr un, yr un peth

**dive** vi ymsuddo, deifio

**diverse** adj gwahanol; annhebyg

**diversion** n difyrrwch, adloniant; dargyfeiriad

**divert** vt dargyfeirio, difyrru

**divide** vb rhannu, dosbarthu, gwahanu ♦ n gwahanfa

**divided** adj rhanedig

**dividend** n buddran; difidend

**divine** adj dwyfol ♦ n diwinydd ♦ vb dewinio, dyfalu

**divinity** n duwdod; diwinyddiaeth

**division** n rhan, rhaniad; cyfraniaeth. **long d.** n rhannu hir

**divorce** vt ysgar(u) ♦ n ysgariad

**divorced** adj wedi ysgaru

**divulge** vt datguddio, dadlennu

**dizzy** adj penysgafn, pensyfrdan

**DJ** n troellwr

**do** vb gwneud, gwneuthur

**docile** adj dof, hywedd, hydrin

**dock** n (dail) tafol

**dock** vt tocio, cwtogi

**dock** n doc, porthladd ♦ vt docio; cwtogi

**dockyard** n iard longau

**doctor** n doctor, meddyg; doethor, doethur

**doctrine** n athrawiaeth

**document** n ysgrif, gweithred, dogfen

**documentary** adj dogfennol

**dodge** vb osgoi, twyllo ♦ n cast, ystryw

**doe** n ewig

**dog** n ci ♦ vb dal i ddilyn

**dogged** adj cyndyn, ystyfnig

**dogmatic** adj athrawiaethol; awdurdodol, pendant

**dole** n dôl, dogn. **on the d.** yn ddi-waith, ar y clwt ♦ vt dogni, rhannu

**doleful** adj trist, prudd, galarus

**doll** n dol, doli

**dollar** n doler

**dolphin** n dolffin

**domain** n tiriogaeth, maes

**dome** n cromen, cryndo

**domestic** adj teuluaidd, cartrefol; gwâr, dof

**dominant** adj trech

**dominate** vb dominyddu

**dominion** n rheolaeth; dominiwn, tiriogaeth

**don** vt gwisgo (dilledyn) ♦ n athro (coleg)

**donate** vb rhoddi

**donation** n rhodd

**donkey** n asyn, mul

**donor** n rhoddwr

**doodle** vb dwdlan

**doom** n dedfryd, barn, tynged ♦ vt dedfrydu, tynghedu, collfarnu

**doomsday** n dydd barn

**door** n drws, dôr, porth

**doorkeeper** n porthor

**door-step** n rhiniog, trothwy

**doorway** n porth, drws

**dope** n cyffur ♦ vb rhoi cyffur

**dormant** n ynghwsg; di-rym

**dormitory** n ystafell gysgu, hundy

**dose** n dogn ♦ vt dogni

**dot** n dot ♦ vb dotio

**dote** vi dotio, gwirioni, ffoli, dylu

**double** adj, n dwbl ♦ vb dyblu, plygu. **d. glazing** gwydro dwbl, ffenestri dwbl. **d. flat** meddalnod dwbl

**double-bass** n bas dwbl

**double-dealing** n twyll

**doubt** vb amau, petruso ♦ n amheuaeth, (pl) amheuon

**doubtful** adj amheus, petrus

**doubtless** adv yn ddiamau, diau

**dough** n toes

**doughnut** n toesen

**douse** vb trochi; diffodd

**dove** n colomen

**dowdy** adj aflêr, anniben

**down** n manblu

**down** n gwaun, rhos, mynydd-dir

**down** adv i lawr, i waered. **d. and out** digalon, truenus

**downcast** adj digalon, prudd

**downfall** n cwymp, codwm, dinistr

**downpour** n tywalltiad, pistylliad ♦ vb tywallt, pistyllio

**downright** adj diamheuol

**downstairs** n y llawr ♦ adv ar y llawr
**downwards** adv i lawr, i waered
**dowry** n gwaddol
**doze** vi hepian ♦ n cyntun
**dozen** n deuddeg, dwsin
**drab** adj llwyddaid, salw
**draft** n drafft, braslun ♦ vb drafftio braslunio
**drag** vb llusgo ♦ n car llusg
**dragon** n draig
**dragon-fly** n gwas y neidr
**drain** n traen, carthffos
**drain** vb draenio, diferu, yfed. **draining board** bwrdd diferu
**drainage** n draeniad. **d. basin** dalgylch afon
**drake** n ceiliog hwyad, meilart
**drama** n drama
**dramatic** adj dramatig
**dramatise** vb dramadeiddio, dramodi
**dramatist** n dramodydd
**drape** vt gwisgo, gorchuddio
**draper** n dilledydd
**drastic** adj cryf, llym, trwyadl
**draught** n dracht, llymaid, drafft(en); tynfa (llong)
**draughts** npl drafftiau
**draughtsman** n drafftsmon, lluniadydd
**draw** n atyniad, tynfa ♦ vb tynnu, llusgo; lluniadu, darlunio. **d. to scale** graddluniadu. **drawn game** gêm gyfartal
**drawback** n anfantais
**drawer** n drâr, drôr
**drawing** n lluniad, llun
**drawing room** n ystafell groeso
**drawl** vb llusgo (geiriau)
**dread** vb ofni, arswydo ♦ n ofn, arswyd
**dreadful** adj ofnadwy
**dream** vb breuddwydio ♦ n breuddwyd
**dreamy** adj breuddwydiol
**dreary** adj llwm, diflas, digysur

**dredge** vb glanhau
**dregs** npl gwaddod, gwaelodion, gwehilion
**drench** vt gwlychu; drensio
**dress** vb gwisgo, dilladu ♦ n gwisg
**dresser** n dreser, gwisgwr
**dressing** n dresin. **salad d.** dresin salad. **d. gown** gŵn gwisgo
**dressmaker** n gwniadwraig
**dressmaking** n gwniadwaith ♦ vb gwneud dillad
**dribble** n dribl(ad), drefl ♦ vb driblo, dreflu, glafoerio
**drier** n peiriant sychu
**drift** n drifft, lluwch; tuedd ♦ vb drifftio, lluwchio
**drill** vb drilio ♦ n dril
**drink** vb yfed ♦ n diod, llymaid
**drinker** n yfwr, diotwr
**drinking water** n dŵr yfed
**drip** vb diferu, defnynnu ♦ n diferiad
**dripping** adj diferol ♦ n toddion, saim
**drive** n dreif, gyriant, cymhelliad ♦ vb dreifio, gyrru
**drivel** vi glafoerio, driflan, dreflu ♦ n glafoerion
**driver** n gyrrwr
**driving** adj trwm, â grym y tu ôl iddo, grymus ♦ n gyrru
**driving licence** n trwydded yrru
**drizzle** vb briwlan ♦ n glaw mân
**droll** adj digrif, ysmala
**drone** n gwenynen ormes; diogyn
**droop** vi llaesu, ymollwng; nychu
**drop** n diferyn, dafn, cwympiad ♦ vb diferu, cwympo, gollwng. **d. goal** gôl adlam
**drought** n tywydd sych, sychder, sychdwr
**drover** n porthmon, gyrrwr
**drown** vb boddi
**drowsy** adj cysglyd, marwaidd, swrth
**drudgery** n caledwaith, slafdod
**drug** n cyffur

**druid** n derwydd

**drum** n tabwrdd, drwm ♦ vb tabyrddu

**drunk** adj meddw, brwysg

**drunkard** n meddwyn

**dry** adj sych, hysb, cras ♦ vb sychu. **d. cleaners** n sych lanhawyr

**dryness** n sychder, craster

**dry rot** n sych-bydredd, tyllau pryfed

**dual** adj deuol. **d. carriageway** ffordd ddeuol

**dub** vt urddo, galw, llysenwi; dwbio, lleisio (ffilm)

**dubious** adj amheus, petrus

**Dublin** n Dulyn

**duchess** n duges

**duchy** n dugiaeth

**duck** n hwyad, hwyaden

**duck** vb trochi; gostwng pen, gwyro

**duckling** n cyw hwyaden

**dud** n ffugbeth

**due** adj dyledus, dyladwy ♦ n dyled, haeddiant

**duel** n gornest

**duet** n deuawd

**duke** n dug

**dull** adj dwl, hurt; marwaidd; diflas; cymylog; pŵl ♦ vb pylu, lleddfu

**dumb** adj mud

**dumbfound** vt syfrdanu, drysu

**dummy** n dymi; delw; ffug-bas (rygbi) ♦ vb ffug-basio

**dump** n dymp, storfa ♦ vb dympio

**dumpling** n tymplen, poten

**dunce** n hurtyn, twpsyn, penbwl

**dune** n twyn

**dung** n tom, tail

**dungarees** npl dyngaris

**dungeon** n daeardy, daeargell, dwnsiwn

**dupe** n gwirionyn ♦ vt twyllo

**duplex** adj dwplecs

**duplicate** adj dyblyg ♦ n copi ♦ vt dyblygu

**duplicity** n dichell, rhagrith

**durable** adj parhaol, parhaus, cryf

**duration** n parhad

**duress** n gorfodaeth

**during** prep yn ystod

**dusk** n cyfnos, gwyll

**dust** n llwch ♦ vt taenu neu sychu llwch, dwstio

**dustbin** n bin sbwriel

**duster** n cadach, dwster

**dustman** n dyn lludw

**dusty** adj llychlyd

**Dutch** n Iseldireg. **Dutchman** n Iseldirwr

**dutiful** adj ufudd, ufuddgar

**duty** n dyletswydd; toll. **customs d.** tolldal. **import d.** toll fewnforio. **export d.** toll allforio

**dwarf** n cor, corrach ♦ adj corachaidd

**dwell** vi trigo, preswylio

**dwelling** n annedd, preswyl

**dwindle** vi darfod, lleihau, dirywio

**dye** vb lliwio, llifo ♦ n lliw, lliwur

**dyke** n morglawdd, cob

**dynamic** adj dynamig

**dynamics** n dynameg

# E

**each** adj, pron pob, pob un. **e. other** ei gilydd

**eager** adj awyddus, awchus

**eagle** n eryr

**ear** n clust, dolen; tywysen. **earache** clust dost

**earl** n iarll

**early** adj cynnar, bore, boreol ♦ adv yn fore

**earmark** n clustnod, nod clust ♦ vb clustnodi, neilltuo

**earn** vt ennill, elwa

**earnest** adj difrif, difrifol, taer

**earnest** n ern, ernes ♦ vb gwystl

**earnings** npl enillion

**earphone** *n* ffôn clust
**earring** *n* clustlws
**earshot** *n* clyw
**earth** *n* daear, pridd ♦ *vt* priddo
**earthenware** *npl* llestri pridd
**earthly** *adj* daearol, ar wyneb daear
**earthquake** *n* daeargryn
**ease** *n* esmwythdra, esmwythyd; rhwyddineb ♦ *vb* esmwytho
**easel** *n* isl
**east** *n* dwyrain ♦ *adj* dwyreiniol. **E. Germany** Dwyrain yr Almaen
**Easter** *n* y Pasg
**eastern** *adj* dwyreiniol
**eastwards** *adj, adv* tua'r dwyrain
**easy** *adj* hawdd, rhwydd
**easy-chair** *n* cadair esmwyth
**easy-going** *adj* didaro, di-hid
**eat** *vt* bwyta, ysu
**eaves** *npl* bargod, bondo
**eavesdrop** *vb* clustfeinio
**ebb** *n* trai ♦ *vi* treio
**eccentric** *adj* od, hynod; echreiddig
**ecclesiastic** *adj* eglwysig ♦ *n* clerigwr
**echo** *n* atsain, carreg ateb ♦ *vb* atseinio
**eclipse** *n* eclips, diffyg, clip ♦ *vb* tywyllu
**ecology** *n* ecoleg
**economic** *adj* economaidd
**economical** *adj* cynnil, darbodus
**economics** *n* economeg
**economize** *vb* cynilo
**economy** *n* cynildeb, darbodaeth, economi
**ecstacy** *n* gorfoledd, gorawen, hwyl
**edge** *n* min, ymyl ♦ *vb* minio, hogi; symud. **to be on e.** bod ar bigau'r drain
**edible** *adj* bwytadwy
**edict** *n* cyhoeddiad, gorchymyn
**Edinburgh** *n* Caeredin
**edit** *vt* golygu, paratoi i'r wasg

**edition** *n* argraffiad
**editor** *n* golygydd
**editorial** *adj* golygyddol
**educate** *vt* addysgu
**education** *n* addysg
**educational** *adj* addysgol
**eel** *n* llysywen
**eerie** *adj* iasol, annaearol
**effect** *n* effaith; canlyniad ♦ *vt* effeithio. **after-effects** sgil-effeithiau
**effective** *adj* effeithiol
**effectiveness** *n* effeithiolrwydd
**effeminate** *adj* merchetaidd
**efficiency** *n* effeithlonrwydd
**efficient** *adj* effeithiol, cymwys
**effort** *n* ymdrech, ymgais
**effusive** *adj* teimladol, arddangosiadol
**e.g.** *adv abbr* er enghraifft, e.e.
**egg** *n* wy. **scrambled e.** cymysgwy
**egg** *vt* annog, annos
**egg cup** *n* cwpan wy
**egg shell** *n* masgl/plisgyn wy
**ego** *n* ego, yr hunan
**egoism** *n* myfiaeth, egoistiaeth
**egotism** *n* hunanoldeb
**egotist** *n* un hunanol
**Egypt** *n* yr Aifft
**eiderdown** *n* cwrlid plu
**eight** *adj, n* wyth
**eighteen** *adj, n* deunaw, un deg wyth
**eighth** *adj* wythfed
**eighty** *adj, n* pedwar ugain, wyth deg
**Eire** *n* Iwerddon Rydd, Gweriniaeth Iwerddon
**either** *adj* un o'r ddau ♦ *conj* naill ai ♦ *adv, conj* na, nac, ychwaith
**ejaculate** *vb* saethu; gweiddi; ebychu
**eject** *vt* bwrw allan; diarddel
**eke** *vt* estyn allan; hel neu grafu
**elaborate** *adj* llafurfawr, manwl
**elaborate** *vb* manylu
**elapse** *vi* mynd heibio, treiglo

**elastic** *adj* hydwyth, ystwyth. **e. band** *n* cylch lastig
**elated** *adj* gorawenus, calonnog
**elation** *n* gorawen
**elbow** *n* elin, penelin
**elder** *n* henuriad, hynafgwr ♦ *adj* hŷn
**elderly** *adj* oedrannus
**eldest** *adj* hynaf
**elect** *vt* ethol, dewis ♦ *adj* etholedig
**election** *n* etholiad; etholedigaeth
**elector** *n* etholwr
**electorate** *n* etholaeth
**electric** *adj* trydanol, electrig. **e. blanket** *n* blanced drydan. **e. fire** *n* tân trydan
**electrician** *n* trydanwr
**electricity** *n* trydan
**electrify** *vt* gwefreiddio, trydanu
**electronic** *adj* electronig
**elegant** *adj* cain, dillyn, lluniaidd
**elegy** *n* marwnad, galarnad
**element** *n* elfen
**elementary** *adj* elfennol
**elephant** *n* cawrfil, eliffant
**elevate** *vt* dyrchafu, codi
**eleven** *adj*, *n* un ar ddeg
**eleventh** *adj* unfed ar ddeg
**elf** (**elves**) *n* ellyll, coblyn
**elicit** *vb* mynnu gan
**eligible** *adj* cymwys, etholadwy, dewisol
**eliminate** *vt* dileu, deol
**elm** *n* llwyf, llwyfen
**elongate** *vt* hwyhau, estyn
**elongated** *adj* hirgul
**eloquent** *adj* huawdl
**else** *adv* arall, amgen, pe amgen
**elsewhere** *adv* mewn lle arall
**elude** *vt* osgoi
**elusive** *adj* di-ddal, gwibiog, ansafadwy
**emaciate** *vt* teneuo, culhau, curio
**emaciated** *adj* tenau, curiedig
**emanate** *vi* deillio, tarddu, llifo
**emancipate** *vt* rhyddfreinio, rhyddhau

**embankment** *n* clawdd, cob
**embargo** *n* gwaharddiad
**embark** *vb* mynd neu osod ar long; hwylio. **to e. on** ymgymryd â, dechrau
**embarrass** *vt* rhwystro, drysu
**embarrassed** *adj* mewn penbleth, trafferthus
**embarrassing** *adj* dyrys, anffodus
**embarrassment** *n* chwithedd, embaras
**embassy** *n* llysgenhadaeth
**embed** *vb* mewnosod
**embers** *npl* marwor, marwydos
**embezzle** *vt* celcio, darnguddio, lladrata
**embitter** *vt* chwerwi
**emblem** *n* arwyddlun
**embody** *vt* corffori
**emboss** *vt* boglynnu
**embrace** *vt* cofleidio; cynnwys ♦ *n* cofleidiad
**embroider** *vt* brodio
**embroidery** *n* brodwaith
**embryo** *n* cynelwad, embryo
**emend** *vt* cywiro, diwygio
**emerald** *n* emrallt
**emerge** *vi* dyfod allan, dyfod i'r golwg, ymddangos
**emergence** *n* ymddangosiad
**emergency** *n* cyfyngder, taro, argyfwng. **in an e.** mewn taro
**emigrate** *vi* allfudo, ymfudo
**eminent** *adj* enwog, amlwg, o fri
**emit** *vt* rhoddi neu fwrw allan
**emotion** *n* cyffro, teimlad, emosiwn
**emotional** *adj* emosiynol
**empathy** *n* empathi
**emperor** *n* ymerawdwr, ymherodr
**emphasis** *n* pwys, pwyslais
**emphasize** *vt* pwysleisio
**emphatic** *adj* pwysleisiol, pendant
**empire** *n* ymerodraeth
**empirical** *adj* empeiraidd
**employ** *vt* cyflogi; arfer, defnyddio ♦ *n* gwasanaeth

**employee** n gŵr cyflog
**employer** n cyflogwr
**employment** n cyflogaeth, gwaith
**empower** vt awdurdodi, galluogi
**empress** n ymerodres
**empty** adj gwag, coeg ♦ vb gwagu, arllwys, gwacáu, dihysbyddu
**empty-handed** adj gwaglaw
**emulate** vt ymgystadlu â; efelychu
**emulsion** n emwlsiwn
**enable** vt galluogi
**enact** vt deddfu, ordeinio; cyflawni
**enchant** vt swyno, cyfareddu, hudo
**enclose** vt amgau
**enclosed** adj amgaeëdig
**enclosure** n lle caeëdig, lloc
**encompass** vt amgylchu, cylchynu
**encore** n encôr ♦ adv eto
**encounter** vt cyfarfod, taro ar ♦ n ymgyfarfod, brwydr
**encourage** vt cefnogi, calonogi, annog
**encouragement** n cefnogaeth, calondid, anogaeth
**encroach** vi llechfeddiannu
**encyclopaedia** n gwyddoniadur
**end** n diwedd; diben ♦ vb diweddu, dibennu, terfynu. **e. point** pwynt terfyn. **from e. to e.** o ben bwy gilydd
**endanger** vt peryglu
**endear** vt anwylo
**endeavour** vi ymdrechu ♦ n ymdrech
**ending** n diwedd, dibeniad, terfyniad
**endless** adj diddiwedd
**endorse** vt cefnogi, arnodi, ardystio
**endorsement** n arnodiad, ardystiad
**endow** vt gwaddoli, cynysgaeddu, donio
**endowment** n gwaddol, cynhysgaeth
**endurance** n dygnwch
**endure** vb parhau; dioddef,

goddeff
**enemy** n gelyn
**energetic** adj grymus, egnïol
**energy** n ynni, egni
**enforce** vt gorfodi
**enforcement** n gorfodaeth
**engage** vb ymrwymo, dyweddïo; cyflogi; ymladd
**engaged** adj ymrwymedig, wedi dyweddïo; prysur
**engagement** n ymrwymiad, dyweddïad; brwydr
**engaging** adj deniadol
**engender** vt achosi, peri
**engine** n peiriant, injan
**engineer** n peiriannydd
**engineering** n peirianneg
**England** n Lloegr
**English** adj Saesneg, Seisnig ♦ n Saesneg. **E. Channel** Môr Udd
**Englishman** (-men) n Sais (pl Saeson)
**engrave** vt ysgythru
**engraving** n ysgythrad
**engulf** vt llyncu
**enhance** vb chwanegu, mwyhau, chwyddo, hyrwyddo
**enjoy** vt mwynhau; meddu
**enjoyable** adj pleserus
**enjoyment** n mwynhad
**enkindle** vt ennyn
**enlarge** vt ehangu, helaethu
**enlighten** vt goleuo; hysbysu
**enlightened** adj goleuedig; golau
**enlist** vb ymrestru, listio; ennill
**enmity** n gelyniaeth
**enormity** n anfadrwydd, ysgelerder
**enormous** adj dirfawr, anferth, enfawr
**enough** adj, n, adv digon
**enquire** vb ymofyn, ymholi, gofyn, holi
**enquiry** n ymholiad
**enrage** vt ffyrnigo, cynddeiriogi
**enrich** vt cyfoethogi
**enrol** vt cofrestru

enrolment *n* cofrestrad
ensign *n* lluman, baner; llumanwr
enslave *vt* caethiwo
ensue *vi* dilyn, canlyn
ensure *vt* diogelu, sicrhau
entail *vt* gorfodi, gofyn
entangle *vt* drysu, maglu, rhwydo
enter *vb* mynd i mewn, treiddio;
cofnodi
enterprise *n* anturiaeth, menter
enterprising *adj* anturiaethus,
mentrus
entertain *vt* difyrru, adlonni;
croesawu
entertainer *n* difyrrwr, diddanwr
entertaining *adj* difyrrus, diddan
entertainment *n* difyrrwch,
adloniant
enthrall *vb* swyno
enthrone *vt* gorseddu
enthusiasm *n* brwdfrydedd
enthusiastic *adj* brwdfrydig,
eiddgar
entice *vb* hudo, denu, llithio
entire *adj* cyfan, hollol, llwyr
entirely *adv* yn gyfan gwbl, yn
llwyr
entirety *n* cyfanrwydd
entrails *npl* perfedd, ymysgaroedd
entrance *n* mynediad, mynedfa. e.
fee tâl mynediad
entrance *vt* swyno
entreat *vt* erfyn, ymbil, deisyf
entrust *vt* ymddiried
entry *n* mynediad, mynedfa;
cofnodiad
envelop *vt* amgáu
envelope *n* amlen
envious *adj* cenfigennus
environment *n* amgylchedd,
amgylchfyd
environmental *adj* amgylchol
envisage *vb* rhagweld
envoy *n* cennad, negesydd
envy *n* cenfigen, eiddigedd ♦ *vt*
cenfigennu, eiddigeddu
epic *adj* arwrol, arwraidd ♦ *n*

arwrgerdd, epig
epidemic *adj* heintus ♦ *n* haint
epiglottis *n* epiglotis
epilepsy *n* epilepsi
Epiphany *n* Yr Ystwyll
episcopate *n* esgobaeth
episode *n* digwyddiad, gogyfran,
episôd
epistle *n* epistol, llythyr
epitaph *n* beddargraff
epitome *n* crynodeb, talfyriad
equable *adj* gwastad, cyson, tawel
equal *adj* cyfartal ♦ *n* cydradd ♦ *vt*
bod yn gyfartal. without e. heb ei
ail
equality *n* cydraddoldeb,
cyfartaledd
equalize *vb* cydraddoli, cyfartalu
equally *adv* yn ogystal â, yn llawn,
yn gyfartal
equanimity *n* tawelwch, anghyffro
equate *vt* cyfartalu, cymharu
equation *n* hafaliad. simple e. *n*
hafaliad syml. quadratic e. *n*
hafaliad dwyradd. simultaneous e.
*n* hafaliad cydamserol
equator *n* y cyhydedd
equatorial *adj* cyhydeddol
equestrian *adj* marchogol ♦ *n*
marchog
equilateral *adj* hafalochrog
equilibrium *n* cydbwysedd,
cymantoledd
equip *vt* taclu, paratoi, cymhwyso,
cyfarparu
equipment *n* cyfarpar, offer
equipoise *n* cydbwysedd
equivalent *adj* cyfwerth, cyfartal
equivocal *adj* amwys
era *n* cyfnod
eradicate *vt* difodi, difa
erase *vt* dileu, rhwbio allan
eraser *n* dilëydd, rwber
erect *adj* syth, unionsyth ♦ *vt* codi,
adeiladu
ermine *n* carlwm
erode *vb* ysu, treulio, erydu

**erosion** n erydiad

**erotic** adj serchol, nwydol, erotig

**err** vi cyfeiliorni

**errand** n neges, cenadwri

**erratic** adj ansefydlog, crwydraidd

**error** n cyfeiliornad, camgymeriad; bai, gwall. **in e.** ar gam

**erupt** vb echdorri, torri allan

**eruption** n echdoriad, tarddiad

**escalator** n escaladur

**escapade** n pranc, direidi

**escape** vb dianc, osgoi ♦ n dihangfa

**escort** vt hebrwng ♦ n gosgordd

**especial** adj arbennig, neilltuol

**especially** adv yn arbennig, yn enwedig

**espionage** n ysbiaeth

**esquire** n yswain, ysgwier

**essay** n ymgais; traethawd, ysgrif

**essay** vt profi, ymgeisio

**essence** n hanfod; rhinflas

**essential** adj hanfodol, anhepgor ♦ n hanfod, anghenraid

**essentially** adv yn hanfodol

**essentials** npl hanfodion, anhepgorion

**establish** vt sefydlu

**establishment** n sefydliad

**estate** n stad, ystad, eiddo. **industrial e.** stad ddiwydiannol

**esteem** vt parchu, edmygu, cyfrif ♦ n parch, bri

**estimate** vt, n amcangyfrif

**estimation** n amcangyfrif, parch, bri

**estrange** vt dieithrio

**estuary** n aber

**et cetera** adv ac yn y blaen

**eternal** adj tragwyddol, bythol

**eternally** adv yn dragwyddol, yn oes oesoedd, byth bythoedd

**eternity** n tragwyddoldeb

**ethical** adj moesegol

**ethics** npl moeseg

**Ethiopia** n Ethiopia

**ethnic** adj ethnig, cenhedlig

**ethos** n ethos, naws, natur

**etiquette** n moesau, arfer

**etymology** n geirdarddiad

**eucharist** n cymun, cymundeb

**Europe** n Ewrob, Ewrop

**European** adj Ewropeaidd ♦ n Ewropead

**evacuate** vt ymgilio, ymadael (â)

**evade** vt gochelyd, osgoi

**evangelical** adj efengylaidd

**evangelist** n efengylydd

**evangelize** vt efengylu

**evaporate** vb ymageru, anweddu

**evaporated milk** n llaeth anwedd(og)

**evasion** n osgoad, gocheliad

**eve** n min nos, noswyl

**even** adj gwastad, llyfn; cyfartal ♦ adv hyd yn oed. **e. number** eilrif

**evening** n noswaith, yr hwyr, min nos. **e. class** n dosbarth nos. **e. dress** n gwisg ffurfiol

**evensong** n prynhawnol weddi, gosber

**event** n digwyddiad. **in the e. of** os bydd

**eventful** adj llawn digwyddiadau

**eventuality** n achlysur, digwyddiad posibl

**eventually** adv o'r diwedd

**ever** adv bob amser, erioed, byth. **e. and anon** byth a hefyd

**evergreen** n, adj bythwyrdd, anwyw

**everlasting** adj tragwyddol, bythol

**evermore** adv byth, byth bythoedd

**every** adj pob

**everybody** pron pawb, pob un

**everyday** adj bob dydd, beunyddiol

**everyone** pron pawb, pob un

**everything** pron popeth

**everywhere** adv ym mhobman

**evict** vt troi allan, dadfeddiannu

**evidence** n tystiolaeth, prawf

**evident** adj amlwg, eglur

**evil** adj drwg, drygionus ♦ n drwg, drygioni

**evoke** *vt* galw neu dynnu allan; gwysio
**evolution** *n* esblygiad
**evolve** *vb* datblygu; esblygu
**ewe** *n* dafad, mamog
**ex-** *prefix* allan o; cyn-
**exact** *adj* manwl, cywir, union
**exact** *vt* hawlio, mynnu
**exacting** *adj* manwl, gorthrymus
**exactly** *adv* yn union, i'r dim
**exaggerate** *vt* chwyddo, gorliwio
**exaggeration** *n* gormodiaith, gorliwiad
**exalt** *vt* dyrchafu, mawrygu
**examine** *vt* arholi, archwilio
**examination** *n* arholiad, archwiliad
**examiner** *n* arholwr, archwiliwr
**example** *n* esiampl, enghraifft
**exasperate** *vt* llidio, cythruddo
**exasperation** *n* llid, cythrudd
**excavate** *vt* cloddio
**exceed** *vt* rhagori ar, bod yn fwy na
**exceedingly** *adv* tros ben, tra
**excel** *vb* rhagori
**excellent** *adj* rhagorol, ardderchog, godidog, campus
**except** *prep* ac eithrio, eithr, namyn, oddieithr, heblaw
**exception** *n* eithriad
**exceptional** *adj* eithriadol
**excerpt** *n* dyfyniad, detholiad
**excess** *n* gormod, gormodedd
**excessive** *adj* gormodol, eithafol
**exchange** *vt* cyfnewid, ffeirio ♦ *n* cyfnewid, cyfnewidfa. **e. rate** cyfradd cyfnewid
**exchequer** *n* trysorlys
**excise** *n* toll ♦ *vt* gosod toll
**excite** *vt* cynhyrfu, cyffroi
**excited** *adj* cynhyrfus
**excitement** *n* cynnwrf
**exciting** *adj* cyffrous
**exclaim** *vt* llefain, gweiddi, bloeddio, ebychu
**exclamation** *n* llef, gwaedd,

ebychiad. **e. mark** ebychnod
**exclude** *vt* cau allan, bwrw allan
**exclusion** *n* gwaharddiad, gwrthodiad
**exclusive** *adj* cyfyngedig
**excommunicate** *vt* esgymuno
**excrement** *n* carth, tom, baw
**excrete** *vt* ysgarthu
**excruciating** *adj* dirdynnol
**excursion** *n* gwibdaith, pleserdaith
**excuse** *vt* esgusodi ♦ *n* esgus
**execute** *vt* cyflawni, gweithredu; dienyddio
**execution** *n* cyflawniad, dienyddiad
**executioner** *n* dienyddiwr
**executive** *adj* gweithiol, gweithredol ♦ *n* gweithredwr. **e. committee** pwyllgor gwaith
**executor** *n* ysgutor
**exemplify** *vt* egluro, dangos, enghreifftio
**exempt** *adj* rhydd, esgusodol ♦ *vt* rhyddhau, esgusodi
**exercise** *n* ymarfer, ymarferiad ♦ *vb* ymarfer. **e. book** llyfr ysgrifennu, ymarfer
**exert** *vt* ymegnïo, ymdrechu
**exertion** *n* ymdrech, ymroddiad
**exhale** *vb* anadlu allan
**exhaust** *vt* disbyddu, diffygio, gwacáu ♦ *n* disbyddwr, gwacáwr. **e. (pipe)** *n* pibell nwyon
**exhausted** *adj* lluddedig, blin, disbyddedig, wedi ymlâdd
**exhaustion** *n* gorludded
**exhaustive** *adj* trwyadl
**exhibit** *vt* dangos, arddangos
**exhibition** *n* arddangosfa; ysgoloriaeth
**exhilarate** *vt* llonni, sirioli, bywiogi
**exile** *n* alltud; alltudiaeth ♦ *vt* alltudio
**exist** *vi* bod, bodoli
**existence** *n* bod(olaeth), hanfod. **in e.** mewn bod, ar glawr
**exit** *n* allanfa ♦ *vb* mynd allan,

ymadael
**exodus** *n* ymadawiad
**exonerate** *vt* esgusodi
**exorbitant** *adj* afresymol,
gormodol
**exotic** *adj* estron, egsotig
**expand** *vb* lledu, ehangu, datblygu
**expanse** *n* ehangder
**expansion** *n* ehangiad, ymlediad
**expect** *vb* disgwyl
**expectancy** *n* disgwyliad
**expectation** *n* disgwyliad
**expediency** *n* hwylustod
**expedient** *adj* hwylus, cyfleus ♦ *n*
ystryw
**expedite** *vt* hyrwyddo, hwyluso
**expedition** *n* ymgyrch, alldaith
**expel** *vt* bwrw allan, diarddel
**expend** *vt* gwario, treulio
**expenditure** *n* gwariant
**expense** *n* traul, cost
**expenses** *npl* treuliau
**expensive** *adj* drud, costus
**experience** *n* profiad ♦ *vt* profi
**experienced** *adj* profiadol
**experiment** *n* arbrawf ♦ *vi* arbrofi
**expert** *n* arbenigwr ♦ *adj* medrus,
deheuig
**expertise** *n* medr, dawn,
arbenigaeth
**expire** *vb* anadlu allan; darfod,
marw
**expiry** *n* diwedd, terfyn
**explain** *vt* egluro, esbonio
**explanation** *n* eglurhad, esboniad
**explanatory** *adj* eglurhaol,
esboniadol
**explicit** *adj* eglur, manwl, echblyg
**explode** *vb* ffrwydro, chwalu
**exploit** *n* camp, gorchest ♦ *vt*
gweithio, gwneud elw o, ymelwa
ar
**exploitation** *n* ymelwad
**explore** *vt* fforio, chwilio
**explorer** *n* fforiwr
**explosion** *n* ffrwydriad; tanchwa
**explosive** *n* ffrwydrydd/yn ♦ *adj*

ffrwydrol
**exponent** *n* esboniwr, dehonglwr
**export** *vt* allforio ♦ *n* allforyn
**exporter** *n* allforiwr
**expose** *vt* amlygu, dinoethi
**expound** *vt* esbonio
**express** *vt* mynegi, datgan ♦ *adj*
cyflym, clir ♦ *n* trên cyflym
**expression** *n* mynegiant
**expressly** *adv* yn unig swydd, yn
benodol
**expulsion** *n* diarddeliad
**exquisite** *adj* odiaeth, rhagorol;
coeth
**extempore** *adv, adj* byrfyfyr, o'r
frest
**extend** *vb* estyn, ymestyn; ehangu
**extension** *n* helaethiad, ehangiad,
(ym)estyniad
**extensive** *adj* ymestynnol, helaeth
**extent** *n* ehangder, maint, hyd,
mesur. **to some e.** i raddau
**extenuate** *vt* lleihau, lleddfu;
esgusodi
**exterior** *adj* allanol ♦ *n* tu allan
**exterminate** *vt* difodi, dileu
**external** *adj* allanol
**extinct** *adj* wedi diffodd, wedi
darfod, diflanedig
**extinguish** *vt* diffodd; diddymu,
dileu
**extinguisher** *n* diffoddwr
**extol** *vt* moli, moliannu, clodfori
**extort** *vt* cribddeilio, gwasgu
**extortionate** *adj* gormodol
**extra** *adj* ychwanegol ♦ *adv* tu
hwnt, dros ben ♦ *n* peth dros ben,
ychwanegiad
**extract** *vt* echdynnu, tynnu;
dyfynnu, rhinio ♦ *n* echdyniad;
dyfyniad; rhin, darn
**extracurricular** *adj* allgyrsiol
**extramural** *adj* allanol
**extraordinary** *adj* hynod,
anghyffredin
**extravagant** *adj* gwastraffus,
afradlon

**extreme** adj i'r eithaf, eithafol ♦ n
eithaf
**extremely** adv dros ben, gor-
**extremity** n pen, eithaf; cyfyngder
**extrovert** adj allblyg, alltro ♦ n
alltröedydd, person allblyg
**eye** n llygad; crau; dolen ♦ vt
llygadu, sylwi ar, gwylio
**eyeball** n cannwyll y llygad
**eyebrow** n ael
**eyelashes** npl blew yr amrant
**eye-level** n llinell orwel
**eyelid** n amrant
**eye-opener** n agoriad llygad
**eyesight** n golwg
**eyesore** n hyllbeth
**eyewitness** n llygad-dyst

# F

**fable** n chwedl, dameg; anwiredd
**fabric** n adail, adeilad, defnydd
**fabricate** vt llunio, dyfeisio, ffugio
**fabrication** n ffug, anwiredd
**fabulous** adj chwedlonol, diarhebol
**face** n wyneb, wynepryd ♦ vb
wynebu. f. cloth n clwtyn
ymolchi. f. value wynebwerth
**facilitate** vt hwyluso, hyrwyddo
**facility** n hwylustod, cyfleustra,
rhwyddineb
**fact** n ffaith, gwirionedd. as a
matter of f. mewn gwirionedd
**factor** n ffactor, elfen, nodwedd.
prime f. ffactor cysefin
**factory** n ffatri
**factual** adj ffeithiol
**faculty** n cynneddf; cyfadran
**fad** n mympwy, chwilen
**fade** vb diflannu, gwywo; colli ei
liw
**fag** vb slafio, ymládd, blino ♦ n
caledwaith, lludded; gwas bach
**fail** vi ffaelu, methu, pallu,
diffygio. without f. yn ddi-ffael
**failure** n methiant, pall,

aflwyddiant
**faint** adj llesmeiriol, gwan, llesg ♦
vi llewygu ♦ n llesmair, llewyg
**fair** n ffair
**fair** adj teg, glân; gweddol; golau
**fairly** adv yn deg/lân, yn weddol
**fairness** n glendid, tegwch
**fairy** n un o'r tylwyth teg
**fairy-tale** n stori hud, chwedl werin
**faith** n ffydd, cred, coel
**faithful** adj ffyddlon, cywir
**faithfully** adv yn fyddlon, yn
gywir. yours f. yr eiddoch yn
gywir
**fake** n ffug ♦ vb ffugio
**falcon** n hebog, curyll
**fall** vi cwympo, syrthio ♦ n cwymp.
f. out cweryla. f. through methu
**fallacy** n cyfeiliornad, gwall
**fallow** n braenar ♦ vt braenaru
**false** adj gau, ffug, ffals,
twyllodrus. f. teeth dannedd
gosod/dodi
**falter** vb petruso, methu, pallu
**fame** n enwogrwydd, clod, bri
**familiar** adj cynefin, cyfarwydd
**familiarity** n cynefindra
**family** n teulu, tylwyth
**famine** n newyn
**famish** vb newynu, llwgu
**famous** adj enwog
**fan** n gwyntyll; ffan ♦ vt
gwyntyllio, chwythu
**fanatic** n penboethyn, ffanatig
**fanaticism** n penboethni,
ffanatigiaeth
**fanciful** adj ffansïol
**fancy** n dychymyg, ffansi, serch ♦
vt dychmygu, ffansïo, serchu. f.
dress gwisg ffansi
**fang** n ysgithr, dant, pig, blaen
**fantastic** adj ffantastig, rhyfeddol
**fantasy** n ffantasi
**far** adj pell(ennig) ♦ adv ymhell. as
f. as hyd at
**farce** n ffars
**fare** n cost, pris; ymborth ♦ vi bod,

dod ymlaen byw
**farewell** *excl* yn iach, ffarwel ♦ *n*
ffarwel. **to bid f.** canu'n iach
**farm** *n* fferm ♦ *vt* amaethu,
ffarmio
**farmer** *n* ffarmwr, ffermwr,
amaethwr. **Young Farmers' Club**
Clwb y Ffermwyr Ifainc
**farmhouse** *n* ffermdy
**farming** *n* ffermio. **intensive f.**
ffermio dwys
**farmyard** *n* buarth, clos
**fascinate** *vt* hudo, swyno
**fascinating** *adj* hudol, swynol
**fascism** *n* ffasgaeth
**fashion** *n* ffasiwn, arfer, dull ♦ *vt*
llunio, gwneud
**fashionable** *adj* ffasiynol
**fast** *vi* ymprydio ♦ *n* ympryd
**fast** *adj* tyn, sownd; buan, cyflym,
clau
**fasten** *vb* sicrhau, cau, clymu,
ffasno
**fastener** *n* ffasnydd
**fastening** *n* ffasnin
**fastidious** *adj* cysetlyd
**fat** *adj* tew, bras ♦ *n* braster,
bloneg, saim
**fatal** *adj* angheuol, marwol;
andwyol
**fatality** *n* trychineb, marwolaeth
**fate** *n* tynged, ffawd ♦ *vt* tynghedu
**fateful** *adj* tyngedfennol
**father** *n* tad ♦ *vt* tadogi
**father-in-law** *n* tad-yng-nghyfraith
**fatherly** *adj* tadol
**fathom** *n* gwryd ♦ *vt* plymio
**fatigue** *n* lludded, blinder ♦ *vt*
lluddedu, blino
**fatten** *vb* tewhau, pesgi
**fatty** *adj* seimlyd, brasterog
**fatuous** *adj* ynfyd, ffôl
**fault** *n* bai, diffyg, nam, anaf. **at f.**
ar fai
**faultless** *adj* di-fai, perffaith
**faulty** *adj* gwallus, diffygiol
**favour** *n* ffafr, cymwynas ♦ *vt*

ffafrio. **in f. of** o blaid
**favourable** *adj* ffafriol
**favourite** *adj*, *n* ffefryn ♦ *adj* hoff
**fawn** *n* elain ♦ *adj* llwyd
**fawn** *vi* cynffonna, gwenieithio
**fear** *n* ofn, braw, arswyd ♦ *vb* ofni,
arswydo
**fearful** *adj* ofnus, brawychus,
arswydus
**feasible** *adj* dichonadwy
**feast** *n* gwledd, gŵyl ♦ *vb* gwledda
**feat** *n* camp, gorchest
**feather** *n* pluen, plufyn ♦ *vt* pluo,
plufio
**feature** *n* arwedd, nodwedd
**February** *n* Chwefror, Mis Bach
**federal** *adj* cynghreiriol, ffederal
**fee** *n* ffi, tâl, cyflog
**feeble** *adj* gwan, eiddil
**feed** *vb* porthi, ymborthi, bwydo ♦
*n* porthiant, ffid, ymborth, gwledd
**feedback** *n* adborth, ymateb ♦ *vb*
adborthi
**feel** *vb* teimlo, clywed, profi
**feeler** *n* teimlydd; ymchwiliad
**feeling** *n* teimlad, synhwyriad
**feign** *vb* cymryd arno, ffugio
**fell** *vb* cwympo, cymynu ♦ *n* croen;
ffridd, rhos
**fellow** *n* cymar; cymrawd ♦ *prefix*
cyd-
**fellowship** *n* cymdeithas,
cyfeillach; cymrodoriaeth
**felt** *n* ffelt ♦ *vb* ffeltio
**female** *adj*, *n* benyw
**feminine** *adj* benywaidd, benywol
**feminist** *n* ffeminist
**femur** *n* ffemwr
**fence** *n* clawdd, ffens ♦ *vb* cau,
amgáu
**fencing** *n* ffensio, cleddyfaeth
**fend** *vb* cadw draw; ymdaro,
ymdopi
**ferment** *n* eples, cynnwrf ♦ *vb*
eplesu, cynhyrfu
**fermentation** *n* eplesiad
**fern** *n* rhedynen, rhedyn

**ferocious** *adj* ffyrnig, gwyllt, milain
**ferret** *n* ffured ♦ *vt* ffuredu, chwilota
**ferry** *n* porth, fferi ♦ *vb* cludo dros
**ferry-boat** *n* ysgraff
**fertile** *adj* ffrwythlon, toreithiog
**fertilisation** *n* ffrwythloniad
**fertility** *n* ffrwythlonder
**fertilize** *vb* ffrwythloni; gwrteithio
**fertilizer** *n* gwrtaith
**fervent** *adj* brwd, gwresog, tanbaid, taer
**fester** *vi* crawni, gori, crynhoi
**festival** *n* gŵyl, dydd gŵyl. **singing f.** cymanfa ganu
**festive** *adj* llawen, llon
**festivity** *n* rhialtwch, miri, ysbleddach
**fetch** *vt* cyrchu, hôl, ymofyn, nôl
**fête** *n* gŵyl, miri ♦ *vi* gwledda
**feud** *n* cynnen, ffiwd
**feudal** *adj* ffiwdal
**feudalism** *n* ffiwdaliaeth
**fever** *n* twymyn, clefyd, gwres
**feverish** *adj* â thwymyn
**few** *adj* ychydig, prin, anaml
**fiancé(e)** *n* darpar-ŵr/wraig
**fib** *n* anwiredd, celwydd
**fibre** *n* edefyn, ffibr
**fibreglass** *n* ffibr gwydrog
**fickle** *adj* anwadal, oriog, gwamal
**fiction** *n* ffuglen
**fictitious** *adj* ffug, ffugiol
**fiddle** *n* ffidil, crwth ♦ *vi* canu'r ffidl; ffidlan
**fidelity** *n* ffyddlondeb, cywirdeb
**fidget** *vt* ffwdanu, aflonyddu ♦ *n* un ffwdanus, un aflonydd
**field** *n* cae, maes ♦ *vb* maesu
**field marshal** *n* maeslywydd
**field work** *n* gwaith maes
**fiend** *n* cythraul, ellyll, ysbryd drwg
**fierce** *adj* ffyrnig, milain; tanbaid
**fiery** *adj* tanllyd, tanbaid
**fifteen** *adj*, *n* pymtheg

**fifth** *adj*, *n* pumed
**fifty** *adj*, *n* hanner cant, deg a deugain
**fig** *n* ffigysen
**fight** *vb* ymladd, cwffio, brwydro, rhyfela ♦ *n* ymladdfa, brwydr
**fighter** *n* ymladdwr, brwydrwr
**fighting** *n* ymladd
**figment** *n* creadigaeth (y dychymyg)
**figurative** *adj* ffigurol, cyffelybiaethol
**figure** *n* ffigur; llun, ffurf ♦ *vb* cyfrif; llunio; ymddangos. **f. of speech** troad ymadrodd
**figurehead** *n* arweinydd (mewn enw)
**file** *n* ffeil, rhathell; rhes ♦ *vb* ffeilio, rhathu
**fill** *vb* llenwi ♦ *n* llenwad, llonaid, gwala
**fillet** *n* llain, ffiled. **f. steak** *n* stêc ffiled
**filling** *n* llenwad, mewnyn
**filly** *n* eboles
**film** *n* pilen, caenen; ffilm ♦ *vb* ffilmio, gwneud ffilm. **f. strip** stribed ffilm
**filter** *n* hidl, hidlydd ♦ *vb* hidlo, ffiltro. **f. tip** *n* hidl difaco
**filth** *n* brynti, budreddi, baw
**filthy** *adj* brwnt, budr, aflan
**filtrate** *n* hidlif ♦ *vb* hidlo
**fin** *n* adain, asgell, ffin
**final** *adj* terfynol, olaf. **semi-f.** cynderfynol
**finale** *n* ffinale, diweddglo
**finally** *adv* o'r diwedd, yn olaf
**finance** *n* cyllid ♦ *vb* cyllido, codi arian
**financial** *adj* cyllidol, ariannol
**find** *vt* darganfod ♦ *n* darganfyddiad
**finding** *n* darganfyddiad, dedfryd
**fine** *adj* main; mân; gwych; braf
**fine** *n* dirwy ♦ *vt* dirwyo
**finery** *n* gwychder

**finger** n bys ♦ vt bysio, bodio. **little
f.** bys bach. **third f.** bys y fodrwy.
**middle f.** y bys canol
**fingerprint** n bysbrint, ôl bys
**finicky** adj cysetlyd, gorfanwl
**finish** vb diweddu, gorffen,
cwblhau ♦ n diwedd; gorffeniad
**finished** adj gorffenedig
**finite** adj meidrol
**Finland** n y Ffindir
**fir** n ffynidwydden
**fire** n tân ♦ vb tanio, ennyn. **wild f.**
tân gwyllt. **f. precautions**
rhagodion tân
**firearm** n arf-tân
**firebrigade** n brigâd dân
**fire engine** n peiriant tân
**fire escape** n grisiau tân
**fire-extinguisher** n diffoddydd tân
**fireguard** n sgrin dân
**fireman** n taniwr, diffoddwr tân
**fireplace** n lle tân
**fireside** n aelwyd
**firewood** n coed tân, cynnud
**fireworks** npl tân gwyllt
**firm** n cwmni, ffyrm ♦ adj cadarn,
diysgog
**firmly** adv yn gadarn, yn ddiysgog
**first** adj cyntaf, blaenaf, prif ♦ adv
yn gyntaf. **f. aid** n cymorth
cyntaf. **f. class** adj dosbarth
cyntaf. **f. floor** n llawr cyntaf. **f.-
hand** adj o lygad y ffynnon. **f.-rate**
adj campus, ardderchog, rhagorol
**fish** n pysgodyn, pysgod ♦ vb
pysgota. **f. and chips** pysgodyn a
sglodion
**fisherman** n pysgotwr
**fishing** n pysgota
**fishing rod** n genwair, gwialen
bysgota
**fishmonger** n gwerthwr pysgod
**fishy** adj amheus; pysgodol
**fist** n dwrn
**fit** n llewyg, ffit, mesur
**fit** adj ffit, addas, cymwys,
gweddus; abl, iach ♦ vb ffitio,

gweddu, taro
**fitful** adj anwadal, gwamal
**fitment** n cynhalydd
**fitness** n ffitrwydd, addasrwydd
**fitter** n ffitiwr
**fitting** n ffitiad ♦ vb ffitio ♦ adj
priodol, gweddus, addas. **fittings**
mân daclau, ffitiadau
**five** adj pum ♦ n pump
**fix** vb sicrhau, sefydlu, gosod ♦ n
cyfyngder, cyfyng-gyngor
**fixation** n sefydlogiad, sefydledd
**fixed** n sefydlog
**fixture** n gosodyn, peniant (byd
chwarae)
**fizz** vi sïo
**fizzle** vb hisian, sïo
**fizzy** adj byrlymog
**flabbergast** vt synnu, syfrdanu
**flabby** adj llipa, llac, llaes
**flag** n baner, lluman; fflagen ♦ vb
llumanu; llaesu
**flake** n fflaw, caenen; pluen (eira)
**flamboyant** adj coegwych
**flame** n fflam ♦ vi fflamio, ffaglu
**flame-resistant** adj gwrthfflam
**flan** n fflan
**flank** n ystlys, ochr ♦ vb ymylu,
ystlysu
**flannel** n gwlanen
**flap** n llabed, fflap ♦ vb fflapio
**flare** vb fflêr, fflach; fflerio, fflachio
**flash** vb fflachio ♦ n fflach
**flashback** n ôl-fflach
**flashlight** n fflachlamp
**flashy** adj gorwych
**flask** n costrel, fflasg
**flat** n fflat, gwastad; meddalnod ♦
adj fflat, gwastad, lleddf ♦ vb
fflattio
**flatten** vb gwastatáu
**flatter** vt gwenieithio
**flattery** n gweniaith
**flatulence** n gwynt (yn y cylla)
**flaunt** vb fflawntio, rhodresa
**flavour** n blas, cyflas ♦ vt blasu,
cyflasu

**flavouring** n cyflasyn

**flaw** n bai, diffyg, nam

**flax** n llin

**flaxen** adj golau, o lin

**flay** vt blingo

**flea** n chwannen

**flee** vb ffoi, cilio, dianc, diflannu

**fleece** n cnu ♦ vt cneifio; ysbeilio

**fleet** n llynges, fflyd ♦ adj cyflym, buan

**fleeting** adj diflanedig

**flesh** n cig, cnawd. **f. and blood** cig a gwaed. **f. and bones** cnawd ac esgyrn

**flex** n fflecs

**flexible** adj hyblyg, ystwyth

**flick** vt cyffwrdd â blaen chwip, cnithio

**flier** n ehedwr

**flight** n hediad, ffo, rhes

**flighty** adj gwamal, penchwiban

**flimsy** adj tenau, simsan, bregus

**flinch** vi cilio yn ôl, gwingo, llwfrhau

**fling** vt taflu, bwrw, lluchio ♦ n rhwysg, tafliad

**flint** n callestr, carreg dân, fflint

**flip** vb cnithio ♦ n cnith

**flippant** adj tafodrydd, gwamal

**flipper** n asgell

**flirt** vb cellwair caru, fflyrtan ♦ n fflyrten, fflyrtyn

**flit** vi gwibio

**float** n arnofyn, fflôt, trol ♦ vb arnofio

**flock** n diadell, praidd ♦ vi heidio

**flog** vt fflangellu, chwipio

**flood** n llif, dilyw, cenllif ♦ vt llifo, gorlifo

**floodlight** n llifolau ♦ vb llifoleuo

**floor** n llawr ♦ vt llorio; methu. **ground f.** daearlawr. **first f.** llawr cyntaf

**flop** n methiant, ymollwng

**flora** n fflora, planhigion

**floral** adj fflurol

**florid** adj blodeuog

**florist** n tyfwr neu werthwr blodau

**flounce** vi swalpio, ysboncio ♦ n llam, ysbonc

**flounder** n lleden fach ♦ vb ymdrybaeddu, ffwndro

**flour** n blawd, can

**flourish** vb blodeuo; ffynnu; ysgwyd ♦ n rhwysg; cân cyrn

**flout** vb gwawdio, wfftio, diystyru

**flow** vi llifo, llifeirio ♦ n llif, llanw

**flow chart** n siart rhediad

**flower** n blodeuyn, blodyn ♦ vi blodeuo. **flowerpot** pot blodau

**flowery** adj blodeuog

**flu** n ffliw, anwydwst

**fluctuate** vi codi a gostwng, amrywio, anwadalu

**flue** n pibell simnai, ffliw

**fluency** n huodledd, llithrigrwydd

**fluent** adj llithrig, rhugl

**fluff** n fflwcs, fflwff ♦ vb bwnglera, methu

**fluid** adj hylif, llifol ♦ n hylif, llifydd

**fluke** n pry'r afu; ffliwc, lwc

**fluoride** n ffliworid

**flurry** n cyffro, ffwdan

**flush** n gwrid; rhuthr dŵr ♦ adj cyfwyneb, gorlawn ♦ vb gwrido, cochi; gorlifo

**fluster** vb ffwdanu, cyffroi ♦ n ffwdan, cyffro

**flute** n ffliwt

**flutter** vb dychlamu, siffrwd ♦ n dychlamiad, siffrwd

**fly** n gwybedyn, cleren, pryf

**fly** vb ehedeg, ehedfan; ffoi ♦ n pryf, cleren, copis. **f. into a passion** ymwylltio, gwylltu

**flying** adj hedegog, cyflym

**flyover** n pontffordd, trosffordd

**foal** n ebol, eboles ♦ vb bwrw ebol. **in f.** cyfebol

**foam** n ewyn ♦ vi ewynnu, glafoerio

**focus** n canolbwynt, ffocws ♦ vb canolbwyntio

**fodder** n porthiant, ebran
**foe** n gelyn
**fog** n niwl
**foggy** adj niwlog
**foil** vt rhwystro, trechu ♦ n ffoil, ffwyl, dalen
**fold** n plyg; corlan ♦ vb plygu, corlannu
**folder** n plygell
**folding** n plygiant
**foliage** n dail, deiliant
**folio** n ffolio
**folk** npl pobl, gwerin
**folklore** n llên gwerin
**folk song** n cân werin
**follow** vb canlyn, dilyn
**follower** n dilynwr, canlynwr
**following** adj dilynol, canlynol ♦ n dilyniad, canlynwyr
**folly** n ffolineb, ynfydrwydd
**fond** adj hoff, annwyl
**fondle** vt anwylo, anwesu
**font** n bedyddfaen
**food** n bwyd, ymborth, lluniaeth.
tinned f. bwyd tun. f. **poisoning** n gwenwyn bwyd
**fool** n ffŵl, ynfytyn ♦ vb ynfydu, twyllo
**foolhardy** adj rhyfygus
**foolish** adj ffôl, ynfyd, annoeth
**foot** (feet) n troed; troedfedd ♦ vb troedio. f. **and mouth disease** n clwyf y traed a'r genau. f. **rot** clwy'r traed
**football** n pêl droed
**footballer** n peldroediwr
**footbrake** n brêc troed
**footbridge** n pont gerdded, pompren
**foothold** n gafael troed, troedle
**footing** n sylfaen, safle
**footlights** npl golau'r godre
**footman** n gwas (â lifrai)
**footmark** n ôl troed
**footnote** n troednodiad
**footpath** n llwybr troed
**footprint** n ôl troed

**footstep** n cam, ôl troed
**footway** n troedffordd
**footwear** n troedwisg
**for** prep i, at, am, dros, er ♦ conj canys, oblegid, oherwydd, gan, achos
**forage** n bwyd (anifail), porthiant ♦ vb chwilio am fwyd
**forasmuch** conj yn gymaint ag, am, gan, oherwydd
**foray** n cyrch, rhuthr ♦ vb gwneud cyrch, rhuthro
**forbid** vt gwahardd, gwarafun, gomedd
**forbidden** adj gwaharddedig
**force** n grym; trais ♦ vt gorfodi.
**centrifugal** f. grym allgyrchol.
**centripetal** f. grym mewngyrchol.
**the forces** y lluoedd arfog
**forceful** adj grymus, egnïol
**forceps** n gefel fain
**forcible** adj nerthol, effeithiol
**ford** n rhyd ♦ vt rhydio
**fore** adj blaen, blaenaf ♦ adv ymlaen ♦ prefix cyn-, rhag-, blaen-. **to the** f. amlwg, blaenllaw
**forearm** n elin ♦ vb rhagarfogi
**forebode** vt rhagargoeli, rhagarwyddo, darogan
**foreboding** n rhagargoel
**forecast** n rhagolygon, rhagolwg ♦ vb rhagddweud, darogan
**forefather** n cyndad
**forefinger** n mynegfys
**forefront** n lle blaen ♦ adj blaen
**forego** vb hepgor. **foregone conclusion** penderfyniad ymlaen llaw
**foreground** n blaendir
**forehead** n talcen
**foreign** adj estron, tramor. f. **affairs** materion tramor
**foreigner** n estron, tramorwr
**foreman** n fforman
**foremost** adj blaenaf ♦ adv ym mlaenaf
**forensic** adj fforensig

**forerunner** *n* rhagredegydd
**foresee** *vt* rhagweld, rhagwybod
**foreseeable** *adj* rhagweladwy
**foreshadow** *vb* rhagarwyddo,
rhagargoeli
**foresight** *n* rhagwelediad
**forest** *n* coedwig, fforest ♦ *vt*
coedwigo, fforestu
**forestall** *vt* achub y blaen
**forestry** *n* coedwigaeth. **f.**
**commission** Comiswn Coedwigo
**foretaste** *n* rhagflas ♦ *vb* rhagbrofi
**foretell** *vt* rhagfynegi, darogan
**forever** *adv* am byth
**foreword** *n* rhagair,
rhagymadrodd
**forfeit** *n* fforffed ♦ *vt* fforffedu,
colli
**forge** *n* gefail, ffwrn ♦ *vb* gofannu;
ffugio
**forget** *vt* anghofio
**forgetful** *adj* anghofus
**forgive** *vt* maddau
**forgiveness** *n* maddeuant
**forgo** *vt* gadael, hepgor, mynd heb
**fork** *n* fforch, fforc ♦ *vb* fforchio
**forlorn** *adj* amddifad, truan,
anobeithiol
**form** *n* ffurf; mainc; ffurflen ♦ *vb*
ffurfio. **application f.** ffurflen gais
**formal** *adj* ffurfiol, defodol
**former** *adj* blaenaf, blaenorol
**formerly** *adv* gynt, yn flaenorol
**formidable** *adj* arswydus,
ofnadwy, grymus
**formula** *n* rheol, fformwla
**forsake** *vt* gadael, ymadael â,
gwrthod, cefnu ar
**fort** *n* caer, castell, amddiffynfa
**forte** *n* cryfder ♦ *adj* uchel, cryf
**forth** *adv* allan, ymlaen. **and so f.**
ac felly yn y blaen
**forthcoming** *adj* ar ddod, gerllaw
**forthright** *adj* union, plaen
**forthwith** *adv* yn ddioed, ar
unwaith
**fortify** *vt* cadarnhau, cryfhau

**fortitude** *n* gwroldeb, dewrder
**fortnight** *n* pythefnos
**fortnightly** *adj, adv* bob pythefnos
**fortress** *n* amddiffynfa, caer,
castell
**fortunate** *adj* ffodus, ffortunus
**fortunately** *adv* yn ffodus, yn
lwcus
**fortune** *n* ffawd; ffortun
**fortune teller** *n* un sy'n dweud
ffortun
**forty** *adj, n* deugain
**forum** *n* fforwm
**forward** *n* blaenwr ♦ *adj* eofn, hy;
blaen ♦ *adv* ymlaen ♦ *vb* anfon
ymlaen; hwyluso, hyrwyddo.
**inside f.** mewnwr. **wing f.**
blaenasgellwr
**fossil** *n* ffosil ♦ *adj* ffosilaidd
**fossilise** *vb* ffosileiddio
**foster** *vt* magu, meithrin, coleddu
**foster-child** *n* plentyn maeth
**foster-mother** *n* mamfaeth
**foul** *adj* aflan; annheg; afiach ♦ *n*
ffowl(en) ♦ *vb* ffowlio, llychwino.
**f. play** anfadwaith. **f. throw**
camdaflu
**found** *vt* dechrau, sylfaenu,
sefydlu
**foundation** *n* sail, sylfaen
**founder** *vb* ymddryllio, suddo ♦ *n*
sylfaenydd
**foundry** *n* ffowndri, efail
**fountain** *n* ffynnon, ffynhonnell
**four** *adj, n* pedwar (*f* pedair)
**foursome** *n* pedwarawd
**fourteen** *adj, n* pedwar (pedair) ar
ddeg
**fourth** *adj* pedwerydd (*f*
pedwaredd)
**fowl** *n* dofedn, ffowlyn, ffowl
**fox** *n* cadno, llwynog
**foyer** *n* cyntedd
**fraction** *n* ffracsiwn. **improper f.**
ffracsiwn pendrwm. **vulgar f.**
ffracsiwn cyffredin. **proper f.**
ffracsiwn bondrwm

**fracture** n toriad, drylliad ♦ vt torri, dryllio

**fragile** adj brau, bregus

**fragment** n dryll, darn, briwsionyn

**fragrance** n perarogl, persawr

**frail** adj brau, bregus, gwan, eiddil

**frame** n ffrâm; agwedd ♦ vt fframio, llunio. **f. of mind** agwedd meddwl

**framework** n fframwaith

**franchise** n etholfraint ♦ vb etholfreinio

**frank** adj didwyll, agored

**frankincense** n thus

**frantic** adj cyffrous, gwallgof

**fraternal** adj brawdol

**fraternity** n brawdoliaeth

**fraud** n twyll, hoced

**fraudulent** adj twyllodrus

**fraught** adj llwythog, llawn

**fray** n ymryson, ymgiprys, ffrae, rhaflad ♦ vb treulio, rhaflo

**freak** n mympwy, peth od

**freckle** n brych, brychni

**free** adj rhydd; hael; di-dâl, rhad ♦ vb rhyddhau

**freedom** n rhyddid, rhyddfraint

**free expression** n rhyddfynegiant

**freehold** adj rhydd-ddaliadol

**free kick** n cic rydd

**freely** adv yn rhydd, yn hael

**freemason** n saer rhydd

**free trade** n masnach rydd

**free verse** n mesur rhydd y wers rydd

**free will** n ewyllys rydd, o'i fodd

**freeze** vb rhewi, fferru

**freeze-dry** vb sychrewi

**freezer** n rhewgist, rhewgell

**freezing point** n rhewbwynt

**freight** n llwyth llong ♦ vt llwytho llong

**French** adj Ffrengig ♦ n Ffrangeg. F. **beans** npl ffa Ffrengig

**Frenchman** n Ffrancwr

**Frenchwoman** n Ffrances

**frenzy** n gorffwylltra, cynddaredd

**frequency** n amlder, mynychder

**frequent** adj mynych, aml ♦ vt mynychu

**frequently** adv yn fynych, yn aml

**fresh** adj ffres, crai, cri, croyw, newydd

**freshen** vb ffresáu, ireiddio

**freshness** n ffresni, creider, irder

**fret** vb sorri, poeni ♦ n soriant, tralod, ffret

**friar** n brawd, mynach

**friction** n ffrithiant, ymrafael

**Friday** n dydd Gwener

**fridge** n oergell, rhewadur

**friend** n cyfaill, ffrind

**friendly** adj cyfeillgar

**friendship** n cyfeillgarwch

**frieze** n ffris

**fright** n dychryn, ofn, braw

**frighten** vb dychrynu, brawychu, codi ofn ar

**frightful** adj dychrynllyd, brawychus

**frigid** adj oer, rhewllyd; oeraidd, oerllyd. **f. zone** n cylchfa rew

**frill** n ffril

**fringe** n ymyl, ymylwe, rhidens ♦ vb ymylu, rhidennu. **f. benefits** cilfanteision

**frisk** vt prancio

**fritter** vt afradu, ofera, gwastraffu

**frivolous** adj gwamal; diystyr, disylwedd

**frizzy** adj crychlyd

**fro** adv: **to and f.** yn ôl ac ymlaen

**frock** n ffrog

**frog** n llyffant (melyn), broga; bywyn, ffroga

**frolic** vi prancio, campio ♦ n pranc

**from** prep o, oddi, oddi wrth, gan

**front** n wyneb, blaen, ffrynt, talcen ♦ vb wynebu ♦ adj blaen. **f. door** drws ffrynt. **f. page** tudalen flaen. **f. room** ystafell (ffrynt)

**frontier** n ffin, terfyn, goror

**frost** n rhew

**frostbite** n ewinrhew

**frosty** adj rhewllyd
**froth** n ewyn ♦ vi ewynnu
**frown** vi cuchio, gwgu ♦ n cuwch, gwg
**frozen** adj wedi rhewi
**frugal** adj cynnil, darbodus
**fruit** n ffrwyth, ffrwythau. **f. juice** sudd ffrwyth. **f. salad** salad ffrwythau
**fruiterer** n gwerthwr ffrwythau
**fruitful** adj ffrwythlon, toreithiog
**fruition** n ffrwythloniad
**frustrate** vt rhwystro, llesteirio
**frustration** n llesteiriant
**fry** vb ffrio ♦ n afu, sil, silod. **small f.** n pobl ddibwys
**frying-pan** n ffrimpan, padell ffrio
**fudge** n cyffug
**fuel** n tanwydd; cynnud. **f. cell** cynudydd
**fugitive** adj ar ffo, diflanedig ♦ n ffoadur
**fulfil** vt cyflawni
**fulfilment** n cyflawniad
**full** adj llawn, cyflawn ♦ n llonaid
**full-back** n cefnwr
**fuller** n pannwr
**full stop** n atalnod
**fulltime** adj llawn amser
**fully** adv yn gyfan gwbl, yn gyflawn, yn hollol
**fulsome** adj ffiaidd, diflas (am weniaith, etc)
**fumble** vb palfalu, bwnglera
**fume** n tarth, mwg; llid ♦ vb mygu; llidio, sorri
**fun** n difyrrwch, digrifwch, hwyl
**function** n swydd, swyddogaeth; ffwythiant (mathemateg)
**functional** adj swyddogaethol, ffwythiannol, defnyddiol
**fund** n cronfa, trysorfa
**fundamental** adj sylfaenol
**funeral** n angladd, cynhebrwng, claddedigaeth
**fungus** n ffwng
**funnel** n twmffat, twndis, corn

**funny** adj digrif, ysmala; rhyfedd, hynod
**fur** n blew, ffwr; cen. **f. coat** n cot ffwr
**furious** adj cynddeiriog, ffyrnig, gwyllt
**furlong** n ystad, wythfed ran milltir
**furnace** n ffwrn, ffwrnais
**furnish** vt dodrefnu, rhoddi
**furnishings** npl dodrefn
**furniture** n dodrefn, celfi
**furrow** n cwys, rhych ♦ vt cwyso, rhychu
**furry** adj blewog
**further** adj pellach ♦ adv ymhellach ♦ vt hyrwyddo. **f. education** addysg bellach
**fury** n cynddaredd, ffyrnigrwydd
**fuse** n ffiws, toddyn, diogelydd ♦ vb ffiwsio
**fuss** n ffwdan, helynt, stŵr ♦ vb ffwdanu
**fussy** adj ffwdanus
**futile** adj ofer, di-les
**future** adj, n dyfodol
**fuzzy** adj blewog, aneglur

# G

**gabble** vb bregliach, clebran ♦ n cleber
**gable** n piniwn, talcen tŷ
**gadget** n dyfais
**Gaelic** n Gaeleg ♦ adj Gaelaidd
**gaff** n bach pysgota
**gag** n smaldod; safnglo ♦ vb smalio; safngloi, cau ceg
**gaiety** n llonder, difyrrwch, miri
**gaily** adv yn llawen
**gain** vb ennill, elwa ♦ n ennill, elw, budd
**gait** n cerddediad, osgo
**gale** n awel, gwynt cryf; tymestl
**gall** n bustl, chwydd ♦ vb dolurio, blino. **g. bladder** n coden y bustl.

g. **stones** cerrig y bustl
**gallant** adj gwrol, dewr ♦ n carwr
**gallery** n oriel, llofft
**galley** n rhwyflong; gali
**gallon** n galwyn
**gallop** n carlam ♦ vb carlamu
**gallows** n crocbren
**galore** n, adv digonedd
**galvanize** vt galfaneiddio, galfanu;
   symbylu
**gamble** vb hapchwarae, gamblo ♦
   n gambl
**game** n chwarae, camp;
   helwriaeth ♦ adj calonnog, dewr,
   glew
**game-keeper** n cipar
**gammon** n palfais (mochyn);
   ffwlbri, lol
**gander** n ceiliagwydd, clacwydd
**gang** n mintai, torf, haid, gang
**gangster** n troseddwr
**gangway** n tramwyfa, eil, ale;
   pont
**gaol** n carchar ♦ vt carcharu
**gap** n bwlch, adwy
**gape** vi rhythu, syllu ♦ n rhythiad
**garage** n modurdy, garej
**garbage** n ysgarthion, ysbwriel,
   sothach
**garble** vt darnio, llurgunio
**garden** n gardd ♦ vi garddio
**gardener** n garddwr
**gardening** n garddwriaeth
**gargle** n golch gwddf ♦ vb golchi
   gwddf
**garish** adj coegwych
**garland** n coronbleth, garlant,
   talaith
**garlic** n garlleg
**garment** n dilledyn, gwisg
**garnish** vt addurno, harddu
**garrison** n gwarchodlu, garsiwn
**garrulous** adj tafodrydd, siaradus
**garter** n gardas, gardys ♦ vb
   gardysu
**gas** n nwy ♦ vb gwenwyno â nwy.
   g. **cooker** ffwrn nwy. g. **fire** tân

nwy. g. **ring** cylch nwy
**gash** n archoll, hollt, hac ♦ vt
   archolli, hacio
**gasket** n gasged
**gas-mask** n mwgwd nwy
**gasometer** n tanc nwy
**gasp** vb ebychu, anadlu'n drwm
**gate** n porth, llidiart, clwyd, gât,
   iet ♦ vb porthio, porthellu
**gate-crasher** n ymyrrwr
**gatehouse** n porthordy
**gateway** n mynedfa
**gather** vb casglu, cynnull, crynhoi,
   hel
**gathering** n casgliad, cynulliad
**gaudy** adj coegwych, gorwych
**gauge** n mesur; lled; meidrydd ♦
   vt mesur, meidryddu
**Gaul** n Gâl
**Gaulish** n Galeg
**gaunt** adj llwm, tenau
**gauntlet** n dyrnfol, maneg ddur. **to
   throw down the g.** herio
**gauze** n rhwyllen, gaws, meinwe
**gay** adj llon, bywiog, ofer, hoyw
**gaze** vi edrych, syllu, tremio ♦ n
   golwg, trem
**gazette** n newyddiadur
   (swyddogol)
**gazetteer** n geiriadur daearyddol
**GCSE** n abbr TGAU = Tystysgrif
   Gyffredin Addysg Uwchradd
**gear** n gêr, offer, taclau ♦ vb
   taclu, harneisio
**gearbox** n gergist, blwch gêr,
   gerbocs
**gelignite** n geligneit
**gem** n glain, gem, tlws
**gender** n cenedl
**genealogy** n achau; achyddiaeth
**general** adj cyffredin, cyffredinol ♦
   n cadfridog. g. **election** n etholiad
   cyffredinol
**generalize** vb cyffredinoli
**generally** adv yn gyffredinol
**generate** vt cenhedlu, cynhyrchu,
   generadu

**generation** n cenhedliad; cenhedlaeth, to
**generator** n cynhyrchydd; generadur
**generosity** n haelioni
**generous** adj hael, haelionus, haelfrydig
**genetic** adj genetig
**genetics** n geneteg
**Geneva** n Genefa
**genial** adj hynaws, rhadlon, tyner, tirion
**genital** adj cenhedol. **genitals** npl organau cenhedlu
**genius** n athrylith
**genteel** adj bonheddig, boneddigaidd
**gentle** adj bonheddig; mwyn, tyner
**gentleman** n gŵr bonheddig
**gently** adv yn dyner, addfwyn; gan bwyll
**gentry** npl bonedd
**gents** npl toiledau dynion
**genuine** adj dilys, diffuant, pur
**geography** n daearyddiaeth
**geology** n daeareg
**geometry** n geometreg
**geriatrics** n geriatreg
**germ** n hedyn, eginyn, germ
**German** adj Almaenaidd ♦ n Almaenwr; Almaeneg. **G. measles** y frech Almeinig
**Germany** n yr Almaen
**germinate** vi egino, atyfu
**germination** n eginiad, atyfiant
**gesture** n ystum, arwydd, mosiwn
**get** vb cael, caffael, ennill. **to g. on with it** bwrw arni, bwrw iddi
**geyser** n geyser
**Ghana** n Ghana
**ghastly** adj erchyll, gwelw
**gherkin** n gercin
**ghost** n ysbryd, drychiolaeth, bwgan
**giant** n cawr ♦ adj cawraidd
**gibberish** n cleber, baldordd
**gibe** vb gwawdio ♦ n gwawd

**giblets** npl giblets, syrth, gwŷdd
**Gibraltar** n Gibralter
**giddiness** n pendro
**giddy** adj penfeddw, penchwiban
**gift** n rhodd, dawn, anrheg, gwobr
**gifted** adj dawnus, talentog
**gigantic** adj cawraidd, dirfawr, anferth
**giggle** vb lledchwerthin, giglan
**gill** n tagell; gil, chwarter peint
**gimmick** n gimig
**gin** n jin; hoenyn
**ginger** n sinsir
**gingerly** adj, adv gochelgar, gwyliadwrus
**gipsy, gy-** n sipsi
**giraffe** n siráff
**girder** n trawst
**girdle** n gwregys, rhwymyn ♦ vt gwregysu
**girl** n merch, geneth, hogen
**girlfriend** n cariadferch, anwylyd
**girth** n cengl; cylchfesur, cwmpas
**gist** n cnewyllyn pwnc, ergyd, sylwedd
**give** vb rhoddi, rhoi. **g. up** rhoi'r gorau i
**glacier** n rhewlif, iäen, glasier
**glad** adj llawen, llon, balch
**gladiator** n cleddyfwr, ymladdwr
**gladly** adv yn llawen, â phleser
**glamorous** adj swynol, cyfareddol, hudol
**glamour** n swyn, cyfaredd, hud
**glance** vb ciledrych, tremio ♦ n cipolwg, trem, cip
**gland** n chwarren, cilchwyrnen, gland
**glare** vb disgleirio; rhythu ♦ n disgleirdeb, tanbeidrwydd
**glass** n gwydr; gwydraid; pl gwydrau, sbectol
**glassy** adj gloyw, pŵl
**glaze** vt gwydro; sgleinio ♦ n sglein, gwydredd
**glazier** n gwydrwr
**gleam** n pelydryn, llewyrch ♦ vi

pelydru, llewyrchu
**glean** *vb* lloffa
**glebe** *n* clastir, tir eglwys
**glee** *n* llonder, hoen; rhangan
**glen** *n* glyn, cwm, dyffryn
**glib** *adj* llyfn, llithrig, rhugl, ffraeth
**glide** *vi* llithro, llifo ♦ *n* llithr, llithrad
**gliding** *n, vb* llithran
**glimmer** *vi* llewyrchu'n wan ♦ *n* llewyrchyn, llygedyn
**glimpse** *n* trem, cipolwg
**glint** *vb* fflachio ♦ *n* fflach, llewyrch
**glisten** *vi* disgleirio
**glitter** *vi* tywynnu, pelydru ♦ *n* pelydriad
**gloat** *vb* llawenhau
**global** *adj* hollfydol, cyffredinol
**globe** *n* pêl, pelen
**gloom** *n* caddug, prudd-der, tywyllwch
**gloomy** *adj* prudd, digalon, tywyll
**glorify** *vt* gogoneddu
**glorious** *adj* gogoneddus
**glory** *n* gogoniant ♦ *vi* ymffrostio, gorfoleddu
**gloss** *n* disgleirdeb arwynebol, sglein; glòs, esboniad
**glossary** *n* geirfa
**glossy** *adj* llathraidd
**glove** *n* maneg
**glow** *vi* twymo, gwrido ♦ *n* gwres, gwrid
**glower** *vi* cuchio, gwgu
**glue** *n* glud ♦ *vt* gludio, asio
**glum** *adj* prudd, digalon, trist
**glut** *vt* gorlenwi, glythu ♦ *n* gormodedd, gorlawnder
**glutton** *n* glwth
**gluttony** *n* glythineb
**gnarled** *adj* cnotiog, ceinciog, garw
**gnat** *n* gwybedyn, cylionen
**gnaw** *vb* cnoi, deintio, cnewian
**gnome** *n* gwireb; ysbryd, coblyn
**go** *vi* mynd, cerdded, rhodio ♦ *n*

tro
**goad** *n* swmbwl ♦ *vt* symbylu
**goal** *n* gôl, nod, bwriad. **g. posts** *npl* pyst gôl. **g. shooter** saethwr
**goalkeeper** *n* golgeidwad, golwr
**goat** *n* gafr
**goblin** *n* ellyll, coblyn, bwgan
**god** *n* duw. **G.** Duw
**godchild** *n* mab bedydd, merch fedydd
**goddess** *n* duwies
**godfather** *n* tad bedydd
**godhead** *n* duwdod
**godly** *adj* duwiol
**godmother** *adj* mam fedydd
**godsend** *n* caffaeliad
**goggles** *npl* gwydrau
**gold** *n* aur ♦ *adj* aur, euraid
**golden** *adj* euraid
**goldfish** *npl* eurbysg, pysgod aur
**goldsmith** *n* gof aur, eurych
**golf** *n* golff. **g. links** maes golff. **g. course** *n* maes golffio
**golfer** *n* golffwr
**gong** *n* gong, cloch fwyd
**good** *adj* da, daionus; cryn ♦ *n* da, daioni, lles. **g. morning** bore da. **g. afternoon** prynhawn da. **g. evening** noswaith dda. **g. night** nos da. **g. enough** digon da. **no g.** dim gwerth, da i ddim. **G. Friday** Dydd Gwener y Groglith. **g. humour** natur dda
**good-bye** *excl, n* da bo chi, yn iach! ffarwel
**good-looking** *adj* golygus
**goodly** *adj* hardd, teg
**good-natured** *adj* hynaws, rhadlon
**goodness** *n* daioni
**goods** *npl* nwyddau, eiddo
**goodwill** *n* ewyllys da; braint (masnachol)
**goose** (**geese**) *n* gŵydd
**gooseberry** *n* eirinen Fair, gwsbersen
**gooseflesh** *n* croen gŵydd
**gore** *n* gwaed, gôr ♦ *vb* cornio

**gorge** n hafn, ceunant ♦ vb safnio, traflyncu

**gorgeous** adj ysblennydd, gwych

**gorilla** n gorila

**gorse** n eithin

**gory** adj gwaedlyd

**gosling** n cyw gŵydd

**gospel** n efengyl

**gossip** n clec, clonc, clebryn, clebran ♦ vb clebran, clecian, hel straeon

**gout** n gowt, cymalwst

**govern** vb llywodraethu, rheoli, llywio

**governess** n athrawes

**government** n llywodraeth

**governor** n llywodraethwr

**gown** n gŵn

**grab** vb crafangu, cipio ♦ n gwanc, crap

**grace** n gras, rhad, graslonrwydd; gosgeiddrwydd ♦ vt harddu, prydferthu, addurno

**graceful** adj graslon, rhadlon; gosgeiddig, lluniaidd

**gracious** adj graslon, grasol, rhadlon, hynaws

**grade** n gradd, safon ♦ vb graddio

**gradient** n graddiant

**gradual** adj graddol

**gradually** adv yn raddol

**graduate** vb graddio, graddoli ♦ n gŵr gradd, graddedig

**graduation** n graddedigaeth, graddnod

**graffiti** n graffiti

**graft** n impyn, hunan-les ♦ vt impio, grafftio

**grain** n grawn, gronyn; mymryn; graen ♦ vb graenu, graenio

**gram** n gram

**grammar** n gramadeg. **g. school** n ysgol ramadeg

**grammatical** adj gramadegol

**granary** n ysgubor

**grand** adj mawreddog, ardderchog, crand; prif, uchel

**grandchild** n ŵyr, wyres. **great g.** n gorwyr(es)

**granddaughter** n wyres

**grandfather** n taid, tad-cu. **great g.** n hen daid, hen-dad-cu

**grandmother** n nain, mam-gu

**grandson** n ŵyr

**granite** n gwenithfaen, ithfaen

**grant** vt rhoddi, caniatáu ♦ n rhodd, grant. **to take for granted** cymryd yn ganiataol

**granulated** adj gronynnog

**granule** n gronynnell

**grapefruit** n grawnffrwyth

**grapes** n grawnwin

**graph** n graff

**graphic** adj graffig; byw

**graphics** npl graffigwaith, graffeg

**grapple** n gafl, gafaelfach ♦ vb gafaelyd, mynd i'r afael â

**grasp** vb gafael; amgyffred ♦ n gafael, amgyffrediad

**grasping** adj trachwantus

**grass** n glaswellt, porfa

**grasshopper** n ceiliog y rhedyn, sioncyn y gwair

**grate** n grat ♦ vb rhygnu, crafellu; merwino

**grateful** adj diolchgar; dymunol

**grater** n grater, crafellydd

**gratify** vt boddio, boddhau

**grating** adj garw, cras ♦ n gratin

**gratitude** n diolchgarwch

**gratuity** n cildwrn, rhodd

**grave** adj difrifol, dwys

**grave** n bedd, beddrod

**gravel** n graean, gro, grafel

**gravestone** n beddfaen, carreg fedd

**graveyard** n mynwent

**gravitate** vi disgyrchu, treiglo

**gravity** n disgyrchiant; pwysigrwydd. **centre of g.** craidd disgyrchiant

**gravy** n grefi, isgell, sew

**graze** vb pori; crafu, rhwbio, ysgythru

**grease** n saim, iraid ♦ vt iro, seimio

**greaseproof** adj gwrthsaim

**greasy** adj seimllyd, ireidlyd

**great** adj mawr. **a g. many** llawer iawn

**greatly** adv yn fawr

**Greece** n Groeg

**greed** n trachwant, gwanc

**greedy** adj barus, trachwantus, gwancus

**Greek** n Groeg; Groegwr ♦ adj Groegaidd

**green** adj gwyrdd, glas, ir ♦ vb glasu

**greenery** n gwyrddlesni

**greengrocer** n gringroser, gwerthwr llysiau

**greenhouse** n tŷ gwydr

**Greenland** n Grønland

**greet** vt annerch, cyfarch

**greeting** n cyfarchiad

**grenade** n grenâd

**grey** adj llwyd, llwydwyn, glas

**greyhound** n milgi

**grid** n grid, alch. **g. reference** cyfeirnod grid

**grief** n gofid, galar, hiraeth

**grievance** n cwyn

**grieve** vb gofidio, galaru, hiraethu

**grievous** adj gofidus, poenus, blin, difrifol

**grill** n gril, gridyll ♦ vb grilio, gridyllu. **mixed g.** gril cymysg

**grille** n gril, dellt

**grim** adj sarrug, milain, difrifol

**grimace** n ystum ♦ vi ystumio

**grimy** adj budr, brwnt, diraen

**grin** vb lledwenu ♦ n gwên

**grind** vb malu (ŷd etc); llifo (arf), llifanu

**grip** vb gafael, gwasgu ♦ n gafael, crap

**grisly** adj erch, erchyll, hyll, milain

**gristle** n madruddyn, gwythi

**grit** n grit, grud, graean; pybyrwch

**groan** vi, n griddfan

**grocer** n groser

**groceries** npl nwyddau

**groin** n cesail morddwyd, gwerddyr

**groom** n priodfab; gwastrawd ♦ vb trwsio

**groove** n rhigol, rhych ♦ vt rhigoli, rhychu

**grope** vi ymbalfalu

**gross** n gros; crynswth ♦ adj bras, aflednais. **g. profit** elw gros

**grotto** n groto

**ground** n llawr, daear, tir; sail; gwaelod ♦ vt daearu, llorio. **g. floor** n daearlawr

**groundless** adj di-sail

**groundwork** n sylfaen, sail

**group** n grŵp twr, bagad ♦ vt grwpio. **discussion g.** cylch trafod

**grouse** n grugiar ♦ vb grwgnach

**grove** n llwyn, celli

**grovel** vi ymgreinio

**grow** vb tyfu, prifio, cynyddu, codi

**grower** n tyfwr

**growing** adj yn tyfu

**growl** vi chwyrnu

**growth** n twf, tyfiant, cynnydd

**grub** n pryf, cynrhonyn; bwyd ♦ vb dadwreiddio

**grubby** adj budr, brwnt

**grudge** vt gwarafun, grwgnach ♦ n dig, cenfigen, cas

**gruesome** adj erchyll, hyll, ffiaidd

**gruff** adj sarrug, garw, swta

**grumble** vi grwgnach, tuchan

**grumpy** adj sarrug, diserch

**grunt** vi rhochian ♦ n rhoch

**guarantee** n gwarant, ernes ♦ vt gwarantu, mechnïo

**guard** n gard, gwarchodydd; sgrin ♦ vb gwarchod

**guarded** adj gwyliadurus, gofalus

**guardian** n gwarcheidwad

**guerilla** n herfilwr

**guess** vb dyfalu, dyfeisio ♦ n

amcan
**guesswork** n dyfaliad
**guest** n gwestai, gŵr/gwraig
(g)wadd
**guffaw** n crechwen ♦ vb
crechwenu
**guidance** n cyfarwyddyd
**guide** n arweinydd ♦ vt arwain,
cyfarwyddo
**guide book** n teithlyfr
**guide-dog** n arweingi
**guide-lines** npl canllawiau
**guild** n cymdeithas, corfforaeth,
urdd
**guile** n twyll, dichell, ystryw
**guillotine** n gilotîn
**guilt** n euogrwydd, bai
**guilty** adj euog
**guinea pig** n mochyn cwta
**guise** n dull, modd, rhith, diwyg
**guitar** n gitâr
**gulf** n gwlff, geneufor; gagendor
**gull** n gwylan; gwirionyn ♦ vt
twyllo
**gullet** n corn gwddf, sefnig
**gullible** adj hygoelus
**gully** n rhigol, ffos
**gulp** vt llawcian, traflyncu ♦ n
llawc, traflwnc
**gum** n gwm, glud ♦ vt gymio,
gludio
**gumboots** npl esgidiau rwber
**gums** npl cig y dannedd,
gorcharfanau, crib y dannedd,
gorfant
**gun** n gwn, dryll
**gunner** n gynnwr
**gunpowder** n powdr gwn
**gunshot** n ergyd gwn
**gunsmith** n gof gynnau (bach)
**gurgle** vi byrlymu
**gush** vb ffrydio, llifeirio ♦ n ffrwd,
hyrddwynt
**gust** n chwythwm
**gusto** n awch, blas, sêl
**gut** n perfeddyn, coluddyn ♦ vt
diberfeddu; difrodi, ysbeilio

**gutter** n ffos, cwter, cafn
**guttural** adj gyddfol
**guzzle** vb llawcio, traflyncu
**gym** n campfa
**gymnasium** n gymnasiwm,
campfa
**gymnast** n mabolgampwr
**gynaecologist** n gynaecolegydd
**gynaecology** n gynaecoleg
**gypsy** n sipsi
**gyrate** vi troi, chwyrlïo

# H

**ha** excl ha!
**haberdashery** n dilladach, siop
ddillad
**habit** n arferiad; anian; gwisg ♦ vt
gwisgo, dilladu
**habitable** adj cyfannedd,
cyfanheddol
**habitat** n cartref, cynefin
**habitation** n trigfa, preswylfa
**habitual** adj arferol, cyson
**habituate** vt arfer, cynefino
**hack** vb hacio, torri ♦ n hac
**hack** n hurfarch; cystog, slâf
**hackneyed** adj ystrydebol,
cyffredin
**hades** n annwfn
**haddock** n corbenfras, hadog
**haemorrhage** n gwaedlif
**haemorrhoids** npl clwyf y
marchogion
**haft** n carn
**hag** n gwrach, gwiddon
**haggard** adj gwyllt, curiedig
**haggle** vi bargeinio'n daer
**hail** n cenllysg, cesair ♦ vb bwrw
cesair
**hail** excl henffych well ♦ vb
cyfarch, galw
**hair** n gwallt, blew, rhawn. **hair's
breadth** trwch y blewyn. **h.
splitting** hollti blew
**hairbrush** n brws gwallt

**haircut** n triniaeth gwallt, toriad, crop

**hairdresser** n triniwr gwallt

**hair dryer** n sychwr gwallt

**hair spray** n chwistrelliad gwallt; chwistrellydd gwallt

**hairy** adj blewog

**hake** n cegddu

**hale** adj iach, cryf, hoenus

**half** (halves) n hanner

**half-back** n hanerwr

**half-breed** adj cymysgryw

**half-dead** adj lledfyw

**half-hearted** adj diawydd, llugoer

**halfpenny** n dimai

**halibut** n halibwt

**hall** n llys, neuadd, plas; cyntedd

**hallmark** n dilysnod

**hallo** excl helô

**hallow** vt cysegru, sancteiddio

**Halloween** n nos Galangaeaf

**hallucination** n geuddrych, rhithweledid

**halo** n corongylch, gogoniant, halo, lleugylch

**halt** vb sefyll ♦ n safiad; gorsaf, arosfa

**halter** n cebystr, tennyn

**halve** vt haneru

**ham** n morddwyd, ham

**hames** npl mynci

**hamlet** n pentref

**hammer** n morthwyl, mwrthwl, gordd ♦ vb morthwylio

**hammock** n hamog, gwely crog

**hamper** vt rhwystro, llesteirio

**hamstring** n llinyn y gar

**hand** n llaw; (of clock) bys ♦ vt estyn, trosglwyddo. **hand-off** n hwp llaw. **in-hand** adj ar waith. **to be on h.** bod with law

**handbag** n bag llaw

**handbook** n llawlyfr

**handbrake** n brec llaw

**handcuff** n gefyn llaw

**handful** n dyrnaid, llond llaw

**handicap** n rhwystr, llestair, anfantais; blaen. **handicapped children** plant dan anfantais

**handicraft** n crefft

**handiwork** n gwaithllaw

**handkerchief** n cadach poced, hances, macyn, neisied

**handle** n carn, coes, troed, dolen, clust, dwrn ♦ vt trin, trafod. **to fly off the h.** colli tymer

**handlebars** npl cyrn

**handmade** adj wedi ei wneud â llaw

**handmaid, -en** n llawforwyn

**handrail** n canllaw

**handsome** adj golygus, hardd, prydferth; hael

**handwriting** n llawysgrifen

**handy** adj hylaw, deheuig, cyfleus

**hang** vb crogi, hongian, dibynnu

**hangar** n awyrendy

**hang-gliding** vb barcuta

**hangover** n blinder ddoe, pen mawr

**hank** n cengl

**hanker** vi blysio, crefu, dyheu, hiraethu

**hanky-panky** n twyll, dichell ♦ adj twyllodrus, dichellgar

**hap** n hap, damwain

**haphazard** adj, adv damweiniol, ar siawns

**happen** vi digwydd

**happily** adv yn hapus

**happiness** n dedwyddwch, hapusrwydd

**happy** adj dedwydd, hapus

**happy-go-lucky** adj didaro, di-hid

**harangue** n araith, arawd ♦ vb areithio

**harass** vt poeni, blino, gofidio

**harassment** n poen, blinder

**harbour** n porthladd, harbwr ♦ vb llochesu

**hard** adj caled, anodd. **h. of hearing** trwm ei glyw. **to be h.** done by cael cam. **h. headed** hirben

**hardboard** n caledfwrdd

**harden** vb caledu
**hardener** n caledwr
**hardness** n caledwch
**hardship** n caledi
**hard shoulder** n llain galed
**hard-up** adj prin o arian
**hardware** n nwyddau metel
**hardwood** n pren caled
**hardy** adj caled, cryf, gwydn; hy, eofn
**hare** n ysgyfarnog, ceinach
**harebrained** adj byrbwyll, gwyllt
**harelip** n bylchfin, gwefus fylchog
**hark** excl gwrando! clyw! **h. back** dychwelyd
**harlot** n putain
**harm** n niwed, drwg, cam ♦ vt niweidio, drygu
**harmful** adj niweidiol
**harmless** adj diniwed, diddrwg
**harmonious** adj cytûn
**harmonise** vb cytgordio, cytuno
**harmony** n harmoni, cynghanedd
**harness** n harnais, gêr ♦ vt harneisio
**harp** n telyn ♦ vi canu'r delyn
**harpoon** n tryfer ♦ vt tryferu
**harrow** n og ♦ vt llyfnu; rhwygo, dryllio
**harrowing** adj dychrynllyd, ofnadwy, deifiol
**harry** vt difrodi, blino
**harsh** adj garw, gerwin, aflafar
**harshness** n craster, gerwindeb
**hart** n hydd
**harvest** n cynhaeaf ♦ vt cynaeafu
**harvester** n cynaeafwr. **combine h.** n combein
**hash** n briwgig; cymysgfa, cybolfa
**hasp** n hesben
**haste** n brys, hast ♦ vi brysio, prysuro
**hasten** vb brysio, prysuro, hastu
**hastily** adv yn frysiog
**hasty** adj brysiog, byrbwyll
**hat** n het
**hatch** vb deor, gori ♦ n deoriad

**hatch** n gorddrws, rhagddor, dôr
**hatchery** n deorfa
**hatchet** n bwyell (fach)
**hate** vt casáu ♦ n cas, casineb
**hateful** adj cas, atgas
**hatred** n cas, casineb, digasedd
**haughtiness** n balchder, traha, ffroenucheledd
**haughty** adj balch, ffroenuchel, trahaus
**haul** vb tynnu, llusgo, halio ♦ n dalfa
**haulage** n cludiad, cludiant
**haulier** n haliwr
**haunch** n morddwyd, pedrain
**haunt** vt cyniwair, mynychu; trwblu, aflonyddu ♦ n cyniweirfa, cynefin, cyrchfa
**have** vt cael, meddu. **I h. blue eyes** mae llygaid glas gennyf. **I h. a cold** mae annwyd arnaf
**haven** n hafan, porthladd
**haversack** n ysgrepan
**havoc** n hafog, difrod
**hawk** n hebog, cudyll, curyll ♦ vb heboca
**hawk** vt gwerthu o dŷ i dŷ, pedlera
**haws** npl crawel y moch, criafol y moch
**hawthorn** n draenen wen
**hay** n gwair
**hayfever** n clefyd y gwair
**hayrick** n tas wair
**hazard** n perygl, llestair, antur ♦ vt anturio, peryglu
**hazardous** adj peryglus, enbydus
**haze** n niwl, tarth, tawch
**hazel** n collen ♦ adj gwinau golau
**haziness** n aneglurder
**hazy** adj aneglur, niwlog
**he** pron ef, efe; efo, fo, o
**head** n pen ♦ vb blaenori, penio
**headache** n dolur (cur) yn y pen, pen tost
**header** n peniad
**headgear** n penffest, penwisg

**heading** n pennawd
**headlamp** n lamp fawr
**headland** n pentir, penrhyn; talar
**headline** n pennawd, teitl, hedin
**headlong** adv pendramwnwgl
**headmaster** n prifathro
**headmistress** n prifathrawes
**headphone** n ffôn pen
**headquarters** npl pencadlys
**headstrong** adj cyndyn
**headway** n cynnydd
**heal** vb iacháu, meddyginiaethu
**health** n iechyd. **h. food shop** n
siop bwyd. **H. Service** n y
Gwasanaeth Iechyd
**healthy** adj iach, iachus
**heap** n crug, pentwr ♦ vt crugio,
pentyrru
**hear** vb clywed
**hearing** n clyw
**hearing aid** n cymorth clywed
**hearken** vi gwrando, clustfeinio
**hearsay** n sôn, siarad ♦ adj o ben i
ben, ail-law
**hearse** n hers
**heart** n calon
**heart-ache** n ing, dolur calon
**heart attack** n trawiad
**heartburn** n dŵr poeth
**hearten** vb calonogi
**hearth** n aelwyd
**heartland** n perfeddwlad
**hearty** adj calonnog, cynnes
**heat** n gwres, poethder, (sport)
rhagras ♦ vb twymo, poethi
**heater** n gwresogydd
**heath** n rhos, rhostir
**heathen** adj paganaidd ♦ n pagan
**heather** n grug
**heating** n gwres
**heave** vb codi, dyrchafu;
chwyddo; taflu ♦ n hwb
**heaven** n nef, nefoedd
**heavenly** adj nefol, nefolaidd
**heavily** adv yn drwm, yn drymaidd
**heavy** adj trwm, trymaidd,
trymllyd

**heavyweight** n (SPORT) pwysau
trwm
**Hebrew** n Hebrëwr; Hebraeg ♦ adj
Hebraeg; Hebreig
**heckle** vb ymyrryd
**hectare** n hectar
**hedge** n clawdd, gwrych, perth
**hedgehog** n draenog
**heed** vt ystyried, talu sylw ♦ n
ystyriaeth
**heel** n sawdl ♦ vb sodli
**heifer** n anner, heffer, treisiad
**height** n uchder, uchelder, taldra
**heinous** adj dybryd, anfad, ysgeler
**heir** n etifedd, aer
**heiress** n etifeddes, aeres
**helicopter** n hofrennydd
**hell** n uffern
**hellish** adj uffernol
**hello** excl helô!, hylô!, clyw!,
gwrando!
**helm** n llyw; llywyddiaeth
**helmet** n helm
**help** vt helpu, cymorth,
cynorthwyo ♦ n help, cymorth,
cynhorthwy
**helper** n cynorthwywr, helpwr
**helpful** adj defnyddiol,
cymwynasgar, gwasanaethgar,
buddiol
**helping** n dogn, cyfran (o fwyd)
**helpless** adj diymadferth
**helter-skelter** adv blith-draphlith
**hem** n hem, ymyl ♦ vt hemio
**hemi-** prefix hanner
**hemisphere** n hemisffer
**hemlock** n cegid
**hemp** n cywarch
**hen** n iâr
**hence** adv oddi yma ♦ excl ymaith!
**henceforth, -forward** adv rhag
llaw, mwyach, o hyn ymlaen
**henchman** n gwas, canlynwr,
cefnogydd
**hepatitis** n llif yr afu, hepatitis
**her** pron ei, hi, hithau
**herald** n herald ♦ vt cyhoeddi;

rhagflaenu

**herb** n llysieuyn, sawr-lysieuyn

**herbal** adj llysieuol

**herbicide** n llysleiddiad

**herd** n gyr, cenfaint, gre ♦ vb heidio

**here** adv yma

**hereditary** adj etifeddol

**heredity** n etifeddeg

**heresy** n heresi, gau athrawiaeth

**heretic** n heretic, camgredwr

**heritage** n etifeddiaeth, treftadaeth

**hermit** n meudwy

**hernia** n bors, hernia, torllengig

**hero** n arwr, gwron

**heroic** adj arwrol

**heroine** n arwres

**heron** n crëyr, crychydd

**herring** n pennog, ysgadenyn

**hesitant** adj petrusgar

**hesitate** vi petruso

**hesitation** n petruster

**heterodox** adj anuniongred

**heterodoxy** n anuniongrededd

**heterogeneous** adj anghydryw, afryw, heterogenus

**heterosexual** n anghyfunryw

**hew** vt naddu, torri, cymynu

**hewer** n cymynwr, torrwr

**hexa-** prefix chwech

**heyday** n anterth

**hiatus** n hiatws

**hibernate** vi gaeafu

**hiccup** n yr ig ♦ vi igian

**hide** vb cuddio, celu, ymguddio

**hide** n croen

**hide-and-seek** n chwarae mig

**hideous** adj hyll, erchyll

**hiding place** n cuddfan, lloches

**hierarchy** n gradd, offeiriadaeth

**higgle** vi taeru, bargenna

**high** adj uchel; mawr; cryf; llawn

**highbrow** adj uchel-ael

**high chair** n cadair ar gyfer plentyn

**highland** n ucheldir

**highly** adv yn fawr, yn uchel

**highness** n uchelder

**high-priest** n archoffeiriad

**high-spirited** adj calonnog, nwyfus

**high water** n pen llanw

**highway** n priffordd, ffordd fawr

**highwayman** n lleidr penffordd

**hijack** vb cipio

**hike** vb crwydro ♦ n taith gerdded

**hilarious** adj llawen, llon, siriol, hoenus

**hill** n bryn, allt, gorifyny

**hillock** n bryncyn, ponc, twmpath

**hilly** adj bryniog, mynyddig

**hilt** n carn cleddyf

**him** pron ef, efe, yntau

**hind** adj ôl

**hind** n ewig

**hinder** vt rhwystro, atal, lluddias, llesteirio

**hindrance** n rhwystr, llestair, lludd

**hinge** n colyn drws ♦ vb troi, dibynnu

**hint** n awgrym ♦ vt awgrymu

**hinterland** n cefnwlad

**hip** n clun, pen uchaf y glun

**hippie** n hipi

**hips** npl egroes

**hire** vt cyflogi, hurio, llogi ♦ n cyflog, hur

**hiss** vb chwythu, sïo, hysio, hisian

**historian** n hanesydd

**historic** adj hanesyddol

**historical** adj hanesyddol

**hit** vb taro ♦ n ergyd, trawiad

**hitch** vb bachu ♦ n cwlwm; atalfa, rhwystr

**hitchhike** vb bodio

**hitchhiker** n bodiwr

**hither** adv yma, hyd yma, tuag yma

**hitherto** adv hyd yma, hyd yn hyn

**hive** n cwch gwenyn. **h. off** vb rhannu, trosglwyddo, newid

**hoar** adj llwyd, penllwyd ♦ n llwydrew, barrug

**hoard** n cronfa, cuddfa ♦ vt cronni

**hoarfrost** *n* barrug, llwydrew
**hoarse** *adj* cryg, cryglyd
**hoax** *vt* twyllo ♦ *n* cast, tric, twyll
**hob** *n* pentan
**hobble** *vb* hercian
**hobby** *n* difyrwaith, hobi
**hobby horse** *n* ceffyl pren; hoff
  beth
**hobgoblin** *n* bwbach, bwci, bwgan
**hoe** *n* hof ♦ *vb* hofio
**hog** *n* mochyn
**hoist** *vt* codi, dyrchafu
**hold** *vb* dal, credu; atal; cadw ♦ *n*
  gafael, dalfa
**hold** *n* ceudad llong, howld
**holdall** *n* celsach
**holding** *n* deiliadaeth; tyddyn
**hold up** *n* (*robbery*) lladrad arfog;
  (*in traffic*) rhwystr
**hole** *n* twll, ffau
**holiday** *n* gŵyl, dygwyl
**holiness** *n* sancteiddrwydd
**Holland** *n* Isalmaen
**hollow** *adj* cau, gwag ♦ *n* ceudod,
  pant ♦ *vt* tyllu, cafnio
**holly** *n* celyn, celynnen
**holocaust** *n* lladdfa
**holster** *n* gwain
**holy** *adj* sanctaidd, glân
**Holy Ghost/Spirit** *n* Ysbryd Glân
**homage** *n* gwrogaeth
**home** *n*, *adj* cartref ♦ *adv* adref. **at
  h.** gartref
**homeland** *n* mamwlad
**homeless** *adj* digartref
**homely** *adj* cartrefol
**home rule** *n* ymreolaeth, hunanlywodraeth
**homesick** *adj* hiraethus
**homestead** *n* tyddyn
**homework** *n* gwaith cartref
**homicide** *n* dynleiddiad,
  llofruddiaeth
**homily** *n* pregeth, homili
**homogeneous** *adj* cydryw,
  homogenus
**homosexual** *n* gwrywgydiwr

**homosexuality** *n* gwrywgydiaeth
**hone** *n* carreg hogi, hôn ♦ *vb* hogi
**honest** *adj* (g)onest, didwyll
**honesty** *n* (g)onestrwydd
**honey** *n* mêl
**honeycomb** *n* dil mêl, crwybr ♦ *vt*
  tyllu, britho
**honeymoon** *n* mis mêl
**honeysuckle** *n* gwyddfid
**honorary** *adj* mygedol
**honour** *n* anrhydedd ♦ *vt*
  anrhydeddu
**honourable** *adj* anrhydeddus
**hood** *n* cwfl, cwcwll
**hoodwink** *vt* dallu, twyllo
**hoof** *n* carn
**hook** *n* bach; cryman ♦ *vb* bachu
**hooker** *n* bachwr
**hooligan** *n* adyn, dihiryn
**hoop** *n* cylch, cant ♦ *vt* cylchu,
  cantio
**hoot** *vb* hwtian, hwtio ♦ *n* hŵt
**hop** *vb* hercian ♦ *n* llam, herc
**hope** *n* gobaith ♦ *vb* gobeithio
**horde** *n* torf, haid, mintai
**horizon** *n* gorwel
**horizontal** *adj* llorwedd
**hormone** *n* hormôn
**horn** *n* corn ♦ *vt* cornio, twlcio
**horned** *adj* corniog
**hornet** *n* gwenynen feirch, cacynen
**horoscope** *n* horosgôp
**horrible** *adj* erchyll, ofnadwy
**horrid** *adj* erchyll, echrydus,
  anferth
**horrify** *vt* brawychu
**horror** *n* arswyd, erchylltod
**horse** *n* march, ceffyl
**horsehair** *n* rhawn
**horseman** *n* marchog
**horsemanship** *n* marchogaeth
**horseplay** *n* direidi
**horseshoe** *n* pedol
**horticultural** *adj* garddwriaethol
**horticulture** *n* garddwriaeth
**horticulturist** *n* garddwriaethwr
**hose** (**hose**) *n* hosan; (**hoses**) *n*

pibell ddŵr
**hospitable** adj lletygar, croesawus
**hospital** n ysbyty
**hospitality** n lletygarwch, croeso
**host** n llu, byddin
**host** n lletywr, gwesteiwr
**hostage** n gwystl
**hostel** n llety efrydwyr, neuadd breswyl
**hostess** n croesawferch
**hostile** adj gelyniaethus
**hot** adj poeth, twym, brwd, gwresog
**hotbed** n magwrfa
**hotch-potch** n cymysgfa, cybolfa
**hotel** n gwesty
**hotelier** n gwestywr
**hot-headed** adj penboeth, byrbwyll
**hot-water bottle** n jar/potel dŵr twym
**hound** n bytheiad, helgi ♦ vt hela, erlid, annos
**hour** n awr
**house** n tŷ, annedd ♦ vb lletya
**household** n teulu, tylwyth
**householder** n deiliad tŷ
**housekeeper** n gofalyddes
**housewife** n gwraig tŷ
**housing** n tai
**hovel** n penty, hofel
**hover** vi hofran
**hovercraft** n hofrenfad
**how** adv pa mor, pa fodd, pa sut, sut
**howbeit** adv er hynny
**however** adv pa fodd bynnag, sut bynnag
**howl** vi udo, oernadu ♦ n udiad, oernad
**hoyden** n rhampen, hoeden
**hub** n both olwyn; canolbwynt
**hubbub** n mwstwr
**huddle** vb tyrru, gwthio
**hue** n gwawr
**huff** n sorri, tramgwyddo ♦ n soriant
**hug** vt cofleidio, gwasgu

**huge** adj anferth, enfawr, dirfawr
**hulk** n corff llong, llong foel, hwlc
**hull** n corff llong; cibyn, plisgyn
**hullabaloo** n dadwrdd, helynt, halibalŵ
**hum** vb mwmian ♦ n si, sibrwd
**human** adj dynol
**humane** adj tirion, tosturiol, trugarog
**humanism** n dyneiddiaeth
**humanist** n dyneiddiwr
**humanistic** adj dyneiddiol
**humanitarian** n dyngarwr
**humanitarianism** n dyngaroldeb
**humanity** n dynoliaeth, dynolryw
**humble** adj gostyngedig, ufudd ♦ vt darostwng
**humble-bee** n cacynen
**humbug** n twyll, ffug, hoced; twyllwr ♦ vt twyllo
**humdrum** adj diflas
**humid** adj llaith
**humiliate** vt bychanu, gwaradwyddo, darostwng, iselu
**humiliation** n darostyngiad
**humility** n gostyngeiddrwydd
**humour** n hwyl, donioldeb ♦ vt boddio
**hump** n crwmach, crwmp, crwb
**hunch** n syniad, tybiaeth
**hunch backed** adj cefngrwm
**hundred** adj cant, can ♦ n cant; cantref
**Hungary** n Hwngari
**hunger** n newyn, chwant bwyd ♦ vi newynu
**hungry** adj newynog
**hunk** n cwlff(yn)
**hunt** vb hela, erlid ♦ n helwriaeth, hela
**hunter** n heliwr; ceffyl hela
**hunting** n hela
**hurdle** n clwyd
**hurl** vt hyrddio
**hurly-burly** n hwrli-bwrli, dwndwr
**hurricane** n corwynt
**hurried** adj brysiog

**hurry** vb brysio ♦ n brys
**hurt** vb niweidio, dolurio, brifo ♦ n niwed, dolur
**hurtful** adj niweidiol
**hurtle** vb gwrthdaro, chwyrlïo
**husband** n gŵr, priod ♦ vt cynilo
**husbandry** n amaethyddiaeth, hwsmonaeth
**hush** excl ust ♦ vb distewi ♦ n distawrwydd
**husk** n plisgyn, cibyn ♦ vt plisgo
**husky** adj sych, cryglyd
**hussy** n maeden
**hustings** n hwstyng, llwyfan etholiad
**hustle** vb gwthio, prysuro
**hut** n bwth, caban, cwt
**hutch** n cwt cwningen, cwb
**hyacinth** n croeso haf
**hybrid** adj croesryw
**hydration** n hydradiad
**hydraulic** adj hydrolig
**hydraulics** n hydroleg
**hydro-** prefix dwfr
**hydroelectric** adj hydroelectrig
**hydrophobia** n hydroffobia
**hygiene** n iechydaeth, gwyddor glendid
**hymn** n emyn ♦ vb emynu
**hyper-** prefix gor-, tra-
**hyperbole** n gormodiaith
**hypermarket** n archfarchnad
**hyphen** n cyplysnod, cysylltnod (-)
**hypnotism** n swyngwsg, hypnotiaeth
**hypnotize** vt swyno, rheibio
**hypochondria** n pruddglwyf, y felan
**hypocrisy** n rhagrith
**hypocrite** n rhagrithiwr
**hypothesis** (-theses) n damcaniaeth
**hyssop** n isop
**hysteria** n y famwst, hysteria
**hysterical** adj hysterig

# I

**I** pron mi, myfi; fi, i; minnau, innau
**ice** n iâ, rhew ♦ vt taenu (megis) â rhew
**iceberg** n mynydd rhew
**ice cream** n hufen iâ
**Iceland** n Gwlad yr Iâ
**ice lolly** n loli iâ
**ice rink** n llain iâ
**icicle** n clöyn iâ, cloch iâ, pibonwy
**icing** n eising
**icy** adj rhewllyd
**idea** n drychfeddwl, syniad
**ideal** adj delfrydol, ideal ♦ n delfryd
**idealism** n delfrydiaeth
**idealist** n delfrydiwr
**idealistic** adj delfrydol
**idealize** vb delfrydu
**identical** adj yr un (yn union)
**identify** vt adnabod (fel yr un un); uniaethu
**identikit (picture)** n tebyglun
**identity** n unfathiant, hunaniaeth
**idiocy** n gwiriondeb, penwendid
**idiom** n priod-ddull, idiom
**idiosyncrasy** n tymer, anianawd
**idiot** n gwirionyn, hurtyn
**idle** adj segur, ofer ♦ vb segura, ofera
**idleness** n segurdod, diogi
**idol** n eilun
**idolater** n eilunaddolwr
**idolatry** n eilunaddoliaeth
**idolise** vb addoli, gwirioni
**idyll** n bugeilgerdd; canig
**if** conj os, pe
**igloo** n iglŵ
**ignite** vb ennyn, tanio, cynnau
**ignition** n taniad
**ignoble** adj anenwog, isel, gwael, salw
**ignominious** adj gwarthus,

gwaradwyddus

**ignorance** *n* anwybodaeth

**ignorant** *adj* anwybodus

**ignore** *vt* anwybyddu, diystyru

**il-** *prefix* di-, an-

**ill** *adj* drwg; gwael, claf ♦ *adv* yn ddrwg ♦ *n* drwg, niwed

**ill-advised** *adj* annoeth, ffôl

**illegal** *adj* anghyfreithlon

**illegible** *adj* annarllenadwy, aneglur

**illegitimate, illicit** *adj* anghyfreithlon

**illiterate** *adj* anllythrennog

**illness** *n* afiechyd, anhwylder, anhwyldeb

**illogical** *adj* afresymegol

**ill-timed** *adj* anamserol

**ill-treat** *vb* camdrin

**illuminate** *vt* goleuo, addurno

**illumination** *n* golau, esboniad

**illusion** *n* rhith, lledrith, rhithganfyddiad

**illustrate** *vt* egluro; darlunio

**illustration** *n* eglureb; darlun

**illustrative** *adj* darluniol, eglurhaol

**illustrious** *adj* enwog, hyglod

**ill-will** *n* gelyniaeth, casineb

**im-** *prefix* di, an-

**image** *n* delw, llun; delwedd

**imagery** *n* delweddaeth

**imaginary** *adj* dychmygol

**imagination** *n* dychymyg, darfelydd

**imaginative** *adj* dychmygus

**imagine** *vt* dychmygu, tybio

**imbalance** *n* anghydbwysedd

**imbecile** *adj, n* (un) penwan

**imbue** *vt* trwytho

**imitate** *vt* dynwared, efelychu

**immaculate** *adj* difrycheulyd, pur, glân

**immaterial** *adj* dibwys

**immature** *adj* anaeddfed

**immediate** *adj* agos, presennol

**immediately** *adv* ar unwaith

**immemorial** *adj* er cyn cof

**immense** *adj* anferth, eang, dirfawr

**immerse** *vt* trochi, suddo

**immigrant** *n* mewnfudwr

**immigrate** *vi* mewnfudo

**imminent** *adj* gerllaw, agos, wrth y drws

**immobile** *adj* diymod, disymud

**immoral** *adj* anfoesol

**immortal** *adj* anfarwol

**immortality** *n* anfarwoldeb

**immortalize** *vb* anfarwoli

**immovable** *adj* diysgog, ansymudol

**immune** *adj* rhydd rhag

**immunization** *n* gwrtheintiad

**immunize** *vb* gwrtheintio

**immure** *vt* caethiwo, carcharu

**immutable** *adj* anghyfnewidiol, digyfnewid

**imp** *n* dieflyn, cenau

**impact** *n* ardrawiad, gwrthdrawiad

**impair** *vt* amharu

**impale** *vt* trywanu

**impart** *vt* cyfrannu, rhoddi

**impartial** *adj* diduedd, amhleidiol, teg

**impassable** *adj* na ellir mynd heibio iddo

**impasse** *n* ataliad, pen draw

**impassioned** *adj* brwd, hwyliog, cyffrous

**impassive** *adj* digyffro, didaro

**impatient** *adj* diamynedd

**impeach** *vt* cyhuddo, cwyno yn erbyn, uchelgyhuddo

**impeccable** *adj* di-fai

**impede** *vt* atal, rhwystro, llesteirio

**impediment** *n* atalfa, rhwystr ram

**impel** *vt* gyrru, hyrddio, cymell

**impending** *adj* agos, gerllaw

**imperative** *n* gorchymyn ♦ *adj* gorchmynnol, gorfodol

**imperfect** *adj* amherffaith

**imperial** *adj* ymerodrol

**imperil** *vt* peryglu

**imperious** *adj* awdurdodol, trahaus

**impermeable** *adj* anathraidd
**impersonal** *adj* amhersonol
**impersonate** *vt* personoli, cynrychioli, portreadu (*person*)
**impertinent** *adj* amherthnasol; digywilydd
**imperturbable** *adj* tawel, digyffro
**impervious** *adj* na ellir ei dreiddio, anhydraidd
**impetuous** *adj* byrbwyll, nwydwyllt
**impetus** *n* cymhelliad, symbyliad
**impinge** *vi* taro yn erbyn, gwrthdaro, cyffwrdd â
**impious** *adj* annuwiol, diras
**implacable** *adj* anghymodlon
**implant** *vt* plannu, gwreiddio
**implement** *n* offeryn, arf ♦ *vb* gweithredu
**implication** *n* ymhlygiad, goblygiad
**implicit** *adj* dealledig; ymhlyg, goblygedig
**implore** *vt* atolygu, ymbil, erfyn, crefu
**imply** *vt* arwyddo, awgrymu
**impolite** *adj* anfoesgar
**import** *vt* mewnforio ♦ *n* (*pl*) mewnforion; arwyddocâd; pwys
**importance** *n* pwys, pwysigrwydd
**important** *adj* pwysig
**importer** *n* mewnforiwr
**importune** *vt* dyfal geisio, taer erfyn
**impose** *vb* gosod ar; twyllo
**imposing** *adj* llethol, mawreddog
**impossibility** *n* amhosibilrwydd
**impossible** *adj* amhosibl
**impostor** *n* twyllwr
**imposture** *n* twyll, hoced
**impotence** *n* anallu, analluedd
**impotent** *adj* di-rym, analluog
**impound** *vi* ffaldio; atafaelu
**impoverish** *vt* tlodi, llymhau
**impracticable** *adj* anymarferol
**imprecate** *vt* rhegi, melltithio
**impregnable** *adj* cadarn, di-syfl

**impregnate** *vt* ffrwythloni; trwytho
**impress** *vt* argraffu, pwyso, dylanwadu ♦ *n* argraffiad
**impression** *n* argraff
**impressionable** *adj* hawdd ei argyhoeddi
**impressive** *adj* trawiadol
**imprint** *vt* argraffu ♦ *n* argraff, delw
**imprison** *vt* carcharu
**improbable** *adj* annhebygol
**impromptu** *adj, adv* ar y pryd, byrfyfyr
**improper** *adj* anweddus
**improve** *vb* gwella, diwygio
**improvement** *n* gwelliant
**improvise** *vb* addasu ar y pryd
**impudent** *adj* digywilydd, haerllug
**impulse** *n* cymhelliad, ysgogiad
**impulsive** *adj* byrbwyll
**impunity** *n* bod heb gosb. **with i.** yn ddi-gosb
**impure** *adj* amhur, aflan
**impute** *vt* cyfrif i; priodoli; bwrw ar
**in** *prep* yn, mewn, i mewn, o fewn
**in-** *prefix* di-, an-
**inability** *n* anallu
**inaccessible** *n* anhygyrch
**inaccurate** *adj* anghywir, anfanwl
**inaction** *n* segurdod
**inadequate** *adj* annigonol
**inadmissible** *adj* annerbyniol
**inadvertent** *adj* anfwriadol, amryfus
**inane** *adj* gwag, gwageddus, ofer
**inanimate** *adj* difywyd, dienaid
**inappropriate** *adj* anaddas
**inasmuch** *adv* yn gymaint (â)
**inaudible** *adj* anhyglyw, na ellir ei glywed
**inaugurate** *vt* urddo, cysegru, agor, dechrau
**inauguration** *n* agoriad, dechreuad
**inborn** *adj* cynhenid, greddfol
**inbreed** *vb* mewnfrido

**incandescent** adj gwynias
**incantation** n swyn, swyngyfaredd
**incapable** adj analluog
**incapability** n anallu
**incapacitate** vt anghymhwyso, analluogi
**incarcerate** vt carcharu
**incarnation** n ymgnawdoliad
**incendiary** adj llosg ♦ n bom tân
**incense** n arogldarth
**incense** vt llidio, cythruddo
**incentive** adj cymelliadol ♦ n cymhelliad
**inception** n dechreuad, agoriad
**incessant** adj di-baid, di-dor
**incest** n llosgach
**inch** n modfedd
**incident** n digwyddiad
**incidental** adj digwyddiadol, achlysurol
**incidentally** adv gyda llaw
**incinerate** vb llosgi'n ulw
**incineration** n llosgiad llwyr
**incinerator** n llosgydd, ffwrnais
**incipient** adj dechreuol
**incise** vt torri, trychu
**incisive** adj llym, miniog
**incite** vt annog, cyffroi, annos
**inclement** adj gerwin, garw, drycinog
**inclination** n tuedd, gogwydd
**incline** vb tueddu, gogwyddo ♦ n llethr
**include** vt cynnwys
**including** prep gan gynnwys
**inclusive** adj cynwysedig, gan gynnwys
**incognito** adj yn ddirgel, dan ffugenw
**incoherent** adj digyswllt, anghysylltus
**income** n incwm. **i. tax** treth incwm
**incompatible** adj anghytûn
**incompetent** n anghymwys
**incomplete** adj anghyflawn
**incomprehensible** adj

annealladwy
**incongruous** adj anghydweddol, anaddas
**inconsistency** n anghysondeb
**inconsistent** adj anghyson
**inconspicuous** adj anamlwg
**incontestable** adj diymwad, diamheuol
**inconvenience** n anghyfleustra
**inconvenient** adj anghyfleus
**incorporate** vb corffori, ymgorffori
**incorporated** adj corfforedig
**incorrect** adj anghywir
**incorrigible** adj anwelladwy
**increase** vb cynyddu ♦ n cynnydd
**incredible** adj anhygoel, anghredadwy
**incredulity** n anghrediniaeth
**incredulous** adj anghrediniol
**increment** n cynnydd, ychwanegiad
**incriminate** vt cyhuddo, euogi
**incubate** vb gori, deor
**incubator** n deorydd
**incumbent** adj rhwymedig ar ♦ n periglor, offeiriad, clerigwr
**incur** vt rhedeg i ddyled; achosi
**incursion** n cyrch
**indebted** adj dyledus
**indecent** adj anweddus
**indecision** n petruster
**indecisive** adj amhendant
**indeed** adv yn wir; iawn, dros ben
**indefatigable** adj diflin, dyfal
**indefinite** adj amhenodol, amhendant
**indelible** adj annileadwy
**indelicate** adj aflednais
**indemnify** vb digolledu
**indemnity** n iawn
**indented** adj bylchog, danheddus
**indenture** n cytundeb, cyfamod
**independence** n annibyniaeth
**independent** adj annibynnol ♦ n annibynnwr
**indescribable** adj annisgrifiadwy
**indeterminate** adj amhenodol,

penagored
**index** *n* mynegai; mynegfys
**India** *n* India
**Indian** *adj* Indiaidd ♦ *n* Indiad
**indicate** *vt* dangos, arwyddo
**indicative** *adj* arwyddol, mynegol
**indicator** *n* dangosydd
**indict** *vt* cyhuddo
**indifference** *n* difaterwch,
  difrawder
**indifferent** *adj* difater; dibwys
**indigenous** *adj* cynhenid
**indigent** *adj* anghenus, tlawd,
  rheidus
**indigestion** *n* diffyg traul,
  camdreuliad
**indignant** *adj* dig, digofus, dicllon
**indignation** *n* dig, digofaint, llid
**indignity** *n* amarch, sarhad, anfri
**indirect** *adj* anuniongyrchol
**indiscreet** *adj* annoeth
**indiscriminate** *adj* diwahaniaeth
**indispensable** *adj* anhepgorol
**indisposed** *adj* anhwylus
**indisputable** *adj* diamheuol
**indissoluble** *adj* annatod
**indistinct** *adj* aneglur, anhyglyw,
  bloesg
**indite** *vt* cyfansoddi, traethu
**individual** *adj* unigol ♦ *n* un,
  unigolyn
**indoctrinate** *vb* trwytho (ag
  athrawiaeth), credorfodi
**indoctrination** *n* credorfodaeth
**indolence** *n* seguryd, syrthni
**indolent** *adj* segur, swrth, dioglyd
**indomitable** *adj* anorchfygol, di-
  ildio
**indoor** *adj*, *adv* dan do
**indubitable** *adj* diamheuol
**induce** *vt* darbwyllo, denu, cymell
**inducement** *n* anogiad
**induct** *vt* sefydlu; anwytho
**induction** *n* anwythiad
**indulge** *vb* boddio; maldodi
**indulgence** *n* ymfoddhad; maldod
**indulgent** *adj* ffafriol, maldodus

**industrial** *adj* diwydiannol,
  gweithfaol
**industrialize** *vb* diwydiannu
**industrious** *adj* diwyd, dyfal,
  gweithgar
**industry** *n* diwydrwydd; diwydiant
**inebriate** *vt* meddwi ♦ *n* meddwyn
**inedible** *adj* anfwytadwy
**ineffable** *adj* anhraethol,
  anhraethadwy
**ineffective** *adj* aneffeithiol
**inefficiency** *n* anallu
**inefficient** *adj* analluog
**ineligible** *adj* anghymwys
**inept** *adj* heb fod yn taro, gwrthun,
  gwirion
**inequality** *n* anghysondeb
**inert** *adj* swrth, diynni, diegni
**inertia** *n* anegni, inertia
**inestimable** *adj* amhrisiadwy
**inevitable** *adj* anochel, anesgorol
**inexhaustible** *adj* dihysbydd
**inexorable** *adj* di-ildio, anhyblyg
**inexpensive** *adj* rhad
**inexperience** *n* diffyg profiad
**inexperienced** *adj* amhrofiadol,
  dibrofiad
**infallible** *adj* anffaeledig
**infallibility** *n* anffaeledigrwydd
**infamous** *adj* gwaradwyddus,
  gwarthus
**infancy** *n* mabandod, mebyd,
  maboed
**infant** *n* maban, baban; un dan
  oed
**infantry** *n* gwŷr traed, milwyr
  traed
**infatuate** *vt* gwirioni, ffoli, dwlu
**infatuated** *adj* wedi ffoli, wedi
  gwirioni
**infect** *vt* heintio, llygru
**infection** *n* haint
**infectious** *adj* heintus
**infer** *vt* casglu
**inferior** *adj* is, israddol ♦ *n* isradd
**inferiority** *n* israddoldeb
**inferiority complex** *n* cymhleth y

taeog
**infernal** *adj* uffernol, dieflig
**infertile** *adj* anffrwythlon
**infertility** *n* anffrwythlondeb
**infest** *vt* bod yn bla, heigiannu
**infidel** *n* anffyddiwr
**infidelity** *n* anffyddlondeb
**infield** *adj* mewnfaes
**infinite** *adj* anfeidrol
**infinitesimal** *adj* anfeidrol fach, gorfychan
**infinitive** *adj* annherfynol ♦ *n* berfenw
**infirm** *adj* egwan, gwan, gwanllyd
**infirmary** *n* ysbyty, clafdy
**infirmity** *n* gwendid, llesgedd
**inflame** *vb* ennyn, cyffroi, llidio
**inflamed** *adj* llidus
**inflammable** *adj* hylosg, hyfflam
**inflammation** *n* enyniad, enynfa, llid
**inflatable** *adj* y gellir ei chwyddo neu ei chwythu
**inflate** *vt* chwyddo
**inflation** *n* chwyddiant
**inflect** *vt* ffurfdroi; treiglo
**inflexible** *adj* anhyblyg
**inflexibility** *n* anhyblygrwydd
**inflict** *vt* peri, gweinyddu (cosb, poen, *etc*)
**influence** *n* dylanwad ♦ *vt* dylanwadu
**influenza** *n* ffliw
**influx** *n* dylifiad
**inform** *vb* hysbysu
**informal** *adj* anffurfiol
**information** *n* gwybodaeth, hysbysrwydd
**infra-** *prefix* is-
**infra-red** *adj* is-goch
**infrastructure** *n* seilwaith
**infrequent** *adj* anaml
**infringe** *vt* torri, troseddu
**infuriate** *vt* ffyrnigo, cynddeiriogi
**infuse** *vt* tywallt, arllwys; trwytho
**infusion** *n* trwyth, hydreiddiad
**ingenious** *adj* medrus, cywrain,

celfydd
**ingenuous** *adj* didwyll, diddichell
**ingenuousness** *n* didwylledd, diffuantrwydd
**ingrained** *adj* wedi greddfu; cynhenid
**ingratiate** *vt* ennill ffafr
**ingratitude** *n* anniolchgarwch
**ingredients** *npl* cynhwysion, defnyddiau
**inhabit** *vt* cyfaneddu, trigo, preswylio
**inhabitable** *adj* cyfannedd, trigadwy
**inhabitant** *n* preswyliwr
**inhale** *vt* anadlu
**inhere** *vi* glynu, ymlynu, bod
**inherent** *adj* cynhenid, greddfol
**inherit** *vt* etifeddu
**inheritance** *n* etifeddiaeth
**inheritor** *n* etifedd, etifeddwr
**inhibit** *vt* gwahardd, atal
**inhibition** *n* ataliad, atalnwyd
**inhibitor** *n* atalydd
**inhuman** *adj* annynol, creulon
**inimical** *adj* gelyniaethus
**inimitable** *adj* digyffelyb
**iniquitous** *adj* drwg, traws
**iniquity** *n* anwiredd, camwedd
**initial** *adj* dechreuol ♦ *n* llythyren gyntaf
**initiate** *vt* egwyddori; derbyn; dechrau
**initiative** *n* cynhoredd, menter
**inject** *vt* chwistrellu
**injection** *n* chwistrelliad, pigiad
**injunction** *n* gorchymyn, gwaharddiad
**injure** *vt* niweidio, anafu
**injury** *n* niwed, cam, anaf
**injustice** *n* anghyfiawnder, cam
**ink** *n* inc ♦ *vt* incio
**inkling** *n* awgrym, arwydd
**inland** *adj* canoldirol ♦ *n* canoldir.
l. Revenue *n* Cyllid y Wlad
**inlet** *n* cilfach, bae
**inmate** *n* trigiannydd, preswylydd

**inmost** *adj* nesaf i mewn, dyfnaf
**inn** *n* tafarn, tafarndy, gwesty
**innate** *adj* cynhenid, cynhwynol, greddfol
**inner** *adj* mewnol
**innings** *npl* batiad
**innkeeper** *n* tafarnwr
**innocence** *n* diniweidrwydd
**innocent** *adj* diniwed, gwirion, dieuog
**innocuous** *adj* diniwed, diberygl
**innovate** *vi* newid, cyflwyno
**innovation** *n* newyddbeth
**innuendo** *n* ensyniad
**innumerable** *adj* aneirif, afrifed, dirifedi, di-rif
**inoculate** *vt* brechu
**inoculation** *n* brechiad
**inoffensive** *adj* di-ddrwg
**inordinate** *adj* anghymedrol, di-rôl
**inorganic** *adj* anorganig
**input** *n* mewnbwn, cyfraniad
**inquest** *n* cwest; trengholiad
**inquire** *vb* ymofyn, ymholi, gofyn, holi
**inquiry** *n* ymholiad
**inquisition** *n* ymchwiliad; chwil-lys
**inquisitive** *adj* ymofyngar, holgar
**in-road** *n* cyrch
**insane** *adj* gwallgof, gorffwyll, ynfyd
**insanitary** *adj* aflachus, brwnt
**insatiable** *adj* anniwall
**inscribe** *vt* arysgrifio
**inscription** *n* arysgrif
**inscrutable** *adj* anolrheiniadwy, anchwiliadwy
**insect** *n* pryf, trychfil
**insensibility** *n* dideimladrwydd
**insensible** *adj* dideimlad
**insert** *vb* mewnosod
**in-service** *adj* mewn swydd
**inside** *n* tu mewn ♦ *adj* mewnol ♦ *prep* yn tu mewn i ♦ *adv* i mewn, o fewn
**inside-forward** *n* mewnwr

**inside-half** *n* mewnwr
**inside-out** *adv* o chwith
**inside-right** *n* mewnwr de
**insidious** *adj* llechwraidd
**insight** *n* mewnwelediad
**insignificance** *n* dinodedd
**insignificant** *adj* di-nod, distadl, dibwys
**insincere** *adj* annidwyll, ffuantus, rhagrithiol
**insincerity** *n* annidwylledd
**insinuate** *vb* ensynio
**insipid** *adj* diflas, merfaidd
**insist** *vi* mynnu
**insolence** *n* haerllugrwydd
**insolent** *adj* haerllug
**insolvent** *adj* methdalus, wedi torri
**insomnia** *n* anhunedd
**inspect** *vt* arolygu, archwilio
**inspector** *n* arolygwr
**inspiration** *n* ysbrydoliaeth
**inspire** *vb* ysbrydoli
**instability** *n* ansadrwydd
**install** *vt* sefydlu, gorseddu
**instalment** *n* cyfran, rhandal
**instance** *n* enghraifft ♦ *vt* enwi, nodi
**instant** *adj* taer, ebrwydd ♦ *n* eiliad, moment. **i. coffee** *n* coffi powdr
**instantaneous** *adj* yn y fan; disymwth
**instantly** *adv* ar drawiad
**instead** *adv* yn lle
**instep** *n* mwnwgl troed, cefn troed
**instigate** *vt* annog, cymell
**instil** *vt* argymell
**instinct** *n* greddf
**institute** *n* athrofa
**institution** *n* sefydliad
**instruct** *vt* hyfforddi
**instruction** *n* hyfforddiant
**instructor** *n* hyfforddwr
**instrument** *n* offeryn
**insubordinate** *adj* anufudd, gwrthryfelgar

**insufferable** adj annioddefol
**insufficient** adj annigonol
**insular** adj ynysol, cul
**insulate** vt ynysu, inswleiddio
**insult** vt sarhau ♦ n sarhad
**insuperable** adj anorfod, anorchfygol
**insurance** n yswiriant. **i. policy** n polisi yswiriant
**insure** vb yswirio
**insurgent** adj gwrthryfelgar ♦ n gwrthryfelwr
**insurrection** n terfysg, gwrthryfel
**intact** adj cyfan, dianaf
**integral** adj cyfan, cyflawn
**integrate** vb cyfannu
**integrity** n cywirdeb, gonestrwydd
**intellect** n deall
**intellectual** n deallusyn ♦ adj deallus, deallgar
**intelligence** n deallgarwch, deallusrwydd; hysbysrwydd
**intelligent** adj deallus
**intelligible** adj dealladwy
**intend** vt bwriadu, amcanu, golygu
**intense** adj angerddol, dwys
**intensive care unit** n uned ofal arbennig
**intent** adj dyfal, diwyd, astud
**intent** n bwriad, amcan; ystyr; diben
**intention** n bwriad
**intentional** adj bwriadol
**inter** vt claddu, daearu
**inter-** prefix rhwng, cyd
**interaction** n rhyngweithiad
**interbreed** vb rhyngfridio
**intercede** vi cyfryngu, eiriol
**intercept** vt rhyng-gipio, rhwystro, rhagod
**intercession** n cyfryngdod, eiriolaeth
**interchange** vt cyfnewid, ymgyfnewid
**intercourse** n cyfathrach
**interdict** vt gwahardd ♦ n gwaharddiad

**interest** n budd, buddiant; diddordeb; llog ♦ vt diddori
**interested** adj â chanddo ddidordeb
**interesting** adj diddorol
**interests** npl diddordebau
**interface** n cydwyneb
**interfere** vt cyfryngu, ymyrryd, ymhel
**interference** n ymyrraeth
**interim** adj dros dro ♦ n cyfamser
**interior** adj mewnol ♦ n tu mewn, canol, perfeddwlad
**interject** vt ebychu
**interlock** vb cyd-gloi
**interloper** n ymwthiwr, ymyrrwr
**interlude** n egwyl; anterliwt
**intermediary** n canolwr, cyfryngwr
**intermediate** adj canol, canolradd
**intern** vt carcharu
**internal** adj mewnol
**international** adj cydwladol, rhyngwladol
**interpolate** vt dodi i mewn, rhyngosod
**interpolation** n rhyngosodiad
**interpose** vb gosod rhwng, cyfryngu, rhyngwthio
**interpret** vt dehongli; cyfieithu
**interpretation** n dehongliad; cyfieithiad
**interpreter** n lladmerydd, cyfieithydd
**interrelation** n cydberthynas
**interrogate** vt holi
**interrogative** adj gofynnol
**interrupt** vt torri ar, torri ar draws, ymyrryd
**intersect** vb croesi ei gilydd; croesdorri
**intersection** n croesdoriad
**intersperse** vb gwasgaru, britho
**interval** n egwyl, saib
**intervene** vi ymyrryd
**interview** n cyfweliad ♦ vb cyfweld
**intestines** npl perfedd, coluddion

**intimacy** n agosatrwydd
**intimate** adj cyfarwydd, agos ♦ n cydnabod
**intimate** vt arwyddo, hysbysu
**intimidate** vt dychrynu, brawychu
**into** prep i, i mewn i
**intolerable** adj annioddefol
**intonation** n tonyddiaeth, goslef
**intone** vt llafarganu
**intoxicate** vt meddwi
**intoxication** n meddwdod
**intractable** adj anhydrin, afreolus
**intransitive** adj cyflawn (gramadeg)
**intrepid** adj di-ofn, diarswyd, gwrol, dewr
**intricate** adj dyrys, cymhleth, astrus
**intrigue** vi, n cynllwyn
**intrinsic** adj priodol, hanfodol
**introduce** vt cyflwyno
**introduction** n cyflwyniad, rhagarweiniad
**introductory** adj dechreuol, agoriadol, rhagarweiniol
**introspection** n mewnsylliad
**introvert** adj mewnblyg
**intrude** vb ymyrryd
**intruder** n ymyrrwr, ymwthiwr
**intrusion** n ymwthiad, ymyrraeth
**intuition** n sythwelediad
**inundate** vt gorlifo, boddi
**inundation** n gorlifiad
**inure** vt cyfarwyddo, caledu
**invade** vt goresgyn
**invalid** adj di-rym, annilys
**invalid** n un afiach, un methedig
**invaluable** adj amhrisiadwy
**invariable** adj gwastad, dieithriad
**invariably** adv yn ddieithriad
**invasion** n goresgyniad
**invective** n difrïaeth, cabledd
**invent** vt dyfeisio, dychmygu
**inventory** n rhestr, stocrestr
**inverse** adj (yn y) gwrthwyneb, yn groes
**inversion** n gwrthdro

**invert** vt troi wyneb i waered, gwrthdroi
**inverted commas** npl dyfynodau
**invest** vt buddsoddi; arwisgo
**investigate** vt chwilio, archwilio, ymchwilio
**investigation** n ymchwiliad
**investigator** n ymchwiliwr
**investiture** n arwisgiad
**investment** n buddsoddiad
**investor** n buddsoddwr
**invidious** adj annymunol
**invigilate** vb arolygu
**invigilator** n arolygwr, gwyliwr
**invigorate** vt cryfhau, grymuso
**invincible** adj anorchfygol
**inviolable** adj dihalog, cysegredig
**invisible** adj anweledig, anweladwy
**invitation** n gwahoddiad
**invite** vt gwahodd
**invoice** n anfoneb
**involuntary** adj o anfodd, anfwriadol
**involve** vt drysu; cynnwys, ymwneud
**involvement** n ymwneud, ymglymiad
**inward** adj mewnol
**iodine** n ïodin
**ion** n ïon
**ionisation** n ïoneiddiad
**ionise** vb ïoneiddio
**iota** n mymryn, iod, gronyn
**ir-** prefix di-, an-
**Iran** n Iran
**Iraq** n Iraq
**irate** adj dig, llidiog
**Ireland** n Iwerddon
**iris** n enfys; elestr
**Irish** adj Gwyddelig ♦ n Gwyddeleg
**irksome** adj blin, trafferthus, diflas
**iron** n, adj haearn ♦ vt smwddio
**ironic** adj eironig
**ironing board** n bwrdd smwddio
**ironmonger** n gwerthwr nwyddau haearn
**irony** n eironi

**irradiate** vt arbelydru
**irradiation** n arbelydredd
**irrational** adj direswm, afresymol
**irreconcilable** adj anghymodlon
**irrefutable** adj anatebadwy
**irregular** adj afreolaidd
**irregularity** n afreoleidd-dra
**irrelevant** adj amherthnasol
**irreparable** adj anadferadwy
**irreproachable** adj diargyhoedd,
di-fai
**irresistible** adj anorchfygol
**irretrievable** adj anadferadwy
**irrevocable** adj di-alw-yn-ôl
**irrigate** vt dyfrhau
**irritable** n croendenau, anniddig,
llidiog
**irritate** vt blino, poeni, cythruddo
**is** vi mae, sydd, yw, ydy(w), oes
**island, isle** n ynys
**islet** n ynysig
**isolate** vt neilltuo, gwahanu
**isolated** adj wedi ei neilltuo, wedi
ei wahanu
**isolation** n neilltuaeth,
arwahanrwydd
**Israel** n Israel
**Israelite** n Israeliad
**issue** n llif; agorfa, arllwysfa;
hilogaeth, plant; canlyniad, pwnc
mewn dadl ♦ vb tarddu, deillio;
rhoi allan, cyhoeddi
**isthmus** n culdir
**it** pron efe, fe, ef, efo, fo, o; hi
**Italian** adj Eidalaidd ♦ n Eidalwr;
(LING) Eidaleg
**italic** adj italig
**italicize** vb italeiddio
**italics** npl llythrennau italaidd
**Italy** n Yr Eidal
**itch** vi ysu, cosi ♦ n y crafu, ysfa
**item** n peth, pwnc, darn, tamaid
**iterate** vt ailadrodd
**itinerant** adj teithiol
**itinerary** n taith, teithlyfr
**itinerate** vi teithio, cylchdeithio
**itself** pron ei hun, ei hunan

**ivory** n ifori
**ivy** n eiddew, iorwg

# J

**jab** n jab, pigiad ♦ vb procio,
gwanu
**jabber** vi bragawthan, clebran ♦ n
clebar
**jack** n jac
**jackass** n asyn gwryw; hurtyn
**jackdaw** n corfran, jac-y-do
**jacket** n siaced
**jade** vt blino, lluddedu
**jagged** adj danheddog, ysgithrog
**jail** n carchar
**jam** n jam; tagfa
**jam** vt jamio, tagu
**Jamaica** n Jamaica
**jangle** vi clochdar
**janitor** n porthor
**January** n Ionawr
**Japan** n Nihon, Japán, Siapán
**Japanese** adj Siapaneaidd ♦ n
Siapanead; (LING) Siapaneg
**jar** n anghytsain; anghydfod ♦ vb
rhygnu
**jar** n jar
**jargon** n ffregod, bregiaith, jargon
**jaundice** n y clefyd melyn
**jaunt** vi gwibio, rhodio ♦ n
gwibdaith
**jaunty** adj llon, bywiog, talog
**javelin** n picell, gwaywffon
**jaw** n gên, cern; (pl) safn
**jay** n sgrech y coed
**jazz** n jas
**jealous** adj eiddigus, cenfigennus,
gwenwynllyd
**jealousy** n cenfigen, eiddigedd
**jeans** n jîns
**jeep** n jip
**jeer** vb gwawdio, gwatwar
**jelly** n jeli
**jellyfish** n slefren fôr
**jeopardy** n perygl, enbydrwydd

**jerk** n plwc, ysgytiad ♦ vb plycio, ygytio
**jerkin** n siercyn, siaced
**jersey** n siersi
**Jerusalem** n Caersalem, Jerwsalem
**jest** n cellwair, ysmaldod ♦ vi cellwair, ysmalio
**Jesus** n Iesu
**jet** n ffrwd, jet; muchudd ♦ vb ffrydio, pistyllio
**jettison** vt taflu (llwyth) dros y bwrdd
**jetty** n jeti, glanfa
**Jew** n Iddew
**jewel** n gem, tlws
**jeweller** n gemydd
**jewellery** n gemwaith, gemau
**Jewish** adj Iddewig
**jib** n hwyl flaen llong, jib
**jib** vi nogio, strancio
**jig** n dawns fywiog, jig
**jig-saw** n jig-so
**jilt** vt siomi cariad
**jingle** n rhigwm, tinc ♦ vb tincial
**job** n tasg, gorchwyl, gwaith
**Job Centre** n Canolfan Gwaith
**jobless** adj diwaith
**jockey** n joci
**jocose** adj cellweirus, direidus, ysmala
**jocular** adj ffraeth, ysmala
**jog** vb loncian
**jogger** n lonciwr
**join** vb cydio, cysylltu, uno, ymuno, asio
**joiner** n asiedydd, saer coed
**joint** n cyswllt, cymal ♦ adj cyd. **j. of meat** darn o gig
**joist** n dist, trawst
**joke** n cellwair, maldod ♦ vb cellwair, ysmalio
**jolly** adj braf, difyr, llawen
**jolt** n ysgytiad ♦ vb ysgytio
**Jordan** n Iorddonen
**jostle** n hergwd ♦ vb gwthio
**jot** n iod, tipyn ♦ vt nodi

**jotter** n nodlyfr
**journal** n newyddiadur
**journalism** n newyddiaduraeth
**journalist** n newyddiadurwr
**journey** n taith, siwrnai ♦ vt teithio
**jovial** adj llon, llawen
**joy** n llawenydd, gorfoledd
**joyful** adj llon, llawen, gorfoleddus
**J.P.** Gwêl **justice of the peace**
**jubilant** adj gorfoleddus
**jubilee** n jiwbili
**Judaism** n Iddewaeth
**judge** n barnwr, beirniad ♦ vb barnu, beirniadu
**judg(e)ment** n barn, brawd, dyfarniad; dedfryd
**judicial** adj barnwrol, ynadol
**judiciary** n barnwyr gwlad, barnwriaeth
**judicious** adj call, synhwyrol, doeth
**jug** n jwg
**juggle** vb siwglo
**juggler** n siwglwr
**juice** n sug, sugn, sudd, nodd
**juicy** adj llawn sudd
**July** n Gorffennaf
**jumble** vb cymysgu, cyboli ♦ n cymysgfa, cybolfa
**jumble sale** n ffair sborion
**jump** vb neidio, llamu ♦ n naid, llam
**jumper** n neidiwr; siwmper
**jumpy** adj ofnus
**junction** n cydiad; uniad; cyffordd
**juncture** n cyfwng, cyswllt
**June** n Mehefin
**jungle** n jyngl, coedwig; drysi
**junior** adj iau, ieuengach; ieuaf. **j. school** n ysgol iau
**junk** n sothach
**jurisdiction** n awdurdod
**juror, juryman** n rheithiwr
**jury** n rheithgor
**just** adj cyfiawn, uniawn, teg ♦ adv yn union; prin, braidd; newydd. **j. now** gynnau(fach)

**justice** *n* cyfiawnder; ynad, ustus.
  **j. of the peace** *n* ynad heddwch
**justify** *vt* cyfiawnhau
**jut** *vi* taflu allan, ymwthio
**juvenile** *adj* ieuanc

# K

**kale** *n* cêl, celys
**kangaroo** *n* cangarŵ
**keel** *n* gwaelod llong, trumbren,
  cilbren
**keen** *adj* craff, llym, awchus, brwd
**keep** *vb* cadw, cynnal ♦ *n* cadw;
  amddiffynfa
**keeper** *n* ceidwad
**keepsake** *n* cofrodd
**kennel** *n* cenel, cwb ci, cwt ci
**kerb** *n* cwrbyn
**kerchief** *n* cadach, neisied, hances,
  macyn
**kernel** *n* cnewyllyn
**kestrel** *n* cudyll
**kettle** *n* tegell
**kettle-drum** *n* tympan
**key** *n* agoriad, allwedd; cywair. **k.**
  **ring**, *n* cylch allweddi. **k. worker** *n*
  gweithiwr allweddol
**keyboard** *n* allweddell
**keyhole** *n* twll clo
**khaki** *adj*, *n* caci
**kick** *vb* cicio, gwingo ♦ *n* cic
**kid** *n* myn; hogyn, plentyn, crwt
**kidnap** *vt* herwgipio
**kidney** *n* aren. **k. beans** *npl* ffa
  dringo, cidnebêns
**kill** *vt* lladd
**killer** *n* lladdwr
**killing** *n* lladd
**kiln** *n* odyn
**kilo** *n* cilo
**kilogram** *n* cilogram
**kilometre** *n* cilomedr
**kilowatt** *n* cilowat
**kin** *n* perthynas, tras, carennydd
**kind** *n* rhyw, rhywogaeth, math

**kind** *adj* caredig
**kindergarten** *n* ysgol feithrin
**kindle** *vb* ennyn, cynnau
**kindly** *adj* caredig, hynaws, tirion
**kindness** *n* caredigrwydd
**kindred** *n* perthynas; perthynasau
  ♦ *adj* perthynol
**king** *n* brenin
**kingdom** *n* teyrnas
**kingfisher** *n* glas y dorlan
**kink** *n* cinc
**kiosk** *n* ciosg, bwth
**kipper** *n* ciper, ysgadenyn hallt
  (neu sych)
**kirk** *n* eglwys (Albanaidd)
**kiss** *vt* cusanu ♦ *n* cusan
**kit** *n* cit, pac
**kitchen** *n* cegin. **k. garden** *n* gardd
  lysiau
**kitchenette** *n* cegin fach
**kite** *n* barcut
**kitten** *n* cath fach ♦ *vb* bwrw
  cathod
**kleptomania** *n* ysfa ladrata
**knack** *n* cnac, medr
**knacker** *n* prynwr hen geffylau,
  nacer
**knapsack** *n* ysgrepan
**knave** *n* cnaf, dihiryn
**knead** *vt* tylino
**knee** *n* glin, pen-lin, pen-glin
**kneel** *vi* penlinio
**knell** *n* cnul
**knickers** *npl* nicers
**knife** (**knives**) *n* cyllell
**knight** *n* marchog ♦ *vt* urddo yn
  farchog
**knighthood** *n* urdd marchog
**knit** *vb* gwau; clymu
**knitting needle** *n* gwaell
**knob** *n* cnap, cnwc; dwrn
**knock** *vb* cnocio, taro, curo ♦ *n*
  cnoc, ergyd
**knot** *n* cwlwm; cymal, cwgn,
  cainc ♦ *vt* clymu
**know** *vb* gwybod, adnabod
**knowing** *adj* gwybodus

**knowingly** adv yn fwriadol
**knowledge** n gwybodaeth
**knowledgeable** adj gwybodus
**knuckle** n cymal, migwrn, cwgn

# L

**label** n llabed, label ♦ vt llabedu, enwi
**labial** adj gwefusol
**labialize** vb gwefusoli
**laboratory** n labordy
**laborious** adj llafurus
**labour** n llafur; gwewyr esgor ♦ vb llafurio. **the L. Party** Y Blaid Lafur. **l. force** n llafurlu
**labourer** n gweithiwr, labrwr
**labyrinth** n drysfa
**lace** n las, les; carrai ♦ vb cau (esgidiau)
**lacerate** vt rhwygo, llarpio, dryllio darnio
**lack** n eisiau, diffyg, gwall ♦ vb bod mewn eisiau
**lackadaisical** adj diynni, llipa
**laconic** adj byreiriog, byr, cwta
**lacquer** n lacer ♦ vb lacro
**lad** n bachgen, hogyn, llanc
**ladder** n ysgol; rhwyg (mewn hosan)
**lade** vt llwytho
**ladies** npl toiledau merched
**ladle** n lletwad, llwy
**lady** n arglwyddes; boneddiges, bonesig
**ladybird** n buwch goch gota
**lag** vi llusgo ar ôl, ymdroi, llercian
**lagging** n ynysydd, lagin
**lagoon** n morlyn, lagŵn
**lair** n gwâl, lloches, ffau
**laity** n lleygwyr
**lake** n llyn
**lamb** n oen ♦ vb bwrw ŵyn, wyna
**lame** n cloff ♦ vt cloffi
**lament** vb galaru, cwynfan, cwyno
**lamentation** n galar, galarnad

**laminate** adj haenog ♦ vb haenogi, lamineiddio, laminadu
**lamp** n lamp, llusern
**lampoon** n dychangerdd, gogangerdd ♦ vb dychanu
**lamppost** n polyn lamp
**lampshade** n lamplen
**lance** n gwaywffon, picell ♦ vt lansio, agor dolur
**lance corporal** n is-gorpral
**land** n tir, gwlad ♦ vb tirio, glanio
**landing** n glaniad, glanio; glanfa; pen y grisiau
**landlady** n perchennog llety, gwraig llety
**landlord** n meistr tir; lletywr, tafarnwr
**landscape** n tirlun
**lane** n lôn, wtre, beidr
**language** n iaith. **l. laboratory** n labordy iaith
**languid** adj egwan, llesg
**languish** vi nychu, dihoeni, llesgáu
**languor** n llesgedd, nychdod
**lank** adj cul, tenau, main, llipa
**lanky** adj meindal
**lantern** n llusern
**lap** n arffed, glin
**lap** vb plygu, lapio ♦ n plyg, tro, cylch
**lap** vb llepian, lleibio
**lapel** n llabed
**lapse** n cwymp, methiant, gwall ♦ vi llithro, cwympo, methu
**larceny** n lladrad
**larch** n llarwydden
**lard** n bloneg ♦ vt blonegu
**larder** n bwtri, pantri
**large** adj mawr, helaeth, eang, maith
**largely** adv gan mwyaf
**lark** n ehedydd
**lark** n sbort, difyrrwch, miri ♦ vi cellwair, prancio
**larva (-ae)** n cynrhonyn, larfa
**laryngitis** n gwddf tost, laringitis
**larynx** n afalfreuant, bocs llais

**lascivious** adj anllad, trythyll, anniwair

**lash** n llach, fflangell ♦ vb llachio, fflangellu; rhwymo

**lass** n llances

**lasso** n dolenraff, lasŵ ♦ vt dolenraffu

**last** adj olaf, diwethaf ♦ adv yn olaf, yn ddiwetha. **at l.** o'r diwedd. **l. night** neithiwr. **l. week** yr wythnos ddiwethaf

**last** vi parhau, para

**latch** n clicied ♦ vt clicedu

**late** adj hwyr, diweddar. **l. developers** plant hwyrgynnydd

**lately** adv yn ddiweddar

**latent** adj dirgel, cudd

**later** adv wedyn, eto, yn ddiweddarach

**lateral** adj ochrol

**latest** adj diweddaraf

**lath** n eisen, dellten

**lathe** n turn

**lather** n trochion ♦ vb seboni, trochioni; golchi

**Latin** adj, n Lladin

**Latin America** n America Ladin

**latitude** n lledred; penrhyddid

**latter** adj diwethaf

**lattice** n dellt, rhwyllwaith

**laud** vt canmol, clodfori, moli

**laudable** adj canmoladwy

**laugh** vb chwerthin ♦ n chwerthiniad

**laughable** adj chwerthinllyd, digrif

**laughing stock** n cyff gwawd

**laughter** n chwerthin

**launch** vb lansio

**launderette** n landret, golchdy

**laundry** n golchdy; dillad golch

**laureate** adj llawryfog

**laurel** n llawryf

**lavatory** n tŷ bach, ymolchfa, ystafell ymolchi

**lavender** n lafant

**lavish** adj hael, afradlon, gwastraffus ♦ vb afradu, gwastraffu

**lavishness** n haelioni, afradionedd

**law** n cyfraith, deddf. **l. and order** cyfraith a threfn. **l. of the land** cyfraith gwlad

**lawful** adj cyfreithlon

**lawgiver** adj deddfroddwr

**lawless** adj digyfraith

**lawlessness** n anghyfraith

**lawn** n lawnt, llannerch. **l. tennis** n tenis (lawnt)

**lawnmower** n peiriant torri porfa

**lawsuit** n cyngaws, cyfraith

**lawyer** n cyfreithiwr, twrnai

**lax** adj llac, esgeulus, diofal

**laxative** n carthlyn

**lay** n cân, cerdd

**lay** vt gosod, dodi; dodwy

**lay** adj lleyg

**layby** n gorffwysfan

**layer** n haen

**laze** vb diogi, segura

**laziness** n diogi

**lazy** adj diog, dioglyd

**lea** n doldir, dôl

**lead** n plwm

**lead** vb arwain, tywys ♦ n blaenoriaeth

**leader** n arweinydd; erthygl flaen

**leadership** n arweinyddiaeth

**leaf** (**leaves**) n deilen, dalen

**leaflet** n taflen

**league** n cynghrair ♦ vi cynghreirio

**leak** n agen, coll ♦ vi gollwng, diferu, colli

**lean** adj main, tenau, cul ♦ n cig coch

**lean** vb pwyso, gogwyddo

**leap** vb neidio, llamu ♦ n naid, llam. **l. year** n blwyddyn naid

**leapfrog** n chwarae naid

**learn** vb dysgu

**learned** adj dysgedig, hyddysg

**learner** n dysgwr

**learning** n dysg, dysgeidiaeth

**lease** n prydles ♦ vt prydlesu

**leasehold** n prydles
**leash** n cynllyfan, tennyn ♦ vt cynllyfanu
**least** adj lleiaf. **at l.** o leiaf
**leather** n lledr
**leave** n cennad, caniatâd
**leave** vb gadael, ymadael
**leaven** n lefain ♦ vt lefeinio
**Lebanon** n Libanus
**lecherous** adj trythyll, anllad
**lechery** n trythyllwch, anlladrwydd
**lectern** n darllenfa
**lecture** n darlith ♦ vb darlithio
**lecturer** n darlithydd
**ledge** n silff, ysgafell; crib
**ledger** n llyfr cyfrifon
**lee** n ochr gysgodol, cysgod gwynt
**leech** n gelen
**leek** n cenhinen
**leer** vi cilwenu
**lees** npl gwaddod, gwaelodion
**left** adj aswy, chwith
**left-handed** adj llawchwith
**left-handedness** n llawchwithedd
**left luggage** n lle cadw bagiau
**leg** n coes
**legacy** n etifeddiaeth, cymynrodd
**legal** adj cyfreithiol, cyfreithlon
**legalize** vb cyfreithloni
**legation** n llysgenhadaeth
**legend** n chwedl
**legible** adj darllenadwy, eglur
**legion** n lleng, llu
**legislate** vi deddfu
**legislation** n deddfwriaeth
**legislative** adj deddfwriaethol
**legitimate** adj cyfreithlon
**leisure** n hamdden
**leisurely** adj hamddenol
**lemon** n lemwn
**lemonade** n diod lemwn, lemonêd
**lend** vt benthyca, rhoi benthyg
**length** n hyd, meithder
**lengthen** vb estyn, hwyhau
**lengthy** adj hir, maith
**leniency** n tiriondeb, tynerwch
**lens** n lens. **concave l.** lens

ceugrwm. **convex l.** lens amgrwm
**Lent** n y Grawys
**lentil** n corbysen, lentil
**leonine** adj llewaidd
**leopard** n llewpart
**leper** n dyn gwahanglwyfus, gwahanglaf
**leprosy** n gwahanglwyf
**less** adj, adv llai
**lessee** n prydlesai
**lessen** vb lleihau
**lesson** n gwers; llith
**lest** conj rhag, rhag ofn, fel na
**let** vt gadael, goddef; gollwng; gosod, rhentu
**lethal** adj marwol, angheuol
**lethargy** n cysgadrwydd, syrthni
**letter** n llythyren; llythyr
**letterbox** n bocs llythyrau
**lettering** n llythreniad
**lettuce** n letysen
**level** n, adj lefel, gwastad ♦ vt lefelu, gwastatáu. **spirit l.** n lefelydd
**level crossing** n croesfan
**level-headed** adj pwyllog
**lever** n trosol
**leveret** n ysgyfarnog ieuanc, lefren
**Levite** n Lefiad
**levity** n ysgafnder, gwamalrwydd
**levy** vt codi, trethu ♦ n treth
**lewd** adj anllad, anweddus
**lexicographer** n geiriadurwr
**lexicon** n geiriadur
**liability** n cyfrifoldeb, rhwymedigaeth
**liable** adj atebol
**liaison** n cyswllt
**liar** n gŵr celwyddog, celwyddgi
**libel** n athrod, enllib ♦ vt athrodi, enllibio
**liberal** adj hael, rhyddfrydig, rhyddfrydol ♦ n rhyddfrydwr
**liberate** vt rhyddhau
**liberation** n rhyddhad
**liberty** n rhyddid
**librarian** n llyfrgellydd

**library** *n* llyfrgell
**Libya** *n* Libya
**licence** *n* trwydded; penrhyddid.
  **driving l.** *n* trwydded yrru
**license** *vt* trwyddedu
**licensed** *adj* trwyddedig
**licentious** *adj* penrhydd, ofer,
  anllad
**lick** *vt* llyfu, llyo; curo
**lid** *n* caead, clawr
**lie** *n* celwydd, anwiredd ♦ *vi* dweud
  celwydd
**lie** *vi* gorwedd
**liege** *adj* ffyddlon, ufudd
**lieutenant** *n* is-gapten; rhaglaw
**life** (**lives**) *n* bywyd, einioes, oes,
  buchedd, hoedl
**lifebelt** *n* nofdorch, gwregys achub
**lifeboat** *n* bad achub
**lifeguard** *n* achubwr
**life insurance** *n* yswiriant bywyd
**life jacket** *n* siaced achub
**lifeless** *adj* difywyd, marw(aidd)
**lifetime** *n* oes, einioes, hoedl
**lift** *vt* codi, dyrchafu ♦ *n* codiad;
  llifft
**ligament** *n* giewyn, gewyn
**light** *n* golau, goleuni ♦ *adj* golau ♦
  *vb* goleuo, cynnau
**light** *adj* ysgafn
**light bulb** *n* bwlb golau
**lighter** *n* goleuydd, taniwr
**light-footed** *adj* ysgafndroed
**light-headed** *adj* penchwiban
**light-hearted** *adj* ysgafnfryd
**lighthouse** *n* goleudy
**lightning** *n* mellt, lluched
**lightning conductor** *n* cludydd
  mellt
**lightship** *n* goleulong
**like** *adj* tebyg, cyffelyb
**like** *vb* caru, hoffi
**likeable** *adj* hoffus; dymunol
**likelihood** *n* tebygolrwydd
**likely** *adj, adv* tebygol, tebyg
**liken** *vt* cyffelybu
**likeness** *n* tebygrwydd

**likewise** *adv* yn gyffelyb, yn yr un
  modd
**lilac** *n* lelog
**lily** *n* lili, alaw
**lily-of-the-valley** *n* lili'r
  dyffrynnoedd
**limb** *n* aelod, cainc
**lime** *n* calch
**limekiln** *n* odyn galch
**limelight** *n* amlygrwydd
**limestone** *n* carreg galch
**limit** *n* terfyn, ffin ♦ *vt* cyfyngu
**limited** *adj* cyfyngedig
**limp** *adj* llipa, ystwyth, hyblyg
**limp** *vi* hercian, cloffi
**limpet** *n* brenigen, llygad maharen
**line** *n* llin, llinell, lein, rhes;
  llinach ♦ *vt* llinellu, rhesu
**lineage** *n* ach, llinach
**linear** *adj* llinellog, llinellaidd,
  llinol, unionlin. **l. equation**
  hafaliad llinol
**linen** *n* lliain
**line-out** *n* lein, llinell
**liner** *n* leiner
**linesman** *n* llumanwr
**linger** *vb* ymdroi, aros
**lingo** *n* iaith ddieithr, cleber
**linguist** *n* ieithydd
**linguistics** *n* ieithyddiaeth
**liniment** *n* ennaint, eli
**lining** *n* leinin
**link** *n* dolen, cyswllt ♦ *vb* cydio,
  cysylltu
**linnet** *n* llinos
**lino** *n* leino
**linseed** *n* had llin, llinad
**lintel** *n* capan drws, lintel
**lion** *n* llew
**lip** *n* gwefus, min, gwefl
**lipstick** *n* minlliw
**liquid** *n* llyn, hylif ♦ *adj* gwlyb,
  hylif
**liquidate** *vb* talu, clirio (dyled),
  dirwyn i ben, diddymu, dileu
**liquidize** *vb* hylifo
**liquor** *n* diod, gwirod

**lisp** n bloesgni ♦ vb siarad yn floesg

**list** n rhestr, llechres ♦ vt rhestru

**list** n gogwydd, goledd ♦ vi pwyso, gwyro, gogwyddo

**listen** vi gwrando

**listener** n gwrandawr

**listless** adj llesg, diynni

**listlessness** n llesgedd

**litany** n litani

**literacy** n llythrynnedd

**literal** adj llythrennol

**literary** adj llenyddol

**literature** n llenyddiaeth

**lithe, lithesome** adj ystwyth, hyblyg

**lithograph** n lithograff

**litigate** vb cyfreithio

**litmus** n litmws

**litre** n litr

**litter** n elorweiy; ysbwriel, gwasarn; torllwyth, tor

**little** adj bach, bychan; mân, ychydig ♦ n ychydig, tipyn

**liturgy** n litwrgi

**live** adj byw, bywiol, bywiog

**live** vi byw

**livelihood** n bywoliaeth

**livelong** adj maith, hirfaith

**lively** adj bywiog, hoyw, heini, sionc

**liven** vb bywiogi

**liver** n iau, afu

**livery** n lifrai

**living** n bywoliaeth; personiaeth

**lizard** n madfall, modrchwilen

**load** n llwyth ♦ vb llwytho

**loaf** (**loaves**) n torth

**loaf** vb ystelcian, sefyllian, diogi

**loafer** n diogyn, segurwr

**loam** n tywotglai, marl, priddglai

**loan** n benthyg, benthyciad

**loath, loth** adj anewyllysgar, anfodlon

**loathe** vt ffieiddio, casáu

**loathsome** adj atgas, ffiaidd

**lobby** n cyntedd, porth, lobi

**lobster** n cimwch

**local** adj lleol. **l. government** n llywodraeth leol

**locality** n lle, safle, ardal, cymdogaeth

**locate** vt lleoli, sefydlu, gosod

**location** n lleoliad

**loch** n llyn

**lock** n clo; llifddor ♦ vb cloi, cau

**lock** n cudyn; (pl) gwallt

**locked** adj ar glo, ynghlo, dan glo

**locker** n cwpwrdd clo

**locomotion** n ymsymudiad

**locomotive** adj ymsymudol ♦ n peiriant rheilffordd

**locust** n locust

**lodge** n lluest, lletty; cyfrinfa ♦ vb lletya

**lodger** n lletywr

**lodging** n, **lodgings** npl lletty

**loft** n taflod, llofft

**lofty** adj uchel, aruchel, dyrchafedig

**log** n cyff, boncyff, pren

**loggerheads** npl benben

**logic** n rhesymeg

**logical** adj rhesymegol

**loin** n llwyn, lwyn

**loiter** vi ymdroi, loetran, sefyllian

**loll** vi gorweddian, diogi

**lollipop** n lolipop

**London** n Llundain

**loneliness** n unigrwydd

**lonely** adj unig

**long** adj, adv hir, maith, llaes

**long** vi hiraethu, dyheu

**longevity** n hirhoedledd, hiroes

**long-headed** adj call, hirben

**longing** n hireath, dyhead

**longitude** n hydred

**longitudinal** adj hydredol

**long sight** n golwg hir

**long-suffering** adj hirymarhous ♦ n hirymaros

**long-term** adj yn y tymor hir

**long-winded** adj hirwyntog

**look** vb edrych, syllu ♦ n

edrychiad, golwg
**looking-glass** n drych
**lookout** n gwyliwr
**loom** n gwŷdd
**loom** vi ymrithio, ymddangos
**loon** n gwirionyn, dihiryn
**loop** n dolen ♦ vb dolennu
**loophole** n dihangdwll
**loose** adj rhydd, llac ♦ vt gollwng
**loosen** vb rhyddhau, llacio
**loot** n anrhaith, ysbail ♦ vb
ysbeilio, anrheithio
**looter** n ysbeiliwr, anrheithlwr
**lop** vt tocio
**lopsided** adj unochrog,
anghymesur, anghyfartal
**lord** n arglwydd ♦ vb
arglwyddiaethu
**lord mayor** n arglwydd faer
**lordship** n arglwyddiaeth
**lore** n dysg, llên, traddodiad
**lorry** n lori. l. driver n gyrrwr lori
**lose** vb colli
**loss** n colled
**lost property office** n swyddfa
eiddo coll
**lot** n coelbren, rhan, tynged. a l.
llawer
**lotion** n golchdrwyth, eli
**lottery** n hapchwarae, raffl
**lotus** n alaw'r dŵr
**loud** adj uchel, croch. l. speaker n
corn siarad
**lounge** n lolfa ♦ vi segura,
gorweddian
**louse** (lice) n lleuen
**lousy** adj lleuog, brwnt
**lout** n lleban, llabwst, delff
**love** n cariad, serch ♦ vt caru
**loveliness** n prydferthwch
**lovely** adj hawddgar, teg, hyfryd
**lover** n cariad, carwr
**loving** adj cariadus, serchog
**loving-kindness** n trugaredd,
cariad
**low** adj isel
**low** vi brefu ♦ n bref (buwch)

**lower** vb gostwng, darostwng, iselu
**lower** vi gwgu, duo, hel cymylau
**lowliness** n gostyngeiddrwydd
**lowly** adj isel, iselfrydig,
gostyngedig
**low tide** n llanw isel; trai
**low water** n trai, distyll
**loyal** adj teyrngar
**loyalty** n teyrngarwch, ffyddlondeb
**lozenge** n losin
**lubricate** vt iro, llithrigo, seimio
**lucid** adj eglur, clir
**luck** n lwc, damwain, hap, ffawd
**lucky** adj ffodus, lwcus
**ludicrous** adj chwerthinllyd,
gwrthun
**lug** vb llusgo, tynnu
**luggage** n clud, bagiau, celfi
**luggage rack** n silff eiddo
**lukewarm** adj claear, llugoer
**lull** vt suo, gostegu ♦ n gosteg
**lullaby** n hwiangerdd
**lumbago** n llwynwst
**lumber** n llanastr, anialwch
**lumber** vb pentyrru; llusgo
**luminous** adj golau, disglair,
llachar
**lump** n lwmp, clamp, clap, talp. l.
sum cyfandaliad
**lunacy** n lloerigrwydd,
gwallgofrwydd
**lunatic** n lloerig, gwallgofddyn
**lunch** vb ciniawa (ganol dydd)
**lunch, luncheon** n byrbryd, cinio
canol dydd
**lung** n ysgyfaint
**lunge** n hergwd, gwth, rhuthr
**lurch** n cyfyngder, dryswch, trybini
♦ vi gwegian
**lure** n hud ♦ vt hudo, denu
**lurid** adj erchyll, erchliw,
fflamgoch
**lurk** vi llercian, llechu
**luscious** adj melys
**lush** adj toreithiog, ffrwythlon
**lust** n chwant, trachwant ♦ vi
trachwantu

**lustre** n gloywder, disgleirdeb, llewyrch
**lusty** adj heini, cryf, pybyr, grymus
**Luxembourg** n Luxembourg
**luxuriant** adj toreithiog, bras, ffrwythlon
**luxurious** adj moethus
**luxury** n moeth, moethusrwydd, amheuthun
**lying** adj celwyddog
**lyre** n telyn gron
**lyric** adj telynegol ♦ n telyneg

# M

**mace** n brysgyll, byr-llsyg
**macerate** vb meddalu, mwydo; nychu, curio
**machine** n peiriant
**machinery** n peiriannau
**mackerel** n macrell
**mackintosh** n cot law
**mad** adj cynddeiriog, gwallgof, gwyllt, ynfyd
**madden** vb gwallgofi, ffyrnigo
**made-to-measure** adj wedi ei dorri gan deiliwr
**madman** n ynfytyn, gwallgofddyn
**madness** n ynfydrwydd, gwallgofrwydd
**madrigal** n madrigal
**magazine** n ystorfa, arfdy; cylchgrawn
**maggot** n cynrhonyn
**magic** adj cyfareddol ♦ n hud, dewiniaeth, swyngyfaredd
**magician** n swynwr, dewin
**magistrate** n ynad
**magnanimous** adj mawrfrydig
**magnet** n magned
**magnetic** n magnetig
**magnificent** adj gwych, ysblennydd
**magnify** vt mawrhau, mwyhau, chwyddo

**magnifying-glass** n chwyddwydr
**magnitude** n maint, maintioli
**magpie** n pi, pia, pioden, piogen
**maid** n merch, morwyn
**maiden name** n enw morwynol
**mail** n y post
**mail** n arfwisg
**maim** vt anafu, anffurfio, llurgunio
**main** n prif bibell; prif gebl; cefnfor. **in the m.** yn bennaf, gan mwyaf
**main** adj pennaf, prif, mwyaf. **m. road** n priffordd, ffordd fawr
**mainland** n y tir mawr
**mainly** adv yn bennaf
**mainstay** n prif gynhaliaeth
**maintain** vt dal, cynnal, maentumio
**maintenance** n cynhaliaeth, gofalaeth
**maize** n indrawn, injan corn
**majesty** n mawrhydi, mawredd
**majestic** adj mawreddog, urddasol
**major** adj mwy, mwyaf, pennaf ♦ n uwchgapten
**majority** n mwyafrif; oedran llawn
**make** vt gwneud, gwneuthur, peri ♦ n gwneuthuriad
**maker** n gwneuthurwr, creawdwr
**making** n gwneuthuriad, ffurfiad
**make-up** n colur
**malady** n drwg, anhwyldeb, dolur
**male** n, adj gwryw
**malevolence** n malais
**malevolent** adj drygnaws, maleisus
**malformation** n camffurfiad
**malice** n malais
**malign** vt enllibio, difrïo, pardduo
**malignant** adj llidiog, adwythig, gwyllt
**mallet** n gordd
**malnutrition** n gwallfaethiad, camluniaeth
**malt** n brag ♦ vb bragu
**maltreat** vb cam-drin
**maltreatment** n camdriniaeth

**mammal** n mamal
**mammoth** n mamoth ♦ adj anferth
**man** (men) n dyn, gŵr
**manacle** n gefyn ♦ vt gefynnu
**manage** vb trin, llywodraethu, rheoli; ymdaro, ymdopi, llwyddo
**manageable** adj hydrin
**management** n rheolaeth, goruchwyliaeth
**manager** n goruchwyliwr, rheolwr
**mandate** n gorchymyn, arch
**mane** n mwng
**mange** n clafr, clefri, brech y cŵn
**manger** n mansier, preseb
**mangle** vt llurgunio
**mangle** n mangl
**manhood** n dyndod
**mania** n gwallgofrwydd, gorawydd
**maniac** n gwallgofddyn
**manifest** adj amlwg ♦ vt amlygu, dangos
**manifesto** n datganiad, maniffesto
**manifold** adj amryw, amrywiol
**manipulate** vt trin, trafod
**mankind** n dynolryw
**manly** adj dynol, gwrol
**manner** n modd; moes
**mannerism** n dullwedd
**mannerly** adj boneddigaidd, moesgar
**manners** npl moesau
**manor** n maenor, maenol
**manse** n tŷ gweinidog, mans
**manservant** n gwas
**mansion house** n trigfan y maer
**manslaughter** n dynladdiad
**mantelpiece** n silff ben tân
**mantle** n mantell ♦ vt mantellu
**manual** adj perthynol i'r llaw ♦ n llawlyfr
**manufacture** n gwaith, nwydd ♦ vt gwneuthur, gwneud
**manure** n tail, gwrtaith, achles ♦ vt teilo, gwrteithio, achlesu
**manuscript** n llawysgrif
**many** adj aml, sawl, llawer. **as m.** cymaint, cynifer. **how m.** sawl

**map** n map
**maple** n masarnen
**mar** vt difetha, andwyo, hagru
**maraud** vb ysbeilio, anrheithio
**marble** n marmor, mynor; marblen
**March** n (mis) Mawrth
**march** vb ymdeithio ♦ n ymdaith
**march** n mers, goror, cyffin
**marchionness** n ardalyddes
**mare** n caseg
**margarine** n margarîn
**margin** n ymyl, cwr, goror
**marigold** n gold Mair, gold
**marine** adj morol ♦ n môr-filwr; llynges
**mariner** n morwr, llongwr, mordwywr
**marital** n priodasol
**maritime** adj morol, arforol
**mark** n nod, marc ♦ vt nodi, marcio, carffu, sylwi
**market** n marchnad ♦ vb marchnata
**maroon** vb rhoi a gadael ar ynys anial
**marquis** n ardalydd
**marriage** n priodas
**married** adj priod
**marrow** n mêr. **vegetable m.** n pwmpen
**marry** vb priodi
**Mars** n Mawrth
**marsh** n morfa, cors, mignen
**marshal** n cadlywydd, marsialydd ♦ vt byddino, trefnu
**mart** n mart
**martial** adj milwraidd, milwrol
**martinet** n disgyblwr llym
**martyr** n merthyr ♦ vt merthyru
**martyrdom** n merthyrdod
**marvel** n rhyfeddod ♦ vi rhyfeddu, synnu
**marvellous** adj rhyfeddol, gwych
**marxism** n marcsiaeth
**marxist** adj marcsaidd
**mascara** n masgara, colur llygaid

**masculine** adj gwryw, gwrywaidd
**mash** n cymysg, stwns ♦ vt
stwnsio
**mask** n mwgwd ♦ vt mygydu,
cuddio
**mason** n saer maen, masiwn,
meiswn
**mass** n pentwr, talp, crynswth,
mas; (pl) y werin
**mass** n offeren
**massacre** n cyflafan ♦ vt cyflafanu
**massive** adj anferth
**mast** n hwylbren
**master** n meistr, athro, capten
(llong) ♦ vt meistroli
**masterpiece** n campwaith,
gorchest
**mastery** n meistrolaeth,
goruchafiaeth
**masticate** vt cnoi, malu
**mastiff** n gafaelgi, cystowci, catgi
**mat** n mat ♦ vt matio, plethu
**match** n matsen
**match** n cymar; priodas;
ymrysonfa, gêm ♦ vb cystadlu;
cyfateb
**matchless** n digymar, digyffelyb
**mate** n cymar, cydymaith; mêt ♦
vt cymharu
**material** adj materol; o bwys ♦ n
defnydd
**materialism** n materoliaeth
**maternal** adj mamol; o du'r fam
**maternity** n mamolaeth
**mathematics** npl mathemateg
**matins** npl boreol weddi, plygain
**matriculate** vb ymaelodi mewn
prifysgol, matricwleiddio
**matrimony** n priodas
**matron** n gwraig briod, meistres,
matron, modron
**matter** n mater; crawn ♦ vi bod o
bwys
**mattock** n caib, matog
**mattress** n matras
**mature** adj aeddfed; mewn oed ♦
vb aeddfedu

**maturity** n aeddfedrwydd
**maul** vt baeddu, pwyo ♦ n sgarmes
**mauve** n lliw porffor, piws
**maxim** n dihareb, gwireb, rheol
**maximum** n uchafswm, uchafrif,
uchafbwynt
**May** n Mai. **M. Day** n Calan Mai
**may** n blodau drain gwynion
**maybe** adv efallai, hwyrach,
dichon
**mayor** n maer
**mayoress** n maeres
**me** pron myfi, mi, fi, i; minnau
**mead** n medd
**meadow** n dôl, gwaun, gweirglodd
**meagre** adj cul, tenau, prin,
tlodaidd, llwm
**meal** n blawd
**meal** n pryd o fwyd
**meals on wheels** npl pryd ar glud
**mean** n cyfrwng, modd; canol;
cymedr
**mean** vt meddwl, golygu, bwriadu
**mean** adj gwael, isel, crintach,
iselwael
**meander** n ystum (afon) ♦ vi
dolennu, troelli, ymdroelli
**meaning** n ystyr, meddwl
**meanness** n cybydd-dod,
crintachrwydd
**means** npl cyfrwng, modd(ion),
cyfoeth. **by all m.** ar bob cyfrif,
wrth gwrs
**meantime, -while** adv yn y
cyfamser
**measles** npl y frech goch
**measure** vt, n mesur
**measurement** n mesur, mesuriad
**meat** n ymborth, bwyd; cig
**mechanic** n peiriannydd
**mechanical** adj peiriannol,
peiriannyddol, mecanyddol
**mechanics** npl mecaneg
**mechanism** n peirianwaith
**medal** n bathodyn, medal
**meddle** vi ymyrryd, busnesa,
ymhél

**media** *npl* cyfryngau
**mediaeval** *adj* canoloesol
**medial** *adj* canol, canolog
**mediate** *vi* canoli, cyfryngu
**medical** *adj* meddygol
**medicine** *n* meddyginiaeth; ffisig, moddion
**mediocre** *adj* canolig, cyffredin
**meditate** *vb* myfyrio
**meditation** *n* myfyrdod
**Mediterranean** *n*: the M. y Môr Canoldir
**medium** *n* canol; cyfrwng ♦ *adj* canol, canolig
**medley** *n* cymysgfa, cybolfa; cymysgedd, cadwyn o alawon
**meek** *adj* llariaidd, addfwyn
**meekness** *n* addfwynder
**meet** *vb* cyfarfod, cwrdd ♦ *adj* addas
**meeting** *n* cyfarfod, cyfarfyddiad
**melancholy** *adj* prudd, pruddglwyfus ♦ *n* pruddglwyf, y felan
**mêlée** *n* ymgiprys, ysgarmes
**mellifluous** *adj* melyslais, melysber
**mellow** *adj* aeddfed, meddal ♦ *vb* aeddfedu
**melody** *n* peroriaeth, melodi
**melt** *vb* toddi, ymdoddi
**member** *n* aelod. M. of Parliament *n* Aelod Seneddol
**membership** *n* aelodaeth
**membrane** *n* pilen, croenyn
**memento** *n* cofarwydd
**memoir** *n* cofiant
**memorable** *adj* cofiadwy, bythgofiadwy
**memorandum** *n* cofnod, cofnodiad
**memorial** *adj* coffadwriaethol ♦ *n* coffadwriaeth; cofeb; deiseb
**memorise** *vt* dysgu ar gof
**memory** *n* cof; coffadwriaeth
**menace** *n* bygythiad ♦ *vt* bygwth
**menagerie** *n* milodfa, sioe (siew) anifeiliaid

**mend** *vb* gwella, cyweirio, trwsio, helpu
**mendacity** *n* anwiredd, celwydd
**mendicant** *adj* cardotaidd, cardotlyd ♦ *n* cardotyn
**menial** *adj* gwasaidd, isel ♦ *n* gwas
**meningitis** *n* llid yr ymennydd
**menstruation** *n* y misglwyf
**mensuration** *n* mesureg
**mental** *adj* meddyliol
**mention** *vt* crybwyll, sôn ♦ *n* crybwylliad
**mentor** *n* cynghorwr, cyfarwyddwr
**menu** *n* bwydlen, arlwy
**mercantile** *adj* marchnadol, masnachol
**mercenary** *adj* ariangar, chwannog i elw ♦ *n* huriwr, milwr cyflog
**merchandise** *n* marsiandïaeth
**merchant** *n* masnachwr, marsiandwr
**merciful** *adj* trugarog, tosturiol
**mercifully** *adv* drwy drugaredd
**merciless** *adj* didrugaredd
**mercuric** *adj* mercurig
**mercury** *n* arian byw, mercwri
**mercy** *n* trugaredd
**mere** *adj* unig, pur, moel, noeth, hollol
**mere** *n* llyn, llwch
**merge** *vb* soddi, suddo, colli, ymgolli, uno
**merger** *n* ymsoddiad, cyfuniad, ymdoddiad, uniad
**meridian** *n* nawn; cyhydedd; anterth
**merit** *n* haeddiant, teilyngdod ♦ *vt* haeddu, teilyngu
**mermaid** *n* môr-forwyn
**merriment** *n* digrifwch, difyrrwch
**merry** *adj* llawen, llon
**merry-go-round** *n* ceffylau bach
**mesh** *n* masgl, magl, rhwydwaith
**mess** *n* saig; llanastr, annibendod ♦ *vb* bwyta; ymhel; maeddu
**message** *n* cenadwri, neges
**messenger** *n* cennad, negesydd

**messieurs** (**Messrs**) *npl* meistri
**metabolism** *n* metaboleg, metabolaeth
**metal** *n* metel ♦ *adj* metelaidd
**metamorphosis** (**-ses**) *n* trawsffurfiad, metamorffosis
**metaphor** *n* trosiad
**metaphysics** *n* metaffiseg
**mete** *vb* mesur
**meteor** *n* seren wib
**meter** *n* mesurydd; medr
**method** *n* trefn, method, dull
**meticulous** *adj* gorfanwl
**metonymy** *n* trawsenwad
**metre** *n* mesur, mydr
**metrical** *adj* mydryddol
**metric system** *n* system fedrig
**metropolis** *n* prifddinas
**mettle** *n* metel, anian, ysbryd
**mew** *vi* mewian
**Mexico** *n* México
**miasma** *n* tawch heintus
**Michaelmas** *n* gŵyl Fihangel
**microbe** *n* trychfilyn, meicrob
**micro-chip** *n* meicro-sglodyn
**microphone** *n* meicroffon, meic
**microscope** *n* chwyddwydr, meicrosgop
**microwave** *n* meicrodon. **m. oven** ffwrn meicrodon
**mid** *adj* canol
**midday** *n* canol dydd, hanner dydd
**middle** *n, adj* canol
**middle-aged** *adj* canol oed
**middling** *adj* canolig, gweddol, symol
**midge** *n* gwybedyn
**midget** *n* corrach
**midnight** *n* canol nos, hanner nos
**midriff** *n* llengig
**midst** *n* canol, plith
**midsummer** *n* canol haf. **M. Day** *n* gŵyl Ifan
**midwife** (**-wives**) *n* bydwraig
**mien** *n* golwg, pryd, gwedd, agwedd
**might** *n* nerth, cadernid, gallu

**mighty** *adj* cadarn, galluog, nerthol
**migrant** *n* mudwr, ymfudwr, crwydrwr ♦ *adj* mudol, crwydrol
**migrate** *vi* symud, mudo
**migration** *n* mudiad, ymfudiad
**milch** *adj* blith, llaethog
**mild** *adj* tyner, tirion, mwyn; gwan, ysgafn
**mildew** *n* llwydi, llwydni
**mildness** *n* tynerwch, tiriondeb, mwynder
**mile** *n* milltir
**mileage** *n* milltiredd
**milestone** *n* carreg filltir
**militant** *adj* milwriaethus
**military** *adj* milwrol
**militate** *vi* milwrio
**milk** *n* llaeth, llefrith ♦ *vt* godro
**milkman** *n* dyn llaeth
**milkshake** *n* ysgytlaeth, llaeth 'di guro
**Milky Way** *n*: **the M.W.** Y Llwybr Llaethog, Caer Wydion
**mill** *n* melin ♦ *vt* melino, malu
**millennium** *n* mil blynyddoedd
**miller** *n* melinydd
**millimetre** *n* milimedr
**milliner** *n* hetwraig
**million** *n* miliwn
**millionaire** *n* miliynydd
**millstone** *n* maen melin
**mime** *n* meim
**mimic** *vt* dynwared, gwatwar
**mimicry** *n* dynwarededd
**mince** *vt* malu ♦ *n* briwgig, briwfwyd
**mind** *n* meddwl, bryd, cof ♦ *vb* gofalu, cofio
**mine** *n* mwynglawdd, pwll
**miner** *n* mwynwr, glöwr
**mineral** *adj* mwynol ♦ *n* mwyn
**mineral water** *n* dŵr pistyll
**mingle** *vb* cymysgu, britho
**mingy** *adj* cybyddlyd, crintach
**miniature** *n* mân ddarlun ♦ *adj* bychan

**minimize** vt lleihau, bychanu
**minimum** n lleiafswm, isafrif
**mining** n mwyngloddiaeth.
**opencast m.** n mwyngloddio brig
**minister** n gweinidog ♦ vb
gwasanaethu, gweinidogaethu
**ministry** n gweinidogaeth,
gweinyddiaeth, gwasanaeth
**minnow** n pilcodyn, pilcyn, sildyn,
silcyn
**minor** adj llai, lleiaf, lleddf; un
dan oed
**minority** n maboed, mebyd;
lleiafrif
**minster** n mynachlog; eglwys
gadeiriol
**minstrel** n clerwr, cerddor
**mint** n bathdy ♦ vt bathu
**mint** n mintys
**minus** adj, pron llai, heb, yn fyr o
♦ n minws
**minute** adj bach, bychan, mân;
manwl
**minute** n munud; cofnod. **m. book**
n llyfr cofnodion
**minx** n coegen, mursen, maeden
**miracle** n gwyrth
**miraculous** adj gwyrthiol
**mirage** n rhithlun, lleurith
**mire** n llaid, llaca, tom, baw
**mirror** n drych ♦ vt adlewyrchu
**mirth** n llawenydd, digrifwch,
afiaith
**mis-** prefix cam-
**misadventure** n anffawd,
damwain
**misanthropist** n dyngasâwr
**misapprehension** n
camddealltwriaeth
**misbehave** vi camymddwyn
**misbehaviour** n camymddygiad
**miscarriage** n erthyliad. **m. of
justice** n aflwyddo cyfiawnder
**miscarry** vi erthylu; aflwyddo;
colli
**miscellaneous** adj amrywiol
**mischance** n anffawd, damwain

**mischief** n drwg, drygioni, direidi
**mischievous** adj drygionus,
direidus
**misconception** n camsyniad,
cam-dyb
**misconduct** n camymddygiad ♦ vb
camymddwyn
**misdeed** n drwgweithred,
camwedd
**misdemeanour** n camwedd,
trosedd
**miser** n cybydd
**miserable** adj truenus, gresynus,
anhapus
**misery** n trueni, gresyni, adfyd
**misfortune** n anffawd, aflwydd
**misgivings** npl amheuon, ofnau
**misguide** vb camarwain
**mishandle** vb cam-drin
**mishap** n anap, anffawd, aflwydd
**misinterpret** vb camesbonio
**misjudge** vb camfarnu, camddeall
**mislead** vb camarwain, twyllo
**misnomer** n camenw
**misprint** n cambrint ♦ vb
camargraffu
**misread** vb camddarllen
**misrepresent** vt camddarlunio,
camliwio
**miss** vt methu, ffaelu, colli ♦ n
meth
**missal** n llyfr offeren
**missile** n saethyn, taflegryn
**missing** adj yn eisiau, yngholl, ar
goll
**mission** n cenhadaeth
**missionary** n cenhadwr ♦ adj
cenhadol
**missive** n llythyr
**misspell** vb camsillafu
**mist** n niwl, nudden; tarth; caddug
**mistake** vt camgymryd, methu ♦ n
camgymeriad, gwall
**mistletoe** n uchelwydd
**mistress** n meistres; athrawes;
Mrs
**mistrust** vt drwgdybio, amau

**misty** *adj* niwlog
**misunderstanding** *n* camddealltwriaeth
**mite** *n* hatling; mymryn, tamaid
**mitigate** *vt* lleddfu, lliniaru, lleihau
**mitre** *n* meitr
**mix** *vb* cymysgu
**mixture** *n* cymysgedd, cymysgfa
**moan** *n, vb* ochain, griddfan, udo
**moat** *n* ffos (castell)
**mob** *n* torf, tyrfa, haid ♦ *vt* ymosod ar, baeddu
**mobile** *adj* symudol, symudadwy; mudol (cemeg)
**mobilize** *vt* dygyfor, byddino
**mock** *vb* gwatwar ♦ *adj* gau, ffug
**mockery** *n* gwatwar; ffug
**mode** *n* modd, dull
**model** *n* cynllun, patrwm ♦ *vt* llunio
**moderate** *adj* cymedrol ♦ *vt* cymedroli
**moderation** *n* cymedroldeb
**modern** *adj* modern, diweddar
**modernize** *vb* moderneiddio
**modest** *adj* gwylaidd; diymhongar
**modesty** *n* gwylder, gwyleidd-dra
**modify** *vt* newid, lleddfu
**modulate** *vb* cyweirio neu reoli llais
**moiety** *n* hanner, hanereg
**moist** *adj* llaith, gwlyb
**moisture** *n* lleithder, gwlybaniaeth, gwlybwr
**moisturizer** *n* lleithydd
**molar** *n* cilddant
**mole** *n* man geni
**mole** *n* gwadd, twrch daear
**mole** *n* morglawdd
**molecule** *n* molecwl ♦ *adj* molecylig
**molehill** *n* pridd y wadd
**molest** *vt* molestu, aflonyddu, blino
**mollify** *vt* meddalu, tyneru, dyhuddo
**mollycoddle** *vb* maldodi

**molten** *adj* tawdd
**moment** *n* moment; pwys, pwysigrwydd
**momentum** *n* momentwm
**monarch** *n* brenin, teyrn, penadur
**monarchy** *n* brenhiniaeth
**monastery** *n* mynachlog, mynachdy
**monastic** *adj* mynachaidd
**Monday** *n* dydd Llun
**monetary** *adj* ariannol
**money** *n* arian, pres
**mongrel** *adj* cymysgryw ♦ *n* mwngrel
**monitor** *n* monitor
**monk** *n* mynach
**monkey** *n* mwnci
**mono-** *prefix* un-
**monogamy** *n* unwreigiaeth
**monoglot** *adj* uniaith ♦ *n* person uniaith
**monolith** *n* maen hir
**monologue** *n* ymson
**monopoly** *n* monopoli
**monosyllable** *n* gair unsill
**monotheism** *n* undduwiaeth
**monotone** *adj, n* unsain, un-dôn
**monotonous** *adj* undonog
**monotony** *n* undonedd, unrhywiaeth
**monsoon** *n* monswn
**monster** *n* anghenfil; clamp ♦ *adj* anferth
**monstrous** *adj* angenfilaidd, anferth, gwrthun
**month** *n* mis
**monthly** *adj* misol ♦ *n* misolyn
**monument** *n* cofadail, cofgolofn
**mood** *n* hwyl, tymer; modd
**moody** *adj* oriog, cyfnewidiol
**moon** *n* lleuad, lloer. **harvest m.** *n* lleuad fedi
**moonlight** *n* golau lleuad
**moonshine** *n* ffiloreg, ffwlbri, lol
**moor** *n* morfa, rhos, gwaun
**moor** *vt* angori, bachu, sicrhau
**moorhen** *n* iâr fach y dŵr**

**moorland** *n* rhostir, gweundir
**mop** *n* mop ♦ *vt* mopio, sychu
**mope** *vi* pendrymu, delwi
**moraine** *n* marian
**moral** *adj* moesol ♦ *n* moeswers, addysg
**morality** *n* moesoldeb
**morals** *npl* moesau
**morass** *n* cors, mignen
**morbid** *adj* afiach
**mordant** *adj* brathog, llym
**more** *adj* mwy, ychwaneg, rhagor ♦ *adv* mwy, mwyach
**moreover** *adv* heblaw hynny, hefyd
**moribund** *adj* ar farw, ar dranc
**morning** *n* bore ♦ *adj* bore, boreol
**Morocco** *n* Moroco
**morose** *adj* sur, sarrug, afrywiog, blwng
**morphology** *n* ffurfianneg, morffoleg
**morrow** *n* trannoeth
**morsel** *n* tamaid, tameidyn
**mortal** *adj* marwol, angheuol ♦ *n* dyn marwol
**mortar** *n* cymrwd, morter; breuan, morter
**mortgage** *n* morgais, arwystl ♦ *vt* morgeisio, arwystlo
**mortify** *vb* marwhau; blino, siomi
**mortise** *n* mortais ♦ *vt* morteisio
**mortuary** *n* marwdy
**mosaic** *adj* brith, amryliw ♦ *n* brithwaith, mosaig
**Moscow** *n* Moscow
**mosque** *n* mosg
**moss** *n* mwswgl, mwsogl
**most** *adj* mwyaf, amlaf
**mostly** *adv* gan mwyaf, fynychaf
**mote** *n* brycheuyn, llychyn
**moth** *n* gwyfyn
**mother** *n* mam. **m.-in-law** *n* mam yng nghyfraith, chwegr
**motion** *n* symudiad, ysgogiad; cynigiad
**motive** *adj* symudol, ysgogol ♦ *n*

cymhelliad, amcan, motif
**motley** *adj* brith, cymysg
**motor** *n* modur
**motor cycle** *n* beic modur
**motorist** *n* modurwr
**motorway** *n* traffordd
**mottle** *vt* britho, brychu
**motto** *n* arwyddair
**mould** *n* pridd, daear, gweryd ♦ *vt* priddo
**mould** *n* mold; delw ♦ *vt* moldio, llunio, delweddu
**mould** *n* llwydni, llwydi
**moulder** *vi* malurio, adfeilio
**moult** *vb* bwrw plu, mudo
**mound** *n* twmpath, clawdd, crug
**mount** *n* mynydd, bryn
**mount** *vb* esgyn, dringo, codi, mynd ar gefn; gosod
**mountain** *n* mynydd
**mountaineer** *n* mynyddwr
**mourn** *vb* galaru
**mournful** *adj* galarus, dolefus, alaethus
**mourning** *n* galar; galarwisg
**mouse** (**mice**) *n* llygoden ♦ *vb* llygota
**moustache** *n* trawswch, mwstas
**mouth** *n* genau, safn, ceg ♦ *vb* cegu, safnu
**move** *vb* symud, syflyd; cymell; cynnig; cyffroi
**movement** *n* symudiad; ysgogiad
**mow** *vt* lladd (gwair) ♦ *n* mwdwl, medel
**MP** *n abbr* AS (aelod seneddol)
**much** *adj* llawer ♦ *adv* yn fawr
**mucilage** *n* glud, llys, llysnafedd
**muck** *n* tail, tom, baw ♦ *vt* tomi, baeddu
**mucus** *n* llys, llysnafedd
**mud** *n* mwd, llaid, llaca, baw
**muddle** *vi* drysu ♦ *n* dryswch
**mug** *n* cwpan, godart
**mulberry** *n* morwydden
**mule** *n* mul, bastart mul
**mullion** *n* post ffenestr

**multi-** *prefix* aml, lluosog
**multifarious** *n* amryfath, lluosog
**multiple** *adj* amryfal ♦ *n* cynhwysrif, lluosrif
**multiplicand** *n* lluosrif, lluosyn
**multiplication** *n* amlhad, lluosogiad, lluosiad
**multiplicity** *n* lluosowgrwydd
**multiply** *vb* amlhau, lluosogi, lluosi
**multi-storey** *adj* aml-lawr
**multitude** *n* lliaws, tyrfa
**mumble** *vb* grymial, myngial
**mummy** *n* mwmi
**mumps** *n* clwy'r pennau, y dwymyn doben
**munch** *vt* cnoi
**mundane** *adj* bydol, daearol
**municipal** *adj* dinesig, bwrdeisiol
**munificent** *adj* hael, haelionus
**munitions** *npl* arfau neu offer rhyfel
**mural** *adj* murol ♦ *n* murlun
**murder** *vt* llofruddio ♦ *n* llofruddiaeth
**murderer** *n* llofrudd
**murky** *adj* tywyll, cymylog, dudew
**murmur** *vb, n* murmur, grwgnach
**muscle** *n* cyhyr, cyhyryn
**muscular** *adj* cyhyrog
**muse** *n* awen, awenydd
**muse** *vi* myfyrio, synfyfyrio
**museum** *n* amgueddfa
**mushroom** *n* madarch
**music** *n* miwsig, cerdd, cerddoriaeth, peroriaeth
**musical** *adj* cerddorol
**musician** *n* cerddor
**mussel** *n* misglen. **mussels** *npl* cregyn gleision
**must** *vb def* rhaid
**mustard** *n* mwstart
**muster** *vb* casglu, cynnull, byddino ♦ *n* cynulliad, mwstwr
**musty** *adj* wedi llwydo, hendrwm, mws
**mutable** *adj* anwadal, cyfnewidiol
**mutate** *vb* treiglo (llythrennau)

**mutation** *n* cyfnewidiad, treiglad
**mute** *adj* mud ♦ *n* mudan
**muteness** *n* mudandod
**mutilate** *vt* anafu, hagru, llurgunio
**mutiny** *n* terfysg, gwrthryfel
**mutter** *vb* myngial, grymial, mwmian
**mutton** *n* cig dafad, cig mollt, cig gwedder
**mutual** *adj* cyd, o boptu, y naill a'r llall
**muzzle** *n* genau, ffroen; pennor ♦ *vt* cau safn, rhoi taw ar
**my** *pron* fy
**myriad** *n* myrdd
**myrmidon** *n* anfadwas, dihiryn
**myrrh** *n* myrr
**myrtle** *n* myrtwydd
**myself** *pron* myfi fy hun
**mysterious** *adj* dirgel, rhyfedd, dirgelaidd
**mystery** *n* dirgelwch
**mystic** *n* cyfriniwr, cyfrinydd
**mystify** *vt* synnu, syfrdanu
**myth** *n* dameg, chwedl, myth
**mythology** *n* chwedloniaeth

# N

**nab** *vb* cipio, dal
**nadir** *n* isafbwynt, ory
**nag** *vb* cecru, ffraeo, cadw sŵn ♦ *n* ceffyl
**nail** *n* hoel, hoelen; ewin ♦ *vt* hoelio. **n. file** *n* ffeil/rhathell ewinedd
**naïve** *adj* diniwed, diddichell, gwirion
**naked** *adj* noeth
**namby-pamby** *adj* merf, merfaidd, llipa
**name** *n* enw ♦ *vt* enwi, galw
**namely** *adv* sef, nid amgen
**namesake** *n* cyfenw
**nanny** *n* nani
**nap** *vi* cysgu, pendwmpian ♦ *n*

cyntun

**nape** n gwar, gwegil

**napkin** n napcyn, cadach, cewyn

**nappy** n cewyn, clwt

**narcotic** adj narcotig ♦ n moddion cwsg

**narrate** vt adrodd (hanes)

**narrative** n hanes, chwedl, stori

**narrow** adj cul, cyfyng ♦ vb culhau, cyfyngu

**nasal** adj trwynol

**nasty** adj cas, brwnt, budr, ffiaidd

**natal** adj genedigol

**nation** n cenedl

**national** adj cenedlaethol

**nationalism** n cenedlaetholdeb

**nationalist** n cenedlaetholwr

**nationality** n cenedl, cenedligrwydd

**nationalization** n gwladoliad

**nationalize** vb gwladoli, cenedlaetholi

**native** n brodor ♦ adj brodorol; cynhenid

**nativity** n genedigaeth

**natural** adj anianol, naturiol

**naturalist** n naturiaethwr

**naturalize** vb naturioli, breinio, cywladu, brodori

**nature** n anian, natur; naturiaeth

**naught** n dim

**naughtiness** n drygioni, direidi

**naughty** adj drwg, drygionus

**nausea** n clefyd y môr; cyfog; ffieidd-dod

**nauseous** adj cyfoglyd, ffiaidd, atgas

**nautical** adj morwrol, mordwyol

**naval** adj llyngesol, morol

**nave** n corff eglwys

**nave** n both, bwl

**navel** n bogail

**navigate** vt morio, mordwyo, llywio

**navvy** n cloddiwr, ceibiwr

**navy** n llynges

**nay** adv na, nage; nid hynny yn

unig

**naze** n trwyn, penrhyn, pentir

**neap** adj, n: **n. tide** nêp, llanw isel

**near** adj, adv, prep agos, ger, gerllaw ♦ vb agosáu, nesu

**nearby** adv gerllaw, yn ymyl

**nearly** adv bron

**nearness** n agosrwydd

**neat** adj del, destlus, twt, trefnus; pur

**nebula** (-ae) n niwlen; niwl sêr

**nebulous** adj niwlog

**necessarily** adv o angenrheidrwydd

**necessary** adj angenrheidiol

**necessitate** vt gorfodi, gwneud yn angenrheidiol

**necessitous** adj anghenus, rheidus

**necessity** n angen, anghenraid, rhaid

**neck** n gwddf, mwnwgl, gwar

**necklace** n mwclis

**necromancy** n dewiniaeth

**nectar** n neithdar

**need** n, vb (bod mewn) angen, eisiau

**needful** adj rheidiol, angenrheidiol

**needle** n nodwydd; gwaell

**needlework** n gwniadwaith

**needless** adj afreidiol, dianghenraid

**nefarious** adj anfad, drygionus, ysgeler

**negation** n nacâd, gwadiad, negyddiad

**negative** adj nacaol, negyddol

**neglect** vt esgeuluso ♦ n esgeulustra

**negligence** n esgeulustod

**negligent** adj esgeulus

**negotiate** vb trafod, trefnu, negodi

**negotiation** n trafodaeth, cyd-drafodaeth

**negro** n dyn du, negro

**neigh** vi gweryru ♦ n gweryriad

**neighbour** n cymydog

**neighbourhood** n cymdogaeth

**neither** *conj* na, nac, ychwaith ♦ *adj, pron* na'r naill na'r llall, nid yr un o'r ddau

**Nemesis** *n* dialedd

**neo-** *prefix* newydd, diweddar

**nephew** *n* nai

**nepotism** *n* neigaredd

**nerve** *n* giewyn, gewyn, nerf ♦ *vt* gwroli

**nervous** *adj* gieuol; nerfus, ofnus

**nest** *n* nyth ♦ *vb* nythu

**nestle** *vb* nythu, gwasgu'n glos at

**nestling** *n* aderynbach, cyw

**net** *n* rhwyd, rhwyden

**net** *adj* union, cywir, net ♦ *vt* rhwydo

**netball** *n* pêl rwyd

**nether** *adj* isaf

**Netherlands** *npl:* **the N.** yr Iseldiroedd

**nettle** *n* danadl ♦ *vt* pigo; llidio

**network** *n* rhwydwaith

**neuralgia** *n* gieuwst

**neurasthenia** *n* nerfwst

**neuritis** *n* newritis

**neurosis** *n* newrosis

**neuter** *adj* diryw

**neutral** *adj* amhleidiol ♦ *n* amhleidydd

**neutrality** *n* newtraliaeth, amhleidiaeth

**neutralize** *vt* dieffeithio, dirymu

**never** *adv* ni ... erioed, ni ... byth

**nevertheless** *adv, conj* eto, er hynny

**new** *adj* newydd. **N. Year** *n* Y Calan, Y Flwyddyn Newydd. **N. York** *n* Efrog Newydd. **N. Zealand** *n* Seland Newydd

**newcomer** *n* newydd-ddyfodiad

**newness** *n* newydd-deb

**news** *n* newydd, newyddion, hanes

**newsagent** *n* gwerthwr papurau newyddion

**newspaper** *n* papur newydd, newyddiadur

**newt** *n* madfall, genau-goeg, modrchwilen

**next** *adj* nesaf ♦ *adv* yn nesaf

**nib** *n* blaen, nib

**nibble** *vb* deintio, cnoi

**nice** *adj* neis, hardd, tlws; manwl, cynnil

**niche** *n* cloer, cilfach

**nickname** *n* llysenw ♦ *vt* llysenwi

**niece** *n* nith

**niggard** *n* cybydd ♦ *adj* cybyddlyd, crintach

**nigger** *n* dyn du (mewn dirmyg)

**nigh** *adj, adv* agos

**night** *n* nos; noson, noswaith. **by n.** liw nos. **dead of n.** cefn nos. **n. club** *n* clwb nos

**nightdress** *n* gŵn nos, coban

**nightfall** *n* y cyfnos, yr hwyr

**nightingale** *n* eos

**nightmare** *n* hunllef

**nil** *n* dim

**nimble** *adj* gwisgi, heini, sionc

**nimbleness** *n* sioncrwydd

**nincompoop** *n* penbwl, gwirionyn

**nine** *adj, n* naw

**nineteen** *adj, n* pedwar (pedair) ar bymtheg, un deg naw

**ninety** *adj, n* deg a phedwar ugain, naw deg

**ninth** *adj* nawfed

**nip** *vb* brathu, cnoi; deifio

**nipple** *n* diden, teth; tethan

**nit** *n* nedden

**nitrate** *n* nitrad

**nitre** *n* neitr

**nitrogen** *n* nitrogen

**nitrous** *n* nitrus

**no** *adj* ni ... neb, dim ♦ *adv* ni, *etc* dim; nac oes, nage, naddo

**nobility** *n* bonedd, urddas, mawredd

**noble** *adj* ardderchog, urddasol, pendefigaidd ♦ *n* pendefig

**nobleman** *n* pendefig

**nobody** *n* neb

**nocturnal** *adj* nosol, gyda'r nos

**nod** *vb* amneidio; pendrymu ♦ *n*

amnaid
**noise** n sŵn, twrf, trwst
**noisome** adj niweidiol, atgas,
ffiaidd
**noisy** adj swnllyd
**nomad** n nomad, crwydrwr ♦ adj
crwydrol
**nom de plume** n ffugenw
**nomenclature** n cyfundrefn enwau
**nominal** adj enwol, mewn enw
**nominate** vt enwi, enwebu
**nomination** n enwebiad
**nominative** adj enwol
**non-** prefix an-, di-
**nonagenarian** n un deng mlwydd
a phedwar ugain
**non-alcoholic** adj dialcahol
**nonce** n: **for the n.** am y tro
**nonchalance** n difrawder,
difaterwch
**nonchalant** adj didaro, difater
**nonconformist** n anghydffurfiwr,
ymneilltuwr
**nonconformity** n anghydffurfiaeth,
ymneilltuaeth
**nondescript** adj anodd ei
ddarlunio, od
**none** pron neb, dim, dim un
**nonentity** n dyn dibwys, neb
**nonplus** vt drysu, dymchwelyd
**nonsense** n lol, dyli, gwiriondeb
**non-violence** n didreisedd
**non-violent** adj di-drais, didrais
**noodle** n gwirionyn, ffwlcyn; nwdl
**nook** n congl, cornel, cilfach
**noon** n nawn, hanner dydd, canol
dydd
**noose** n cwlwm rhedeg, magl
**nor** conj na, nac
**normal** adj rheolaidd, cyffredin,
safonol
**normality** n normalrwydd
**north** n gogledd ♦ adj gogleddol. **N.
Pole** n Pegwn y Gogledd. **N. Sea** n
Môr y Gogledd
**northern** adj gogleddol. **N. Ireland**
n Gogledd Iwerddon

**Norway** n Norwy
**nose** n trwyn ♦ vb trwyno, ffroeni,
gwyntio
**nosebleed** n gwaedlif o'r trwyn
**nosegay** n blodeuglwym, pwysi
**nostalgia** n hiraeth
**nostril** n ffroen
**not** adv na, nac, nad, ni, nid
**notable** adj nodedig, hynod, enwog
**notary** n nodiadur, nodiedydd
**notation** n nodiant
**notch** n rhic, bwlch, hecyn, rhwgn,
rhint
**note** n nod, nodyn ♦ vt nodi, sylwi
**noted** adj nodedig, hynod, enwog
**note pad** n pad ysgrifennu
**notepaper** n papur ysgrifennu
**noteworthy** adj nodedig
**nothing** n dim. **n. at all** dim byd,
dim o gwbl
**notice** n sylw, rhybudd ♦ vt sylwi
**noticeboard** n hysbysfwrdd
**notify** vt hysbysu, rhoi rhybudd
**notion** n tyb, amcan, syniad
**notoriety** n enw gwael
**notorious** adj hynod, carn, rhemp
**notwithstanding** conj er ♦ prep er,
er gwaethaf
**nought** n dim; gwagnod (0)
**noun** n enw
**nourish** vt maethu, meithrin
**nourishing** adj maethlon
**nourishment** n maeth
**novel** adj newydd ♦ n nofel
**novelist** n nofelydd
**November** n Tachwedd
**novice** n newyddian, nofis
**now** adv, conj, n yn awr, yr awron,
yrŵan, weithian, bellach. **just n.**
gynnau. **n. and then** yn awr ac yn
y man
**nowadays** adv yn y dyddiau hyn
**nowhere** adv dim yn unlle
**noxious** adj niweidiol, afiach
**nozzle** n ffroenell
**nuclear** adj niwclear
**nucleus** n cnewyllyn, bywyn

**nude** adj noeth, noeth lymun
**nudge** vt pwnio, penelino
**nugatory** adj ofer, disylwedd, dirym
**nugget** n clap aur
**nuisance** n pla, poendod, budreddi
**null** adj diddim, dirym, ofer
**numb** adj diffrwyth, cwsg ♦ vt fferru, merwino
**number** n nifer, rhif, rhifedi; rhifyn ♦ vt rhifo, cyfrif. **n. plate** n plat rhif car, plat cofrestru
**numeral** n rhifol, rhifnod
**numeration** n cyfrifiad
**numerator** n rhifiadur
**numerical** adj rhifiadol
**numerous** adj niferog, lluosog, aml
**nun** n lleian, mynaches
**nurse** n mamaeth, gweinyddes, nyrs ♦ vt magu, meithrin, nyrsio
**nursery** n magwrfa, meithrinfa
**nurture** n maeth, magwraeth, meithriniad ♦ vt maethu, meithrin
**nut** n cneuen; gwain, gweinell
**nutcracker** n gefel gnau
**nutriment** n maeth
**nutrition** n maeth, maethiad
**nutritious** adj maethlon
**nutshell** n plisgyn (masgl) cneuen
**nuzzle** vb trwyno, turio, ymwasgu
**nylon** n neilon

# O

**oaf** n delff, hurtyn, awff, llabwst
**oak** n derwen; derw
**oakum** n carth, breisgion
**oar** n rhwyf
**oat** n ceirchen, (pl) ceirch
**oatcake** n bara ceirch, teisen geirch
**oath** n llw
**oatmeal** n blawd ceirch
**obdurate** adj caled, cyndyn,

ystyfnig, anhyblyg
**obedience** n ufudd-dod
**obedient** adj ufudd
**obese** adj tew, corfful
**obey** vb ufuddhau
**obituary** n marwgoffa
**object** n gwrthrych; amcan ♦ vb gwrthwynebu
**objection** n gwrthwynebiad
**objectionable** adj annymunol
**objective** adj gwrthrychol ♦ n amcan, nod
**obligation** n dyled, rhwymau
**oblige** vt rhwymo; boddio; gorfodi
**obliging** adj caredig, cymwynasgar
**oblique** adj lleddf, gŵyr, ar osgo
**obliterate** vt dileu
**oblivion** n angof, ebargofiant
**oblong** adj hirgul ♦ n oblong
**obnoxious** adj atgas, ffiaidd
**obscene** adj serth, anllad, anniwair, brwnt
**obscure** adj tywyll; anhysbys ♦ vt tywyllu
**obsequious** adj gwasaidd, cynffongar
**observation** n sylw; sylwadaeth
**observatory** n arsyllfa
**observe** vb sylwi, arsyllu; cadw
**observer** n sylwedydd, arsyllwr
**obsolete** adj anarferedig, ansathredig
**obstacle** n rhwystr, atalfa
**obstinate** adj cyndyn, ystyfnig, gwrthnysig
**obstreperous** adj trystiog, afreolus
**obstruct** vt cau, tagu; rhwystro, lluddio
**obtain** vt cael, caffael, ennill
**obtrude** vb gwthio ar, ymwthio
**obtrusive** adj ymwthgar
**obtuse** adj pŵl, di-fin, hurt. **o. angle** ongl aflem
**obvious** adj eglur, amlwg
**occasion** n achlysur ♦ vt achlysuro
**occasional** adj achlysurol, anaml

**occidental** *adj* gorllewinol
**occult** *adj* cudd, dirgel, cêl, cyfrin
**occupation** *n* gwaith,
galwedigaeth; meddiant
**occupy** *vt* meddu, meddiannu;
llenwi; dal
**occur** *vi* digwydd; taro i'r meddwl
**occurrence** *n* digwyddiad
**ocean** *n* môr, cefnfor, cyfanfor,
eigion
**o'clock** *adv* o'r gloch
**octagon** *n* wythongl
**octave** *n* wythawd, octef
**octavo** *adj* wythblyg ♦ *n* llyfr
wythblyg
**October** *n* Hydref
**octogenarian** *n* gŵr pedwar ugain
mlwydd oed
**odd** *adj* od, hynod. **o. number** odrif
**odds** *npl* ots, gwahaniaeth;
mantais
**ode** *n* awdl
**odious** *adj* atgas, cas, ffiaidd
**odium** *n* atgasrwydd;
gwaradwydd; bai
**odour** *n* arogl, aroglau, sawr
**of** *prep* o; gan; am; ynghylch. **o.
course** wrth gwrs
**off** *adv* ymaith, i ffwrdd ♦ *prep*
oddi, oddi wrth, oddi ar. **o. and
on** yn awr ac yn y man
**offal** *n* syrth, gwehilion, perfedd
**offence** *n* tramgwydd, trosedd,
camwedd
**offend** *vb* tramgwyddo, troseddu,
pechu; digio
**offender** *n* troseddwr
**offensive** *adj* tramgwyddus, atgas,
ffiaidd; ymosodol
**offer** *vb* cynnig, cyflwyno; offrymu
♦ *n* cynnig
**offering** *n* offrwm, aberth
**office** *n* swydd; swyddfa
**officer** *n* swyddog, swyddwr
**official** *adj* swyddogol ♦ *n* swyddog
**officiate** *vi* gweinyddu
**officious** *adj* ymyrgar, busneslyd

**offside** *n* camochr, camsefyll ♦ *vb*
camochri, camsefyll
**offspring** *n* hiliogaeth, epil, hil,
plant
**oft, often** *adv* yn aml, yn fynych
**ogle** *vb* cilwenu, ciledrych
**ogre** *n* anghenfil, bwystfil, cawr
**oh** *excl* O!
**oil** *n* olew, oel ♦ *vt* iro, oelio
**oil rig** *n* llwyfan olew
**ointment** *n* ennaint, eli
**okay** *excl* popeth yn iawn
**old** *adj* hen, oedrannus. **of o.** gynt.
**o. age** henaint, henoed. **o. and
infirm** hen a methedig. **o.-
fashioned** *adj* henffasiwn, od. **o.
stager** *n* hen law
**olive** *n* olewydden
**omelette** *n* crempog wyau
**omen** *n* argoel, arwydd,
rhagarwydd
**ominous** *adj* argoelus, bygythiol
**omission** *n* gwall
**omit** *vt* gadael allan, esgeuluso
**on** *prep* ar, ar warthaf ♦ *adv*
ymlaen
**once** *adv* unwaith; gynt
**one** *adj, n* un. **o.-way** *adj* unffordd
(*street, traffic*)
**onion** *n* wynwynyn, wnionyn
**only** *adj* unig ♦ *adv* yn unig; ond
**onset** *n* ymosodiad, cyrch;
cychwyn
**onslaught** *n* ymosodiad, rhuthr,
cyrch
**onus** *n* baich, dyletswydd,
cyfrifoldeb
**onward** *adj, adv*, **onwards** *adv*
ymlaen
**ooze** *n* llaid, llysnafedd ♦ *vi*
chwysu
**opaque** *adj* afloyw, tywyll
**open** *adj* agored ♦ *vb* agor,
ymagor
**open-air** *n, adj* awyr agored
**opencast** *n* (*coal*) (glo) brig
**opening** *n* agoriad, agorfa

**operate** vb gweithredu, gweithio
**operation** n gweithrediad; gweithred, triniaeth lawfeddygol
**operator** n gweithredydd, trafodwr
**opiate** n cysglyn
**opinion** n tyb, meddwl, barn, opiniwn
**opponent** n gwrthwynebydd
**opportune** adj amserol, cyfleus
**opportunity** n cyfle, egwyl
**oppose** vt gwrthwynebu, cyferbynnu
**opposite** adj, adv, prep gwrthwyneb, cyferbyn
**opposition** n gwrthwynebiad, gwrthblaid
**oppress** vt gorthrymu, llethu
**optician** n optegydd
**optimism** n optimistiaeth
**optimist** n optimist
**option** n dewisiad, dewis
**or** conj neu, ai, ynteu, naill ai
**oracle** n oracl
**oral** adj geneuol, llafar, anysgrifenedig
**orally** adv ar lafar
**orange** n oren, oraens ♦ adj melyngoch
**oration** n araith, anerchiad
**orator** n areithiwr, areithydd
**orb** n pêl, pelen, pellen; y llygad
**orbit** n rhod, tro, cylchdro, chwyldro
**orchard** n perllan
**orchestra** n cerddorfa
**ordain** vt ordeinio, urddo
**ordeal** n prawf llym
**order** n trefn; gorchymyn, archeb; urdd ♦ vb ordeinio, trefnu, gorchymyn; archebu; urddo. **in o. that** er mwyn
**orderly** adj trefnus ♦ n gwas milwr
**ordinal** adj trefnol
**ordinarily** adv fel rheol
**ordinary** adj cyffredin, arferol
**ordination** n ordeiniad, urddiad
**ore** n mwyn

**organ** n organ, offeryn
**organist** n organydd
**organization** n trefn; cyfundrefn; trefniadaeth
**organize** vb trefnu
**organized** adj trefnus. **o. by** trefnwyd gan
**organizer** n trefnydd
**orgy** n gloddest, cyfeddach
**oriental** adj dwyreiniol ♦ n dwyreiniwr
**orientate** vb cyfeirio
**orifice** n genau, ceg, agorfa
**origin** n dechreuad, tarddiad
**original** adj, n gwreiddiol
**originality** n gwreiddioldeb
**originate** vb dechrau, tarddu
**ornament** n addurn ♦ vt addurno
**ornate** adj addurnedig, mawrwych
**ornithology** n adaryddiaeth, adareg
**orphan** adj, n amddifad
**orthodox** adj uniongred
**orthography** n orgraff
**oscillate** vb siglo, dirgrynu, osgiladu
**ostensible** adj ymddangosiadol, proffesedig
**ostentation** n rhodres
**ostentatious** adj rhodresgar
**ostracize** vt diarddel, alltudio
**ostrich** n estrys
**other** adj, pron arall, llall, amgen
**otherwise** adv amgen
**otter** n dyfrgi, dwrgi
**ounce** n owns
**our** pron ein, ein ... ni
**oust** vt disodli
**out** adv allan, i maes
**outcast** n alltud, digartref, gwrthodedig
**outcome** n canlyniad, ffrwyth
**outcrop** n brig, cribell ♦ vb brigo
**outcry** n gwaedd; dadwrdd; gwrthdystiad
**outdo** vt rhagori ar, trechu
**outdoor** adj yn yr awyr agored

**outer** adj allanol, nesaf allan, cyrion

**outing** n pleserdaith, gwibdaith

**outlandish** adj dieithr, estronol, anghysbell, diarffordd

**outlast** vb goroesi

**outlaw** n herwr

**outlay** n traul, cost

**outlet** n allfa

**outline** n amlinelliad, braslun; amlinell ♦ vb amlinellu

**outlive** vb goroesi

**outlook** n rhagolwg, argoel; golygfa

**outset** n dechrau, dechreuad

**outside** n tu allan, tu faes ♦ adj, adv allan(ol), oddi allan ♦ prep tu allan i, tu faes i

**outside-forward** n blaenwr mas

**outside-half** n maswr

**outside-left** n asgellwr chwith

**outside-right** n asgellwr de

**outskirts** npl cyrrau, maestrefi

**outstanding** adj amlwg; dyledus

**outward** adj allanol

**outwards** adv tuag allan

**outweigh** vt gorbwyso

**oval** adj hirgrwn

**ovary** n wygell, wyfa, ofari

**ovation** n cymeradwyaeth

**oven** n ffwrn, popty

**over** prep uwch, tros ♦ adv gor, rhy, tra

**overall** adj o ben i ben ♦ n troswisg

**overbearing** adj gormesol

**overcast** adj cymylog

**overcharge** vt gorbrisio, codi gormod

**overcoat** n cot fawr/uchaf

**overcome** vt gorchfygu, trechu, cael y gorau ar

**overdo** vb gorwneud

**overflow** n gorlif(iad) ♦ vb gorlifo

**overhead** adj, adv uwchben

**overheat** vi gorboethi

**overload** vb gorlwytho

**overlook** vb edrych dros; esgeuluso

**overnight** adv dros nos

**overpopulate** vb gorboblogi

**overpower** vb trechu

**overrun** vb goresgyn

**overseas** adv tramor, dros y môr

**overtake** vt goddiweddyd

**overthrow** n dymchweliad ♦ vt dymchwelyd

**overture** n cynnig; agorawd

**overturn** vt troi, dymchwelyd

**overwhelm** vt llethu, gorlethu

**overwork** vb gorweithio

**owe** vt bod mewn dyled

**owl** n tylluan, gwdihŵ

**own** adj eiddo dyn ei hun, priod ♦ vt meddu; arddel, addef

**owner** n perchen, perchennog

**ox** (-en) n ych, eidion

**oxide** n ocsid

**oxygen** n ocsigen

**oyster** n llymarch, wystrysen

# P

**pace** n cam, camre; cyflymdra ♦ vb camu, cerdded

**pacific** adj heddychol, tawel

**Pacific Ocean** n Môr Tawel

**pacifism** n heddychiaeth

**pacifist** n heddychwr

**pacify** vt heddychu, tawelu

**pack** n pac, swp, pwn ♦ vb pacio, pynio

**package** n pecyn, bwndel, sypyn

**packed lunch** n tocyn, pryd wedi ei bacio

**packet** n sypyn, paced

**pact** n cyfamod, cynghrair

**pad** n pad ♦ vt padio

**paddle** n padl, rhodl, rhwyf ♦ vb rhodli, padlo

**paddling pool** n pwll padlo

**paddock** n marchgae, cae bach

**padlock** n clo clap, clo clwt, clo

egwyd
**pagan** *n* pagan ♦ *adj* paganaidd
**page** *n* tudalen
**pageant** *n* pasiant
**pail** *n* ystwc, crwc, bwced
**pain** *n* poen, gwayw, dolur ♦ *vt* poeni
**painful** *adj* poenus
**painkiller** *n* lleddfydd poen, lladdwr poen, dofydd poen
**painstaking** *adj* gofalus, trylwyr, diwyd
**paint** *n* paent, lliw ♦ *vt* peintio, lliwio
**painter** *n* peintiwr; arlunydd
**painting** *n* llun, darlun
**pair** *n* pâr, dau, cwpl ♦ *vb* paru
**Pakistan** *n* Pakistan
**palace** *n* plas, palas, palasty
**palaeo-, paleo-** *prefix* hen, hynafol
**palatable** *adj* archwaethus, blasus
**palate** *n* taflod y genau; blas, archwaeth
**palatial** *adj* palasaidd, gwych
**palaver** *n* cleber, baldordd ♦ *vb* clebran, baldorddi
**pale** *adj* gwelw, llwyd, glas, gwelwlas ♦ *vb* gwelwi
**pale** *n* pawl, cledr; clawdd, ffin
**Palestine** *n* Palestina
**palisade** *n* palis, gwalc
**pall** *vb* diflasu
**pallet** *n* gwely gwellt, matras
**pallid** *adj* gwelw, llwyd
**pallor** *n* gwelwedd
**palm** *n* palf, cledr llaw ♦ *vt* palfu
**palm** *n* palmwydden. **P. Sunday** Sul y Blodau
**palpable** *adj* amlwg, dybryd, teimladwy
**palpitate** *vi* curo, dychlamu
**palsy** *n* parlys ♦ *vt* parlysu, diffrwytho
**paltry** *adj* distadl, gwael, pitw
**pamper** *vt* mwytho, maldodi
**pamphlet** *n* pamffled, llyfryn
**pan-** *prefix* oll-

**pan** *n* padell
**pancake** *n* crempog, cramwythen, ffroisen
**pandemonium** *n* dadwrdd, terfysg, mwstwr
**pander** *vb* porthi, gweini
**pane** *n* cwar, cwarel, paen
**panegyric** *n* molawd
**panel** *n* panel
**pang** *n* gloes, gwasgfa, brath, gwayw
**panic** *n* dychryn, panig
**pansy** *n* trilliw, llysiau'r Drindod
**pant** *vi* dyheu
**pantaloons** *npl* llodrau
**panties** *npl* pantos
**pantomime** *n* pantomeim
**pantry** *n* bwtri, pantri
**pants** *npl* pants
**papacy** *n* pabaeth
**papal** *adj* pabaidd
**paper** *n* papur ♦ *vb* papuro. **blotting p.** *n* papur sugno. **tissue p.** *n* papur sidan. **brown p.** *n* papur llwyd
**paperback** *n* llyfr clawr meddal
**paperclip** *n* clip papur
**papist** *n* pabydd
**papyrus** (-i) *n* papurfrwyn
**par** *n* cyfartaledd, llawn werth
**parable** *n* dameg
**parachute** *n* parasiwt
**parade** *n* rhodfa; rhodres, rhwysg
**paradise** *n* paradwys, gwynfa, gwynfyd
**paradox** *n* gwrthddywediad, paradocs
**paradoxical** *adj* paradocsaidd
**paradoxically** *adv* yn baradocsaidd
**paraffin** *n* paraffin
**paragraph** *n* paragraff
**parallel** *adj* cyfochrog, cyflin, paralel
**paralyze** *vt* parlysu, diffrwytho
**paralysis** *n* parlys
**paralytic** *adj*, *n* claf o'r parlys
**paramount** *adj* pen, pennaf, prif

**paramour** n gordderch
**parapet** n canllaw, rhagfur
**paraphernalia** npl meddiannau, taclau, celfi, petheuach
**paraphrase** n aralleiriad ♦ vt aralleirio
**parasite** n un yn byw ar gefn un arall, cynffonnwr
**parcel** n parsel, swp, sypyn
**parch** vb crasu, deifio, golosgi, sychu
**parched** adj cras, crasboeth
**parchment** n memrwn
**pardon** n maddeuant, pardwn ♦ vt maddau, pardynu
**parent** n tad neu fam, (pl) rhieni
**parenthesis** (-ses) n sangiad, ymadrodd rhwng cromfachau
**pariah** n dyn ysgymun
**parings** npl pilion, creifion
**Paris** n Paris
**parish** n plwyf ♦ adj plwyf, plwyfol
**parishioner** n plwyfolyn, (pl) plwyfolion
**parity** n cydraddoldeb, cyfartaledd
**park** n parc, cae, coetgae ♦ vb parcio
**parking meter** n amserydd parcio, rheolydd parcio
**parking ticket** n tocyn parcio
**parlance** n ymadrodd, iaith
**parliament** n senedd
**parliamentary** adj seneddol
**parlour** n parlwr
**parochial** adj plwyfol
**parody** n parodi ♦ vb gwatwar, dynwared
**parole** n gair, addewid, parôl
**parricide** n tadladdiad; tadleiddiad
**parrot** n parot, perot
**parry** vt osgoi, gochelyd, troi heibio
**parse** vt dosbarthu
**parsimonious** adj crintach, cybyddlyd
**parsimony** n crintachrwydd
**parsley** n persli

**parsnip** n panasen
**parson** n person, offeiriad
**part** n rhan; parth; plaid ♦ vb rhannu, parthu; gwahanu; ymadael
**partake** vb cyfrannu, cyfranogi
**partial** adj rhannol; pleidiol, tueddol
**participate** vb cyfranogi
**participle** n rhangymeriad
**particle** n mymryn, gronyn; geiryn
**particular** adj neilltuol, penodol; manwl ♦ n pwnc, (pl) manylion
**parting** n ymadael
**partisan** n pleidiwr
**partition** n canolfur, gwahanfur, palis
**partly** adv mewn rhan, yn rhannol
**partner** n partner; cymar
**partridge** n petrisen
**part-time** adj rhanamser
**party** n plaid; parti, mintai
**pass** vb myned heibio, llwyddo, pasio; treulio, bwrw ♦ n cyflwr, sefyllfa; bwlch; trwydded. **to p. away** vb marw. **reverse p.** n pas wrthol
**passable** adj y gellir mynd heibio iddo; purion
**passage** n tramwyfa; mordaith; cyfran
**passenger** n teithiwr
**passing** n ymadawiad, tranc, pasio ♦ adj yn pasio, diflannol
**passion** n dioddefaint; gwŷn, nwyd
**passionate** adj angerddol, nwydwyllt
**passive** adj goddefol
**Passover** n y Pasg
**passport** n trwydded deithio, pasbort
**past** adj, n gorffennol ♦ prep wedi ♦ adv heibio
**paste** n past ♦ vt pastio, gludio
**pastern** n egwyd
**pasteurize** vb pasteureiddio
**pasteurized** adj wedi ei

basteureiddio
**pastime** n difyrrwch, adloniant
**pastor** n bugail (eglwys), gweinidog
**pastoral** adj bugeiliol ♦ n bugeilgerdd
**pastry** n pasteiod, pasteiaeth, tarten; crwst
**pasture** n porfa ♦ vb porfelu, pori
**pasty** n pastai
**pat** vt patio, pratio, canmol ♦ adj parod, cymwys, priodol
**patch** n clwt, darn ♦ vt clytio
**patchwork** n clytwaith
**paten** n plat cymundeb
**patent** adj agored, cyhoedd, amlwg; breintiedig ♦ n breintlythyr
**paternal** adj tadol
**paternoster** n pader
**path** n llwybr
**pathetic** adj gresynus, pathetig
**pathological** adj patholegol
**pathos** n teimlad, dwyster
**patience** n amynedd
**patient** adj amyneddgar, dioddefus ♦ n dioddefydd, claf
**patriarch** n patriarch
**patrimony** n treftadaeth; gwaddol
**patriot** n gwladgarwr
**patriotic** adj gwladgarol
**patrol** n gwyliadwriaeth, gwylfa, patrôl
**patron** n noddwr
**patronage** n nawdd, nawddogaeth
**patronize** vt noddi, nawddogi
**patronizing** adj nawddogol
**patronymic** n tadenw
**patter** vb curo (fel glaw ar ffenestr)
**patter** vb padera ♦ n clebar, siaradach
**pattern** n patrwm, cynllun
**paucity** n prinder
**paunch** n bol, cest
**pauper** n dyn tlawd, tlotyn
**pause** n saib, seibiant, hoe ♦ vi

aros, sefyll, ymbwyllo
**pave** vt palmantu
**pavement** n palmant, pafin
**pavilion** n pabell, pafiliwn
**paw** n palf, pawen ♦ vb palfu, pawennu
**pawky** adj direidus
**pawn** n gwystl, (CHESS) gwerin ♦ vt gwystlo
**pay** vb talu ♦ n tâl, cyflog, pae, hur. **back p.** ôl-dâl
**payment** n taliad, tâl
**pea** n pysen
**peace** n heddwch, tangnefedd ♦ excl gosteg!, ust!
**peaceful** adj heddychol, tangnefeddus, llonydd
**peach** n eirinen wlanog
**peacock** n paun
**peak** n pig; crib, copa; uchafbwynt
**peal** n sain clychau; twrf (taran) ♦ vb canu
**peanut** n cneuen ddaear
**pear** n gellygen
**pearl** n perl
**peasant** n gwladwr, gwerinwr
**peasantry** n gwerin
**peat** n mawn
**pebble** n carreg lefn, cerrigyn, gröyn
**peck** vb pigo, cnocellu ♦ n cnoc, pigiad
**peculiar** adj priod, priodol; hynod
**peculiarity** n hynodrwydd
**pecuniary** adj ariannol
**pedagogue** n athro plant, ysgolfeistr
**pedal** n pedal ♦ vb pedalu
**pedant** n pedant
**pedantic** adj pedantig
**peddle** vb pedlera
**pedestal** n troed, bôn, gwaelod
**pedestrian** adj ar draed, pedestrig ♦ n gŵr traed, cerddwr. **p. crossing** n croesfan
**pedigree** n ach, achau, bonedd

**pedlar** *n* pedler

**pee** *n* pisiad ♦ *vb* pisio

**peel** *n* pil, croen, rhisgl ♦ *vb* pilio, plicio, crafu

**peep** *vi* cipedrych, sbio ♦ *n* cipolwg, cip

**peer** *vi* ciledrych, syllu

**peer** *n* gogyfurdd, cydradd; pendefig

**peevish** *adj* anniddig, blin, piwis

**peg** *n* hoel bren, peg ♦ *vt* pegio

**Peking** *n* Peking

**pelf** *n* golud

**pellet** *n* peled, pelen, haelsen

**pelt** *vt* lluchio, taflu, peledu, baeddu

**pelvis** *n* pelfis

**pen** *n* pin, ysgrifbin ♦ *vt* ysgrifennu

**pen** *n* lloc, ffald, cwt ♦ *vt* ffaldio, llocio

**penal** *adj* penydiol

**penalize** *vb* cosbi

**penalty** *n* cosb, cosbedigaeth. **p. (kick)** *n* cic gosb

**penance** *n* penyd

**pence** *npl* ceiniogau, pres

**pencil** *n* pwyntil, pensel, pensil. **p. sharpener** *n* naddwr pensiliau

**pendant** *n* tlws

**pending** *prep* hyd, nes, yn ystod

**pendulous** *adj* yn hongian, yn siglo

**pendulum** *n* pendil

**penetrate** *vb* treiddio; dirnad

**penfriend** *n* cyfaill llythyru

**penguin** *n* pengwin

**penicillin** *n* penisilin

**peninsula** *n* gorynys

**penis** *n* cala, pidyn

**penitence** *n* edifeirwch

**penitent** *adj* edifar, edifarus, edifeiriol

**penitentiary** *n* carchar

**penknife** (**-knives**) *n* cyllell boced

**pen name** *n* ffug enw

**pennant, pennon** *n* penwn, banner

**penniless** *adj* heb geiniog

**penny** (**pence, pennies**) *n* ceiniog

**pension** *n* blwydd-dâl, pensiwn

**pensioner** *n* pensiynwr

**pensive** *adj* synfyfyriol, meddylgar

**pent** *adj* wedi ei gau i mewn, caeth

**Pentateuch** *n* pumllyfr Moses

**penult** *n* goben

**people** *n* pobl, gwerin ♦ *vt* pobli, poblogi

**pepper** *n* pupur

**peppermint** *n* mintys poethion; botwm gwyn

**per** *prep* trwy, wrth, yn ôl

**peradventure** *adv* efallai

**perceive** *vt* canfod, gweld, dirnad, deall

**percentage** *n* hyn a hyn y cant, canran

**perceptible** *adj* canfyddadwy

**perception** *n* canfyddiad, canfod

**perceptive** *adj* yn gallu dirnad

**perch** *n* perc; clwyd ♦ *vb* clwydo

**perchance** *adv* efallai, hwyrach

**percolate** *vb* hidlo, diferu

**percussion** *n* trawiad, gwrthdrawiad. **p. band** seindorf daro

**peremptory** *adj* pendant, awdurdodol

**perennial** *adj* drwy'r flwyddyn; bythol, lluosflwydd

**perfect** *adj* perffaith ♦ *vt* perffeithio

**perfection** *n* perffeithrwydd

**perfectly** *adv* yn berffaith

**perfervid** *adj* brwd, tanbaid

**perfidy** *n* brad, dichell, ffalster

**perforate** *vt* tyllu

**perforated** *adj* tyllog

**perforation** *n* twll

**perforce** *adv* o orfod, drwy drais

**perform** *vb* cyflawni; chwarae, perfformio

**performance** *n* perfformiad

**performer** *n* perfformiwr

**perfume** *n* perarogl, persawr ♦ *vt* perarogli

**perfunctory** *adj* o raid, diofal, esgeulus

**perhaps** *adv* efallai, hwyrach, ond odid, dichon

**peril** *n* perygl, enbydrwydd

**perimeter** *n* amfesur, perimedr

**period** *n* cyfnod; cyfadran (miwsig); diweddnod; misglwyf

**periodic** *adj* cyfnodol

**periodical** *n* cyfnodolyn

**peripatetic** *adj* crwydrol, cylchynol, peripatetig

**peripheral** *adj* ymylol

**periphery** *n* ymylon, cylchfesur

**periphrastic** *adj* cwmpasog

**perish** *vi* colli, trengi, marw, darfod; llygru

**periwinkle** *n* gwichiad

**perjure** *vt:* **p. oneself** tyngu anudon

**perjury** *n* anudon, anudoniaeth

**perk** *n* mantais. **to p. up** bywhau, adfywio

**perky** *adj* bywiog, eofn, hyf

**permanent** *adj* parhaol, arhosol, sefydlog

**permeate** *vt* treiddio, trwytho

**permissible** *adj* wedi ei ganiatáu

**permission** *n* caniatâd, cennad

**permissive** *adj* goddefol. **the p. society** y gymdeithas oddefol

**permit** *vb* caniatáu ♦ *n* trwydded

**peroration** *n* diweddglo araith, perorasiwn

**perpendicular** *adj* syth, unionsyth

**perpetrate** *vt* cyflawni (rhyw ddrwg)

**perpetual** *adj* parhaol, parhaus, bythol

**perpetuate** *vt* parhau, anfarwoli

**perplex** *vt* drysu, cythryblu, tralodi

**persecute** *vt* erlid

**persevere** *vi* dyfalbarhau

**persist** *vi* dal ati; mynnu, taeru, dyfalbarhau

**persistent** *adj* dyfal, taer, cyndyn, parhaus

**person** *n* person

**personable** *adj* golygus, prydweddol, hawddgar

**personal** *adj* personol. **p. assistant** *n* cynorthwyydd personol

**personality** *n* personoliaeth

**personally** *adv* yn bersonol

**perspective** *n* persbectif, safbwynt

**perspiration** *n* chwys

**perspire** *vb* chwysu

**persuade** *vt* darbwyllo, perswadio

**pert** *adj* eofn, tafodrydd

**pertain** *vi* perthyn

**pertinent** *adj* perthynol, cymwys

**perturb** *vt* cyffroi, aflonyddu, cythruddo

**peruse** *vt* darllen, chwilio

**pervade** *vt* treiddio, trwytho

**perverse** *adj* gwrthnysig, trofaus, croes

**pervert** *vt* gwyrdoi, llygru, camdroi ♦ *n* cyfeiliornwr

**pessimism** *n* pesimistiaeth

**pessimist** *n* pesimist

**pest** *n* pla, haint, poendod

**pester** *vt* blino, aflonyddu, poeni

**pestilence** *n* haint, pla

**pet** *n* anwylyn, ffafryn ♦ *adj* llywaeth, swci ♦ *vt* anwesu, canmol

**petal** *n* petal

**petite** *adj* bychan

**petition** *n* deisyfiad; deiseb, petisiwn

**petitioner** *n* deisebwr

**petrel** *n* aderyn drycin

**petrified** *adj* stond

**petrify** *vb* parlysu

**petroleum** *n* petroliwm

**petrol pump** *n* pwmp petrol

**petrol station** *n* gorsaf betrol

**petticoat** *n* pais

**petty** *adj* bach, bychan, mân, gwael

**petulant** *adj* anniddig, anfoddog,
anynad

**pew** *n* eisteddle, côr, sedd

**pewit, peewit** *n* cornicyll,
cornchwiglen

**pewter** *n* piwter

**phantom** *n* rhith, drychiolaeth

**Pharisee** *n* Pharisead

**pharmacy** *n* fferylliaeth; fferyllfa

**pharynx** *n* sefnig

**phase** *n* golwg, gwedd, agwedd;
tro

**pheasant** *n* ceiliog coed, coediar,
ffesant

**phenomenon** (**-na**) *n* ffenomen;
rhyfeddod

**phial** *n* ffiol

**philander** *vi* gwamalio caru

**philanthropist** *n* dyngarwr

**philanthropy** *n* dyngarwch

**Philippines** *n* Pilipinas

**Philistine** *n* Philistiad

**philology** *n* ieitheg

**philosopher** *n* athronydd

**philosophical** *adj* athronyddol

**philosophy** *n* athroniaeth

**phlegm** *n* cornboer, llysnafedd,
fflem

**phlegmatic** *adj* difraw, digyffro,
difywyd

**phobia** *n* ffobia

**phone** *n* ffôn, teleffon ♦ *vb* ffonio.
**p. book** *n* cyfeiriadur ffôn. **p. box**
*n* caban ffôn. **p. call** *n* galwad ffôn

**phonetic** *adj* seinegol

**phonetician** *n* seinegydd

**phonetics** *n* seineg

**phoney** *adj* ffug

**phonology** *n* ffonoleg

**phosphorus** *n* ffosfforws

**photocopier** *n* llungopïydd

**photocopy** *n* llungopi ♦ *vb*
llungopïo

**photograph** *n* llun, ffotograff

**photographer** *n* ffotograffydd

**photography** *n* ffotograffiaeth

**phrase** *n* ymadrodd; cymal ♦ *vt*
geirio

**phraseology** *n* geiriad,
geirweddiad

**physical** *adj* corfforol, materol;
ffisegol. **p. education** *n* addysg
gorfforol

**physician** *n* meddyg, ffisigwr

**physicist** *n* ffisegydd/wr

**physics** *n* ffiseg

**physiology** *n* ffisioleg

**physiotherapy** *n* ffisiotherapi

**physique** *n* corffolaeth,
cyfansoddiad

**piano** *n* piano

**pick** *n* caib ♦ *vb* ceibio

**pick** *vb* pigo, dewis, dethol ♦ *n*
dewis

**pickaxe** *n* caib

**picket** *n* polyn, cledren; gwyliwr,
gwyliadwriaeth, picedwr ♦ *vb*
picedu

**pickle** *n* picl, heli ♦ *vt* piclo, halltu

**picnic** *n* picnic

**pickpocket** *n* pigwr pocedi,
codleidr

**pictorial** *adj* darluniadol

**picture** *n* llun, darlun, pictiwr. **p.
book** *n* llyfr lluniau

**picturesque** *adj* darluniaidd,
gwych, byw

**pie** *n* pastai. **p. chart** *n* siart olwyn

**piebald** *adj* brith; brithryw

**piece** *n* darn, dryll, rhan ♦ *vt*
clytio, asio, uno

**piecemeal** *adv* bob yn damaid

**pied** *adj* brith, brithliw

**pier** *n* piler; pier

**pierce** *vb* brathu, gwanu, trywanu

**piety** *n* duwioldeb

**piffle** *n* lol, oferedd, gwegi

**pig** *n* mochyn ♦ *vb* porchellu, bwrw
perchyll

**pigeon** *n* colomen

**pigeonhole** *n* cloer

**pigeon-house** *n* colomendy

**piggy bank** *n* cadw-mi-gei, blwch
cynilo

**pig-headed** *adj* pendew, ystyfnig
**pigment** *n* paent, lliw
**pigsty** *n* twlc mochyn
**pigtail** *n* pleth
**pike** *n* gwaywffon; penhwyad
**pile** *n* crug, pentwr ♦ *vt* pentyrru
**pile** *n* pawl, cledr
**pile** *n* blew, ceden
**piles** *npl* clwyf y marchogion
**pilfer** *vb* chwiwladrata
**pilgrim** *n* pererin
**pilgrimage** *n* pererindod
**pill** *n* pelen, pilsen
**pillage** *n* ysbail, anrhaith ♦ *vt* ysbeilio, anrheithio
**pillar** *n* colofn, piler. **p. box** *n* bocs postio
**pillion** *n* sgil
**pillory** *n* rhigod, pilwri
**pillow** *n* gobennydd, clustog. **p. case** *n* cas gobennydd
**pilot** *n* cyfarwyddwr llongau, peilot
**pimple** *n* ploryn, tosyn
**pin** *n* pin ♦ *vt* pinio, hoelio
**pinafore** *n* brat, piner
**pincers** *npl* gefel, pinsiwrn
**pinch** *vb* pinsio, gwasgu; cynilo ♦ *n* pins, pinsiad; gwasgfa, cyfyngder
**pincushion** *n* pincas, pincws
**pine** *n* pinwydden
**pine** *vi* dihoeni, nychu, curio
**pineapple** *n* afal pîn
**pinion** *n* asgell, adain ♦ *vt* torri esgyll
**pink** *adj*, *n* pinc
**pinpoint** *vb* pinbwyntio
**pint** *n* peint
**pioneer** *n* arloeswr, arloesydd
**pious** *adj* duwiol, duwiolfrydig, crefyddol
**pip** *n* hedyn afal, *etc*
**pipe** *n* pib, pibell ♦ *vb* canu pibell
**piping** *adj:* **p. hot** chwilboeth
**piquant** *adj* pigog, llym, tost
**pique** *vt* llidio, cyffroi; ymfalchïo ♦ *n* soriant

**pirate** *n* môr-leidr
**piss** *vb* pisio
**pissed** *adj* meddw
**pistol** *n* llawddryll, pistol
**pit** *n* pwll, pydew ♦ *vt* pyllu. **coal p.** pwll glo
**pitch** *n* pyg ♦ *vt* pygu
**pitch** *vb* bwrw; gosod; taro (tôn) ♦ *n* gradd, mesur, traw
**pitcher** *n* piser, ystên, cawg
**pitchfork** *n* picfforch, picwarch; seinfforch
**piteous** *adj* truenus, gresynus
**pitfall** *n* magl, perygl
**pith** *n* bywyn; mwydion; mêr; grym, sylwedd
**pithy** *adj* cryno, cynhwysfawr
**pitiful** *adj* truenus, tosturiol
**pitiless** *adj* didostur, didrugaredd
**pittance** *n* dogn, cyfran (annigonol)
**pity** *n* tosturi, trueni, gresyn ♦ *vt* tosturio, gresynu
**pivot** *n* colyn, pegwn
**placable** *adj* cymodlon, hynaws
**placard** *n* murlen, hysbyslen
**placate** *vt* cymodi, heddychu, dyhuddo
**place** *n* lle, man, mangre ♦ *vt* cyfleu, gosod. **to take p.** digwydd. **in the first p.** yn y lle cyntaf
**placid** *adj* araf, tawel, llonydd
**plagiary** *n* llên-ladrad; llên-leidr
**plague** *n* pla, haint ♦ *vt* poeni, blino
**plaice** *n* lleden
**plaid** *n* plod
**plain** *adj* plaen, eglur ♦ *n* gwastadedd
**plaintiff** *n* achwynwr, hawlydd
**plait** *n* pleth ♦ *vt* plethu
**plan** *n* cynllun, plan ♦ *vt* cynllunio, planio
**plane** *adj*, *n* gwastad, lefel
**plane** *n* plaen; awyren ♦ *vt* plaenio
**planet** *n* planed
**plank** *n* astell, estyllen, planc

**planning** n cynllunio. **p. permission** n caniatâd cynllunio

**plant** n planhigyn, llysieuyn; offer; ffatri ♦ vt plannu

**plaster** n plaster ♦ vt plastro

**plastic** n, adj plastig. **p. bag** cwdyn plastig

**plat** n darn o dir, clwt, lawnt

**plate** n plat; llestri aur, etc ♦ vt golchi â metel

**plateau** n gwastatir uchel

**platform** n llwyfan, esgynlawr

**platitude** n sylw hen a diflas, gwireb

**platoon** n platŵn

**platter** n plat, dysgl, noe

**plaudit** n banllef o gymeradwyaeth

**plausible** adj teg neu resymol yr olwg, ffals

**play** vb chwarae; canu (offeryn) ♦ n chwarae

**player** n chwaraewr

**playful** adj chwareus

**playground** n chwaraele

**playgroup** n grŵp chwarae

**playing field** n maes chwarae

**plaything** n tegan

**playwright** n dramodydd

**plea** n ple, dadl, hawl; esgus

**plead** vb pledio, dadlau, eiriol, ymbil

**pleasant** adj hyfryd, pleserus, difyr, siriol

**please** vb boddhau, boddio, rhyngu bodd. **if you p.** os gwelwch yn dda

**pleased** adj boddhaus, bodlon, hapus. **p. to meet you** mae'n dda gen i gwrdd â chi

**pleasing** adj dymunol

**pleasure** n pleser, hyfrydwch

**pleat** n plet, pleten ♦ vt pletio

**plebeian** n gwerinwr, gwrêng

**plebiscite** n pleidlais y bobl

**pledge** n gwystl, ernes ♦ vt gwystlo

**plenary** adj llawn, cyflawn, diamodol

**plenty** n digon, helaethrwydd

**plethora** n gorgyflawnder

**pleurisy** n eisglwyf, plewrisi

**pliable, pliant** adj ystwyth, hyblyg

**pliers** npl gefel fechan

**plight** n cyflwr, drych, anghyflwr

**plight** vt addo, gwystlo

**plod** vb troedio, ymlafnio, llafurio, slafio

**plot** n darn o dir; brad, cynllwyn; cynllun, plot, ystofiad ♦ vb cynllwyn; cynllunio

**plotter** n cynllwynwr

**plough** n aradr, gwŷdd ♦ vb aredig, troi

**ploy** n cynllun, strategiaeth

**pluck** vt tynnu; pluo ♦ n glewder

**plucky** adj dewr, gwrol, glew

**plug** n topyn, plwg ♦ vt topio, plygio

**plum** n eirinen

**plumage** n plu

**plumber** n plymwr

**plumbing** n gwaith plymwr

**plume** n pluen, plufyn ♦ vt pluo, plufio

**plummet** n plymen

**plump** adj tew, llyfndew, graenus ♦ vb pleidleisio i un (yn unig)

**plunder** n ysbail, anrhaith ♦ vt ysbeilio, anrheithio

**plunge** n plymiad ♦ vb plymio, trochi, bwrw

**pluperfect** adj gorberffaith

**plural** adj lluosog

**plus** n plws, ychwaneg ♦ prep, adj ychwanegol

**plush** n plwsh

**ply** vb arfer, defnyddio, gyrru; poeni

**plywood** n pren haenog (tair-haen, pum-haen)

**pneumatic** adj â'i lond o wynt, awyrog

**pneumonia** n llid yr ysgyfaint, niwmonia

**poach** vb herwhela, potsio

**poach** vt berwi (wy) heb ei blisg
**poacher** n herwheliwr, potsiwr
**pock** n brech, ôl brech
**pocket** n poced, llogell ♦ vt pocedu. **p. knife** cyllell boced. **p. money** arian poced
**pod** n coden, plisgyn, masgl, cibyn
**podgy** adj byrdew
**poem** n cerdd, cân
**poet** n bardd, prydydd
**poetry** n barddoniaeth, prydyddiaeth
**poignant** adj llym, tost, ingol, aethus, awchlym
**point** n pwynt; man; blaen ♦ vb pwyntio; blaenllymu; dangos. **p. of view** n safbwynt. **to be on the p. of doing sth** bod ar fin gwneud rhywbeth. **to get the p.** deall. **there's no p. (in doing)** does dim diben gwneud. **to p. out** nodi
**pointed** adj pigfain
**pointedly** adv yn llym
**pointer** n cyfeirydd; mynegfys
**pointless** adj dibwynt, diystyr, gwag
**poise** vb mantoli; hofran ♦ n ystum, osgo
**poison** n gwenwyn ♦ vt gwenwyno
**poisoning** n gwenwyno
**poisonous** adj gwenwynig
**poke** vb gwthio, pwnio, procio
**poker** n pocer
**poky** adj cyfyng, gwael
**polar** adj pegynol
**pole** n pawl, polyn; pegwn
**polemic** adj dadleuol ♦ n dadl
**police** n heddlu. **p. car** n car heddlu. **p. station** n gorsaf heddlu
**policeman** n heddwas, heddgeidwad, plismon
**policewoman** n heddferch, plismones
**policy** n polisi
**polish** vb cwyro, caboli, gloywi, llathru ♦ n cwyr
**polite** adj moesgar, boneddigaidd

**politic** adj call, cyfrwys, doeth, buddiol
**political** adj gwleidyddol
**politician** n gwleidydd, gwleidyddwr
**politics** n gwleidyddiaeth
**poll** n pen, copa; pôl ♦ vb cneifio; pleidleisio, polio. **p. tax** treth y pen, treth gymunedol
**pollen** n paill
**polling booth** n bwth pleidleisio
**polling day** n dydd pleidleisio
**polling station** n gorsaf bleidleisio
**pollute** vt halogi, difwyno, llygru
**pollution** n llygredd
**polo neck** n jersi polo
**polygamy** n amlwreigiaeth
**polysyllable** n gair lluosill
**polytechnic** n polytechnig
**pomegranate** n pomgranad
**pomp** n rhwysg
**pompous** adj rhwysgfawr, balch
**pond** n llyn, pwll
**ponder** vb ystyried, myfyrio, pwyso
**ponderous** adj pwysfawr, trwm
**pong** n drewdod
**pontiff** n archoffeiriad; y Pab
**pontoon** n ysgraff
**pony** n merlyn, poni, merlen. **p. trekking** merlota
**pooh** excl pw!
**pool** n pwll, llyn
**pool** n cronfa; pwll ♦ vt cydgyfrannu
**poor** adj tlawd, truan, gwael, sâl
**poorly** adj sâl, gwael, claf
**pop** vb ffrwydro, ysgortio; picio, plannu, taro
**pope** n pab
**popery** n pabyddiaeth
**pop-gun** n gwn clats
**poplar** n poplysen
**poppy** n pabi (coch), llygad y bwgan
**populace** n gwerin, gwerinos
**popular** adj poblogaidd

**population** n poblogaeth
**populous** adj poblog
**porcelain** n porslen
**porch** n porth, cyntedd
**porcine** adj mochaidd
**porcupine** n ballasg
**pore** n twll chwys
**pore** vi astudio, myfyrio, synfyfyrio
**pork** n cig moch, porc
**porker** n mochyn, porcyn
**porous** adj tyllog
**porpoise** n llamhidydd
**porridge** n uwd
**port** n porth, porthfa, porthladd
**port** n ochr aswy llong wrth edrych ymlaen
**port** n gwin Oporto, gwin coch
**portable** adj cludadwy
**portcullis** n porthcwlis
**portent** n argoel; rhyfeddod, gwyrth
**porter** n porthor
**portfolio** n cas papurau, portffolio; swydd
**porthole** n ffenestr llong; gyndwll
**portion** n rhan, cyfran, gwaddol
**portly** adj tew, corffol
**portrait** n llun, darlun
**portray** vt portreadu, darlunio
**Portugal** n Portiwgal
**pose** vb sefyll, ymddangos, cymryd ar ♦ n ystum, rhodres
**posh** adj hardd, coeth
**position** n safle, sefyllfa, swydd
**positive** adj cadarnhaol, pendant, posidiol
**posse** n mintai, torf
**possess** vt meddu, meddiannu
**possession** n meddiant
**possessor** n perchen, perchennog
**possibility** n posibilrwydd
**possible** adj posibl, dichonadwy
**possibly** adv dichon, efallai
**post** n post, cledr ♦ vt gosod, cyhoeddi
**post** n post, llythyrfa; safle, swydd

♦ vb postio
**post-** prefix wedi, ar ôl
**postage** n cludiad (llythyr, etc.)
**postal** adj post
**postal order** n archeb bost
**postbox** n bocs postio
**postcard** n cerdyn post
**postcode** n côd post
**poster** n hysbyslen, poster
**posterior** adj ar ôl, ôl
**posterity** n cenedlaethau'r dyfodol, hiliogaeth
**postgraduate** adj graddedig
**posthumous** adj ar ôl marw
**postman** n postmon
**postmark** n postfarc
**postmaster** n postfeistr
**post office** n llythyrdy, swyddfa'r post
**postpone** vt gohirio, oedi
**postscript** n ôl-ysgrif
**posture** n agwedd, ystum, osgo
**postwar** adj ar ôl y rhyfel
**posy** n blodeuglwm, pwysi
**pot** n pot, potyn; crochan ♦ vb potio
**potato** (-oes) n taten, pytaten
**potency** n nerth, grym
**potent** adj cryf, galluog, grymus, nerthol
**potential** adj dichonadwy, dichonol ♦ n potensial
**pothole** n ceubwll
**potion** n dogn, llymaid, llwnc
**pottage** n cawl, potes
**potter** n crochenydd
**potter** vb diogi, ymdroi, sefyllian, swmera
**pottery** n llestri pridd; gwaith llestri pridd; priddweithfa
**potty** n pot
**pouch** n cod, coden, cwd ♦ vb cydu
**poultice** n powltis
**poultry** n dofednod, ffowls
**pounce** vb disgyn ar, dyfod ar warthaf
**pound** n pwys; punt

**pound** n ffald ♦ vt ffaldio
**pound** vb pwyo, pwnio, malu, malurio
**pour** vb tywallt, arllwys; bwrw
**pout** vi pwdu, sorri, terru, monni
**poverty** n tlodi
**poverty-stricken** adj tlawd, llwm
**powder** n powdr, llwch, pylor ♦ vt powdro
**powdered milk** n llaeth powdr
**powder room** n ystafell bincio
**power** n gallu, nerth, grym, awdurdod; pŵer
**power cut** n toriad yn y cyflenwad
**power failure** n pall ar y cyflenwad
**powerful** adj nerthol, grymus
**powerless** adj dirym
**power station** n pŵerdy
**pox** n crynodeb
**practicable** adj dichonadwy
**practical** adj ymarferol
**practice** n arfer, arferiad, ymarferiad
**practise** vb arfer, ymarfer
**practising** adj ymarferol; yn dilyn ei swydd
**practitioner** n meddyg; cyfreithiwr
**prairie** n gwastatir, gweundir, paith
**praise** vt canmol, moli ♦ n canmoliaeth, mawl
**pram** n coets, pram
**prance** vi prancio
**prank** n cast, ystranc, pranc
**prawn** n corgimwch
**pray** vb gweddïo. **I p. thee** atolwg
**prayer** n gweddi
**pre-** prefix cyn-, rhag-, blaen-
**preach** vb pregethu
**preacher** n pregethwr
**preamble** n rhagymadrodd, rhaglith
**precarious** adj ansicr, peryglus, enbyd
**precaution** n rhagofal, rhagocheliad, gofal

**precede** vb blaenori, blaenu, rhagflaenu
**precedence** n blaenoriaeth
**precedent** n cynsail
**precentor** n arweinydd y gân, codwr canu
**preceptor** n athro, hyfforddwr
**precinct** n cyffin, rhodfa
**precious** adj gwerthfawr, prid, drud
**precipice** n dibyn, diffwys, clogwyn
**precipitate** vt bwrw, hyrddio ♦ vi gwaddodi, gwaelodi ♦ adj byrbwyll, anystyriol
**précis** n crynodeb
**precise** adj penodol, manwl
**preclude** vt cau allan, atal, rhwystro
**precocious** adj hen o'i oed, henaidd, henffel
**precondition** n rhagamod
**precursor** n rhagredegydd, rhagflaenydd
**predatory** adj anrheithgar, ysglyfaethus
**predecessor** n rhagflaenydd
**predestination** n rhagarfaethiad
**predicament** n cyflwr, helynt, sefyllfa
**predicate** vt haeru, honni ♦ n traethiad
**predict** vt rhagfynegi, rhagddywedyd, proffwydo
**predilection** n hoffter, tuedd, tueddfryd
**predominate** vi bod yn bennaf neu yn fwyaf, arglwyddiaethu, rhagori
**pre-eminent** adj ar y blaen i bawb
**preen** vb pincio, harddu
**preface** n rhagymadrodd, rhaglith
**prefect** n rhaglaw; swyddog
**prefer** vt dewis yn hytrach, bod yn well gan
**preferable** adj gwell
**preference** n dewis, hoffter,

ffafraeth, blaenoriaeth
**preferential** *adj* ffafriol
**preferment** *n* dyrchafiad, codiad
**prefix** *vt* rhagddodi ♦ *n*
rhagddodiad
**pregnancy** *n* beichiogaeth
**pregnant** *adj* beichiog, llawn
**prehistoric** *adj* cynhanesiol
**prejudice** *n* rhagfarn; niwed ♦ *vt*
rhagfarnu, niweidio
**prejudiced** *adj* rhagfarnllyd
**prelate** *n* esgob, prelad
**preliminary** *adj* arweiniol,
rhagarweiniol
**prelude** *n* rhagarweiniad; preliwd
(cerdd.)
**premarital** *adj* cyn priodi
**premature** *adj* anaeddfed,
cynamserol
**premier** *adj* blaenaf, pennaf, prif ♦
*n* prifweinidog
**première** *n* blaenberfformiad
**premise** *n* rhagosodiad; (*pl*)
adeiladau, *etc* ♦ *vt* rhagosod
**premium** *n* gwobr, tâl, taliad
**preoccupied** *adj* wedi ymgolli
**preoccupy** *vt* rhagfeddiannu;
llenwi, ymgolli
**prepaid** *adj* wedi ei dalu ymlaen
llaw, rhagdalwyd
**preparation** *n* paratoad,
darpariaeth
**preparatory** *adj* rhagbaratoawl
**prepare** *vb* paratoi, darparu,
darbod, arlwyo
**prepared** *adj* parod; effro
**preposition** *n* arddodiad
**preposterous** *adj* afresymol,
gwrthun
**prerequisite** *n* rhaganghenraid
**prerogative** *n* braint, rhagorfraint
**presage** *n* argoel, rhagargoel ♦ *vt*
argoeli
**presbyter** *n* henuriad, offeiriad
**Presbyterian** *adj* Henadurol,
Presbyteraidd ♦ *n* Presbyteriad
**presbytery** *n* henaduriaeth; tŷ

offeiriad Pabyddol
**prescience** *n* rhagwybodaeth
**prescribe** *vb* gorchymyn,
cyfarwyddo
**prescription** *n* cyngor,
cyfarwyddyd, presgripsiwn
**presence** *n* gŵydd, presenoldeb
**present** *adj*, *n* presennol
**present** *n* anrheg ♦ *vt* anrhegu;
cyflwyno; dangos
**presentiment** *n* rhagargoel
**presently** *adv* yn fuan
**preserve** *vt* cadw, diogelu ♦ *n* jam
**preside** *vi* llywyddu
**president** *n* llywydd, arlywydd
**press** *vb* gwasgu ♦ *n* gwasg;
gwrŷf; cwpwrdd
**pressing** *adj* taer, dwys
**pressure** *n* gwasgiad, gwasgfa,
pwys
**prestige** *n* bri, dylanwad, braint
**presumable** *adj* y gellir ei dybio
**presumably** *adv* yn ôl pob tebyg,
gellid tybio
**presume** *vb* tybio, tebygu; beiddio,
rhyfygu
**presumption** *n* rhyfyg; tyb
**presumptuous** *adj* rhyfygus
**pretence** *n* rhith, esgus, ffug
**pretend** *vb* ffugio, cymryd ar,
cogio; proffesu; honni hawl
**pretension** *n* honiad, hawl
**preter-** *prefix* tu hwnt i, mwy na
**pretext** *n* esgus, cochl
**pretty** *adj* tlws, del, pert ♦ *adv*
cryn, go
**prevail** *vi* tycio, ffynnu; gorfod,
trechu
**prevalent** *adj* cyffredin; nerthol
**prevent** *vt* rhagflaenu; atal,
rhwystro
**preview** *n* rhagolwg
**previous** *adj* blaenorol, cynt
**prey** *n* ysglyfaeth, aberth ♦ *vi*
ysglyfaethu
**price** *n* pris, gwerth ♦ *vt* prisio. **p.**
**list** *n* rhestr prisiau, taflen

brisiau; telerau *npl*

**prick** *n* pigyn, swmbwl ♦ *vb* pigo; picio, codi

**prickle** *n* draen ♦ *vb* pigo, tymhigo

**pride** *n* balchder ♦ *vt* balchïo, ymfalchïo

**priest** *n* offeiriad

**priesthood** *n* offeiriadaeth

**prig** *n* sychfoesolyn, mursennwr, coethyn

**prim** *adj* cymen, cymhenllyd

**primary** *adj* prif, cyntaf, cysefin; cynradd. **p. school** *n* ysgol gynradd

**primate** *n* archesgob

**prime** *adj* prif, cyntaf; gorau ♦ *n* anterth

**prime** *vt* llwytho, llenwi, cyflenwi

**primer** *n* llyfr cyntaf, cynlyfr

**primeval** *adj* cynoesol, cyntefig

**primitive** *adj* cyntefig; garw, amrwd

**primordial** *adj* cyntefig, cysefin

**primrose** *n* briallen, (*pl*) briallu

**prince** *n* tywysog

**principal** *adj* prif ♦ *n* pen; prifathro; corff

**principality** *n* tywysogaeth

**principle** *n* egwyddor, elfen

**print** *n* argraff, print, ôl ♦ *vb* argraffu, printio

**printed** *adj* argraffedig, wedi ei argraffu

**prior** *adj* cynt, blaenorol ♦ *n* prior, priol

**priority** *n* blaenoriaeth

**priory** *n* priordy, mynachdy

**prise, prize** *vt* dryllio'n agored â throsol

**prism** *n* prism

**prison** *n* carchar, carchardy

**prisoner** *n* carcharor

**pristine** *adj* hen, cyntefig, cysefin

**private** *adj* preifat, cyfrinachol, personol. **p. enterprise** *n* ymroddiad unigol

**privation** *n* amddifadrwydd, diffyg

**privilege** *n* braint, rhagorfraint

**privy** *adj* dirgel, cudd, cyfrin ♦ *n* geudy

**prize** *n* gwobr ♦ *vt* prisio, gwerthfawrogi

**prize** *n* ysbail, caffaeliad, gwobr

**pro-** *prefix* am, yn lle; o blaid

**probability** *n* tebygolrwydd

**probable** *adj* tebygol, tebyg

**probate** *n* prawf ewyllys

**probation** *n* prawf

**probe** *n* profiedydd ♦ *vt* profi, chwilio

**probity** *n* uniondeb, cywirdeb

**problem** *n* pwnc, drysbwnc, problem

**procedure** *n* trefn, arfer, defod, dull

**proceed** *vi* myned, deillio, tarddu; erlyn ♦ *n* (*pl*) enillion, elw

**process** *n* gweithrediad, goruchwyliaeth, dull

**procession** *n* gorymdaith; deilliad

**proclaim** *vt* cyhoeddi, datgan

**proclamation** *n* cyhoeddiad, proclamasiwn

**proclivity** *n* gogwydd, tuedd

**proconsul** *n* rhaglaw

**procrastinate** *vi* oedi, gohirio

**procreate** *vt* cenhedlu

**procure** *vb* ceisio, caffael, cael

**prod** *vt* procio, pwnio, symbylu

**prodigal** *adj* afradlon, hael

**prodigious** *adj* aruthrol, anferth

**prodigy** *n* rhyfeddod, gwyrth

**produce** *vt* cynhyrchu, epilio; dwyn ♦ *n* cynnyrch, ffrwyth

**product** *n* cynnyrch, ffrwyth

**production** *n* cynhyrchiad; (*pl*) cynhyrchion

**profane** *adj* anghysegredig, halogedig ♦ *vt* anghysegru, halogi

**profess** *vb* proffesu, arddel

**profession** *n* proffes, galwedigaeth

**professional** *adj* proffesiynol

**professor** *n* proffeswr; athro

**proffer** *vt, n* cynnig

**proficient** *adj* hyddysg, cyfarwydd
**profile** *n* ystlyslun, cernlun
**profit** *n* budd, lles, elw, proffid ♦ *vb* llesáu, proffidio
**profiteer** *vi* gwneud elw
**profligate** *adj* afradlon, ofer
**profound** *adj* dwfn, dwys, angerddol
**profundity** *n* dyfnder
**profuse** *adj* hael, helaeth, toreithiog
**progenitor** *n* cyndad
**progeny** *n* hil, epil, hiliogaeth
**prognostic** *n* argoel, rhagarwydd
**programme** *n* rhaglen
**progress** *n* cynnydd; taith ♦ *vi* cynyddu
**progressive** *adj* cynyddgar, progresif
**prohibit** *vt* gwahardd
**project** *n* bwriad, cynllun; project
**project** *vb* bwrw; bwriadu; ymestyn; taflunio (ffilm)
**projectile** *n* teflyn
**projector** *n* taflunydd
**proletariat** *n* gwerin, gwrêng
**prolific** *adj* epiliog, ffrwythlon, toreithiog
**prolix** *adj* maith, amleiriog
**prologue** *n* rhagair, prolog
**prolong** *vt* hwyhau, estyn
**promenade** *n* rhodfa ♦ *vb* rhodianna
**prominent** *adj* yn sefyll allan, amlwg
**promise** *n* addewid ♦ *vb* addo, argoeli
**promissory** *adj* addewidiol
**promontory** *n* pentir, penrhyn
**promote** *vt* hyrwyddo, meithrin, dyrchafu
**promoter** *n* hyrwyddwr
**prompt** *adj* parod, buan ♦ *vt* cofweini; cymell
**promptitude** *n* parodrwydd
**promulgate** *vt* cyhoeddi, lledaenu
**prone** *adj* â'i wyneb i waered; tueddol

**prong** *n* fforch, pig fforch
**pronominal** *adj* rhagenwol
**pronoun** *n* rhagenw
**pronounce** *vb* cynanu, yngan; cyhoeddi, datgan
**pronunciation** *n* cynaniad
**proof** *n* prawf; proflen
**prop** *n* ateg, post, prop ♦ *vt* ategu
**propaganda** *n* propaganda
**propagate** *vt* epilio, cenhedlu; lledaenu
**propel** *vt* gyrru ymlaen, gwthio
**propensity** *n* tuedd, tueddfryd, gogwydd
**proper** *adj* priod, priodol, gweddus
**property** *n* priodoledd; eiddo; priodwedd (cemeg)
**prophecy** *n* proffwydoliaeth
**prophesy** *vb* proffwydo
**prophet** *n* proffwyd
**propinquity** *n* agosrwydd, cyfnesafrwydd
**propitiate** *vt* cymodi, dyhuddo
**propitiation** *n* cymod, iawn
**propitious** *adj* tirion, ffafriol
**proportion** *n* cyfartaledd, cyfrannedd
**proportional** *adj* cyfrannol
**proportionate** *adj* cymesur
**proposal** *n* cynnig
**propose** *vb* cynnig, bwriadu
**proposition** *n* cynigiad; gosodiad
**propound** *vt* cynnig, gosod gerbron
**proprietor** *n* perchen, perchennog
**propriety** *n* priodoldeb, gwedduster
**propulsion** *n* gwthiad, gyriad
**prorogue** *vt* gohirio
**prosaic** *adj* rhyddieithol, cyffredin
**proscribe** *vt* deol, diarddel, gwahardd
**prose** *n* rhyddiaith
**prosecute** *vt* erlyn, dilyn, dwyn ymlaen
**prosecutor** *n* erlynydd
**proselyte** *n* proselyt

**prosody** *n* mydryddiaeth
**prospect** *n* rhagolwg, golwg, golygfa
**prospectus** *n* rhaglen, hysbyslen, prosbectws
**prosper** *vb* llwyddo, tycio, ffynnu
**prosperity** *n* llwyddiant, hawddfyd, ffyniant
**prostitute** *n* putain ♦ *vt* darostwng
**prostrate** *adj* yn gorwedd ar ei wyneb; ar lawr yn lân ♦ *vt* bwrw i lawr; ymgrymu
**protect** *vt* amddiffyn, noddi
**protection** *n* amddiffyn, nawdd, diogelwch
**protective** *adj* amddiffynnol
**protector** *n* amddiffynnydd
**protest** *vb* gwrthdystio ♦ *n* gwrthdystiad
**prototype** *n* cynddelw, cynllun
**protract** *vt* estyn, hwyhau
**protrude** *vb* gwthio allan
**protuberance** *n* chwydd
**proud** *adj* balch
**prove** *vb* profi
**provender** *n* ebran, gogor, porthiant
**proverb** *n* dihareb
**provide** *vt* darparu
**providence** *n* rhagluniaeth, darbodaeth
**provident** *adj* darbodus
**providential** *adj* rhagluniaethol
**province** *n* talaith, tiriogaeth; cylch, maes
**provision** *n* darpariaeth. **provisions** *npl* darbodion; ymborth
**proviso** *n* amod
**provocation** *n* anogaeth, cyffroad, cythrudd
**provoke** *vt* annog, cyffroi, cythruddo, profocio
**provost** *n* maer, profost
**prow** *n* pen blaen bad neu long
**prowess** *n* dewrder, glewder, grymuster
**prowl** *vi* ysglyfaetha, prowlan

**proximate** *adj* nesaf, agos at; agos
**proximity** *n* agosrwydd
**proxy** *n* dirprwy
**prude** *n* mursen, coegen
**prudence** *n* pwyll, synnwyr, callineb
**prudent** *adj* pwyllog, synhwyrol, call, doeth
**prune** *n* eirinen sech
**Prussia** *n* Prwsia
**pry** *vi* chwilota, chwilenna
**psalm** *n* salm
**psalmody** *n* caniadaeth y cysegr, salmyddiaeth
**psalter** *n* llyfr salmau, sallwyr
**pseudo-** *prefix* gau, ffug
**pseudonym** *n* ffugenw
**pshaw** *excl* wfft, pw, och, ffei
**psychiatrist** *n* seiciatrydd
**psychological** *adj* seicolegol, meddyliol
**psychology** *n* seicoleg
**puberty** *n* aeddfedrwydd oed, blaenlencyndod, puberdod
**public** *adj* cyhoeddus ♦ *n* y cyhoedd. **p. house** *n* tŷ tafarn. **p. library** *n* llyfrgell gyhoeddus
**publican** *n* publican; tafarnwr
**publicity** *n* cyhoeddusrwydd
**publish** *vt* cyhoeddi
**pucker** *vb* crychu, crybachu
**pudding** *n* pwdin
**puddle** *n* corbwll; pydew, llaca
**puerile** *adj* bachgennaidd, plentynnaidd
**puff** *n* pwff, chwa, chwyth ♦ *vb* pwffio, chwythu
**pugilist** *n* paffiwr, ymladdwr
**pugnacious** *adj* ymladdgar, cwerylgar
**puissant** *adj* galluog, grymus, nerthol
**pull** *vt* tynnu ♦ *n* tynfa, tyniad
**pullet** *n* cywen
**pulley** *n* chwerfan, troell, pwli
**pullover** *n* gwasgod wlân
**pulmonary** *adj* ysgyfeiniol

**pulp** *n* bywyn, mwydion

**pulpit** *n* pulpud

**pulsate** *vb* curo (megis y galon)

**pulse** *n* curiad y galon, curiad y gwaed

**pulse** *n* pys, ffa, *etc*

**pulverize** *vt* malu yn llwch, chwilfriwio

**pummel** *vt* pwnio, dyrnodio, curo

**pump** *n* sugnedydd, pwmp ♦ *vb* pwmpio

**pumpkin** *n* pwmpen

**pun** *n* gair mwys, mwysair

**punch** *n* pwns; dyrnod ♦ *vb* pwnsio, dyrnodio

**punctilious** *adj* cysetlyd, gorfanwl

**punctual** *adj* prydlon

**punctuate** *vt* atalnodi

**puncture** *n* twll ♦ *vt* tyllu

**pundit** *n* ysgolhaig, doethwr

**pungent** *adj* llym, llymdost, siarp

**punish** *vt* cosbi, ceryddu; poeni

**punishment** *n* cosb, cosbedigaeth

**punitive** *adj* cosbol

**puny** *adj* eiddil, bychan, tila, pitw

**pupil** *n* ysgolhaig, ysgolor, disgybl; cannwyll llygad

**puppet** *n* delw, dol, pyped; gwas

**puppy** *n* ci bach

**purblind** *adj* cibddall, coegddall

**purchase** *vt* prynu, pwrcasu ♦ *n* pryniant, pwrcas

**pure** *adj* pur, noeth

**purgative** *adj* carthol ♦ *n* carthlyn

**purgatory** *n* purdan

**purge** *vt* puro, glanhau, carthu, coethi ♦ *n* carthlyn

**purification** *n* puredigaeth

**purify** *vt* puro, coethi, glanhau

**Puritan** *n* Piwritan

**purity** *n* purdeb

**purl** *vi* crychleisio, byrlymu

**purlieu** *n* cyffin, ffin, cymdogaeth

**purloin** *vt* lladrata, dwyn

**purple** *adj, n* porffor

**purport** *n* ystyr, rhediad, ergyd ♦ *vt* arwyddo, proffesu, honni

**purpose** *n* pwrpas, bwriad, arfaeth ♦ *vt* bwriadu, arfaethu

**purr** *vb* canu crwth, grwnan

**purse** *n* pwrs, cod ♦ *vb* crychu

**pursue** *vb* dilyn, erlyn, erlid, ymlid

**pursuit** *n* ymlidiad; ymchwil, gorchwyl

**purulent** *adj* crawnllyd, gorllyd

**purvey** *vb* darparu lluniaeth, darmerth

**purview** *n* amcan, maes, cylch

**pus** *n* crawn, gôr

**push** *vb* gwthio ♦ *n* gwth, ysgŵd; ymdrech

**pushchair** *n* coets

**puss** *n* titw, pws; ysgyfarnog

**pustule** *n* ploryn, llinoryn

**put** *vb* gosod, dodi, rhoddi, rhoi

**putative** *adj* tybiedig, cyfrifedig

**putrefaction** *n* pydredd, madredd

**putrefy** *vb* pydru, madru

**putrid** *adj* pwdr, mall

**putty** *n* pwti ♦ *vt* pwtïo

**puzzle** *n* dryswch, penbleth, pos ♦ *vb* drysu, pyslo

**pygmy** *n* corrach

**pyjamas** *npl* gwisg nos, gŵn nos

**pyramid** *n* pyramid, bera

**pyre** *n* cynnau angladdol, coelcerth

**pyrotechnic** *adj, n* (o natur) tân gwyllt

# Q

**quack** *n* crachfeddyg, cwac

**quack** *vi* cwacian

**quadrangle** *n* pedrongl

**quadrant** *n* cwadrant

**quadruped** *n* pedwarcarnol

**quadruple** *adj* pedwarplyg

**quadruplet** *n* pedrybled

**quaff** *vb* drachtio, cofftio, yfed

**quagmire** *n* siglen, cors, mignen, sybwll

**quail** *n* sofliar

**quaint** *adj* od, hen-ffasiwn
**quake** *vi* crynu
**Quaker** *n* Crynwr
**qualification** *n* cymhwyster; cymhwysiad
**qualified** *adj* cymwys
**qualify** *vt* cymhwyso, cyfaddasu
**quality** *n* ansawdd, rhinwedd
**qualm** *n* petruster, amheuaeth
**quandary** *n* penbleth, cyfyng-gyngor
**quantity** *n* swm, maint, mesur
**quarantine** *n* cwarant, neilltuaeth
**quarrel** *n* ymrafael, ffrae, cweryl ♦ *vi* ffraeo
**quarry** *n* chwarel, cloddfa, cwar ♦ *vb* cloddio
**quarry** *n* ysglyfaeth
**quart** *n* chwart, cwart
**quarter** *n* chwarter, cwarter; cwr, man; trugaredd; (*pl.*) llety. **a q. of an hour** chwarter awr. **q. final** rownd gogynderfynol. **quarter-sessions** *n* llys chwarter
**quartet, -te** *n* pedwarawd
**quarto** *adj*, *n* (llyfr) pedwarplyg
**quartz** *n* creigrisial, cwarts
**quash** *vt* diddymu, dirymu
**quaver** *vi* cwafrio, crynu ♦ *n* cwafer
**quay** *n* cei
**queen** *n* brenhines
**queer** *adj* od, hynod, digrif, ysmala
**quell** *vt* llonyddu, gostegu, darostwng
**quench** *vt* diffodd, dofi, torri
**quern** *n* llawfelin, breuan
**querulous** *adj* cwynfanllyd, blin
**query** *n* holiad, gofyniad ♦ *vb* holi, amau
**quest** *n* ymchwil, ymchwiliad, cwest
**question** *n* gofyniad, cwestiwn ♦ *vt* holi, amau
**questionable** *adj* amheus
**question mark** *n* gofynnod

**questionnaire** *n* holiadur
**queue** *n* cynffon, cwt, ciw
**quibble** *n* geirddadl, mân-ddadl ♦ *vi* geirddadlau, mân-ddadlau, hollti blew
**quick** *adj* byw; buan, cyflym, clau. **to the q.** i'r byw
**quicken** *vb* cyflymu
**quicksilver** *n* arian byw
**quid** *n* punt
**quiescent** *adj* distaw, llonydd, digyffro
**quiet** *adj* llonydd, tawel, distaw ♦ *n* llonyddwch, tawelwch ♦ *vt* llonyddu, tawelu
**quill** *n* pluen, plufyn, cwilsyn
**quilt** *n* cwilt, cwrlid ♦ *vt* cwiltio
**quintet** *n* pumawd
**quintuplet** *n* pumled
**quip** *n* gair ffraeth, ateb parod
**quit** *vt* gadael, symud ♦ *adj* rhydd
**quits** *adj* yn gyfartal
**quite** *adv* cwbl, llwyr, hollol
**quiver** *n* cawell saethau
**quiver** *vi* crynu, dirgrynu
**quixotic** *adj* mympwyol, gwyllt
**quiz** *vt* holi, pyslo, profocio
**quoit** *n* coeten, coetan
**quondam** *adj* wedi bod, gynt, hen
**quorum** *n* nifer gofynnol, corwm
**quota** *n* rhan, cyfran, dogn, cwota
**quotation** *n* dyfyniad; prisiant
**quote** *vt* dyfynnu; nodi (prisiau)
**quoth** *vt* meddai, ebe

# R

**rabbi** *n* rabi
**rabbit** *n* cwningen
**rabble** *n* ciwed, tyrfa ddireol
**rabid** *adj* cynddeiriog
**rabies** *n* y gynddaredd
**race** *n* ras, gyrfa, rhedfa ♦ *vi* rasio
**race** *n* hil
**racial** *adj* hiliol
**racism** *n* hiliaeth

**rack** n rac, clwyd, rhestl;
arteithglwyd ♦ vt arteithio,
dirdynnu
**racket** n twrf, mwstwr; raced
(tennis etc.)
**racy** adj blasus; arab, ffraeth
**radiant** adj disglair, llachar,
tanbaid
**radiate** vb pelydru, rheiddio
**radiation** n ymbelydredd
**radiator** n rheiddiadur
**radical** adj gwreiddiol, cynhenid;
trylwyr ♦ n rhyddfrydwr, radical
**radio** n radio
**radioactive** adj ymbelydrol
**radio station** n gorsaf radio
**radish** n rhuddygl, radis
**radius** (-ii) n cylch; radius
**raffle** n raffl
**raft** n cludair, ysgraff, rafft
**rafter** n tulath, ceibren, trawst
**rag** n carp, clwt
**rag doll** n doli glwt
**rage** n cynddaredd ♦ vi terfysgu,
cynddeiriogi
**ragged** adj carpiog, bratiog
**raid** n rhuthr, cyrch ♦ vb
anrheithio, ysbeilio
**rail** n canllaw, cledren, rheilen ♦ vb
cledru
**rail** vi difrïo, difenwi, cablu
**raillery** n difyrrwch, cellwair
**railway** n rheilffordd. **r. station** n
gorsaf reilffordd
**raiment** n dillad, gwisg
**rain** n glaw ♦ vb glawio, bwrw
glaw
**rainbow** n enfys
**raincoat** n cot law
**rainy** adj glawog
**raise** vt codi, cyfodi, dyrchafu
**raisin** n rhesinen
**rake** n cribin, rhaca ♦ vb cribinio,
crafu, rhacanu
**rally** vb atgynnull; adgyfnerthu,
gwella ♦ n cynulliad
**ram** n hwrdd, maharen ♦ vt

hyrddio, pwnio
**ramble** vi gwibio, crwydro ♦ n
gwib
**rampant** adj uchel ei ben, rhonc
**rampart** n caer, rhagfur,
gwrthglawdd
**ramshackle** adj bregus, candryll
**rancid** adj â blas cryf arno,
drewllyd
**rancour** n digasedd, chwerwder
**random** n antur, siawns, damwain
♦ adj damweiniol
**range** n amrediad; cwmpas;
ystod; lle tân â ffwrn ♦ vb
rhestru, cyfleu; crwydro
**ranger** n coedwigwr, ceidwad parc
**rank** n rheng, gradd ♦ vb rhestru.
**the r. and file** y bobl gyffredin
**rank** adj mws; gwyllt, bras; rhonc,
noeth
**rankle** vi gori, madru; cnoi, llidio
**ransack** vt chwilio, chwilota,
ysbeilio
**ransom** n pridwerth ♦ vt prynu,
gwaredu
**rant** vi bragaldian, brygawthan
**rap** n cnoc, ergyd ♦ vt cnocio, curo
**rap** n gronyn, mymryn, blewyn
**rapacious** adj rheibus,
ysglyfaethus
**rape** vt treisio ♦ n trais
**rapid** adj cyflym, buan, chwyrn,
gwyllt
**rapist** n treisiwr
**rapture** n perlewyg, gorawen,
afiaith
**rare** adj anaml, prin; godidog;
tenau
**rascal** n dihiryn, cnaf, gwalch,
cenau
**rash** adj byrbwyll, rhyfygus,
anystyriol
**rash** n brech, tarddiant
**rasher** n ysglisen, sleisen, tafell,
golwyth
**rasp** vb rhasglio, crafu, rhygnu
**raspberry** n afanen, mafonen

**rat** *n* llygoden fawr, llygoden ffrengig ♦ *vi* llygota
**rate** *vt* ffraeo, dwrdio, dweud y drefn
**rate** *n* cyflymder; treth; cyfradd (*of interest*)
**rateable value** *n* gwerth trethiannol
**ratepayer** *n* trethdalwr
**rather** *adv* braidd, hytrach, go, lled
**ratify** *vt* cadarnhau
**ratio** *n* cyfartaledd; cymhareb
**ration** *n* dogn, saig ♦ *vt* dogni
**rational** *adj* rhesymol
**rationale** *n* rhesymwaith
**rationalization** *n* rhesymoliad
**rationalize** *vb* rhesymoli
**rattle** *vb* rhuglo, trystio ♦ *n* rhugl, rhwnc
**raucous** *adj* cryg, garw, aflafar
**ravage** *vt* anrheithio, diffeithio, difrodi
**rave** *vi* gwallgofi, ynfydu, gwynfydu
**ravel** *vb* drysu; dad-weu, datod
**raven** *n* cigfran
**ravenous** *adj* rheibus, gwancus
**ravine** *n* hafn, ceunant
**raving** *adj* ynfyd, dwl, gwallgof
**ravish** *vt* treisio, cipio; swyno, hudo
**ravishing** *adj* deniadol iawn
**raw** *adj* amrwd; crai, cri; noeth, dolurus, garw; dibrofiad ♦ *n* cig noeth, dolur
**ray** *n* paladr, pelydryn
**ray** *n* cath fôr
**raze** *vt* llwyr ddymchwelyd, dileu
**razor** *n* ellyn, rasal ♦ *vt* eillio. **r. blade** *n* llafn ellyn
**re** *prep* ym mater, mewn perthynas â
**re-** *prefix* ad-, ail-
**reach** *vb* cyrraedd, estyn ♦ *n* cyrraedd
**react** *vi* adweithio
**reaction** *n* adwaith

**reactionary** *adj* adweithiol
**reactor** *n* adweithydd
**read** *vb* darllen
**readable** *adj* darllenadwy
**reader** *n* darllenydd
**readily** *adv* yn barod, yn ddiffwdan
**reading** *n* darllen
**readjustment** *n* atgywiriad, addasiad
**ready** *adj* parod, rhwydd
**reafforestation** *n* ailfforestiad
**real** *adj* gwir, real, go-iawn
**reality** *n* gwirionedd, sylwedd; dirwedd, realiti
**realize** *vt* sylweddoli; troi yn arian
**really** *adv* gwir, hollol, mewn difrif
**realm** *n* teyrnas, gwlad, bro
**reap** *vb* medi
**reappear** *vb* ailymddangos
**rear** *n* cefn, pen ôl, ôl
**rear** *vb* codi, magu; codi ar ei draed ôl
**reason** *n* rheswm ♦ *vb* rhesymu
**reasonable** *adj* rhesymol
**reassurance** *n* calondid
**reassure** *vt* calonogi, cysuro
**rebate** *n* ad-daliad
**rebel** *vi* gwrthryfela ♦ *n* gwrthryfelwr
**rebellion** *n* gwrthryfel
**rebound** *vi* adlamu ♦ *n* adlam
**rebuff** *n* nacâd, sen ♦ *vt* nacáu, sennu
**rebuke** *vt* ceryddu ♦ *n* cerydd, sen
**rebut** *vt* gwrthbrofi, gwrthddywedyd
**recall** *vt* galw yn ôl; galw i gof, cofio
**recant** *vb* datgyffesu
**recapitulate** *vt* ailadrodd (yn gryno)
**recede** *vi* encilio, cilio yn ôl
**receipt** *n* derbyniad; derbynneb
**receive** *vt* derbyn
**receiver** *n* derbynnydd
**recent** *adj* diweddar
**receptacle** *n* llestr; cynheiliad

(llysieueg)

**reception** n derbyniad, croeso. **r. desk** n man croeso, man derbyn

**receptionist** n croesawferch, croesawydd

**recess** n cil, encil; cilfach; gwyliau

**recessional** adj, n (emyn) ymadawol

**recipe** n cyfarwyddyd; rysáit

**recipient** n derbyniwr, derbynnydd

**reciprocal** adj cilyddol

**reciprocate** vb talu'n ôl, cydgyfnewid; cilyddu

**recital** n adroddiad, datganiad

**recitation** n adroddiad

**recite** vb adrodd

**reck** vb gofalu, ystyried

**reckless** adj anystyriol, rhyfygus, dibris

**reckon** vb cyfrif, barnu, bwrw

**reclaim** vt adennill, diwygio

**recline** vb lledorwedd, gorwedd, gorffwys

**recluse** n meudwy, ancr

**recognition** n adnabyddiaeth, cydnabyddiaeth

**recognize** vt adnabod, cydnabod

**recoil** vi adlamu, gwrthneidio, cilio

**recollect** vt galw i gof, atgofio, cofio

**recommend** vt cymeradwyo, argymell

**recompense** vt ad-dalu, gwobrwyo, talu

**reconcile** vt cymodi, cysoni

**recondite** adj dwfn, cudd, cêl, tywyll

**recondition** vt atgyflyru, ailwneud

**reconnaissance** n rhagchwiliad

**reconnoitre** vt chwilio, archwilio

**record** vt cofnodi, recordio ♦ n cofnod, record

**recorder** n (LAW) cofiadur; (MUS) recordydd

**recording** n recordiad

**recount** vt adrodd

**re-count** vb ailgyfrif

**recoup** vb digolledu

**recourse** n cyrchfa. **to have r. to** mynd at, defnyddio

**recover** vb cael yn ôl, adennill; ymadfer; adferiad

**recreation** n difyrrwch, adloniant

**recruit** n recriwt; newyddian ♦ vt codi gwŷr; adennill

**rectangle** n petryal

**rectangular** adj petryalog

**rectify** vt unioni, cywiro; puro, coethi

**rectilinear** adj unionlin

**rector** n rheithor

**rectory** n rheithoriaeth; rheithordy

**recuperate** vb adfer, ymadfer, cryfhau, gwella

**recur** vi ailddigwydd, dychwelyd

**recurrence** n ail-ddigwyddiad, ail-ymddangosiad

**recurring** adj cylchol

**recusant** n anghydffurfiwr

**red** adj, n coch, rhudd

**redeem** vt prynu (yn ôl), gwaredu

**redemption** n prynedigaeth

**redeploy** vb adleoli

**redeployment** n adleoliad, trawsgyflogaeth

**red herring** n (met) ysgyfarnog

**redirect** vb ailgyfeirio

**redo** vb ailwneud

**redolent** adj yn sawru o

**redoubtable** adj i'w ofni; pybyr

**redress** vt unioni ♦ n iawn (am gam)

**Red Sea** n: **the R.S.** y Môr Coch

**reduce** vt lleihau, gostwng; rhydwytho

**reduced** adj gostyngol

**reduction** n lleihad, gostyngiad

**redundancy** n anghyflogaeth

**redundant** adj gormodol; anghyflog, digyflog

**reed** n cawnen, corsen, calaf; pibell

**reef** n plyg hwyl, riff ♦ vt plygu

hwyl

**reef** *n* creigl (yn y môr), creigfa, rîff

**reek** *n* mwg, tarth, drewdod ♦ *vb* mygu, drewi

**reel** *n* ril ♦ *vb* dirwyn

**reel** *vi* troi, chwyldroi ♦ *n* dawns

**refectory** *n* ffreutur

**refer** *vb* cyfeirio, cyfarwyddo

**reference** *n* cyfeiriad; geirda

**refill** *n* adlenwad ♦ *vt* adlenwi

**refine** *vb* puro, coethi

**reflect** *vb* adlewyrchu; myfyrio

**reflection** *n* adlewyrchiad, myfyrdod, ailfeddwl

**reflex** *n* adweithred, atgyrch

**reflexive** *adj* atblygol

**reform** *vb* diwygio, gwella ♦ *n* diwygiad

**reformation** *n* diwygiad

**reformatory** *n* ysgol ddiwygio

**refrain** *vb* ymatal

**refrain** *n* byrdwn

**refresh** *vt* adfywio, dadebru, adlonni

**refresher course** *n* cwrs adolygu

**refreshing** *adj* adfywiol

**refreshments** *npl* ymborth, lluniaeth

**refrigerate** *vt* rheweiddio, cadw'n oer

**refrigerator** *n* rhewgell, oergell

**refuge** *n* noddfa, lloches

**refugee** *n* ffoadur

**refund** *n* ad-daliad ♦ *vb* ad-dalu

**refurbish** *vb* adnewyddu

**refusal** *n* gwrthodiad, nacâd

**refuse** *vb* gwrthod

**refuse** *n* ysbwriel, gwehilion, sothach

**refute** *vt* gwrthbrofi, datbrofi

**regal** *adj* brenhinol

**regard** *vt* edrych ar, ystyried ♦ *n* sylw, parch, hoffter

**regarding** *prep* ynglŷn â, ynghylch

**regardless** *adj* heb ofal, diofal

**regenerate** *vt* aileni

**régime** *n* trefn, cyfundrefn

**regiment** *n* catrawd

**region** *n* ardal, bro, gwlad

**regional** *adj* rhanbarthol

**register** *n* cofrestr ♦ *vt* cofrestru

**registered** *adj* cofrestredig

**registrar** *n* cofrestrydd

**registration** *n* cofrestriad. **r. number** *n* rhif cofrestru, rhif trethiant

**registry** *n* cofrestrfa

**regret** *vt* gofidio, edifaru ♦ *n* gofid

**regular** *adj* rheolaidd, cyson

**regulate** *vt* rheoleiddio, llywio, rheoli

**regulation** *n* rheol, trefniant

**rehabilitate** *vt* adfer i fri neu fraint, ailsefydlu

**rehabilitation** *n* adferiad

**rehearsal** *n* rihyrsal, practis

**rehearse** *vt* adrodd; ymarfer ymlaen llaw

**reign** *vi* teyrnasu ♦ *n* teyrnasiad

**reimburse** *vt* talu yn ôl, ad-dalu

**rein** *n* afwyn, awen ♦ *vt* ffrwyno

**reindeer** *n* carw

**reinforce** *vt* atgyfnerthu

**reinstate** *vt* adfer i safle neu fraint

**reiterate** *vt* ailadrodd, mynychu

**reject** *vt* gwrthod, bwrw ymaith

**rejection** *n* gwrthodiad

**rejoice** *vb* llawenhau, gorfoleddu

**rejoin** *vb* ateb, gwrthateb

**rejoinder** *n* ateb, gwrthateb

**rejuvenate** *vb* adfywiogi, adnewyddu

**relapse** *vi* ailglafychu, ailymhoelyd, atglafychu

**relate** *vb* adrodd, mynegi; perthyn

**related** *adj* yn perthyn; wedi ei ddweud

**relating to** *prep* yn ymwneud â

**relation** *n* adroddiad; perthynas

**relationship** *n* perthynas

**relative** *adj* perthnasol ♦ *n* perthynas. **r. pronoun** rhagenw perthynol

**relax** vb llacio, llaesu, ymollwng
**relaxing** adj ymlaciol
**relay** n cyflenwad newydd, cyfnewid; darlledu ♦ vb ailosod. **r. race** n ras gyfnewid
**release** vt rhyddhau, gollwng ♦ n rhyddhad
**relegate** vt alltudio, deol, darostwng
**relent** vi tyneru, tirioni, llaesu
**relevant** adj perthnasol
**reliable** adj y gellir dibynnu arno, dibynadwy
**reliance** n ymddiried, dibyniaeth, hyder, pwys
**relic** n crair, (pl) gweddillion
**relief** n cynhorthwy; gollyngdod, ymwared; tirwedd
**relieve** vt cynorthwyo; esmwytho, ysgafnhau; rhyddhau, gollwng
**religion** n crefydd
**religious** adj crefyddol
**relinquish** vt gollwng, gildio, gwadu
**relish** n blas; ennyn, mwyniant ♦ vb blasio, hoffi
**reluctance** n amharodrwydd, anfodlonrwydd
**reluctant** adj anfodlon, anewyllysgar
**rely** vi hyderu, ymddiried, dibynnu
**remain** vi aros, parhau, gorffwys
**remainder** n gweddill, rhelyw
**remains** npl olion, gweddillion
**remand** vt aildraddodi. **r. home** n cartref i droseddwyr ifanc
**remark** vb sylwi ♦ n sylw
**remarkable** adj nodedig, hynod, rhyfedd, syn
**remedial** n adferol; meddyginiaethol
**remedy** n meddyginiaeth ♦ vt meddyginiaethu, gwella
**remember** vt cofio
**remembrance** n cof, coffa, coffadwriaeth
**remind** vt atgofio, atgoffa, cofio

**reminiscence** n atgof
**remiss** adj esgeulus, diofal, llac
**remission** n maddeuant
**remit** vb maddau; arafu, peidio; anfon
**remittance** n taliad
**remnant** n gweddill, gwarged
**remonstrance** n cwyn, gwrthdystiad
**remonstrate** vi ymliw, gwrthdystio
**remorse** n edifeirwch, gofid, atgno
**remote** adj pell, pellennig, anghysbell
**remotely** adv o bell
**removable** adj symudadwy, y gellir ei symud
**removal** n symudiad, diswyddiad
**remove** vb symud, dileu; mudo
**remunerate** vt talu, gwobrwyo
**renaissance** n dadeni
**rend** vb rhwygo, dryllio, llarpio
**render** vb talu; datgan; gwneud; troi, cyfieithu
**rendezvous** n cyrchfa, man cyfarfod
**renegade** n gwrthgiliwr
**renew** vt adnewyddu
**renounce** vt ymwrthod, ymwadu, gwadu
**renovate** vt adnewyddu
**renown** n clod, bri, enwogrwydd
**rent** n rhwyg
**rent** n ardreth, rhent ♦ vt ardrethu, rhentu
**rental** n rent
**repair** vi cyrchu, mynd
**repair** vi atgyweirio, trwsio ♦ n cywair
**reparation** n iawn, ad-daliad
**repartee** n ateb parod
**repatriate** vb adfer i'w wlad ei hun
**repeal** vt diddymu ♦ n diddymiad
**repeat** vb ailadrodd, ailgyflawni
**repel** vt bwrw yn ôl
**repent** vb edifarhau, edifaru
**repentance** n edifeirwch

**repetition** *n* ailadroddiad
**repetitive** *adj* ailadroddus
**replace** *vb* ailosod, dodi'n ôl;
cymryd lle (arall)
**replacement** *n* un sy'n cymryd lle
arall
**replay** *vb* ailchwarae
**replenish** *vt* ail-lenwi, diwallu
**replete** *adj* llawn, cyflawn, gorlawn
**replica** *n* copi cywir, cyflun
**reply** *vi* ateb ♦ *n* ateb, atebiad
**report** *vt* adrodd, hysbysu ♦ *n*
adroddiad; swn ergyd
**reporter** *n* gohebydd
**repose** *vb* gorffwys ♦ *n* gorffwys
**repository** *n* ystorfa, trysorfa
**reprehend** *vt* ceryddu, argyhoeddi
**represent** *vt* portreadu,
cynrychioli
**representative** *adj* yn cynrychioli
♦ *n* cynrychiolydd
**repress** *vt* atal, gostegu, llethu
**repression** *n* ataliad, darostyngiad,
gwrthodiad
**reprimand** *n* cerydd ♦ *vt* ceryddu
**reprisal** *n* dial
**reproach** *vt* ceryddu,
gwaradwyddo, edliw ♦ *n*
gwaradwydd
**reproduce** *vt* atgynhyrchu, epilio
**reproduction** *n* atgynhyrchiad,
copi; epiliad
**reproof** *n* cerydd
**reprove** *vt* ceryddu, argyhoeddi
**reptile** *n* ymlusgiad
**republic** *n* gweriniaeth,
gwerinlywodraeth
**repudiate** *vt* diarddel, diarddelwi,
gwadu
**repugnant** *adj* croes, atgas,
gwrthun
**repulse** *vt* bwrw'n ôl; nacáu ♦ *n*
gwrthergyd
**repulsion** *n* gwrthnysedd
**repulsive** *adj* atgas, ffiaidd
**reputable** *adj* parchus, cyfrifol
**reputation** *n* gair, cymeriad, enw

da
**repute** *vt* cyfrif, tybied ♦ *n* parch,
bri
**request** *n* cais ♦ *vt* ceisio, gofyn
**requiem** *n* offeren dros y meirw;
galargerdd
**require** *vt* gofyn, mynnu
**requisite** *adj* gofynnol,
angenrheidiol
**requisition** *n* archeb ♦ *vb* hawlio
**requite** *vt* talu, gwobrwyo, talu'r
pwyth
**rescind** *vt* diddymu, dirymu
**rescue** *vt* achub ♦ *n* achubiad
**research** *n* ymchwil, ymchwiliad ♦
*vb* ymchwilio
**resemblance** *n* tebygrwydd
**resemble** *vt* tebygu i
**resent** *vt* tramgwyddo, digio,
cymryd yn chwith
**resentful** *adj* digofus, llidiog
**resentment** *n* dig, dicter
**reservation** *n* cadw, cadfa
**reserve** *vt* cadw yn ôl, cadw wrth
gefn ♦ *n* yr hyn a gedwir, cronfa;
swildod
**reserved** *adj* swil; wedi ei gadw;
**r. seat** sedd gadw
**reservoir** *n* cronfa, llyn
**reshuffle** *vb* aildrefnu
**reside** *vi* preswylio
**residential** *adj* preswyl
**residue** *n* gweddill
**resign** *vb* rhoi i fyny,
ymddiswyddo, ymddeol
**resignation** *n* ymddiswyddiad;
ymostyngiad
**resilience** *n* hydwythder,
ystwythder
**resilient** *adj* hydwyth, ystwyth
**resin** *n* ystor, rhwsin
**resist** *vb* gwrthsefyll, gwrthwynebu
**resistance** *n* gwrthwynebiad,
gwrthsafiad
**resolute** *adj* penderfynol
**resolution** *n* penderfyniad
**resolve** *vb* penderfynu ♦ *n*

penderfyniad
**resonant** adj atseiniol
**resort** vi cyrchu ♦ n cyrchfa;
ymwared
**resound** vb atseinio, diasbedain
**resource** n sgil, dyfais; (pl)
adnoddau
**respect** vt parch ♦ n golwg; parch
**respectable** adj parchus
**respectful** adj boneddigaidd, yn
dangos parch
**respective** adj priodol, ar wahân
**respite** n oediad, saib, seibiant,
hamdden
**resplendent** adj disglair,
ysblennydd
**respond** vi ateb, ymateb; porthi
**response** n ateb, atebiad
**responsibility** n cyfrifoldeb
**responsible** adj atebol, cyfrifol
**responsive** adj ymatebol
**rest** n, vb gorffwys ♦ n (music)
tawnod
**rest** vi aros, parhau ♦ n gweddill
**restaurant** n tŷ bwyta, bwyty
**restful** adj tawel, llonydd, esmwyth
**restitution** n adferiad; iawn
**restive** adj ystyfnig, ystranclyd,
noglyd, diamynedd
**restless** adj aflonydd, rhwyfus
**restore** vt adfer; atgyweirio
**restrain** vt atal, ffrwyno
**restrained** adj cynnil, gochelgar,
cymhedrol
**restraint** n atalfa, ffrwyn,
caethiwed
**restrict** vt cyfyngu, caethiwo
**restriction** n cyfyngiad
**result** vi deillio, canlyn ♦ n
canlyniad
**resume** vt ailddechrau
**résumé** n crynodeb
**resumption** n ailddechreuad
**resurgent** adj yn ailgodi, yn ailfyw
**resurrection** n atgyfodiad
**resuscitate** vb adfywhau, dadebru
**retail** vt manwerthu, adwerthu ♦ n

adwerth
**retailer** n manwerthwr
**retain** vb cadw, dal; llogi
**retaliate** vb talu'n ôl, talu'r pwyth,
dial
**retaliation** n dial
**retard** vb rhwystro, oedi
**retch** vi cyfogi, chwydu
**retentive** adj yn dal heb ollwng;
gafaelgar
**reticent** adj tawedog, distaw
**retina** n rhwyden y llygad, retina
**retinue** n gosgordd, gosgorddlu
**retire** vi ymneilltuo, encilio, cilio,
ymddeol
**retired** adj wedi ymddeol
**retirement** n ymddeoliad
**retiring** adj swil
**retort** vb gwrthateb ♦ n ateb
parod; ritort (cemeg)
**retrace** vb mynd yn ôl dros yr un
ffordd, dychwelyd
**retract** vb tynnu'n ôl
**retrain** vb ailhyfforddi
**retreat** vi cilio, encilio, ffoi ♦ n
encil, ffo
**retrench** vb cwtogi, cynilo
**retribution** n ad-daledigaeth, cosb,
dial
**retrieve** vt olrhain; adennill, adfer
**retrogress** vi mynd yn ôl, dirywio
**retrospect** n ad-drem, adolwg
**return** vb dychwelyd ♦ n
dychweliad; elw, enillion. **r.**
**(ticket)** n tocyn dwyffordd
**reveal** vt datguddio, amlygu,
dangos
**revel** vi gloddesta; ymhyfrydu ♦ n
gloddest
**revelry** n miri
**revenge** vb, n dial
**revenue** n cyllid, enillion, incwm
**reverberate** vb taro'n ôl; atseinio
**revere** vt parchu, anrhydeddu
**reverence** n parch, parchedigaeth
**reverend** adj parchedig
**reverent** adj parchus, gŵyl,

gwylaidd
**reversal** *n* dymchweliad, cwymp
**reverse** *adj* gwrthwyneb, chwith ♦
*vb* troi, gwrthdroi ♦ *n* gwrthdro,
aflwydd. **r. charge call** *n* galwad y
telir amdani'r pen arall. **r. (gear)**
*n* gêr ôl
**revert** *vb* troi yn ôl, dychwelyd
**review** *vt* adolygu ♦ *n* adolygiad
**reviewer** *n* adolygydd
**revile** *vt* difenwi, cablu,
gwaradwyddo
**revise** *vt* cywiro, diwygio
**revision** *n* cywiriad; adolygiad
**revival** *n* adfywiad, diwygiad
**revive** *vb* adfywio, adnewyddu
**revoke** *vb* galw yn ôl, diddymu,
dirymu
**revolt** *vb* gwrthryfela ♦ *n*
gwrthryfel
**revolting** *adj* gwrthnaws, atgas,
ffiaidd
**revolution** *n* chwyldro, chwyldroad
**revolutionary** *adj* chwildroadol ♦ *n*
chwildrowr
**revolve** *vb* troi, amdroi, cylchdroi
**revolver** *n* llawddryll
**revulsion** *n* atgasedd
**reward** *n* gwobr ♦ *vt* gwobrwyo
**reword** *vb* ailysgrifennu,
ailddweud
**rhapsody** *n* hwyl, ymfflamychiad
**rhetoric** *n* rhetoreg, rhethreg
**rheumatism** *n* cryd cymalau,
gwynegon
**rhinoceros** *n* rhinoseros
**rhombus** *n* rhombws
**rhubarb** *n* rhiwbob
**rhyme** *n* odl, rhigwm ♦ *vb* odli,
rhigymu
**rhythm** *n* rhythm, rhediad
**rib** *n* asen, eisen
**ribald** *n* masweddwr ♦ *adj*
masweddol
**ribbon** *n* rhuban, ysnoden
**rice** *n* reis
**rich** *adj* cyfoethog, goludog, bras

**riches** *npl* cyfoeth, golud
**richness** *n* cyfoethogrwydd,
braster, ffrwythlonrwydd
**rick** *n* tas
**rickets** *npl* y llech(au)
**rickety** *adj* simsan, bregus
**rid** *vt* gwared
**riddle** *n* dychymyg, pos
**riddle** *n* rhidyll ♦ *vt* rhidyllio,
gogrwn
**ride** *vb* marchogaeth, marchocáu
**rider** *n* marchogwr; atodiad
**ridge** *n* grwn, trum, cefn, crib
**ridicule** *n* gwawd ♦ *vt* gwawdio,
chwerthin am ben
**ridiculous** *adj* chwerthinllyd
**riding** *n* marchogaeth
**riding school** *n* ysgol farchogaeth
**rife** *adj* aml, cyffredin, rhemp
**riff-raff** *n* gwehilion y bobl, dihirod
**rifle** *vt* anrheithio, ysbeilio
**rifle** *n* dryll, reiffl
**rift** *n* agen, hollt, rhwyg
**rig** *vb* rigio, taclu ♦ *n* rig
**right** *adj* iawn, uniawn; deau ♦ *adv*
yn iawn ♦ *vt* unioni, cywiro ♦ *n*
iawnder, hawl. **r. angle** *n* ongl
sgwâr. **rights and customs** braint
a defod. **r. wing** (*POL*) asgell dde
**righteous** *adj* cyfiawn
**righteousness** *n* cyfiawnder
**rightful** *adj* cyfreithlon, iawn, teg
**rigid** *adj* anhyblyg, manwl, caeth
**rigmarole** *n* ffregod, rhibidirês
**rigour** *n* llymder
**rile** *vt* cythruddo, ffyrnigo, llidio
**rim** *n* ymyl, cylch, cant
**rind** *n* pil, croen, crawen, rhisgl
**ring** *n* modrwy, cylch ♦ *vb*
modrwyo
**ring** *vb* canu cloch, atseinio;
modrwyo ♦ *n* sŵn cloch, tinc.
**wedding r.** *n* modrwy briodas. **r.
road** *n* cylchffordd
**rinse** *vt* golchi, trochi
**riot** *n* terfysg, gloddest ♦ *vi*
terfysgu

**rip** *vb* rhipio, rhwygo, datod ♦ *n* rhwyg. **r.-off** *n* lladrad amlwg
**ripe** *adj* aeddfed
**ripple** *n* crych ♦ *vb* crychu
**rise** *vi* codi, cyfodi ♦ *n* codiad
**risk** *n* perygl, enbydrwydd ♦ *vt* peryglu, anturio, mentro
**rite** *n* defod
**ritual** *adj* defodol ♦ *n* defod
**rival** *n* cydymgeisydd ♦ *vb* cystadlu
**river** *n* afon
**rivet** *n* rhybed, hem, rifet ♦ *vb* rhybedu, hemio, rifetio
**rivulet** *n* afonig, nant, cornant
**road** *n* ffordd, heol; angorfa. **r. map** *n* map ffyrdd, map moduro. **r. works** *n* gwaith cynnal y ffordd
**roam** *vi* crwydro, gwibio
**roar** *vi* rhuo ♦ *n* rhu, rhuad
**roast** *vb* rhostio, crasu, pobi, digoni
**rob** *vt* lladrata, ysbeilio
**robber** *n* lleidr, ysbeiliwr
**robbery** *n* lladrad
**robe** *n* gwisg, gŵn
**robin** *n* brongoch
**robust** *adj* cadarn, cryf, grymus
**rock** *vb* siglo
**rock** *n* craig
**rockery** *n* gardd gerrig
**rocket** *n* roced
**rocky** *adj* creigiog; sigledig
**rod** *n* gwialen, llath
**rodent** *n* cnofil
**roe** *n* iyrches, ewig
**roe** *n* grawn pysgod, gronell
**roebuck** *n* iwrch
**rogue** *n* gwalch, cnaf
**role** *n* rhan, tasg, cymeriad
**roll** *vb* rholio, treiglo ♦ *n* rhôl. **r. call** *n* galw enwau (ar restr)
**rolling** *adj* tonnog. **r. pin** *n* rholbren. **r. stock** *n* rholstoc
**Roman** *n* Rhufeiniwr ♦ *adj* Rhufeinaidd, Rhufeinig. **R. Catholic** *n* Pabydd
**romance** *n* rhamant ♦ *vi* rhamantu

**Romania** *n* România
**romantic** *adj* rhamantus
**Rome** *n* Rhufain
**romp** *vi* rhampio ♦ *n* rhamp; rhampen
**rood** *n* rhwd; y grog, y groes
**roof** *n* to, nen ♦ *vt* toi
**rook** *n* ydfran, brân
**room** *n* lle; ystafell. **r. service** *n* gwasanaeth ystafell
**roomy** *adj* helaeth, eang
**roost** *n* clwyd ♦ *vi* clwydo
**rooster** *n* ceiliog
**root** *n* gwraidd, gwreiddyn ♦ *vb* gwreiddio; dadwreiddio
**rope** *n* rhaff ♦ *vt* rhaffu, rhwymo
**rosary** *n* paderau, llaswyr
**rose** *n* rhosyn. **r. hips** *npl* egroes
**rosette** *n* ysnoden
**rostrum** *n* llwyfan, areithfa
**rosy** *adj* rhosynnaidd, gwritgoch, disglair
**rot** *vb* pydru, braenu ♦ *n* pydredd; lol
**rota** *n* rhod, trefn
**rotate** *vi* troi, cylchdroi, chwyldroi
**rote** *n* tafod-leferydd
**rotten** *adj* pwdr, pydredig, sâl
**rouge** *n* lliw coch, gruddliw
**rough** *adj* garw, gerwin, bras
**round** *adj* crwn ♦ *n* crwn, cylch, tro, rownd ♦ *adv, prep* o glych, o amgylch ♦ *vb* crynio, rowndio
**roundabout** *n* cylchdro, cylchfan, cylch ogylch; ceffylau bach ♦ *adj* o amgylch, cwmpasog
**rouse** *vb* dihuno, deffroi, cyffroi
**rout** *n* rhawt; ffo, dymchweliad ♦ *vb* ymlid, dymchwelyd
**route** *n* ffordd, llwybr, hynt
**routine** *n* defod, arfer
**rove** *vb* crwydro, gwibio
**roving** *adj* crwydrol
**row** *n* rhes, rhestr
**row** *vb* rhwyfo
**row** *n* terfysg, cythrwfl, ffrae
**rowan** *n* criafol

**rowdy** *adj* trystiog, afreolus
**rowel** *n* troell ysbardun, rhywel
**rowing boat** *n* cwch rhwyfo
**royal** *adj* brenhinol
**royalty** *n* brenhiniaeth; toll, tâl, breindal
**rub** *vb* rhwbio, rhathu, iro, crafu
**rubber** *n* rwber
**rubbish** *n* ysbwriel, sothach; lol. **r. bin** *n* bin ysbwriel. **r. dump** *n* tomen ysbwriel
**rubble** *n* rhwbel
**ruby** *n* rhuddem ♦ *adj* coch, rhudd
**ruck** *n* pentwr, crynswth, haid, ysgarmes
**rucksack** *n* rhychsach
**ruction** *n* helynt, terfysg
**rudder** *n* llyw
**ruddy** *adj* coch, gwridog, gwritgoch
**rude** *adj* anfoesgar; anghelfydd, garw
**rudiment** *n* egwyddor, elfen
**rue** *vt* galaru, gofidio, edifaru
**rueful** *adj* trist, truenus, gresynus
**ruffian** *n* adyn, anfadyn, dihiryn
**ruffle** *vb* crychu, cyffroi, aflonyddu
**rug** *n* hugan
**rugby** *n* rygbi
**rugged** *adj* garw, gerwin, clogyrnog
**ruin** *n* distryw, dinistr; adfail ♦ *vb* difetha, andwyo
**rule** *n* rheol, llywodraeth; riwl ♦ *vb* rheoli, llywodraethu; llinellu
**ruler** *n* llywodraethwr; pren mesur, rhiwl
**ruling** *n* dyfarniad, barn ♦ *adj* llywodraethol, mewn grym
**rum** *n* rym ♦ *adj* od, rhyfedd
**rumble** *vi* trystio, tyrfu, godyrfu
**rummage** *vb* chwalu a chwilio, chwilota
**rumour** *n* chwedl, gair, sôn, achlust
**rump** *n* tin, bôn, cwman, cloren
**rumple** *vt* crychu, sybachu

**rumpus** *n* helynt, terfysg
**run** *vb* rhedeg, llifo ♦ *n* rhediad, rhedfa. **in the long r.** yn y pen draw
**rung** *n* ffon ysgol
**rupture** *n* rhwyg; tor llengig ♦ *vb* rhwygo
**rural** *adj* gwledig, gwladaidd
**ruse** *n* ystryw, dichell
**rush** *n* brwynen, pabwyryn
**rush** *vb* rhuthro ♦ *n* rhuthr. **r. hour** *n* awr brysur
**russet** *adj* llwytgoch
**Russia** *n* Rwsia
**rust** *n* rhwd ♦ *vb* rhydu
**rustic** *adj* gwladaidd, gwledig ♦ *n* gwladwr
**rusticate** *vt* anfon adref am dymor
**rustle** *vi* siffrwd, chwithrwd, rhuglo
**rusty** *adj* rhydlyd
**rut** *n* rhych, rhigol
**ruthless** *adj* didostur, diarbed, creulon
**rye** *n* rhyg

# S

**Sabbath** *n* Sabath, Saboth
**sabotage** *n* difrod bwriadol ♦ *vb* difrodi
**sacerdotal** *adj* offeiriadol
**sack** *n* sach, ffetan ♦ *vt* sachu; difrodi; diswyddo
**sackcloth** *n* sachlen, sachliain
**sacrament** *n* sacrament, ordinhad
**sacred** *adj* cysegredig, glân, sanctaidd
**sacrifice** *n* aberth, offrwm ♦ *vb* aberthu
**sacrilege** *n* halogiad, cysegrysbeiliad
**sad** *adj* trist, athrist, prudd, digalon
**saddle** *n* cyfrwy ♦ *vt* cyfrwyo; beichio

**saddler** n cyfrwywr
**sadness** n tristwch, prudd-der
**safe** adj diogel, dihangol, saff ♦ n cell, cist, cloer
**safety** n diogelwch. **s. belt** gwregys diogelwch. **s. pin** pin cau
**saffron** n saffrwm ♦ adj melyn
**sag** vb segio, segian, sagio, ymollwng
**sage** adj doeth ♦ n gŵr doeth
**sage** n saets
**Sahara** n Sahara
**sail** n hwyl ♦ vb hwylio, morio, mordwyo
**sailing** n hwylio. **s. boat** n llong hwylio
**sailor** n morwr, llongwr
**saint** n sant
**sake** n mwyn. **for the s. of** er mwyn
**salary** n cyflog
**sale** n gwerth, gwerthiant, arwerthiant
**salient** adj amlwg
**saline** adj heliaidd, hallt ♦ n heli
**saliva** n haliw, poer, dŵr anadl
**sallow** adj melyn afiach
**salmon** n eog, gleisiad, samwn
**saloon** n neuadd, salŵn
**salt** n halen, halwyn (cemeg) ♦ adj hallt ♦ vt halltu. **s. cellar** n llestr halen. **s. water** n dŵr hallt, dŵr y môr
**salty** adj hallt
**salute** vt cyfarch; saliwtio ♦ n cyfarchiad; saliwt
**salvation** n iachawdwriaeth. **S. Army** Byddin yr Iachawdwriaeth
**salve** n eli, ennaint ♦ vt elio, lleddfu; achub
**same** adj yr un, yr unrhyw, yr un fath
**sample** n sampl, enghraifft ♦ vt samplu, samplo
**sanctify** vt sancteiddio
**sanctimonious** adj ffug-sanctaidd, sych-dduwiol

**sanction** n caniatâd; cosb; sancsiwn (moeseg) ♦ vt caniatáu; cosbi
**sanctity** n sancteiddrwydd
**sanctuary** n cysegr; noddfa, nawdd
**sand** n tywod ♦ vt tywodi. **s. castle** n castell tywod
**sandpaper** n papur gwydrog
**sandpit** n pwll tywod
**sandwich** n brechdan
**sandy** adj tywodlyd; melyngoch
**sane** adj iach, call, synhwyrol
**sanitary** adj iechydol. **s. towel** n tywel misglwyf, tywel iechydol
**sanitation** n iechydiaeth
**sanity** n iechyd meddwl, iawn bwyll
**Santa Claus** n Siôn Corn
**sap** n nodd, sudd, sugn ♦ vt sugno, hysbyddu
**sap** vb tangloddio, diseilio
**sapling** n pren ieuanc
**sapphire** n saffir ♦ adj glas
**sarcasm** n gwawdiaith, coegni, gair du
**sarcastic** adj gwawdlym, coeglyd, brathog
**sardine** n sardîn
**sash** n gwregys; ffrâm ffenestr
**satchel** n sachell, cod lyfrau
**sate** vt digoni, llenwi, diwallu
**satellite** n canlynwr, cynffonnwr; lleuad; lloeren
**satiate** vt digoni, diwallu, syrffedu
**satin** n satin, pali
**satire** n dychan, gogan
**satirize** vb dychan, goganu
**satisfaction** n bodlonrwydd; iawn
**satisfactory** adj boddhaol; iawnol
**satisfy** vt bodloni, diwallu, digoni
**saturate** vt trwytho, mwydo
**Saturday** n dydd Sadwrn
**sauce** n saws; haerllugrwydd
**saucepan** n sosban
**saucer** n soser
**saucy** adj digywilydd, haerllug

**Saudi Arabia** n Saudi Arabia
**saunter** vi rhodianna, ymdroi, swmera
**sausage** n selsig, selsigen
**savage** adj gwyllt, ffyrnig, milain, anwar ♦ n dyn gwyllt, anwariad, anwarddyn
**save** vb achub, arbed, gwaredu; cynilo ♦ prep oddieithr, ond
**saving** adj achubol, darbodus
**savings** npl cynilion
**saviour** n achubwr, gwaredwr, iachawdwr
**savour** n sawr, blas ♦ vb sawru
**savoury** n blasusfwyd; adj sawrus
**saw** n llif ♦ vb llifio
**sawdust** n blawd llif
**sawmill** n melin lifio
**say** vb dywedyd, dweud
**saying** n dywediad, ymadrodd, gair
**scab** n crachen, cramen; clafr
**scabies** n y crafu
**scaffold** n ysgaffald; dienyddle
**scald** vt ysgaldio, sgaldan(u) ♦ n ysgaldiad
**scale** n clorian, tafol, mantol
**scale** n graddfa ♦ vb dringo
**scale** n cen ♦ vb cennu; digennu, pilio
**scallop** n gylfgragen; gwlf ♦ vt gylfu, minfylchu
**scalp** n copa, croen y pen ♦ vt penflingo
**scamp** n cnaf, gwalch, dihiryn
**scamper** vi ffoi, carlamu, brasgamu
**scan** vb corfannu; sganio, edrych, chwilio
**scandal** n tramgwydd, gwarth, enllib
**Scandinavia** n Llychlyn
**scanner** n sganydd
**scant, -y** adj prin
**scapegoat** n bwch dihangol
**scapegrace** n dyn diras, oferwr, dihiryn

**scar** n craith ♦ vt creithio
**scarce** adj, adv prin
**scarcely** adv prin, braidd, odid, nemor
**scare** vt brawychu, tarfu ♦ n dychryn
**scared** adj wedi cael ofn, wedi rhuso, wedi brawychu
**scarf** n crafat, sgarff
**scarlatina** n y dwymyn goch
**scarlet** adj ysgarlad
**scarp** n llethr
**scathe** vt deifio, anafu, niweidio
**scathing** adj deifiol, miniog
**scatter** vb gwasgaru, chwalu, taenu
**scavenger** n carthwr, carthydd
**scene** n lle; golwg, golygfa
**scenery** n golygfa
**scenic** adj hardd, golygfaol
**scent** n arogl, aroglau, trywydd; perarogl ♦ vt arogli
**sceptic** n amheuwr
**sceptical** adj amheugar
**sceptre** n teyrnwialen
**schedule** n atodlen, cofrestr, taflen
**scheme** n cynllun; cynllwyn ♦ vb cynllunio
**schism** n rhwyg, ymraniad, sism
**scholar** n ysgolhaig, ysgolor
**scholarly** adj ysgolheigaidd
**scholarship** n ysgolheictod; ysgoloriaeth
**scholastic** adj athrofaol
**school** n ysgol, ysgoldy ♦ vt disgyblu
**schoolbook** n llyfr ysgol
**schoolboy** n bachgen ysgol
**schoolchildren** npl plant ysgol
**schooldays** npl dyddiau ysgol
**schoolgirl** n merch ysgol
**schoolmaster** n athro
**schoolmistress** n athrawes
**schooner** n ysgwner
**sciatica** n clunwst
**science** n gwyddor, gwyddoniaeth
**scientific** adj gwyddonol

**scientist** *n* gwyddonydd
**scissors** *npl* siswrn
**scoff** *n* gwawd ♦ *vi* gwawdio, gwatwar
**scold** *vb* dwrdio, tafodi, ceryddu, cymhennu ♦ *n* cecren
**scone** *n* sgon
**scoop** *n* lletwad ♦ *vt* cafnu, cafnio
**scope** *n* ergyd, bwriad; cylch, cwmpas, lle
**scorch** *vb* deifio, llosgi, greidio, rhuddo
**score** *n* hac, rhic; cyfrif, dyled; sgôr; ugain
**score** *vb* rhicio, cyfrif, sgori(o)
**scorn** *n* dirmyg ♦ *vb* dirmygu, gwatwar
**scorpion** *n* ysgorpion
**Scot** *n* Ysgotyn, Albanwr
**scotch** *vt* hacio, darnio, trychu
**Scotch** *adj* Ysgotaidd, Albanaidd
**scot-free** *adj* croeniach, dianaf
**Scotland** *n* Yr Alban
**Scottish** *adj* Albanaidd
**scoundrel** *n* cnaf, dihiryn
**scour** *vt* carthu, ysgwrio
**scour** *vb* rhedeg; chwilio
**scourge** *n* fflangell, pla ♦ *vt* fflangellu
**scout** *n* sgowt, ysbïwr ♦ *vt* sgowta, ysbïo
**scowl** *vb* cuchio, gwgu ♦ *n* cilwg, gwg
**scraggy** *adj* esgyrnog, tenau, cul, salw
**scramble** *vi*, *n* ciprys, ymgiprys.
**scrambled egg** *n* cymysgwy
**scrap** *n* tamaid, tameidyn, dernyn
**scrapbook** *n* llyfr lloffion
**scrape** *vb* crafu ♦ *n* helynt, helbul, crafiad
**scratch** *vb* crafu, cripio
**scrawl** *vb* ysgriblo, ysgriblan
**scream** *vi* ysgrechain ♦ *n* ysgrech, gwawch
**screech** *vi* ysgrechain ♦ *n* ysgrech
**screen** *n* llen, cysgod; sgrin ♦ *vt*

cysgodi
**screw** *n* sgriw, hoel dro ♦ *vb* ysgriwio
**screwdriver** *n* tyrnsgriw
**scribble** *n* ysgribl ♦ *vb* ysgriblo, ysgriblan
**script** *n* llawysgrif, ysgrif, sgript
**scripture** *n* ysgrythur
**scroll** *n* rhòl, plyg llyfr
**scrub** *n* prysgwydd; ysgwrfa ♦ *vt* ysgwrio
**scruff** *n* gwar, gwegil
**scrum(mage)** *n* sgrym, ysgarmes
**scruple** *n* petruster (moesol) ♦ *vi* petruso
**scrupulous** *adj* gwyliadwrus, manwl
**scrutinize** *vt* chwilio, archwilio
**scrutiny** *n* archwiliad
**scuffle** *vi*, *n* ymgiprys, ymryson
**scull** *n* rhwyf unllaw, rhodl ♦ *vb* rhodli
**scullery** *n* cegin fach, cegin gefn
**sculptor** *n* cerflunydd
**sculpture** *n* cerfluniaeth; cerflun ♦ *vb* cerfio, torri
**scum** *n* sgum; gwehilion, sorod
**scurf** *n* cen, mardon
**scurrilous** *adj* bustlaidd, brwnt, difrïol
**scurry** *vi* ffrystio ♦ *n* ffrwst, ffwdan
**scurvy** *adj* crachlyd, crach ♦ *n* llwg
**scutter** *vi* ffoi, diengyd
**scuttle** *n* llestr glo
**scuttle** *vt* tyllu llong i'w suddo
**scuttle** *vi* heglu ffoi, dianc
**scythe** *n* pladur
**sea** *n* môr, cefnfor; moryn. **s. water** *n* dŵr y môr
**seaboard** *n* morlan, glan y môr
**seafood** *n* bwyd môr
**seagull** *n* gwylan
**seal** *n* morlo
**seal** *n* sêl, insel ♦ *vt* selio
**sea level** *n* lefel y môr

**seam** *n* gwnïad, gwrym; haen, gwythïen; craith

**seaman** *n* morwr, llongwr

**seamstress** *n* gwniadwraig, gwniadyddes

**seamy** *adj* annymunol

**seance** *n* seawns

**seaplane** *n* awyren fôr

**sear** *adj* sych, crin, gwyw ♦ *vt* serio, deifio

**search** *vb* chwilio, profi ♦ *n* ymchwil

**seashore** *n* glan y môr

**seasickness** *n* salwch y môr

**seaside** *n* glan y môr

**season** *n* tymor, amser, pryd, adeg ♦ *vb* tymheru; halltu. **high/ low s.** *n* tymor prysur/llac

**seasonal** *adj* tymhorol

**season ticket** *n* tocyn tymor

**seat** *n* sedd, sêt, eisteddle ♦ *vi* eistedd

**seat belt** *n* gwregys diogelwch

**seaweed** *n* gwymon, gwmon

**seaworthy** *adj* addas i'r môr, diogel

**secede** *vi* ymneilltuo, encilio; torri'n rhydd, ymwahanu

**secession** *n* ymneilltuad, enciliad; ymwahaniad

**seclude** *vt* cau allan, neilltuo

**second** *adj* ail ♦ *n* ail; eiliad ♦ *vt* eilio. **s. class** *adj* ail ddosbarth, isradd

**secondary** *adj* eilradd, uwchradd. **s. school** *n* ysgol uwchradd

**second-hand** *adj* ail law

**secret** *adj* dirgel, cyfrinachol ♦ *n* cyfrinach

**secretary** *n* ysgrifennydd. **S. of State** *n* Ysgrifennydd Gwladol

**secretive** *adj* yn celu, tawedog

**sect** *n* sect, enwad

**sectarian** *adj* enwadol, cul

**section** *n* toriad, trychiad; rhan, adran

**sector** *n* sector

**secular** *adj* bydol; lleygol; seciwlar

**secure** *adj* sicr, diogel ♦ *vt* sicrhau, diogelu

**security** *n* diogelwch, sicrwydd, gwystl

**sedate** *adj* tawel, digyffro ♦ *vb* rhoi i gysgu, tawelu

**sedative** *adj* lleddfol, lliniarol

**sedge** *n* hesg

**sediment** *n* gwaelodion, gwaddod

**sedition** *n* terfysg, brad, gwrthryfel

**seduce** *vt* llithio, hudo, twyllo

**seductive** *adj* llithiol, deniadol

**see** *n* esgobaeth

**see** *vb* gweld, canfod

**seed** *n* had, hedyn ♦ *vb* hadu, hedeg

**seedy** *adj* hadog; salw; sâl, anhwylus

**seek** *vb* ceisio, ymofyn, chwilio

**seem** *vi* ymddangos

**seemly** *adj* gweddus, gweddaidd, addas

**seep** *vb* diferu, gollwng

**seer** *n* gweledydd

**seesaw** *n* siglenydd

**seethe** *vb* berwi, byrlymu

**segment** *n* darn, rhan, segment

**segregate** *vt* didoli, neilltuo, gwahanu

**seize** *vb* gafael mewn, atafaelu, dal, achub

**seizure** *n* daliad; strôc

**seldom** *adv* anfynych, anaml

**select** *vt* dewis, dethol

**self** (**selves**) *n* hun, hunan ♦ *prefix* hunan-, ym-

**self-catering** *adj* hunan arlwy

**self-conscious** *adj* hunanymwybodol, swil

**self-contained** *adj* annibynnol, ar wahân

**self-control** *n* hunanlywodraeth

**self-employed** *adj* hunangyflogedig

**self-evident** *adj* amlwg, eglur

**self-government** *n* ymreolaeth
**self-interest** *n* hunan-les
**selfish** *adj* hunanol
**self-possessed** *adj* hunanfeddianol
**self-respect** *n* hunan barch
**self-sacrifice** *n* hunanaberth
**selfsame** *adj* yr un, yr unrhyw
**self-satisfied** *adj* hunanddigonol
**self-service** *n* hunanwasanaeth
**self-sufficient** *adj* hunanddigonol, hy
**sell** *vb* gwerthu; siomi ♦ *n* siom
**seller** *n* gwerthwr
**sellotape** *n* selotâp
**semblance** *n* tebygrwydd, rhith
**semi-** *prefix* hanner, lled, go
**semicolon** *n* gwahannod (;)
**seminary** *n* athrofa, ysgol
**sempiternal** *adj* bythol, tragwyddol
**senate** *n* senedd
**send** *vt* anfon, danfon, gyrru
**senile** *adj* hen a methedig, heneiddiol
**senior** *adj* hŷn ♦ *n* hynaf
**seniority** *n* blaenoriaeth
**sensation** *n* ymdeimlad, teimlad; cyffro, ias, syndod
**sensational** *adj* iasol, cyffrous
**sense** *n* synnwyr, pwyll, ystyr
**senseless** *adj* dienaid, disynnwyr, hurt
**sensible** *adj* synhwyrol; teimladwy
**sensitive** *adj* teimladwy, croendenau; hydeiml
**sensual** *adj* cnawdol; trythyll, chwantus
**sensuous** *adj* teimladol, synhwyrus
**sentence** *n* brawddeg; barn, dedfryd ♦ *vt* dedfrydu
**sententious** *adj* doetheiriog
**sentiment** *n* syniad, teimlad
**sentry** *n* gwyliwr, gwyliedydd
**separate** *adj* ar wahân ♦ *vb* gwahanu, neilltuo, ysgar; ymwahanu

**separation** *n* gwahaniad
**sept-** *prefix* saith, seith-
**September** *n* Medi
**septic** *adj* braenol, pydrol, madreddol
**sepulchre** *n* bedd, beddrod
**sequel** *n* canlyniad
**sequence** *n* trefn, dilyniad
**sequester** *vt* neilltuo; atafaelu
**serenade** *n* hwyrgan, nosgan ♦ *vt* hwyrganu
**serene** *adj* teg; tawel, digynnwrf
**sergeant** *n* rhingyll, sarsiant
**serial** *adj* cyfresol, bob yn rhifyn ♦ *n* stori gyfres
**series** *n* rhes, cyfres
**serious** *adj* difrifol
**seriously** *adv* yn ddifrifol
**sermon** *n* pregeth
**serpent** *n* sarff
**serrated** *adj* danheddog
**serum** *n* serwm
**servant** *n* gwas; morwyn
**serve** *vb* gwasanaethu, gweini
**service** *n* gwasanaeth, oedfa; llestri. **s. charge** *n* tâl am wasanaeth
**serviceable** *adj* gwasanaethgar, defnyddiol
**serviette** *n* napcyn
**servile** *adj* gwasaidd
**session** *n* eisteddiad; sesiwn; tymor
**set** *vb* gosod, dodi; plannu; sadio; sefydlu; machlud ♦ *n* set; impyn, planhigyn
**settee, settle** *n* sgiw, setl
**setting** *n* lleoliad, safle; machludiad
**settle** *vb* sefydlu; penderfynu; cytuno, setlo; plwyfo; talu
**settlement** *n* cytundeb; gwladfa
**seven** *adj*, *n* saith
**seventeen** *adj*, *n* dau (dwy) ar bymtheg, un deg saith
**seventh** *adj* seithfed
**seventy** *adj*, *n* deg a thrigain,

saith deg
**sever** *vb* gwahanu, datod, torri
**several** *adj* amryw; gwahanol
**severance** *n* gwahaniad, datgysylltiad
**severe** *adj* caled, tost, llym, gerwin
**severity** *n* llymder, gerwindeb
**sew** *vb* gwnïo, pwytho
**sewage** *n* carthffosiaeth, carthion
**sewer** *n* ceuffos, carthffos
**sewing machine** *n* peiriant gwnïo
**sex** *n* rhyw
**sex education** *n* addysg ryw
**sextet** *n* chwechawd
**sexton** *n* clochydd; torrwr beddau
**sexual** *adj* rhywiol
**shabby** *adj* carpiog, gwael, aflêr
**shack** *n* caban
**shackle** *n* hual, gefyn, llyffethair
**shade** *n* cysgod; ysbryd ♦ *vt* cysgodi
**shadow** *n* cysgod ♦ *vt* cysgodi
**shadowy** *adj* cysgodol, rhithiol
**shady** *adj* cysgodol; amheus
**shaft** *n* paladr, saeth; llorp; braich; pwll; gwerthyd
**shaggy** *adj* cedenog, blewog
**shake** *vb* ysgwyd, siglo, crynu
**shaky** *adj* ansad, crynedig
**shallow** *adj* bas ♦ *n* basle, beisle
**sham** *vb* ffugio ♦ *adj* ffug, gau, coeg ♦ *n* ffug, ffugbeth
**shambles** *npl* galanastra
**shame** *n* cywilydd, gwaradwydd, gwarth ♦ *vb* cywilyddio, gwaradwyddo
**shamefaced** *n* swil, gwylaidd
**shameful** *adj* cywilyddus, gwarthus
**shampoo** *vt* golchi pen ♦ *n* siampŵ
**shank** *n* coes, gar, esgair; paladr
**shanty** *n* caban, bwthyn, penty
**shape** *n* siâp, llun ♦ *vt* siapio, llunio
**shapeless** *adj* afluniaidd, di-lun

**shapely** *adj* siapus, lluniaidd, gosgeiddig
**share** *n* rhan, cyfran ♦ *vb* rhannu; cyfranogi
**share** *n* swch aradr
**shareholder** *n* cyfranddaliwr
**shark** *n* siarc, morgi; twyllwr
**sharp** *adj* siarp, llym, miniog ♦ *n* llonnod (cerdd)
**sharpen** *vb* hogi, minio, awchlymu
**sharpener** *n* naddwr
**sharper** *n* siarpwr
**sharply** *adv* yn sydyn
**shatter** *vb* dryllio, chwilfriwio; ysigo
**shave** *vb* eillio, torri barf; rhasglio
**shavings** *npl* naddion
**shawl** *n* siôl
**she** *pron* hi ♦ *adj, prefix* benyw
**sheaf** (**sheaves**) *n* ysgub
**shear** *vt* cneifio; morgi; siero
**shears** *npl* gwellau
**sheath** *n* gwain; (*contraceptive*) maneg atal cenhedlu
**sheathe** *vt* gweinio
**shed** *n* penty, sied
**shed** *vt* tywallt; gollwng; colli; dihidlo, bwrw
**sheen** *n* disgleirdeb, llewyrch, gwawr
**sheep** (**sheep**) *n* dafad
**sheer** *vi* gwyro o'r ffordd, cilio
**sheer** *adj* pur, glân, noeth, syth, serth
**sheet** *n* llen; cynfas; hwylraff; taflen
**shekel** *n* sicl
**shelf** (**shelves**) *n* silff, astell
**shell** *n* cragen; plisgyn, masgl; tân-belen
**shellfish** *npl* cregynbysg
**shelter** *n* cysgod, lloches ♦ *vb* cysgodi, llochesu; ymochel; llechu
**shelve** *vi* llechweddu, llethru
**shelve** *vt* gosod naill ochr, troi o'r neilltu

**shepherd** *n* bugail ♦ *vt* bugeilio
**sheriff** *n* sirydd, siryf
**sherry** *n* sieri
**Shetland** *n* Shetland
**shield** *n* tarian ♦ *vt* cysgodi, amddiffyn
**shift** *vb* newid, symud; ymdaro ♦ *n* newid; tro, stem, shifft
**shilling** *n* swllt
**shilly-shally** *n* anwadalwch
**shimmer** *vi* tywynnu, caneitio, rhithio
**shin** *n* crimog, crimp coes
**shindy** *n* helynt, ffrwgwd, terfysg
**shine** *vb* disgleirio, llewyrchu, tywynnu ♦ *n* disgleirdeb, sglein, llewyrch
**shingle** *n* graean, gro
**shingle** *n* peithynen; estyllen
**shingles** *npl* yr eryr, yr eryrod
**shiny** *adj* gloyw, disglair
**ship** *n* llong ♦ *vt* trosglwyddo
**shipping** *n* llongau (gwlad)
**shipshape** *adj*, *adv* taclus, trefnus, twt
**shipwreck** *n* llongddrylliad
**shire** *n* sir
**shirk** *vt* gochel, osgoi
**shirt** *n* crys
**shiver** *vi* crynu
**shiver** *vb* dryllio, chwilfriwio
**shoal** *n* haig ♦ *vi* heigio
**shoal** *n* basle, beisle
**shock** *n* sioc, ergyd, ysgytiad ♦ *vt* ysgytio; tramgwyddo
**shocking** *adj* arswydus, ysgytiol
**shoddy** *n* brethyn eilban ♦ *adj* ffug, gwael
**shoe** *n* esgid; pedol ♦ *vt* pedoli
**shoehorn** *n* seisbin, siasbi
**shoelace** *n* carrai/lasen esgid
**shoemaker** *n* crydd
**shoe shop** *n* siop esgidiau
**shoot** *vb* tarddu, blaguro; saethu ♦ *n* ysbrigyn, blaguryn
**shooting** *n* saethu
**shop** *n* masnachdy, siop ♦ *vb* siopa

**shopkeeper** *n* siopwr
**shopper** *n* prynwr
**shopping** *n* siopa
**shore** *n* glan, traeth
**short** *adj* byr, cwta, prin
**shortage** *n* prinder, diffyg
**short circuit** *n* cylchedd byr
**shortcoming** *n* diffyg, bai
**short cut** *n* llwybr tarw, llwybr llygad, ffordd fer
**shorthand** *n* llaw-fer
**shorts** *npl* trowsus cwta
**shot** *n* ergyd; saethwr
**shoulder** *n* ysgwydd, palfais ♦ *vt* ysgwyddo. **s. blade** *n* sgapwla, pont yr ysgwydd
**shout** *vb* bloeddio, gweiddi ♦ *n* bloedd, gwaedd
**shove** *vb* gwthio
**shovel** *n* llwyarn ♦ *vt* rhofio
**show** *vb* dangos, arddangos ♦ *n* arddangosfa, sioe, siew
**shower** *n* cawod, cawad ♦ *vb* cawodi, bwrw
**shred** *n* llarp, cerpyn ♦ *vb* rhwygo, torri'n fân
**shrew** *n* cecren, gwraig anynad; llyg
**shrewd** *adj* ffel, craff, call, cyfrwys
**shriek** *vb* ysgrechian ♦ *n* ysgrech
**shrill** *adj* llym, main, meinllais
**shrimp** *n* berdysen ♦ *vi* berdysa
**shrine** *n* ysgrîn; creirfa; cysegr, seintwar
**shrink** *vb* crebachu, tynnu ato, cilio
**shrivel** *vb* crychu, crebachu
**shroud** *n* amdo, amwisg; (*pl*) rhaffau hwylbren ♦ *vt* amdoi, cuddio, celu
**Shrove Tuesday** *n* Mawrth Ynyd
**shrub** *n* prysgwydden, llwyn
**shrug** *vb* codi'r ysgwyddau
**shudder** *n* crynfa, echryd, arswyd ♦ *vi* crynu, arswydo
**shuffle** *vb* siffrwd; llusgo; gwingo,

gwamalu

**shun** *vt* gochelyd, osgoi

**shunt** *vb* troi o'r neilltu, symud o'r ffordd, siyntio

**shut** *vb* cau ♦ *adj* caeëdig

**shutter** *n* caead, clawr, gwerchyr

**shuttle** *n* gwennol (gwëydd)

**shuttlecock** *n* gwennol

**shy** *adj* swil ♦ *vi* osgoi, rhusio

**siblings** *npl* plant

**sick** *adj* claf; yn chwydu, â chyfog arno; wedi diflasu

**sickbay** *n* canolfan iechyd

**sickening** *adj* atgas, diflas, cyfoglyd

**sickle** *n* cryman

**sickly** *adj* afiach, nychlyd

**side** *n* ochr, ystlys; tu, plaid ♦ *vi* ochri

**sidestep** *vb* ochrgamu

**sidetrack** *vb* troi o'r neilltu

**sideways** *adv* tua'r ochr, yn wysg ei ochr

**sidle** *vi* cerdded yn wysg ei ochr, gwyro

**siege** *n* gwarchae

**sieve** *n* gogr, gwagr, rhidyll, sife

**sift** *vt* gogrwn, nithio, hidlo, rhidyllio

**sigh** *vb* ochneidio ♦ *n* ochenaid

**sight** *n* golwg, golygfa ♦ *vt* gweld

**sightseeing** *n* taith i weld y wlad

**sign** *n* arwydd, argoel ♦ *vb* arwyddo, llofnodi

**signal** *adj* hynod ♦ *n* arwydd

**signatory** *adj* arwyddol ♦ *n* arwyddwr

**signature** *n* llofnod

**significance** *n* arwyddocâd, ystyr

**significant** *adj* arwyddocaol; o bwys

**signify** *vb* arwyddo, arwyddocáu

**signpost** *n* mynegbost, arwyddbost

**silence** *n* taw, distawrwydd ♦ *vt* rhoi taw ar

**silent** *adj* distaw, tawedog, mud

**silhouette** *n* llun du, cysgodlun,

silwet

**silicon** *n* silicon. **s. chip** sglodyn silicon

**silk** *n* sidan

**silky** *adj* sidanaidd

**sill** *n* sil

**silly** *adj* gwirion, ffôl, disynnwyr

**silt** *n* gwaelodion, llaid ♦ *vb* gwaelodi, tagu

**silver** *n* arian ♦ *vt* ariannu. **s. paper** *n* papur arian

**silversmith** *n* gof arian

**silvery** *adj* ariannaid(d)

**similar** *adj* tebyg, cyffelyb

**simile** *n* cyffelybiaeth, cymhariaeth

**simmer** *vi* lledferwi, goferwi

**simper** *vi* cilwenu, glaswenu

**simple** *adj* syml, unplyg; gwirion, diniwed

**simplicity** *n* symlrwydd, unplygrwydd

**simplify** *vt* symleiddio

**simulate** *vt* ffugio, dynwared

**simultaneous** *adj* cyfamserol, ar y pryd

**sin** *n* pechod ♦ *vb* pechu

**since** *conj* gan, yn gymaint ♦ *prep* er, er pan

**sincere** *adj* diffuant, didwyll, pur

**sinew** *n* gewyn, giewyn

**sing** *vb* canu

**singe** *vt* deifio

**singer** *n* canwr, cantwr, cantores

**singing** *n* canu

**single** *adj* sengl, dibriod, gweddw. **s. bed** *n* gwely sengl. **s.-minded** *adj* unplyg, cywir. **s. room** *n* ystafell sengl

**singlet** *n* gwasgod wlanen, crys isaf

**singular** *adj* unigol; hynod

**sinister** *adj* ysgeler; chwithig

**sink** *vb* soddi, suddo ♦ *n* sinc

**sinner** *n* pechadur

**sinuous** *adj* dolennog, troellog

**sip** *vt* llymeitian ♦ *n* llymaid,

llymeidyn
**siphon** n siffon
**sir** n syr
**siren** n corn, seiren
**sirloin** n llwyn eidion
**sissy** n cadi(ffan)
**sister** n chwaer
**sister-in-law** n chwaer yng nghyfraith
**sit** vb eistedd
**site** n safle, lle ♦ vb lleoli
**sitting** n eisteddiad
**situated** adj yn sefyll, wedi ei leoli
**situation** n lle, safle; sefyllfa
**six** adj, n chwech
**sixteen** adj, n un ar bymtheg, un deg chwech
**sixth** adj chweched
**sixty** adj, n trigain, chwe deg
**sizable** adj gweddol fawr
**size** n maint, maintioli
**sizzle** vb ffrïo
**skate** n cath fôr
**skate** n sgêt ♦ vb ysglefrio
**skateboard** n bwrdd sglefrio
**skein** n cengl, sgain
**skeleton** n ysgerbwd; amlinelliad
**sketch** n llun, braslun ♦ vb braslunio, tynnu
**skewer** n gwaell, gwachell
**ski** n sgi ♦ vb sgïo
**skid** vb llithro (naill ochr)
**skier** n sgïwr
**skiff** n ysgafnfad, ceubal, sgiff
**skill** n medr, medrusrwydd
**skilled** adj medrus, crefftus
**skim** vb tynnu, codi (hufen)
**skimmed milk** n llaeth glas, llaeth sgim
**skimp** vb crintachu, cybydda
**skimpy** adj crintach
**skin** n croen ♦ vb blingo
**skinny** adj tenau; prin, crintach
**skip** vi llamu, sgipio
**skipper** n capten llong
**skipping-rope** n rhaff sgipio
**skirmish** n ysgarmes

**skirt** n godre, sgyrt ♦ vt dilyn gyda godre
**skit** n gogan
**skittish** adj nwyfus, gwantan, anwadal
**skittles** npl ceilys
**skulk** vi llechu, techu
**skull** n penglog
**skunk** n drewgi
**sky** n wybren, wybr, awyr
**skylark** n ehedydd
**skylight** n ffenestr do
**slab** n llech
**slack** adj llac, diofal, esgeulus ♦ n glo mân
**slacken** vb llacio, llaesu
**slag** n sorod, slag
**slake** vt torri (syched), slecio
**slam** vb cau yn glats, clepian
**slander** n enllib ♦ vt enllibio
**slang** n iaith sathredig, slang ♦ vt difrïo
**slant** vb gwyro, gogwyddo ♦ n gogwydd
**slanting** adj ar oledd/osgo
**slap** vt clewtian ♦ n clewt(en), palfod
**slapdash** adj ffwrdd-â-hi, rhywsut-rywfodd
**slash** n slaes, hac ♦ vt slasio, chwipio
**slate** n llech, llechen
**slate** vt sennu, difrïo
**slattern** n slwt, slebog, sopen
**slaughter** n lladdedigaeth, lladdfa ♦ vt lladd
**slaughterhouse** n lladd-dy
**slave** n slaf, caethwas ♦ vi slafio
**slavery** n caethiwed, caethwasanaeth
**slay** vt lladd
**sled, sledge, sleigh** n car llusg, sled
**sledgehammer** n gordd
**sleek** adj llyfn, llyfndew, graenus
**sleep** vb cysgu, huno ♦ n cwsg, hun

**sleeper** n (*person*) cysgwr; pren neu ddefnydd arall i ddal y cledrau

**sleeping bag** n sach gysgu

**sleeping pill** n pilsen gysgu

**sleepy** adj cysglyd

**sleet** n eirlaw

**sleeve** n llawes

**sleight** n deheurwydd, cyfrwystra, dichell

**slender** adj main, eiddil, prin

**slice** n tafell, ysglisen ♦ vt tafellu, ysglisio

**slick** adj llyfn, tafodrydd, slic

**slide** vb llithro, sglefrio ♦ n llithren, sleid

**slight** adj ysgafn, eiddil, prin ♦ vt diystyru ♦ n diystyrwch, sarhad

**slightly** adj yn fain; ychydig

**slim** adj main, eiddil

**slime** n llaid, llaca; llys, llysnafedd

**sling** vt taflu, lluchio ♦ n ffon dafl

**slip** vb llithro, dianc; gollwng ♦ n slip

**slipper** n llopan, sliper

**slippery** adj llithrig, diafael, di-ddal

**slipshod** adj anniben

**slipway** n llithrfa

**slit** vb hollti, agennu, rhwygo ♦ n hollt

**slither** vb ymlusgo, llithro

**slobber** vb glafoerio, slobran

**sloe** n eirinen ddu fach, draenen ddu

**slog** vb gweithio'n galed

**sloop** n slŵp

**slop** n (*pl*) golchion ♦ vb gwlychu, trochi

**slope** n llethr, gogwydd ♦ vb gogwyddo

**sloppy** adj lleidiog, tomlyd; meddal, masw; anniben

**slot** n agen, twll

**sloth** n diogi, seguryd, syrthni

**slouch** vb llaesu, ymollwng; cerdded yn aflêr

**sloven** n dyn aflêr, slebog

**slovenly** adj anniben

**slow** adj araf, hwyrfrydig, hwyrdrwm ♦ vb arafu

**slowly** adv yn araf (deg)

**sludge** n llaid, llaca

**slug** n gwlithen, malwoden

**sluggish** adj diog, dioglyd, swrth

**sluice** n llifddor

**slum** n slym

**slumber** vb hepian, cysgu ♦ n cwsg

**slump** n cwymp, gostyngiad; dirwasgiad

**slur** vb difrïo ♦ n llithriad, cyflusg (cerdd.); anfri

**slush** n llaid, llaca, eira gwlyb

**slut** n slwt, slebog

**sly** adj cyfrwys, ffals, dichellgar, tan din

**smack** n blas ♦ vi blasu, blasio, archwaethu

**smack** n smac, palfod ♦ vb smacio, chwipio

**smack** n llongan, smac

**small** adj bach, bychan, mân, main

**smallholder** n tyddynnwr

**small-pox** n y frech wen

**smart** vi gwynio, dolurio, llosgi ♦ n gwŷn, dolur ♦ adj llym, bywiog; ffel, ffraeth; crand

**smash** vb torri, malu, chwilfriwio

**smattering** n gwybodaeth fas, crap

**smear** vt iro, dwbio

**smell** n arogl, aroglau ♦ vb arogli

**smile** vb gwenu ♦ n gwên

**smirch** vt llychwino, difwyno

**smirk** vi cilwenu, glaswenu ♦ n cilwen

**smith** n gof

**smithy** n gefail (gof)

**smog** n smog, mwgwl

**smoke** n mwg ♦ vb mygu, ysmygu, smocio

**smoked** adj wedi ei fygu

**smoky** adj myglyd

**smooth** *adj* llyfn, esmwyth ♦ *vt* llyfnhau

**smother** *vb* mygu, llethu

**smoulder** *vi* mudlosgi

**smudge** *n* baw, staen, smotyn ♦ *vb* difwyno, trochi

**smug** *adj* hunanol, cysetlyd

**smuggle** *vt* smyglio

**smut** *n* parddu, huddygl, smotyn; siarad aflan

**smutty** *adj* aflan, brwnt

**snack** *n* tamaid, byrbryd. **s. bar** *n* lle am damaid

**snag** *n* rhwystr, maen tramgwydd

**snail** *n* malwoden, malwen

**snake** *n* neidr

**snap** *vb* clecian, torri'n glats; tynnu llun ♦ *n* clec

**snare** *n* magl, croglath ♦ *vt* maglu, rhwydo

**snarl** *vi* ysgyrnygu, chwyrnu

**snatch** *vb* cipio ♦ *n* cip, crap; tamaid

**sneak** *vi* llechian ♦ *n* llechgi

**sneaking** *adj* llechwraidd, cachgïaidd

**sneer** *vb* gwawdio, glaswenu ♦ *n* gwawd, glaswen

**sneeze** *vi* tisian

**sniff** *vb* ffroeni, gwyntio

**snigger** *vb* glaschwerthin

**snip** *vb* torri, cynhinio ♦ *n* demyn, toriad

**snipe** *n* giach

**snippet** *n* tamaid, cynhinyn

**snob** *n* crechyn (*pl.* crachach), snob

**snobbish** *adj* crachaidd, snoblyd

**snooker** *n* snwcer

**snooze** *vb* hepian ♦ *n* cyntun

**snore** *vi* chwyrnu

**snort** *vi* ffroeni, ffroenochi

**snotty** *adj* cas

**snout** *n* trwyn anifail, duryn

**snow** *n* eira, ôd ♦ *vb* bwrw eira, odi

**snowball** *n* pelen eira

**snowdrift** *n* lluwch

**snowflake** *n* pluen eira

**snow plough** *n* aradr eira

**snub** *vt* sennu ♦ *n* sen

**snub** *adj* pwt, smwt

**snub-nosed** *adj* trwyn smwt

**snuff** *vb* ffroeni, snwffian ♦ *n* trwynlwch, snisyn

**snug** *adj* cryno, clyd, diddos

**snuggle** *vb* ymwasgu at; llochi, anwesu

**so** *adv, conj* fel, felly; mor, cyn

**soak** *vb* mwydo, sucio; slotian

**soap** *n* sebon ♦ *vb* seboni. **s. opera** *n* opera sebon. **s. powder** *n* powdr golchi

**soapy** *adj* sebonllyd

**soar** *vi* ehedeg, esgyn

**sob** *vi* igian, beichio ♦ *n* ig, ebwch

**sober** *adj* sobr, sad ♦ *vb* sobri

**sobriety** *n* sobrwydd

**so-called** *adj* dywededig

**soccer** *n* pêl-droed, y bêl gron

**sociable** *adj* cymdeithasgar

**social** *adj* cymdeithasol. **s. club** *n* clwb cymdeithasol. **s. security** *n* nawdd cymdeithasol. **s. work** *n* gwaith cymdeithasol

**socialism** *n* sosialaeth

**socialist** *n* sosialydd

**society** *n* cymdeithas, cyfeillach

**sociology** *n* cymdeithaseg

**sock** *n* hosan

**socket** *n* twll, crau, soced

**sod** *n* tywarchen

**soda water** *n* dŵr soda

**sodden** *adj* wedi mwydo, soeglyd

**sofa** *n* glwth, esmwythfainc, soffa

**soft** *adj* meddal, tyner; distaw; gwirion. **s. drink** *n* diod ysgafn

**software** *n* meddalwedd

**soggy** *adj* gwlyb, lleidiog

**soil** *n* pridd, daear, gweryd

**soil** *vt* difwyno, baeddu ♦ *n* baw, tom

**solace** *n* cysur, diddanwch ♦ *vt* cysuro, diddanu

**solar** *adj* heulog, solar
**solder** *n* sawdring, sawdur, sodr ♦ *vt* asio, sawdurio, sodro
**soldier** *n* milwr
**sole** *adj* unig, unigol, un
**sole** *n* gwadn ♦ *vt* gwadnu
**sole** *n* (*fish*) lleden chwithig
**solemn** *adj* difrifol, dwys
**sol-fa** *n* sol-ffa ♦ *vb* solffeuo
**solicit** *vt* erfyn, ymofyn; llithio
**solicitor** *n* cyfreithiwr
**solid** *adj* caled, sylweddol, solet, cadarn
**solid** *n* solid
**solidarity** *n* undod
**solitary** *adj* unig; anghyfannedd
**solitude** *n* unigedd
**solo** *n* unawd
**soloist** *n* unawdydd
**soluble** *adj* toddadwy, hydawdd
**solution** *n* dehongliad, esboniad; toddiant
**solve** *vt* datrys, dehongli
**solvent** *adj* yn gallu talu, di-ddyled ♦ *n* toddfa
**sombre** *adj* tywyll, prudd
**some** *adj* rhai, rhyw, peth, ychydig ♦ *pron* rhywrai, rhywfaint ♦ *adv* ynghylch, tua, rhyw
**somebody** *pron* = **someone**
**somehow** *adv* rywfodd, rhywsut
**someone** *pron* rhywun
**somersault** *n* trosben ♦ *vb* troi tin tros ben, pen dra mwnwgl
**something** *n* rhywbeth
**sometime** *adv* rywbryd, gynt
**sometimes** *adv* weithiau, ar brydiau, ambell waith
**somewhat** *adv* go, lled, braidd
**somewhere** *adv* (yn) rhywle
**son** *n* mab
**song** *n* cân, cathl, cerdd
**sonic** *adj* sonig
**son-in-law** *n* mab yng nghyfraith
**sonnet** *n* soned
**soon** *adv* buan, ebrwydd, clau
**sooner** *adv* (*time*) ynghynt, yn

gynt; (*preference*): **I would s. do** byddai'n well gennyf wneud; **s. or later** yn hwyr neu'n hwyrach
**soot** *n* huddygl, parddu
**soothe** *vt* lliniaru, lleddfu, dofi, tawelu
**sop** *n* tamaid (wedi ei wlychu)
**sophism** *n* soffyddiaeth
**sophist** *n* soffydd
**sophistical** *adj* soffyddol
**sophisticated** *adj* soffistigedig
**sopping** *adj* gwlyb diferu
**soppy** *adj* teimladol; mwydlyd
**soprano** *n* soprano
**sorcerer** *n* swynwr, dewin
**sorcery** *n* swyngyfaredd, dewiniaeth
**sordid** *adj* brwnt, cybyddlyd, gwael
**sore** *adj* tost, blin, dolurus ♦ *n* dolur
**sorrow** *n* tristwch, gofid, galar ♦ *vi* tristáu, gofidio
**sorry** *adj* drwg gan, edifar; salw
**sort** *n* modd; math, bath ♦ *vt* trefnu, dosbarthu
**sortie** *n* cyrch
**sorting office** *n* swyddfa ddosbarthu
**so-so** *adv* gweddol
**sot** *n* diotyn, meddwyn
**soul** *n* enaid
**soul-destroying** *adj* yn fwrn llethol
**sound** *n* sain, sŵn, trwst ♦ *vb* seinio
**sound** *vb* plymio, chwilio
**sound** *n* culfor, swnt
**sound** *adj* iach, iachus, dianaf, cyfan, dilys. **s. effects** *npl* effeithiau sain
**soundboard** *n* seinfwrdd
**soundly** *adv* yn drwm, yn llwyr
**soundproof** *adj* yn gwrthsefyll sŵn
**soup** *n* potes, cawl
**sour** *adj* sur ♦ *vb* suro
**source** *n* ffynhonnell, tarddiad

**south** n deau, de. **S. Africa** n De
Affrica
**southern** adj deheuol
**souvenir** n cofrodd
**sovereign** adj pen ♦ n penadur;
sofren
**Soviet** adj Sofietaidd
**Soviet Union** n: **the S.U.** yr
Undeb Sofietaidd
**sow** n hwch
**sow** vt hau
**soya** n soya. **s. beans** npl ffa soya
**space** n lle, gwagle, gofod, encyd,
ysbaid
**spaceman** n gofodwr
**spaceship** n llong ofod
**spacious** adj eang, helaeth
**spade** n rhaw, pâl
**Spain** n Hisbaen
**span** n rhychwant ♦ vt rhychwantu
**spaniel** n adargi, sbaniel
**Spanish** adj Sbaenaidd ♦ n
Sbaeneg
**spank** vt slapio, smacio, palfodi,
chwipio tin
**spanner** n sbaner
**spar** vi cwffio, paffio
**spar** n polyn, cledren, ceibren
**spare** adj prin; tenau; sbâr ♦ vt
arbed; hepgor
**sparerib** n sbarib, asen-frân
**sparing** adj cynnil, prin
**spark** n gwreichionen
**sparkle** vi gwreichioni, serennu,
pefrio
**sparkling** adj gloyw, llachar;
byrlymog
**sparrow** n aderyn y to
**sparse** adj tenau, prin, gwasgarog
**spasm** n pwl, gwayw, brath
**spate** n llifeiriant sydyn
**spatter** vb tasgu
**spawn** n grawn, gronell; grifft; sil
♦ vb silio, bwrw grawn
**speak** vb llefaru, siarad
**speaker** n llefarydd, siaradwr
**spear** n gwaywffon, picell ♦ vt

trywanu
**special** adj neillltuol, arbennig
**specialist** n arbenigwr
**speciality** n arbenigrwydd
**species** (species) n rhywogaeth
**specific** adj priodol, penodol,
pendant
**specify** vt enwi, penodi
**specimen** n enghraifft, cynllun
**specious** adj teg yr olwg, rhithiol
**speck** n brycheuyn, ysmotyn
**speckle** vt britho, brychu
**spectacle** n drych, golygfa; (pl)
sbectol
**spectator** n edrychwr, gwyliwr
**spectre** n drychiolaeth
**spectrum** (-ra) n spectrwm
**speculate** vi dyfalu; anturio,
mentro
**speculation** n dyfaliad; antur,
menter
**speech** n llafar, lleferydd, parabl,
ymadrodd; araith
**speed** n cyflymder, buander ♦ vb
prysuro, cyflymu. **s. limit** n
ataliad cyflymder
**speedometer** n mesurydd
cyflymdra
**spell** n cyfaredd, swyn
**spell** n sbel, hoe, ysbaid
**spell** vt sillafu
**spend** vb treulio, gwario, bwrw
**spendthrift** n afradwr, oferwr,
gwastraffwr
**sperm** n had
**spew** vb chwydu
**sphere** n cronnell, sffêr, pêl;
cylch, maes
**spice** n perlysiau, peraroglau,
sbeis
**spick-and-span** adj fel y pin
**spicy** adj blasus; ffraeth, diddorol;
coch
**spider** n cor corryn, pryf copyn
**spike** n pig, hoel, cethren
**spikenard** n ysbignard, nard
**spill** vb colli, tywallt

**spin** *vb* nyddu, troi, troelli

**spinach** *n* pigoglys, sbinais

**spindle** *n* gwerthyd; echel

**spin-dryer** *n* trowasgwr

**spine** *n* asgwrn cefn; draen, pigyn

**spinner** *n* nyddwr

**spinning top** *n* top tro

**spinning-wheel** *n* troell

**spin-off** *n* mantais

**spinster** *n* merch ddibriod, hen ferch

**spiral** *adj* fel cogwrn tro, troellog

**spirant** *adj* llaes ♦ *npl* llaesion

**spire** *n* meindwr, pigwrn, pigdwr

**spirit** *n* ysbryd; gwirod

**spirited** *adj* calonnog, nwyfus, ysbrydol

**spiritual** *adj* ysbrydol

**spiritualist** *n* ysbrydegydd

**spit** *n* bêr

**spit** *vb* poeri

**spite** *n* sbeit, malais ♦ *vt* sbeitio

**spiteful** *adj* maleisus, sbeitlyd

**spittle** *n* poer, poeryn

**spittoon** *n* llestr poeri

**splash** *vb* sblasio, tasgu

**spleen** *n* y ddueg; pruddglwyf; natur ddrwg, gwenwyn

**splendid** *adj* ysblennydd, gwych, campus

**splendour** *n* ysblander, gwychder

**splint** *n* dellten, ysgyren, sblint

**splinter** *vb* ysgyrioni ♦ *n* ysgyren, fflaw

**split** *vb* hollti, rhannu, gwahanu

**spoil** *n* ysbail, anrhaith ♦ *vb* ysbeilio, ysbwylio, difetha

**spoke** *n* adain olwyn, sbogen, braich

**spokesman** *n* llefarwr, llefarydd

**spoliation** *n* ysbeiliad, ysbwyliad

**sponge** *n* sbwng ♦ *vb* ysbyngu

**sponsor** *n* mach, hyrwyddwr, noddwr; tad bedydd, mam fedydd

**spontaneous** *adj* gwirfoddol, digymell

**spook** *n* ysbryd, bwgan, bwci

**spool** *n* gwerthyd

**spoon** *n* llwy ♦ *vb* llwyo; caru

**spoonful** *n* llwyaid

**spoor** *n* brisg, ôl

**sporadic** *adj* achlysurol, gwasgarog

**spore** *n* had (rhedyn, *etc*)

**sport** *n* sbort, chwarae, difyrrwch, cellwair, hwyl

**sportive** *adj* chwareus, nwyfus

**sports** *npl* mabolgampau, chwaraeon

**spot** *n* man, lle, llecyn; brycheuyn, ysmotyn ♦ *vt* mannu, brychu, ysmotio ♦ *adj* ar y pryd

**spotless** *adj* difrycheulyd, glân

**spotted** *adj* brith, brych

**spouse** *n* priod

**spout** *vt* pistyllio, ffrydio ♦ *n* pistyll

**sprain** *vt* ysigo

**sprawl** *vi* ymdaenu, ymdreiglo, ymrwyfo

**spray** *n* gwlith, tawch, trochion ♦ *vt* taenellu; chwistrellu

**spray** *n* ysbrigyn, cainc; chwystrellydd

**spread** *vb* lledu, taenu, lledaenu, gwasgaru

**spree** *n* sbri

**sprig** *n* brigyn, ysbrigyn

**sprightly** *adj* bywiog, hoenus, nwyfus

**spring** *vb* tarddu, codi, deillio; llamu, neidio ♦ *n* ffynnon; llam; sbring; gwanwyn. **s.-clean** *n* glanhau'r gwanwyn

**springy** *adj* sbringar

**sprinkle** *vb* taenellu, ysgeintio

**sprint** *vb* gwibio

**sprinter** *n* gwibiwr

**sprit** *n* sbryd

**sprite** *n* ysbryd, bwgan, bwci

**sprout** *vb* tarddu, egino, glasu

**sprouts** *npl* (*Brussels*) ysgewyll Brysel

**spruce** *adj* twt, taclus, smart,

crand ♦ n pyrwydden

**spry** adj sionc, heini, hoyw

**spur** n ysbardun, swmbwl ♦ vb ysbarduno, symbylu

**spurious** adj ffug, gau, annilys

**spurn** vb cicio, dirmygu, tremygu

**spurt** n ysbonc

**sputter** vb poeri siarad, baldorddi

**spy** n ysbïwr ♦ vb ysbïo

**squabble** vi cweryla, ffraeo ♦ n ffrwgwd, ffrae

**squad** n carfan, mintai

**squadron** n sgwadron

**squalid** adj brwnt, bawlyd, budr

**squall** vi ysgrechain ♦ n gwawch; storm o wynt

**squalor** n brynti

**squander** vt gwastraffu, afradu

**square** adj, n sgwâr, petryal

**squash** vt gwasgu, llethu ♦ n sboncen. **orange s.** sudd oren

**squat** vi swatio, cyrcydu

**squawk** vi gwawchio ♦ n gwawch

**squeak** vi gwichian ♦ n gwich

**squeal** vi gwichian

**squeamish** adj dicra, misi

**squeeze** vb gwasgu

**squelch** vt llethu, gostegu, rhoi taw ar

**squib** n tanen wyllt, fflachen; gogan, dychan

**squint** vb ciledrych, cibedrych ♦ n llygaid croes

**squire** n ysgweier, yswain

**squirm** vb gwingo

**squirrel** n gwiwer

**squirt** vb chwistrellu, tasgu ♦ n chwistrell, gwn dŵr

**stab** vb brathu, gwanu, trywanu

**stable** n ystabl

**stable** adj diysgog, sefydlog, safadwy, sad

**stack** n tas, bera; corn simnai, stac

**staff** n ffon; erwydd; staff

**stag** n carw, hydd

**stage** n pwynt; gradd, lefel; llwyfan

**stage-coach** n y goets fawr

**stagger** vb honclan, gwegian; syfrdanu

**stagnant** adj llonydd, marw

**stagnate** vi cronni, sefyll

**staid** adj sad, sobr

**stain** vb ystaenio, llychwino ♦ n staen

**stained glass window** n ffenestr liw

**stainless** adj difrycheulyd, gloyw

**stair** n gris, staer

**stake** n polyn, pawl, ystanc; cyngwystl

**stale** adj hen, hendrwm; diflas, mws

**stalk** vb torsythu, rhodio'n benuchel, mynd ar drywydd

**stalk** n paladr, gwelltyn, coes

**stall** n côr; stondin; talcen glo ♦ vb stolio

**stalls** npl (in cinema, theatre) seddau; stondinau

**stallion** n march, stalwyn

**stalwart** adj cadarn, pybyr, dewr

**stamen** n brigeryn

**stamina** n saf, ynni

**stammer** vb bloesgi, siarad ag atal arno

**stamp** n stamp, delw, argraff ♦ vb stampio; curo traed

**stampede** n chwalfa, rhuth

**stanch** vt atal, sychu (gwaed)

**stanchion** n annel, ateg, post, gwanas

**stand** vb sefyll, bod, aros ♦ n safiad; eisteddle; stondyn

**standard** n lluman, baner; post; safon

**stanza** n pennill

**staple** n prif nwydd; edefyn (gwlân, etc)

**staple** n ystwffwl, stapal

**stapler** n styffylwr

**star** n seren ♦ vb serennu

**starch** n starts

**stare** vb llygadrythu, synnu

**stark** adj syth, moel, rhonc ♦ adv hollol

**starling** n aderyn drudwy, drudwen, aderyn yr eira

**starry** adj serennog

**start** vb dechrau, cychwyn, codi, rhusio, tasgu

**startle** vt brawychu, dychrynu, rhusio

**starvation** n newyn

**starve** vb newynu; fferru, rhynnu

**state** n ystad, cyflwr, ansawdd; rhwysg; gwladwriaeth; talaith

**state** vt mynegi, datgan; penodi

**stately** adj urddasol, mawreddog

**statement** n mynegiad, datganiad, haeriad

**statesman (men)** n gwladweinydd

**station** n gorsaf, stesion; safle, sefyllfa

**stationary** adj sefydlog

**stationer** n gwerthwr papurau

**stationer's** n (shop) siop bapurau

**stationmaster** n gorsaf-feistr

**statistics** npl ystadegau

**statue** n delw, cerfddelw, cerflun

**stature** n uchder, taldra, corffolaeth

**status** n safle, braint, statws

**statute** n deddf, cyfraith, ystatud

**staunch** adj pybyr, cywir

**stave** n estyllen, erwydd ♦ vt astellu; dryllio. **s. off** cadw draw

**stay** vb aros; ategu; atal ♦ n arhosiad; ateg; (pl) staes

**stead** n lle

**steadfast** adj diysgog

**steadily** adv yn bwyllog, yn gyson

**steady** adj sad, diysgog; cyson, gwastad

**steak** n golwyth, stec

**steal** vb dwyn, lladrata, cipio

**stealth** n lladrad. **by s.** yn ddistaw bach

**stealthy** adj lladradaidd

**steam** n ager, anwedd, stêm, tarth

♦ vb ageru

**steamer** n agerlong, stemar

**steed** n march, ceffyl

**steel** n dur ♦ vt caledu

**steelworks** n gwaith dur

**steep** adj serth ♦ n dibyn, clogwyn, llethr

**steep** vt rhoi yng ngwlych, mwydo, sucio

**steeple** n clochdy

**steer** n bustach

**steer** vb llywio; cyfeirio

**steering** n llywio

**steering wheel** n llyw

**stem** n paladr, corsen, coes, bôn; ach; pen blaen

**stem** vt gwrthsefyll, gwrthladd, atal

**stench** n drewdod, drycsawr

**stenography** n llaw-fer

**step** vi camu; cerdded ♦ n cam; gris

**step-** prefix llys-

**stepdaughter** n llysferch

**stepfather** n llystad

**stepmother** n llysfam, mam wen

**stepsister** n llyschwaer

**stepson** n llysfab

**stereotype** n ystrydeb ♦ vt ystrydebu

**sterile** adj diffrwyth, sych

**sterilize** vb diffrwythloni, diheintio

**sterling** adj ysterling; diledryw, diffuant

**stern** adj llym, penderfynol

**stern** n starn, pen ôl llong

**stethoscope** n corn meddyg

**stevedore** n llwythwr a dadlwythwr llongau

**stew** vb araf ferwi, stiwio ♦ n stiw

**steward** n stiward, goruchwyliwr, distain

**stick** n pren, ffon, pric, gwialen

**stick** vb glynu; gwanu, brathu

**sticky** adj gludiog, glynol; anodd

**stiff** adj syth, anystwyth, anhyblyg, ystyfnig

**stiffen** vb sythu, ystyfnigo

**stifle** vt mygu, tagu, diffodd

**stigma** n gwarthnod, stigma

**stile** n camfa, sticil, sticill

**still** n distyllfa, stil

**still** adj llonydd; marw ♦ vb
llonyddu

**still** adv eto, er hynny; byth

**stilt** n ystudfach

**stilted** adj annaturiol; mawreddog

**stimulant** n symbylydd; gwirod

**stimulate** vt symbylu

**stimulus** (-li) n symbyliad,
swmbwl

**sting** vb pigo, brathu, colynnu ♦ n
colyn

**stingy** adj crintach, cybyddlyd

**stink** vi, n drewi

**stinking** adj drewllyd

**stint** vt cynilo, cybydda ♦ n
prinder

**stipend** n cyflog, tâl

**stipulate** vb amodi, mynnu

**stir** vb cyffroi, cynhyrfu, symud ♦
n stŵr, cynnwrf

**stirrup** n gwarthol

**stitch** n pwyth; gwayw, pigyn ♦ vt
pwytho, gwnïo

**stoat** n carlwm

**stock** n cyff; stoc, ystôr. **stocks** npl
cyffion

**stock exchange** n cyfnewidfa stoc

**stocking** n hosan

**stocky** adj cadarn, cryf, cydnerth

**stodgy** adj toeslyd, trymllyd, diflas

**stoke** vb edrych ar ôl tân, tanio

**stole** n ystola

**stolid** adj swrth, digyffro

**stomach** n cylla, stumog

**stone** n carreg, maen ♦ vt
llabyddio

**stool** n ystôl

**stoop** vb plygu, crymu,
gwargrymu, ymostwng

**stop** vb atal, rhwystro; stopio,
cau; aros, sefyll ♦ n atalfa;
atalnod

**stoppage** n (pay) ataliad, (strike)
streic

**stopper** n topyn, caead

**storage** n stôr, storfa

**store** n ystôr, ystorfa ♦ vt ystorio

**storey, story** n uchdwr, llofft,
llawr

**stork** n ciconia, chwibon

**storm** n (y)storm, tymestl

**stormy** adj stormus, tymhestlog,
garw

**story** n hanes, chwedl, stori;
celwydd

**stout** adj tew, ffyrf; pybyr, gwrol,
glew

**stove** n stof, ffwrn

**stow** vt pacio, dodi o'r neilltu

**stowaway** n teithiwr cudd

**straddle** vi bongamu, lledu'r traed

**straggle** vi crwydro, gwasgaru

**straggler** n crwydryn

**straight** adj union, syth

**straighten** vb unioni

**straightforward** adj syml; didwyll,
gonest

**straightway** adv yn y fan, yn syth

**strain** vb straenio, streifio, ysigo;
tynhau; hidlo ♦ n straen

**strainer** n hidl(en)

**strait** adj cyfyng, cul, caeth ♦ n
cyfyngder; culfor

**strand** n traeth, traethell, tywyn

**strand** n cainc (rhaff), edau

**strange** adj dieithr, estronol,
rhyfedd

**stranger** n dyn dieithr, estron

**strangle** vt tagu, llindagu

**strap** n strap, cengl

**strategic** adj strategol

**strategy** n strategaeth

**stratum** (-ta) n haen

**straw** n gwellt; gwelltyn, blewyn

**strawberry** n mefysen, syfien

**stray** vi crwydro, cyfeiliorni

**streak** n llinell, rhes, rhesen;
stremp ♦ vb gwibio

**stream** n ffrwd ♦ vb ffrydio, llifo

**streamer** *n* rhuban, baner
**street** *n* heol, ystryd
**strength** *n* cryfder, nerth, grym
**strengthen** *vb* cryfhau, nerthu
**strenuous** *adj* egnïol, ymdrechgar
**stress** *n* pwys, straen, caledi
**stretch** *vb* estyn, tynhau ♦ *n* estyniad
**stretcher** *n* trestl, stretsier
**strew** *vt* gwasgaru, sarnu, chwalu, taenu
**strict** *adj* cyfyng, caeth, llym
**stricture** *n* cyfyngiad; cerydd, sen
**stride** *vb* camu, brasgamu ♦ *n* cam
**strife** *n* cynnen, ymryson, ymrafael
**strike** *vb* taro; gostwng ♦ *n* taro, streic
**striker** *n* streiciwr
**striking** *adj* trawiadol, hynod
**string** *n* llinyn, tant, cortyn
**stringent** *adj* caeth, llym, tyn
**strip** *n* llain, llafn, llefnyn. **film s.** striplun, stribed ffilm
**strip** *vb* diosg, ymddiosg, ymddihatru
**stripe** *n* rhes, rhesen; gwialennod
**striped** *adj* rhengog, rhesenog; â llinellau amlïw ar hyd-ddo
**stripling** *n* glaslanc, llanc, llencyn
**strive** *vi* ymdrechu; ymryson
**stroke** *n* dyrnod, ergyd, trawiad; llinell
**stroke** *vt* llochi, dylofi, pratio, canmol
**stroll** *vi* crwydro, rhodianna
**strong** *adj* cryf, grymus, cadarn
**stronghold** *n* amddiffynfa, cadarnle
**structure** *n* adail, adeilad, saernïaeth, adeiledd, strwythur
**struggle** *vi* gwingo; ymdrechu ♦ *n* ymdrech
**strut** *vi* torsythu
**stub** *n* bonyn
**stubble** *n* sofl
**stubborn** *adj* cyndyn, ystyfnig
**stuck-up** *adj* ffroenuchel

**stud** *n* boglwm, boglyn, styden
**stud** *n* gre
**student** *n* myfyriwr, efrydydd
**studio** *n* stiwdio
**study** *n* astudiaeth, efrydiaeth, *npl* efrydiau; myfyrgell, stydi ♦ *vb* myfyrio, efrydu, astudio
**stuff** *n* defnydd, stwff ♦ *vb* stwffio, gwthio
**stuffing** *adj* (*bed*) fflocys; (*CULIN*) stwffin
**stuffy** *adj* myglyd, trymllyd, trymaidd
**stumble** *vb* tramgwyddo, baglu, syrthio
**stump** *n* bonyn, boncyff
**stun** *vt* syfrdanu, byddaru, hurtio
**stunt** *vt* crabio
**stunted** *adj* crablyd
**stupefy** *vt* syfrdanu, hurtio
**stupendous** *adj* aruthrol
**stupid** *adj* hurt, pendew, dwl, twp
**stupor** *n* syfrdandod, syrthni
**sturdy** *adj* talgryf, pybyr, cadarn, cryf
**stutter** *vi* siarad ag atal arno, bloesgi
**sty** *n* cwt, cut, twlc
**style** *n* dull, arddull; cyfenw, teitl ♦ *vt* cyfenwi
**stylish** *adj* dillyn, trwsiadus
**stylus** *n* (*of record player*) nodwydd
**suave** *adj* mwyn, tirion, hynaws, rhadlon
**sub-** *prefix* tan-, is-, go-
**subconscious** *n* isymwybod ♦ *adj* isymwybodol
**subdue** *vt* darostwng; lleddfu
**subject** *adj* darostyngedig; caeth; ufudd ♦ *n* deiliad; pwnc, testun; goddrych
**subject** *vt* darostwyn, dwyn dan
**subjective** *adj* goddrychol
**subjugate** *vt* darostwng
**subjunctive** *adj* dibynnol
**sublime** *adj* aruchel, arddunol
**submarine** *adj* tanforol ♦ *n* llong

danfor
**submerge** vb soddi, suddo
**submission** n ymostyngiad;
ufudd-dod; cyflwyniad
**submissive** adj gostyngedig, ufudd
**submit** vb ymostwng,
ymddarostwng; datgan barn;
cyflwyno
**subnormal** adj isnormal
**subordinate** adj israddol ♦ vt
darostwng
**subpoena** n gwŷs
**subscribe** vb tanysgrifio, cyfrannu
**subscription** n tanysgrifiad,
cyfraniad
**subsequent** adj canlynol, dilynol
**subsequently** adv wedyn, ar ôl
hynny
**subside** vi soddi, ymollwng;
darfod
**subsidiary** adj israddol;
ychwanegol, atodol
**subsidy** n arian cymorth,
cymhorthdal
**subsist** vb byw, bod, bodoli,
ymgynnal
**subsistence** n cynhaliaeth
**subsoil** n isbridd
**substance** n sylwedd, defnydd; da
**substantial** adj sylweddol
**substantiate** vt profi, gwirio
**substitute** n eilydd, dirprwy, un
yn lle arall ♦ vt rhoi yn lle
**subterfuge** n ystryw, cast
**subterranean** adj tanddaearol
**subtle** adj cyfrwys, craff
**subtract** vt tynnu ymaith
**suburb** n maestref
**subvert** vt dymchwelyd, gwyrdroi
**subway** n isffordd
**succeed** vb dilyn, canlyn, llwyddo,
ffynnu
**success** n llwyddiant, llwydd,
ffyniant
**successful** adj llwyddiannus
**successfully** adv yn llwyddiannus
**succession** n dilyniad, olyniaeth

**successive** adj dilynol, olynol
**succinct** adj byr, cryno
**succour** vt swcro, ymgeleddu ♦ n
swer, ymgeledd
**succulent** adj ir, iraidd, noddlyd
**succumb** vi ymollwng dan, ildio,
marw
**such** adj cyfryw, y fath, cyffelyb
**suck** vb sugno, dyfnu; llyncu, yfed
**suckle** vt rhoi bron, sugno
**suction** n sugn, sugniad,
sugndyniad
**sudden** adj sydyn, disymwth,
disyfyd
**suds** npl trochion sebon, sucion
**sue** vb erlyn; erfyn, deisyf
**suede** n swêd
**suet** n gwêr, swyf, siwed
**suffer** vb goddef, dioddef, gadael
**sufferer** n dioddefydd
**suffering** n dioddef
**suffice** vb bod yn ddigon, digoni
**sufficient** adj digon, digonol
**suffix** n olddodiad
**suffocate** vb mygu, tagu
**suffrage** n pleidlais
**suffuse** vt taenu, gwasgaru,
ymledu
**sugar** n siwgr ♦ vt siwgro
**suggest** vt awgrymu
**suggestion** n awgrym, awgrymiad
**suicide** n hunanladdiad
**suit** n cwyn, cyngaws, hawl;
deisyfiad, cais; siwt, pâr ♦ vb
ateb, siwtio, gweddu, taro
**suitable** adj addas, cyfaddas,
cymwys
**suitably** adv yn addas
**suitcase** n bag dillad
**suite** n cyfres; gosgordd, nifer
**suitor** n cwynwr; cariadfab
**sulk** vi sorri, pwdu, mulo
**sullen** adj sarrug, cuchiog, blwng
**sully** vt difwyno, llychwino
**sulphur** n sylffwr
**sultan** n swltan
**sultry** adj mwrn, mwll, clòs

**sum** *n* swm ♦ *vt* crynhoi, symio
**summarize** *vb* crynhoi
**summary** *adj* byr, cryno ♦ *n* crynodeb
**summer** *n* haf
**summerhouse** *n* tŷ haf
**summit** *n* pen, copa, crib
**summon** *vt* gwysio, dyfynnu
**summons** *n* gwŷs, dyfyn
**sump** *n* swmp
**sumptuous** *adj* moethus
**sun** *n* haul ♦ *vt* heulo
**sunbathe** *vb* torheulo, bolaheulo
**sunbeam** *n* pelydryn
**sunburn** *n* llosg haul
**Sunday** *n* dydd Sul
**sunder** *vt* ysgaru, gwahanu
**sundry** *adj* armryw, amrywiol
**sunflower** *n* blodyn yr haul
**sunglasses** *npl* sbectol haul
**sunny** *adj* heulog
**sunshine** *n* heulwen
**sunstroke** *n* ergyd (yr) haul
**suntan** *n* lliw haul
**sup** *vb* llymeitian; swpera, swperu ♦ *n* llymaid
**super-** *prefix* uwch, goruwch, gor-, tra-, ar-
**superannuation** *n* ymddeolaeth, pensiwn
**superb** *adj* ysblennydd, godidog
**supercilious** *adj* balch, ffroenuchel
**superficial** *adj* arwynebol, bas
**superfine** *adj* coeth
**superfluous** *adj* gormodol, afreidiol
**superintend** *vt* arolygu
**superintendent** *n* arolygwr, arolygydd
**superior** *adj* uwch, gwell, rhagorach; uwchraddol ♦ *n* uchafiad, uwchradd
**superiority** *n* rhagoriaeth
**superlative** *adj* uchaf; eithaf
**supermarket** *n* archfarchnad
**supernatural** *adj* goruwchnaturiol
**supersede** *vt* disodli

**superstition** *n* coelgrefydd, ofergoeliaeth
**superstitious** *adj* coelgrefyddol, ofergoelus
**supervene** *vi* digwydd
**supervise** *vt* arolygu
**supervision** *n* arolygiaeth
**supine** *adj* diofal, didaro, swrth
**supper** *n* swper
**supplant** *vt* disodli
**supple** *adj* ystwyth, hyblyg
**supplement** *n* atodiad ♦ *vt* atodi
**supplementary** *adj* atodol, ychwanegol
**suppliant** *n* ymbiliwr, erfyniwr
**supplicate** *vb* erfyn, ymbil, deisyf
**supplier** *n* cyflenwr, cyflenwydd
**supply** *vt* cyflenwi, cyflawni ♦ *n* cyflenwad
**support** *vt* cynnal ♦ *n* cynhaliaeth
**supporter** *n* cefnogwr, cefnogydd
**suppose** *vt* tybio, tybied, bwrw
**suppository** *n* tawddgyffur
**suppress** *vt* llethu, gostegu; atal; celu
**suppurate** *vi* crawni, gori
**supreme** *adj* goruchaf, prif, pennaf
**sur-** *prefix* gor-
**surcharge** *n* gordal, gordoll ♦ *vb* codi gormod
**sure** *adj, adv* siwr, sicr; diamau, diau
**surely** *adv* yn sicr, yn ddiau
**surety** *n* mach, meichiau, gwystl
**surf** *n* traethfor, beiston; gorewyn ♦ *vb* brigo, brigdonni
**surface** *n* wyneb, arwynebedd, caen
**surfeit** *n* syrffed ♦ *vb* alaru, syrffedu
**surge** *vi* ymchwyddo ♦ *n* ymchwydd
**surgeon** *n* llawfeddyg
**surgery** *n* llawfeddygaeth; meddygfa, llys meddyg
**surgical** *adj* llawfeddygol
**surly** *adj* sarrug, afrywiog

**surmise** n tyb ♦ vt tybied, amau
**surmount** vt mynd dros, gorchfygu, trechu
**surname** n cyfenw ♦ vt cyfenwi
**surpass** vt rhagori ar, trechu
**surplice** n gwenwisg
**surplus** n gweddill, gormod, gwarged
**surprise** n syndod ♦ vt synnu
**surprising** adj syn, rhyfedd
**surrender** vb traddodi, ildio
**surreptitious** adj lladradaidd, llech-wraidd
**surrogate** n dirprwy, rhaglaw esgob
**surround** vt amgylchu, amgylchynu
**surroundings** npl amgylchoedd
**surveillance** n arolygiaeth, gwyliadwriaeth
**survey** vt edrych, arolygu; mesur ♦ n arolwg
**survival** n goroesiad
**survive** vb goroesi
**survivor** n goroeswr
**susceptible** adj parod i, tueddol i
**suspect** vt drwgdybio, amau ♦ n un a ddrwgdybir
**suspend** vt crogi; gohirio, atal
**suspended sentence** n dedfryd wedi'i gohirio
**suspense** n pryder, petruster, oediad
**suspension** n ataliad. **s. bridge** n pont grog
**suspicion** n drwgdybiaeth, amheuaeth
**suspicious** adj drwgdybus, amheus
**sustain** vt cynnal; dioddef, goddef
**sustained** adj parhaus, cyson
**sustenance** n cynhaliaeth, ymborth, bwyd
**swagger** vb rhodresa, torsythu, swagro
**swallow** n gwennol
**swallow** vt llyncu ♦ n llwnc
**swamp** n cors ♦ vt gorlifo, boddi

**swan** n alarch
**swank** vi bocsachu, rhodresa ♦ n bocsach
**swap** vb ffeirio
**swarm** n haid ♦ vi heidio, heigio
**swarm** vb dringo
**swarthy** adj melynddu, croenddu, tywyll
**swat** vb taro
**swathe** vt rhwymo, rhwymynnu
**sway** vb siglo, gwegian; llywio ♦ n llywodraeth, swae
**swear** vb tyngu, rhegi
**sweat** n chwys ♦ vb chwysu
**sweater** n cot wlan, sweter
**sweaty** adj chwyslyd
**swede** n rwden, sweden
**Swede** n Swediad
**Sweden** n Sweden
**Swedish** adj Swedaidd
**sweep** vb ysgubo ♦ n ysgubiad; ysgubwr
**sweeping** adj ysgubol
**sweet** adj melys, pêr, peraidd ♦ n pwdin
**sweeten** vb melysu; pereiddio
**sweetheart** n cariad
**sweetmeat** n fferin, melysyn
**swell** vb chwyddo ♦ n chwydd, ymchwydd; gŵr mawr
**swelling** n chwydd(i)
**swelter** vi crasu; lluddedu, dyddfu
**sweltering** adj llethol, tesog
**swerve** vi gwyro, osgoi, cilio, troi
**swift** adj cyflym, buan, chwyrn, clau
**swift** n gwennol ddu
**swig** n llymaid, dracht ♦ vb drachtio
**swill** n golchion; bwyd sur ♦ vb golchi; slotian
**swim** vb nofio ♦ n nawf
**swimmer** n nofiwr
**swimming** n nofio
**swimmingly** adv yn braf, yn hwylus
**swimming pool** n pwll nofio

**swimsuit** n dillad nofio, gwisg nofio

**swindle** vb twyllo, hocedu ♦ n twyll

**swine (swine)** n mochyn

**swing** vb siglo ♦ n sigl, siglen, swing

**swinge** vt llachio, baeddu

**swirl** vb troi, chwyldroi, chwyrndroi

**swish** vb chwipio

**switch** n swits, botwm ♦ vb troi, newid

**swivel** n bwylltid ♦ vb troi

**swollen** adj chwyddedig, wedi chwyddo

**swoon** vt llewygu, llesmeirio ♦ n llewyg

**swoop** vb dyfod ar warthaf, disgyn

**swop** vt cyfnewid, ffeirio

**sword** n cleddyf, cleddau, cledd

**sycamore** n sycamorwydden

**syllable** n sillaf

**syllabus** n rhaglen, maes llafur

**syllogism** n cyfresymiad

**symbol** n arwyddlun, symbol, symlen (estheteg)

**symbolism** n symboliaeth

**symmetrical** adj cymesur

**symmetry** n cymesuredd

**sympathetic** adj cydymdeimladol

**sympathize** vi cydymdeimlo

**sympathy** n cydymdeimlad

**symphony** n symffoni

**symposium (-ia)** n trafodaeth, cynhadledd

**symptom** n arwydd

**synagogue** n synagog

**synchronize** vb cyfamseru, cydamseru

**syncopation** n trawsacen (cerdd)

**syncope** n marwlewyg; syncopé

**syndicate** n cwmni

**synod** n cymanfa, senedd, synod

**synonym** n (gair) cyfystyr

**synopsis (-ses)** n cyfolwg;

crynodeb

**syntax** n cystrawen

**synthesis (-ses)** n cyfosodiad, synthesis

**Syria** n Syria

**syringe** n chwistrell ♦ vt chwistrellu

**syrup** n sudd; triagl (melyn)

**system** n cyfundrefn; trefn, system

**systematic** adj cyfundrefnol

**systematize** vb cyfundrefnu

# T

**tab** n tafod, llabed

**tabby** n cath frech, cath fenyw

**tabernacle** n tabernacl, pabell

**table** n bwrdd, bord; tabl, taflen

**tableau** n golygfa (ddramatig)

**table-cloth** n lliain bord (bwrdd)

**tableful** n bordaid, byrddaid

**tablespoon** n llwy fwrdd

**tablet** n llechen, llech; tabled

**table tennis** n tennis bwrdd, ping pong

**taboo** n ysgymunbeth; gwaharddiad, tabŵ

**tabular** adj taflennol

**tabulate** vt tablu, taflennu

**tacit** adj dealledig (ond heb ei grybwyll)

**taciturn** adj tawedog

**tack** n tac, pwyth, brasbwyth ♦ vb tacio

**tackle** n taclau, offer, tacl (mewn rygbi), taclad ♦ vb ymosod ar, taclo

**tackler** n taclwr

**tact** n tact, callineb, doethineb

**tactful** adj doeth, pwyllog, synhwyrol

**tactician** n tactegydd

**tactics** npl cynlluniau, tactegau

**tactile** adj cyffyrddol

**tactless** adj di-dact, annoeth

**tadpole** *n* penbwl, penbwla

**tag** *n* pwyntl; clust, dolen

**tail** *n* cynffon, llosgwrn, cwt

**tailback** *n* cwt, tagfa

**tailor** *n* teiliwr

**taint** *vb* llygru, heintio, difwyno ♦ *n* llwgr, ystaen, mefl

**take** *vb* cymryd, derbyn, cael

**talcum** *n* talcwm

**tale** *n* chwedl, hanes, stori, clec, clep

**talent** *n* talent

**talisman** *n* swynbeth, swyn, cyfaredd

**talk** *vb, n* siarad

**talkative** *adj* siaradus

**tall** *adj* tal, hir, uchel

**tallness** *n* taldra

**tallow** *n* gwêr

**tally** *n* cyfrif ♦ *vb* cyfateb, cytuno

**talon** *n* ewin, crafanc (aderyn)

**tambourine** *n* tambwrîn

**tame** *adj* dof, gwâr ♦ *vt* dofi

**temper** *vi* ymhél(â), ymyrryd(â)

**tampon** *n* tampwn

**tan** *vb* trin lledr; llosgi, melynu

**tangent** *n* tangiad, llinell gyffwrdd

**tangible** *adj* cyffyrddadwy, sylweddol

**tangle** *vb* drysu, cymysgu ♦ *n* dryswch, cymhlethdod

**tank** *n* dyfrgist, tanc

**tankard** *n* diodlestr, tancr

**tanker** *n* tancer, llong olew

**tannery** *n* barcerdy, crwynfa, tanerdy

**tantalize** *vt* poeni, poenydio, pryfocio

**tantamount** *adj* cyfwerth, cyfystyr

**tantrums** *npl* stranciau, nwydau

**tap** *vb* taro yn ysgafn

**tap** *n* tap, feis ♦ *vt* tapio, gollwng

**tape** *n* tâp, incil

**tape measure** *n* tâp mesur

**tape-recorder** *n* recordydd tâp, peiriant recordio, arnodydd

**taper** *n* cannwyll gwyr, tapr ♦ *vb*

meinhau, tapro

**tapestry** *n* tapestri

**tape-worm** *n* llyngeren

**tapioca** *n* tapioca

**tar** *n* tar; llongwr, morwr

**tardy** *adj* hwyrfrydig, araf, diweddar, ymarhous

**target** *n* nod, targed

**tariff** *n* toll; rhestr taliadau, rhestr prisiau

**tarmac** *n* tarmac

**tarnish** *vb* pylu, cymylu, llychwino

**tarpaulin** *n* tarpolin

**tarry** *vb* aros, oedi, tario; trigo, preswylio

**tart** *n* tarten, pastai

**tart** *adj* sur, surllyd

**tartan** *n* brithwe, plod

**task** *n* gorchwyl, tasg ♦ *vt* rhoi tasg, trethu, llethu

**tassel** *n* tusw, tasel

**taste** *vb* chwaethu, blasu, profi ♦ *n* blas; chwaeth

**tatter** *n* rhecsyn, cerpyn

**tattered** *adj* carpiog

**tattle** *vb* clebran, clegar ♦ *n* cleber, baldordd

**tattoo** *n* tatŵ ♦ *vb* torri llun (yn y croen)

**taunt** *vt* edliw, dannod, gwatwar ♦ *n* gwaradwydd, sen

**taut** *adj* tyn

**tautologous** *adj* ailadroddol, cyfystyrol

**tautology** *n* tawtologaeth, ailadrodd, cyfystyredd

**tavern** *n* tafarn, tafarndy, tŷ tafarn

**tawdry** *adj* coegwych

**tawny** *n* melynddu, melyn

**tax** *n* treth ♦ *vt* trethu; cyhuddo

**taxi** *n* tacsi. **t. rank** *n* lloc dacsi

**taxidermist** *n* stwffiwr anifeiliaid

**tea** *n* te

**tea-bag** *n* bag te, cwdyn te

**teacup** *n* disgl de, cwpan te

**tea-leaves** *n* dail te

**tea-party** n téparti
**teach** vt dysgu, addysgu
**teacher** n athro
**teaching** n dysgeidiaeth; dysgu
**teak** n tîc
**team** n gwedd, pâr, tîm
**teapot** n tebot
**tear** n deigryn, deigr
**tear** vb rhwygo, llarpio ♦ n rhwyg
**tearful** adj dagreuol
**tease** vt pryfocio, plagio, poeni
**teaser** n poenwr, poenydiwr
**teaspoon** n llwy de
**teaspoonful** n llond llwy de
**teat** n teth, diden, bron
**technical** adj technegol
**technician** n technegydd
**technique** n techneg
**technological** adj technolegol
**technology** n technoleg
**teddy (bear)** n arth anwes, tedi
**tedious** adj blin, anniben, poenus
**tedium** n diflastod, blinder
**teem** vb epilio, hilio, heigio
**teenager** n un yn yr arddegau
**teens** n arddegau
**teethe** vi torri dannedd
**teetotaller** n llwyrymwrthodwr, titotal
**telecast** n telediad
**telecommunication** n cysylltiad trwy'r teliffon, telegyfathrebaeth
**telegram** n teligram
**telegraph** n teligraff ♦ vb teligraffio
**teleology** n dibenyddiaeth
**telepathy** n telepathi
**telephase** n olgyflwr
**telephone** n teliffon, ffôn. **t. box** n bocs ffonio. **t. call** n galwad ffôn. **t. directory** cyfeirlyfr ffôn
**telescope** n ysbienddrych, telisgob
**televise** vb teledu
**television** n teledu
**tell** vb dweud, traethu, adrodd, mynegi; cyfrif, rhifo
**telltale** n clepgi, clepiwr, clepwraig

**temerity** n rhyfyg, hyfdra
**temper** n tymer, naws ♦ vt tymheru
**temperament** n anianawd
**temperamental** adj gwamal, oriog, di-ddal
**temperance** n dirwest
**temperate** adj cymedrol; tymherus
**temperature** n tymheredd
**tempest** n tymestl
**tempestuous** adj tymhestlog
**temple** n teml
**temple** n arlais
**temporal** adj tymhorol
**temporary** adj dros amser, tymhoroi
**temporize** vi oedi, anwadalu
**tempt** vt temtio, profi
**tempter** n temtiwr
**temptation** n temtiad, temtasiwn
**ten** adj, n deg
**tenable** adj daliadwy, y gellir ei ddal; diffynadwy
**tenacious** adj tyn ei afael, gwydn, gludiog, cyndyn
**tenacity** n cyndynrwydd
**tenant** n deiliad, tenant
**tench** n tens
**tend** vb tendio, gweini
**tend** vi tueddu, cyfeirio, symud
**tendance** n sylw, gofal, tendans
**tendency** n tuedd, gogwydd
**tendentious** adj pleidiol, pleidgar
**tender** adj tyner, tirion, mwyn; meddal
**tender** vb cynnig, cyflwyno ♦ n cynnig
**tenderness** n tynerwch
**tendon** n gewyn
**tendril** n tendril
**tenement** n annedd, rhandy
**tenet** n daliad, barn, tyb
**tenfold** adj dengwaith
**tennis** n tennis. **t. ball** n pêl dennis. **t. court** n cwrt tennis. **t. racket** n

raced tennis
**tenon** n tyno
**tenor** n cyfeiriad, tuedd, rhediad; tenor
**tense** adj tyn, dirdynnol, dwys, angerddol
**tense** n amser (berf)
**tension** n tyndra, pwys, tyniant
**tent** n pabell
**tentacle** n tentacl, braich
**tentative** adj arbrofiadol, dros dro; ansicr
**tenter-hook** n bach deintur. **on tenter-hooks** ar bigau'r drain
**tenth** adj degfed
**tenuous** adj tenau, main, prin
**tenure** n deiliadaeth
**tepid** adj claear
**tercentenary** n trichanmlwyddiant
**term** n terfyn; term; teler, amod; tymor ♦ vt galw, enwi
**terminal** adj terfynol, termol
**terminate** vb terfynu
**termination** n terfyniad
**terminology** n termynoleg
**terminus** n terfyn
**termites** npl morgrug gwynion
**tern** n môr-wennol
**terrace** n rhes dai, teras
**terrain** n tir, bro, ardal
**terrestrial** adj daearol
**terrible** adj dychrynllyd, ofnadwy, arswydus
**terrier** n daeargi
**terrific** adj dychrynllyd, arswydus
**terrify** vt brawychu, dychrynu
**terrifying** adj brawychus, dychrynllyd
**territorial** adj tiriogaethol
**territory** n tir, tiriogaeth
**terror** n dychryn, braw, arswyd, ofn
**terrorise** vb dychrynu, brawychu
**terrorist** n terfysgwr, brawychwr
**terror-stricken** adj wedi ei ddychrynu
**terse** adj byr a chryno

**terseness** n byrdra
**test** n prawf ♦ vt profi
**testament** n testament, cyfamod, ewyllys
**testator** n cymynnwr
**tester** n profwr
**testicle** n caill, carreg
**testify** vb tystio
**testimonial** n tysteb, tystlythyr
**testimony** n tystiolaeth; profiad
**testy** adj afrywiog, ffrom, croes
**tetanus** n gên glo, tetanws
**tether** n rhaff, tennyn ♦ vt clymu
**text** n testun, adnod
**textbook** n gwerslyfr
**textile** adj gweol
**textual** adj testunol
**texture** n gwe, gwead, cyfansoddiad
**Thailand** n Gwlad Thai
**than** conj na, nag
**thank** vt, n diolch
**thankful** adj diolchgar
**thankless** adj diddiolch
**thanks** npl diolch, diolchiadau
**thanksgiving** n diolchgarwch
**that** pron dem hwn (hon) yna (acw), hwnnw, honno, hynny ♦ rel a, y(r) ♦ adj hwn, hon, yma, yna, acw ♦ conj mai, taw
**thatch** n to, to gwellt ♦ vt toi
**thatcher** n tôwr (â gwellt, etc)
**thaw** vb dadlaith, dadmer, meirioli, toddi
**the** adj yr, y
**theatre** n theatr, chwaraedy; maes, golygfa
**theatrical** adj theatraidd
**thee** pron ti, tydi, tithau
**theft** n lladrad
**their** pron eu
**theirs** pron yr eiddynt, eiddynt hwy
**theism** n duwiaeth, theistiaeth
**theist** n un sy'n credu yn Nuw
**them** pron hwy, hwynt, hwythau
**theme** n testun, pwnc, thema
**themselves** pron eu hunain

**then** adv y pryd hwnnw, yna ♦ conj yna

**thence** adv oddi yno, o hynny

**thenceforth** adv o'r amser hwnnw ymlaen

**theocracy** n theocratiaeth

**theologian** n diwinydd

**theological** adj diwinyddol

**theology** n diwinyddiaeth

**theorem** n theorem

**theoretical** adj damcaniaethol, mewn theori

**theorise** vb damcaniaethu

**theory** n damcaniaeth, tyb

**therapeutic** adj iachaol, meddygol

**therapy** n therapi

**there** adv yna, yno, acw; dyna, dacw

**thereafter** adv wedyn

**thereat** adv ar hynny, yna

**thereby** adv trwy hynny

**therefore** conj gan hynny, am hynny

**therefrom** adv oddi yno

**therein** adv yno, ynddo

**thereupon** adv ar hynny

**therewith** adv gyda hynny

**thermal** adj thermol, gwresol, brwd

**thermometer** n thermomedr, mesurydd gwres

**these** adj pl y rhai hyn, y rhai yma

**thesis** (-ses) n gosodiad; traethawd, thesis

**they** pron hwy, hwynt, hwynt-hwy

**thick** adj tew, praff, trwchus

**thicken** vb tewhau, tewychu

**thicket** n prysglwyn, llwyn

**thick-headed** adj pendew, hurt, twp

**thickness** n trwch, tewder

**thick-skinned** adj croendew

**thief** (**thieves**) n lleidr

**thieve** vi lladrata, dwyn

**thigh** n clun, morddwyd

**thimble** n gwniadur

**thin** adj tenau, cul, main; anaml, prin ♦ vb teneuo

**thine** pron eiddot ti; dy

**thing** n peth, dim

**think** vb meddwl

**thinker** n meddyliwr

**third** adj trydydd, trydedd

**thirst** n syched ♦ vi sychedu

**thirteen** adj, n tri (tair) ar ddeg, un deg tri (tair)

**thirty** adj, n deg ar hugain, tri deg

**this** adj, pron hwn, hon, hyn

**thistle** n ysgallen

**thither** adv yno, tuag yno

**thong** n carrai

**thorax** n y ddwyfron, y frest, thoracs

**thorn** n draen, draenen; pigyn, swmbwl

**thorny** n dreiniog, pigog

**thorough** adj trwyadl, trylwyr

**thoroughbred** adj tryryw, o rywogaeth dda

**thoroughfare** n tramwyfa

**thorough-going** adj trwyadl

**thoroughness** n trylwyredd

**those** adj pl y rhai hynny, y rhai yna

**thou** pron ti, tydi, tithau

**though** conj er, pe, cyd

**thought** n meddwl

**thoughtful** adj meddylgar, ystyriol

**thoughtless** adj difeddwl, anystyriol

**thousand** adj, n mil

**thraldom** n caethiwed

**thrall** n caethwr, caethwas

**thrash** vt dyrnu, ffusto, curo

**thread** n edau, edefyn

**threadbare** adj llwm, treuliedig, wedi treulio

**threat** n bygwth, bygythiad

**threaten** vt bygwth

**threatening** adj bygythiol

**three** adj, n tri, tair

**three-cornered** adj trichornel

**threefold** adj triphlyg

**three-legged** *adj* teircoes
**threepence** *n* tair ceiniog, pisyn tair
**thresh** *vt* dyrnu, ffusto
**thresher** *n* dyrnwr, ffustwr
**threshold** *n* trothwy, rhiniog, hiniog
**thrice** *adv* teirgwaith
**thrift** *n* darbodaeth, cynildeb
**thriftless** *adj* gwastraffus
**thrifty** *adj* darbodus, cynnil, diwastraff
**thrill** *vb* gwefreiddio ♦ *n* ias, gwefr
**thriller** *n* stori iasoer
**thrilling** *adj* cyffrous, gwefreiddiol
**thrive** *vi* llwyddo, ffynnu; prifio
**throat** *n* gwddf
**throb** *vi* dychlamu, curo
**throe** *n* dolur, poen, gloes, gwewyr
**thrombosis** *n* clot mewn gwythïen, thrombosis
**throne** *n* gorsedd, gorseddfainc
**throng** *n* tyrfa, torf ♦ *vb* tyrru, heidio
**throstle** *n* bronfraith
**throttle** *n* corn gwynt, corn gwddf, sbardun ♦ *vt* llindagu
**through** *prep* trwy ♦ *adv* trwodd
**throughout** *prep* trwy, trwy gydol ♦ *adv* trwodd
**throw** *n* tafliad ♦ *vb* taflu, bwrw, lluchio
**thrower** *n* taflwr
**thrush** *n* bronfraith
**thrush** *n* llindag, gân
**thrust** *vb* gwthio, gwanu, brathu ♦ *n* gwth
**thud** *n* twrf, sŵn trwm
**thug** *n* llindagwr, dihiryn
**thumb** *n* bawd ♦ *vt* bodio
**thump** *vb* dyrnodio, pwnio, dulio
**thumping** *adj* aruthrol
**thunder** *n* taran(au), tyrfau, trystau ♦ *vb* taranu
**thunderbolt** *n* llucheden
**thunderstorm** *n* storm dyrfau
**Thursday** *n* dydd Iau

**thus** *adv* fel hyn, felly
**thwart** *vt* croesi, gwrthwynebu
**thwart** *vb* rhwystro
**thy** *pron* dy, 'th
**thyme** *n* teim
**thyroid** *n* thiroid
**tiara** *n* talaith, coron, coronig
**tibia** *n* asgwrn y grimpog
**tick** *vi* tipian, ticio ♦ *n* tipian, tic
**tick** *vt* marcio, ticio ♦ *n* nod, marc, tic
**tick** *n* lliain gwely, tic
**ticket** *n* tocyn, ticed. **t. collector** *n* tocynnwr. **t. office** *n* swyddfa docynnau
**tickle** *vb* goglais, gogleisio ♦ *n* goglais
**ticklish** *n* gogleisiol; anodd, dyrys
**tide** *n* llanw, teid; amser, pryd. **high/low t.** *n* penllanw, trai
**tidiness** *n* taclusrwydd
**tidings** *npl* newyddion, chwedlau
**tidy** *adj* taclus, twt, trefnus, destlus
**tie** *vt* clymu, rhwymo ♦ *n* cwlwm, cadach
**tier** *n* rhes, rheng
**tiff** *n* ffrae fach
**tiger** *n* teigr, dywalgi
**tight** *adj* tyn, cryno, twt; cyfyng
**tighten** *vb* tynhau
**tightness** *n* tyndra
**tights** *npl* teits
**tigress** *n* teigres
**tile** *n* priddlech, teilsen
**till** *prep, conj* hyd
**till** *vt* trin, amaethu, llafurio
**tiller** *n* coes llyw; llafurwr, triniwr
**tilt** *vb* gogwyddo; gosod (â gwayw)
**tilth** *n* triniaeth tir, âr
**timber** *n* coed, pren
**time** *n* amser ♦ *vt* amseru
**timely** *adj* amserol, prydlon
**timepiece** *n* cloc, wats
**timetable** *n* amserlen
**timid** *adj* ofnus, ofnog, llwfr
**timidity** *n* ofnusrwydd

**timing** *n* amseriad
**timorous** *adj* ofnus, ofnog
**tin** *n* alcam, tyn
**tincture** *n* lliw
**tinfoil** *n* ffoel alcam
**tinge** *vt* lliwio, arlliwio ♦ *n* arlliw, gwawr
**tingle** *vi* ysu, llosgi, merwino
**tinker** *n* tincer; eurych ♦ *vb* tincera
**tinkle** *vb* tincian
**tinned** *adj* mewn tun, tun
**tint** *n* lliw, arlliw, gwawr ♦ *vt* lliwio
**tinted** *adj* wedi ei liwio
**tinworker** *n* gweithiwr tun, gweithiwr alcam
**tiny** *adj* bychan, bach, pitw
**tip** *n* blaen, pen ♦ *vt* blaenu
**tip** *vb* troi, dymchwelyd; gwobrwyo ♦ *n* tip, tomen; cyngor; gwobr, cil-dwrn
**tipple** *vb* llymeitian, diota
**tippler** *n* diotwr, meddwyn
**tipsy** *adj* meddw, penfeddw, brwysg
**tiptoe** *n:* **on t.** ar flaenau ei draed
**tip-top** *adj* campus, penigamp
**tirade** *n* araith lem
**tire** *vb* blino, lluddedu, diffygio
**tire, tyre** *n* cant, cylch, teiar
**tired** *adj* blinedig
**tiredness** *n* blinder
**tireless** *adj* diflino
**tiresome** *adj* blin, diflas, plagus
**tiro, tyro** *n* newyddian, dechreuwr
**tissue** *n* gwe, meinwe; defnydd cnawd
**tissue paper** *n* papur sidan
**titanic** *adj* cawraidd, anferth, aruthrol
**titbit** *n* tamaid blasus, amheuthun
**tithe** *n* degwm ♦ *vt* degymu
**titivate** *vb* pincio, ymbincio
**title** *n* teitl, hawl, hawlfraint
**titled** *adj* â theitl
**title-deed** *n* dogfen hawlfraint

**title-page** *n* wyneb-ddalen
**titmouse** *n* gwas y dryw, yswidw
**titter** *vi* cilchwerthin, chwerthinial
**tittle** *n* gronyn, mymryn, tipyn
**tittle-tattle** *n* cleber
**titular** *adj* yn rhinwedd teitl; mewn enw
**to** *prep* i, at, hyd, er mwyn, wrth, yn
**toad** *n* llyffant du dafadennog
**toadstool** *n* caws llyffant, bwyd y boda, madarch
**toady** *n* cynffonnwr ♦ *vt* cynffonna
**toast** *n* tost; llwncdestun ♦ *vb* tostio, crasu
**toaster** *n* tostiwr
**tobacco** *n* tybaco, baco
**tobacconist** *n* gwerthwr tybaco
**toboggan** *n* tybogan, sled fach, car llusg
**today** *adv* heddiw
**toddle** *vi* cropian
**toddler** *n* plentyn bach
**toe** *n* bys troed; blaen carn ceffyl
**toe-cap** *n* blaen esgid
**toffee** *n* taffi, cyflaith
**together** *adv* ynghyd, gyda'i gilydd
**toil** *vi* llafurio, poeni ♦ *n* llafur
**toilet** *n* trwsiad, gwisgiad; ystafell ymolchi, tŷ bach. **t. paper** *n* papur tŷ bach. **t. water** *n* dŵr Groeg
**token** *n* arwydd, argoel; tocyn
**tolerable** *adj* goddefol; gweddol, symol, cymhedrol
**tolerant** *adj* goddefgar
**tolerate** *vt* goddef
**toleration** *n* goddefgarwch
**toll** *n* toll, treth
**toll** *vb* canu (cloch, cnul)
**tollbooth** *n* tollfa
**tomato** *n* tomato
**tomb** *n* bedd, beddrod
**tomboy** *n* hoeden, rhampen
**tom-cat** *n* gwrcath, cwrcyn
**tome** *n* cyfrol (fawr)
**tomfool** *n* ynfytyn, pen-ffŵl

**tomfoolery** n ynfydrwydd, ffwlbri
**tomorrow** adv yfory
**tomtit** n gwas y dryw, yswidw
**ton** n tunnell
**tonality** n tonyddiaeth
**tone** n tôn, oslef ♦ vb tyneru, lleddfu
**tongs** npl gefel
**tongue** n tafod; tafodiaith, iaith
**tonic** n meddyginiaeth gryfhaol, tonic. **t. water** n dŵr tonig
**tonnage** n pwysau llwyth (llong); toll
**tonsil** n tonsil
**tonsillitis** n llid y tonsil
**tonsure** n corun, tonsur
**tonight** adv heno
**too** adv rhy; hefyd. **t. much** gormod
**tool** n arf, erfyn
**toot** vb canu corn
**tooth** (**teeth**) n dant
**toothache** n dannoedd
**toothbrush** n brws dannedd
**toothed** adj danheddog
**toothless** adj diddanedd, mantach
**toothpaste** n sebon dannedd, past dannedd
**toothpick** n pic dannedd
**toothsome** adj danteithiol, blasus
**top** n pen, brig, copa ♦ vt tocio; rhagori ar
**top** n cogwrn, top
**top-heavy** adj pendrwm
**topic** n pwnc
**topical** adj amserol
**topography** n daearyddiaeth leol
**topple** vb syrthio, cwympo, dymchwel
**topsyturvy** adv wyneb i waered, yn bendramwnwgl
**torch** n fflach, tors, ffagl
**torch-light** n golau tors
**torment** n poen, poenedigaeth ♦ vt poeni, poenydio
**tormentor** n poenydiwr
**torn** adj wedi ei rwygo, rhwygedig

**tornado** n hyrddwynt, corwynt
**torpedo** n torpedo
**torpid** adj marwaidd, cysglyd, swrth
**torrent** n cenllif, llifeiriant, rhyferthwy
**torrential** adj llifeiriol, trwm
**torrid** adj poeth, crasboeth
**torso** n corff (heb y pen a'r aelodau), torso
**tortoise** n crwban
**tortoise-shell** n cragen crwban, trilliw (am gath)
**tortuous** adj troellog, trofaus
**torture** n dirboen, artaith ♦ vt arteithio
**torturer** n arteithiwr
**tory** n tori, ceidwadwr ♦ adj torïaidd
**toryism** n toriaeth
**toss** vb taflu, lluchio, bwrw
**total** adj hollol, cyflawn ♦ n cyfan, cyfanswm
**totalitarian** adj totalitaraidd
**totalitarianism** n totalitariaeth
**totality** n cyfanrwydd
**totally** adv yn llwyr, yn gyfan, yn ei grynswth
**totter** vi honcian, siglo, gwegian
**touch** vb teimlo, cyffwrdd ♦ n teimlad
**touched** adj dan deimlad
**touching** adj teimladwy
**touch-line** n yr ystlys
**touchstone** n maen prawf, safon
**touchy** adj croendenau
**tough** adj gwydn, caled, cyndyn
**toughen** vb gwneud yn wydn, cryfhau
**tour** n tro, taith
**tourism** n twristiaeth
**tourist** n teithiwr, ymwelydd, twrist. **t. office** n swyddfa twristiaid
**tournament** n twrnamaint
**tourniquet** n offeryn i atal gwaed
**tousle** vt dragio, anhrefnu

**tousled** adj anniben
**tout** vi poeni pobl am archebion, gwasgu ar
**tow** n carth
**tow** vt llusgo, tynnu
**toward, -s** prep tua, tuag at
**towel** n lliain sychu, tywel
**tower** n twr ♦ vi esgyn, ymgodi, sefyll yn uchel
**town** n tref. **t. centre** n canol(y) dref. **t. clerk** n clerc y dref. **t. council** n cyngor y dref. **t. hall** n neuadd y dref
**township** n trefgordd
**toxic** adj gwenwynig
**toy** n tegan ♦ vi chwarae, maldodi
**trace** n tres; ôl, trywydd
**trace** vt olrhain, dilyn ♦ n ôl
**tracery** n rhwyllwaith (maen, etc)
**trachea** n breuant, corn gwynt, pibell wynt
**track** n ôl, brisg; llwybr ♦ vt olrhain
**tracksuit** n tracwisg
**tract** n ardal, rhandir
**tract** n traethodyn
**tractable** adj hydyn, hydrin, hywedd
**traction** n tyniad, tyniant, llusgiad
**trade** n masnach; crefft ♦ vb masnachu
**trade-mark** n nod masnach
**trader** n masnachwr
**trade-union** n undeb llafur
**trade-wind** n gwynt y dwyrain, cylchwynt
**tradition** n traddodiad
**traditional** adj traddodiadol
**traduce** vt cablu, difenwi, enllibio
**traffic** vb masnachu, trafnidio ♦ n masnach, trafnidiaeth. **t. jam** n tagfa. **t. warden** n warden traffig
**traffic-lights** npl goleuadau traffig
**tragedy** n trasiedi, trychineb
**tragic** adj trychinebus, alaethus
**trail** n llusg, brisg, ôl ♦ vb llusgo
**trailer** n ôl-gerbyd, ôl-gart, cart;

rhaglun (ffilm)
**train** vb hyfforddi, ymarfer ♦ n gosgordd; godre; trên, cerbydres
**trained** adj hyfforddedig, cymwys, wedi ei hyfforddi
**trainer** n hyfforddwr
**training** n hyfforddiant, disgyblaeth. **t. shoes** npl esgidiau ymarfer
**trait** n nodwedd, (pl) teithi
**traitor** n bradwr, teyrnfradwr
**trajectory** n taflwybr
**trammel** n rhwyd; hual ♦ vt llyffetheirio, hualu
**tramp** vb crwydro, trampio ♦ n crwydryn
**trample** vb sathru, sangu, mathru
**trance** n llewyg, llesmair, perlewyg
**tranquil** adj tawel, llonydd, digyffro
**tranquility** n tawelwch, llonyddwch
**tranquillizer** n tawelyn, tawelydd
**trans- tran-, tra-** prefix tros-, tra-
**transact** vt trafod, gwneud, trin
**transaction** n trafodaeth
**transactions** n trafodion
**transcend** vt rhagori ar, trarhagori
**transcendent** adj tra-rhagorol
**transcendental** adj trosgynnol
**transcribe** vt copio
**transcriber** n adysgrifiwr, copïwr, copïydd
**transcript** n copi, adysgrifiad
**transept** n croes (eglwys)
**transfer** vt trosglwyddo ♦ n trosglwyddiad
**transference** n trosglwyddiad
**transfiguration** n gweddnewidiad
**transfigure** vt gweddnewid
**transfix** vt trywanu, gwanu
**transform** vt trawsffurfio
**transformation** n trawsffurfiad
**transformer** n newidydd
**transfusion** n trosglwyddiad (gwaed), trallwysiad (gwaed)

**transgress** vt troseddu
**transgression** n trosedd, camwedd
**transgressor** n troseddwr
**transient** adj diflanedig, darfodedig
**transit** n mynediad dros, trosiad
**transition** n trosiad,
  trawsgyweiriad
**transitional** adj ar newid, tros dro
**transitive** adj anghyflawn (gram)
**transitory** adj diflanedig,
  darfodedig
**translate** vt cyfieithu
**translation** n cyfieithiad
**transliterate** vt trawslythrennu
**translucent** adj tryloyw
**transmigrate** vi trawsfudo
**transmission** n trosglwyddiad
**transmit** vt anfon, trosglwyddo
**transmitter** n trosglwyddydd
**transmitting-station** n gorsaf
  drosglwyddo
**transmute** vt trawsnewid
**transparency** n tryloywder
**transparent** adj tryloyw
**transpire** vb dyfod yn hysbys,
  digwydd
**transplant** vt trawsblannu
**transport** vt trosglwyddo; alltudio
  ♦ n trosglwyddiad; cludiant;
  perlewyg, gorawen
**transpose** vt trawsddodi,
  trawsgyweirio
**transubstantiation** n traws-
  sylweddiad
**transverse** adj croes, traws
**trap** n trap, magl; car bach ♦ vt
  dal, maglu
**trapeze** n trapis
**trappings** npl harnais, gêr
**trash** n sothach, gwehilion, ffwlbri,
  ysbwriel
**travail** vi trafaelu ♦ n trafael,
  llafur
**travel** vb teithio, trafaelio ♦ n
  teithio, (pl) teithiau. **t. agent** n
  asiant teithio
**traveller** n teithiwr, trafaeliwr. **t.'s**

**cheque** n siec deithio
**travelling** adj teithiol
**traverse** vb mynd ar draws, croesi
**travesty** n parodi
**trawl** vb llusgrwydo ♦ n llusgrwyd
**trawler** n llong bysgota
**tray** n hambwrdd
**treacherous** adj twyllodrus
**treachery** n brad, bradwriaeth
**treacle** n triagl
**tread** vb sathru, sengi, troedio ♦ n
  sang
**treadmill** n troell droed
**treason** n brad, bradwriaeth
**treasonable** adj bradwrus
**treasure** n trysor ♦ vt trysori
**treasurer** n trysorydd
**treasury** n trysorfa, trysordy, y
  Trysorlys
**treat** vb trin; tretio; traethu ♦ n
  gwledd, amheuthun
**treatise** n traethawd
**treatment** n triniaeth, ymdriniaeth
**treaty** n cyfamod, cytundeb
**treble** adj triphlyg ♦ n trebl ♦ vb
  treblu
**tree** n pren, coeden
**trefoil** n meillionen, meillion
**trek** vi mudo ♦ n mud, mudo
**trellis** n delltwaith
**tremble** vi crynu, echrydu,
  arswydo
**tremendous** adj dychrynllyd,
  ofnadwy, anferth
**tremor** n crynfa, crynod, ias
**tremulous** adj crynedig
**trench** n ffos, rhigol, rhych ♦ vb
  ffosi
**trenchant** adj llym, miniog
**trencher** n trensiwr, treinsiwr, plat
**trend** vi tueddu ♦ n tuedd,
  gogwydd
**trepidation** n cryndod, ofn,
  dychryn
**trespass** vi troseddu ♦ n trosedd
**trespasser** n tresmaswr
**tress** n cudyn gwallt, tres

**trestle** n trestl
**tri-** prefix tri
**triad** n tri, (pl) trioedd
**trial** n prawf, profedigaeth, treial
**triangle** n triongl
**triangular** adj trionglog
**tribal** adj llwythol
**tribe** n llwyth, tylwyth, gwehelyth
**tribulation** n trallod, cystudd
**tribunal** n brawdle, llys, tribiwnlys
**tributary** adj dan deyrnged ♦ n
  rhagafon, isafon, cainc
**tribute** n teyrnged, treth
**trice** n munudyn, chwinciad
**trick** n tric, cast, ystryw ♦ vt
  castio
**trickery** n dichell, twyll, ystryw
**trickle** vi diferu, diferynnu
**trickster** n twyllwr, castiwr
**tricky** adj ystrywgar; anodd
**tricycle** n treisigl
**trident** n tryfer
**triennial** adj bob tair blynedd
**trifle** n gronyn, mymryn;
  gwaelbeth ♦ vt ofera, cellwair
**trifling** adj diwerth, dibwys
**trigger** n cliced, triger
**trigonometry** n trigonomeg
**trill** vb crychleisio, cwafrio ♦ n
  crychlais
**trillion** n triliwn
**trilogy** n cyfres o dair (nofel,
  drama etc)
**trim** adj taclus, twt, del ♦ vb taclu,
  trwsio ♦ n diwyg, trefn
**trinity** n trindod
**trinket** n tegan, tlws
**trio** n triawd
**trioxide** n triocsid
**trip** vb tripio, maglu; disodli ♦ n
  trip, tro
**tripartite** adj teiran
**tripe** n tripa
**triple** adj triphlyg
**triplet** n tripled
**tripod** n trybedd
**trite** adj cyffredin, sathredig

**triumph** n gorfoledd, buddugoliaeth
  ♦ vi gorfoleddu; buddugoliaethu
**triumphal** adj buddugol
**triumphant** adj buddugoliaethus
**triumvirate** n llywodraeth tri
  (Rhufain)
**trivet** n trybedd
**trivial** adj distadl, dibwys, diwerth
**trolley, -y** n troli
**troop** n byddin, torf, mintai ♦ vb
  tyrru. **troops** npl lluoedd,
  minteioedd
**trooper** n milwr (ar farch)
**trophy** n gwobr, tlws
**tropic** n trofan
**tropical** adj trofannol
**trot** vb tuthio, trotian ♦ n tuth, trot
**troubadour** n trwbadŵr, bardd
  telynegol
**trouble** vt blino, trafferthu ♦ n
  blinder, trallod, helbul, trafferth
**troubled** adj aflonydd, anesmwyth,
  pryderus, ofnus, dyrys
**troubles** npl trafferthion, helbulon,
  pryderon, ofnau
**troublesome** adj blinderus,
  trafferthus
**trough** n cafn
**trounce** vt ffonodio, cystwyo,
  baeddu
**troupe** n mintai o berfformwyr
**trousers** npl llodrau, trowsus,
  trwser
**trousseau** n dillad priodasferch
**trout** n brithyll
**trow** vb tybied, meddylied, credu
**trowel** n trywel
**truant** n triawnt, mitsiwr
**truce** n cadoediad
**truck** n trwc, gwagen
**truck** vb cyfnewid, ffeirio
**truckle** vi plygu, ymostwng,
  ymgreinio
**truculent** adj ffyrnig, milain
**trudge** vb cerdded yn ffwdanus,
  trwmgerdded
**true** adj gwir, cywir

**truism** *n* gwireb, gwiredd

**truly** *adv* yn wir, yn ddiau, yn gywir

**trump** *vb* utganu; twyllo, ffugio ♦ *n* trwmp

**trumpery** *n* sothach, ffwlbri ♦ *adj* coeg, gwacsaw

**trumpet** *n* utgorn, corn, trwmped

**truncheon** *n* pastwn, trensiwn

**trundle** *vb* treiglo, rholio

**trunk** *n* cyff, cist; corff; duryn, trwnc

**trunks** *npl* trons

**truss** *vb* gwneud bwndel; gwâellu (ffowlyn)

**trust** *n* ymddiried, ymddiriedaeth, coel; ymddiriedolaeth ♦ *vb* hyderu, ymddiried, coelio

**trustee** *n* ymddiriedolwr

**trusteeship** *n* ymddiriedolaeth

**trustworthy** *adj* y gellir dibynnu arno

**trusty** *adj* ffyddlon, cywir, teyrngar

**truth** *n* gwir, gwirionedd

**truthful** *adj* geirwir

**truthfulness** *n* geirwiredd

**try** *vb* profi, cynnig, ceisio, treio

**trying** *adj* poenus, anodd, blin

**tryst** *n* oed

**T-shirt** *n* crys-T

**tub** *n* twba, twb, baddon

**tuba** *n* tiwba

**tube** *n* pib, pibell, tiwb, corn

**tuber** *n* cloronen, taten

**tuberculosis** *n* darfodedigaeth, dicáu, dicléin

**tubular** *adj* tiwbaidd. **t. bridge** ceubont

**tuck** *vt* cwtogi, plygu ♦ *n* plyg, twc

**Tuesday** *n* dydd Mawrth

**tuft** *n* cogyn, tusw, cudyn

**tug** *vb* llusgo, tynnu

**tuiton** *n* addysg, hyfforddiant

**tulip** *n* tiwlip

**tumble** *vb* cwympo ♦ *n* codwm, cwymp

**tumbler** *n* gwydryn

**tumid** *adj* chwyddedig

**tummy** *n* bola

**tumour** *n* chwydd, casgliad, cornwyd

**tumult** *n* terfysg, cynnwrf

**tumultuous** *adj* terfysglyd

**tuna** *n* tiwna

**tune** *n* tôn, tiwn, cywair ♦ *vb* cyweirio

**tuneful** *adj* soniarus

**tunic** *n* crysbais, siaced

**Tunisia** *n* Tunisia

**tunnel** *n* ceuffordd, twnnel

**turban** *n* twrban

**turbid** *adj* afloyw, cymysglyd, lleidiog

**turbine** *n* twrbin

**turbot** *n* twrbot

**turbulence** *n* terfysg, cynnwrf

**turbulent** *adj* terfysglyd, afreolus

**turf** *n* tywarchen

**turgid** *adj* chwyddedig

**Turk** *n* Twrc

**turkey** *n* twrci

**Turkey** *n* Twrci

**Turkish** *adj* Twrcaidd

**turmoil** *n* trafferth, ffwdan, berw

**turn** *vb* troi ♦ *n* tro, trofa

**turncoat** *n* gwrthgiliwr

**turner** *n* turniwr

**turning** *n* tro; trõedigaeth

**turning point** *n* trobwynt

**turnip** *n* erfinen, meipen

**turnout** *n* cynulliad

**turnover** *n* cyfanswm busnes

**turnpike** *n* tollborth, tyrpeg

**turnstyle** *n* camfa dro

**turntable** *n* trofwrdd

**turpentine** *n* twrpant, turpant

**turpitude** *n* gwarth, ysgelerder

**turquoise** *n* maen glas (gwerthfawr)

**turret** *n* twred, tyryn

**turtle** *n* crwban môr

**turtle, -dove** *n* turtur

**tusk** *n* ysgithrddant, ysgithr

**tussle** *n* ymgiprys, ysgarmes
**tut** *excl* twt!
**tutelage** *n* hyfforddiant, nawdd
**tutor** *n* athro, hyfforddwr ♦ *vt*
  hyfforddi
**tutorial** *adj* tiwtorial
**twaddle** *n* lol, ffiloreg
**twang** *vb* clecian, swnio ♦ *n* sŵn,
  llediaith
**tweed** *n* brethyn gwlân, twid
**tweezers** *n* gefel fach
**twelfth** *adj* deuddegfed
**twelve** *adj, n* deuddeg, un deg dau
**twentieth** *adj* ugeinfed
**twenty** *adj, n* ugain
**twice** *adv* dwywaith
**twiddle** *vt* chwarae bodiau,
  cellwair
**twig** *n* brigyn, ysbrigyn, impyn
**twilight** *n* cyfnos, cyfddydd
**twill** *n* brethyn caerog
**twin** *n* gefell
**twine** *n* llinyn ♦ *vb* cyfrodeddu,
  cordeddu
**twinge** *n* cnofa, brath, gwayw
**twinkle** *vi* serennu, pefrio
**twinkling** *n* chwinciad, amrantiad
**twirl** *vb* chwyrndroi, chwyldroi,
  nydd-droi
**twist** *vb* nyddu, nydd-droi,
  cyfrodeddu; troi, gwyrdroi ♦ *n*
  tro; edau gyfrodedd
**twit** *n* dannod, edliw; un ffôl
**twitch** *vb* tymhigo, brathgnoi ♦ *n*
  tymig
**twitch** *n* gwayw, brath, plwc ♦ *vb*
  brathu, tynnu'n sydyn, plycio
**twitter** *vi* trydar
**two** *adj, n* dau, dwy
**two-faced** *adj* dauwynebog
**twofold** *adv* deublyg
**two piece** *n* deuddarn
**tympan** *n* tabwrdd, tympan
**type** *n* math, teip
**typescript** *n* teipysgrif
**typewriter** *n* teipiadur, peiriant
  teipio

**typhoid** *n* twymyn yr
  ymysgaroedd
**typhoon** *n* corwynt
**typhus** *n* twymyn heintus, teiffws
**typical** *adj* arwyddol, nodweddiadol
**typify** *vt* arwyddo, nodweddu
**typist** *n* teipydd
**typographical** *adj* argraffyddol
**typography** *n* argraffwaith
**tyranny** *n* tra-arglwyddiaeth,
  gormes
**tyrannize** *vb* gormesu, treisio
**tyrant** *n* gormesteyrn, gormeswr
**tyre** *n* teiar
**tyro** *n* newyddian, dechreuwr

# U

**ubiquitous** *adj* ym mhob man,
  hollbresennol
**udder** *n* pwrs, cadair, piw
**ugh** *excl* ach! ych y fi!
**ugly** *adj* hagr, hyll
**ugliness** *n* hagrwch, hylldra
**ulcer** *n* casgliad, cornwyd, wlser
**Ulster** *n* Ulster
**ulterior** *adj* tu draw i, tu hwnt i,
  pellach; cudd
**ultimate** *adj* diwethaf, olaf, eithaf
**ultimately** *adv* o'r diwedd
**ultimatum** *n* y gair olaf, y
  rhybudd olaf
**ultra** *adj* eithafol ♦ *prefix* tu hwnt i,
  gor-
**ultramodern** *adj* modern iawn
**umbrage** *n* tramgwydd
**umbrella** *n* ymbrelo, brela,
  ambarél, ymbarél
**umpire** *n* dyfarnwr, canolwr
**un-** *prefix* an-, am-, ang-, af-, di-,
  heb
**unable** *adj* analluog
**unaccented** *adj* diacen
**unacceptable** *adj* anghymeradwy,
  annerbyniol
**unaccompanied** *adj* heb gwmni;

heb gyfeiliant
**unaccountable** adj anesboniadwy
**unaccustomed** adj anghyfarwydd,
anghynefin
**unacquainted** adj anghyfarwydd
**unadulterated** adj pur, digymysg
**unaffected** adj naturiol; heb ei
effeithio gan
**unanimity** n unfrydedd
**unanimous** adj unfrydol
**unanimously** adv yn unfryd
**unarmed** adj diamddiffyn, heb
arfau
**unassailable** adj diysgog
**unassuming** adj diymhongar
**unattainable** adj anghyraeddadwy
**unavoidable** adj anorfod
**unaware** adj anymwybodol
**unawares** adv yn ddiarwybod
**unbearable** adj annioddefol
**unbecoming** adj anweddus,
anweddaidd
**unbeliever** n anghredadun,
anffyddiwr
**unbelieving** adj anghrediniol
**unbiassed** adj diduedd
**unblemished** adj di-nam, dinam
**unbounded** adj diderfyn
**unbridled** adj heb ei ffrwyno
**unbroken** adj di-dor
**unbutton** vb datod, datfotymu
**uncalled (for)** adj di-alw-amdano
**uncanny** adj rhyfedd, dieithr,
annaearol
**uncle** n ewythr
**unclean** adj brwnt, aflan
**uncomfortable** adj anghysurus
**uncommon** adj anghyffredin
**uncompromising** adj di-ildio,
digyfaddawd, cyndyn
**unconcerned** adj difater, didaro
**unconditional** adj diamod
**unconfirmed** adj heb ei gadarnhau
**unconquerable** adj anorchfygol
**unconscionable** adj digydwybod,
afresymol
**unconscious** adj anymwybodol

**unconstitutional** adj
anghyfansoddiadol
**uncontaminated** adj di-lwgr, pur
**uncontrollable** adj aflywodraethus
**unconventional** adj
anghonfensiynol
**uncouth** adj trwsgl, lletchwith,
garw, amrwd
**uncover** vb datguddio
**unction** n eli; eneiniad, arddeliad,
hwyl
**unctuous** adj seimlyd; rhagrithiol
**uncultivated** adj heb ei feithrin
**undamaged** adj heb ei niweidio
**undecided** adj petrus, mewn
penbleth
**undefended** adj diamddiffyn
**undefiled** adj dihalog, pur
**undefined** adj amhenodol,
annelwig
**undeniable** adj anwadadwy
**under** prep tan, is, islaw ◆ adv
tanodd, oddi tanodd ◆ prefix is-,
tan-
**undercurrent** n islif
**underestimate** vb prisio'n rhy isel
**undergraduate** n myfyriwr
israddedig
**underground** adj tanddaearol
**underhand** adj llechwraidd, tan
din
**underline** vb tanlinellu, pwysleisio
**undermine** vb tanseilio
**underneath** adv oddi tanodd ◆ prep
tan
**underpass** n ffordd danddaearol,
tanffordd
**underrate** vb tanbrisio, iselbrisio
**understand** vt deall, dirnad
**understanding** n amgyffred,
dealltwriaeth
**undertake** vb ymgymryd
**undertaker** n ymgymerydd; saer
(coffinau)
**undertaking** adj ymrwymiad
**undertone** n islais
**underworld** n annwn

**undeserved** *adj* anhaeddiannol
**undesirable** *adj* annymunol
**undeveloped** *adj* heb ei ddatblygu
**undeviating** *adj* diwyro
**undignified** *adj* anurddasol, diurddas
**undisciplined** *adj* diddisgyblaeth
**undisputed** *adj* diamheuol
**undisturbed** *adj* llonydd, tawel, digyffro
**undo** *vt* dadwneud; datod; andwyo, difetha
**undoing** *n* distryw, dinistr
**undoubted** *adj* diamheuol
**undress** *vb* dadwisgo
**undue** *adj* amhriodol
**undulate** *vi* tonni
**unearned** *adj* heb ei ennill
**unearthly** *adj* annaearol
**uneasiness** *n* anesmwythder, pryder
**uneasy** *adj* anesmwyth, aflonydd, pryderus
**unedifying** *adj* di-fudd, anadeiladol
**uneducated** *adj* annysgedig
**unemployed** *adj* di-waith, segur
**unemployment** *n* diweithdra, anghyflogaeth
**unending** *adj* diddiwedd
**unendurable** *adj* annioddefol
**unequal** *adj* anghyfartal
**unequalled** *adj* digymar, dihafal
**unequivocal** *adj* diamwys
**unerring** *adj* sicr
**uneven** *adj* anwastad
**uneventful** *adj* diddigwyddiad
**unexpected** *adj* annisgwyliadwy
**unfailing** *adj* di-feth
**unfair** *adj* annheg
**unfairness** *n* annhegwch
**unfaithful** *adj* anffyddlon
**unfamiliar** *adj* anghyfarwydd
**unfasten** *vb* datod
**unfathomable** *adj* annealladwy
**unfavourable** *adj* anffafriol
**unfeeling** *adj* dideimlad
**unfettered** *adj* dilyffethair

**unfinished** *adj* anorffenedig
**unfit** *adj* anghymwys; afiach
**unfitting** *adj* amhriodol
**unflinching** *adj* diysgog, dewr
**unfold** *vb* datblygu
**unforseen** *adj* heb ei ragweld
**unforgiving** *adj* anfaddeugar
**unfortunate** *adj* anffodus
**unfortunately** *adj* yn anffodus
**unfounded** *adj* di-sail
**unfrequented** *adj* anhygyrch, unig
**unfriendly** *adj* anghyfeillgar
**unfrock** *vb* diarddel
**unfulfilled** *adj* heb ei gyflawni
**unfurnished** *adj* diddodrefn
**ungainly** *adj* afrosgo, trwsgl
**ungentlemanly** *adj* anfoneddigaidd
**ungodly** *adj* annuwiol, drwg
**ungrammatical** *adj* anramadegol
**ungrateful** *adj* anniolchgar
**unguarded** *adj* ar awr wan
**unguent** *n* ennaint, eli
**unhallowed** *adj* halogedig
**unhappiness** *n* anhapusrwydd
**unhappy** *adj* anhapus
**unharmed** *adj* dianaf
**unhealthy** *adj* afiach
**unheeding** *adj* diofal
**unhesitating** *adj* dibetrus
**unhorse** *vb* taflu oddi ar geffyl
**unicorn** *n* uncorn, unicorn
**unification** *n* uniad
**uniform** *adj* unffurf ♦ *n* gwisg swyddogol
**uniformity** *n* unffurfiaeth
**unify** *vt* unoli, uno
**unilateral** *adj* unochrog
**unimpaired** *adj* dianaf
**unimpeded** *adj* dirwystr
**unimportant** *adj* dibwys
**uninspired** *adj* diawen
**unintelligent** *adj* anneallus
**unintelligible** *adj* annealladwy
**unintentional** *adj* anfwriadol
**uninteresting** *adj* anniddorol
**union** *n* undeb; uniad
**unionism** *n* undebaeth

**unionist** n undebwr; unoliaethwr (Iwerddon)

**unique** adj dihafal, digymar

**unison** n unsain, unseinedd

**unit** n un, rhif un; uned; undod

**Unitarian** n Undodwr ♦ adj Undodaidd

**Unitarianism** n Undodiaeth

**unite** vb uno, cyfuno, cyduno, cydio

**united** adj unol, unedig. **U. States (of America)** n yr Unol Daleithiau

**United Kingdom** n: **the U.K.** y Deyrnas Unedig

**unity** n undod

**universal** adj cyffredinol

**universe** n bydysawd

**university** n prifysgol

**unjust** adj anghyfiawn, annheg

**unjustly** adv ar gam

**unkempt** adj heb ei gribo, aflêr, anniben

**unkind** adj angharedig

**unknown** adj anadnabyddus, anenwog

**unlace** vb datod

**unlawful** adj anghyfreithlon

**unlearned** adj annysgedig

**unless** conj oni, onid

**unlettered** adj anllythrennog

**unlike** adj annhebyg

**unlikely** adj annhebygol

**unlimited** adj diderfyn

**unload** vb dadlwytho

**unlock** vb datgloi

**unlucky** adj anlwcus

**unmanageable** adj aflywodraethus

**unmannerly** adj anfoesgar

**unmarried** adj dibriod

**unmask** vb dinoethi

**unmatched** adj digymar

**unmerciful** adj didrugaredd

**unmistakable** adj digamsyniol

**unmixed** adj digymysg

**unnatural** adj annaturiol

**unnecessary** adj dianghenraid

**unobserved** adj heb ei weld

**unobtrusive** adj anymwthiol

**unoccupied** adj gwag

**unopened** adj heb ei agor

**unopposed** adj yn ddiwrthwynebiad

**unorthodox** adj anarferol, anuniongred

**unpack** vb dadbacio

**unpaid** adj di-dâl, didal

**unparalleled** adj digyffelyb

**unpardonable** adj anfaddeuol

**unpatriotic** adj anwlatgar

**unpleasant** adj annymunol

**unpolluted** adj dihalog, pur

**unpopular** adj amhoblogaidd

**unpopularity** n amhoblogrwydd

**unpractical** adj anymarferol

**unprejudiced** adj diragfarn

**unprepared** adj amharod

**unprincipled** adj diegwyddor

**unprofitable** adj amhroffidiol

**unprotected** adj diamddiffyn

**unpublished** adj anghoeddledig

**unqualified** adj heb gymhwyster

**unquestionable** adj diamheuol

**unready** adj amharod

**unreasonable** adj afresymol

**unrelated** adj amherthnasol; heb berthyn

**unremitting** adj dyfal

**unrestrained** adj dilywodraeth

**unripe** adj anaeddfed

**unrivalled** adj digymar

**unruffled** adj tawel

**unruly** adj afreolus

**unsafe** adj anniogel

**unsatisfactory** adj anfoddhaol

**unsatisfied** adj anfodlon

**unsatisfying** adj annigonol

**unscathed** adj dianaf

**unscrew** vt agor; llacio; datroi

**unscrupulous** adj diegwyddor

**unseasonable** adj annhymorol

**unseat** vb troi o'i swydd; taflu (ceffyl)

**unseemly** adj anweddaidd

**unseen** adj anweledig

**unsettled** adj ansefydlog
**unshaken** adj diysgog, cadarn
**unsighted** adj heb allu gweld
**unsightly** adj diolwg, blêr
**unskilful** adj anfedrus
**unskilled** adj anghelfydd
**unsociable** adj anghymdeithasgar
**unsolicited** adj heb ei ofyn
**unsound** adj diffygiol, cyfeitiornus
**unsparing** adj diarbed, hael
**unspeakable** adj anhraethol
**unstable** adj ansefydlog
**unstained** adj dilychwin
**unsteadiness** n ansadrwydd
**unsteady** adj ansefydlog
**unsubstantial** adj ansylweddol
**unsuccessful** adj aflwyddiannus
**unsuitable** adj anaddas
**unsullied** adj dilychwin
**unsurmountable** adj anorchfygol
**unsurpassed** adj diguro
**unsuspecting** adj heb amau dim
**untainted** adj di-lwgr, pur
**untangle** vb datrys
**unthankful** adj anniolchgar
**unthinking** adj difeddwl
**untidy** adj anniben
**untie** vb datod
**until** prep, conj hyd, hyd oni, nes, tan
**untimely** adj anamserol
**untiring** adj diflino
**unto** prep i, at, hyd at, wrth
**untold** adj di-ben-draw
**untoward** adj anffodus, cyndyn
**untrodden** adj disathr
**untrue** adj celwyddog
**unusual** adj anarferol, anghynefin; anghyffredin; newydd; dieithr
**unutterable** adj anhraethadwy
**unvarying** adj digyfnewid, cyson
**unveil** vb dadorchuddio
**unversed** adj anhyddysg
**unwarranted** adj heb ei warantu
**unwary** adj diofal
**unwell** adj anhwylus
**unwholesome** adj afiach

**unwieldy** adj afrosgo
**unwilling** adj anfodlon, amharod
**unwise** adj annoeth
**unwittingly** adv yn ddiarwybod
**unworthiness** n annheilyngdod
**unworthy** adj annheilwng
**unwounded** adj dianaf, cyfan
**unyielding** adj di-ildio
**up** adj, prep i fyny, i'r lan
**upbringing** n magwraeth
**upheaval** n cyffro, terfysg
**uphill** adj i fyny
**uphold** vb cynnal
**upholsterer** n dodrefnwr, clustogwr
**upkeep** n cynhaliaeth
**upland** n ucheldir, blaenau
**uplifting** adj dyrchafol
**upon** prep ar, ar warthaf, ar uchaf
**upper** adj uwch, uchaf
**uppermost** adj, adv uchaf
**upright** adj syth, union, unionsyth
**uprising** n terfysg, gwrthryfel
**uproar** n terfysg, cythrwfl, dadwrdd
**uproot** vt diwreiddio
**upset** vb troi, dymchwelyd, cyffroi, gofidio
**upshot** n swm, canlyniad, diwedd
**upside-down** adj, adv (â'i) wyneb i waered
**upstairs** n llofft
**upstart** n crach fonheddwr
**upward** adj, adv, **upwards** adv i fyny
**uranium** n wraniwm
**urban** adj dinasol, dinesig
**urbane** adj hynaws, mwyn, boneddigaidd
**urbanize** vb gwneud yn drefol
**urchin** n draenog; crwtyn
**urethra** n pibell ddŵr o'r bledren
**urge** vt cymell, annog
**urgency** n brys
**urgent** adj taer, pwysig, yn gofyn brys
**urine** n troeth, trwnc, piso

**urn** *n* wrn
**us** *pron* ni, nyni, ninnau; 'n
**usage** *n* arfer, defod, triniaeth
**use** *n* iws, arfer, defnydd,
gwasanaeth, diben ♦ *vb* iwsio,
arfer, defnyddio
**used** *adj* arferedig, mewn arfer,
cynefin; *(car)* ail-law
**useful** *adj* defnyddiol
**useless** *adj* diwerth
**user** *n* defnyddiwr
**usher** *n* rhingyll; isathro;
tywysydd ♦ *vt* arwain i mewn,
dwyn ymlaen
**usual** *adj* arferol, cynefin
**usurer** *n* usuriwr
**usurp** *vt* trawsfeddiannu
**usurper** *n* trawsfeddiannwr
**usury** *n* usuriaeth, ocraeth
**utensil** *n* offeryn, llestr
**uterus** *n* croth, bru
**utilitarian** *adj* defnyddiol
**utilitarianism** *n* llesyddiaeth
**utility** *n* defnyddioldeb, budd, lles
**utilization** *n* defnydd
**utilize** *vt* defnyddio
**utmost** *adj* eithaf, pellaf
**utopia** *n* gwlad ddelfrydol
(ddychmygol)
**utopian** *adj* defrydol, anymarferol
**utter** *adj* eithaf, pellaf; hollol,
llwyr
**utter** *vt* yngan, traethu, dywedyd
**utterance** *n* parabl, ymadrodd,
lleferydd
**uttermost** *adj* eithaf, pellaf
**U-turn** *n* tro pedol
**uvula** *n* tafod bach, tafodig
**uvular** *adj* tafodigol

# V

**vacancy** *n* lle gwag, swydd wag,
gwacter
**vacant** *adj* gwag; syn, synfyfyriol,
hurt

**vacate** *vt* ymadael â, gadael yn
wag
**vacation** *n* seibiant, gwyliau
**vaccinate** *vt* brechu, bufrechu,
torri'r frech
**vaccination** *n* y frech, brechiad
**vaccine** *n* brech
**vacillate** *vi* anwadalu, bwhwman
**vacuous** *adj* gwg, syn, hurt
**vacuum** *n* gwag, gwagle, gwactod
**vacuum cleaner** *n* sugnydd llwch
**vacuum flask** *n* thermos, jac
**vagabond** *n* crwydryn, dihiryn
**vagary** *n* mympwy
**vagrancy** *n* crwydro
**vagrant** *adj* crwydrol ♦ *n* crwydryn
**vague** *adj* amwys, amhenodol
**vagueness** *n* amwysedd
**vain** *adj* balch, coegfalch; ofer
**vale** *n* dyffryn, glyn, bro, cwm,
ystrad
**valediction** *n* ffarwel
**valentine** *n* falant, folant
**valet** *n* gwas
**valiant** *adj* dewr, dewrwych, gwrol,
glew
**valid** *adj* digonol, dilys, cyfreithlon,
iawn
**validate** *vb* cadarnhau, dilysu
**validity** *n* dilysrwydd
**valley** *n* dyffryn, cwm, glyn
**valour** *n* dewrder, gwroldeb,
glewder
**valuable** *adj* gwerthfawr
**valuation** *n* prisiad
**value** *n* gwerth ♦ *vt* gwerthfawrogi,
prisio
**valuer** *n* prisiwr
**valve** *n* falf
**vampire** *n* sugnwr gwaed
**van** *n* blaen cad, y rheng flaenaf
**van** *n* men, fan
**vandal** *n* fandal
**vandalism** *n* fandaliaeth
**vane** *n* ceiliog gwynt
**vanguard** *n* blaen cad, blaenfyddin
**vanilla** *n* fanila

**vanish** vi diflannu, darfod
**vanity** n gwagedd, gwegi,
coegfalchder
**vanquish** vt gorchfygu, trechu
**vanquisher** n gorchfygwr
**vantage** n mantais
**vapid** adj diflas, merf, marwaidd,
egr
**vaporize** vb anweddu
**vaporous** adj llawn tarth
**vapour** n tawch, tarth, ager,
anwedd
**variable** adj cyfnewidiol, anwadal,
oriog
**variable** n newidyn (rhifyddiaeth)
**variance** n anghytundeb,
anghydfod, amrywioldeb
**variant** n amrywiad
**variation** n amrywiad
**varicose** adj chwyddedig (am
wythiennau)
**varied** adj amrywiol
**variegated** adj brith, brithliw
**variety** n amrywiaeth
**various** adj gwahanol, amrywiol
**varnish** n barnais, farnais ♦ vt
barneisio, farneisio
**varnisher** n farneisiwr
**vary** vb amrywio; newid
**vase** n cwpan, cawg
**vaseline** n faselin, eli
**vassal** n caethddeiliad, taeog, aillt,
deiliad
**vast** adj dirfawr, anferth
**vastness** n mawredd, ehangder
**vat** n cerwyn
**Vatican** n plas y Pab
**vaticinate** vb proffwydo, darogan
**vaticination** n proffwydoliaeth,
darogan
**vault** n daeargell, claddgell;
cromen ♦ vb neidio, llamu
**vaulted** adj bwaog
**vaunt** vb ymffrostio, bostio, brolio
**veal** n cig llo
**vector** n fector
**veer** vb troi, cylchdroi;

trawshwylio
**vegetable** adj llysieuol ♦ n
llysieuyn ymborth
**vegetarian** n llysieuwr
**vegetate** vi tarddu, tyfu; ofera
**vegetation** n tyfiant llysiau,
llystyfiant
**vehemence** n angerdd
**vehement** adj angerddol, tanbaid
**vehicle** n cerbyd; cyfrwng,
moddion
**veil** n gorchudd, llen ♦ vt
gorchuddio
**vein** n gwythïen
**velar** adj felar
**veldt** n anialdir, maestir
**vellum** n memrwn
**velocity** n buander, cyflymder,
buanedd (mathemateg)
**velvet** n melfed
**venal** adj llygredig, anonest
**vend** vt gwerthu
**vendor** n gwerthwr
**veneer** n argaen, wynebiad; rhith,
ffug
**venerable** adj hybarch
**venerate** vt parchu, anrhydeddu
**venereal** adj gwenerol
**Venetian blind** n llen Fenis
**vengeance** n dial, dialedd
**vengeful** adj dialgar
**venial** adj maddeuadwy, esgusodol
**venison** n cig carw, fenswn
**venom** n gwenwyn
**venomous** adj gwenwynig
**venous** adj gwythennol
**vent** n agorfa, twll, arllwysfa ♦ vt
arllwys, gollwng
**ventilate** vt awyru, gwyntyllu
**ventilation** n awyriad, gwyntylliad
**ventilator** n awyrydd, gwyntyllydd
**ventriloquism** n tafleisiaeth
**ventricle** n bolgell y galon, fentrigl
**venture** n anturiaeth, mentr ♦ vb
anturio, mentro
**venturesome** adj mentrus, anturus
**venue** n man cyfarfod

**Venus** n Gwener, duwies serch
**veracious** adj cywir, geirwir, gwir
**veracity** adj geirwiredd
**verandah** n feranda
**verb** n berf
**verbal** adj berfol; geiriol
**verbally** adv mewn geiriau, gair am air
**verbatim** adv air am air, air yng ngair
**verbiage** n amleiraeth, geiriogrwydd
**verb-noun** n berfenw
**verbose** adj amleiriog
**verbosity** n geiriogrwydd
**verdant** adj gwyrddlas, gwyrdd
**verdict** n dyfarniad, dedfryd, rheithfarn
**verdure** n gwyrddlesni
**verge** n min, ymyl ♦ vi ymylu
**verger** n byrllysgydd, eglwyswas
**verfication** n gwireddiad
**verify** vt gwiro, gwireddu
**verily** adv yn wir, yn ddiau
**verisimilitude** n tebygolrwydd
**veritable** adj gwirioneddol
**verity** n gwir, gwirionedd
**vermilion** n fermiliwn, lliw cochlyd
**vermin** npl pryfed, pryfetach; llygod, etc
**vernacular** adj cynhenid, brodorol ♦ n iaith y wlad
**vernal** adj gwanwynol
**veronica** n feronica, llysiau Llywelyn
**versatile** adj amryddawn
**versatility** n amlochredd
**verse** n gwers, adnod, pennill; prydyddiaeth
**versed** adj cyfarwydd, hyddysg
**versify** vb mydru, prydyddu, prydu
**version** n cyfieithiad, trosiad; esboniad
**vers libre** n gwers rydd
**versus** prep yn erbyn
**vertebra** (-brae) n un o gymalau'r asgwrn cefn

**vertebrate** n anifail ag asgwrn cefn
**vertex** (-tices) n pen, crib, copa
**vertical** adj syth, unionsyth, plwm
**vertigo** n y bendro, y ddot
**vervain** n llysiau hudol, y ferfain
**verve** n bywyd, egni, asbri
**very** adj, adv iawn, pur, tra; diamheuol
**vespers** npl gosber
**vessel** n llestr
**vest** n gwasgod, crys isaf ♦ vb arwisgo, cynysgaeddu
**vestal** adj gwyryfol ♦ n lleian, gwyry
**vested** adj yn ymwneud ag eiddo
**vestibule** n porth, cyntedd
**vestige** n ôl, ôl troed, brisg
**vestigial** adj gweddilliol, ôl
**vestment** n gwisg, defodwisg
**vestry** n festri
**vesture** n gwisg, dilledyn, dillad
**vet** vb arholi, archwilio ♦ n meddyg anifeiliaid
**vetch** n pys llygod
**veteran** n un hen a chyfarwydd
**veterinary** adj milfeddygol. **v. surgeon** meddyg anifeiliaid, milfeddyg
**veto** (-oes) n gwaharddiad ♦ vt gwahardd
**vex** vt blino, poeni, poenydio, cythruddo
**vexation** n blinder, gofid
**vexed** adj blin, dig
**vexing** adj blin, plagus
**via** prep trwy, ar hyd
**viable** adj abl i fodoli, dichonadwy
**viaduct** n pontffordd, fforddbont
**vial** n ffiol
**viand** n bwyd, ymborth
**vibrant** adj dirgrynol
**vibrate** vb crynu, dirgrynu
**vibration** n dirgryniad
**vicar** n ficer
**vicarage** n ficeriaeth; ficerdy
**vicarious** adj dirprwyol, mechnïol

**vice** n drygioni, drygedd, bai, gwŷd
**vice** n gwasg, feis
**vice-** prefix rhag-, is-
**vice-admiral** n is-lyngesydd
**vice-chairman** n is-gadeirydd
**vice-chancellor** n is-ganghellor
**vice-president** n is-lywydd
**viceroy** n rhaglaw
**vice-versa** adv i'r gwrthwyneb
**vicinity** n cymdogaeth
**vicious** adj drygionus, gwydus
**viciousness** n drygioni, sbeit
**vicissitude** n cyfnewidiad, tro
**victim** n aberth, ysglyfaeth
**victimise** vb erlid, gormesu
**victor** n gorchfygwr
**victorious** adj buddugol, buddugoliaethus
**victory** n buddugoliaeth
**victual** n (pl) bwyd, lluniaeth ♦ vt bwydo
**victualler** n gwerthwr bwyd. **licensed v.** n tafarnwr
**vide** vb gwêl
**videlicet** (**viz**) adv sef, h.y.
**vie** vi cystadlu, cydymgais
**Vienna** n Wien
**Vietnam** n Fietnam
**view** n golygfa, barn ♦ vt edrych
**viewer** n gwyliwr (teledu)
**viewpoint** n safbwynt
**vigil** n noswyl, gwylnos
**vigilant** adj gwyliadwrus
**vignette** n addurn, llun
**vigorous** adj grymus, egnïol
**vigour** n grym, nerth, egni, ynni
**viking** n môr-leidr (o Lychlyn gynt)
**vile** adj gwael, brwnt
**vileness** n brynti
**vilify** vt pardduo, difrïo
**villa** n fila
**village** n pentref
**villager** n pentrefwr
**villain** n cnaf, adyn, dihiryn
**villainous** adj anfad, ysgeler

**villainy** n anfadwaith
**vim** n grym, ynni
**vindicate** vt amddiffyn, cyfiawnhau
**vindication** n cyfiawnhad
**vindictive** adj dialgar
**vindictiveness** n dialedd
**vine** n gwinwydden
**vinegar** n finegr
**vineyard** n gwinllan
**vintage** n cynhaeaf gwin
**vintner** n gwinwr, gwinydd
**viola** n fiola
**violate** vt torri, troseddu, treisio, trochi
**violation** n treisiad, trosedd
**violence** n ffyrnigrwydd, trais
**violent** adj gwyllt, tanbaid, angerddol
**violet** n fioled, crinllys
**violin** n ffidil
**violinist** n feiolinydd, ffidler
**violoncello** n basgrwth
**viper** n gwiber
**viper's bugloss** n tafod y bwch
**virago** n cecren
**virgin** n gwyry, morwyn
**virginal** n fyrginal ♦ adj gwyryfol, morwynol
**virile** adj gwrol, egnïol
**virility** n gwrolaeth, gwroldeb
**virtual** adj rhinweddol
**virtually** adv i bob pwrpas
**virtue** n rhinwedd
**virtuoso** n un celfydd, carwr celfyddyd
**virulence** n gwenwyn, casineb
**virulent** adj gwenwynig, ffyrnig
**virus** n gôr, crawn; gwenwyn, firws
**visa** n fisa
**visage** n wyneb, wynepryd
**vis-à-vis** adv wyneb yn wyneb, gyferbyn
**viscid** adj gwydn, gludiog
**viscount** n is-iarll
**visible** adj gweladwy, gweledig
**vision** n gweledigaeth; golwg,

gweled

**visionary** n breuddwydiwr ♦ adj breuddwydiol

**visit** vt ymweld, gofwyo ♦ n ymweliad

**visitation** n ymweliad, archwiliad

**visitor** n ymwelwr, ymwelydd

**visor** n miswrn, mwgwd

**vista** n golygfa

**visual** adj gweledol, golygol. **v. aids** cyfarpar gweld

**visualise** vb gwneud yn weledig, disgrifio, dychmygu

**vital** adj bywiol, bywydol, hanfodol

**vitality** n bywyd, bywiogrwydd

**vitalize** vb bywiocáu, bywiogi

**vitamin** n fitamin

**vitiate** vt llygru, difetha, dirymu

**vitreous** adj gwydrol, gwydraidd

**vitriol** n fitriol, asid sylffurig

**vitriolic** adj fitriolaidd, atgas, chwerw

**vituperate** vt cablu, difenwi, difrïo

**vituperative** adj difriol

**vivacious** adj bywiog, heini, nwyfus

**vivacity** n hoen, nwyf

**viva voce** adv ar lafar

**vivid** adj byw, clir, llachar, tanbaid

**vividness** n eglurder

**vivify** vt bywhau, bywiocáu

**vivisection** n bywdrychiad, bywddifyniad

**vixen** n cadnawes, llwynoges

**viz.** adv sef (talfyriad o *videlicet*)

**vizier** n swyddog gwlad (Mohametanaidd)

**vocable** n gair

**vocabulary** n geirfa

**vocal** adj lleisiol, llafarol, llafar

**vocalist** n lleisiwr, cantor

**vocalize** vt llafarseinio; llafarogi

**vocally** adv â'r llais

**vocation** n galwad, galwedigaeth

**vocative** adj cyfarchol

**vociferate** vb crochlefain, gweiddi

**vodka** n fodca

**vogue** n arfer, ffasiwn, bri

**voice** n llais, lleferydd; stad (*gram.*)

**voiced** adj llafarog, lleisiol

**voiceless** adj dilais, mud

**void** adj gwag; ofer, di-rym ♦ n gwagle ♦ vt gwagu, gollwng; gwacau

**volatile** adj hedegog, anwadal, gwamal, ysgafn, cyfnewidiol

**volcanic** adj folcanig

**volcano** n llosgfynydd, mynydd tân

**vole** n llygoden y maes

**volition** n ewyllysiad, ewyllys

**volley** n cawod o ergydion; taro pêl yn yr awyr

**volt** n uned grym trydan, folt

**voltage** n grym trydan

**voluble** adj rhugl, ymadroddus

**volume** n cyfrol; swm, crynswth, folum (cemeg), cyfaint (mathemateg)

**voluminous** adj mawr, helaeth

**voluntary** adj gwirfoddol

**volunteer** n gwirfoddolwr ♦ vb gwirfoddoli

**voluptuary** n pleserwr, glythwr

**voluptuous** adj glwth, trythyll

**voluptuousness** n trythyllwch

**vomit** vb chwydu, cyfogi

**voracious** adj gwancus, rheibus

**vortex** n trobwll, chwyldro

**votary** n addunwr, diofrydwr; pleidiwr

**vote** n pleidlais ♦ vb pleidleisio

**voter** n pleidleisiwr

**votive** adj addunedol, addunol

**vouch** vb gwirio, gwarantu

**vouchsafe** vt caniatáu, rhoddi

**vow** n adduned, diofryd ♦ vb addunedu

**vowel** n llafariad. **v. affection** affeithiad. **v. mutation** gwyriad

**voyage** n mordaith ♦ vb mordeithio, mordwyo

**voyager** n mordeithiwr

**vulcanize** vb caledu rwber

**vulgar** *adj* cyffredin; isel, di-foes, aflednais

**vulgarism** *n* ymadrodd aflednais

**vulgarity** *n* diffyg moes

**Vulgate** *n* Y Fwlgat

**vulnerable** *adj* archolladwy, hyglwyf, hawdd ei niweidio

**vulture** *n* fwltur

# W

**wad** *n* sypyn, wad

**wadding** *n* wadin

**waddle** *vi* siglo, honcian

**wade** *vb* beisio, rhydio

**wader** *n* rhydiwr

**wadi** *n* gwely afon (sy'n dueddol i sychu)

**wafer** *n* afrlladen

**waft** *vt* chwifio, cludo, dygludo

**wag** *vb* ysgwyd, siglo, honcian

**wag** *n* cellweiriwr, wag

**wage** *vt* gwneuthur, dwyn ymlaen

**wage** *n* cyflog, hur

**wager** *n* cyngwystl ♦ *vt* cyngwystlo

**waggish** *adj* cellweirus

**waggle** *vb* siglo

**wagon** *n* men, gwagen

**wagtail** *n* sigl-i-gwt

**waif** *n* plentyn digartref

**wail** *vb* cwynfan, wylofain, udo

**wainscot** *n* palis

**waist** *n* gwasg, canol

**waistcoat** *n* gwasgod

**wait** *vb* aros; gweini ♦ *n* arhosiad

**waiter** *n* gweinydd

**waiting** *n* aros, sefyll

**waiting room** *n* ystafell aros

**waitress** *n* gweinyddes

**wake** *vb* deffro ♦ *n* gwylmabsant; gwylnos

**wake** *n* ôl, brisg

**wakefulness** *n* anhunedd

**waken** *vb* deffro, dihuno

**Wales** *n* Cymru

**walk** *vb* cerdded, rhodio ♦ *n* rhodfa; tro

**walker** *n* cerddwr

**walkie-talkie** *n* set radio symud a siarad

**walking** *n* cerddediad; cerdded. **w. stick** ffon gerdded

**walkover** *n* goruchafiaeth hawdd, digystadleuaeth

**wall** *n* mur, gwal, pared ♦ *vt* murio

**wallaby** *n* cangarŵ bach

**wall-cress** *n* berwr y fagwyr

**wallet** *n* ysgrepan, gwaled

**wallflower** *n* llysiau'r fagwyr, blodau'r fagwyr, blodau mamgu

**wallop** *vt* curo, llachio, wado

**wallow** *vi* ymdreiglo, ymdrybaeddu

**wallpaper** *n* papur wal

**walnut** *n* cneuen Ffrengig

**walrus** *n* morfarch

**waltz** *n* wols

**wan** *adj* gwelw, gwelwlas, llwyd

**wand** *n* gwialen, llath, hudlath

**wander** *vb* crwydro, gwibio, cyfeiliorni

**wanderer** *n* crwydryn

**wandering** *adj* ar grwydr

**wanderlust** *n* elfen grwydro

**wane** *vi* darfod, treio, cilio, lleihau

**wangle** *vb* dyfeisio

**want** *n* angen, eisiau, diffyg ♦ *vb* bod mewn angen

**wanting** *adj* yn eisiau

**wanton** *adj* anllad, trythyll; diachos

**wantonness** *n* anlladrwydd

**war** *n* rhyfel ♦ *vb* rhyfela

**warble** *vb* telori

**warbler** *n* telor

**ward** *n* gwart, gward; gwarchodaeth ♦ *vt* gwarchod, amddiffyn

**warden** *n* gwarden, gwarcheidwad

**wardenship** *n* gwardeniaeth

**warder** *n* gwarchodwr, gwyliwr

**wardrobe** *n* cypwrdd dillad,

gwardrob
**ware** n nwydd; llestri, wâr
**warehouse** n ystordy, ystorfa,
warws
**warfare** n milwriaeth, rhyfel
**wariness** n pwyll, gwyliadwriaeth
**warlike** adj rhyfelgar, milwraidd,
milwrol
**warm** adj cynnes ♦ vb cynhesu
**warmonger** n rhyfelgi
**warmth** n cynhesrwydd
**warn** vt rhybuddio
**warning** n rhybudd
**warp** n ystof, dylif ♦ vb gwyro,
lleddfu
**warrant** n gwarant, awdurdod ♦ vt
gwarantu, cyfreithloni
**warrantor** n gwarantydd
**warren** n cwningar, parc cwningod
**warrior** n rhyfelwr
**warship** n llong rhyfel
**wart** n dafad, dafaden
**wary** adj gwyliadwrus, gochelgar
**was** vi oedd, bu
**wash** vb golchi ♦ n golchiad,
golchfa; golchion
**washable** adj golchadwy
**washing** n golch
**washing machine** n peiriant
golchi
**washing powder** n powdr golchi
**washing-up liquid** n sebon golchi
llestri
**wasp** n cacynen, gwenynen feirch
**wassail** n gwasael
**waste** vb difrodi, gwastraffu,
treulio ♦ n gwastraff, traul
**wasteful** adj gwastraffus
**wastepaper basket** n basged
sbwriel
**wastrel** n oferwr, oferddyn
**watch** vb gwylio, gwylied,
gwarchod ♦ n gwyliadwriaeth;
oriawr, oriadur, wats
**watchful** adj gwyliadwrus
**watchmaker** adj oriadurwr,
trwsiwr watsys

**watchman** n gwyliwr
**watch-night** n gwylnos
**watchword** n arwyddair,
cyswynair
**water** n dwfr, dŵr ♦ vb dyfrhau
**water-cock** n tap
**watercolour** n paent (i'w gymysgu
â dŵr); dyfrlliw
**watercress** n berwr dŵr
**waterfall** n rhaeadr, pistyll,
cwymp dŵr, sgwd
**waterhen** n iâr fach y dŵr
**watering place** n lle i anifeiliaid
gael dŵr; tref ffynhonnau
**waterlogged** adj llawn dŵr
**watermark** n dyfrnod
**waterproof** adj diddos
**watershed** n trum, gwahanfa
ddŵr
**water skiing** n sglefrioar ddŵr
**watertight** adj diddos, heb ollwng
dŵr neu leithder
**water wagtail** n sigwti fach y dŵr
**watt** n wat, uned pŵer trydan
**wattle** n clwyd, pleiden; tagell
ceiliog
**wave** vb chwifio; tonni ♦ n ton
**waver** vi anwadalu, petruso,
gwamalu
**wax** n cwyr ♦ vt cwyro
**wax** vi cynyddu, tyfu
**wax-candle** n cannwyll gŵyr
**waxworks** npl arddangosfa delwau
cŵyr
**way** n ffordd, modd, arfer
**wayfarer** n fforddolyn, teithiwr,
tramwywr
**wayfaring tree** n ysgawen y gors
**waylay** vt cynllwyn, rhagod
**wayside** n ymyl y ffordd
**wayward** adj cyndyn, ystyfnig,
gwrthnysig
**we** pron ni, nyni, ninnau
**weak** adj gwan, egwan
**weaken** vb gwanhau, gwanychu
**weakling** n un gwan, edlych,
ewach

**weakly** *adj* gwanllyd
**weak-minded** *adj* diniwed, gwirion
**weakness** *n* gwendid
**weal** *n* llwydd, llwyddiant, lles
**weald** *n* fforest; gwlad agored
**wealth** *n* golud, cyfoeth, da
**wealthy** *adj* cyfoethog
**wean** *vt* diddyfnu
**weapon** *n* arf
**wear** *vb* gwisgo, treulio ♦ *n* traul; gwisg
**weariness** *n* blinder
**weary** *adj* blin, blinedig ♦ *vb* blino
**weasel** *n* gwenci, bronwen
**weather** *n* tywydd, hin ♦ *vt* dal, dioddef
**weather-beaten** *adj* ag ôl y tywydd arno
**weatherglass** *n* baromedr
**weathervane** *n* ceiliog gwynt
**weave** *vb* gwau, gweu
**weaver** *n* gwehydd
**web** *n* gwe
**webbing** *n* webin
**web-footed** *adj* â thraed gweog
**wed** *vb* priodi, ymbriodi
**wedding** *n* priodas
**wedge** *n* cŷn, gaing, lletem ♦ *vt* cynio; gwthio i mewn
**wedlock** *n* ystad priodas, priodas
**Wednesday** *n* dydd Mercher
**wee** *adj* bach, bychan, pitw
**weed** *n* chwynnyn, chwyn ♦ *vb* chwynnu
**week** *n* wythnos
**weekday** *n* diwrnod gwaith
**weekend** *n* dros y Sul, penwythnos
**weekly** *n* wythnosolyn (cylchgrawn) ♦ *adj* wythnosol ♦ *adv* yn wythnosol
**weep** *vb* wylo, wylofain, llefain
**weevil** *n* gwyfyn yr ŷd
**weft** *n* anwe
**weigh** *vb* pwyso; codi (angor)
**weight** *n* pwys, pwysau
**weighty** *adj* pwysig, trwm
**weir** *n* cored

**weird** *adj* annaearol, iasol
**welcome** *excl*, *n* croeso ♦ *vt* croesawu ♦ *adj* derbyniol, dymunol
**weld** *vt* asio
**welfare** *n* llwydd, lles
**welfare state** *n* gwladwriaeth les
**well** *adv* yn dda ♦ *adj* da, iach ♦ *excl* wel
**well** *n* ffynnon, pydew
**well-balanced** *adj* cytbwys
**wellbeing** *n* lles, budd
**well-bred** *adj* boneddigaidd
**well-fed** *adj* mewn cas cadw da
**wellingtons** *npl* esgidiau glaw
**well-off** *adj* cefnog, da ei fyd
**Welsh** *adj* Cymreig (o ran teithi); Cymraeg (o ran iaith) ♦ *n* Cymraeg
**Welshman** *n* Cymro
**Welshwoman** *n* Cymraes
**welt** *n* gwald, gwaldas
**welter** *vi* ymdrybaeddu
**wen** *n* wen
**wench** *n* geneth, llances
**wend** *vt* mynd, cerdded
**werewolf** *n* bleidd-ddyn
**Wesleyan** *adj* Wesleaidd
**west** *n* gorllewin ♦ *adj* gorllewinol. **W. Germany** *n* Gorllewin yr Almaen. **W. Indies** *npl:* **the W.I.** India'r Gorllewin
**westerly** *adj* gorllewinol, o'r gorllewin
**western** *adj* gorllewinol
**westwards** *adv* tua'r gorllewin
**wet** *adj* gwlyb ♦ *vt* gwlychu ♦ *n* gwlybaniaeth
**wetness** *n* gwlybaniaeth
**wetting** *n* gwlychfa
**wether** *n* mollt, gwedder
**whack** *vb* llachio, baeddu, ffonodio
**whale** *n* morfil
**wharf** *n* porthfa, llwythfa
**what** *adj*, *pron* yr hyn; pa beth, pa faint
**whatever** *pron* beth bynnag

**whatsoever** *pron* pa beth bynnag
**wheat** *n* gwenith
**wheedle** *vt* denu, hudo, llithio, truthio
**wheel** *n* olwyn, rhod, troell ♦ *vt* olwyno, powlio
**wheelbarrow** *n* berfa (drol), whilber
**wheelchair** *n* cadair olwyn
**wheelwright** *n* saer troliau
**wheeze** *vi* gwichian ♦ *n* gwich
**wheezy** *adj* gwichlyd
**whelk** *n* chwalc, gwalc
**whelp** *n* cenau
**when** *adv* pan, pa bryd
**whence** *adv* o ba le, o ba un
**whenever** *adv* pa bryd bynnag
**where** *adv* ym mha le; yn y lle, lle
**whereabouts** *adv* ymhle
**whereas** *conj* gan, yn gymaint â
**whereby** *adv* trwy yr hyn
**wherefore** *adv* paham, am hynny
**wherein** *adv* yn yr hyn
**whereof** *adv* y ... amdano
**whereon** *adv* ar yr hwn
**wheresoever, wherever** *adv* pa le bynnag
**whereto** *adv* y ... iddo
**whereupon** *adv* ar hynny
**wherewithal** *n* modd, arian
**wherry** *n* ysgraff, ceubal, porthfad
**whet** *vt* hogi, minio, awchlymu
**whether** *conj* ai, pa un ai
**whetstone** *n* carreg hogi, hogfaen, agalen
**whey** *n* maidd, gleision
**which** *pron* pa un, pa rai; a ♦ *adj* pa
**whichever** *pron, adj* pa un bynnag
**whiff** *n* chwiff, pwff, chwyth, chwa
**Whig** *n* Chwig, Rhyddfrydwr
**while** *n* ennyd, talm, amser ♦ *vt* treulio ♦ (hefyd **whilst**) *adv* cyhyd, tra
**whim** *n* mympwy, chwim
**whimper** *vb* swnian crio

**whimsical** *adj* ysmala, mympwyol
**whimsicality** *n* bod yn fympwyol
**whin** *n* eithin
**whinchat** *n* clochdar yr eithin
**whine** *vb* swnian crio, cwynfan
**whinny** *vi* gweryru
**whip** *vb* chwipio, ffrewyllu, fflangellu ♦ *n* chwip, ffrewyll, fflangell
**whiphand** *n* llaw uchaf
**whippet** *n* corfilgi
**whipping** *n* chwipiad, fflangelliad
**whir** *vi* chwyrndroi, chwyrnu
**whirl** *vb* chwyrlïo, chwyrnellu, chwyrndroi
**whirligig** *n* chwyrligwgan, chwyrnell
**whirlpool** *n* pwll tro, trobwll
**whirlwind** *n* trowynt, corwynt
**whisk** *n* tusw ♦ *vb* ysgubo; chwyrlïo
**whiskered** *adj* blewog, barfog
**whiskers** *npl* blew, barf
**whisky** *n* chwisgi
**whisper** *vb, n* sibrwd, sisial
**whist** *n* chwist
**whistle** *vb* chwibanu ♦ *n* chwiban, chwibanogl, chwît
**whit** *n* tipyn, gronyn, mymryn
**white** *adj* gwyn, can, cannaid
**whiten** *vb* gwynnu, cannu
**whiteness** *n* gwynder, gwyndra
**whitewash** *n* gwyngalch ♦ *vb* gwyngalchu
**whither** *adv* i ba le
**whiting** *n* gwyniad
**whitlow** *n* ffelwm, ffalwm, ewinor, bystwn
**whitlow grass** *n* llysiau'r bystwn
**Whit Monday** *n* Llungwyn
**Whitsun(day)** *n* Sulgwyn
**Whitsuntide** *n* dros y Sulgwyn
**whittle** *vt* naddu, lleihau
**whiz** *vi* sïo, chwyrnellu, chwyrlïo
**who** *pron* a, pwy
**whoever** *pron* pwy bynnag
**whole** *adj* cyfan, holl; iach,

holliach ♦ *n* cyfan
**wholehearted** *adj* â'i holl galon
**wholemeal** *adj* â'r grawn cyfan, cyflawn
**wholeness** *n* cyfanrwydd
**wholesale** *n* cyfanwerth ♦ *adj* yn y crynswth
**wholesaler** *n* cyfanwerthwr
**wholesome** *adj* iach, iachus, iachusol
**wholly** *adv* yn hollol, yn gyfan gwbl, yn llwyr
**whom** *pron* a (y, yr)
**whomsoever** *pron* pwy bynnag
**whoop** *vi* bloeddio, banllefain ♦ *n* bloedd
**whooping cough** *n* pas
**whop** *vt* ffusto, baeddu
**whopper** *n* un mawr
**whopping** *adj* mawr iawn
**whore** *n* putain, hŵr
**whorl** *n* tro, troell, sidell
**whortleberry** *n* llus, llusi duon bach
**whose** *pron* y ... ei, eiddo pwy? pwy biau?
**whosoever** *pron* pwy bynnag
**why** *adv* paham, pam
**wick** *n* pabwyr, pabwyryn, wic
**wicked** *adj* drwg, drygionus, ysgeler
**wickedness** *n* drygioni
**wicker** *n* gwaith gwiail
**wickerwork** *n* plethwaith, basgedwaith
**wicket** *n* wiced, clwyd, llidiart
**wide** *adj* llydan, eang, helaeth; rhwth
**wide-awake** *adj* effro, ar ddihun
**widely** *adj* yn eang
**widen** *vb* lledu, llydanu
**widespread** *adj* cyffredinol
**widgeon** *n* wiwell
**widow** *adj* gweddw ♦ *n* gwraig weddw, gwidw
**widowed** *adj* gweddw
**widower** *n* gwidman

**widowhood** *n* gweddwdod
**width** *n* lled, ehangder
**wield** *vt* llywio, rheoli; ysgwyd, arfer, trin
**wife** (**wives**) *n* gwraig, gwraig briod, priod
**wig** *n* gwallt gosod, perwig, wig
**wigging** *n* cerydd
**wild** *adj* gwyllt ♦ *n* diffeithle
**wilderness** *n* anialwch
**wildfire** *n* tân gwyllt
**wildness** *n* gwylltineb
**wile** *n* dichell, ystryw, cast
**wilful** *adj* gwirfoddol, bwriadol; ystyfnig
**wilfully** *adj* o fwriad
**wilfulness** *or U.S.* **willfulness** *n* ystyfnigrwydd
**wiliness** *n* dichell, cyfrwystra
**will** *vt* ewyllysio, mynnu ♦ *n* ewyllys
**willing** *adj* ewyllysgar, bodlon
**willingly** *adj* o wirfodd
**willingness** *n* parodrwydd
**will-o-the-wisp** *n* jacolantern
**willow** *n* helygen, pren helyg
**willowherb** *n* helyglys
**willowy** *adj* helygaidd, gosgeiddig
**willpower** *n* grym ewyllys
**willy-nilly** *adv* bodlon neu beidio, o fodd neu anfodd
**wily** *adj* cyfrwys, dichellgar
**wimple** *n* gwempl
**win** *vb* ennill
**wince** *vi* gwingo
**winch** *n* wins
**wind** *n* gwynt
**wind** *vb* dirwyn, troi
**windbag** *n* clebryn
**windfall** *n* lwc, ffawd dda
**windflower** *n* anemoni, blodyn y gwynt
**windless** *adj* di-wynt, llonydd
**windmill** *n* melin wynt
**window** *n* ffenestr
**windowpane** *n* cwarel
**windpipe** *n* breuant, y bibell wynt

**windscreen** *n* ffenestr flaen
**windscreen wiper** *n* braich law
**windward** *adj* tua'r gwynt
**windy** *adj* gwyntog
**wine** *n* gwin
**wineglass** *n* gwydr gwin
**wing** *n* adain, asgell; asgellwr
(rygbi)
**wing-commander** *n* asgell-
gomander
**winged** *adj* adeiniog
**wing-forward** *n* blaenasgellwr
**wink** *vb* wincio, cau llygad ♦ *n*
winc; hunell
**winner** *n* enillydd
**winning** *adj* enillgar, deniadol
**winnings** *npl* enillion
**winnow** *vt* nithio, gwyntyllio
**winnower** *n* nithiwr
**winsome** *adj* serchog, deniadol
**winter** *n* gaeaf ♦ *vb* gaeafu
**wintry** *adj* gaeafol
**wipe** *vt* sychu
**wire** *n* gwifr, gwifren
**wireless** *n* radio
**wirepulling** *n* cynllwyn,
dylanwadu, 'tynnu gwifrau'
**wiring** *n* weiro
**wiry** *adj* gwydn, caled
**wisdom** *n* doethineb
**wise** *adj* doeth
**wiseacre** *n* doethyn, ffwlcyn
**wish** *vb* dymuno, chwennych ♦ *n*
dymuniad
**wishbone** *n* asgwrn tynnu
**wishful** *adj* awyddus. **w. thinking**
breuddwyd gwrach
**wishywashy** *adj* gwan, di-asgwrn-
cefn
**wisp** *n* tusw
**wistful** *adj* awyddus, hiraethus
**wit** *vb*: **to w.** sef, hynny yw, nid
amgen
**wit** *n* synnwyr; arabedd; gŵr
ffraeth
**witch** *n* dewines, gwrach
**witchcraft** *n* dewiniaeth

**with** *prep* â, ag, gyda, gydag, efo,
gan
**withdraw** *vb* tynnu yn ôl, encilio;
codi arian
**withdrawal** *n* enciliad
**withe** *n* gwden, gwialen helyg
**wither** *vb* gwywo, crino
**withering** *adj* gwywol, crin
**withers** *npl* ysgwydd march
**withhold** *vt* atal, cadw yn ôl
**within** *adv*, *n*, *prep* i mewn, o fewn
**without** *prep* heb, di- ♦ *adv*, *n* tu
allan
**withstand** *vt* gwrthsefyll
**witless** *adj* disynnwyr, ynfyd, ffôl
**witness** *n* tyst; tystiolaeth ♦ *vb*
tystio
**wits** *npl* synhwyrau
**witticism** *n* ffraethair, ffraetheb
**wittiness** *n* ffraethineb
**wittingly** *adv* trwy wybod, yn
fwriadol
**witty** *adj* arab, arabus, ffraeth
**wizard** *n* swynwr, dewin
**wizardry** *n* dewiniaeth, hud
**wizened** *adj* gwyw, crin, sybachog
**woad** *n* glaslys
**wobble** *vi* siglo, honcian,
anwadalu
**wobbly** *adj* sigledig
**woe** *n* gwae
**woebegone** *adj* athrist
**wolf** (**wolves**) *n* blaidd
**wolfsbane** *n* llysiau'r blaidd
**woman** (**women**) *n* gwraig, merch
**womanliness** *n* rhinweddau
benywaidd
**womanly** *adj* gwreigaidd,
benywaidd
**womb** *n* croth, bru
**wonder** *n* rhyfeddod, syndod ♦ *vi*
rhyfeddu, synnu
**wonderful, wondrous** *adj*
rhyfeddol
**wont** *vb*, *n* arfer ♦ *adj* arferol
**woo** *vt* caru; deisyf
**wood** *n* coed, coedwig; pren

**woodbine** *n* gwyddfid
**woodcock** *n* cyffylog
**woodcutter** *n* torrwr coed
**wooded** *adj* coedog
**wooden** *adj* o goed, o bren; trwsgl, trwstan
**woodland** *n* coetir
**woodlark** *n* ehedydd y coed
**wood-louse** (-**lice**) *n* gwrach y lludw, mochyn y coed, tyrchyn llwyd
**woodpecker** *n* taradr y coed
**wood-pigeon** *n* ysguthan
**wood sage** *n* chwerwlys yr eithin, saets gwyllt
**wood sorrel** *n* surran y coed
**woodwind** *npl* chwythoffer pren
**woodwork** *n* gwaith coed, gwaith saer
**woof** *n* anwe
**wool** *n* gwlân
**woollen** *adj* gwlanog, gwlân
**woolly** *adj* gwlanog
**woolsack** *n* sedd yr Arglwydd Ganghellor
**word** *n* gair ♦ *vt* geirio
**wording** *n* geiriad
**wordy** *adj* geiriog, amleiriog
**work** *n* gwaith, gweithred, gorchwyl ♦ *vb* gweithio
**worker** *n* gweithiwr
**workhouse** *n* tloty, wyrcws
**working** *adj* yn gweithio, gwaith
**workman** *n* gweithiwr
**workmanlike** *n* gweithgar, diwyd
**workmanship** *n* saerniaeth, crefft
**workshop** *n* gweithdy
**world** *n* byd
**worldly** *adj* bydol
**worldwide** *adj* byd-eang
**worm** *n* pryf, abwydyn; llyngyren ♦ *vb* ymnyddu
**wormwood** *n* wermod
**worn-out** *adj* wedi blino; wedi treulio
**worried** *adj* pryderus, gofidus
**worry** *vb* cnoi, baeddu, blino, poeni, poenydio ♦ *n* pryder, blinder
**worse** *adj* gwaeth
**worsen** *vb* gwaethygu
**worship** *n* addoliad ♦ *vb* addoli
**worshipper** *n* addolwr
**worst** *vt* gorchfygu, trechu
**worsted** *n* edafedd hirwlan, wstid
**worth** *n* gwerth, teilyngdod
**worthless** *adj* diwerth
**worthy** *adj* teilwng ♦ *n* gŵr o fri
**wound** *n* archoll, clwyf ♦ *vt* archolli, clwyfo
**wraith** *n* cyhiraeth, cyheuraeth
**wrangle** *vb* cecru, cweryla, ffraeo ♦ *n* ffrae, ymryson
**wrap** *vt* plygu, amdoi, lapio
**wrapping paper** *n* papur lapio
**wrasse** *n* gwrachen y môr
**wrath** *n* llid, digofaint, soriant
**wrathful** *adj* digofus, llidiog, dig
**wreak** *vt* tywallt, dial (llid)
**wreath** *n* torch
**wreck** *n* llongddrylliad ♦ *vb* llongddryllio
**wren** *n* dryw, dryw bach
**wrench** *vt* rhwygo ymaith, tyndroi ♦ *n* tyndro
**wrestle** *vi* ymgodymu, ymaflyd codwm
**wrestler** *n* ymgodymwr, taflwr codwm
**wretch** *n* adyn, truan; gwalch, dihiryn
**wretched** *adj* truan, truenus, gresynus
**wriggle** *vb* gwingo, ymnyddu
**wright** *n* saer
**wring** *vt* troi, gwasgu
**wrinkle** *n* crych, crychni ♦ *vb* crychu
**wrinkle** *n* awgrym, hysbysrwydd
**wrinkled** *n* crychiog
**wrist** *n* arddwrn
**wristband** *n* rhwymyn llawes
**wristwatch** *n* wats arddwrn, wats fraich, oriawr

**writ** *n*: Holy W. yr Ysgrythur Lân
**write** *vb* ysgrifennu
**writer** *n* ysgrifennwr, awdur
**writhe** *vb* ymnyddu, gwingo
**writing** *n* ysgrifen; ysgrifennu
**writing paper** *n* papur ysgrifennu
**wrong** *adj* cyfeiliornus, cam, anghywir, o'i le ♦ *n* cam ♦ *vt* gwneud cam â, niweidio, drygu
**wrongdoing** *n* trosedd, camwedd
**wrongful** *adj* anghyfiawn, ar gam
**wroth** *adj* dig, dicllon, digofus, llidiog
**wrought** *adj*: w. iron haearn gyr
**wry** *adj* cam, gwyrgam

# X

**xenophobia** *n* senoffobia
**X-rays** *npl* pelydrau X
**xylophone** *n* seiloffon

# Y

**yacht** *n* llong bleser, iot
**yachtsman** *n* hwyliwr iot
**yap** *vi* clepian cyfarth
**yard** *n* llath, llathen; hwyl-lath
**yard** *n* iard, buarth, cadlas, clos
**yarn** *n* edau, edafedd; stori, chwedl
**yawl** *n* bad mawr, cwch llong
**yawn** *vi* dylyfu gên, agor ceg
**ye** *pron* chwi, chwychwi; chwithau
**yea** *adv* ie, yn wir
**year** *n* blwyddyn, blwydd
**yearling** *n* anifail blwydd
**yearly** *adv* blynyddol
**yearn** *vi* hiraethu, dyheu
**yearning** *n* hiraeth
**yeast** *n* burum, berem, berman
**yell** *vb* ysgrechain ♦ *n* ysgrech, nâd
**yellow** *adj*, *n* melyn
**yellowhammer** *n* y benfelen, melyn yr eithin

**yelp** *vi* cyfarth, gogyfarth, cipial
**yeoman** *n* gwrêng, iwmon; amaethwr
**yeomanry** *n* meirchfilwyr
**yes** *adv* ie, do, oes, *etc*
**yesterday** *n*, *adv* doe
**yet** *conj*, *adv* er hynny, eto
**yew** *n* yw, ywen
**Yiddish** *n* Almaeneg Iddewaidd
**yield** *vb* ildio, gildio, ymroddi, rhoddi ♦ *n* cynnyrch
**yoghurt** *n* iogwrt
**yoke** *n* iau, gwedd ♦ *vb* ieuo
**yokefellow** *n* cymar
**yokel** *n* lleban, gwladwr, taeog
**yolk** *n* melyn wy, melynwy
**yonder** *adj* acw, draw ♦ *adv* dacw, acw, draw
**yore** *n* y dyddiau gynt, y cynfyd
**you** *pron* chi, chwi, 'ch; chwychwi; chwithau
**young** *adj* ifanc, ieuanc
**younger** *adj* iau
**youngest** *adj* ieuaf, ifancaf
**youngster** *n* bachgennyn, plentyn
**your** *pron* eich, 'ch
**yours** *pron* eiddoch, yr eiddoch
**yourself** *pron* eich hun(an)
**yourselves** *pron* eich hunain
**youth** *n* ieuenctid, mebyd; llanc. y. hostel *n* gwesty ieuenctid
**youthful** *adj* ieuanc, ieuengaidd
**Yugoslavia** *n* Iwgoslafia
**Yule** *n* Nadolig
**Yuletide** *n* tymor y Nadolig

# Z

**Zambia** *n* Zambia
**zeal** *n* sêl, aidd, eiddgarwch, brwdfrydedd
**zealot** *n* gwynfydwr, penboethyn
**zealous** *adj* selog, eiddgar, brwdfrydig
**zebra** *n* sebra
**zenana** *n* gwragedd-dy, gwreicty

**zenith** n entrych; anterth
**zephyr** n awel dyner (o'r gorllewin)
**zero** n dim, diddim, gwagnod (0), sero
**zest** n awch, blas, afiaith
**zigzag** adj, n igam-ogam
**Zimbabwe** n Zimbabwe
**zinc** n sinc

**zip** n sip
**zither** n sither
**zodiac** n sidydd
**zone** n gwregys, cylch, rhanbarth
**zoo** n sw
**zoological** adj swolegol
**zoologist** n swolegydd
**zoology** n milofyddiaeth, swoleg